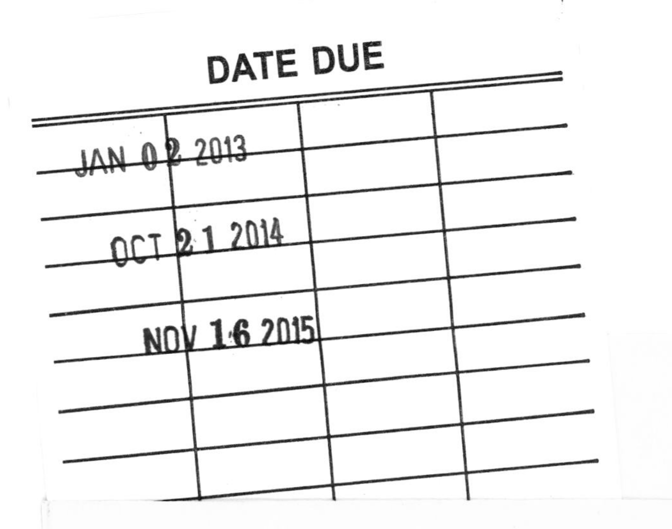

Principles of

Cost Accounting

PRINCIPLES OF

COST ACCOUNTING

15E

EDWARD J. VANDERBECK

Professor Emeritus
Department of Accountancy
Xavier University

SOUTH-WESTERN
CENGAGE Learning™

Australia • Brazil • Japan • Korea • Mexico • Singapore • Spain • United Kingdom • United States

Principles of Cost Accounting, 15th Edition
Edward J. VanDerbeck

Vice President of Editorial, Business: Jack W. Calhoun
Acquisitions Editor: Matt Filimonov
Developmental Editor: Lauren Athmer
Marketing Manager: Kristen Hurd
Marketing Coordinator: Heather McAuliffe
Content Project Manager: Corey Geissler
Production Technology Analyst: Starratt Alexander
Media Editor: Scott Fidler
Sr. Manufacturing Coordinator: Doug Wilke
Production Service: Cadmus
Sr. Art Director: Stacy Shirley
Internal Designer: Jennifer Lambert, Jen2Design, LLC
Cover Designer: cmiller design
Cover Image: ©Getty Images

Library of Congress Control Number: 2009935270

ISBN-10: 0-8400-3703-1

ISBN-13: 978-0-8400-3703-9

South-Western Cengage Learning,
5191 Natorp Boulevard
Mason OH 45040,
USA

Cengage Learning products are represented in Canada by Nelson Education, Ltd.

For your course and learning solutions, visit www.cengage.com
Purchase any of our products at your local college store or at our preferred online store www.ichapters.com

Printed in the United States of America
1 2 3 4 5 6 7 13 12 11 10 09

Preface

Why Study Cost Accounting?

The 15th edition of *Principles of Cost Accounting*, in an easily accessible presentation, applies cost concepts, cost behavior, and cost accounting techniques to manufacturing, merchandising, and service businesses. Students learn how to determine costs of products and services more accurately; use the knowledge of product and service costs to set selling prices, to bid on contracts, and to analyze the relative profitability of various products and services; use techniques to measure the performance of managers and subunits within an organization; design an accounting system to fit the production and distribution system of an organization; and use the accounting system as a tool to motivate managers towards the organization's goals.

What Does the 15th Edition Offer?

- Appropriate content for a one-quarter or one-semester cost accounting course.
- A ten-chapter format—a distinguishing feature of the text that makes it most appropriate for shorter courses.
- Directed assignments at intervals within each chapter.
- A very readable and relevant text that covers the essentials of cost accounting in a logical sequence and concise manner.
- The inclusion of cost accounting techniques for service businesses.
- A discussion of the special purpose reports and analytical techniques used for management decision making.
- Emphasis on nonfinancial performance measures via the balanced scorecard.
- An increase in the number of end-of-chapter exercises, problems, and Self-Study Problems.

What Is New in the 15th Edition?

The 15th edition includes the following changes:

- All new chapter-opening vignettes with real-world applications.
- Increased use of graphics, including Excel spreadsheet "screen shots" and flow diagrams.
- An increase in the number of end-of-chapter self-study problems.
- An increased emphasis on ethical decision making in the end-of-chapter Mini-Cases.
- Newly added "real company" examples throughout the text.
- First-time inclusion of corporate governance, lean manufacturing, demand software, and Web-based budgeting.
- An integrated illustration of materials control procedures.
- An illustration of the least squares regression method using Microsoft Excel.

What Are the Features of the 15th Edition?

The 15th edition includes several features that facilitate the learning process for the student and allow the instructor to teach with ease.

Directed Assignments

At specific points within each chapter, students are directed to appropriate end-of-chapter assignments. This allows students to work practice items without completing the entire chapter.

Self-Study Problems

Two demonstration problems are included at the end of each chapter, with a step-by-step explanation of how to solve them. These Self-Study Problems are constructed from difficult concepts in the chapter and reinforce the techniques and procedures discussed in the chapter. An added feature is end-of-chapter problems that reference students back to Self-Study Problems that are similar in topic and difficulty.

End-of-Chapter Materials

The end-of-chapter questions, exercises, problems, mini-cases, and Internet activities have been carefully written, revised, added to, and verified to reflect the coverage as it appears in the chapters. There has been a concerted effort to provide the instructor with a wide choice of subject matter and degree of difficulty when assigning end-of-chapter materials. Where appropriate, comprehensive review problems have been added that cover concepts from more than one chapter. Additionally, selected problems may be solved using spreadsheet software.

Integrated Learning Objectives

Learning objectives begin each chapter. Each learning objective is indicated in the text where first discussed. All end-of-chapter exercises, problems, mini-cases, and Internet activities are identified by learning objectives.

Key Terms

Key terms are highlighted as they are introduced. They are listed, along with page references, at the end of each chapter. A comprehensive glossary is included at the end of the book, providing definitions for all the key terms. Actual companies are highlighted where their practices are discussed in the chapters.

Appendixes

The Institute of Management Accountants "Statement of Ethical Professional Practice" is included in an appendix at the end of Chapter 1. An appendix at the end of Chapter 9 illustrates the four-variance and three-variance methods of analyzing factory overhead.

What Supplementary Materials Are Available?

A complete package of supplementary materials is available with the 15th edition of *Principles of Cost Accounting* to assist both instructors and students. The package includes materials that have been carefully prepared and reviewed.

Available to Instructors

All instructor resources are available online on the Instructor Companion Web Site (www.cengage.com/accounting/vanderbeck), as well as on the Instructor Resource CD-ROM (IRCD).

Solutions Manual. This manual contains the answers to all end-of-chapter questions, exercises, problems, Internet exercises, and mini-cases.

Test Bank. The test bank is available in a computerized version for Windows. The user may select, mix, edit, and add questions or problems to create the type of test or problem set needed.

ExamView Pro™ Testing Software. The printed test bank is available in a computerized version for Windows. The user may select, mix, edit, and add questions or problems to create the type of test or problem set needed. ExamView is available on the Instructor's Resource CD.

PowerPoint Presentations. This resource provides presentations for each chapter, created specifically for this edition; thus, they follow along closely with the text. The presentations for each chapter are also available online for students to use as an additional study resource.

Instructor Resource CD-ROM (IRCD). This convenient resource includes the Test Bank, ExamView, the Solutions Manual, PowerPoint Presentations, and the Instructor Spreadsheet Templates (with solutions).

Instructor Spreadsheet Templates. The Instructor Spreadsheet Templates show the completed spreadsheet solutions for exercises within the end-of-chapter materials. These files are available on the IRCD, or they can be downloaded from the Instructor Companion Web Site.

Instructor Companion Web Site (www.cengage.com/accounting/vanderbeck). The text-specific Web site provides access to all instructor resources organized by chapter and topic, and are password protected. All of these resources are also available on the IRCD: Test Bank, ExamView, Solutions Manual, PowerPoint Presentations, and the Instructor Spreadsheet Templates (with solutions).

Available to Students

All student resources are available online on the Student Companion Web Site (www.cengage.com/accounting/vanderbeck).

Study Guide. The study guide provides a review summary for each chapter as well as questions and problems to test comprehension of chapter material. Solutions for all questions and problems are included in a separate section at the end of the study guide.

Student Spreadsheet Templates. The Student Spreadsheet Templates correlate to exercises within the end-of-chapter materials. These files are available for downloading on the Student Companion Web Site.

PowerPoint Presentations. This study resource provides presentations for each chapter, created specifically for this edition; thus, they follow along closely with the text.

Experience Accounting Videos. Highlight progressive companies and allow you to effectively visualize critical chapter concepts—enhancing what you learn in class! The Experience Accounting Videos can be bundled at *no additional cost with new copies of the text* or can be purchased separately. You can access the videos at www.cengage.com/accounting/eav.

Acknowledgments

We would like to thank all of those individuals who have helped during the revision of this text by providing constructive comments and suggestions.

Josephine M. Mathias
Mercer County Community College

Joanne E. Shurbert
Concord's Community College and Manchester Community College

Ann Bikofsky
College of West Chester

Theresa Laws-Dahl
Blackhawk Technical College

Sam Lester
Middle Georgia Technical College

Edward Kufuor
ASA Institute

Jim Murray
Western Technical College

David A. Flannery
Bryant & Stratton College, Virginia Beach

James Emig
Villanova University

About the Author

Ed VanDerbeck has been a professor of accounting for 32 years and was Chair of the Department of Accountancy at Xavier University, Cincinnati, Ohio, for 24 years. Before retiring in 2008, Professor VanDerbeck specialized in teaching cost accounting to accounting majors and managerial accounting to undergraduate and MBA students. He has taught at the two-year college level at SUNY–Delhi. He has a BA in Accounting from Binghamton University (formerly SUNY–Binghamton) and an MS in Business Administration from the University of Albany (formerly SUNY–Albany). He is licensed as a CPA (inactive) in the state of Ohio. Professor VanDerbeck has worked as an internal revenue agent, performed a faculty internship at what was formerly the Big Eight accounting firm of Touche-Ross. He has served as a developmental editor and marketing manager for accounting publications with South-Western College Publishing. Professor VanDerbeck is an avid tennis player and a student of casino gaming strategies.

BRIEF CONTENTS

Contents

9 Cost Accounting for Service Businesses and the Balanced Scorecard 447

10 Cost Analysis for Management Decision Making 481

Principles of
Cost Accounting

CHAPTER 1

Introduction to Cost Accounting

Learning Objectives

After studying this chapter, you should be able to:

LO1 Explain the uses of cost accounting information.

LO2 Describe the ethical responsibilities and certification requirements for management accountants, as well as corporate governance.

LO3 Describe the relationship of cost accounting to financial and management accounting.

LO4 Identify the three basic elements of manufacturing costs.

LO5 Illustrate basic cost accounting procedures.

LO6 Distinguish between the two basic types of cost accounting systems.

LO7 Illustrate a job order cost system.

An article in the August 22, 2008 *Wall Street Journal,* "Burger King Battles Costs with Small Whopper Jr.," describes Burger King's attempt to "overcome high ingredient costs that are eating into its profit." Chief Executive John Chidsey said, "To combat costs, Burger King is testing its $1 Whopper Jr. with smaller hamburger pattie—down to two ounces apiece from 2.2 ounces—in some markets and experimenting with different beverage sizes." The article went on to explain that "McDonald's is testing modifications to its $1 double cheeseburger, including selling a different version and raising the price of the traditional double cheeseburger."

- What is the total cost to make and sell each Whopper Jr. or McDonald's double cheeseburger?
- How many burgers must be sold and at what prices to cover costs and to provide shareholders with an acceptable return on their investment?
- Given that fast-food prices are constrained by competitors' prices, what other cost-cutting measures might Burger King employ to return operations to normal profit margins?

These questions can be best answered with the aid of cost information introduced in this and the following chapters.

The importance of cost accounting information to the successful operation of a business has long been recognized. However, in the current global economic environment, such information is more

Figure 1-1 Production Process for Goods and Services

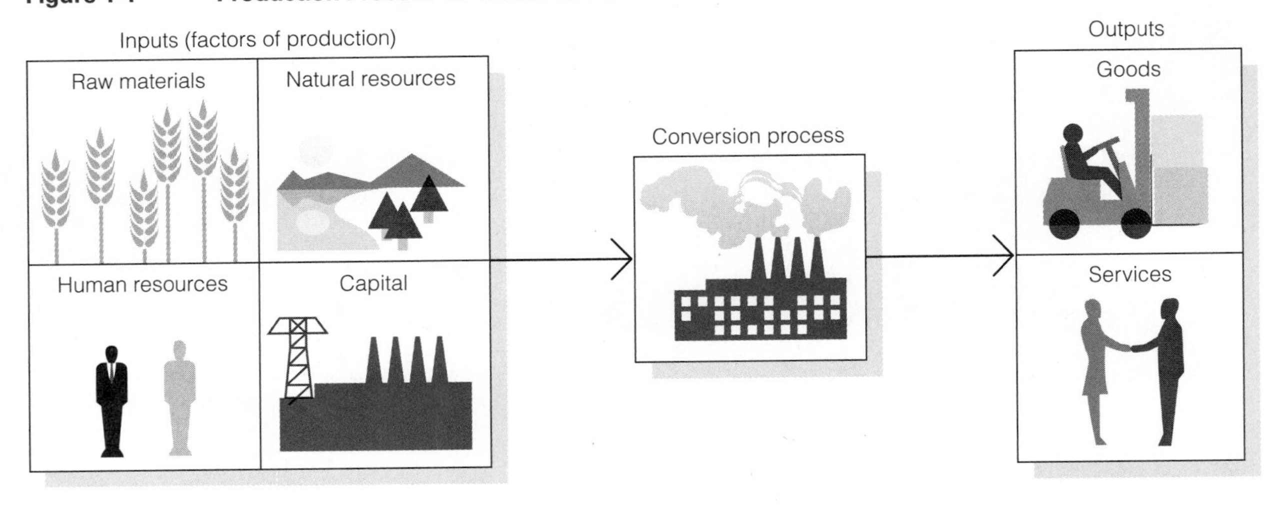

crucial than ever. Automobiles from Korea, clothing from China, electronic equipment from Japan, and laptop computers from Poland are just a few examples of foreign-made products that have provided stiff competition to U.S. manufacturers both at home and abroad. As a result of these pressures, companies today are placing more emphasis on controlling costs in an attempt to keep their products competitive. For example, U.S. companies are outsourcing production and service activities to other countries, such as production operations in Honduras and Indonesia and technical support call centers in India.

Cost accounting provides the detailed cost information that management needs to control current operations and plan for the future. Figure 1-1 illustrates the production process for goods and services for which cost accounting provides information. Management uses this information to decide how to allocate resources to the most efficient and profitable areas of the business.

All types of business entities—manufacturing, merchandising, and service businesses—require cost accounting information systems to track their activities. **Manufacturers** convert purchased raw materials into finished goods by using labor, technology, and facilities. **Merchandisers** purchase finished goods for resale. They may be **retailers**, who sell products to individuals for consumption, or **wholesalers**, who purchase goods from manufacturers and sell to retailers. **For-profit service businesses**, such as health clubs, accounting firms, and NBA basketball teams, sell services rather than products. **Not-for-profit service agencies**, such as charities, governmental agencies, and some health care facilities, provide services at little or no cost to the user.

The nature of the manufacturing process requires that the **accounting information systems** of manufacturers be designed to accumulate detailed cost data relating to the production process. It is common today for manufacturers of all sizes to have **cost accounting systems** that track the costs incurred to produce and sell their diverse product lines. While the cost accounting principles and procedures discussed in the text mostly emphasize manufacturers, many of the same principles apply to merchandising and service businesses. Cost accounting is essential to the efficient operation of fast-food restaurants, athletic teams, fine arts groups, hospitals, social welfare agencies, and numerous other entities. Chapter 9 and various other sections throughout the text illustrate cost accounting procedures for service businesses.

In many ways, the activities of a manufacturer are similar to those of a merchandiser. They purchase, store, and sell goods; both must have efficient management and adequate sources of capital; and they may employ hundreds or thousands of workers. The manufacturing process itself highlights the differences between the two: merchandisers, such as **Target,** buy goods in marketable form to resell to their customers; manufacturers, such as **Procter & Gamble,** must make the goods they sell. Once a merchandiser has acquired goods, it can perform the marketing function. The purchase of raw materials by a manufacturer, however, is only the beginning of a long and sometimes complex chain of events that results in a finished product for sale.

The **manufacturing process** requires the conversion of raw materials into finished goods through the use of labor and various other factory resources. A manufacturer must make a major investment in physical assets, such as property, plant, and equipment. To produce finished goods, a manufacturer must purchase appropriate quantities of raw materials and supplies, and develop a workforce. In addition to the cost of materials and labor, the manufacturer incurs other expenses in the production process. Many of these costs, such as depreciation, taxes, insurance, and utilities, are similar to those incurred by a merchandising concern. Costs such as machine maintenance and repair, materials handling, production setup, production scheduling, and inspection are unique to manufacturers. Other costs, such as selling and administrative expenses, are similar to those incurred by merchandisers and service businesses. The methods of accounting for sales, cost of goods sold, and selling and administrative expenses for a manufacturer are similar to those of merchandisers. Service businesses, by comparison, have no inventories because the service is consumed at the time it is provided. Service businesses have revenue and operating expenses, but no cost of goods sold.

Note that product quality is as important a competitive weapon as cost control in the global arena. Originally issued for companies marketing products in Europe, a set of international standards for quality management, known as the **ISO 9000 family**, was designed by the International Organization for Standardization, based in Switzerland. The standards require that manufacturers have a well-defined quality control system, that they consistently maintain a high level of product quality to enhance customer satisfaction, and that they achieve continual improvement of their performance in pursuit of these objectives. The standards are accepted in 158 countries, 106 of which are "member bodies" with full voting rights on technical and policy issues.[1] Major U.S. companies such as **General Electric** and **Procter & Gamble** require their suppliers to obtain ISO 9000 certification.

Uses of Cost Accounting Information

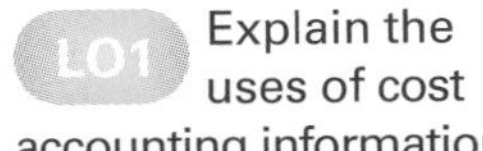

Explain the uses of cost accounting information.

Principles of cost accounting have been developed to enable manufacturers to process the many different costs associated with manufacturing and to provide built-in control features. The information produced by a cost accounting system provides a basis for determining product costs and selling prices, and it helps management to plan and control operations.

Determining Product Costs and Pricing

Cost accounting procedures provide the means to determine product costs that enable the preparation of meaningful financial statements and other reports needed to manage a business. The cost accounting information system must be designed to permit the determination of **unit costs** as well as total product costs. For example, the fact that a manufacturer spent $100,000 for labor in a certain month is not, in itself, meaningful; but if this labor produced 5,000 finished units, the fact that the cost of labor was $20 per unit is significant. This figure can be compared to the company's unit labor cost for prior periods and, often, to the labor cost of major competitors.

Unit cost information is also useful in making a variety of important marketing decisions such as:

1. *Determining the selling price of a product.* Knowing the manufacturing cost of a product aids in determining the desired selling price. It should be high enough to cover the cost of producing the item and the marketing and administrative expenses attributable to it, as well as to provide a satisfactory profit to the owners.
2. *Meeting competition.* If a product is being undersold by a competitor, detailed information regarding unit costs can be used to determine whether the problem can be resolved by reducing the selling price, by reducing manufacturing and selling expenses attributable to the product, or by some combination of the above that will still result in profitable sales.
3. *Bidding on contracts.* Many manufacturers must submit competitive bids in order to be awarded contracts. Knowledge of the unit costs attributable to a particular product is of great importance in determining the bid price.
4. *Analyzing profitability.* Unit cost information enables management to determine the amount of profit that each product earns, thereby allocating the company's scarce resources to those that are most profitable.

1 International Organization for Standardization, "ISO Members," www.iso.org.

It is not uncommon, however, for some companies to retain a certain product line, known as a **loss leader**, that yields a very low profit, or even a loss, in order to maintain the product variety that will attract those customers who also purchase the more profitable items.

Planning and Control

One of the most important aspects of cost accounting is the preparation of reports that management can use to plan and control operations.

Planning is the process of establishing objectives or goals for the firm and determining the means by which they will be met. Effective planning is facilitated by the following:

1. *Clearly defined objectives of the manufacturing operation.* These objectives may be expressed in terms of the number of units to be produced, the desired quality, the estimated unit cost, the delivery schedules, and the desired inventory levels.

2. *A production plan that will assist and guide the company in reaching its objectives.* This detailed plan includes a description of the manufacturing operations to be performed, a projection of human resource needs for the period, and the coordination of the timely acquisition of materials and facilities.

Cost accounting information enhances the planning process by providing historical costs that serve as a basis for future projections. Management can analyze the data to estimate future costs and operating results and to make decisions regarding the acquisition of additional facilities, any changes in marketing strategies, and the availability of capital.

The word "control" is used in many different ways, but from the viewpoint of the manufacturing concern, **control** is the process of monitoring the company's operations and determining whether the objectives identified in the planning process are being accomplished. Effective control is achieved as follows:

1. Assigning Responsibility. Responsibility should be assigned for each detail of the production plan. All managers should know precisely what their responsibilities are in terms of efficiency, operations, production, and costs. The key to proper control involves the use of responsibility accounting and cost centers.

The essence of **responsibility accounting** is the assignment of accountability for costs or production results to those individuals who have the most authority to influence them. It requires a cost information system that traces the data to cost centers and their managers.

A **cost center** is a unit of activity within the factory to which costs may be practically and equitably assigned. A cost center may be a department or a group of workers; it could represent one job, one process, or one machine. The criteria for a cost center are (1) a reasonable basis on which manufacturing costs can be traced or allocated and (2) a person who has control over and is accountable for many of the costs charged to that center.

With responsibility accounting, the manager of a cost center is accountable only for those costs that the manager controls. For example, labor and materials costs will be charged to the cost center, but the manager may be responsible only for the quantity of materials used and the number of labor hours worked. This manager would probably not be accountable for the unit cost of raw materials or the hourly rate paid to employees. These decisions are normally beyond the manager's control and are the responsibility of the purchasing and human resource departments, respectively. The manager may be responsible for the cost of machinery maintenance and repair due to misuse in the cost center, but not responsible for the costs of depreciation, taxes, and insurance on the machinery if the decision to purchase the machinery was made at a higher level in the organization. If production in the cost center for a given period is lower than planned, this could be due to poor supervision of production workers, which is the manager's responsibility. If the decrease in production is caused by less-skilled workers being hired by Human Resources, however, that would be beyond the manager's control.

Cost and production reports for a cost center reflect its costs, in dollars, and its production activity, in units. In a responsibility accounting system, the specific data for which the manager is responsible would be highlighted for the purpose of performance evaluation. Quite often, both a cost and production report and a separate performance report will be prepared for a cost center. The **performance report** will include only those costs and production data that the center's manager can control. An illustration of a performance report appears in Figure 1-2. Note the "variance columns" that appear in the illustration. A **variance** represents the amount by which the actual result differs from the budgeted or planned amount. If the actual amount spent is less than the amount budgeted for, the variance is *favorable (F)*; if more than budgeted, it is *unfavorable (U)*. An in-depth discussion of budgeting and variance analysis appears in Chapters 7 and 8.

These reports must be furnished at regular intervals (monthly, weekly, or daily) on a timely basis. To provide the maximum benefit, the reports should be available as soon as possible after the end of the period being reported. Reports not produced in a timely fashion are not effective in controlling future operations.

2. Periodically Measuring and Comparing Results. Actual operating results should be reviewed periodically and compared to the objectives established in the planning process. This analysis, which may be made monthly, weekly, daily, or even hourly in the case of production and scrap reports, is a major part of cost control because it compares current performance with the overall plan. The actual dollars, units produced, hours worked, or materials used are compared with the **budget**, which is management's operating plan expressed in quantitative terms (units and dollars). This comparison is a primary feature of cost analysis. The number of dollars spent or the quantity of units produced has little significance until compared with the budgeted amounts. Note that the appropriateness of the

Figure 1-2 Performance Report

	A	B	C	D	E	F	G	H	I	J	K	L	M	N
1						Leonardo's Italian Café								
2						Performance Report—Kitchen								
3						September 30, 2011								
4				*Budgeted*				*Actual*				*Variance*		
5	*Expense*		*September*		*Year-to-*		*September*		*Year-to-*		*September*		*Year-to-*	
6					*Date*				*Date*				*Date*	
7	Kitchen wages		$5,500		$47,000		$5,200		$46,100		$300	F	$900	F
8	Food		17,700		155,300		18,300		157,600		600	U	2,300	U
9	Supplies		3,300		27,900		3,700		29,100		400	U	1,200	U
10	Utilities		1,850		15,350		1,730		16,200		120	F	850	U
11	Total		$28,350		$245,550		$28,930		$249,000		$580	U	$3,450	U
12														

F = Favorable; U = Unfavorable

$157,600 actual year-to-date expenditure for "Food" in Figure 1-2 can be evaluated only when compared to the budgeted amount of $155,300.

3. Taking Necessary Corrective Action. The performance reports may identify problem areas and deviations from the business plan. Appropriate corrective action should be implemented where necessary. A significant variance from the plan is a signal for attention. An investigation may reveal a weakness to be corrected or a strength to be better utilized. Management wants to know not only the results of operations, but also how the results—whether favorable or unfavorable—compare with the plan, why things happened, and who was responsible. For example, management may want to determine the causes of the unfavorable year-to-date variance of $2,300 for "Food" in Figure 1-2. The variance may be due to an uncontrollable rise in food prices or to a controllable waste of food at the restaurant, or a combination of both. Based on the variance analysis, management must be prepared to improve existing conditions by such means as implementing more economical purchasing methods and standard portion sizes. Otherwise, the periodic measurement of activity has little value. The relationship of planning and control is illustrated in Figure 1-3.

Figure 1-3 Relationship of Planning and Control for Leonardo's Italian Café

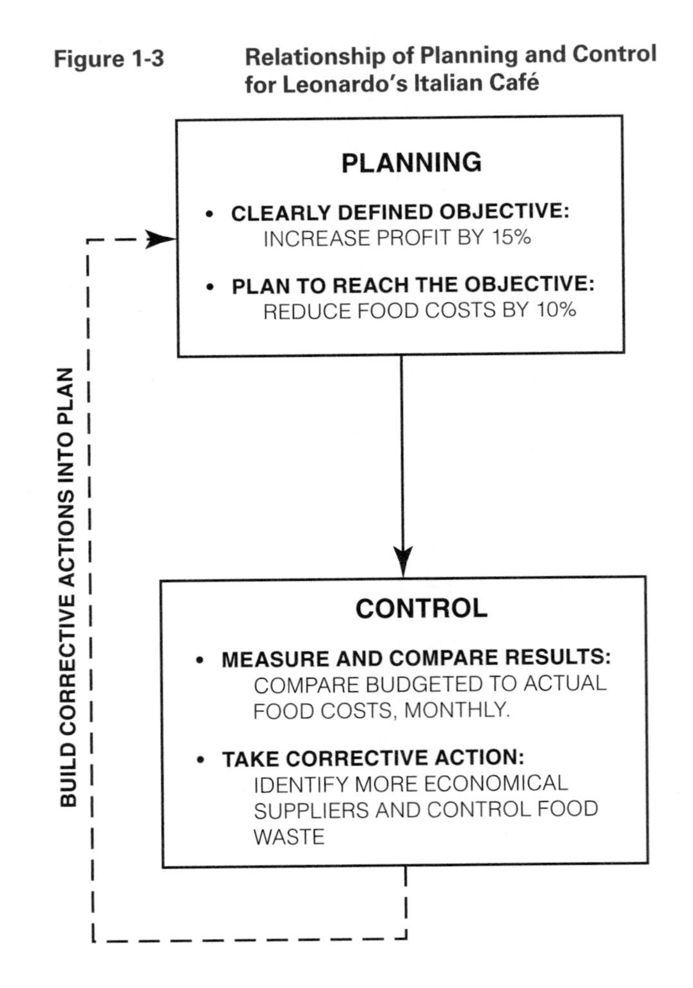

Professional Ethics, CMA Certification, and Corporate Governance

LO2 Describe the ethical responsibilities and certification requirements for management accountants, as well as corporate governance.

The Institute of Management Accountants (IMA) is the largest organization of accountants in industry in the world. Comparable to the CPA certification for public accountants, the Certified Management Accountant (CMA) certificate—which is awarded by the IMA after the candidate completes a four-year college degree, two years of relevant professional experience in management accounting and financial management, and a rigorous four-part examination whose topics include business analysis, management accounting and reporting, strategic management, and business applications with a strong emphasis on ethics—evidences a high level of competency in management accounting.

In addition to competency, the need for ethical conduct in managing corporate affairs has never been greater. Individual employees, investors, and the economy as a whole have been negatively impacted by recent accounting scandals where management, including controllers and chief financial officers, has "cooked the books" to make reported financial results seem better than actual. Enron, WorldCom, Health South, Tyco International, Rite Aid, and AOL Time Warner are just a few examples of firms that have had major accounting scandals in recent years. To help curb future abuses, the **Sarbanes-Oxley Act** of 2002 was written to protect shareholders and other stakeholders of publicly-traded companies by improving *corporate governance*. **Corporate governance** is the means by which a company is directed and controlled. Key elements of the act include:

- certification by the CEO and CFO that the financial statements fairly represent the results of business operations.
- the establishment of the Public Company Accounting Oversight Board (PCAOB) to provide oversight of the accounting profession.
- prohibiting a public accounting firm from providing many nonauditing services to a company that it audits.
- the requirement that a company's annual report contain an internal control report that includes management's opinion on the effectiveness of its internal controls.
- the placement of responsibility for hiring, compensating, and terminating the audit firm in the hands of the board of directors' audit committee, not top management.
- severe criminal penalties for the destruction or alteration of business documents and for retaliation against "whistleblowers."[2]

2 American Institute of Certified Public Accountants, "The Sarbanes-Oxley Act," www.aicpa.org.

It is equally important that the internal accounting reports prepared by management accountants be as accurate and unbiased as possible. To that end, the IMA has issued a Statement of Ethical Professional Practice that must be adhered to by its members. These standards address members' responsibility in areas such as maintaining appropriate levels of professional competence, refraining from disclosing confidential information, avoiding conflicts of interest, and communicating information fairly and objectively. The second part of the document provides guidance for resolving ethical conflicts. The complete IMA Statement of Ethical Professional Practice may be found in the appendix to this chapter and at the IMA Web site, which is linked to the text Web site at http://www.cengage.com/accounting/vanderbeck.

Relationship of Cost Accounting to Financial and Management Accounting

LO3 Describe the relationship of cost accounting to financial and management accounting.

The objective of accounting is to accumulate financial information for use in making economic decisions. **Financial accounting** focuses on gathering historical financial information to be used in preparing financial statements that meet the needs of investors, creditors, and other external users of financial information. The statements include a balance sheet, income statement, retained earnings statement, and statement of cash flows. Although these financial statements are useful to management as well as to external users, additional reports, schedules, and analyses are required for management's use in planning and controlling operations. Management spends most of its time evaluating the problems and opportunities of individual departments and divisions of the company rather than looking at the entire company at once. As a result, the external financial statements for the whole company are of little help to management in making day-to-day operating decisions.

Management accounting focuses on both historical and estimated data that management needs to conduct ongoing operations and do long-range planning. **Cost accounting** includes those parts of both financial and management accounting that collect and analyze cost information. It provides the product cost data required for special reports to management (management accounting) and for inventory costing in the financial statements (financial accounting). For example, cost accounting information is needed to determine: whether to make or buy a product component; whether to accept a special order at a discounted price; the amount at which cost of goods sold should be reported on the income statement; and the valuation of inventories on the balance sheet. The various users and uses of cost accounting data are illustrated in Figure 1-4, and Figure 1-5 shows how cost accounting intersects both financial and management accounting. "What Is Management Accounting?", a description prepared by the Institute of Management Accountants as to the role performed by management accountants, appears on the following page.

WHAT IS MANAGEMENT ACCOUNTING?[1]

Management accounting is the internal business building role of accounting and finance professionals who work inside organizations. These professionals are involved in designing and evaluating business processes, budgeting and forecasting, implementing and monitoring internal controls, and analyzing, synthesizing, and aggregating information—to help drive economic value.

The role of management accounting differs from that of public accounting, since management accountants work at the "beginning" of the value chain, supporting decision making, planning, and control, while audit and tax functions involve checking the work after the fact. Management accountants are valued business partners, directly supporting an organization's strategic goals. With a renewed emphasis on good internal controls and sound financial reporting, the role of the management accountant is more important than ever.

It obviously takes more people to "do" the work than it does to "check" the work. In fact, of the five million finance function professionals in the U.S., more than 90% work inside organizations as management accountants and finance professionals. Some common job titles for management accountants in organizations of all sizes and structure include:

- Staff Accountant
- Cost Accountant
- Senior Accountant
- Corporate or Division Planner
- Financial Analyst
- Budget Analyst
- Internal Auditor
- Finance Manager
- Controller
- Vice President, Finance
- Treasurer
- Chief Financial Officer (CFO)
- Chief Executive Officer (CEO)

To learn more about IMA and the management accounting profession, please visit Frequently Asked Questions.

1 Reprinted with permission from IMA, Montvale, N.J., "About Management Accounting" from www.imanet.org.

Figure 1-4 Users and Uses of Cost Accounting Information

Cost Accounting System
(Accumulates Cost Information)

Characteristics	Financial Accounting	Managerial Accounting
Users:	• External Parties (Shareholders, Creditors, Governments) • Managers	• Internal Parties (Managers)
Focus:	Entire Business	Segments of the Business
Uses of Cost Information:	Product Costs for Calculating Cost of Goods Sold (Income Statement) and Finished Goods, Work in Process, and Raw Materials Inventories (Balance Sheet) Using Historical Costs and Generally Accepted Accounting Principles	• Budgeting • Special Decisions Such as Make or Buy a Component, Keep or Replace a Facility, and Sell a Product at a Special Price • Nonfinancial Information Such as Defect Rates, Percentage of Products Returned, and Percentage of On-Time Deliveries (All of the Above Using a Combination of Historical Data, Estimates, and Future Projections)

Figure 1-5 Uses of Product Cost Data in Financial and Management Accounting

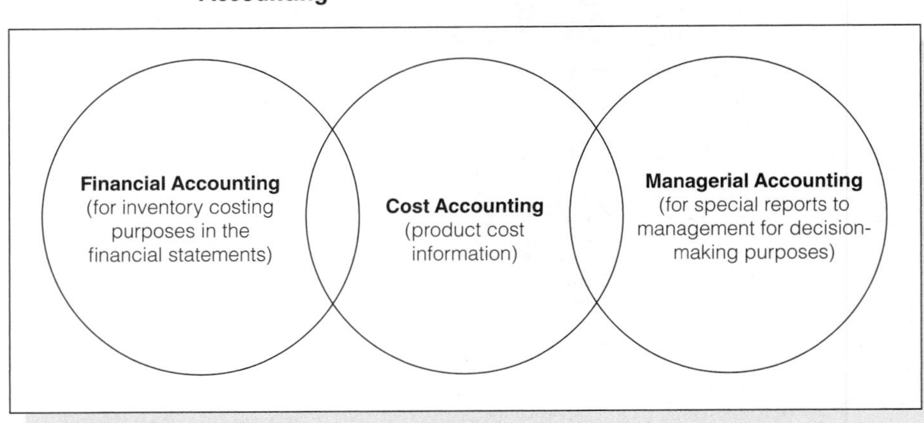

Costs of Goods Sold

Merchandising concerns compute cost of goods sold as follows (the amount of purchases represents the cost of goods acquired for resale during the period):

Beginning merchandise inventory
Plus **purchases** (merchandise)
Merchandise available for sale
Less ending merchandise inventory
Cost of goods sold

Because a manufacturer makes, rather than buys, the products it has available for sale, the term *finished goods inventory* replaces *merchandise inventory*, and the term *cost of goods manufactured* replaces *purchases* in determining the cost of goods sold, as shown below (the cost of goods manufactured amount is supported by a schedule detailing the costs of material and labor and the expenses of maintaining and operating a factory.):

Beginning finished goods inventory
Plus **cost of goods manufactured**
Finished goods available for sale
Less ending finished goods inventory
Cost of goods sold

The format of the income statement for a manufacturer is not significantly different from that of a merchandiser. However, the cost accounting procedures needed to determine the cost of goods manufactured are considerably more complex than the procedures needed to determine the cost of merchandise purchased in its finished form. Note that the income statements for service businesses do not have a cost of goods sold section, because they provide a service rather than a product.

Inventories

If a merchandiser has unsold items on hand at the end of an accounting period, the cost of the merchandise is reflected in the current assets section of the balance sheet in the following manner:

Current assets:
Cash
Accounts receivable
Merchandise inventory

On the balance sheet of a manufacturing concern, the current assets section is expanded as follows:

Current assets:
Cash
Accounts receivable
Inventories:
Finished goods
Work in process
Materials

The balance of the **finished goods** account represents the total cost incurred in manufacturing goods completed but still on hand at the end of the period. The balance of the **work in process** account includes all manufacturing costs incurred to date for goods in various stages of production but not yet completed. The balance of the **materials** account represents the cost of all materials purchased and on hand to be used in the manufacturing process, including raw materials, prefabricated parts, and other factory materials and supplies. Raw materials for one company are often the finished product of another company. For example, rolled steel to be used in the production of **Honda** Accord automobiles in its Marysville, Ohio plant would be the final product of **A.K. Steel**, the steel mill in Middletown, Ohio, but raw materials to Honda. Prefabricated parts would include units, such as electric motors, produced by another manufacturer to be used in the assembly of a product such as copying machines. Other materials and supplies might include screws, nails, rivets, lubricants, and solvents.

Service entities do not have inventories on their balance sheets because they provide a service rather than a product. A summary comparison of manufacturing, merchandising, and service businesses appears in Figure 1-6.

Valuation of Inventories. Many procedures used to gather costs are unique to manufacturers. Manufacturers' inventories are valued for external financial reporting purposes by using inventory costing methods—such as first-in, first-out (FIFO); last-in, first-out (LIFO); and moving average—that are also used by merchandisers. Most manufacturers maintain a **perpetual inventory system** that provides a continuous record of purchases, issues, and balances of all goods in stock. Generally, these data are verified by

Figure 1-6 Comparison of Service, Merchandising, and Manufacturing Businesses

Business Sector	Examples	Product or Service	Inventory Account(s)
Service	Hotels, accountants, hair stylists, sports franchises	Intangible benefits such as lodging, tax preparation, grooming, entertainment	None
Merchandising	Bookstores, electronics stores, sports memorabilia shops, beverage wholesalers	Tangible products purchased from suppliers in finished form	Merchandise inventory
Manufacturing	Segway producers, manufacturers of electronic games, home builders	Physical products created by the application of labor and technology to raw materials	Finished Goods, Work in Process, Materials

periodic counts of selected items throughout the year. Under a perpetual system, inventory valuation data for financial statement purposes are available at any time, as distinguished from a **periodic inventory system** that requires estimating inventory during the year for interim financial statements and shutting down operations to count all inventory items at the end of the year.

In addition to providing inventory valuation data for the financial statements, the detailed cost data and perpetual inventory records provide the information necessary to control inventory levels, to ensure the timely availability of materials for production, and to detect pilferage, waste, and spoilage. Inventory valuation and control are discussed in detail in Chapter 2.

Inventory Ledgers. Generally, both merchandisers and manufacturers maintain various subsidiary ledgers, such as those for accounts receivable and accounts payable. In addition, manufacturers usually maintain subsidiary ledgers for the general ledger inventory control accounts: Finished Goods; Work in Process; and Materials. These subsidiary ledgers are necessary to track the individual raw materials, jobs in process, and finished jobs on hand. They support the balances in the control accounts, as illustrated in Figure 1-7, and aid in managing the business on a daily basis.

Figure 1-7 Relationship between General and Subsidiary Ledgers

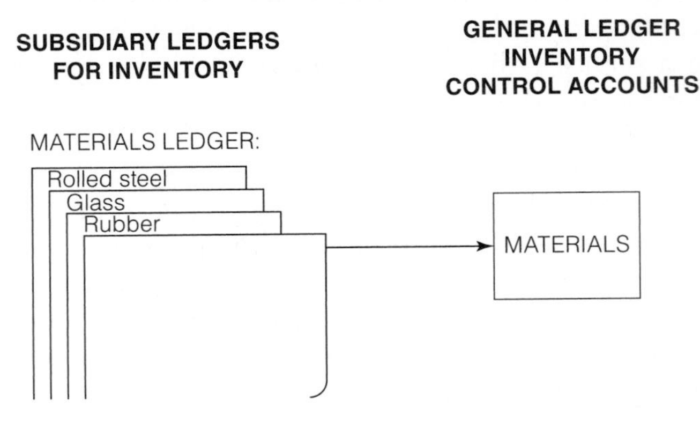

Figure 1-7 **Continued**

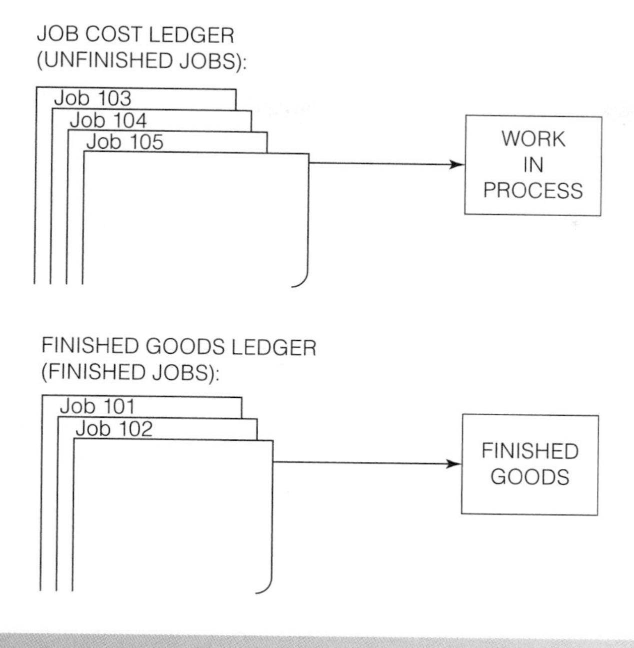

Recall and Review 1

The Recall and Review exercises are aimed at testing your understanding of a key concept in the reading before you proceed to the end-of-chapter materials. Work the exercises independently and then check your solutions at the designated pages.

Samson Manufacturing had finished goods inventory of $45,000 on March 1, March cost of goods manufactured of $228,000, and March 31 finished goods of $53,000. Compute the cost of goods sold for the month of March. $________

(After working this exercise, see page 39 for the solution.)

You should now be able to work the following:
Questions 1–21; Exercises 1-1 to 1-3; Problems 1-1 and 1-2; Mini-Case; and Internet Exercises 1 and 2.

Elements of Manufacturing Costs

Manufacturing or **production costs** are classified into three basic elements: (1) direct materials, (2) direct labor, and (3) factory overhead.

Direct Materials

The materials that become part of a certain manufactured product and can be readily identified with that product are classified as **direct materials.** Examples include lumber used in making furniture, fabric used in the production of clothing, iron ore used in the manufacture of steel products, and rubber used in the production of athletic shoes.

Many types of materials and supplies necessary for the manufacturing process either cannot be readily identified with any particular manufactured item or have a relatively insignificant cost. Items such as sandpaper used in sanding furniture, lubricants used on machinery, and other items for general factory use are classified as **indirect materials**. Similarly classified are materials that actually become part of the finished product, such as thread, screws, rivets, nails, and glue, but whose costs are relatively insignificant, making it not cost effective to trace them to specific products.

Direct Labor

The labor of employees who work directly on the product manufactured, such as machine operators or assembly-line workers, is classified as **direct labor**. The employees who are required for the manufacturing process but who do not work directly on the units being manufactured are considered **indirect labor**. This classification includes department heads, inspectors, materials handlers, and maintenance personnel. Payroll-related costs, such as payroll taxes, group insurance, sick pay, vacation and holiday pay, retirement program contributions, and other fringe benefits are usually treated as indirect costs. Some companies, however, more appropriately, treat the fringe benefits paid for direct laborers as additional direct labor cost for the purpose of more precisely determining how much each hour of direct labor really costs.

As manufacturing processes have become increasingly automated, direct labor cost as a percentage of total product cost has decreased for many companies. Harley-Davidson, the motorcycle manufacturer, stopped tracking direct labor as a separate cost category because it was only 10% of total product cost but required an inordinate amount of time to trace directly to the individual products manufactured.[3]

Factory Overhead

Factory overhead, also known as manufacturing overhead and factory burden, includes all costs related to the manufacture of a product except direct materials and direct labor. Thus, factory overhead includes the previously mentioned indirect materials and indirect labor, plus other manufacturing expenses, such as depreciation on the factory building and the machinery and equipment, heat, light, power, maintenance, insurance, and taxes. As factories have become more automated, factory overhead as a percentage of total manufacturing cost has increased dramatically.

Summary of Manufacturing Costs

The costs of direct materials and direct labor are sometimes combined and described as the **prime cost** of manufacturing a product. Prime cost plus

3 W. Turk, "Management Accounting Revitalized: The Harley-Davidson Experience," *Journal of Cost Management*, Vol. 3, No. 4, 1990, 28–39.

Figure 1-8 Prime Cost and Conversion Cost

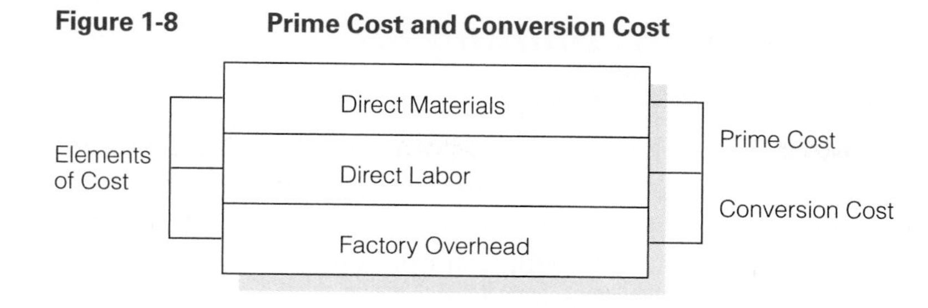

factory overhead equals the total manufacturing cost. Direct labor cost and factory overhead, which are necessary to convert the direct materials into finished goods, can be combined and described as **conversion cost**. These relationships are illustrated in Figure 1-8.

Marketing expenses, general administrative costs, and other nonfactory expenditures are not included in the costs of manufacturing. Some costs incurred by a manufacturer, however, may benefit both factory and nonfactory operations. Examples include depreciation, insurance, and property taxes on a building that houses both the factory and the administrative offices. In this situation, an allocation of cost must be made to each business function.

Flow of Costs

All three elements of manufacturing cost flow through the work in process inventory account. The costs of direct materials and direct labor used in production are charged (debited) directly to Work in Process. All other factory costs—indirect labor, indirect materials, and other factory expenses—are charged to the factory overhead account and later transferred to Work in Process. When goods are completed, the total costs incurred in producing the goods are transferred from Work in Process to Finished Goods. When goods are sold, the costs incurred to manufacture the goods are transferred from Finished Goods to Cost of Goods Sold. Figure 1-9 illustrates the flow of manufacturing costs.

Figure 1-9 Flow of Manufacturing Costs

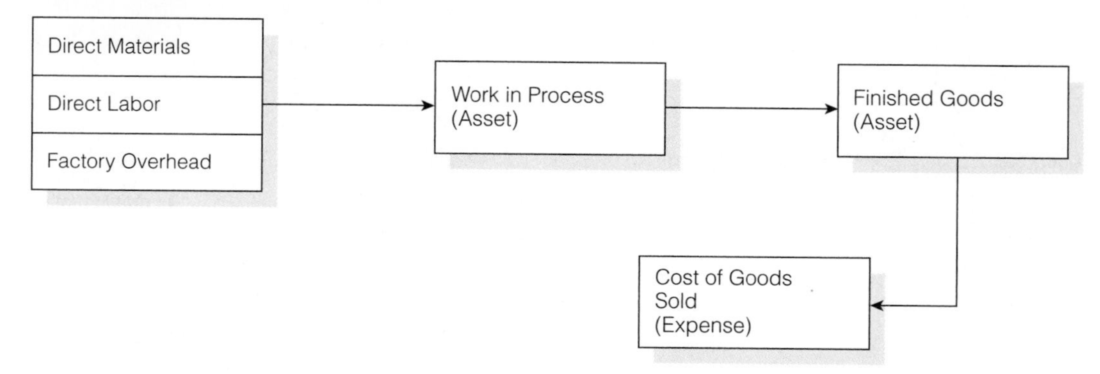

Illustration of Accounting for Manufacturing Costs

LO5 Illustrate basic cost accounting procedures.

Cost accounting procedures are used to accumulate and allocate all elements of manufacturing cost in a manner that will produce meaningful data for the internal use of management and for the preparation of external financial statements. The following example illustrates basic cost accounting procedures, utilizing the terminology and principles that were discussed previously.

Wicker Works, Inc., a small, newly organized corporation, manufactures wicker furniture—both tables and chairs. The firm sells products directly to retailers. The basic steps in the company's production process are as follows:

1. Pieces of rattan, a natural fiber grown in Asia, are purchased in precut specifications. The pieces are assembled to form the frame of the table or chair.
2. The legs and back uprights of the chair and the legs and the outline of the tabletop are then wrapped in binding cane.
3. The seat and back of the chair and the tabletop are now ready to be woven into place, and the chair or table is finished.

All of the previous steps are performed in a single department. The flow of manufacturing costs for Wicker Works is illustrated in Figure 1-10.

Figure 1-10 **Flow of Costs Related to the Production Process**

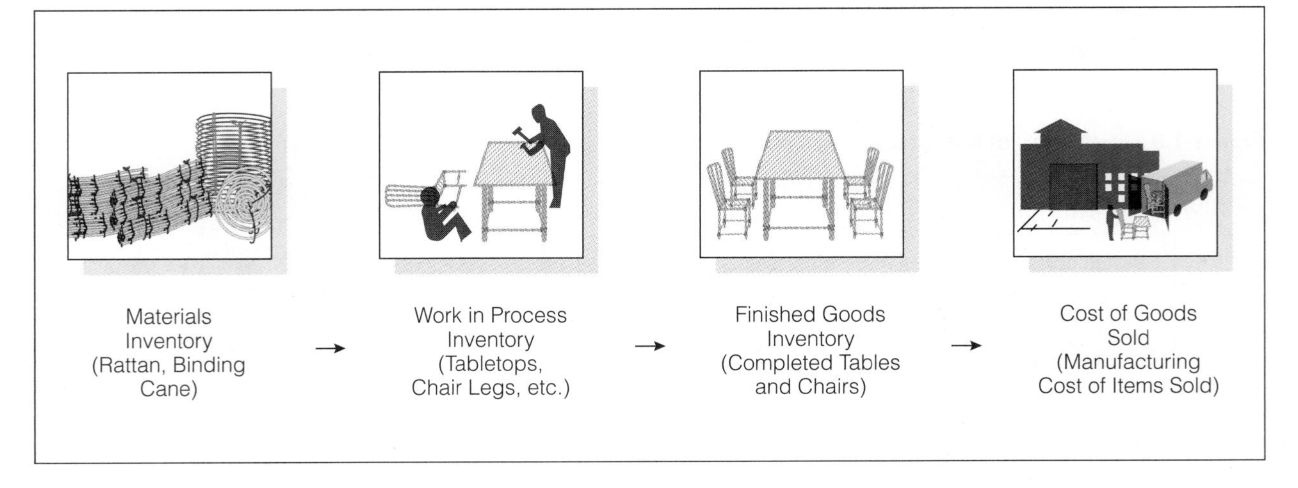

The beginning balance sheet for the company on January 1 of the current year is presented as follows:

Wicker Works, Inc.
Balance Sheet January 1, 2011

Assets		Liabilities and Stockholders' Equity	
Cash	$ 40,000	Liabilities	$ -0-
Building	250,000	Capital stock	365,000
Machinery and equipment	75,000		
Total assets	$365,000	Total liabilities and stockholders' equity	$365,000

Assume, for the purpose of simplification, in the following example, that the company is currently making only one style of table and no chairs. During January the following transactions are completed and recorded, in summary form:

1. Materials (rattan, binding cane, nails, tacks, staples, glue, and solvents) are purchased on account at a cost of $25,000.

Materials	25,000	
Accounts Payable		25,000

The cost of materials purchased on credit increases the asset account, Materials, and the liability account, Accounts Payable. Note that only a single materials control account that contains both the cost of direct and indirect materials appears in the general ledger.

2. During the month, direct materials (rattan and binding cane) costing $20,000 and indirect materials (nails, tacks, staples, glue, and solvents for cleaning) costing $995 are issued into production.

Work in Process (Direct Materials)	20,000	
Factory Overhead (Indirect Materials)	995	
Materials		20,995

Direct materials issued are charged directly to the work in process control account because they can be readily traced to the individual jobs, but the indirect materials are charged to the factory overhead account because they cannot be easily identified with specific jobs. The factory overhead account will be used to accumulate various factory expenses that will later be allocated to individual jobs using some equitable formula.

3. Total gross wages and salaries for the month were: factory employees working on the product, $10,000; factory supervision, maintenance, and custodial employees, $3,500; and sales and administrative employees, $6,500. The entries to record the payroll and the payments to employees (ignoring payroll deductions) would be as follows:

Payroll	20,000	
Wages Payable		20,000
Wages Payable	20,000	
Cash		20,000

4. The entry to distribute the payroll to the appropriate accounts would be as follows:

Work in Process (Direct Labor)	10,000	
Factory Overhead (Indirect Labor)	3,500	
Selling and Administrative Expenses (Salaries)	6,500	
Payroll		20,000

The wages earned by employees working directly on the product are charged to Work in Process, while the salaries and wages of the factory supervisor and the maintenance and custodial personnel, who do not work directly on the product, are charged to Factory Overhead as indirect labor. The salaries of nonfactory employees are debited to the selling and administrative expenses account.

In order to focus on specific cost accounting procedures as distinguished from general accounting procedures, the general ledger account Selling and Administrative Expenses will be used to accumulate all nonmanufacturing expenses. Usually, separate general ledger control accounts would be established for individual selling and administrative expenses.

5. Depreciation expense for the $250,000 building is 6% of the building cost per year. The sales and administrative offices occupy one-tenth of the total building, and the factory operation is contained in the other nine-tenths. The expense for one month is recorded as follows:

Factory Overhead (Depreciation of Building)	1,125**	
Selling and Administrative Expenses (Depreciation of Building)	125**	
Accumulated Depreciation—Building		1,250*

*($250,000 × 0.06 × 1/12 = $1,250;
**$1,250 × 0.90 = $1,125; $1,250 × 0.10 = $125)

The cost accounting principle illustrated here is that only those costs directly related to production should be charged to Factory Overhead. Depreciation on the portion of the building used for office space is an administrative expense and should not be treated as an element of manufacturing cost for inventory costing purposes.

6. Depreciation expense for the $75,000 of factory machinery and equipment is 20% of original cost per year.

Factory Overhead (Depreciation of Machinery and Equipment)	1,250	
Accumulated Depreciation—Machinery and Equipment		1,250

($75,000 × 0.20 × 1/12 = $1,250)

7. The cost of heat, light, and power for the month was $1,500.

Factory Overhead (Utilities)	1,350	
Selling and Administrative Expenses (Utilities)	150	
Accounts Payable		1,500

Because one-tenth of the building is used for office purposes, it was decided that 10% of the total utilities cost should be allocated to Selling and Administrative Expenses. If there were separate meters for each part of the building, the usage could be determined directly rather than by allocation.

8. Miscellaneous selling and administrative expenses for telephone and fax, copying charges, office supplies, travel, and rental of office furniture and equipment totaled $3,750, on account.

Selling and Administrative Expenses	3,750	
Accounts Payable		3,750

A manufacturer may incur many other expenses, but for simplicity it is assumed that Wicker Works incurred no other expenses. After posting the journal entries to the appropriate ledger accounts, Factory Overhead will reflect the following debits:

Transaction	Description	Amount
2.	Indirect materials	$ 995
4.	Indirect labor	3,500
5.	Depreciation of building	1,125
6.	Depreciation of machinery and equipment	1,250
7.	Utilities	1,350
	Total	$8,220

9. The balance in Factory Overhead is transferred to Work in Process by the following entry:

Work in Process	8,220	
Factory Overhead		8,220

The three elements of manufacturing cost—direct materials, direct labor, and factory overhead—are now accumulated in Work in Process. The debits in the account are as follows:

Transaction	Description	Amount
2.	Direct materials	$20,000
4.	Direct labor	10,000
9.	Factory overhead	8,220
	Total	$38,220

10. If we assume that all goods started in process have been finished by the end of the month, then the following entry transfers the cost of these goods from Work in Process to Finished Goods:

Finished Goods	38,220	
Work in Process		38,220

Assuming that 500 tables were produced during the month, we find that the unit cost is $76.44 ($38,220/500). The unit cost for each element of manufacturing cost is calculated as follows:

	Total	Units Produced	Unit Cost
Direct materials	$20,000	500	$40.00
Direct labor	10,000	500	20.00
Factory overhead	8,220	500	16.44
	$38,220		$76.44

If the same type of table is produced in future periods, the unit costs of those periods can be compared with the unit costs for this month. Any significant differences can be analyzed so that management might take appropriate action.

The unit cost also serves as a basis for establishing the selling price of the tables. After also considering the selling and administrative expenses, management establishes a selling price that should provide a reasonable profit. The selling price may be determined by adding a **mark-on percentage**, which is a percentage of the manufacturing cost per unit. For example, if management decides that a 50% mark-on percentage is necessary to cover the product's share of selling and administrative expenses and to earn a satisfactory profit, the selling price per unit, rounded to the nearest cent, would be calculated as follows:

Manufacturing cost	$ 76.44
Mark-on percentage (50%)	38.22
Selling price	$114.66

In later periods, owing to intense competition, it might be found that this particular item cannot be sold at a price that will be high enough to cover all of its costs and provide a normal profit margin. Through analysis of the unit costs, management might effect cost-cutting measures or perhaps even discontinue production of the item.

From this example, it is apparent that, at any given time, the cost of each item in inventory is available. It should be reemphasized that one function of cost accounting is the accurate determination of the cost of manufacturing a unit of product. This knowledge of unit cost helps management to plan and control operations and to make marketing decisions.

To continue with the example, assume that the following additional transactions take place in January:

11. Invoices of $25,000, representing costs of materials, utilities, and selling and administrative expenses, are paid.

Accounts Payable	25,000	
Cash		25,000

12. A total of 400 tables are sold to retailers at a net price of $114.66 each.

Accounts Receivable (400 × $114.66)	45,864	
Sales		45,864
Cost of Goods Sold (400 × $76.44)	30,576	
Finished Goods		30,576

13. Cash totaling $33,000 is collected on accounts receivable.

Cash	33,000	
Accounts Receivable		33,000

The accounts in the general ledger will reflect the entries as follows:

Cash

1/1 Bal.	40,000	3.	20,000
13.	33,000	11.	25,000
	73,000		*45,000*
28,000			

Accounts Receivable

12.	45,864	13.	33,000
12,864			

Finished Goods

10.	38,220	12.	30,576
7,644			

Work in Process

2. Direct materials	20,000	10.	38,220
4. Direct labor	10,000		
9. Factory overhead	8,220		
	38,220		

Materials

1.	25,000	2.	20,995
4,005			

Building

1/1 Bal.	250,000		

Accumulated Depreciation—Building

		5.	1,250

Machinery and Equipment

1/1 Bal.	75,000		

Accumulated Depreciation—Machinery and Equipment

		6.	1,250

Accounts Payable

11.	25,000	1.	25,000
		7.	1,500
		8.	3,750
			30,250
		5,250	

Wages Payable

3.	20,000	3.	20,000

Capital Stock

		1/1 Bal.	365,000

Sales

		12.	45,864

Cost of Goods Sold

12.	30,576		

Payroll

3.	20,000	4.	20,000

Factory Overhead

2. Indirect materials	995	9.	8,220
4. Indirect labor	3,500		
5. Depreciation of building	1,125		
6. Depreciation of machinery & equip.	1,250		
7. Utilities	1,350		
	8,220		

Selling and Administrative Expenses

4. Salaries	6,500		
5. Depreciation of building	125		
7. Utilities	150		
8. Other	3,750		
	10,525		

After calculating the balance of each general ledger account, the equality of the debits and credits is proven by preparing a trial balance, as follows.

Wicker Works, Inc.		
Trial Balance		
January 31, 2011		
Cash	$28,000	
Accounts Receivable	12,864	
Finished Goods	7,644*	
Work in Process	-0-	
Materials	4,005	
Building	250,000	
Accumulated Depreciation—Building		$1,250
Machinery and Equipment	75,000	
Accumulated Depreciation—Mach. and Eq.		1,250
Accounts Payable		5,250
Wages Payable		-0-
Capital Stock		365,000
Sales		45,864
Cost of Goods Sold	30,576	
Payroll	-0-	
Factory Overhead	-0-	
Selling and Administrative Expenses	10,525	
Total	$418,614	$418,614

*The finished goods control account reflects the cost of the 100 units still on hand—100 × $76.44 = $7,644.

From an analysis of the general ledger accounts and the trial balance, a statement of cost of goods manufactured, an income statement, and a balance sheet can be prepared:

Wicker Works, Inc.		
Statement of Cost of Goods Manufactured		
For the Month Ended January 31, 2011		
Direct Materials:		
Inventory, January 1	$-0-	
Purchases	25,000	
Total cost of available materials	$25,000	
Less inventory, January 31	4,005	
Cost of materials used	$20,995	
Less indirect materials used	995	
Cost of direct materials used in production		$20,000
Direct labor		10,000
Factory overhead:		
Indirect materials	$995	
Indirect labor	3,500	
Depreciation of building	1,125	
Depreciation of machinery and equipment	1,250	
Utilities	1,350	
Total factory overhead		8,220
Cost of goods manufactured during the month		$38,220

The cost of goods manufactured includes the manufacturing costs related to the goods that were finished during the period. The figures in the cost of goods manufactured statement were obtained by analyzing the appropriate general ledger accounts. The materials inventory account had no beginning balance but had an ending balance of $4,005. The amount of purchases during the period was determined by analyzing the debits to the materials account. The cost of direct materials used of $20,000 and the direct labor cost of $10,000 were obtained from the work in process account. All other items in the statement of cost of goods manufactured represent factory overhead and are determined from the factory overhead account in the general ledger. If there had been beginning or ending work in process, it would have appeared in the statement of cost of goods manufactured.

	A	B	C	D	E	F	G
1				Wicker Works, Inc.			
2				Income Statement			
3				For the Month Ended January 31, 2011			
4							
5	Net sales:						$45,864
6	Cost of goods sold:						
7		Finished goods inventory, January 1				$-0-	
8		Add cost of goods manufactured				38220	
9		Goods available for sale				$38,220	
10		Less finished goods inventory, January 31				7,644	30,576
11	Gross profit on sales:						$15,288
12	Selling and administrative expenses						10,525
13	Net income						$4,763
14							
15							

	A	B	C	D	E	F	G
1				Wicker Works, Inc.			
2				Balance Sheet			
3				January 31, 2011			
4							
5				Assets			
6	Current assets:						
7		Cash					$28,000
8		Accounts receivable					12,864
9	Inventories:						
10		Finished goods				$7,644	
11		Work in process				-0-	
12		Materials				4,005	11,649
13		Total current assets					$52,513
14	Plant and equipment:						
15		Building				$250,000	
16		Less accumulated depreciation				1,250	$248,750
17		Machinery and equipment				$75,000	
18		Less accumulated depreciation				1,250	73,750
19		Total plant and equipment					$322,500
20	Total assets						$375,013
21							
22				Liabilities and Stockholders' Equity			
23	Current liabilities:						
24		Accounts payable					$5,250
25	Stockholders' equity						
26		Capital stock				$365,000	
27		Retained earnings				4,763	
28		Total stockholders' equity					369,763
29	Total liabilities and stockholders' equity						$375,013
30							

Figure 1-11 **Flow of Costs through the Ledger Accounts**

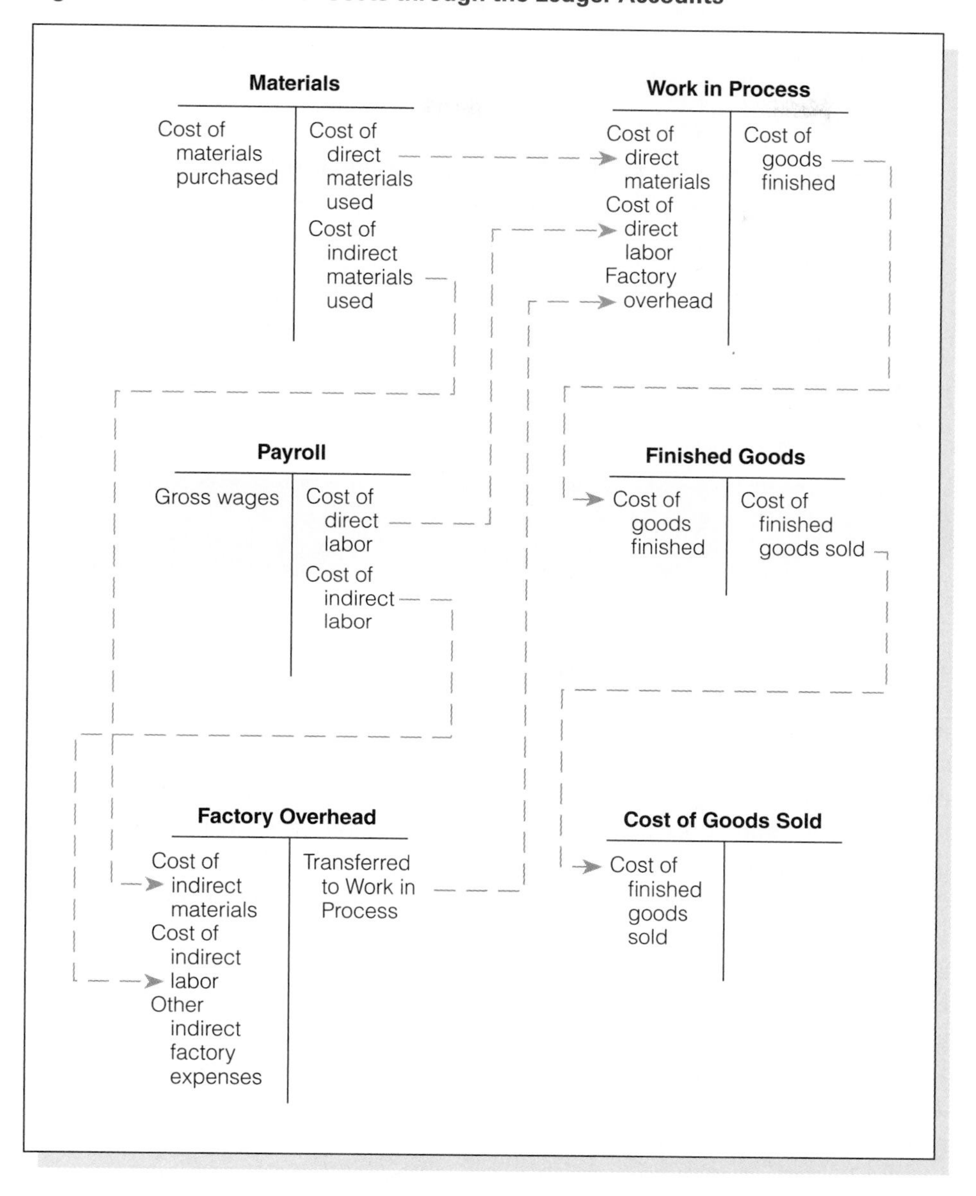

Note that the retained earnings on the balance sheet represent the amount of net income for the period, $4,763, because this was the first month of business operations.

This discussion has presented a complete cycle in cost accounting procedures. Before proceeding, carefully review the basic elements of terminology and the flow of costs. A firm grasp of the fundamentals already covered is necessary to comprehend the more complex material in subsequent chapters. Figure 1-11 presents a graphic illustration of the flow of costs through the ledger accounts. You should study this illustration carefully, following each line to trace the flow of costs.

Recall and Review 2

Classify each of the following items as direct materials (DM), direct labor (DL), factory overhead (FO), or selling and administrative expense (SA):

Electricity used in heating a factory.______________

Automobile expense for customer service representatives.______________

Wages of a bricklayer employed by a home builder.______________

Car batteries used by an automobile manufacturer.______________

Supplies used to clean the factory floor.______________

Wages of a forklift operator in a plant that makes auto parts.______________

(After working this exercise, see page 39 for the solution.)

You should now be able to work the following:
Questions 22–28; Exercises 1-4 to 1-8; Problems 1-3 to 1-7; and Self-Study Problem 1.

Cost Accounting Systems

LO6 Distinguish between the two basic types of cost accounting systems.

The previous example presented the basic foundation of a cost accounting system. In that illustration, costs were accumulated for one month. At the end of the month, the costs were divided by the total units produced to determine the cost per unit. This accomplished one function of cost accounting: the determination of product costs—both total costs for the period and unit cost. However, another important objective of a cost accounting system—cost control—could not be satisfactorily achieved with this information alone. For example, assume that in a subsequent month the cost of direct labor had risen from $20 to $22 per unit. Labor costs went up, but did they go up because of a general rise in wages or because of worker inefficiency? Did labor costs increase throughout the manufacturing process or only for a particular department or job? Answers to such questions would not be readily available using the procedures described in the earlier example.

To provide management with the data needed for effective cost control, two basic types of cost accounting systems have been developed: the process cost system and the job order cost system. Both systems are used to gather cost data and to allocate costs to goods manufactured. The selection of one method or the other depends on the type of manufacturing operation used by a given company. To determine the appropriate method, manufacturing operations are classified into two types: special order and continuous or mass production.

Special Order

In a **job order cost system** the output consists of special or custom-made products; in other words, each product is made to order. Special-order industries include those manufacturing or producing ships, aircraft, custom-

Figure 1-12 Flow of Costs in a Job Order Cost System

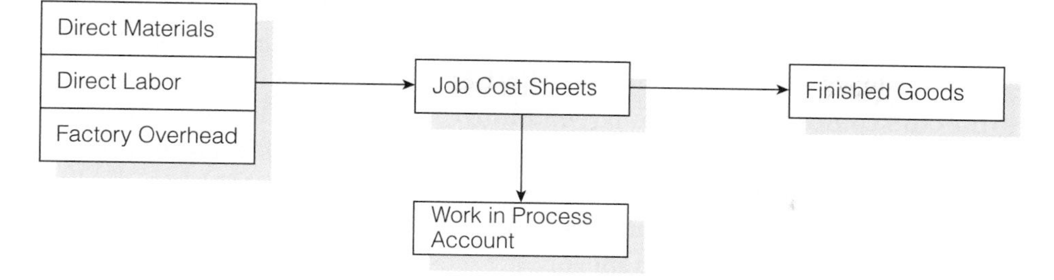

built homes, machine tools, engines, structural steel, books and magazines, directories and catalogs, and specialty shops producing custom-made products such as clothing, shoes, and hats.

A job order cost system provides a separate record for the cost of each special-order job, as illustrated by the block for "Job Cost Sheets" in Figure 1-12. Each job would have its costs tracked on a separate cost sheet or computer file. Job order cost accounting techniques are also used by firms, such as accounting, architecture, and law, that provide a service rather than a product. It is important for these firms to be able to track the various costs of serving different clients. For example, a law firm would expend many more resources defending a client in a capital murder case than it would in defending another client against petty theft charges.

Continuous or Mass Production

This type of operation produces a continuous output of homogeneous products. Such a factory may produce a single product, such as a Toyota Prius automobile, or many different products, such as Pepsi, Diet Pepsi, and Pepsi One soft drinks. The factory generally is departmentally organized. Continuous or mass production industries include those manufacturing automobiles, tires, cement, chemicals, canned goods, lumber, paper, candy, foodstuffs, flour, glass, soap, toothpaste, chewing gum, petroleum products, textiles, plastics, paints, and firms engaged in such processes as rubber compounding and vulcanizing. A **process cost system** accumulates costs for each department or process in the factory as illustrated in Figure 1-13.

Process cost accounting is appropriate for manufacturing situations in which all units of the final product are substantially identical. Wicker Works

Figure 1-13 Flow of Costs in a Process Cost System

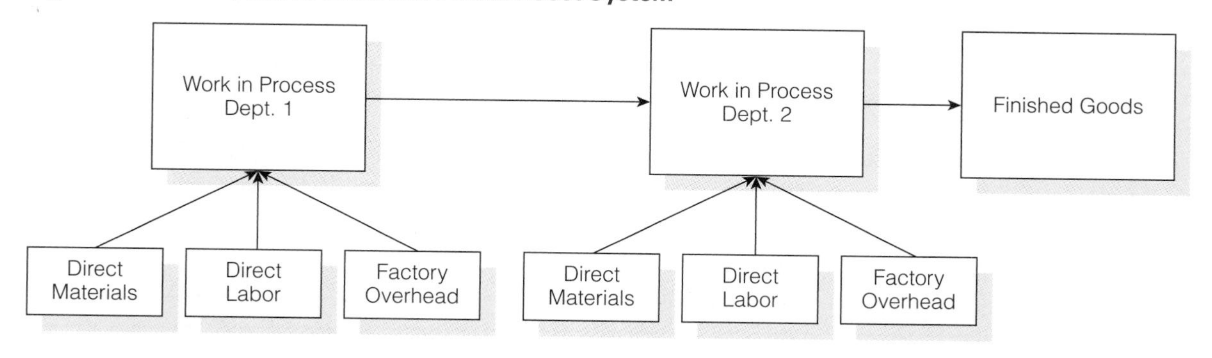

utilized a process cost system in the preceding example to account for its only product, a single style of table. Finished units are placed in stock and removed as needed to fill customer orders. There are no separate jobs presenting substantially different characteristics. Rather, the company (or a department within the company) produces large numbers of virtually identical items that are sold (or transferred to other departments) as orders are received. Process cost accounting techniques also may be used by organizations that provide a service such as for determining the cost of a particular type of MRI in a hospital's radiology department or the cost per passenger-mile for an airline. Chapters 5 and 6 cover process cost accounting. Figure 1-14 shows examples of the use of job order cost and process cost systems in service, merchandising, and manufacturing businesses.

Combination of Systems

Some companies use both a job order cost and a process cost system. For example, a company that manufactures equipment on specific order but also produces, on a continuous basis, a number of small motors that are component parts of many of the equipment orders, may benefit from combining the systems. The costs of making these motors would be accumulated on a process cost basis, while the costs for each unique piece of equipment would be gathered using job order costing. Similarly, although the cost of making a basic Toyota Prius would be tracked using process costing, the optional equipment added to an individual Prius would be tracked using job order costing.

Standard Costing

The job order and process cost accounting systems are the principal systems used by manufacturing organizations. However, as useful as they are in providing cost data, these systems are still limited with regard to cost control. Although they make it possible to determine what a product actually costs, they provide no means to determine what the product should have cost. A **standard cost system**, which is not a third system but may be used with either a job order or a process cost system, uses predetermined standard costs to furnish a measurement that helps management make decisions regarding the efficiency of operations.

Standard costs are costs that would be incurred under efficient operating conditions and are forecast before the manufacturing process begins. During operations, an organization compares the actual costs incurred with

Figure 1-14 **Uses of Cost Systems**

Cost System	Service Business	Merchandising Business	Manufacturing Business
Job Order	Accounting firm, management consultant	Lumber company, personal computer retailer	Custom home builder, printer
Process	Hospital X-ray department, hotel housekeeping	Newspaper publishing, agricultural wholesaler	Soft drink bottler, Paper producer

these predetermined standard costs. "Variances," or differences, are then calculated. These variances reveal which performances deviate from the standard, and thus they provide a basis on which management can take appropriate action to eliminate inefficient operating conditions. Standard cost accounting will be discussed in depth in Chapter 8.

Illustration of a Job Order Cost System

LO7 Illustrate a job order cost system.

With a job order cost system, costs are accumulated by job (or lot). One advantage of a job order cost system is that the accumulation of costs for a particular job helps to determine its selling price. Or, if a job is done under contract with a set price, the profit or loss on the job can be readily determined by comparing the cost with the contract price. At the same time, costs that have been accumulated for a certain type of work will assist management in preparing bids for similar jobs in the future.

To illustrate the use of a job order cost accounting system, assume that Wicker Works, Inc. is now manufacturing custom tables and chairs and that it accepts two orders to manufacture certain items during the month of February. These special orders are as follows:

1. From Strictly Wicker: to manufacture 500 chairs to their specifications; contract price, $36,000. Job No. 101 is assigned to this order.
2. From Patio Providers: to manufacture 500 tables to their specifications; contract price, $59,300. Job No. 102 is assigned to this order.

After accepting these orders and planning the manufacturing requirements as to materials, labor, and overhead, the cost accounting department sets up a job cost sheet for each job. A **job cost sheet**, also known as a job cost record in an automated accounting system, records and accumulates all the costs assigned to a specific job. Figure 1-15 illustrates this form for the Strictly Wicker order. All costs applicable to each job will be accumulated on these forms. Note that Wicker Works has changed from process costing to job order costing now that it is making custom products for specific customers.

Transactions and journal entries for the month of February appear as follows. To highlight job order cost accounting procedures, only those entries relating to the manufacture of goods will be illustrated. Routine entries, such as those for recording the purchase of materials, the incurrence of selling and administrative expenses, or payments to creditors, will be ignored. Those entries are made in the same way as previously illustrated, regardless of the cost system used.

1. Indirect materials with a cost of $5,250 are issued to the factory, and direct materials are issued as follows:

	Job 101	Job 102
Rattan	$ 8,200	$16,000
Binding Cane	4,000	2,000
	$12,200	$18,000

Figure 1-15 Job Cost Sheet

	A	B	C	D	E	F	G	H	I
1	WICKER WORKS INC.								
2	Job Cost Sheet								
3	Customer Name: Strictly Wicker						Job No: 101		
4	Address: 5525 Skyway Dr.						Date Started: 2/24/11		
5	Houston, TX 77057								
6	Quantity: 500						Date Completed: 2/28/11		
7	Product: CHAIRS								
8	Description: 39" wicker								
9									
10	DIRECT MATERIALS			DIRECT LABOR			FACTORY OVERHEAD		
11	Date	Mat'l Req. No.	Amount	Date	Time Tkt. No.	Amount	Date	Basis Applied	Amount
12									
13	2/24	5505	8,200	2/25	2101	2,500		40% of	
14	2/26	6211	4,000	2/27	2826	1,500		total	
15				2/28	3902	2,000	2/28	over-head	5,262
16									
17	Total		12,200			6,000			5,262
18	SUMMARY						Remarks:		
19	Direct materials		$12,200	Selling price		$36,000			
20	Direct labor		6,000	Mfg. cost		23,462			
21	Factory overhead		5,262	Gross profit		$12,538			
22	Total cost		$23,462						
23	Unit cost		$ 46.92						

The entry at the end of the month to record the issues of materials appears as:

Work in Process (Jobs 101 and 102)	30,200	
Factory Overhead (Indirect Materials)	5,250	
Materials		35,450

Note that in the previous entry the $30,200 debit to Work in Process comprises $12,200 of direct materials issued to Job 101 and $18,000 of direct materials issued to Job 102. There is only one general ledger work in process account, but the individual amounts of direct materials issued to each job would appear on the respective job cost sheets in the subsidiary job cost ledger.

If the indirect materials could be directly traced to a specific job, the cost could be charged to that job. However, it is often difficult and not cost effective to determine which job benefited from the use of various supplies such as glue, nails, and cleaning fluid. Thus, indirect materials costs are usually charged to Factory Overhead and later distributed among the various jobs in some equitable way.

2. Indirect labor costs of $4,360 and direct labor costs are incurred as follows:

	Job 101	Job 102
Direct Labor	$6,000	$7,500

The monthly entry to distribute these costs is recorded as follows:

Work in Process (Jobs 101 and 102)	13,500	
Factory Overhead (Indirect Labor)	4,360	
Payroll		17,860

The debit of $13,500 to Work in Process comprises $6,000 of direct labor issued to Job 101 and $7,500 of direct labor issued to Job 102. The explanation for why indirect labor costs are charged to Factory Overhead rather than to Work in Process is similar to the previous explanation for indirect materials.

3. Monthly depreciation expense for the building, allocated according to the square footage used by manufacturing (90%) and selling and administrative (10%), is recorded as follows:

Factory Overhead (Depreciation of Building)	1,125	
Selling and Administrative Expenses (Depreciation of Building) . . .	125	
Accumulated Depreciation—Building		1,250

4. The entry to record monthly depreciation for machinery and equipment, all of which is used for manufacturing operations, is recorded as follows:

Factory Overhead (Depreciation of Machinery and Equipment)	1,250	
Accumulated Depreciation—Machinery and Equipment		1,250

5. The cost of utilities for the month of February is $1,300, again allocated by building square footage, recorded as follows:

Factory Overhead (Utilities)	1,170	
Selling and Administrative Expenses (Utilities)	130	
Accounts Payable		1,300

6. Total charges to Factory Overhead for the month are shown as follows:

Indirect materials	$ 5,250
Indirect labor	4,360
Depreciation of building	1,125
Depreciation of machinery and equipment	1,250
Utilities	1,170
Total	$13,155

Assume that Jobs 101 and 102 are the only jobs worked on during the period and that factory overhead is allocated as follows: 60% to Job 101, 40% to Job 102.

	40%	**60%**
Total Factory Overhead	**Job 101**	**Job 102**
$13,155	$5,262	$7,893

The distribution of factory overhead would then be recorded as follows:

Work in Process (Jobs 101 and 102)	13,155	
Factory Overhead		13,155

The debit of $13,155 to Work in Process comprises $5,262 of overhead allocated to Job 101 and $7,893 of overhead charged to Job 102. At the end of the month, the work in process and factory overhead accounts would appear as follows:

Work in Process

1. Direct materials	30,200		
2. Direct labor	13,500		
6. Factory overhead	13,155		
	56,855		

Factory Overhead

1. Indirect materials	5,250	6. Transfer to Work in Process	13,155
2. Indirect labor	4,360		
3. Depreciation of building	1,125		
4. Depreciation of mach. and equip.	1,250		
5. Utilities	1,170		
	13,155		

The costs shown in the work in process account represent monthly totals (summary entries) for each element of manufacturing cost for both jobs combined. These same costs are shown for each individual job in a **job cost ledger**. It is a subsidiary ledger that has a record of each job. The details on the job cost sheets in the job cost ledger support the balance of the work in process control account in the general ledger.

7. Assuming that both jobs were completed by the end of the month, the costs of the completed jobs would be transferred to the finished goods inventory control account:

Finished Goods	56,855	
Work in Process		56,855

8. When the goods are shipped and billed to the customers, the following entries are made to record the sale and the cost of the jobs:

Accounts Receivable	95,300	
Sales		95,300
Cost of Goods Sold	56,855	
Finished Goods		56,855

The costs of producing the two jobs can be summarized as follows:

	Job 101 (500 Chairs)		Job 102 (500 Tables)	
	Total Cost	**Unit Cost**	**Total Cost**	**Unit Cost**
Direct materials	$12,200	$24.40	$18,000	$36.00
Direct labor	6,000	12.00	7, 500	15.50
Factory overhead	5,262	10.52	7,893	15.79
Total	$23,462	$46.92	$33.393	$67.29

The gross profit realized on each job is determined as follows:

	Job 101 (500 Chairs)		Job 102 (500 Tables)	
	Total	Per Unit	Total	Per Unit
Selling price	$36,000	$72.00	$59,300	$118.60
Cost	23,462	46.92	33,393	67.29
Gross profit	$12,538	$25.08	$25,907	$ 51.31

The job cost sheets would reflect the previous information in more detail, so that a short time after each job was completed, the gross profit could be determined. In addition, if management bids on similar jobs in the future, an accurate record of all costs would be available to assist management in determining contract prices.

Work in Process in the Manufacturing Statement

If there is work in process at the beginning and at the end of the month, it will be shown in the statement of cost of goods manufactured. To illustrate, assume that Wicker Works, Inc.'s statement for June is as follows:

	A–E	F	G
1	**Wicker Works, Inc.**		
2	**Statement of Cost of Goods Manufactured**		
3	**For the Month Ended June 30, 2011**		
4			
5	Direct Materials:		
6	Inventory, June 1	$15,000	
7	Purchases	310,000	
8	Total cost of available materials	$325,000	
9	Less inventory, June 30	25,000	
10	Cost of materials used	$300,000	
11	Less indirect materials used	10,000	
12	Cost of direct materials used in production		$290,000
13	Direct labor		240,000
14	Factory overhead:		
15	Indirect materials	$10,000	
16	Indirect labor	47,000	
17	Depreciation of building	35,000	
18	Depreciation of machinery and equipment	15,000	
19	Utilities	23,000	
20	Total factory overhead		130,000
21	Total manufacturing cost during the month		$660,000
22	**Add work in process inventory, June 1**		**85,000**
23			$745,000
24	**Less work in process inventory, June 30**		**125,000**
25	Cost of goods manufactured during the month		$620,000
26			
27			

In the above statement of cost of goods manufactured, the total manufacturing cost of $660,000 represents the cost of direct materials, direct labor, and factory overhead used during the month of June. Wicker Works, Inc., incurred costs of $85,000 during the previous month for goods that were not completed at the end of that month. The cost of these goods constitutes June's beginning work in process. The total of $745,000 represents manufacturing cost that the company must account for. Work in Process at the end of June is $125,000, which represents the cost incurred to date for items that were not finished at the end of June. Therefore, the cost of goods manufactured (completed) in June, some of which were started in production the previous month, is $620,000. The work in process ledger account, in T-account form, would appear as follows at the end of the month:

Work in Process

6/1 Balance	85,000	To Finished Goods	620,000
Direct materials	290,000		
Direct labor	240,000		
Factory overhead	130,000		
	745,000		
125,000			

Recall and Review 3

The following information was taken from the books of Sunrise Manufacturing after all postings had been completed at the end of July, its first month of operations: direct materials cost, $7,200; direct labor cost, $8,000; factory overhead, consisted of indirect materials of $1,800 and indirect labor of $1,400. All jobs worked on during the month were completed and sold by the end of the month. Prepare the journal entries to: (1) charge the July cost of materials to work in process and factory overhead; (2) charge the July cost of labor to work in process and factory overhead; (3) record the closing of factory overhead to work in process; and (4) record the completion of all jobs.

(After working this exercise, see page 40 for the solution.)

You should now be able to work the following:
Questions 29–34; Exercises 1-9 and 1-10; Problems 1-8 to 1-10; and Self-Study Problem 2.

Appendix

IMA Statement of Ethical Professional Practice

Members of IMA shall behave ethically. A commitment to ethical professional practice includes: overarching principles that express our values, and standards that guide our conduct.

PRINCIPLES

IMA's overarching ethical principles include: Honesty, Fairness, Objectivity, and Responsibility. Members shall act in accordance with these principles and shall encourage others within their organizations to adhere to them.

STANDARDS

A member's failure to comply with the following standards may result in disciplinary action.

I. Competence

Each member has a responsibility to:

1. Maintain an appropriate level of professional expertise by continually developing knowledge and skills.
2. Perform professional duties in accordance with relevant laws, regulations, and technical standards.
3. Provide decision support information and recommendations that are accurate, clear, concise, and timely.
4. Recognize and communicate professional limitations or other constraints that would preclude responsible judgment or successful performance of an activity.

II. Confidentiality

Each member has a responsibility to:

1. Keep information confidential except when disclosure is authorized or legally required.
2. Inform all relevant parties regarding appropriate use of confidential information. Monitor subordinates' activities to ensure compliance.
3. Refrain from using confidential information for unethical or illegal advantage.

III. Integrity

Each member has a responsibility to:

1. Mitigate actual conflicts of interest. Regularly communicate with business associates to avoid apparent conflicts of interest. Advise all parties of any potential conflicts.
2. Refrain from engaging in any conduct that would prejudice carrying out duties ethically.
3. Abstain from engaging in or supporting any activity that might discredit the profession.

IV. Credibility

Each member has a responsibility to:

1. Communicate information fairly and objectively.
2. Disclose all relevant information that could reasonably be expected to influence an intended user's understanding of the reports, analyses, or recommendations.

3. Disclose delays or deficiencies in information, timeliness, processing, or internal controls in conformance with organization policy and/or applicable law.

RESOLUTION OF ETHICAL CONFLICT

In applying the Standards of Ethical Professional Practice, you may encounter problems identifying unethical behavior or resolving an ethical conflict. When faced with ethical issues, you should follow your organization's established policies on the resolution of such conflict. If these policies do not resolve the ethical conflict, you should consider the following courses of action:

1. Discuss the issue with your immediate supervisor except when it appears that the supervisor is involved. In that case, present the issue to the next level. If you cannot achieve a satisfactory resolution, submit the issue to the next management level. If your immediate superior is the chief executive officer or equivalent, the acceptable reviewing authority may be a group such as the audit committee, executive committee, board of directors, board of trustees, or owners. Contact with levels above the immediate superior should be initiated only with your superior's knowledge, assuming he or she is not involved. Communication of such problems to authorities or individuals not employed or engaged by the organization is not considered appropriate, unless you believe there is a clear violation of the law.
2. Clarify relevant ethical issues by initiating a confidential discussion with an IMA Ethics Counselor or other impartial advisor to obtain a better understanding of possible courses of action.
3. Consult your own attorney as to legal obligations and rights concerning the ethical conflict.

Source: Institute of Management Accountants, "IMA's Statement of Ethical Professional Practice," www.imanet.org.

KEY TERMS

Accounting information systems, 2
Budget, 6
Control, 5
Conversion cost, 17
Corporate governance, 9
Cost accounting systems, 2
Cost accounting, 2
Cost and production reports, 6
Cost center, 5
Direct labor, 16
Direct materials, 15
Factory overhead, 16
Financial accounting, 10
Finished goods, 13
For-profit service businesses, 2
Indirect labor, 16
Indirect materials, 16
ISO 9000 family, 3
Job cost ledger, 34
Job cost sheet, 31
Job order cost system, 28
Loss leader, 5

ANSWERS TO RECALL AND REVIEW EXERCISES

R&R 1

Finished goods inventory 3/1	$ 45,000
Cost of goods manufactured	228,000
Finished goods available for sale	$ 273,000
Finished goods inventory 3/31	53,000
Cost of goods sold	$ 220,000

R&R 2

Item	Direct Materials	Direct Labor	Factory Overhead	Selling and Administrative
Electricity used in heating factory			X	
Automobile expense for customer service reps.				X
Wages of a bricklayer employed by a home builder		X		
Car batteries used by an automobile manufacturer	X			
Supplies used to clean the factory floor			X	
Wages of a forklift operator in a plant that makes auto parts			X	

R&R 3

Work in Process	7,200	
Factory Overhead	1,800	
Materials		9,000
Work in Process	8,000	
Factory Overhead	1,400	
Payroll		9,400
Work in Process	3,200	
Factory Overhead		3,200
Finished Goods	18,400	
Work in Process		18,400

SELF-STUDY PROBLEM 1

Basic Cost System; Journal Entries; Financial Statements

Lone Star Manufacturing Co.

The post-closing trial balance of Lone Star Manufacturing Co. at September 30 is reproduced as follows.

Lone Star Manufacturing Co.
Post-Closing Trial Balance
September 30, 2011

Cash	15,000	
Accounts Receivable	18,000	
Finished Goods	25,000	
Work in Process	4,000	
Materials	8,000	
Building	156,000	
Accumulated Depreciation—Building		23,400
Factory Equipment	108,000	
Accumulated Depreciation—Factory Equipment		54,000
Office Equipment	12,000	
Accumulated Depreciation—Office Equipment		2,000
Accounts Payable		30,000
Capital Stock		175,000
Retained Earnings		61,600
	346,000	346,000

During the month of October, the following transactions took place:

a. Raw materials at a cost of $50,000 and general factory supplies costing $8,000 were purchased on account. (Materials and supplies are recorded in the materials account.)
b. Raw materials to be used in production costing $41,000 and miscellaneous factory supplies costing $5,500 were issued.
c. Wages and salaries incurred and paid for the month were as follows: factory wages (including $2,500 indirect labor), $34,000, and selling and administrative salaries, $5,000. (Ignore payroll withholdings and deductions.)
d. Distributed the payroll in (c).
e. Depreciation was recorded for the month at an annual rate of 5% on the building and 20% on the factory equipment and office equipment. The sales and administrative staff uses approximately one-fifth of the building for its offices.
f. During the month, various other expenses totaling $5,200 were incurred on account. The company has determined that one-fourth of this amount is allocable to the office function.
g. Total factory overhead costs were transferred to Work in Process.
h. During the month, goods with a total cost of $79,000 were completed and transferred to the finished goods storeroom.
i. Sales for the month totaled $128,000 for goods costing $87,000 to manufacture. (Assume that all sales were made on account.)
j. Accounts receivable in the amount of $105,000 were collected.
k. Accounts payable totaling $55,000 were paid.

Required:

1. Prepare journal entries to record the transactions.
2. Set up T-accounts for all accounts listed in the September 30, 2011, Post-Closing Trial Balance and for Cost of Goods Sold, Factory Overhead, Selling and Administrative Expenses, Sales, and Wages Payable. Post the beginning trial balance and the journal entries prepared in Part 1 to the accounts and calculate the balances in the accounts on October 31.
3. Prepare a statement of cost of goods manufactured, an income statement, and a balance sheet.

SOLUTION TO SELF-STUDY PROBLEM

Suggestions:

Read the entire problem thoroughly, keeping in mind what you are required to do:

1. Journalize the transactions.
2. Post the beginning trial balance and the journal entries to the T-accounts that you set up and calculate the ending balance for each account.
3. Using the ending account balances, prepare a cost of goods manufactured statement, an income statement, and a balance sheet.

The Specifics in the Problem Highlight the Following Facts:

1. The company is a manufacturer; therefore, three inventory accounts, Materials, Work in Process, and Finished Goods, will be used.
2. A temporary account, Factory Overhead, will be used to record all of the indirect materials, indirect labor, and other manufacturing expenses for the period.

Preparing the Journal Entries:

a. and **b.** Note that there is only one inventory account for materials, which includes the cost of both direct and indirect materials. When the materials are issued into production, the direct materials are charged to Work in Process and the indirect materials are charged to Factory Overhead.

a. Materials	58,000	
Accounts Payable		58,000
b. Work in Process	41,000	
Factory Overhead (Indirect Materials)	5,500	
Materials		46,500

c. The entries to record the payroll and the payments to employees use the payroll and wages payable accounts.

Payroll	39,000	
Wages Payable		39,000
Wages Payable	39,000	
Cash		39,000

d. The entry to distribute the payroll requires the use of the work in process account for the wages of employees who work directly on the product, the factory overhead account for the wages of employees who work in the factory but not directly on the product, and the selling and administrative expenses account for the wages of salespeople and administrative personnel.

Work in Process	31,500	
Factory Overhead (Indirect Labor)	2,500	
Selling and Administrative Expenses (Salaries)	5,000	
Payroll		39,000

e., f., and **g.** The depreciation on the building and equipment and the other expenses are divided between Factory Overhead and Selling and Administrative Expenses, depending on the portion of the expense that relates to the factory and the portion that relates to the selling and administrative function. The balance in the factory overhead account at the end of the month is transferred to Work in Process.

e. Factory Overhead (Depreciation of Building)	520
Factory Overhead (Depreciation of Factory Equipment)	1,800
Selling and Administrative Expenses (Depreciation of Building)	130

Selling and Administrative Expenses (Depreciation of Office Equipment)	200	
Accumulated Depreciation—Building		650
Accumulated Depreciation—Factory Equipment		1,800
Accumulated Depreciation—Office Equipment		200
f. Factory Overhead (Miscellaneous)	3,900	
Selling and Administrative Expenses (Miscellaneous)	1,300	
Accounts Payable		5,200
g. Work in Process	14,220	
Factory Overhead		14,220

h., i., j., and **k.** When goods are completed, the cost of the goods is taken out of Work in Process and recorded in Finished Goods. When the completed goods are sold, the cost of these goods is removed from the finished goods inventory account and recorded in the cost of goods sold expense account, the receivable and revenue are recorded for the amount of the sale, and accounts payable are paid.

h. Finished Goods	79,000	
Work in Process		79,000
i. Accounts Receivable	128,000	
Sales		128,000
Cost of Goods Sold	87,000	
Finished Goods		87,000
j. Cash	105,000	
Accounts Receivable		105,000
k. Accounts Payable	55,000	
Cash		55,000

Posting the Beginning Trial Balance and the Journal Entries to the T-Accounts:

Cash

9/30	15,000	c.	39,000
j.	105,000	k.	55,000
	120,000		
26,000			

Accounts Receivable

9/30	18,000	j.	105,000
i.	128,000		
	146,000		
41,000			

Finished Goods

9/30	25,000	i.	87,000
h.	79,000		
	104,000		
17,000			

Work in Process

9/30	4,000	h.	79,000
b.	41,000		
d.	31,500		
g.	14,220		
	90,720		
11,720			

Materials

9/30	8,000	b.	46,500
a.	58,000		
	66,000		
19,500			

Building

9/30	156,000		

Accumulated Depreciation—Building

		9/30	23,400
		e.	650
			24,050

Factory Equipment

9/30	108,000		

Accumulated Depreciation—Factory Equipment

		9/30	54,000
		e.	1,800
			55,800

Office Equipment

9/30	12,000		

Accumulated Depreciation—Office Equipment

		9/30	2,000
		e.	200
			2,200

Accounts Payable

k.	55,000	9/30	30,000
		a.	58,000
		f.	5,200
			93,200
		38,200	

Wages Payable

c.	39,000	c.	39,000

Capital Stock

		9/30	175,000

Retained Earnings

		9/30	61,600

Sales

		i.	128,000

Cost of Goods Sold

i.	87,000		

Payroll

c.	39,000	d.	39,000

Factory Overhead			
b.	5,500	g.	14,220
d.	2,500		
e.	520		
e.	1,800		
f.	3,900		
	14,220		

Selling and Administrative Expenses		
d.	5,000	
e.	130	
e.	200	
f.	1,300	
	6,630	

Preparing a Statement of Cost of Goods Manufactured, an Income Statement, and a Balance Sheet:
The total manufacturing cost of $86,720 represents the cost of direct materials, direct labor, and factory overhead incurred during the month of October. Note that the cost of the indirect materials is subtracted in calculating the cost of direct materials used in production because it is included as a separate item under factory overhead. To determine the cost of goods manufactured for October, which really means the cost of the goods completed for the month, you have to add the cost of the beginning work in process inventory, $4,000, and subtract the cost of the ending work in process inventory, $11,720, from the total manufacturing cost for October:

Lone Star Manufacturing Co.
Statement of Cost of Goods Manufactured
For the Month Ended October 31, 2011

Direct materials:		
Inventory, October 1	$ 8,000	
Purchases	58,000	
Total cost of available materials	$66,000	
Less inventory, October 31	19,500	
Cost of materials used	$46,500	
Less indirect materials used	5,500	
Cost of direct materials used in production		$41,000
Direct labor		31,500
Factory overhead:		
Indirect materials	$ 5,500	
Indirect labor	2,500	
Depreciation of building	520	
Depreciation of factory equipment	1,800	
Miscellaneous expenses	3,900	
Total factory overhead		14,220
Total manufacturing cost during October		$86,720
Add work in process inventory, October 1		4,000
		$90,720
Less work in process inventory, October 31		11,720
Cost of goods manufactured		$79,000

In preparing an income statement for a manufacturer, remember that the beginning finished goods inventory for the month must be added to the cost of goods manufactured to obtain the cost of goods available for sale. Then the ending finished goods inventory must be subtracted to obtain the cost of goods sold:

Lone Star Manufacturing Co.
Income Statement
For the Month Ended October 31, 2011

Net sales		$128,000
Cost of goods sold:		
Finished goods inventory, October 1	$ 25,000	
Add cost of goods manufactured	79,000	
Goods available for sale	$104,000	
Less finished goods inventory, October 31	17,000	87,000
Gross profit on sales		$ 41,000
Selling and administrative expenses:		
Selling and administrative salaries	$ 5,000	
Depreciation of building	130	
Depreciation of office equipment	200	
Miscellaneous	1,300	6,630
Net income		$ 34,370

In preparing a balance sheet for a manufacturer, note that there are three separate inventory accounts, rather than the single inventory account used by a merchandiser:

Lone Star Manufacturing Co.
Balance Sheet
October 31, 2011

Assets

Current assets:			
Cash			$ 26,000
Accounts receivable			41,000
Inventories:			
Finished goods		$ 17,000	
Work in process		11,720	
Materials		19,500	48,220
Total current assets			$115,220
Plant and equipment:			
Building	$156,000		
Less accumulated depreciation	24,050	$131,950	
Factory equipment	$108,000		
Less accumulated depreciation	55,800	52,200	
Office equipment	$ 12,000		
Less accumulated depreciation	2,200	9,800	
Total plant and equipment			193,950
Total assets			$309,170

Liabilities and Stockholders' Equity

Current liabilities:		
Accounts payable		$ 38,200
Stockholders' equity:		
Capital stock	$175,000	
Retained earnings*	95,970	
Total stockholders' equity		270,970
Total liabilities and stockholders' equity		$309,170

*$61,600 (bal. on 9/30) + $34,370 (Net income for Oct.) = $95,970

SELF-STUDY PROBLEM 2

Job Cost; Journal Entries; Inventory Analysis; Manufacturing Statement

Mesa Manufacturing Co. manufactures engines that are made only on customers' orders and to their specifications. During January, the company worked on Jobs 2525, 2526, 2527, and 2528. The following figures summarize the cost records for the month:

	Job 2525 (200 units)	Job 2526 (120 units)	Job 2527 (50 units)	Job 2528 (200 units)
Direct materials put into process:				
July 2	$ 30,000	$10,000	—	—
18	40,000	32,000	$10,000	—
22	30,000	2,000	20,000	$12,000
28	—	—	7,000	4,000
Direct labor cost (week ending):				
July 2	$ 2,000	$ 2,000	—	—
9	54,000	18,000	—	—
16	64,000	54,000	—	—
23	40,000	6,000	$10,000	$ 1,000
30	—	—	36,000	23,000
Factory overhead	$120,000	$64,000	$35,000	$21,000
Engines completed	100	60	25	—

Jobs 2525 and 2526 have been completed and delivered to the customers at a total selling price of $852,000, on account. Job 2527 is finished but has not yet been delivered. Job 2528 is still in process. There was no work in process at the beginning of the month.

Required:

1. Prepare the summary journal entries for the month to record the distribution of materials, labor, and overhead costs.

2. Prepare a summary showing the total cost of each job completed during the month or in process at the end of the month. Also, determine the cost of the inventories of completed engines and engines in process at the end of the month.
3. Prepare the journal entries to record the completion of the jobs and the sale of the jobs.
4. Prepare a statement of cost of goods manufactured.

SOLUTION TO SELF-STUDY PROBLEM

Read the entire problem thoroughly, keeping in mind what you are required to do:

1. Prepare the summary journal entries to record the distribution of materials, labor, and overhead costs.
2. Prepare a summary that shows the total cost of each job and then determine the cost of the end-of-month finished goods and work in process inventories.
3. Journalize the cost and sales price of the completed jobs.
4. Prepare a statement of cost of goods manufactured for the month of January.

The Specifics in the Problem Highlight the following Facts:

1. The company is a manufacturer; therefore, three inventory accounts, Materials, Work in Process, and Finished Goods, will be used.
2. Four jobs were in process during the month: three of which were finished (Jobs 2525, 2526, and 2527); two of which were sold (Jobs 2525 and 2526); and one of which was still in process at the end of the month (Job 2528).

1. Preparing the Journal Entries:

The cost of direct materials issued to production increases the inventory account, work in process, and decreases the inventory account, materials:

Work in Process	197,000	
Materials		197,000

The cost of direct labor worked during the period also increases the inventory account, work in process:

Work in Process	310,000	
Payroll		310,000

The cost of factory overhead incurred during the period is allocated to the various jobs and summarized in work in process:

Work in Process	240,000	
Factory Overhead		240,000

2. Prepare a Summary Showing the Total Cost of each Job

Job	Direct Materials Cost	Direct Labor Cost	Factory Overhead	Total Production Cost
2525	$100,000	$160,000	$120,000	$380,000
2526	44,000	80,000	64,000	188,000
2527	37,000	46,000	35,000	118,000
2528	16,000	24,000	21,000	61,000
Total	$197,000	$310,000	$240,000	$747,000

The cost of direct materials issued to production increase the inventory account, work in process, and decreases the inventory account, materials:

Determine the Cost of The Ending Finished Goods and Work in Process Inventories

Job 2527 was completed but not sold by the end of the month:

Finished Goods Inventory (Job 2527)	$118,000

Job 2528 was the only job that was still in process at the end of the month:

Work in Process Inventory (Job 2528)	$ 61,000

3. Journalize the Cost of Jobs Finished and the Cost and Sales Price of Jobs Sold

Finished Goods	686,000	
Work in Process (Jobs 2525, 2526, 2527)		686,000
Accounts Receivable	852,000	
Sales (Jobs 2525 and 2526)		852,000
Cost of Goods Sold (Jobs 2525 and 2526)	568,000	
Finished Goods		568,000

4. Preparing a Statement of Cost of Goods Manufactured

The total manufacturing cost of $747,000 represents the cost of direct materials, direct labor, and factory overhead incurred during the month of January. To determine the cost of goods manufactured for January, which really means the cost of the goods completed for the month, you have to subtract the cost of the ending work in process inventory of $61,000. (There was no beginning work in process inventory.)

Mesa Manufacturing Co.
Statement of Cost of Goods Manufactured
For the Month Ended January 31, 2011

Direct materials used	$197,000
Direct labor	310,000
Factory overhead	240,000
Total manufacturing cost	$747,000
Less work in process inventory, January 31	61,000
Cost of goods manufactured	$686,000

QUESTIONS

1. How does the cost accounting function assist in the management of a business?
2. What is ISO 9000, and why is it an important designation for competing globally?
3. How do the activities of manufacturers, merchandisers, and service businesses differ?
4. In what ways does a typical manufacturing business differ from a merchandising concern? In what ways are they similar?
5. How is cost accounting information used by management?
6. Why is unit cost information important to management?
7. For a manufacturer, what does the planning process involve, and how is cost accounting information used in planning?
8. How is effective control achieved in a manufacturing concern?
9. Define "responsibility accounting."
10. What criteria must be met for a unit of activity within the factory to qualify as a cost center?
11. What are the requirements for becoming a Certified Management Accountant?
12. What are the four major categories of ethical conduct that must be adhered to by CMAs? (Appendix)
13. What actions should a CMA take when the established policies of the organization do not resolve an ethical conflict? (Appendix)
14. Define the term *corporate governance* and explain why good corporate governance is important to shareholders and other corporate stakeholders.
15. What circumstances created the need for the Sarbanes-Oxley Act, and how are CEOs and CFOs affected by it?
16. Name five key elements of the Sarbanes-Oxley Act.
17. How is cost accounting related to: financial accounting?; managerial accounting?
18. How does the computation of cost of goods sold for a manufacturer differ from that of a merchandiser?
19. How would you describe the following accounts—Finished Goods, Work in Process, and Materials?
20. Compare the manufacturing, merchandising, and service sectors. How do they differ as to the kinds of businesses in each category, the nature of their output, and type of inventory, if any?
21. What is the difference between a perpetual inventory system and a periodic inventory system?
22. What are the basic elements of production cost?
23. How would you define the following costs: direct materials, indirect materials, direct labor, indirect labor, and factory overhead?
24. Distinguish prime cost from conversion cost. Does prime cost plus conversion cost equal the total manufacturing cost?
25. In what way does the accounting treatment of factory overhead differ from that of direct materials and direct labor costs?
26. How do "cost of goods sold" and "cost of goods manufactured" differ for a manufacturer?
27. How are nonfactory costs and costs that benefit both factory and nonfactory operations accounted for?
28. What is a mark-on percentage?
29. When is job order costing appropriate, and what types of businesses use it?

30. When is process costing appropriate, and what types of businesses use it?
31. What are the advantages of accumulating costs by departments or jobs rather than for the factory as a whole?
32. What is a job cost sheet, and why is it useful?
33. What are standard costs, and what is the purpose of a standard cost system?
34. If the factory operations and selling and administrative offices are housed in the same building, what would be a good cost allocation basis to use in dividing the depreciation expense between the two areas? Why would it be important to make this allocation?

EXERCISES

E1-1 **Performance report**

LO0

Study the performance report for Leonardo's Italian Café in Figure 1-2 of the chapter and write a brief explanation of the strengths and weaknesses of September and year-to-date operations.

E1-2 **Cost of goods sold—merchandiser**

LO3

The following data were taken from the general ledger of Thornton Merchandisers on January 31, the end of the first month of operations in the current fiscal year:

Merchandise inventory, January 1	$ 22,000
Purchases	183,000
Merchandise inventory, January 31	17,000

Compute the cost of goods sold for the month of January.

E1-3 **Cost of goods sold—manufacturer**

LO3

The following data were taken from the general ledger and other data of Thomas Manufacturing on July 31:

Finished goods, July 1	$ 85,000
Cost of goods manufactured in July	343,000
Finished goods, July 31	93,000

Compute the cost of goods sold for the month of July.

E1-4 **Cost classification**

LO4

Classify the following as direct materials, direct labor, factory overhead, or selling and administrative expense.

a. Steel used in an overhead door plant.
b. Cloth used in a shirt factory.
c. Fiberglass used by a sailboat builder.
d. Cleaning solvent for the factory floor.
e. Wages of a binder employed in a printing plant.
f. Insurance on factory machines.
g. Rent paid for factory buildings.

h. Wages of the Machining Department supervisor.
i. Leather used in a shoe factory.
j. Wages of a factory janitor.
k. Electric power consumed in operating factory machines.
l. Depreciation on corporate offices.
m. Fuel used in heating a factory.
n. Paint used in the manufacture of jet skis.
o. Wages of an ironworker in the construction business.
p. Electricity used in lighting sales offices.

E1-5 **Cost flow**

LO4

Explain in narrative form the flow of direct materials, direct labor, and factory overhead costs through the ledger accounts.

E1-6 **Statement of cost of goods manufactured; cost of goods sold**

LO5

The following data are taken from the general ledger and other records of Black Hills Manufacturing Co. on January 31, the end of the first month of operations in the current fiscal year:

Sales	$75,000
Materials inventory (January 1)	25,000
Work in process inventory (January 1)	24,000
Finished goods inventory (January 1)	32,000
Materials purchased	21,000
Direct labor cost	18,000
Factory overhead (including $1,000 of indirect materials used and $3,000 of indirect labor cost)	12,000
Selling and administrative expenses	10,000
Inventories at January 31:	
Materials	22,000
Work in process	20,000
Finished goods	30,000

a. Prepare a statement of cost of goods manufactured.
b. Prepare the cost of goods sold section of the income statement.

E1-7 **Determining materials, labor, and cost of goods sold**

The following inventory data relate to Niagara Corp.:

LO4

LO5

	Inventories	
	Ending	**Beginning**
Finished goods	$75,000	$110,000
Work in process	80,000	70,000
Direct materials	95,000	90,000
Revenues and Costs for the Period:		
Sales		$900,000
Cost of goods available for sale		775,000
Total manufacturing costs		675,000
Factory overhead		175,000
Direct materials used		205,000

Calculate the following for the year:

a. Direct materials purchased.
b. Direct labor costs incurred.
c. Cost of goods sold.
d. Gross profit.

(*Hint:* The answers to subsequent parts may require using solutions from earlier parts.)

E1-8 Journal entries

LO5

The following is a list of manufacturing costs incurred by Orleans Products Co. during the month of July:

Direct materials used	$21,000
Indirect materials used	5,000
Direct labor employed	15,000
Indirect labor employed	3,000
Rent expense	4,000
Utilities expense	1,200
Insurance expense	500
Depreciation expense (machinery and equipment)	1,500

Prepare the journal entries to record the preceding information and to transfer Factory Overhead to Work in Process.

E1-9 Journal entries for job order costing; total and unit cost computation

LO7

Bristol Manufacturing, Inc., uses the job order cost system of accounting. The following information was taken from the company's books after all posting had been completed at the end of May:

Jobs Completed	Direct Materials Cost	Direct Labor Cost	Factory Overhead	Units Completed
1040	$3,600	$4,000	$1,600	400
1065	2,380	2,500	1,000	240
1120	1,800	1,700	680	200

a. Prepare the journal entries to charge the costs of materials, labor, and factory overhead to Work in Process.
b. Compute the total production cost of each job.
c. Prepare the journal entry to transfer the cost of jobs completed to Finished Goods.
d. Compute the unit cost of each job.
e. Compute the selling price per unit for each job, assuming a mark-on percentage of 40%.

E1-10 Journal entries for job order costing

Marine World manufactures goods on a job order basis. During the month of June, three jobs were started in process. (There was no work in process at the beginning of the month.) Jobs Racers and Cruisers were completed and sold, on account, during the month (selling prices: Racers, $22,000; Cruisers, $ 27,000); Job Floaters was still in process at the end of June.

The following data came from the job cost sheets for each job. The factory overhead includes a total of $1,200 of indirect materials and $900 of indirect labor.

	Racers	Cruisers	Floaters
Direct materials	$5,000	$6,000	$3,500
Direct labor	4,000	5,000	2,500
Factory overhead	3,000	4,500	2,000

Prepare journal entries to record the following:

a. Materials used.
b. Factory wages and salaries earned.
c. Factory Overhead transferred to Work in Process.
d. Jobs completed.
e. Jobs sold.

PROBLEMS

P1-1 LO1

Performance report

Prepare a performance report for the dining room of Leonardo's Italian Café for the month of February 2011, using the following data:

Budgeted Data:	January	February
Dining room wages	$4,300	$4,150
Laundry and housekeeping	1,650	1,500
Utilities	2,200	2,050
Depreciation	1,500	1,500
Actual Data:	**January**	**February**
Dining room wages	$4,700	$4,400
Laundry and housekeeping	1,600	1,400
Utilities	2,350	2,100
Depreciation	1,500	1,500

P1-2 LO3

Cost of goods sold—merchandiser and manufacturer

The following data were taken from the general ledgers and other data of Alpha Manufacturing, Inc., and Bravo Merchandising Co. on April 30 of the current year:

Merchandise inventory, April 1	$ 38,000
Finished goods, April 1	67,000
Purchases	121,000
Cost of goods manufactured	287,000
Merchandise inventory, April 30	33,000
Finished goods, April 30	61,000

Required:

1. Compute the cost of goods sold for Bravo Merchandising Co., selecting the appropriate items from the previous list.
2. Compute the cost of goods sold for Alpha Manufacturing, Inc., selecting the appropriate items from the previous list.

P1-3 **Statement of cost of goods manufactured; income statement; balance sheet**

The adjusted trial balance for Indy Furniture Company on November 30, the end of its first month of operation, is as follows:

Indy Furniture Company
Trial Balance
November 30, 2011

Cash	$21,800	
Accounts Receivable	16,200	
Finished Goods	13,900	
Work in Process	—	
Materials	7,400	
Building	300,000	
Accumulated Depreciation—Building		$3,000
Machinery and Equipment	88,000	
Accumulated Depreciation—Mach. and Equip.		2,200
Accounts Payable		8,900
Payroll	—	
Capital Stock		422,550
Sales		68,300
Cost of Goods Sold	42,450	
Factory Overhead	—	
Selling and Administrative Expenses	15,200	
	$504,950	$504,950

The general ledger reveals the following additional data:

a. There were no beginning inventories.
b. Materials purchases during the period were $33,000.
c. Direct labor cost was $18,500.
d. Factory overhead costs were as follows:

Indirect materials	$ 1,400
Indirect labor	4,300
Depreciation—building	3,000
Depreciation—machinery and equipment	2,200
Utilities	2,750
	$13,650

Required:

1. Prepare a statement of cost of goods manufactured for the month of November.

2. Prepare an income statement for the month of November. (*Hint:* Check to be sure that your figure for Cost of Goods Sold equals the amount given in the trial balance.)
3. Prepare a balance sheet as of November 30. (*Hint:* Do not forget Retained Earnings.)

P1-4 **Basic cost system; journal entries; financial statements similar to Self-Study Problem 1**

LO5

The post-closing trial balance of Beamer Manufacturing Co. on April 30 is reproduced as follows:

Beamer Manufacturing Co.
Post-Closing Trial Balance
April 30, 2011

Cash	$ 25,000	
Accounts Receivable	65,000	
Finished Goods	120,000	
Work in Process	35,000	
Materials	18,000	
Building	480,000	
Accumulated Depreciation—Building		$ 72,000
Factory Equipment	220,000	
Accumulated Depreciation—Factory Equipment		66,000
Office Equipment	60,000	
Accumulated Depreciation—Office Equipment		36,000
Accounts Payable		95,000
Capital Stock		250,000
Retained Earnings		504,000
	$ 1,023,000	$ 1,023,000

During the month of May, the following transactions took place:

a. Purchased raw materials at a cost of $45,000 and general factory supplies at a cost of $13,000 on account (recorded materials and supplies in the materials account).
b. Issued raw materials to be used in production, costing $47,000, and miscellaneous factory supplies, costing $15,000.
c. Recorded the payroll, the payments to employees, and the distribution of the wages and salaries earned for the month as follows: factory wages (including $12,000 indirect labor), $41,000; and selling and administrative salaries, $7,000. Additional account titles include Wages Payable and Payroll. (Ignore payroll withholdings and deductions.)
d. Recognized depreciation for the month at an annual rate of 5% on the building, 10% on the factory equipment, and 20% on the office equipment. The sales and administrative staff uses approximately one-fifth of the building for its offices.
e. Incurred various other expenses totaling $11,000. One-fourth of this amount is allocable to the office function.
f. Transferred total factory overhead costs to Work in Process.

g. Completed and transferred goods with a total cost of $91,000 to the finished goods storeroom.
h. Sold goods costing $188,000 for $362,000. (Assume that all sales were made on account.)
i. Collected accounts receivable in the amount of $345,000.
j. Paid accounts payable totaling $158,000.

Required:

1. Prepare journal entries to record the transactions.
2. Set up T-accounts. Post the beginning trial balance and the journal entries prepared in (1) to the accounts and determine the balances in the accounts on May 31.
3. Prepare a statement of cost of goods manufactured, an income statement, and a balance sheet. (Round amounts to the nearest whole dollar.)

P1-5 Journal entries; account analysis

LO5

Selected account balances and transactions of Alpine Manufacturing Co. follow:

	Account Balances	
	May 1	**May 31**
Raw materials	$ 6,000	$ 5,500
Factory supplies	800	900
Work in process	3,500	6,500
Finished goods	12,000	13,200

May Transactions:

a. Purchased raw materials and factory supplies on account at costs of $45,000 and $10,000, respectively. (One inventory account is maintained.)
b. Incurred wages during the month of $65,000 ($15,000 was for indirect labor).
c. Incurred factory overhead costs in the amount of $42,000 on account.
d. Made adjusting entries to record $10,000 of factory overhead for items such as depreciation (credit Various Credits). Factory overhead was closed to Work in Process. Completed jobs were transferred to Finished Goods, and the cost of jobs sold was charged to Cost of Goods Sold.

Required:

Prepare journal entries for the following:

1. The purchase of raw materials and factory supplies.
2. The issuance of raw materials and supplies into production. (*Hint:* Be certain to consider the beginning and ending balances of raw materials and supplies as well as the amount of the purchases.)
3. The recording of the payroll.
4. The distribution of the payroll.
5. The payment of the payroll.
6. The recording of factory overhead incurred.

7. The adjusting entry for factory overhead.
8. The entry to transfer factory overhead costs to Work in Process.
9. The entry to transfer the cost of completed work to Finished Goods. (*Hint:* Be sure to consider the beginning and ending balances of Work in Process as well as the costs added to Work in Process this period.)
10. The entry to record the cost of goods sold. (*Hint:* Be sure to consider the beginning and ending balances of Finished Goods as well as the cost of the goods finished during the month.)

P1-6 **Data analysis, manufacturing statement, cost terminology**

O'Reilly Manufacturing, Inc.'s cost of goods sold for the month ended July 31 was $345,000. The ending work in process inventory was 90% of the beginning work in process inventory. Factory overhead was 50% of the direct labor cost. Other information pertaining to O'Reilly's inventories and production for the month of July is as follows:

Beginning inventories, July 1:	
Direct materials	$ 20,000
Work in process	40,000
Finished goods	102,000
Purchases of direct materials during July	110,000
Ending inventories, July 31:	
Direct materials	26,000
Work in process	?
Finished goods	105,000

Required:

1. Prepare a statement of cost of goods manufactured for the month of July. (*Hint:* Set up a statement of cost of goods manufactured, putting the given information in the appropriate spaces and solving for the unknown information.)
2. Prepare a schedule to compute the prime cost incurred during July.
3. Prepare a schedule to compute the conversion cost charged to Work in Process during July.

P1-7 **Data analysis; manufacturing statement**

Fayetteville Manufacturing Co. produces only one product. You have obtained the following information from the corporation's books and records for the year ended December 31, 2011:

a. Total manufacturing cost during the year was $1,000,000, including direct materials, direct labor, and factory overhead.
b. Cost of goods manufactured during the year was $970,000.
c. Factory overhead charged to work in process was 75% of direct labor cost and 27% of the total manufacturing cost.
d. The beginning work in process inventory, January 1, was 40% of the ending work in process inventory, December 31.

Required:

Prepare a statement of cost of goods manufactured for the year ended December 31 for Fayetteville Manufacturing. (*Hint:* Set up a statement of cost of goods manufactured, putting the given information in the appropriate spaces and solving for the unknown information.)

P1-8 **Job order cost; journal entries; ending work in process; inventory analysis**

Hidalgo Company manufactures goods to special order and uses a job order cost system. During its first month of operations, the following selected transactions took place:

a. Materials purchased on account	$37,000
b. Materials issued to the factory:	
Job 101	$ 2,200
Job 102	5,700
Job 103	7,100
Job 104	1,700
For general use in the factory	1,350
c. Factory wages and salaries earned:	
Job 101	$ 2,700
Job 102	6,800
Job 103	9,200
Job 104	2,100
For general work in the factory	2,250
d. Miscellaneous factory overhead costs on account	$ 2,400
e. Depreciation of $2,000 on the factory machinery recorded.	
f. Factory overhead allocated as follows:	
Job 101	$ 1,200
Job 102	2,000
Job 103	3,800
Job 104	1,000
g. Jobs 101, 102, and 103 completed.	
h. Jobs 101 and 102 shipped to the customer and billed at $39,000.	

Required:

1. Prepare a schedule reflecting the cost of each of the four jobs.
2. Prepare journal entries to record the transactions.
3. Compute the ending balance in Work in Process.
4. Compute the ending balance in Finished Goods.

P1-9 LO7

Job order cost; journal entries; profit analysis

Spokane Manufacturing Co. obtained the following information from its records for the month of July:

	Jobs Completed and Sold		
	230	**320**	**560**
Direct materials cost	$ 25,000	$ 15,000	$ 29,000
Direct labor cost	70,000	60,000	55,000
Factory overhead	50,000	40,000	63,000
Units manufactured	10,000	5,000	14,000
Selling price	152,000	120,000	175,250

Required:

1. Prepare, in summary form, the journal entries that would have been made during the month to record the distribution of materials, labor, and overhead costs; the completion of the jobs; and the sale of the jobs.
2. Prepare schedules showing the gross profit or loss for July for the following:
   - **a.** The business as a whole.
   - **b.** Each job completed and sold.
   - **c.** Each unit manufactured and sold. (Round to the nearest cent.)

P1-10 LO7

Job cost; journal entries; inventory analysis; manufacturing statement similar to Self-Study Problem 2

St. Lawrence Manufacturing Co. manufactures engines that are made only on customers' orders and to their specifications. During January, the company worked on Jobs 007, 008, 009, 010. The following figures summarize the cost records for the month:

	Job 007 (100 units)	Job 008 (60 units)	Job 009 (25 units)	Job 010 (100 units)
Direct materials put into process:				
Jan. 2	$15,000	$ 5,000	—	—
18	20,000	16,000	$ 5,000	—
22	15,000	1,000	10,000	$ 6,000
28	—	—	3,500	2,000
Direct labor cost: Week ending				
Jan. 2	$ 1,000	$ 1,000	—	—
9	27,000	9,000	—	—
16	32,000	27,000	—	—
23	20,000	3,000	$ 5,000	$ 500
30	—	—	18,000	11,500
Factory overhead	$60,000	$32,000	$17,500	$10,500
Engines completed	100	60	25	—

Jobs 007 and 008 have been completed and delivered to the customer at a total selling price of $426,000, on account. Job 009 is finished but has not yet been delivered. Job 010 is still in process. There was no work in process at the beginning of the month.

Required:

1. Prepare the summary journal entries for the month to record the distribution of materials, labor, and overhead costs.
2. Prepare a summary showing the total cost of each job completed during the month or in process at the end of the month. Also, determine the cost of the inventories of completed engines and engines in process at the end of the month.
3. Prepare the journal entries to record the completion of the jobs and the sale of the jobs.
4. Prepare a statement of cost of goods manufactured.

MINI-CASE

Required Ethics

LO2

Marta Johns is the Division Controller and Kevin Deere is the Division Vice President of Tuffy Tractor, Inc. Due to pressures to meet earnings estimates for 2011, Deere instructs Johns to record as revenue $5,000,000 of orders for tractors that are still in production and will not be shipped until January 2012.

Required:

1. Using the IMA's Standards of Ethical Conduct as a guide, what are Johns's ethical responsibilities in this matter?
2. What should Johns do if Deere does not acquiesce and still insists that she record the revenue in 2011?

INTERNET EXERCISE 1

Ethics
Required:

LO2

Accounting organizations, such as the Institute of Management Accountants, encourage ethical conduct. Go to the companion Website at www.cengage.com/accounting/vanderbeck and click on the link to "Ethics Articles/Strategic Finance." Choose a recent ethics article, and write a one-page summary of it.

INTERNET EXERCISE 2

Ethics, Corporate Governance
Required:

Go to the companion Website at www.cengage.com/accounting/vanderbeck and click on the link to "The Sarbanes-Oxley Act." Read the accompanying PowerPoint presentation, and write a one-page summary of it.

Chapter 2

Accounting for Materials

Learning Objectives

After studying this chapter, you should be able to:

- LO1 Recognize the two basic aspects of materials control.
- LO2 Specify internal control procedures for materials.
- LO3 Account for materials and relate materials accounting to the general ledger.
- LO4 Account for inventories in a just-in-time (lean production) system.
- LO5 Account for scrap materials, spoiled goods, and defective work.

Raw materials costs are not just a concern of manufacturers. An article, "Restaurant Costs Harder to Stomach," in the June 7, 2008 *Cincinnati Enquirer,* explained how rapidly food costs were rising and how difficult it was to pass those costs on to diners in a sluggish economy. Bob Conway Jr., vice president of Bistro Group, which operates Friday's, McAlister's, and Karlo's in the Greater Cincinnati area, said that in the past six months, "Food prices increased more than anyone in the industry thought they would. Pasta went up 130 percent. Other big jumps have been eggs up 73 percent and rice up 39 percent ... flour jumped 87 percent in the first three months of 2008 and fats and oils were up 49 percent."

What cost management techniques must purchasers of raw materials employ to survive in such a difficult environment? This chapter will discuss basic aspects of materials control, internal control procedures for materials, and adoption of a lean production manufacturing system to maximize efficiency and minimize waste.

The total inventory cost of a manufactured product consists of the expenditures made for raw materials, direct labor, and its fair share of factory overhead. The principles and procedures for controlling and accounting for these cost elements are discussed in Chapters 2, 3, and 4, respectively. Each chapter examines the accounting procedures and controls that apply to one of the cost elements. Certain procedures and controls, however, pertain to all of the cost elements. The major function of a cost control system is to keep expenditures within the limits of a preconceived plan. The control system should also encourage cost reductions by eliminating waste and operational inefficiencies. An effective system of cost control is designed to control the actions of people responsible for the expenditures, because people control costs. Costs do not control themselves.

An effective cost control system should include the following:

1. A specific assignment of duties and responsibilities.
2. A list of individuals who are authorized to approve expenditures.
3. An established plan of objectives and goals.
4. Regular reports showing the differences between goals and actual performance.
5. A plan of corrective action designed to prevent unfavorable variances from recurring.
6. Follow-up procedures for corrective measures.

Recall from Chapter 1 that responsibility accounting is an integral part of a cost control system because it focuses attention on specific individuals who have been designated to achieve the established goals. Of the three major objectives of cost accounting—cost control, product costing, and inventory pricing—cost control is often the most difficult to achieve. A weakness in cost control can often be overcome by placing more emphasis on responsibility accounting. This makes the people who incur costs accountable for those costs.

Materials Control

LO1 Recognize the two basic aspects of materials control.

The two basic aspects of **materials control** are (1) the physical control or safeguarding of materials and (2) control over the investment in materials, as illustrated in Figure 2-1. Physical control protects materials from misuse or misappropriation. Controlling the investment in materials maintains appropriate quantities of materials in inventory.

Figure 2-1 Physical Control and Controlling the Investment in Materials

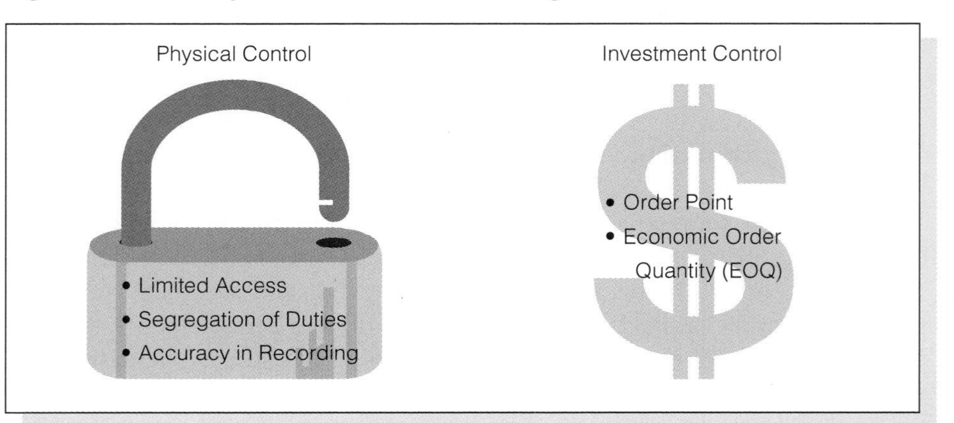

Physical Control of Materials

Every business requires a system of internal control that includes procedures for the safeguarding of assets. Because highly liquid assets, such as cash and marketable securities, are particularly susceptible to misappropriation, the protection provided for such assets is usually more than adequate. However, other assets, including inventories, must also be protected from unauthorized use or theft.

Because raw materials usually represent a significant portion of a manufacturer's current assets and often comprise more than 50% of a product's manufacturing cost, a business must control its materials from the time they are ordered until the time they are shipped to customers in the form of finished goods. In general, to effectively control materials, a business must maintain: (1) limited access, (2) segregation of duties, and (3) accuracy in recording. Note that manufacturers are not the only ones who have direct materials. Although **Taco Bell**, for example, is considered a service business, it has direct materials such as ground beef, tortillas, and salsa that are used in the preparation of its meals, over which physical control must be exercised.

Limited Access. Only authorized personnel should have access to materials storage areas. Raw materials should be issued for use in production only if requisitions are properly documented and approved. Also, procedures should be established within each production area for safeguarding work in process. Finished goods should be safeguarded in limited-access storage areas and not released for shipment in the absence of appropriate documentation and authorization.

Segregation of Duties. A basic principle of internal control is the segregation of employee duties to minimize opportunities for misappropriation of assets. With respect to materials control, the following functions should be segregated: purchasing, receiving, storage, use, and recording. The independence of personnel assigned to these functions does not eliminate the danger of misappropriation or misuse because the possibility of collusion still exists. However, the appropriate segregation of duties limits an individual employee's opportunities for misappropriation and concealment. In smaller organizations, it is frequently not possible to achieve optimum segregation of duties due to the limited number of employees. Small businesses must therefore rely on specially designed control procedures to compensate for the lack of independence of assigned functions.

Accuracy in Recording. An effective materials control system requires the accurate recording of the purchase and issuance of materials. Inventory records should document the inventory quantities on hand, and cost records should provide the data needed to assign a cost to inventories for the preparation of financial statements. Periodically, recorded inventories should be compared with a physical inventory count, and any significant discrepancies should be investigated. Differences may be due to recording errors or to inventory losses through theft or spoilage. Once the cause has been determined, appropriate corrective action should be taken.

Controlling the Investment in Materials

Maintaining an appropriate level of raw materials inventory is one of the most important objectives of materials control. An inventory of sufficient size and variety for efficient operations must be maintained, but the size should not be excessive in relation to scheduled production needs.

Because funds invested in inventories are unavailable for other uses, management should consider other working capital needs in determining inventory levels. In addition to the alternative uses of funds that otherwise would be invested in inventories, management should consider the materials costs of handling, storage, personal property taxes, and casualty insurance. Also, higher than needed inventory levels may increase the possibility of loss from the damage, deterioration, or obsolescence of materials. The planning and control of the materials investment requires that all of these factors be carefully studied to determine (1) when orders should be placed and (2) how many units should be ordered.

Order Point. A minimum level of inventory should be determined for each type of raw material, and inventory records should indicate how much of each type is on hand. A subsidiary **materials ledger,** in which a separate account is maintained for each material, is needed.

The point at which an item should be ordered, called the **order point,** occurs when the predetermined minimum level of inventory on hand is reached. Calculating the order point is based on the following data:

1. **Usage**—the anticipated rate at which the material will be used.
2. **Lead time**—the estimated time interval between the placement of an order and the receipt of the material.
3. **Safety stock**—the estimated minimum level of inventory needed to protect against **stockouts** (running out of stock). Stockouts may occur due to inaccurate estimates of usage or lead time or various other unforeseen events, such as the receipt of damaged or inferior materials from a supplier or a work stoppage at a supplier's plant.

Assume that a company's expected daily usage of an item of material is 100 lb, the anticipated lead time is five days, and the desired safety stock is 1,000 lb. The following calculation shows that the order point is reached when the inventory on hand reaches 1,500 lb:

100 lb (daily usage) × 5 days (lead time)	500 lb
Safety stock required	1,000 lb
Order point	1,500 lb

If estimates of usage and lead time are accurate, the level of inventory when the new order is received would be equal to the safety stock of 1,000 lb. If, however, the new order is delivered three days late, the company would need to issue 300 lb of material from its safety stock to maintain the production level during the delay.

Economic Order Quantity (EOQ). The order point establishes the time when an order should be placed, but it does not indicate the most economical number of units to be ordered. To determine the quantity to be ordered, the cost of placing an order (**order costs**) and the cost of carrying inventory in stock (**carrying costs**) must be considered, as illustrated in Figure 2-2.

Order costs and carrying costs move in opposite directions—annual order costs decrease when the order size increases, while annual carrying costs increase when the order size increases. The optimal quantity to order at one time, called the **economic order quantity**, is the order size that minimizes the total order and carrying costs over a period of time, such as one year.

The factors to be considered in determining order and carrying costs for a particular company vary with the nature of operations and the organizational structure. Special analyses are usually required to identify relevant costs, because these data are not normally accumulated in an accounting system. Care must be exercised in determining which costs are relevant. For example, a company may have adequate warehouse space to carry a large additional quantity of inventory. If the space cannot be used for some other profitable purpose, the cost of the space is not a relevant factor in determining carrying costs. If, however, the space in the company warehouse could be leased to others or if additional warehouse space must be leased to accommodate increased inventories, then the costs associated with the additional space are relevant in determining carrying costs.

The interest cost associated with carrying an inventory in stock should be considered whether or not funds are borrowed to purchase the inventory. If these funds were not used to purchase inventory, they could have been profitably invested in other alternatives. The rate of interest to be used in the calculations will vary depending on the cost of borrowing or the

Figure 2-2 Order Costs and Carrying Costs

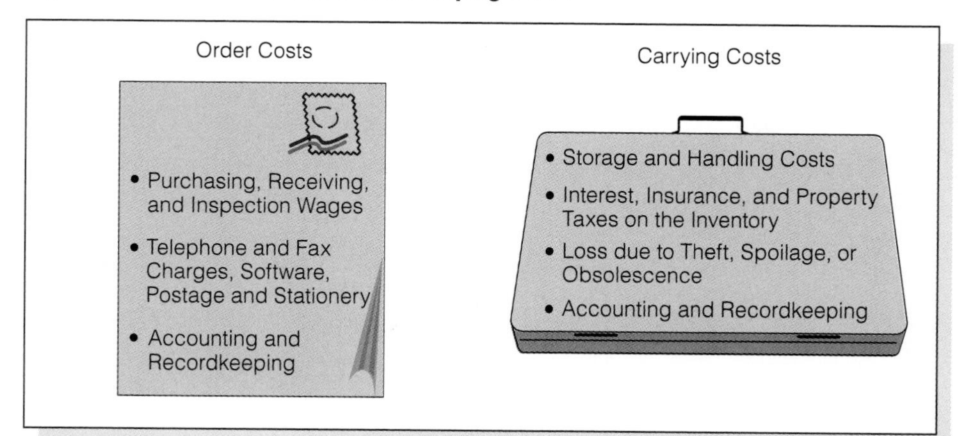

rate that could be earned by the funds if they were used for some other purpose.

Quantitative models or formulas have been developed for calculating the economic order quantity. One formula that can be used is the following:

$$EOQ = \sqrt{\frac{2CN}{K}}$$

where
EOQ = economic order quantity
C = cost of placing an order
N = number of units required annually
K = annual carrying cost per unit of inventory

To illustrate this formula, assume that the following data have been determined by analyzing the factors relevant to materials inventory for Pacific Paint Company:

Number of gallons of material required annually	10,000
Cost of placing an order	$ 10.00
Annual carrying cost per gallon of inventory	$ 0.80

Using the EOQ formula, 500 gallons should be ordered at one time:

$$EOQ = \sqrt{\frac{2 \times \text{cost of order} \times \text{number of units required annually}}{\text{carrying cost per unit}}}$$

$$= \sqrt{\frac{2 \times \$10 \times 10{,}000}{\$0.80}}$$

$$= \sqrt{\frac{\$200{,}000}{\$0.80}}$$

$$= \sqrt{250{,}000}$$

$$= 500 \text{ gal.}$$

The EOQ can also be determined by constructing a table using a range of order sizes. A tabular presentation of the data from the previous example, assuming no safety stock, follows:

(1) Order Size	(2) Number of Orders	(3) Total Order Cost	(4) Average Inventory	(5) Total Carrying Cost	(6) Total Order & Carrying Cost
100	100	$1,000	50	$ 40	$1,040
200	50	500	100	80	580
300	33	330	150	120	450
400	25	250	200	160	410
500	**20**	**200**	**250**	**200**	**400**
600	17	170	300	240	410
700	14	140	350	280	420
800	13	130	400	320	450
900	11	110	450	360	470
1,000	10	100	500	400	500

In this table, the amounts in each column are determined as follows:

1. Number of gallons per order
2. 10,000 annual gallons / order size in column (1)
3. Number of orders × \$10 per order
4. Order size / 2 = average inventory on hand during the year
5. Average inventory × \$0.80 per gal. carrying cost for one year
6. Total order cost in column (3) + total carrying cost in column (5)

The graph in Figure 2-3 shows the total annual order cost decreasing as the order size increases because the order cost is a function of the number of orders placed, not the number of units ordered. Meanwhile, the total annual carrying cost increases as the order size increases because of the necessity to maintain a large quantity of inventory in stock. At the 500-gallon level, the combined carrying and order costs are at their minimum point of \$400. This is always the point at which the total carrying costs equal the total order costs, as demonstrated by their intersection in Figure 2-3, when no safety stock is provided for.

Figure 2-3 **Costs of Ordering and Carrying Inventory**

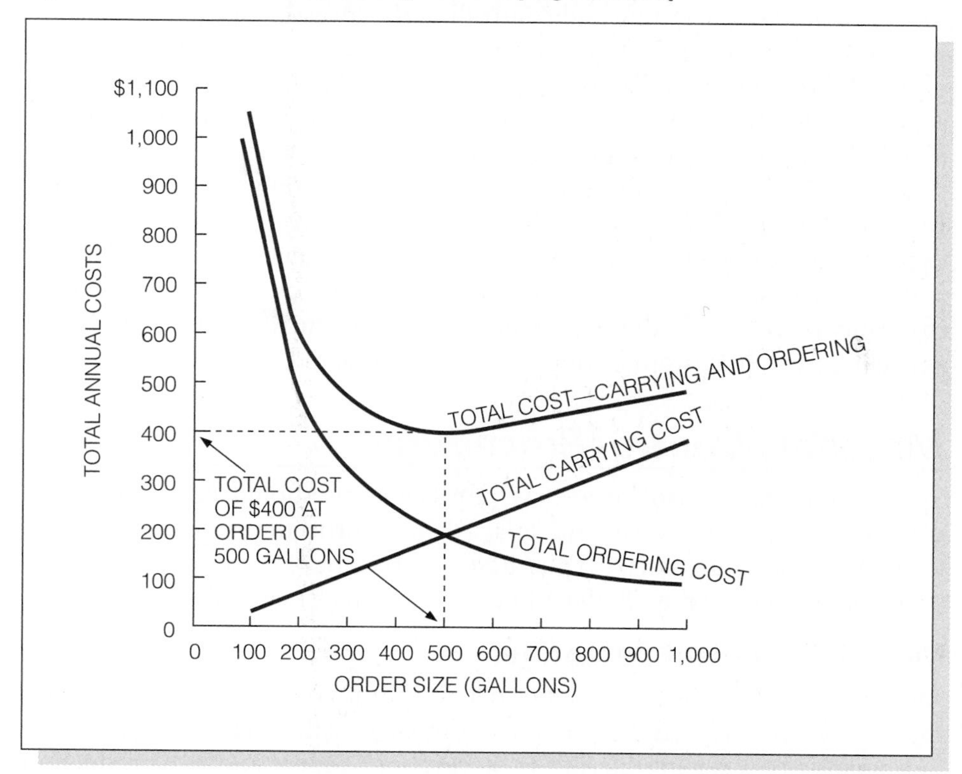

Assume in the preceding example that the company desires a safety stock of 400 gallons to protect against stockouts. The average number of gallons in inventory then would be calculated as follows:

$$\begin{aligned}\text{Average number of}\\ \text{gallons in inventory} &= (1/2 \times \text{EOQ}) + \text{Safety stock}\\ &= (1/2 \times 500) + 400\\ &= 650 \text{ gal.}\end{aligned}$$

The total carrying cost then would be

$$\begin{aligned}\text{Carrying cost} &= \text{Average inventory} \times \text{Carrying cost per unit}\\ &= 650 \times \$0.80\\ &= \$520\end{aligned}$$

Note that the order cost of $200, which doesn't change in this example because the number of orders is the same as before, is significantly less than the carrying cost of $520 when safety stock is present.

Limitations of Order Point and EOQ Calculations. The techniques illustrated for determining when to order (order point) and how much to order (EOQ) may give a false impression of exactness. However, because these calculations are based on estimates of factors such as production volume, leadtime, and order and carrying costs, they are really approximations that serve as a guide to planning and controlling the investment in materials.

In addition, other factors may influence the time for ordering or the quantity ordered. Such factors include the availability of materials from suppliers, the proximity of suppliers, fluctuations in the purchase price of materials, and trade (volume) discounts offered by suppliers.

Companies often increase safety stock due to strong expected demand. In recent years, both the automotive and electronics industries have experienced occasional shortages of parts due to such increased demand and/or work slowdowns or strikes at certain plants. The cost of such stockouts may include the lost revenue from the current sale, as well as a permanent loss of customers due to the ill will created.

Materials Control Procedures

Specify internal control procedures for materials.

Specific internal control procedures for materials should be tailored to a company's needs. However, materials control procedures generally relate to the following functions: (1) purchase and receipt of materials, (2) storage of materials, and (3) requisition and consumption of materials.

Materials Control Personnel

Although actual job titles and duties may vary from one company to another, the personnel involved in materials control usually include (1) purchasing agent, (2) receiving clerk, (3) storeroom keeper, and (4) production department supervisor.

Purchasing Agent. The **purchasing agent** is responsible for buying the materials needed by a manufacturer. In a small plant, the employee who does the buying may also perform other duties, while in a large plant, the purchasing agent may head a department established to perform buying activities. The duties of a purchasing agent and staff may include the following:

1. Working with the production manager to prevent delays caused by the lack of materials.
2. Compiling and maintaining information that identifies where the desired materials can be obtained at the most economical price.
3. Placing purchase orders.
4. Supervising the order process until the materials are received.
5. Verifying purchase invoices and approving them for payments.

Receiving Clerk. The **receiving clerk** is responsible for supervising the receipt of incoming shipments. All incoming materials must be checked as to quantity and quality and sometimes as to price.

Storeroom Keeper. The **storeroom keeper**, who has charge of the materials after they have been received, must see that the materials are properly stored and maintained. The materials must be placed in stock and issued only on properly authorized requisitions. The purchasing agent should be informed of the reorder point and economic order quantity as a guide to purchasing additional materials.

Production Department Supervisor. Each production department has a person who is responsible for supervising the operational functions within the department. This individual may be given the title of **production department supervisor** or another similar designation. One of the assigned duties of a department supervisor is to prepare or approve the requisitions designating the quantities and kinds of material needed for the work to be done in the department.

Control during Procurement

Materials are ordered to maintain the adequate levels of inventory necessary to meet scheduled production needs. The storeroom keeper is responsible for monitoring quantities of materials on hand. When the order point is reached for a particular material, the procurement process is initiated. In most companies, computers store data pertaining to inventories on hand, predetermined order points, and economic order quantities. When properly programmed, computers can simplify the task of maintaining appropriate inventory levels.

Supporting documents are essential to maintaining control during the procurement process. In general, the documents should be prenumbered and protected from unauthorized use. The documents commonly used in procuring materials include: (1) purchase requisitions, (2) purchase orders, (3) vendor's invoices, (4) receiving reports, and (5) debit-credit memoranda. Increasingly, the supporting documents are in the form of computer files, which will be discussed at the appropriate points in the following narrative.

Purchase Requisitions. The form used to notify the purchasing agent that additional materials are needed is known as a **purchase requisition**. It is an important part of the materials control process because it authorizes the agent to buy. Purchase requisitions should originate with the storeroom keeper or some other individual with similar authority and responsibility.

Purchase requisitions should be prenumbered serially to help detect the loss or misuse of any of these forms. They are generally prepared in duplicate. The first copy goes to the purchasing agent, and the storeroom keeper retains the second copy. Figure 2-4 shows a purchase requisition for Hawke Mfg., a company that manufactures skateboards and needs to purchase lumber for use in production.

Purchase Order. The purchase requisition gives the purchasing agent authority to order the materials described in the requisition. The purchasing agent should maintain or have access to an up-to-date list of vendors, which includes prices, available discounts, estimated delivery time, and any

Figure 2-4 **Purchase Requisition. (Notifies purchasing agent that additional materials should be ordered.)**

HAWKE MFG

PURCHASE REQUISITION No. **3246**

Date January 3, 2011

Date wanted February 1, 2011

For { Job No. 300 / Account No. 1482 }

Authorization No. 3313

QUANTITY	DESCRIPTION
20,000 BD.FT.	Hard Rock Maple Plywood

Approved by L. Merz Signed by G. Thomas

Purchase order no. 1982 Date ordered January 6, 2011

Ordered from Forrest Corporation

other relevant information. From this list, the purchasing agent selects a vendor from whom high-quality materials can be obtained when needed at a competitive price. If this information is not available from the list for a particular type of material, the purchasing agent may communicate with several prospective vendors and request quotations on the materials needed.

The purchasing agent then completes a **purchase order**, as shown in Figure 2-5 below, and addresses it to the chosen vendor, describing the materials wanted, stating price and terms, and fixing the date and method of delivery. This purchase order should be prenumbered serially and prepared in quadruplicate. The first copy goes to the vendor, one copy goes to the accounting department, one copy goes to the receiving clerk, and the purchasing agent retains a copy.

The purchasing agent's copy of the order should be placed in an unfilled orders file. Before the order is filed, the purchase requisition on which it is based should be attached to it. This last important step begins the assembly of a complete set of all the forms pertaining to the purchase

Figure 2-5 **Purchase Order. (Prepared by purchasing agent and sent to vendor to order materials.)**

HAWKE MFG

PURCHASE ORDER

Order No. **1982**

Mark Order No. on invoice and on all packages

To: Forrest Corporation
Adirondack, NY

Date January 6, 2011
Terms 3/10 eom n/60
Ship Via Truck (to arrive January 21, 2011)

QUANTITY	DESCRIPTION	PRICE	
20,000 BD.FT.	Hard Rock Maple Plywood	$105,000	00

By a. Lauren
Purchasing Agent

transaction. To identify each document relating to a transaction with all others of the same set, the purchase order number should be shown on each of the documents. The sets can then be compiled according to the respective purchase order numbers.

A computerized purchasing system greatly simplifies the process previously described. The necessary computer files include an inventory file, a supplier file, and an open purchase order file. The storeroom keeper would initiate the process by transmitting a purchase requisition electronically to the purchasing agent. The purchasing agent would then browse the supplier file to choose the most appropriate supplier for the material requested. The purchase order would be prepared electronically, and the open purchase order file would be updated. The transmission of the electronic purchase order to the supplier's computer is an example of **Electronic Data Interchange (EDI)**, which is the process of business-to-business electronic communication for the purpose of expediting commerce and eliminating paperwork.

Vendor's Invoice. The company should receive a **vendor's invoice** before the materials arrive at the factory. As soon as it is received, the vendor's invoice goes to the purchasing agent, who compares it with the purchase order, noting particularly that the description of the materials is the same as what was ordered, that the price and the payment terms agree with the purchase order, and that the method of shipment and the date of delivery conform to the instructions on the order. When satisfied that the invoice is correct, the purchasing agent initials or stamps the invoice indicating that it has been reviewed and agrees with the purchase order. The invoice is then filed together with the purchase order and the purchase requisition in the unfilled orders file until the materials arrive.

Receiving Report. As noted previously, a copy of the purchase order goes to the receiving clerk to give advance notice in preparation for the arrival of the materials ordered. This is done to facilitate planning and to provide space for the incoming materials. The receiving clerk works in the receiving department where all incoming materials are received, opened, counted or weighed, and tested for conformity with the order. If the materials received are of too technical a nature to be tested by the receiving clerk, an engineer from the production manager's office may perform the inspection, or the materials may be sent to the plant laboratory for testing.

The receiving clerk counts and identifies the materials received and prepares a **receiving report** similar to the one presented in Figure 2-6. Each report is numbered serially and shows the vendor, when the materials were received, what the shipment contained, and the number of the purchase order that identifies the shipment. If prepared manually, the report should be prepared in quadruplicate. Two copies go to the purchasing agent, one copy goes with the materials or supplies to the storeroom keeper to ensure that all of the materials that come to the receiving department are put into the storeroom, and the receiving clerk retains one copy. In some plants, the

Figure 2-6 **Receiving Report. (Incoming materials opened, counted, weighed, or tested for conformity with purchase order.)**

HAWKE MFG

RECEIVING REPORT

No. **496**

Date January 21, 2011

To the purchasing agent:

RECEIVED FROM Forrest Corporation

Via Ace Trucking Transportation Charges $210.85

QUANTITY	DESCRIPTION
20,000 BD.FT.	Hard Rock Maple Plywood

Counted by R. S. Inspected by D. P.

Purchase order no. 1982

receiving clerk is given a copy of the purchase order with the quantity ordered omitted, thus ensuring that the items received will be counted.

The purchasing agent compares the receiving report with the vendor's invoice and the purchase order to determine that the materials received are those ordered and billed. If the documents agree, the purchasing agent initials or stamps the two copies of the receiving report. One copy is then attached to the other forms already in the file, and the entire set of forms is sent to the accounting department where the purchase of merchandise on account is recorded. The other copy of the receiving report is sent to the person in the accounting department who maintains inventory records. A summary of the document flows in the purchasing system is illustrated in Figure 2-7.

In the previously mentioned computerized purchasing system, the receiving clerk would enter the quantity of the materials counted into the system. The computer program would then compare the items in the open purchase order file with the items received and generate a receiving report as well as update the inventory file, supplier file, and open purchase order file.

Figure 2-7 **Materials Procurement Document Flows**

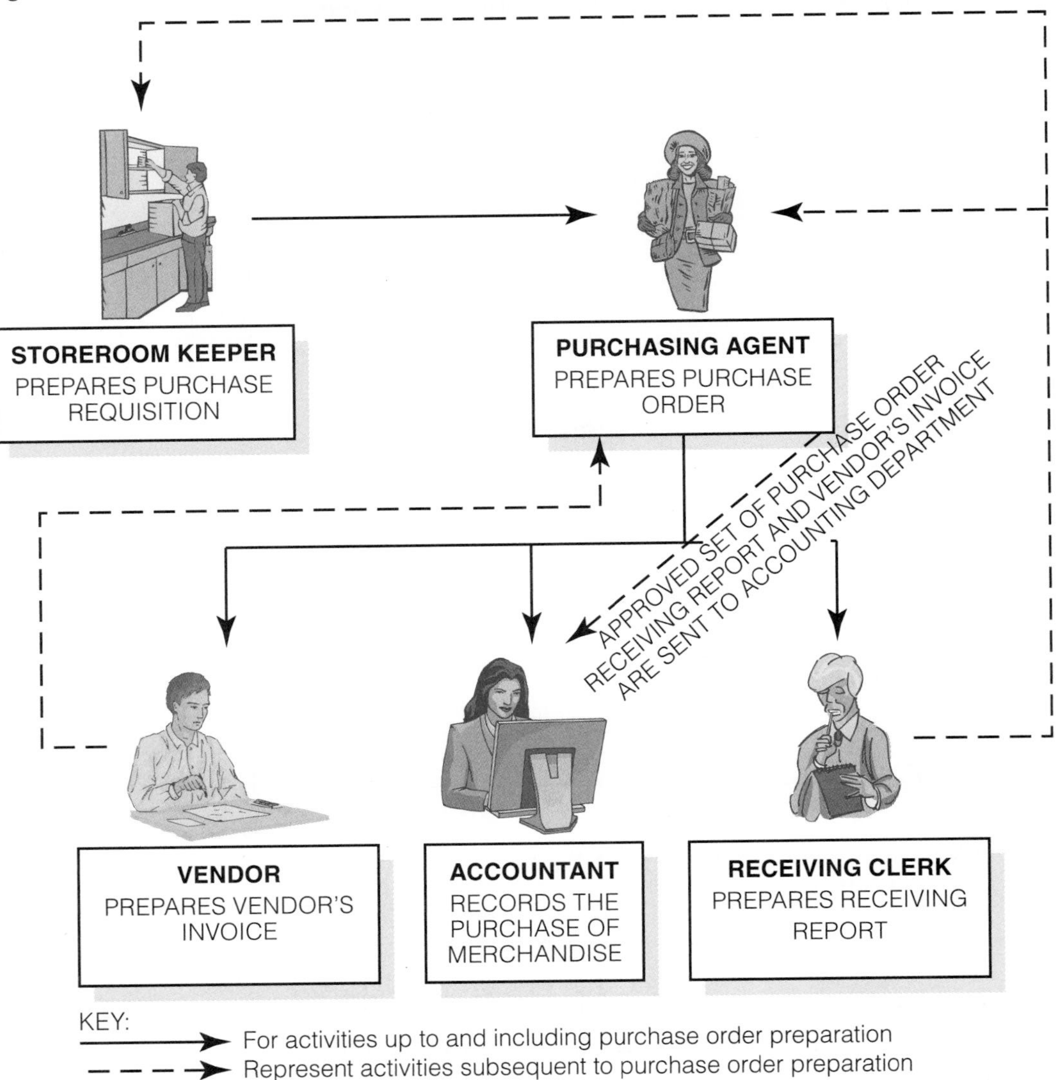

Debit-Credit Memorandum. Occasionally, a shipment of materials does not match the order and the invoice. The purchasing agent will discover this discrepancy when comparing the receiving report with the purchase order and the vendor's invoice. Whatever the cause, the difference will lead to correspondence with the vendor, and copies of the letters should be added to the file of forms relating to the transaction. If a larger quantity has been received than has been ordered and the excess is to be kept for future use, a **credit memorandum** is prepared notifying the vendor of the amount of the increase (to accounts payable) in the invoice.

If, on the other hand, the shipment is short, one of two courses of action may be taken. If the materials received can be used, they may be retained and a **debit memorandum** (decrease to accounts payable) prepared notifying the vendor of the amount of the shortage. If the materials

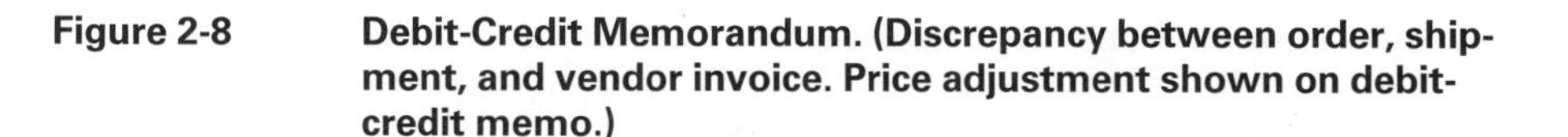

Figure 2-8 **Debit-Credit Memorandum. (Discrepancy between order, shipment, and vendor invoice. Price adjustment shown on debit-credit memo.)**

HAWKE MFG

(DEBIT) / CREDIT MEMORANDUM

Date January 23, 2011

To: Forrest Corporation
Adirondak, NY

We have today (Debited) / Credited your account for the following:

Explanation Poor Quality

QUANTITY	DESCRIPTION	UNIT PRICE	AMOUNT	
500 BD.FT.	Hard Rock Maple Plywood	$5.25	$2,625	00

Purchase order no. 1982
Your invoice date January 15, 2011

By A. Lauren
Purchasing Agent

received cannot be used, perhaps due to a defect, a **return shipping order** is prepared and the materials are returned.

Figure 2-8 shows one form of debit-credit memorandum. This memo shows that the vendor has delivered 500 board feet of lumber that do not meet the buyer's specifications. The purchasing agent will prepare a return shipping order and return the materials to the vendor. In our computerized purchasing system example, the receiving clerk would enter the purchase order number of the returned items into the system, and the computer would generate a credit or debit memorandum and a return shipping order, if necessary.

Control during Storage and Issuance

The preceding discussion outlined ways to maintain the control of materials during the procurement process. The procedures and forms described are necessary for control of the ordering and receiving functions and the transfer of incoming materials to the storeroom. The next step to be considered is the storage and issuance of materials and supplies.

Materials Requisition. As discussed earlier, materials should be protected from unauthorized use. To lessen the chance of theft, carelessness, or misuse, no materials should be issued from the storeroom except on written authorization. The form used to provide this control is known as the **materials requisition**, illustrated in Figure 2-9, and is prepared by factory personnel authorized to withdraw materials from the storeroom. The personnel authorized to perform this function may differ from company to company, but such authority must be given to someone of responsibility. Often, department supervisors are required to sign materials requisitions that are issued by their respective departments. When the storeroom keeper receives a properly signed requisition, the requisitioned materials are released. Both the storeroom keeper and the employee to whom materials are issued should be required to sign the requisition. (Note that in a computerized system, signatures are replaced with passwords and other security codes.)

Figure 2-9 Materials Requisition. (Authorization to withdraw materials from storeroom.)

HAWKE MFG

MATERIALS REQUISITION

Date January 24, 2011 No. **834**

To: D. Graham

QUANTITY	DESCRIPTION	UNIT PRICE	AMOUNT	
1000 BD.FT.	Hard Rock Maple Plywood	$5.25	$5,250	00

Approved by E. B. Issued by B. W.

Received by L. M.

Charged to Job/Dept. 320 Factory Overhead Expense Account ______

In a paper-based system, the materials requisition is usually prepared in quadruplicate. Two copies go to the accounting department for recording; one copy goes to the storeroom keeper and serves as authorization for issuing the materials; and the department supervisor who approved it retains one copy.

Identification is an important factor in the control of materials. For this reason, the materials requisition should indicate the job number, such as Job 320 in Figure 2-9, or the department (in process costing) to which the materials are issued. When indirect materials, such as cleaning materials, lubricants, and paint that cannot be identified with a specific job are issued, the requisition will indicate the name or number of the factory overhead account to be charged.

Returned Materials Report. After materials are requisitioned, occasionally some or all of the materials must be returned to the storeroom. Perhaps more materials were requested than were needed, or the wrong type of materials was issued. Whatever the reason, a written report, called a **returned materials report**, describing the materials and the reason for the return, must accompany the materials to the storeroom.

Recall and Review 1

Dennis Company predicts that it will use 200,000 lb of material during the year. Dennis anticipates that it will cost $25 to place each order. The annual carrying cost per lb is $10.

1. Determine the most economical order quantity, using the EOQ formula. ______
2. Determine the total annual order and carrying cost at this level. ________

(After working this exercise, see page 102 for the solution.)

You should now be able to work the following:
Questions 1–16; Exercises 2-1 to 2-3; Problems 2-1 to 2-3; and Self-Study Problem 1.

Accounting for Materials

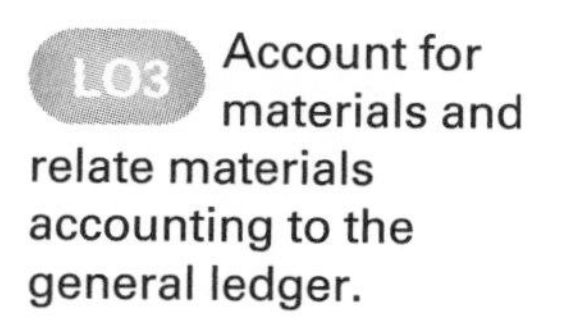

Account for materials and relate materials accounting to the general ledger.

A company's inventory records should show (1) the quantity of each kind of material on hand and (2) its cost. The most desirable method of achieving this result is to integrate the materials accounting system with the general ledger accounts. All purchases of materials on account are recorded as a debit to Materials in the general ledger. (The corresponding credit is to Accounts Payable.) The materials account is a control account that is supported by a subsidiary materials ledger containing an individual account for each type of material carried in stock. Periodically, the balance of the control account and the total of the subsidiary ledger accounts are compared, and any significant variation between the two is investigated.

Each of the individual materials accounts in the materials ledger shows (1) the quantity on hand and (2) the cost of the materials. To keep this information current, it is necessary to record in each individual account, on a timely basis, the quantity and the cost of materials received, issued, and on hand. The materials ledger accounts are usually maintained on computer files similar in design to the one shown in Figure 2-10.

Copies of the purchase order and receiving report are approved by the purchasing agent and sent to the accounting department. Upon receiving the purchase order, the accountant enters the date, purchase order number, and quantity in the "On Order" columns of the appropriate materials ledger account. When materials arrive, the accounting department's copy of the receiving report serves as the basis for posting the receipt of the materials to the materials ledger account. The posting shows the date of receipt, the number of the receiving report, the quantity of materials received, and their unit and total cost.

When materials are issued, two copies of the materials requisition go to the accounting department. One copy is used in posting the cost of requisitioned materials to the appropriate accounts in the job cost ledger (individual jobs in process) and factory overhead ledger (individual factory overhead accounts). Direct materials are charged to the job to which they were issued, and indirect materials are charged to the appropriate factory overhead account. The other copy of the materials requisition becomes the basis for posting to the materials ledger accounts. The posting shows the date of issue, the number of the requisition, the quantity of materials issued, and their unit and total cost.

When materials are returned to the storeroom, a copy of the returned materials report goes to the accounting department. The cost of the returned materials is entered on the report and posted to the appropriate materials ledger account. The cost assigned to the returned materials should be the same as that recorded when the materials were issued to the factory.

The copy of the returned materials report is then routed to the cost accountant in charge of the job cost and factory overhead ledgers. Direct materials returned are credited to the specific job for which they were initially issued, and indirect materials returned are credited to the appropriate factory overhead account.

After each receipt and issue of materials is posted to the materials ledger accounts, the balances are updated. These updates could be made at the end of the accounting period, when ending inventories are determined for financial reporting purposes. However, to wait until then would not make it possible to determine when stock of individual items were falling below minimum requirements. Most companies now have automated inventory systems that utilize online information processing, such as bar coding and optical scanning technology to update the inventory records on a "real-time" basis.

Determining the Cost of Materials Issued

An important area of materials accounting is the costing of materials requisitioned from the storeroom for factory use. The unit cost of incoming materials is known at the time of purchase. The date of each purchase is

Figure 2-10 **Materials Ledger Account**

Description Hard Rock Maple Plywood **Location in Storeroom** Bin 8

Maximum 30,000 BD.FT. **Minimum** 10,000 BD.FT. **Stores Ledger Acct. No.** 1411

Date	ON ORDER		RECEIVED				ISSUED				BALANCE		
	Purchase Order No.	Quantity	Receiving Report No./ (Returned Shipping Order No.)	Quantity	Unit Price	Amount	Materials Requisition/ (Returned Materials Report No.)	Quantity	Unit Price	Amount	Quantity	Unit Price	Amount
Jan. 1											10,000	5 25	52,500 00
5							825	500	5 25	2,625 00	9,500	5 25	49,875 00
6	1982	20,000											
21				20,000	5 25	105,000 00					29,500	5 25	154,875 00
23							(234)	500	5 25	2,625 00	29,000	5 25	152,250 00
24							834	1,000	5 25	5,250 00	28,000	5 25	147,000 00

also known, but the materials on hand typically include items purchased on different dates and at different prices. Items that look alike usually are commingled in the storeroom. As a result, it may be difficult or impossible to identify an issue of materials with a specific purchase when determining what unit cost should be assigned to the materials being issued.

Several practical methods of solving this problem are available. In selecting the method to be employed, the accounting policies of the firm and the federal and state income tax regulations must be considered. As the methods are discussed, it is important to remember that the flow of materials does not dictate the flow of costs. The **flow of materials** is the order in which materials are actually issued for use in the factory. The **flow of costs** is the order in which unit costs are assigned to materials issued. The following examples assume the use of a perpetual inventory system where the materials ledger accounts are updated each time materials are received or issued.

First-In, First-Out Method. The **first-in, first-out (FIFO)** method of costing has the advantage of simplicity. The FIFO method assumes that materials issued are taken from the oldest materials in stock. Therefore, the materials are costed at the prices paid for the oldest materials. In many companies, the flow of costs using FIFO closely parallels the physical flow of materials. For example, if materials have a tendency to deteriorate in storage, the oldest materials would be issued first. However, as noted previously, the flow of costs does not have to be determined on the basis of the flow of materials. As a result, any organization may use FIFO.

The FIFO method can be illustrated using the data below. (Note that, for simplicity, the "On Order" columns were omitted from the following materials ledger accounts.)

Dec. 1	Balance, 1,000 lb @ $20
10	Issued 500 lb
15	Purchased 1,000 lb @ $24
20	Issued 250 lb
26	Issued 500 lb
28	Purchased 500 lb @ $26
30	Issued 500 lb
31	Balance, 750 lb

Using FIFO, we would assign costs to materials issued during the month and to materials on hand at the end of the month as follows (also see Figure 2-11: First-In, First-Out Method):

Dec. 10	Issued from the December 1 balance: 500 lb @ $20, total cost, $10,000.
20	Issued from the December 1 balance: 250 lb @ $20, total cost, $5,000.
26	Issued from the December 1 balance: 250 lb @ $20, total cost, $5,000.
	Issued from the December 15 purchase: 250 lb@ $24, total cost, $6,000.
	Total cost of materials issued: $5,000 + $6,000 = $11,000.
30	Issued from the December 15 purchase: 500 lb @ $24, total cost, $12,000.
31	The ending inventory of materials, 750 lb, consists of the following:

Figure 2-11 **Comparison of Inventory Valuation Methods**

	A	B	C	D	E	F	G	H	I	J
1										
2										
3						**First-In, First-Out Method**				
4			**Received**			**Issued**			**Balance**	
5	**Date**	**Quantity**	**Unit Price**	**Amount**	**Quantity**	**Unit Price**	**Amount**	**Quantity**	**Unit Price**	**Amount**
6										
7	Dec. 1							1,000	20.00	20,000.00
8	10				500	20.00	10,000.00	500	20.00	10,000.00
9	15	1,000	24.00	24,000.00				500	20.00	
10								1,000	24.00	34,000.00
11	20				250	20.00	5,000.00	250	20.00	
12								1,000	24.00	29,000.00
13	26				250	20.00				
14					250	24.00	11,000.00	750	24.00	18,000.00
15	28	500	26.00	13,000.00				750	24.00	
16								500	26.00	31,000.00
17	30				500	24.00	12,000.00	250	24.00	
18								500	26.00	19,000.00
19										
20						**Last-In, First-Out method**				
21			**Received**			**Issued**			**Balance**	
22	**Date**	**Quantity**	**Unit Price**	**Amount**	**Quantity**	**Unit Price**	**Amount**	**Quantity**	**Unit Price**	**Amount**
23										
24	Dec. 1							1,000	20.00	20,000.00
25	10				500	20.00	10,000.00	500	20.00	10,000.00
26	15	1,000	24.00	24,000.00				500	20.00	
27								1,000	24.00	34,000.00
28	20				250	24.00	6,000.00	500	20.00	
29								750	24.00	28,000.00
30	26				500	24.00	12,000.00	500	20.00	
31								250	24.00	16,000.00
32	28	500	26.00	13,000.00				500	20.00	
33								250	24.00	
34								500	26.00	29,000.00
35	30				500	26.00	13,000.00	500	20.00	
36								250	24.00	16,000.00
37										
38						**Moving Average Method**				
39			**Received**			**Issued**			**Balance**	
40	**Date**	**Quantity**	**Unit Price**	**Amount**	**Quantity**	**Unit Price**	**Amount**	**Quantity**	**Unit Price**	**Amount**
41										
42	Dec. 1							1,000	20.00	20,000.00
43	10				500	20.00	10,000.00	500	20.00	10,000.00
44	15	1,000	24.00	24,000.00				1,500	22.6667	34,000.00
45	20				250	22.6667	5,666.67	1,250	22.6667	28,333.33
46	26				500	22.6667	11,333.33	750	22.6667	17,000.00
47	28	500	26.00	13,000.00				1,250	24.00	30,000.00
48	30				500	24.00	12,000.00	750	24.00	18,000.00

Date of Purchase	Lb	Unit Cost	Total Cost
December 15	250	$24	$ 6,000
December 28	500	26	13,000
	750		$ 19,000

As illustrated in the example, ending inventories using FIFO are costed at the prices paid for the most recent purchases. With an ending inventory of 750 lb, 500 lb are assigned a unit cost of $26, the unit cost of the December 28 purchase. The remaining 250 lb on hand are priced at $24 per lb, the unit cost of the next most recent purchase on December 15.

Last-In, First-Out Method. The **last-in, first-out (LIFO)** method of costing materials, as the name implies, assumes that materials issued for manufacturing are the most recently purchased materials. Thus, materials issued are costed at the most recent purchase prices, and inventories on hand at the end of the period are costed at prices paid for the earliest purchases. The LIFO method of costing closely approximates the physical flow of materials in some industries. For example, in the smelting of iron ore, the raw material is stored in mountainous piles. As ore is needed for production, it is drawn from the pile in such a way that the material being used is the last ore to have been received. As emphasized previously, however, physical flow does not have to determine the costing method used.

Using the same data given to illustrate the FIFO method, we determine costs under the LIFO method as follows (also see Figure 2-11: Last-In, First-Out Method):

Dec. 10	Issued from the December 1 balance: 500 lb @ $20, total cost, $10,000.
20	Issued from the December 15 purchase: 250 lb @ $24, total cost, $6,000.
26	Issued from the December 15 purchase: 500 lb @ $24, total cost, $12,000.
30	Issued from the December 28 purchase: 500 lb @ $26, total cost, $13,000.
31	The ending inventory of materials, 750 lb, consists of the following:

Date of Purchase	Lb	Unit Cost	Total Cost
Balance, December 1	500	$20	$10,000
December 15	250	24	6,000
	750		$16,000

As illustrated in the example, ending inventories under LIFO are costed at the prices paid for the earliest purchases. With an ending inventory of 750 lb, 500 lb are priced at the beginning inventory unit cost of $20 per lb and the remaining 250 lb are costed at the $24 per lb price of the earliest purchase.

Moving Average Method. The **moving average** method assumes that the materials issued at any time are simply withdrawn from a mixed group of like materials in the storeroom and that no attempt is made to identify the materials as being from the earliest or the latest purchases. This method has the disadvantage of requiring more frequent computations than the other methods. However, the use of software packages has overcome this disadvantage, and many firms have adopted this method. A basic requirement of the moving average method is that an average unit price must be computed every time a new lot of materials is received, and this average unit price must be used to cost all issues of materials until another lot is purchased. Therefore, the issuances in the illustration would be computed as follows (also see Figure 2-11, Moving Average Method):

Dec. 10	Issued from the December 1 balance: 500 lb @ $20, total cost, $10,000.
15	The balance of materials on hand on December 15 consists of 500 lb from December 1 and 1,000 lb acquired on December 15, for a total of 1,500 lb that cost $34,000. The average cost is $22.6667 per lb ($34,000/1,500).
20	Issued 250 lb @ $22.6667, total cost, $5,666.67.
26	Issued 500 lb @ $22.6667, total cost, $11,333.33.
28	The balance of materials on hand on December 28 consists of 750 lb costing $17,000 (purchased prior to December 28) and 500 lb @ $26 (purchased on December 28) costing $13,000. The total cost is $30,000 for 1,250 lb, representing an average cost of $24 per lb ($30,000/1,250).
30	Issued 500 lb @ $24, total cost, $12,000.
31	The ending inventory of materials is $18,000, consisting of 750 lb at $24 per lb.

Analysis of FIFO, LIFO, and Moving Average. FIFO, LIFO, and moving average are the most commonly used methods of inventory costing. Any of these methods may be adopted to maintain the materials ledger. Because no one method best suits all situations, the method chosen should be the one that most accurately reflects the income for the period in terms of the current economic conditions. One factor to consider is the effect the costing method has on reported income for tax purposes. A higher taxable income will subject a firm to higher taxes.

In an inflationary environment, LIFO is sometimes adopted so that the higher prices of the most recently purchased materials may be charged against the increasingly higher sales revenue. The resulting lower gross margin is assumed to reflect a more accurate picture of earnings because the firm will have to replace its inventory at the new higher costs. Also, the lower gross margin, brought about by the use of the LIFO method, results in a smaller tax liability for the firm.

To illustrate the effects that the different costing methods have on profit determination, assume that A, B, and C are competing companies that use FIFO, moving average, and LIFO, respectively. The companies have no beginning inventories, and they purchase identical materials at the same time, as follows (assume also that each purchase is for one unit):

Purchase No. 1 @ $0.10

Purchase No. 2 @ $0.50

Purchase No. 3 @ $0.90

Assume that one unit of material is used and sold at a price of $1.00 after the last purchase has been made, that operating expenses are $.08, and that the tax rate is 50%. The net income is calculated as follows:

	Co. A FIFO (Per Unit)	Co. B Moving Avg. (Per Unit)	Co. C LIFO (Per Unit)
Net sales	$1.00	$1.00	$1.00
Less cost of goods sold	0.10	0.50*	0.90
Gross margin on sales	$0.90	$0.50	$0.10
Operating expenses	0.08	0.08	0.08
Income before income taxes	$0.82	$0.42	$0.02
Less income taxes (50%)	0.41	0.21	0.01
Net income	$0.41	$0.21	$0.01

*$0.10 + $0.50 + $0.90 = $1.50/3 units = $0.50 per unit.

As shown in the example, LIFO costing has a definite tax advantage when prices are rapidly rising. Notice that Company C pays $0.01 per unit for taxes, while Companies A and B pay taxes per unit of $0.41 and $0.21, respectively. Thus, Company C has after-tax cash flow of $0.99 ($1.00 – $0.01) from each sales dollar to pay for replacement merchandise, operating expenses, and dividends, while Company A has only $0.59 after-tax cash flow ($1.00 – $0.41) and Company B has only $0.79 after-tax cash flow ($1.00 – $0.21) available from each dollar of sales.

As previously mentioned, each unit of material currently costs $0.90 (Purchase No. 3). Therefore, Company A requires additional funding of $0.31 ($0.90 – $0.59) and Company B requires additional funding of $0.11 ($0.90 – $0.79) just to replace a unit of material. Only Company C can replace materials and still have a positive cash flow of $0.09 ($0.99 – $0.90). The companies, using their respective costing methods and the data for the three purchases, have the following ending materials inventory balances for the two remaining units:

Company A (FIFO)	$1.40 ($0.50 + $0.90)
Company B (moving average)	$1.00 ($0.50 + $0.50)
Company C (LIFO)	$0.60 ($0.10 + $0.50)

Company C has the most conservatively valued inventory at $0.60, and Company A shows the highest inventory value at $1.40. The Company A inventory value also may be detrimental because inventory often is subject to state and local property taxes that are based on the inventory valuation chosen by the company. It is important to realize that differences between the three methods usually will not be as extreme as they were in this example. Companies that turn their inventory over very rapidly will not be as concerned with the choice of methods as will companies that hold their inventory for a longer time.

Many companies have adopted the LIFO method to match current materials costs with current revenue as well as to minimize the effect of income taxes in periods of rising prices. Companies considering the adoption of the LIFO method, however, should carefully analyze economic conditions and examine the tax regulations that pertain to LIFO. If there should be a downward trend of prices, these companies would probably desire to change to the FIFO method to have the same competitive advantages that were gained by using LIFO when prices were rising. However, the LIFO election cannot be rescinded for tax purposes unless authorized or required by the Internal Revenue Service.

Accounting Procedures

The purpose of materials accounting is to provide a summary from the general ledger of the total cost of materials purchased and used in manufacturing. The forms commonly used in assembling the required data have already been discussed. The purchase invoices provide the information needed to prepare the entry in the purchases journal. Note that for illustrative purposes in this text, all entries are recorded in general journal format. At the end of the month, the total of the materials purchased on account during the month is posted as a debit to Materials and as a credit to Accounts Payable. The materials account in the general ledger serves as a control account for the subsidiary materials ledger.

All materials issued during the month and materials returned to stock are recorded on a **Summary of Materials Issued and Returned** form (Figure 2-12). When the summary is completed at the end of the month, the total cost of direct materials issued, $22,660.50 in Figure 2-12, is recorded by debiting Work in Process and crediting Materials. The total cost of indirect materials issued, $1,139.50 in this example, is recorded by debiting Factory Overhead and crediting Materials.

Any undamaged materials returned to the storeroom should also be recorded on the Summary of Materials Issued and Returned so that the totals may be recorded at the end of the month. The entries required to record undamaged materials returned are the reverse of the entries required to record materials requisitioned. Thus, the total cost of direct materials returned to the storeroom, $779.20 in Figure 2-12, should be debited to Materials and credited to Work in Process, while the total cost of indirect materials returned, $27.50 in this example, should be debited to Materials and credited to Factory Overhead.

Any materials returned to the original vendors should be debited to Accounts Payable and credited to Materials. All transactions relating to materials should be recorded so that the balance of the materials account in the general ledger will represent the cost of materials on hand at the end of a period. The balance of the materials account in the general ledger may be proven by comparing it to the total of the individual materials ledger account balances. A summary of the procedures involved in accounting for materials is shown in Figure 2-13, which presents the recordings required for the more typical materials transactions, both at the time of the transaction and at the end of the period. At the time of the transaction, the recordings to be made affect the subsidiary ledgers, such as the materials ledger and the job cost ledger. At the end of the period, the recordings to be made affect the control accounts for materials, work in process, and factory overhead in the general ledger. Note that in most computerized accounting systems the general ledger accounts are updated during the period, at the same time that transactions are recorded in the subsidiary ledgers.

Figure 2-12 **Summary of Materials Issued and Returned**

SUMMARY OF MATERIALS ISSUED AND RETURNED Month Ending Jan. 31 2011

Date	Materials Issued					Materials Returned to Storeroom				
	Req. No.	Direct Materials		Indirect Materials		Report No.	Direct Materials		Indirect Materials	
		Job	Amount	Overhead Acct. No.	Amount		Job	Amount	Overhead Acct. No.	Amount
Jan. 5	825	315	$2,150.00							
8	826	316	3,210.00	3121	$ 440.00					
11	827	317	280.00	3121	132.50				3121	$ 12.50
14	828	317	415.00							
17	829	316	340.00							
17	830	317	820.00							
18	831	318	290.00	3121	135.00				3121	15.00
19	832	319	224.20			232	319	$ 12.10		
20	833	319	975.90							
24	834	320	5,250.00			233	320	448.90		
27	835	321	6,500.00	3121	432.00	234	321	318.20		
29	836	322	550.00							
30	837	321	785.40							
31	838	320	870.00							
			$22,660.50		$1,139.50			$ 779.20		$ 27.50

Figure 2-13 Summary of Materials Transactions

	Entry at Time of Transaction			Entry at End of Accounting Period		
Transaction	**Source Document**	**Book of Original Entry**	**Subsidiary Ledger Posting**	**Source of Data**	**Book of Original Entry**	**Journal Entry**
Purchase of materials	Vendor's Invoice Receiving Report	Purchases Journal	Materials Ledger	Purchases Journal	None	Materials Accounts Payable
Materials returned to vendor	Return Shipping Order	General Journal	Materials Ledger	General Journal	None	Accounts Payable Materials
Payment of invoices	Approved Voucher	Cash Payments Journal	None	Cash Payments Journal	None	Accounts Payable Cash
Direct materials issued	Materials Requisitions	None	Materials Ledger Job Cost Ledger	Materials Summary	General Journal	Work in Process Materials
Indirect materials issued	Materials Requisitions	None	Materials Ledger Factory Overhead Ledger	Materials Summary	General Journal	Factory Overhead Materials
Direct materials returned from factory to storeroom	Returned Materials Report	None	Materials Ledger Job Cost Ledger	Materials Summary	General Journal	Materials Work in Process
Indirect materials returned from factory to storeroom	Returned Materials Report	None	Materials Ledger Factory Overhead Ledger	Materials Summary	General Journal	Materials Factory Overhead
Inventory adjustment:						
(a) Materials on hand less than materials ledger balance	Inventory Report	General Journal	Factory Overhead Ledger Materials Ledger	General Journal	None	Factory Overhead Materials
(b) Materials on hand more than materials ledger balance	Inventory Report	General Journal	Factory Overhead Ledger Materials Ledger	General Journal	None	Factory Overhead Materials

Inventory Verification. The materials ledger contains an account for each material used in the manufacturing process. Each account shows the number of units on hand and their cost. The materials ledger provides a perpetual inventory of the individual items of material in the storeroom.

Errors in recording receipts or issues of materials in the materials ledger may affect the reliability of the inventory totals. To guard against error, the materials on hand should be checked periodically against the individual materials ledger account balances. The usual practice is to count one lot of materials at a time, spacing the time of the counts so that a complete check of all inventories in the storeroom can be made within a fixed period of time, such as three months. These periodic checks have the advantage of eliminating the costly and time-consuming task of counting the entire inventory at one time. To guard against carelessness or dishonesty, the count should be made by someone other than the storeroom keeper or the stores ledger clerk.

The person making the count should prepare an **inventory report** similar to the one shown in Figure 2-14. If the total indicated in the count differs from the balance in the materials ledger account, an immediate correcting entry should be made in the affected materials ledger account. The correcting entries in the general ledger accounts may be made in total at the end of the month, prior to the preparation of the monthly financial statements. If the materials on hand exceed the balance in the materials control account, the balance should be increased by the following entry:

Materials	xxx	
Factory Overhead (Inventory Short and Over)		xxx

Figure 2-14 **Inventory Report. (Compares book inventory and physical inventory quantities.)**

HAWKE MFG

INVENTORY REPORT

Material Hard Rock Maple Plywood

Location in storeroom Bin 8

Stores ledger acct. no. 1411

Date of verification January 31, 2011

Units in storeroom 7,940 BD.FT.

Units in receiving department 20,000 BD.FT.

Total number units on hand 27,940 BD.FT.

Balance per stores ledger 28,000 BD.FT.

Difference 60 BD.FT.

Counted by P. Valence

Supervised by W. Cox

If the amount of materials on hand is less than the balance in the materials control account, as was the case in Figure 2-14, the balance should be decreased by the following entry:

Factory Overhead (Inventory Short and Over)	xxx	
Materials		xxx

Such inventory differences are almost always a shortage and may arise from damage or shrinkage during handling, theft, or issuing quantities to production that are in excess of those called for and recorded. Shortages (or overages) are recorded in a factory overhead account, usually entitled Inventory Short and Over, because they cannot be easily identified with specific jobs.

Visual Aid. For a cost accounting system to function properly, each employee must understand the assigned duties and the purpose of the various forms and records. Figure 2-15 shows the interrelationship of the accounts and how internal control procedures can be established.

Figure 2-15 Interrelationship of Materials Documents and Accounts

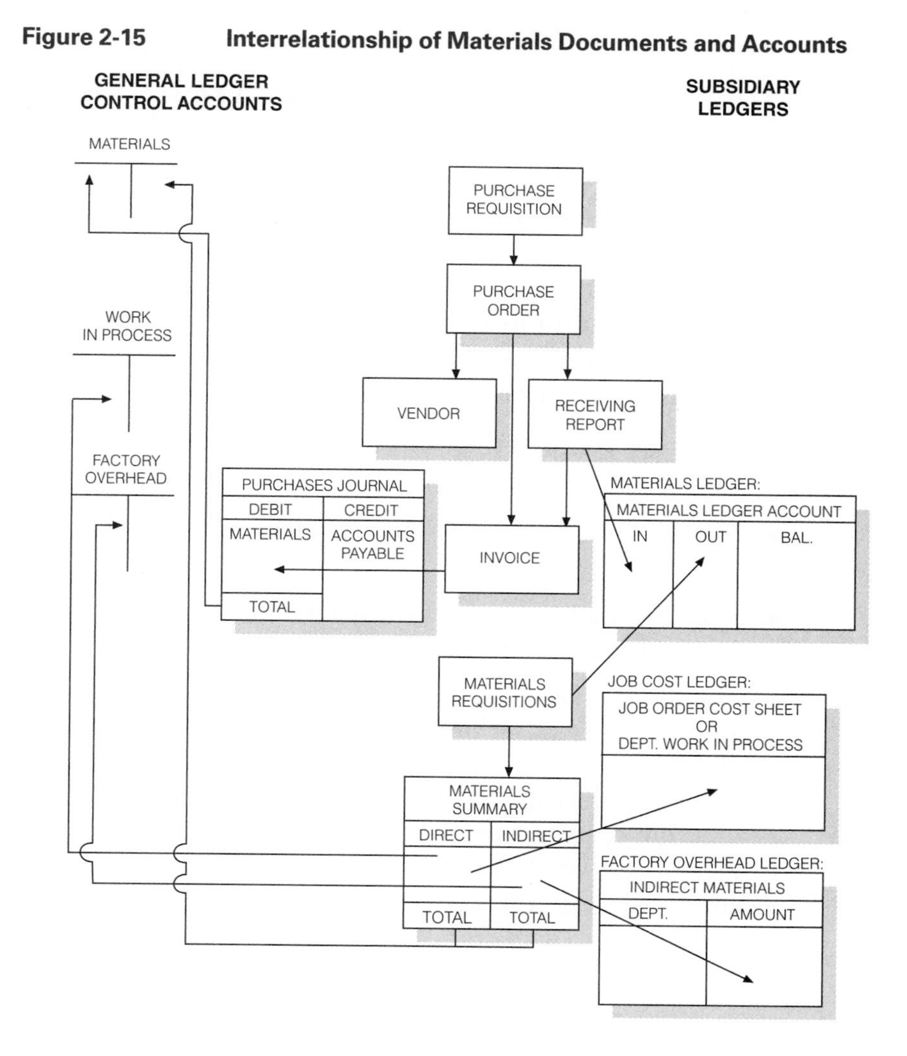

Recall and Review 2

Using FIFO, LIFO, and moving average perpetual inventory costing, and the following information, determine the cost of the May 31 inventory under each of the above inventory costing methods:

May 1	Beginning inventory 500 yards @ $5.00 per yard
10	Purchased 250 yards @ $5.25 per yard
20	Issued 350 yards into production
30	Issued 250 yards into production

FIFO________; LIFO________; Moving Average____________

(After working this exercise, see page 102 for the solution.)

You should now be able to work the following:
Questions 17–20; Exercises 2-4 to 2-11; Problems 2-4 to 2-8 and P2-14R, the review problem for Chapters 1 and 2.

Just-in-Time Materials Control

Boston Company is trying to decide whether or not to change from a traditional inventory system to a just-in-time (JIT) system. The president, Teresa Francona, wants to know whether this change merely will affect how goods are ordered and produced, or if it will also impact the financial health of the company, as well as the accounting system itself. The controller, Donna Ortiz, is preparing a report estimating any expected cost savings and changes to the accounting system resulting from a move to JIT.

- **What are some of the costs that should be affected by the introduction of a JIT system?**
- **Should Francona's customers reap any benefits from the change to JIT?**
- **Will Donna have to make any changes to the way that inventory is accounted for under a JIT system?**

These are some of the questions that will be answered in this section of the chapter and in Mini-Case 2 at the end of the chapter.

LO4 Account for inventories in a just-in-time (lean production) system.

In a **just-in-time (JIT) inventory system**, also known as a **lean production system**, materials are delivered to the factory immediately prior to their use in production. A lean production system significantly reduces inventory carrying costs by requiring that the raw materials be delivered just in time to be placed into production. Also, many manufacturing functions that

Figure 2-16 **Traditional "Push" System of Production Flow**

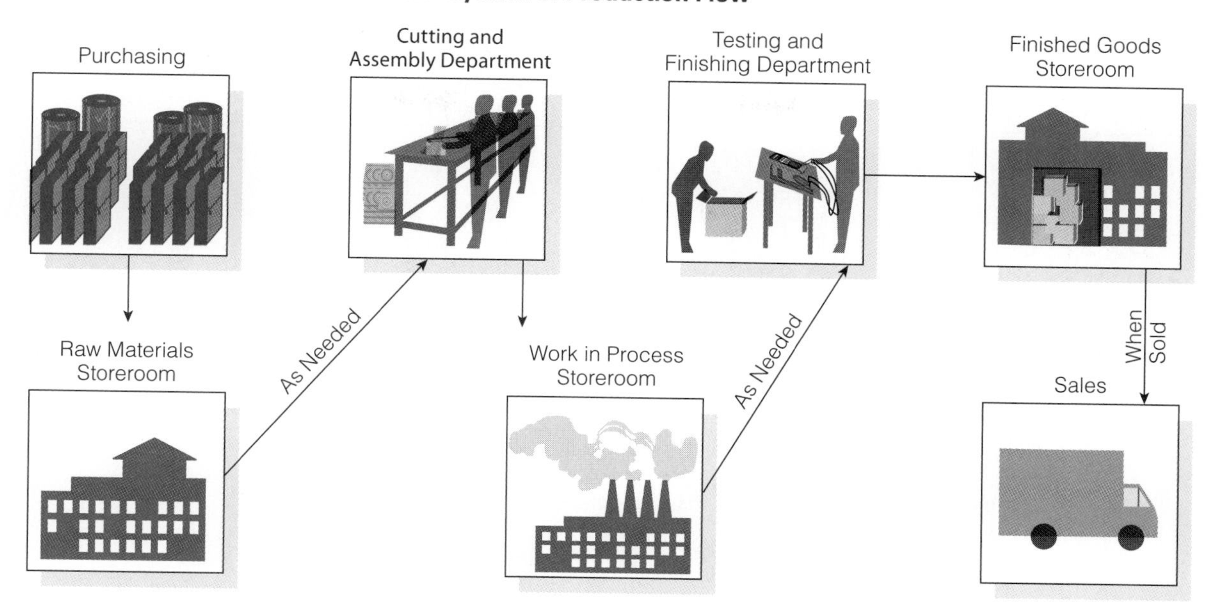

were performed in individual departments in a traditional manufacturing system are combined into work centers, called **manufacturing cells**.

Work in process inventory is minimized by eliminating inventory buffers between manufacturing cells. For example, the work is performed on a unit in Manufacturing Cell 1 only after the department receives the request from Manufacturing Cell 2 for a certain number of the units. This contrasts with traditional **"push" manufacturing systems**, as illustrated in Figure 2-16, which produce goods for inventory with the hope that the demand for these goods then will be created. Disadvantages of a "push" manufacturing system include having too many dollars invested in inventory; defects not being detected, because partially completed goods are inventoried rather than completed immediately; and obsolete products due to the long lead time from start to finish.

The JIT **"pull" manufacturing system** credo is, "Don't make anything for anybody until they ask for it." For JIT to work successfully, a high degree of coordination and cooperation must exist between the supplier and the manufacturer, among manufacturing work centers, and between the manufacturer and the customer. For example, **Wal-Mart** works closely with its major suppliers, such as **Procter & Gamble** and **Lever Brothers**, sharing sales data as to the quantity and timing of sales, so that goods arrive for shelving just in time to meet customer demand. This coordination between supplier, shipper, manufacturer, and customer is known as **supply chain management**. An illustration of a JIT "pull" production system appears in Figure 2-17.

Performing all of the production in one or two manufacturing cells has many advantages. These include fewer and shorter movements of materials, production in smaller lot sizes because other products do not also have to

Figure 2-17 **JIT "Pull" System of Production Flow**

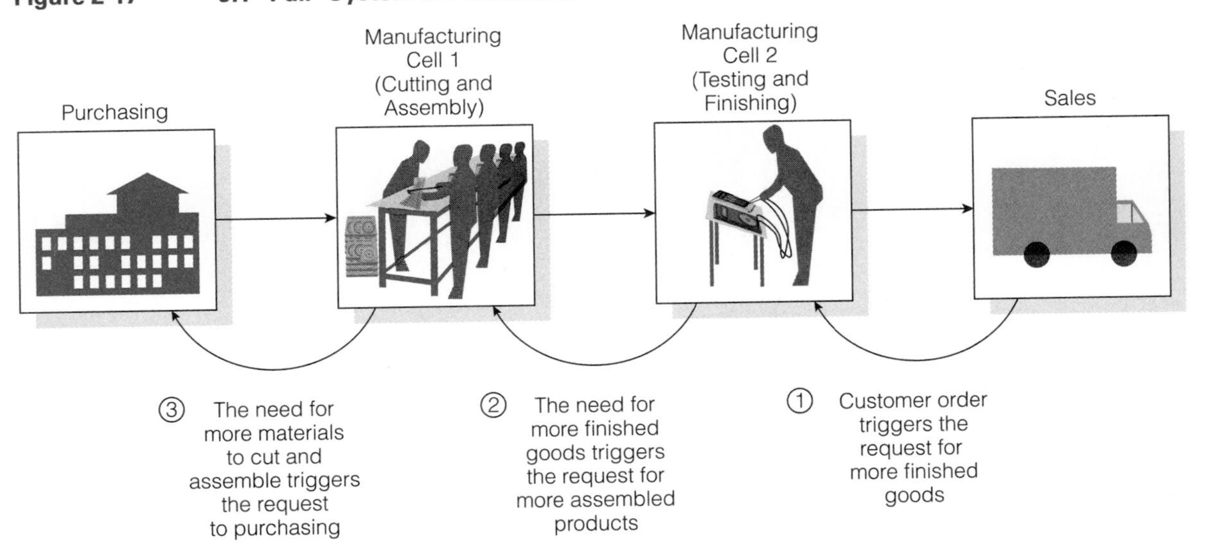

be produced in the same cell, and more worker motivation and satisfaction due to the teamwork approach within the cell. The workers within a cell learn all of the tasks performed in the cell, and they also perform maintenance when "pull" production results in downtime.

Just-in-time production techniques first were utilized by **Toyota Motors** where a **kanban** (card) indicated a manufacturing cell's need for more raw materials or component parts. These techniques have become popular with U.S. manufacturers in recent years. **Dell, General Electric, Harley-Davidson, Hewlett-Packard, IBM, John Deere, and Xerox** are just a few examples of the many U.S. companies that have adopted the principles of lean production. For example, Dell can produce and ship a customized computer to the customer within 36 hours, without ordering components or doing any assembly until the customer's order is received.[1]

Although lean production has its roots in the Toyota Production System of the 1950s, it took decades to catch on with U.S. manufacturers. Today, the service sector's adoption of lean techniques is moving at a much faster pace. "Lean experts" in manufacturing companies are being hired by hospitals and banks at 30 to 40% pay increases. Banks, for example, are using these experts for projects such as identifying bottlenecks in mortgage processing so that decisions on the prospective loans can be made in one day.[2]

JIT and Cost Control

Reducing inventory levels through the use of lean production techniques may increase processing speed, thereby reducing the time it takes for a unit

1 "Inside Dell's Lean Machine," *Works Management*, December 2002.
2 "Toyota's Success Pleases Proponents of 'Lean,'" *USA Today*, April 4, 2007.

to make it through production. For example, if 10,000 units are produced each day and the average number of units in work in process is 40,000, then the **throughput time**, or time that it takes a unit to make it through the system, is 40,000/10,000, or four days. If the same daily output can be achieved while reducing the work in process by 75% or 30,000 units, the throughput time will be reduced to one day, 10,000/10,000, and the **velocity**, or speed with which units are produced in the system, will have quadrupled. If production speed can be increased dramatically, all products may be made to order, thus eliminating the need for finished goods inventory. Also, reducing throughput time can lower costs because there will be fewer **nonvalue-added activities**—operations that include costs but do not add value to the product, such as moving, storing, and inspecting the inventories.

If the velocity of production is quadrupled, as in the preceding example, the inventory carrying costs can be reduced. For example, assume an annual inventory carrying cost percentage of 20% and an average work in process inventory of $400,000, resulting in annual carrying costs of $80,000 (20% × $400,000). Further assume that through the use of JIT production techniques, the velocity of production is quadrupled without changing the total annual output, thus necessitating only one-fourth as much work in process (WIP). The new annual carrying costs would be calculated as follows:

Carrying cost percentage × Average WIP = Annual carrying cost

20% × (1/4 × $400,000) = $20,000

or a $60,000 reduction from the previous level of $80,000.

Another advantage of reduced throughput time is increased customer satisfaction due to quicker delivery. Studies have shown that delivery speed and delivery reliability improve by 70 to 90% in a lean production system.[3] Also, production losses are reduced due to not having great quantities of partially completed units piling up at the next workstation before an error in their production is detected and corrected.

JIT and Cost Flows

Figure 2-18 contrasts the journal entries made in a traditional manufacturing cost accounting system with the entries made in a JIT system. **Backflush costing** is the name for the accounting system used with lean manufacturing. It derives its name from the fact that costs are not "flushed out" of the accounting system and charged to the products until the goods are completed and sold.

3 "How Customers Benefit from Lean Manufacturing Strategies," page 1, http://www.strategosinc.com/lean_benefits_5.htm (visited February 10, 2009).

Figure 2-18 **Journal Entries for Traditional and Backflush Accounting**

Transaction	Journal Entries: Traditional System			Journal Entries: Backflush System		
A. Purchase of raw materials	Materials	50,000		Raw and In-Process	50,000	
	Accounts Payable ...		50,000	Accounts Payable		50,000
B. Raw materials requisitioned to production	Work in Process	50,000		No Entry		
	Materials		50,000			
C. Direct labor cost	Work in Process	25,000		Conversion Costs	25,000	
	Payroll		25,000	Payroll		25,000
D. Manufacturing overhead costs incurred	Factory Overhead	75,000		Conversion Costs	75,000	
	Various Credits		75,000	Various Credits		75,000
E. Transfer of factory overhead costs to work in process	Work in Process	75,000		No Entry		
	Factory Overhead ...		75,000			
F. Completion of all products	Finished Goods	150,000		Finished Goods	150,000	
	Work in Process		150,000	Raw and In-Process ...		50,000
				Conversion Costs		100,000
G. Sale of all products	Cost of Goods Sold	150,000		Cost of Goods Sold	150,000	
	Finished Goods		150,000	Finished Goods		150,000

Entries A and B in Figure 2-18 indicate that a single account, Raw and In-Process, is used in backflush costing for both raw materials and work in process inventories. This is done because, in a lean production system, raw materials are issued to production as soon as they are received from the supplier, thus negating the need for storing materials and creating a separate raw materials inventory account. Also, note that a single journal entry, entry A in Figure 2-18, reflects both the purchase and the issuance of materials into production using backflush costing. Entries C and D illustrate that a single account, Conversion Costs, contains both direct labor and factory overhead costs in a backflush system. This is because direct labor usually is so insignificant in a highly automated JIT setting that it is not cost effective to account for it as a separate category of manufacturing cost.

Entry F, and the "No Entry" in E, illustrate that materials, labor, and overhead costs are not attached to products in a backflush system until they are completed. The rationale for this approach is that products move through the system so rapidly in a lean production environment that it would not be cost effective to track production costs to them while in process. Critics of backflush costing argue that it is not consistent with Generally Accepted Accounting Principles (GAAP) because it does not accurately account for inventories. Proponents of backflush costing argue that Work in Process and Finished Goods are immaterial in a lean

Figure 2-19 **Three Trigger Points: Purchase of Materials, Completion of Goods, Sale of Goods**

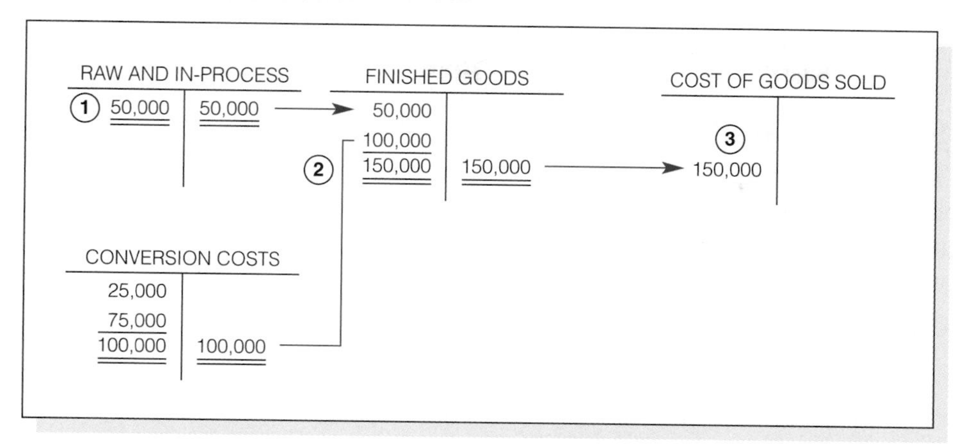

production environment and, therefore, their omission does not materially misstate the financial statements.

Note that different companies choose different points in the production process, called **trigger points,** from the purchase of raw materials to the sale of finished goods, at which to record journal entries in a backflush system. Accountants make this decision based on what points adequately describe the product flows with the least amount of recording. In Figure 2-19, the three trigger points are: (1) the purchase of materials; (2) the completion of work in process; and(3) the sale of finished goods. If the only trigger points were the purchase of materials and the sale of finished goods, entries F and G in Figure 2-18 would be:

F. No entry		
G. Cost of Goods Sold	150,000	
Raw and In-Process		50,000
Conversion Costs		100,000

Scrap, Spoiled Goods, and Defective Work

LO5 Account for scrap materials, spoiled goods, and defective work.

Manufacturing operations usually produce some imperfect units that cannot be sold as regular items. The controls over imperfect items and operations that waste materials are important elements of inventory control. **Scrap materials** may result naturally from the production process, or they may be spoiled or defective units that result from avoidable or unavoidable mistakes during production. Because the sale of imperfect items tends to damage a company's reputation, most companies introduce quality control techniques that prevent imperfect items from being sold. Also, many companies are helping the environment by recycling and reducing waste. For example, 99% of scrap steel generated by **Toyota** plants is now recycled, and total recycling at its Georgetown, KY, plant alone is in excess of 100,000 tons per year, as well as 40,000 light bulbs.[4] Since scrap, spoiled goods, and defective work usually have some value, each of their costs is accounted for separately.

Scrap Materials

The procedures to use in accounting for scrap are determined by the expected sales value of the scrap. When the scrap value is small, no entry is made for it until the scrap is sold, at which time the following journal entry would be made:

Cash (or Accounts Receivable)	xxx	
Scrap Revenue		xxx

The revenue from scrap sales is usually reported as "Other Income" in the income statement. If the accountant chooses to treat the revenue from scrap as a reduction in manufacturing costs, rather than as "Other Income," Work in Process and the individual job in the job cost ledger may be credited if the scrap can be readily identified with a specific job. If the scrap cannot be identified with a specific job, Factory Overhead may be credited.

When the value of the scrap is relatively high, an inventory file should be prepared and the scrap transferred to a controlled materials storage area. If both the quantity and the market value of the scrap are known, the following journal entries are made to record the inventory and the subsequent sale:

Scrap Materials	xxx	
Scrap Revenue (or Work in Process or Factory Overhead)		xxx
Transferred scrap to inventory.		
Cash (or Accounts Receivable)	xxx	
Scrap Materials		xxx
Sold scrap at inventoried market value.		

If the market value of the scrap is not known, no journal entry is made until the scrap is sold. At the time of sale, the following entry is then recorded:

Cash (or Accounts Receivable)	xxx	
Scrap Revenue (or Work in Process or Factory Overhead)		xxx
Sold scrap.		

Spoiled and Defective Work

Scrap is an unexpected by-product of the production of the primary product. Spoiled or defective goods are not by-products but imperfect units of the primary product. **Spoiled units** have imperfections that cannot be economically corrected. They are sold as items of inferior quality or

4 "Steel Recycling," www.toyotageorgetown.com/envsteel.asp (visited February 16, 2009).

"seconds." **Defective units** have imperfections considered correctable because the increase in market value by correcting the unit exceeds the cost to correct it.

Spoiled Work. The loss associated with spoiled goods may be treated as part of the cost of the job or department that produced the spoiled units, or the loss may be charged to Factory Overhead and allocated among all jobs or departments. Generally, Factory Overhead is charged unless the loss results from a special order and the spoilage is due to the type of work required on that particular order. In both cases, the spoiled goods are recorded in Spoiled Goods Inventory at the expected sales price.

To illustrate, assume a garment manufacturer using job order costing completes an order for 1,000 jackets (Job 350) at the following unit costs:

Materials	$20
Labor	20
Factory overhead	10
Total cost per unit	$50

The journal entry to record the costs of production is as follows:

Work in Process (Job 350)	50,000	
Materials		20,000
Payroll		20,000
Factory Overhead		10,000
Recognized production costs for Job 350.		

During the final inspection, 50 jackets are found to be inferior and are classified as irregulars or seconds. They are expected to sell for $10 each. If the unrecovered costs of spoilage are to be charged to Factory Overhead, the following entry is recorded:

Spoiled Goods Inventory	500	
Factory Overhead	2,000	
Work in Process (Job 350)		2,500
Recognized spoiled goods at market value of $500 (50 jackets @ $10), charged Factory Overhead for loss of $2,000 (50 jackets @ $40), and reduced cost of Job 350 by $2,500 (50 jackets @ $50 because the loss is charged to all jobs).		

If the loss from spoilage is caused by the unique production requirements of Job 350, the entry to record the market value is as follows:

Spoiled Goods Inventory	500	
Work in Process (Job 350)		500
Recognized spoiled goods at market value and reduced the cost of Job 350 by the $500 sales price of spoiled goods.		

Spoilage costs charged to Factory Overhead are allocated among all jobs in production. When spoilage is attributed to a specific job, however, the entire cost of spoilage is reflected in the cost of that job. In the example, Job 350 will be charged with only a portion of the $2,000 loss from spoilage when Factory Overhead is allocated to all of the jobs worked on during the period. When Factory Overhead is not charged for the spoilage costs, however, the entire $2,000 loss is included in the total cost of Job 350. (Note how the credit to Work in Process in the previous entry reduces the spoilage loss from the $2,500 cost of the 50 jackets included in Work in Process to $2,000, after considering the $500 sales value of the spoiled goods.)

Defective Work. The procedures used in recording the cost of defective work are similar to those employed in accounting for spoiled goods. There are, however, additional costs for correcting the imperfections in defective units. If these costs are incurred on orders that the company regularly produces, they are charged to Factory Overhead. For special orders, the additional costs are charged to the specific job on which the defective work occurs. An inventory account is not established for goods classified as defective because the defects are corrected and the units become first-quality merchandise.

As in the previous illustration, assume that it costs $50 to manufacture each jacket. Upon final inspection of the 1,000 jackets completed, 50 jackets are defective because one sleeve is a slightly different shade of blue than the other parts of the jacket. Management decides to recut the sleeves from a bolt of material identical in color to the rest of the jacket. The costs of correcting the defect on the 50 jackets are $500 for materials, $400 for labor, and $300 for factory overhead, representing a total cost of $1,200.

If the additional costs are charged to Factory Overhead, the cost of correcting defective work is spread over all jobs that go through the production cycle. The journal entry is as follows:

Factory Overhead	1,200	
Materials		500
Payroll		400
Factory Overhe		300
Recognized costs of correcting defective units.		

If the order for 1,000 jackets was a special order and the defects resulted from the exacting specifications of the order, the additional costs would be charged to the specific job as follows:

Work in Process (Job 350)	1,200	
Materials		500
Payroll		400
Factory Overhead		300
Charged Job 350 with cost of correcting defective work.		

In this instance, the total cost of Job 350 will be higher because the additional costs to correct the defects were charged to the order rather than to the factory overhead account. The unit cost of each completed jacket is increased from $50 ($50,000/1,000) to $51.20 ($51,200/1,000) because of the additional costs charged to the work in process account.

Recall and Review 3

Angel Industries produces 25,000 units each day, and the average number of units in work in process inventory is 50,000.

1. If it is determined that the same daily output can be achieved while reducing the work in process by 50%, determine (a) the current throughput time________ and (b) the projected new throughput time___________.
2. Assuming the above doubling of the velocity of production, an average annual carrying cost of 15%, and an average work in process inventory of $500,000, determine (a) the current annual carrying cost____________ and (b) the projected new annual carrying cost______________.

(After working this exercise, see page 102 for the solution.)

You should now be able to work the following:
Questions 21–28; Exercises 2-12 to 2-17; Problems 2-9 to 2-13; Mini-Cases 1 and 2; Internet Exercise; and Self-Study Problem 2.

KEY TERMS

ANSWERS TO RECALL AND REVIEW EXERCISES

R&R 1

1.

$$\begin{aligned} EOQ &= \sqrt{(2 \times \$25 \times 200{,}000)/\$10} \\ &= \sqrt{1{,}000{,}000} \\ &= 1{,}000 \text{ lb} \end{aligned}$$

2.

Ordering cost = 200,000 lb/1,000 lb per order = 200 orders
= 200 orders × $25 per order = $5,000

Carrying Cost = 1,000 lb/2 = 500 lb average inventory
= 500 lb × $10 = $5,000

R&R 2

Using FIFO:

Dec. 20, Issued from the Dec. 1 inventory 350 yd @ $5.00, $1,750

Dec. 30, Issued 250 yd from:

Dec. 1 inventory 150 yd @ $5.00, $750

Dec. 10 purchase 100 yd @ $5.25, $525

The ending inventory consists of 150 yd @ $5.25, $787.50

Using LIFO:

Dec. 20, Issued 350 yd from:

Dec. 10 purchase 250 yd @ $5.25, $1,312.50

Dec. 1 inventory, 100 yd @ $5.00, $500

Dec. 30, Issued 250 yd from Dec. 1 inventory @ $5.00, $1,250

The ending inventory consists of 150 yd @ $5.00, $750

Using moving average:

Dec. 20, Issued 350 yd @ the moving average cost of $5.08 ($3,812.50/750 yd), $1,778

Dec. 30, Issued 250 yd @ the moving average cost of $5.08, $1,270

The ending inventory consists of 150 yd @ $5.08, $762

R&R 3

1. (a) 50,000/25,000 = 2 days
   (b) (50,000 × .50)/25,000 = 1 day

2. (a) $500,000 × .15 = $75,000
   (b) ($500,000 × ½) × .15 = $37,500

SELF-STUDY PROBLEM 1

Order Point; Economic Order Quantity; Ordering and Carrying Costs

Brooklyn Bat Company

Brooklyn Bat Company, manufacturer of top-of-the-line baseball bats from Northern white ash, predicts that 8,000 billets of lumber will be used during the year. (A billet is the quantity of rough lumber needed to make one bat.) The expected daily usage is 32 billets. The expected lead time is 10 days, and there is a safety stock of 500 billets. The company expects the lumber to cost $4 per billet. It anticipates that it will cost $40 to place each order. The annual carrying cost is $0.25 per billet.

Required:

1. Calculate the order point.
2. Calculate the most economical order quantity (EOQ).
3. Calculate the total cost of ordering and carrying at the EOQ point.

SOLUTION TO SELF-STUDY PROBLEM

Suggestions:

Read the entire problem thoroughly, keeping in mind that you are required to calculate (1) order point, (2) EOQ, and (3) total ordering and carrying costs. The specifics in the problem highlight the following facts relevant to computing the order point:

Expected daily usage is 32 billets.
Expected lead time is 10 days.
Required safety stock is 500 billets.

The order point is the inventory level at which an order should be placed. It is determined by adding the estimated number of billets to be used between placement and receipt of the order:

Estimated usage during lead time
= 32 billets (daily usage) x 10 days (lead time) = 320

Add the number of billets of safety stock (500 in this problem) needed to protect against abnormally high usage and unforeseen delays in receiving good materials from the supplier:

Order Point = Expected usage during lead time + safety stock
= 320 + 500
= 820 billets

The specifics in the problem highlight the following facts relevant to computing the EOQ:

Estimated annual usage of materials	8,000 billets
Cost of placing an order	$40
Annual carrying cost per billet	$0.25

The EOQ is the order size that minimizes total order and carrying costs. It can be calculated by using the EOQ formula:

$$\text{EOQ} = \sqrt{\frac{2 \times \text{order cost} \times \text{annual demand}}{\text{annual carrying cost per unit}}}$$
$$= \sqrt{\frac{2 \times \$40 \times 8{,}000}{\$0.25}}$$
$$= \sqrt{\frac{\$640{,}00}{\$0.25}}$$
$$= \sqrt{2{,}560{,}000}$$
$$= 1{,}600 \text{ billets}$$

The specifics in the problem highlight the following facts that are relevant to computing the total ordering and carrying costs at the EOQ point:

Annual usage	8,000 billets
EOQ	1,600 billets
Ordering costs	$40 per order
Carrying cost	$0.25 per billet
Safety stock	500 billets

To determine the annual ordering cost, you must first determine the number of orders by dividing the annual usage by the EOQ:

$$\text{Number of orders} = \text{annual usage} \ / \ \text{EOQ}$$
$$= 8{,}000 \text{ billets} \ / \ 1{,}600 \text{ billets}$$
$$= 5$$

The annual order cost is determined by multiplying the number of orders by the cost per order:

$$5 \text{ orders} \times \$40 \text{ per order} = \$200$$

To determine the annual carrying cost, you must first determine the average number of billets in inventory:

$$(1/2 \times \text{EOQ}) + \text{safety stock}$$
$$(1/2 \times 1{,}600) + 500 = 1{,}300 \text{ billets}$$

The average number of billets in inventory would consist of one-half of the amount ordered plus the 500 billets that are kept as a cushion against unforeseen events. The total carrying cost would then be as follows:

$$\text{Average inventory} \times \text{carrying cost per billet}$$
$$1{,}300 \times \$0.25 = \$325$$

Total cost of ordering and carrying:

$$\text{Order costs} + \text{carrying costs}$$
$$\$200 + \$325 = \$525$$

SELF-STUDY PROBLEM 2

Journal Entries for Backflush Costing

Speedy Manufacturing Company

Speedy uses backflush costing to account for its manufacturing costs. The trigger points for recording inventory transactions are the purchase of materials, the completion of products, and the sale of completed products. The following transactions occurred during the period:

a. Purchased raw materials on account, $75,000.
b. Requisitioned raw materials to production, $75,000.
c. Distributed direct labor costs, $12,500.
d. Incurred manufacturing overhead costs, $50,000. (Use Various Credits for the credit part of the entry.)
e. Cost of products completed, $137,500.
f. Completed products sold for $200,000, on account.

Required:
Prepare the necessary journal entries to record the above transactions.

SOLUTION TO SELF-STUDY PROBLEM

Suggestions:
Read the entire problem thoroughly, keeping in mind that you are required to prepare journal entries for a JIT manufacturer using backflush costing. The specifics in the problem highlight the following relevant facts:

- Speedy uses backflush costing to account for its manufacturing costs.
- The trigger points for the recording of inventory transactions are:
  the purchase of materials
  the completion of products
  the sale of products

Preparing the Journal Entries:

a.	Raw and In-Process	75,000	
	Accounts Payable		75,000

Raw and In-Process is the single account that is used in backflush costing for both the purchase of raw materials and the issuance of those materials into production.

b. No entry required.

Note that the debit in a. above to Raw and In-Process reflects both the purchase of materials and their issuance into production, thus negating the need for a separate entry here.

c.	Conversion Costs	12,500	
	Payroll		12,500

Because direct labor is usually immaterial in a JIT system, a single account, Conversion Costs, is usually debited for both direct labor and factory overhead.

d. Conversion Costs	50,000	
Various Credits		50,000

(See the explanation in c. above.)

e. Finished Goods	137,500	
Raw and In-Process		75,000
Conversion Costs		62,500

All products started in this JIT system were completed during the period; therefore all materials, labor, and overhead costs should be closed to finished goods.

f. Cost of Goods Sold	137,500	
Finished Goods		137,500

As in a traditional costing system, the sale of completed products causes the product cost to be transferred from an asset account, Finished Goods, to an expense account, Cost of Goods Sold.

Accounts Receivable	200,000	
Sales		200,000

Revenue from the sale is recorded in an asset account, Accounts Receivable, and in a revenue account, Sales.

QUESTIONS

1. What are the two major objectives of materials control?
2. Materials often represent a substantial portion of a company's assets; therefore, they should be controlled from the time orders are placed to the time finished goods are shipped to the customer. What are the control procedures used for safeguarding materials?
3. What factors should management consider when determining the amount of investment in materials?
4. What is the meaning of the term *order point*?
5. What kind of information and data are needed to calculate an order point?
6. How would you define the term *economic order quantity*?
7. What kind of information and data are needed to calculate the economic order quantity?
8. What factors should be considered when determining the cost of placing an order?
9. What are the costs associated with carrying materials in stock?
10. Briefly, what are the duties of the following employees?
    a. Purchasing agent
    b. Receiving clerk
    c. Storeroom keeper
    d. Production supervisor
11. Proper authorization is required before orders for new materials can be placed. What is the difference between a purchase requisition and a purchase order?
12. Purchasing agents are responsible for contacting vendors from which to purchase materials required by production. Why is the purchasing agent also responsible for reviewing and approving incoming vendors' invoices?

13. Illustrations of forms for requisitioning, ordering, and accounting for materials are presented in the chapter. Would you expect these forms, as shown, to be used by all manufacturers? Discuss.

14. What internal control procedures should be established for incoming shipments of materials purchased?

15. What is the purpose of a debit-credit memorandum?

16. Who originates each of the following forms?
    a. Purchase requisition
    b. Purchase order
    c. Receiving report
    d. Materials requisition
    e. Debit-credit memorandum

17. Normally, a manufacturer maintains an accounting system that includes a materials ledger and a general ledger account for Materials. What is the relationship between the materials ledger and the materials account in the general ledger?

18. A company may select an inventory costing method from a number of commonly used procedures. Briefly, how would you describe each of the following methods?
    a. First-in, first-out
    b. Last-in, first-out
    c. Moving average

19. Why do companies adopt the LIFO method of inventory costing? Your discussion should include the effects on both the income statement and balance sheet.

20. Which of the forms shown in the chapter is the source for the following entries to subsidiary ledger accounts?
    a. Debits in materials ledger to record materials purchased
    b. Credits in materials ledger to record materials requisitioned
    c. Debits in job cost ledger to record materials placed in process

21. How does the just-in-time approach to production differ from the traditional approach?

22. Explain the meaning of the terms *push* manufacturing and *pull* manufacturing.

23. List three disadvantages of the "push" manufacturing approach to production.

24. What is the difference between throughput time and velocity?

25. List three advantages to producing all units of a specific product in a single manufacturing cell?

26. What are the arguments for and against "backflush" costing?

27. A manufacturing process may produce a considerable quantity of scrap material because of the nature of the product. What methods can be used to account for the sales value of scrap material?

28. After a product is inspected, some units may be classified as spoiled and others as defective. What distinguishes a product as being spoiled or defective?

EXERCISES

E2-1 Order Point

Aztec Company expects daily usage of 500 pounds of material Inca, an anticipated lead time of seven days, and a desired safety stock of 2,500 pounds.

a. Determine the order point.

b. Determine the number of pounds to be issued from safety stock if the new order is four days late.

LO1

E2-2 Economic order quantity; order cost; carrying cost

Patriot Company predicts that it will use 360,000 gallons of material during the year. The material is expected to cost $5 per gallon. Patriot anticipates that it will cost $72 to place each order. The annual carrying cost is $4 per gallon.

a. Determine the most economical order quantity by using the EOQ formula.

b. Determine the total cost of ordering and carrying at the EOQ point.

LO2

E2-3 Materials control procedures

Match the materials control form in the left column with the person responsible for its preparation in the right column. (A selection may be used more than once.)

a. Purchase requisition	1. Production department supervisor
b. Purchase order	2. Storeroom keeper
c. Receiving report	3. Purchasing agent
d. Debit-credit memo	4. Receiving clerk
e. Materials requisition	5. Accountant

LO3

E2-4 Journalizing materials requisitions

Catskill Manufacturing, Inc., records the following use of materials during the month of June:

			Materials Requisitions	
Date	Req. No.	Use	Direct Materials	Indirect Materials
1	110	Material A, Job 10	$20,000	
5	111	Material B, Job 11	18,000	
9	112	Material B, Job 12	16,000	
12	113	Factory supplies		$ 1,800
18	114	Material C, Job 10	3,000	
21	115	Material D, Job 10	9,000	
23	116	Material D, Job 11	2,000	
28	117	Factory supplies		1,300
30	118	Factory supplies		1,700

Prepare a summary journal entry for the materials requisitions.

LO3

E2-5 Recording materials transactions

Prepare a journal entry to record each of the following materials transactions:

a. Total materials purchased on account during the month amounted to $200,000.

b. Direct materials requisitioned for the month totaled $175,000.

c. Indirect materials requisitioned during the month totaled $12,000.

d. Direct materials returned to the storeroom from the factory amounted to $2,500.
e. Total materials returned to vendor during the month amounted to $1,800.
f. Payment during the month for materials purchases totaled $165,000.

E2-6 **FIFO costing**

LO3

Using first-in, first-out; perpetual inventory costing; and the following information, determine the cost of materials used and the cost of the July 31 inventory:

July 1	Balance on hand, 1,000 yd of linen @ $4.00 each.
3	Issued 250 yd.
5	Received 500 yd@ $4.50 each.
6	Issued 150 yd.
10	Issued 110 yd.
11	Factory returned 10 yd, which were issued on the 10th, to the storeroom.
15	Received 500 yd @ $5.00 each.
20	Returned 300 yd to the vendor from the July 15 purchase.
26	Issued 600 yd.

E2-7 **LIFO costing**

Using last-in, first-out; perpetual inventory costing; and the information presented in E2-6, compute the cost of materials used and the cost of the July 31 inventory.

E2-8 **Moving average costing**

Using the moving average method of perpetual inventory costing and the information presented in E2-6, compute the cost of materials used and the cost of the July 31 inventory. (Round unit prices to four decimal places and totals to the nearest whole dollar.)

E2-9 **Comparison of FIFO, LIFO, and moving average methods**

In tabular form, compare the total materials cost transferred to Work in Process and the cost of the ending inventory for each method used in E2-6, E2-7, and E2-8. Discuss the effect that each method will have on profits, depending on whether it is a period of rising prices or a period of falling prices.

E2-10 **Impact of costing methods on net income**

LO3

Benson Company was franchised on January 1, 2011. At the end of its third year of operations, December 31, 2013, management requested a study to determine what effect different materials inventory costing methods would have had on its reported net income over the three-year period.

The materials inventory account, using LIFO, FIFO, and moving average, would have had the following ending balances:

Materials Inventory Balances

December 31	LIFO	FIFO	Average
2010	$20,000	$22,000	$21,000
2011	20,000	24,000	23,000
2012	20,000	30,000	27,667

a. Assuming the same number of units in ending inventory at the end of each year, were material costs rising or falling from 2011 to 2013?
b. Which costing method would show the highest net income for 2011?
c. Which method would show the lowest net income for 2013?
d. Which method would show the highest net income for the three years combined?

LO3

E2-11 Recording materials transactions

Mystic Manufacturing Company maintains the following accounts in the general ledger: Materials, Work in Process, Factory Overhead, and Accounts Payable. On June 1, the materials account had a debit balance of $5,000. Following is a summary of materials transactions for the month of June:

1. Materials purchased, $23,750.
2. Direct materials requisitioned to production, $19,250.
3. Direct materials returned to storeroom, $1,200.
4. Indirect materials requisitioned to production, $2,975.
5. Indirect materials returned to storeroom, $385.
   a. Prepare journal entries to record the materials transactions.
   b. Post the journal entries to ledger accounts (in T-account form).
   c. What is the balance of the materials inventory account at the end of the month?

E2-12 JIT and cost control

Iwamura Industries produces 10,000 units each day, and the average number of units in work in process is 40,000.

1. Determine the throughput time.
2. If the same daily output can be achieved while reducing the work in process by 75%, determine the new throughput time.

LO4

E2-13 Backflush costing

RDI Company uses backflush costing to account for its manufacturing costs. The trigger points are the purchase of materials, the completion of goods, and the sale of goods. Prepare journal entries to account for the following:

a. Purchased raw materials, on account, $80,000.
b. Requisitioned raw materials to production, $80,000.
c. Distributed direct labor costs, $10,000.

d. Manufacturing overhead costs incurred, $60,000. (Use Various Credits for the account in the credit part of the entry.)
e. Completed all of the production started.
f. Sold the completed production for $225,000, on account.

(*Hint:* Use a single account for raw materials and work in process.)

E2-14 Backflush costing

In E2-13, prepare any journal entries that would have been different if the only trigger points had been the purchase of materials and the sale of finished goods.

E2-15 Scrap materials

LO5

A machine shop manufactures a stainless steel part that is used in an assembled product. Materials charged to a particular job amounted to $600. At the point of final inspection, it was discovered that the material used was inferior to the specifications required by the engineering department; therefore, all units had to be scrapped.

Record the entries required for scrap under each of the following conditions:

a. The revenue received for scrap is to be treated as a reduction in manufacturing cost but cannot be identified with a specific job. The value of stainless steel scrap is stable and estimated to be $125 for this job. The scrap is sold two months later for cash at the estimated value of $125.
b. Revenue received for scrap is to be treated as a reduction in manufacturing cost but cannot be identified with a specific job. A firm price is not determinable for the scrap until it is sold. It is sold eventually for $75 cash.
c. The production job is a special job, and the $85 received on account for the scrap is to be treated as a reduction in manufacturing cost. (A firm price is not determinable for the scrap until it is sold.)
d. Only $40 cash was received for the scrap when it was sold in the following fiscal period. (A firm price is not determinable for the scrap until it is sold, and the amount to be received for the scrap is to be treated as other income.)

E2-16 Spoiled work

LO5

Venus, Inc., manufactures tennis clothing. During the month, the company cut and assembled 8,000 skirts. One hundred of the skirts did not meet specifications and were considered "seconds." Seconds are sold for $9.95 per skirt, whereas first-quality skirts sell for $39.95. During the month, Work in Process was charged $108,000: $36,000 for materials, $48,000 for labor, and $24,000 for factory overhead.

Record the entries to first charge production costs for the period and to then record the loss due to spoiled work, under each of the following conditions:

a. The loss due to spoiled work is spread over all jobs in the department.
b. The loss due to spoiled work is charged to the specific job because it is a special order.

E2-17 Defective work

LO5

David Mfg. Company manufactures an integrated transistor circuit board for repeat customers but also accepts special orders for the same product. Job No. MS1 incurred the following unit costs for 1,000 circuit boards manufactured:

Materials	$ 6.00
Labor	3.00
Factory overhead	2.00
Total cost per unit	$11.00

When the completed products were tested, 50 circuit boards were found to be defective. The costs per unit of correcting the defects follow:

Materials	$3.00
Labor	2.00
Factory overhead	1.00

Record the journal entry for the costs to correct the defective work:

a. If the cost of the defective work is charged to factory overhead.
b. If the cost of the defective work is charged to the specific job.

PROBLEMS

P2-1 Economic order quantity; ordering and carrying costs. similar to Self-Study Problem 1

LO1

Marino Company predicts that it will use 25,000 units of material during the year. The expected daily usage is 200 units, and there is an expected leadtime of five days and a desired safety stock of 500 units. The material is expected to cost $5 per unit. Marino anticipates that it will cost $50 to place each order. The annual carrying cost is $0.10 per unit.

Required:

1. Compute the order point.
2. Determine the most economical order quantity by use of the formula.
3. Calculate the total cost of ordering and carrying at the EOQ point.

P2-2 Economic order quantity; tabular computation

Cortez Chemical, Inc., requires 20,000 gallons of material annually; the cost of placing an order is $20, and the annual carrying cost per gallon is $5.

Required:
Determine the EOQ from potential order sizes of 300, 400, 500, 600, 700, and 800 gallons by constructing a table similar to the one appearing on page 68.

P2-3 **Economic order quantity; safety stock**
In P2-2, assume that the company desires a safety stock of 500 gallons.

Required:
1. Compute the average number of gallons in inventory.
2. Compute the total carrying cost.
3. Compute the total order cost. Did it differ from your answer in P2-2 above?

P2-4 **Inventory costing methods**
The purchases and issues of rubber gaskets (Materials Ledger #11216) as shown in the records of HD Corporation for the month of November follow:

LO3

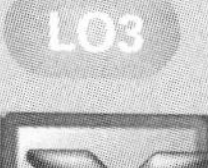

		Units	Unit Price
Nov. 1	Beginning balance	30,000	$3.00
4	Received, Rec. Report No. 112	10,000	3.10
5	Issued, Mat. Req. No. 49	30,000	
8	Received, Rec. Report No. 113	50,000	3.30
15	Issued, Mat. Req. No. 50	20,000	
22	Received, Rec. Report No. 114	25,000	3.50
28	Issued, Mat. Req. No. 51	30,000	

Required:
1. Complete a materials ledger account similar to Figure 2-10 (the "On Order" columns should be omitted) for each of the following inventory costing methods, using a perpetual inventory system:
   a. FIFO
   b. LIFO
   c. Moving average (carrying unit prices to five decimal places)
2. For each method, prepare a schedule that shows the total cost of materials transferred to Work in Process and the cost of the ending inventory.
3. If prices continue to increase, would you favor adopting the FIFO or the LIFO method? Explain.
4. When prices continue to rise, what is the effect of FIFO versus LIFO on the inventory balance for materials reported in the balance sheet? Discuss.

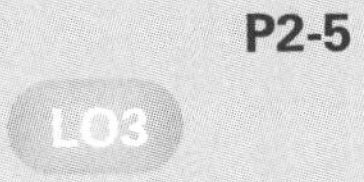

P2-5 **Inventory costing methods**

The following transactions affecting materials occurred in February:

Feb.	1	Balance on hand, 1,200 ft @ $2.76, $3,312.00 (plastic tubing, materials ledger account #906).
	5	Issued 60 ft to production on Materials Requisition No. 108.
	11	Issued 200 ft on Materials Requisition No. 210.
	14	Received 800 ft from a supplier, Receiving Report No. 634, price $2.80 per ft.
	15	Issued 400 ft, Materials Requisition No. 274.
	16	Returned to a supplier for credit, 90 ft purchased on February 14, which were found to be defective.
	18	Received 1,000 ft, Receiving Report No. 712, price $2.83 per ft.
	21	Issued 640 ft, Materials Requisition No. 318.

Required:

Record the transactions on materials ledger accounts similar to Figure 2-10. (The "On Order" columns should be omitted.) Use the following inventory methods, assuming the use of a perpetual inventory system. Carry unit prices to four decimal places.

1. FIFO
2. LIFO
3. Moving average

LO3

P2-6 **Journalizing materials transactions**

Milano's Specialty Clothing, Inc., uses a job order cost system. A partial list of the accounts being maintained by the company, with their balances as of November 1, follows:

Cash	$82,250
Materials	29,500
Work in process	27,000
Accounts payable (credit)	21,000
Factory overhead	none

The following transactions were completed during the month of November:

a. Materials purchases on account during the month, $74,000.
b. Materials requisitioned during the month:
   1. Direct materials, $57,000.
   2. Indirect materials, $11,000.
c. Direct materials returned by factory to storeroom during the month, $1,100.
d. Materials returned to vendors during the month prior to payment, $2,500.
e. Payments to vendors during the month, $68,500.

Required:

1. Prepare general journal entries for each of the transactions.
2. Post the general journal entries to T-accounts.
3. Balance the accounts and report the balances of November 30 for the following:
   a. Cash
   b. Materials
   c. Accounts Payable

P2-7 **Analyzing materials and other transactions**

LO3

Scarlatta's Manufacturing Company uses a job order cost system. The following accounts have been taken from the books of the company:

Materials

Bal. Inventory	7,000	b. Requisitions for month	19,000
a. Purchases for month	22,000		

Work in Process

Bal. Inventory	3,600	e. To finished goods	47,500
b. Material Requisitions	19,000		
c. Direct Labor	17,000		
d. Factory Overhead	12,000		

Finished Goods

Bal. Inventory	11,650	f. Cost of Goods Sold	55,000
e. Goods Finished	47,500		

Required:

1. Analyze the accounts and describe in narrative form what transactions took place. (Use the reference letters a. through f. in your explanations and note that some accounts needed in your explanation have been purposely omitted.)
2. List the supporting documents or forms required to record each transaction involving the receipt or issuance of materials.
3. Determine the ending balances for Materials, Work in Process, and Finished Goods.

P2-8 **Comprehensive analysis of materials accounting procedures**

LO2 LO3

The following actions occurred at Sanibel Sheet Metal Company relative to accounting for materials costs for April.

Mar. 31 The factory manager informs the storeroom keeper that for the month of April, 2,000 sheets of aluminum are the forecasted usage. A check of the stock shows 500 aluminum sheets, costing $23 each, on hand. A minimum stock of 300 sheets must be maintained, and the purchasing agent is notified of the need for 1,800 sheets. This quantity will cover the April production requirements and, at the same time, maintain the minimum inventory level.

Apr. 1 After checking with a number of different vendors, the purchasing agent orders the requested number of sheets at $25 each.

6	The shipment of aluminum sheets is received, inspected, and found to be in good condition. However, the order is short 100 sheets, which are backordered and expected to be shipped in five days. The invoice from the vendor covering the aluminum sheets is also received, and it is approved for later payment.
Apr. 11	The aluminum sheets that were backordered are received and approved.
11	The vendor's invoice for the backordered shipment is received and approved for payment.
16	The April 6 invoice is paid, less a cash discount of 2%.
30	During the month, 1,900 sheets are issued to the factory. The company uses FIFO costing and a job order cost system.
30	The factory returns 20 unused sheets to the storeroom. The returned sheets have a cost of $25 each.
30	At the end of the day, 398 sheets are on hand.

Required:

1. In tabular form, answer the following questions pertaining to each of the preceding decisions and transactions:

a. What forms, if any, were used?

b. What journal entries, if any, were made?

c. What books of original entry, if any, were used to record the data?

d. What subsidiary records were affected?

(*Hint:* To solve a. through d., use a columnar format with columns for Date, Form, Journal Entry, Book of Original Entry, and Subsidiary Ledger—see Figure 2-13.)

2. Calculate and show your computations for the following:

a. The materials inventory balance as of April 30.

b. The cost of materials used in production during April.

P2-9 LO4

JIT and cost control

Yusane Bolts, Inc., produces 50,000 units each day, and the average number of units in work in process is 200,000. The average annual inventory carrying cost percentage is 25%, and the average work in process is $1,000,000.

Required:

1. Determine the throughput time.

2. Compute the annual carrying costs.

3. If the same daily output can be achieved while reducing the work in process by 50%, determine the new throughput time.

4. What has happened to the velocity of production in part 3?

5. Compute the annual carrying costs for part 3.

P2-10 LO4

Backflush costing
similar to Self-Study Problem 2

T. Hilliary, Inc., uses backflush costing to account for its manufacturing costs. The trigger points for recording inventory transactions are the purchase of materials, the completion of products, and the sale of completed products.

Required:

1. Prepare journal entries, if needed, to account for the following transactions.
   a. Purchased raw materials on account, $150,000.
   b. Requisitioned raw materials to production, $150,000.
   c. Distributed direct labor costs, $25,000.
   d. Incurred manufacturing overhead costs, $100,000. (Use Various Credits for the credit part of the entry.)
   e. Cost of products completed, $275,000.
   f. Completed products sold for $400,000, on account.
2. Prepare any journal entries that would be different from the above, if the only trigger points were the purchase of materials and the sale of finished goods.

P2-11 Materials inventory shortage; returns; scrap; spoiled goods

LO3 LO5

An examination of Frosty Corporation's records reveals the following transactions:

a. On December 31, the physical inventory of raw material was 9,950 gallons. The book quantity, using the moving average method, was 10,000 gal @ $0.52 per gal.
b. Production returned to the storeroom materials that cost $775.
c. Materials valued at $770 were charged to Factory Overhead (Repairs and Maintenance), but should have been charged to Work in Process.
d. Defective material, purchased on account, was returned to the vendor. The material returned cost $234, and the return shipping charges (our cost) of $35 were paid in cash.
e. Goods sold to a customer, on account, for $5,000 (cost $2,500) were returned because of a misunderstanding of the quantity ordered. The customer stated that the goods returned were in excess of the quantity needed.
f. Materials requisitioned totaled $22,300, of which $2,100 represented supplies used.
g. Materials purchased on account totaled $25,500. Freight on the materials purchased was $185.
h. Direct materials returned to the storeroom amounted to $950.
i. Scrap materials sent to the storeroom were valued at an estimated selling price of $685 and treated as a reduction in the cost of all jobs worked on during the period.
j. Spoiled work sent to the storeroom valued at a sales price of $60 had production costs of $200 already charged to it. The cost of the spoilage is to be charged to the specific job worked on during the period.
k. The scrap materials in (i) were sold for $685 cash.

Required:

Record the entries for each transaction.

LO5

P2-12 Spoiled goods; loss charged to factory overhead; loss charged to job

One of the tennis racquets that Set Point manufactures is a titanium model (Ace) that sells for $149. The cost of each Ace consists of:

Materials	$35
Labor	15
Factory overhead	25
Total	$75

Job 100 produced 100 Aces, of which 6 racquets were spoiled and classified as seconds. Seconds are sold to discount stores for $50 each.

Required:

1. Under the assumption that the loss from spoilage will be distributed to all jobs produced during the current period, use general journal entries to (a) record the costs of production, (b) put spoiled goods into inventory, and (c) record the cash sale of spoiled units.
2. Under the assumption that the loss due to spoilage will be charged to Job 100, use general journal entries to (a) record the costs of production, (b) put spoiled goods into inventory, and (c) record the cash sale of spoiled units.

LO5

P2-13 Spoiled goods and defective work

Torre, Inc., manufactures electrical equipment from specifications received from customers. Job X10 was for 1,000 motors to be used in a specially designed electrical complex. The following costs were determined for each motor:

Materials	$117
Labor	100
Factory overhead	83
Total	$300

At final inspection, Torre discovered that 33 motors did not meet the exacting specifications established by the customer. An examination indicated that 18 motors were beyond repair and should be sold as spoiled goods for $75 each. The remaining 15 motors, though defective, could be reconditioned as first-quality units by the addition of $1,650 for materials, $1,500 for labor, and $1,200 for factory overhead.

Required:

Prepare the journal entries to record the following:

1. The scrapping of the 18 motors, with the income from spoiled goods treated as a reduction in the manufacturing cost of the specific job.
2. The correction of the 15 defective motors, with the additional cost charged to the specific job.

3. The additional cost of replacing the 18 spoiled motors with new motors.
4. The sale of the spoiled motors for $75 each.

P2-14R Review Problem for Chapters 1 and 2

Lift It, Inc., manufactures chain hoists. The raw materials inventories on hand on October 1 were as follows:

Chain	12,000 pounds, $24,000
Pulleys	4,000 sets, $20,000
Bolts and taps	10,000 pounds, $5,000
Steel plates	4,000 units, $2,000

The balances in the ledger accounts on October 1 were as follows:

Cash	$ 12,000	
Work in process	35,000	
Materials	51,000	
Prepaid insurance	3,000	
Machinery	125,000	
Accumulated depreciation—machinery		$ 10,500
Office equipment	30,000	
Accumulated depreciation—office equipment		4,800
Office furniture	20,000	
Accumulated depreciation—office furniture		2,500
Accounts payable		30,000
Capital stock		182,200
Retained earnings		46,000
	$276,000	$276,000

Transactions during October were as follows:

a. Payroll recorded during the month: direct labor, $28,000; indirect labor, $3,000.
b. Factory supplies purchased for cash, $1,000. (Use a separate inventory account, Factory Supplies.)
c. Materials purchased on account: chain—4,000 pounds, $8,800; pulleys—2,000 sets, $10,200; steel plates—5,000 units, $3,000.
d. Sales on account for the month, $126,375.
e. Accounts receivable collected, $72,500.
f. Materials used during October (FIFO costing): chain, 14,000 pounds; pulleys, 4,400 sets; bolts and taps, 4,000 pounds; steel plates, 3,800 units.
g. Payroll paid, $31,000.
h. Factory supplies on hand, October 31, $350.
i. Factory heat, light, and power costs for October, $3,000 (not yet paid).
j. Office salaries paid, $6,000.

k. Advertising paid, $2,000.
l. Factory superintendence paid, $1,800.
m. Expired insurance—on office equipment, $100; on factory machinery, $300.
n. Factory rent paid, $2,000.
o. Depreciation on office equipment, $400; on office furniture, $180; on machinery, $1,200.
p. Factory overhead charged to jobs, $11,950.
q. Work in Process, October 31, $31,000. (*Hint:* The difference between the sum of the beginning balance in Work in Process plus the total charges to it during the period less the ending balance in Work in Process represents the cost of the goods completed during the period.)
r. Cost of goods sold during the month, $84,250.
s. Accounts payable paid, $33,750.

Required:

1. Set up T-accounts and enter the balances as of October 1.
2. Prepare journal entries to record each of the previous transactions.
3. Post the journal entries to the accounts, setting up any new ledger accounts necessary. Only controlling accounts are to be maintained; however, show the calculation for the cost of materials used.
4. Prepare a statement of cost of goods manufactured for October.
5. Prepare an income statement.
6. Prepare a balance sheet showing the classifications of current assets, plant and equipment, current liabilities, and stockholders' equity.

MINI-CASE 1

Financial and Nonfinancial Aspects of Changing to JIT

LO1 LO4

Katy, Inc., manufactures "smart phones." It is considering the implementation of a JIT system. Costs to reconfigure the production line will amount to $200,000 annually. Estimated benefits from the change to JIT are as follows:

- The quality advantages of JIT should reduce current rework cost of $300,000 by 25%.
- Materials storage, handling, and insurance costs of $250,000 would be reduced by an estimated 40%.
- Average inventory is expected to decline by 300,000 units, and the carrying cost per unit is $0.35.

Required:

1. What is the estimated financial advantage (disadvantage) of changing to a JIT system?
2. Are there any nonfinancial advantages (disadvantages) of changing to a JIT system?

MINI-CASE 2

Changing from a Traditional System to a JIT System

In the scenario on page 91, Boston Company was trying to decide whether or not to change from a traditional inventory system to a just-in-time (JIT) system. The president, Teresa Francona, wanted to know whether this change would merely affect how goods were ordered and produced, or if it would also impact the financial health of the company, as well as the accounting system itself. The controller, Donna Ortiz, was asked to prepare a report estimating any expected cost savings and changes to the accounting system resulting from a move to JIT.

Required:

1. What costs should be affected by the introduction of a JIT system?
2. Should Francona's customers reap any benefits from the change to JIT?
3. Will Ortiz have to make any changes in the way that inventory is accounted for under a JIT system?

INTERNET EXERCISE 1

Just-in-Time Inventory Systems

LO4

Go to the text Website at *http://www.cengage.com/accounting/vanderbeck* and click on the link to the following article: Benefits From Lean and Cellular Manufacturing, by Strategos, Inc.-Consultants, Engineers, Strategists

Required:

Read the article and answer the following questions:

1. Name some general principles for using "lean metrics."
2. What are some materials handling benefits that result from applying lean manufacturing principles?
3. Why do lot sizes tend to be larger in a functional manufacturing environment?
4. How do employees benefit from a lean manufacturing environment?
5. Why is it difficult to make quality improvements in a functional manufacturing environment?
6. How do customers benefit when their suppliers adopt lean manufacturing principles?

CHAPTER 3

Accounting for Labor

Learning Objectives

After studying this chapter, you should be able to:

LO1 Distinguish between the features of hourly rate and piece-rate plans.

LO2 Specify procedures for controlling labor costs.

LO3 Account for labor costs and payroll taxes.

LO4 Prepare accruals for payroll earnings and taxes.

LO5 Account for special problems in labor costing.

Why has **Toyota** been much more profitable than **General Motors** (GM) in recent years? Part of the explanation lies in a comparison of total hourly labor costs. The difference does not lie in the average hourly wage rate where the average Toyota worker holds a slight advantage over the average GM worker—$30 per hour versus $29.78 per hour. It is explained by the difference in pension and health care costs for both active workers and retirees that caused the total hourly labor cost in 2008 to be, on average, $69 for a GM worker and $48 for a Toyota worker. The United Auto Workers union has negotiated much richer benefits over the years for GM, Ford, and Chrysler workers than have been provided by nonunion, foreign automakers in the United States, such as Toyota and Honda.[1]

Note that filings for bankruptcy protection in 2009 by both GM and Chrysler have helped shed some of these expensive labor agreements, in an effort to make both companies more competitive with their foreign rivals. For example, an article in the July 6, 2009 *Wall Street Journal* discussed GM's plan to build its first U.S.-made compact in its Orion, Michigan plant by 2011. Relative to the labor costs at the plant, the article stated: "The UAW agreed to allow GM to employ lower-cost workers making $14 to $16.23 an hour, compared with the current base wage of $28 an hour, with less-expensive benefits than traditional assembly-line personnel."

---

1 "GM Vs. Toyota Wages and Benefits," December 12, 2008, www.topix.com (visited 3/10/2009) and "More on Total Hourly Labor Costs: GM Vs. Toyota," November 24, 2008, www.dailymarkets.com (visited 3/10/2009).

How can companies control labor costs in a highly competitive, global environment? What incentive wage plans can be put in place to ensure that workers are compensated for providing value-added activity? How should bonuses, holiday pay, and vacation pay be accounted for? These are some of the major issues that will be discussed in the chapter.

Factory payroll costs are divided into two categories: direct labor and indirect labor. **Direct labor**, also known as **touch labor,** represents payroll costs traced directly to an individual job. Direct labor costs include the wages of machinists, assemblers, and other workers who physically convert raw materials to finished goods—thus the term *touch*. For example, a painter on the production line at the Toyota plant in Georgetown, Kentucky is a direct laborer. The cost of direct labor is debited to Work in Process. Indirect labor consists of labor costs incurred for a variety of jobs related to the production process but not readily traceable to the individual jobs worked on during the period. Indirect labor costs include the salaries and wages of the factory superintendent, supervisors, janitors, clerks, and factory accountants who support all jobs worked on during the period. For example, the plant manager of the Toyota manufacturing facility is an indirect laborer. Indirect labor costs are charged to Factory Overhead. As was mentioned in Chapter 1, robotics, illustrated in Figure 3-1, is increasingly replacing humans on the production line. This results in a trend of direct labor becoming a smaller percentage of total production costs while indirect manufacturing costs such as maintenance, depreciation, insurance, and personal property taxes on the robots are increasing as a percentage of total product cost.

You may also think of the distinction between direct labor and indirect labor relative to service firms. For example, auditors with a public accounting firm would be considered direct labor relative to the individual jobs that they worked on, whereas the salary of the managing partner would be indirect labor that should be allocated to all of the clients audited in determining the total cost of servicing clients. Other examples of indirect labor in an accounting firm would include the human resources function, the technical support staff, and the secretarial function.

The accounting system of a manufacturer must include the following procedures for recording payroll costs:

1. Recording the hours worked or quantity of output by employees in total and by job, process, or department.
2. Analyzing the hours worked by employees to determine how labor time is to be charged.
3. Charging payroll costs to jobs, processes, departments, and factory overhead accounts.
4. Preparing the payroll, which involves computing and recording employee gross earnings, withholdings and deductions, and net earnings.

Figure 3-1 **The Use of Robotics in Manufacturing (© Photodisc/Getty Images)**

Wage Plans

Stacey Womack is considering the implementation of an incentive wage plan to increase productivity in her small manufacturing plant. The plant is nonunion, and employees have been compensated with only an hourly rate plan. Jane Moore, Vice President–Manufacturing, is concerned that the move to an incentive compensation plan will cause direct laborers to speed up production and, thus, compromise quality.

How might Womack accomplish her goals while alleviating Moore's concerns? Does the compensation have to be all hourly rate or all incentive compensation? Can incentive compensation also apply to service businesses? These are some of the questions that will be answered in this section of the chapter and in Mini-Case 1 at the end of the chapter.

LO1 Distinguish between the features of hourly rate and piece-rate plans.

Employees' wages are based on plans that have been established by management, approved by the unions, if present, and that comply with the regulations of governmental agencies. A manufacturer may use many variations of wage plans. This chapter covers the wage plans most frequently encountered, including hourly rate, piece-rate, and modified wage plans.

Hourly Rate Plan

An **hourly rate plan** establishes a definite rate per hour for each employee. An employee's wages are computed by multiplying the number of hours worked in the payroll period by the established rate per hour. The hourly rate plan is widely used and is simple to apply. Critics argue that it provides no incentive for the employee to maintain or achieve a high level of productivity. An employee is paid for merely "being on the job" for an established period of time. The plan gives no extra recognition or reward for doing more than the minimum required of the position. Proponents of the plan argue that because productivity is not an important factor of such a plan, employees will not be tempted to sacrifice the quality of the product by speeding up production to earn a higher wage. **Productivity** is measured as the amount of output per hour of work. In the 12 months ended December 2008, worker productivity in manufacturing increased 2.8% over the previous 12-month period—the nation's largest productivity increase since 2003.[2]

To illustrate the hourly rate plan, assume that an employee earns $15 per hour and works 40 hours per week. The employee's gross earnings would be $600 (40 × $15 per hour).

Piece-Rate Plan

A company that gives a high priority to the quantity produced by each worker should consider using an **incentive wage plan**, such as a **piece-rate plan**, that bases earnings on the employee's quantity of production. To illustrate, assume that a machine operator will earn $0.30 for each part (or "piece") finished. If the operator finishes 2,200 parts in a week, he or she will earn $660 ($0.30 × 2,200 parts). The plan provides an incentive for employees to produce a high level of output, thereby maximizing their earnings and also increasing the company's revenue. However, a serious shortcoming of such plans is that they may encourage employees to sacrifice quality in order to maximize their earnings, unless the plan is based on only the production of good units. Also, piece rates are not appropriate if machines, rather than people, control production speed.

Modified Wage Plans

Modified wage plans combine some features of the hourly rate and piece-rate plans. An example of a modified wage plan would be to set a base hourly wage that the company will pay if an employee does not attain an established quota of production. If the established quota is exceeded, an additional payment per piece would be added to the wage base. This type of plan rewards high-performing employees and directs management's attention to employees unable to meet the established quotas.

---

2 U.S. worker productivity rose 2.8% in 2008 (according to figures released by the Labor Department), www.bloomberg.com (visited March 2, 2009).

Labor–management negotiations create many variations of the hourly rate and piece-rate plans. These variations occur because management wishes to minimize costs and maximize profits, while labor attempts to maximize employee earnings. To illustrate a modified wage plan, assume that an employee earns $15 per hour for up to 400 units of production per day. The employee who produces more than 400 units per day will receive an additional piece rate of $0.30 per unit. When the employee produces fewer than 400 units, the difference, referred to as a **make-up guarantee**, will be charged to Factory Overhead rather than to Work in Process because it represents the cost of inefficient production, rather than a necessary cost of the specific jobs worked on.

Assume that an employee's production and earnings for one week are as follows:

	Hours Worked	Pieces Finished (Quota 400)	Earnings @ $15 per Hour	Earnings @ $0.30 per Unit	Make-Up Guarantee	Payroll Earnings
Mon.	8	400	$120	$120		$120
Tues.	8	360	120	108	$12	120
Wed.	8	420	120	126		126
Thurs.	8	450	120	135		135
Fri.	8	340	120	102	18	120
	40		$600	$591	$30	$621

Note that the employee's daily earnings are the larger of the amounts in column (3) or column (4). The employee earned $591 for the week on a piece-rate basis, but the daily guarantee of $120 per day compensated for the days when the employee did not reach the quota. A make-up guarantee of $30 is charged to Factory Overhead because the employee did not meet the quota on Tuesday ($12) and Friday ($18). The payroll distribution for the week would be as follows:

Work in Process	591	
Factory Overhead	30	
Payroll		621
Distributed payroll.		

If the number of pieces finished depends on a group effort, then a single incentive plan for the group would be appropriate. In recent years, U.S. manufacturers have adopted the concept of **production work teams**, where output is dependent on contributions made by all members of the work crew or department. The wages may be computed in a manner similar to the previous illustration, except that all members of the group would share the piece-rate bonus.

Incentive compensation plans are not limited to manufacturing workers. Salespersons in service businesses often are paid on a commission or salary-plus-commission basis. Managers and other employees may also participate in incentive wage plans. For example, at the restaurant chain **P. F. Chang's**, "restaurant general managers and chefs are eligible to receive monthly incentive payments based upon the profitability of the restaurant, as well as participate in an incentive program that rewards long-term improvements in the operating performance of the restaurant."[3]

Controlling Labor Cost

LO2 Specify procedures for controlling labor costs.

The timekeeping and payroll departments have the responsibility of maintaining labor records. The timekeeping and payroll functions may be established as separate departments or organized as subdivisions of a single department. Increasingly, automated timekeeping technology has replaced "timekeeping" as a separate department. For example, many companies issue magnetic cards to direct laborers who use them to "log on" and "log off" to specific job assignments. They slide the card through a magnetic card reader connected to a remote computer terminal, much as you would do to pay for your groceries at the supermarket. The computer sends this labor time information to the accounting department for preparation of the payroll and distribution of labor costs to the appropriate jobs.

The payroll department, or payroll function within the accounting department, uses the labor time records, whether manually or electronically generated, to compute each employee's gross earnings, the amount of withholdings and deductions, and the net earnings to be paid to the employee. The payroll function includes completing and maintaining the payroll records, the employees' earnings records, and the payroll summaries.

Labor Time Records

The **labor time record**, illustrated in Figure 3-2, shows the employee's time spent on each job, as well as the time spent as indirect labor on machine repair. Given the magnetic card-reading technology mentioned earlier, the time record typically takes the form of a computer file. Nonetheless, a production supervisor should review the labor hours recorded on the time record for accuracy, because the time record is the source document for allocating the cost of labor to jobs or departments in the job cost ledger and factory overhead ledger, as shown by the arrows to the job cost sheets in Figure 3-2.

The employer must compensate the employee for the time spent on assigned jobs. When time is not fully utilized, the employer suffers a loss just as if a theft of some tangible good had occurred. Therefore, if time spent in the factory has been unproductive, the idle time, along with the reason for it, should be recorded and charged to Factory Overhead. Just as

3 P. F. Chang's China Bistro, Inc., 2007 Annual Report.

Figure 3-2 **Labor Time Record**

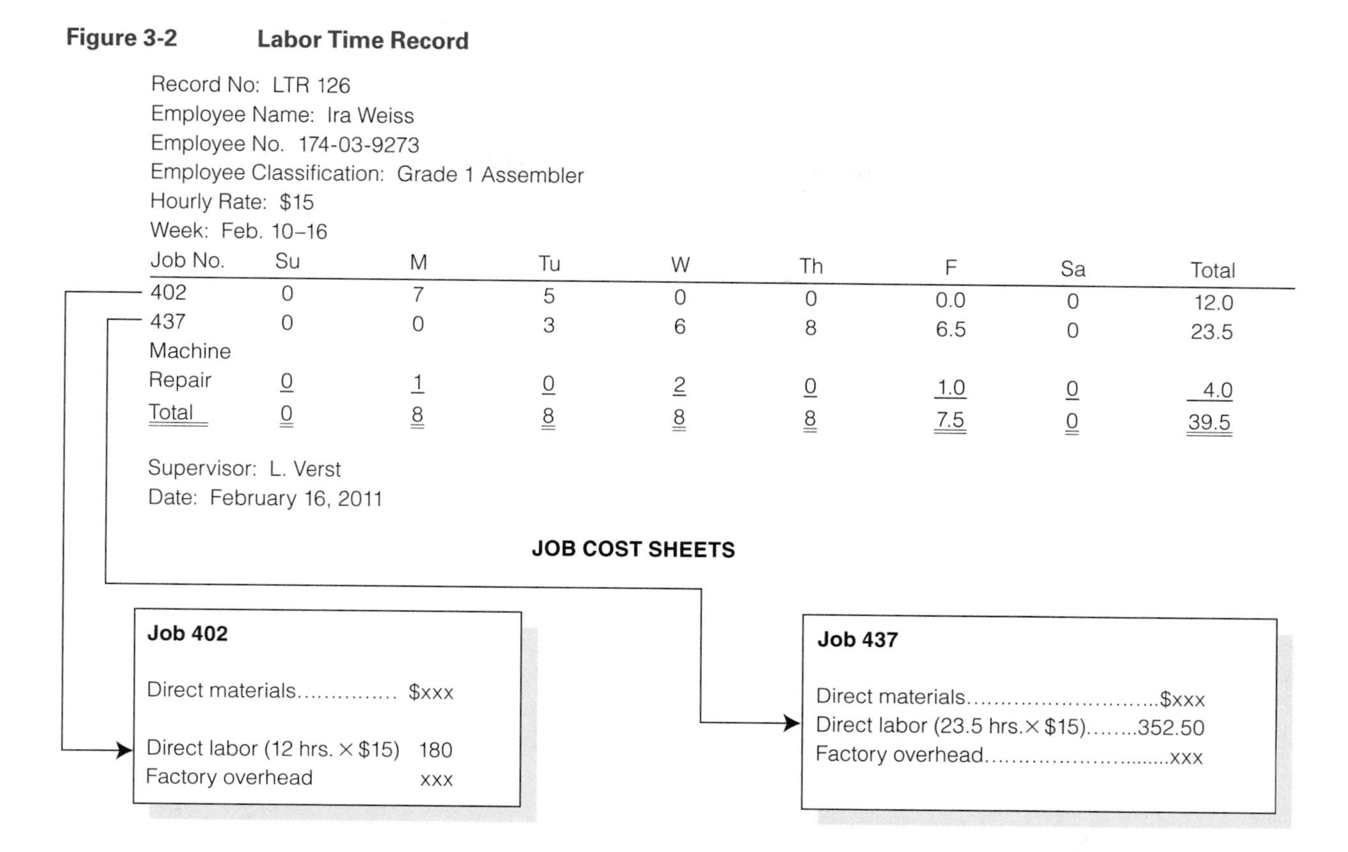

Record No: LTR 126
Employee Name: Ira Weiss
Employee No. 174-03-9273
Employee Classification: Grade 1 Assembler
Hourly Rate: $15
Week: Feb. 10–16

Job No.	Su	M	Tu	W	Th	F	Sa	Total
402	0	7	5	0	0	0.0	0	12.0
437	0	0	3	6	8	6.5	0	23.5
Machine Repair	0	1	0	2	0	1.0	0	4.0
Total	0	8	8	8	8	7.5	0	39.5

Supervisor: L. Verst
Date: February 16, 2011

JOB COST SHEETS

Job 402

Direct materials	$xxx
Direct labor (12 hrs. × $15)	180
Factory overhead	xxx

Job 437

Direct materials	$xxx
Direct labor (23.5 hrs. × $15)	352.50
Factory overhead	xxx

the make-up guarantee discussed earlier was charged to Factory Overhead because it did not add value to any specific jobs, the unproductive idle time spent in the factory should also be charged to Factory Overhead.

Payroll Function

The payroll function's primary responsibility is to compute the employees' wages and salaries. It involves combining the daily wages, determining the total earnings, and computing deductions and withholdings for each employee. Payroll is often a function within a single accounting department, as opposed to being a separate department. Also, many companies now outsource their payroll function to payroll preparation services such as **ADP** or **Paychex, Inc.**

The department must maintain current information concerning regulatory requirements regarding wages and salaries because a specified amount of the employee's wages are subject to social security (FICA) and income tax deductions. Additional deductions, approved by the employee, can be taken for group insurance premiums, union dues, contributions to a tax-sheltered annuity, and so on.

Payroll Records. Forms used to record earnings information may vary considerably from company to company; however, all forms possess some common characteristics. The **payroll record** shown in Figure 3-3, for the

Figure 3-3 Payroll Record

	A	B	C	D	E	F	G	H	I	J
1										
2	**For Period Ending 2/16/2011**							**Earnings**		
3		**Employee**		**No. of**		**Regular**		**Overtime**		**Total**
4	**Name**	**No.**	**M/s**	**Allow.**	**Rate**	**Hours**	**Amount**	**Hours**	**Amount**	**Earnings**
5	Donovan, F	123-45-9876	M	0	14.00	40.0	560.00	0	00.00	560.00
6	Fry, R.	987-65-1234	M	2	16.00	40.0	640.00	2	48.00	688.00
7	Weiss I.	174-03-9273	S	1	15.00	39.5	592.50	0	00.00	592.50
8							1,792.50		48.00	1,840.50
9										
10			**Withholdings**				**Deductions**		**Net Pay**	
11	**FICA**	**FICA**			**Income Taxes**		**Health**		**Check**	**Check**
12	**Earnings**	**Tax**		**Federal**	**State**	**Local**	**Insurance**	**Other**	**No.**	**Amount**
13	560.00	44.80		84.00	28.00	5.60	40.00		8441	357.60
14	688.00	55.04		103.20	34.00	6.88	40.00	50.00 Repay advance	8442	398.88
15	592.50	47.40		88.88	29.62	5.93	40.00		8443	380.67
16	1,840.50	147.24		276.08	91.62	18.41	120.00			1,137.15
17										

period ending February 16, provides typical information. It assembles and summarizes each period's payroll data and serves as a subsidiary record for the preparation of a general journal entry. For example, the entry to record the payroll data in Figure 3-3 would be as shown below.

Payroll	1,840.50	
FICA Tax Payable		147.24
Employees Income Tax Payable		386.11
Health Insurance Payable		120.00
Employee Receivable		50.00
Wages Payable		1,137.15
Recorded payroll liability		

Note that the distribution of the gross payroll between Work in Process (for direct labor) and Factory Overhead (for indirect labor) will be illustrated in the next section. Also note that a prior cash advance was deducted from the paycheck this period, reducing the asset account Employee Receivable.

Employees' Earnings Records. In addition to the payroll record, payroll keeps a record of the earnings for each employee. Figure 3-4 shows an **employee earnings record**. This cumulative record of employee earnings is needed to compute the amount of employee earnings subject to FICA and other payroll taxes. It also serves as the basis for reporting payroll information to governmental agencies, such as individual employee earnings to the Social Security Administration and Wage and Tax Statements (Form W-2) to employees for the purpose of preparing their individual tax returns.

Payment of Net Earnings. The accounting department sends the payroll record (Figure 3-3) to the treasurer's office, which is responsible for making the payments to the employees. The earnings usually are paid by check.

Figure 3-4 Employee Earnings Record

Employee Name: Ira Weiss | Social Security No.: 174-03-9273 | 02/16/2011

Mar. St.: S | No. Allow.: 1 | Sex: M | Department: Grinding | Occupation: Machinist | Date of Birth: 4/4/57

Period	Date	Regular			Overtime		Total	FICA	Income Taxes			Health		Check	
No.	2011	Rate	Hours	Amount	Hours	Amount	Earnings	Tax	Federal	State	Local	Ins	Other	No.	Amount
1	1/05	14.40	40	576.00			576.00	43.20	86.40	28.80	5.76	40.00		7971	371.84
7	2/16	15.00	39.5	592.50			592.50	47.40	88.88	29.62	5.93	40.00		8443	380.67
QtrTtl				4096.00		306.00	4402.00	330.15	660.30	220.10	44.02	280.00	50.00		2817.43
YrlTtl				4096.00		306.00	4402.00	330.15	660.30	220.10	44.02	280.00	50.00		2817.43

A check for the total amount to be paid is drawn to create a special payroll fund from which the employees will be paid. The special account is used only for payroll, and the individual payroll checks, when cashed, are charged to the special account. A new payroll account may be established for each payroll period, numbering the accounts sequentially. The checks drawn for each payroll period can then be identified as belonging to a specific payroll period. This system facilitates the reconciliation of bank statements. The entry to record the payment of net pay to employees for the period ending February 16, 2011, would be as follows:

Wages Payable	1,137.15	
Cash		1,137.15
Paid employees		

In the rare instance where employees are paid cash, a check is cashed for the total amount of net earnings. The cash is then divided into amounts earned by individual employees. These cash amounts are placed in envelopes and distributed to the employees. The employee's receipt or signature acknowledges the payment. Most employers now allow employees to authorize the direct electronic deposit of their net pay to their checking accounts.

Recall and Review 1

An employee earns $20 per hour for up to 200 units of production per day. An employee who produces more than 200 units per day receives an additional piece rate of $.50 per unit. Assume that an employee worked eight hours per day with the following unit production for the week: Monday, 200; Tuesday, 175; Wednesday, 225; Thursday, 250; and Friday, 150. Calculate the employee's gross earnings for the week. $____

(After working this exercise, see page 149 for the solution.)

You should now be able to work the following:
Questions 1–8; Exercises 3-1 to 3-3; Problems 3-1 and 3-2; and Mini-Case 1.

Accounting for Labor Costs and Employers' Payroll Taxes

LO3 Account for labor costs and payroll taxes.

For all regular hourly employees, the hours worked should be recorded on a labor time record. The payroll department enters pay rates and gross earnings and forwards the reports to accounting. Cost accountants examine the labor time records and charge the labor costs to the appropriate jobs or department and to factory overhead. This analysis of labor costs is recorded on a **labor cost summary** (Figure 3-5) that summarizes the direct labor and indirect labor charges to a department for the period.

Figure 3-5 Labor Cost Summary

LABOR COST SUMMARY

Dept. Grinding Month Ending May 31, 2011

Date	Dr. Work in Progress (Direct labor-regular time)		Dr. Factory Overhead (Indirect labor and overtime premium)		Cr. Payroll (Total)	
5/14	11,050	00	1,950	00	13,000	00
5/28	13,000	00	2,600	00	15,600	00
5/31	3,900	00	780	00	4,680	00
Totals	27,950	00	5,330	00	33,280	00

Salaried employees, such as department supervisors, are often not required to prepare labor time records. Payroll sends a list of salaried employees to accounting showing the names of employees, the nature of work performed, and the salaries. The accounting department records the earnings on the labor cost summary and in factory overhead ledger accounts, because the salaried factory employees are supervisors and other factory managers who do not physically convert the raw materials to finished goods, and therefore their salaries are indirect labor.

The labor cost summary becomes the source for making a general journal entry, shown below, to distribute payroll to the appropriate accounts.

Work in Process	27,950	
Factory Overhead	5,330	
Payroll		33,280
Distributed payroll		

The entry is then posted to the control accounts, Work in Process and Factory Overhead, in the general ledger. The labor time records have been used to record the labor costs in both the subsidiary job cost ledger and factory overhead ledger, as well as in the labor cost summary. Therefore, the debit to the work in process control account must equal the total direct labor cost charged to the individual jobs, and the debit to the factory overhead control account must equal the total indirect labor costs recorded in the factory overhead ledger. The flow of costs to and from the labor cost summary is illustrated in Figure 3-6.

In preparing the labor cost summary from the labor time records, any overtime must be separated from an employee's regular time because the

Figure 3-6 **Flow of Costs from Subsidiary Records to General Ledger**

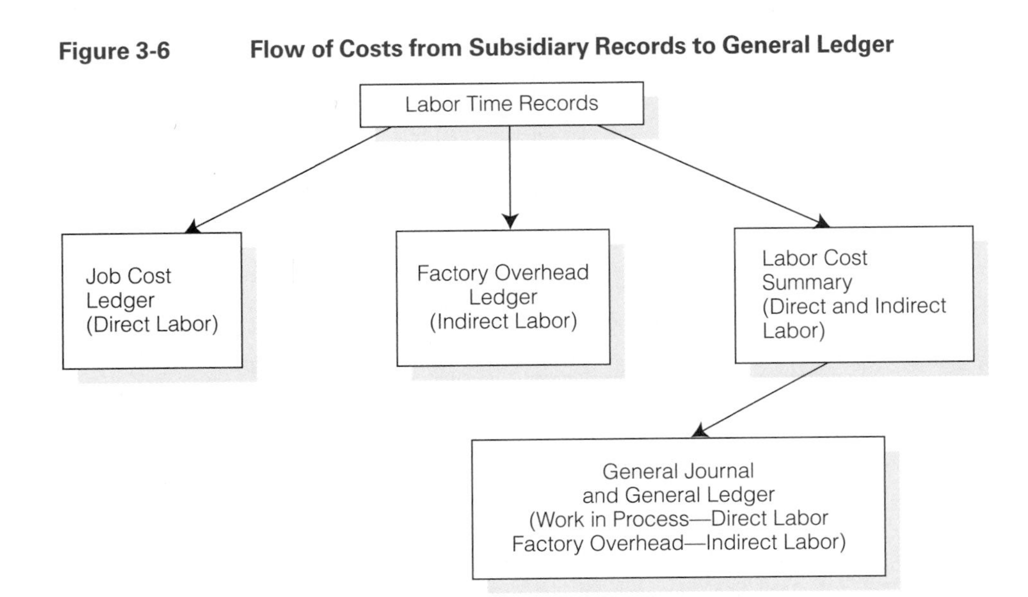

accounting treatment may be different for each type of pay. Regular time worked by direct laborers is charged to Work in Process. Overtime pay may be charged to Work in Process, to Factory Overhead, or allocated partly to Work in Process and partly to Factory Overhead. Overtime distribution depends on the conditions creating the need for overtime hours as the following explains.

If an employee works beyond the regularly scheduled time but is paid at the regular hourly rate, the extra pay is called **overtime pay**. If an additional rate is allowed for the extra hours worked, the additional rate earned is referred to as an **overtime premium**. The premium pay rate is added to the employee's regular rate for the additional hours worked. The premium rate is frequently one-half the regular rate, resulting in a total hourly rate for overtime that is 150% of the regular rate. Under these circumstances, overtime pay is often referred to as "time-and-a-half" pay. In some cases, such as work done on Sundays and holidays, the overtime premium may be equal to the regular rate, resulting in "double-time" pay.

To illustrate how a payroll is computed where an overtime premium is a factor, assume that an employee regularly earns $15 per hour for an 8-hour day. If called upon to work more than 8 hours in a working day, the company pays time-and-a-half for overtime hours. Assuming that the employee works 12 hours on Monday, the earnings would be computed as follows:

Direct labor—8 hours @ $15		$120
Overtime wages:		
Direct labor—4 hours @ $15	60	
Factory overhead (overtime premium)—4 hours @ $7.50	30	90
Total earnings		$210

Work in Process would be charged with the direct labor cost of $180 ($120 + $60), earned at the regular rate of $15 per hour. The additional rate of $7.50 was used to compute the $30 cost of the overtime premium, which was charged to Factory Overhead because the job worked on during the overtime period was a result of the random scheduling of jobs. By charging the overtime premium to the factory overhead account, all jobs worked on during the period share the cost of overtime premiums paid. If an individual job contract stipulated that it was a rush order and the overtime premium resulted from the time limitation in the contract, it would be appropriate to charge the premium pay to Work in Process for the specific job worked on during the overtime period instead of to a factory overhead account.

Employers' Payroll Taxes

Payroll taxes imposed on employers include social security tax and federal and state unemployment taxes. Employers must periodically report and pay the taxes to the appropriate government agencies. Employers who fail to file required reports or pay taxes due are subject to civil and, in some cases, criminal penalties.

The **Federal Insurance Contributions Act (FICA)** requires employers to pay social security taxes on wages and salaries equal to the amount withheld from employees' earnings. The employers and employees, therefore, share equally in the cost of the social security program. FICA includes a tax to finance the Federal Old Age, Survivors, and Disability Insurance program (OASDI) and the Medicare program. The legislation that governs FICA is frequently amended. These amendments change the wage base subject to FICA and the percentage rate of tax to be charged. For example, in 1980 the tax rate for the employer was 6.13% and the wage base was $25,900. For 2009, the FICA tax rate was 7.65% on the first $106,800 in annual earnings; earnings beyond $106,800 were taxed 1.45% for Medicare. (Due to the uncertainty that surrounds both the rate and the base wage, an arbitrary FICA tax rate of 8% will be applied to the first $100,000 of earnings in all discussions, examples, and problems in this text. Earnings beyond $100,000 will not be taxed. The selected arbitrary rate and wage base will simplify the tax calculations related to FICA, but they are not predictive of future legislation that may alter the social security system.)

The **Federal Unemployment Tax Act (FUTA)** requires employers to pay an established rate of tax on wages and salaries to provide for compensation to employees if they are laid off from their regular employment. For 2009, employers were subject to a tax of 6.2%, which may be reduced to 0.8% for credits for state unemployment compensation tax, on the first $7,000 of wages or salaries paid to each employee during the calendar year.

Unemployment benefits, however, are actually paid by individual states and not the federal government, which merely administers the program. As of 2009, the maximum state rate recognized by the federal unemployment system was 5.4% of the first $7,000 of each employee's annual earnings, which goes to the state government to accumulate funds for paying unemployment compensation. Each state has its own unemployment tax laws, although such laws must conform to certain requirements established under FUTA. Both tax rates and wage bases vary among states, and the actual amount of combined federal and state unemployment taxes paid depends on a number of factors, including an experience rating for an employer who provides steady employment that may result in a state rate substantially below the 5.4% federal credit maximum. For example, the state of Texas has a taxable wage base of $9,000 and a maximum and minimum tax rate of 6.26% and 0.26%, respectively. (Because of the variation among states and because FUTA taxes are subject to amendments, the examples, exercises, and problems in the text will assume a 4% rate for state unemployment taxes and a 1% rate for federal unemployment taxes. These tax rates will be applied to the first $8,000 of an employee's annual earnings.)

The employer's payroll taxes are directly related to the costs of direct labor and indirect labor, and theoretically should be charged to these categories of labor cost. However, due to the additional expense and time such allocations would require, it is usually more practical to record all factory-related payroll taxes as factory overhead. The entry to record the payroll taxes for the payroll in Figure 3-3 (page 130), assuming that no employee had exceeded the maximum for unemployment taxes, would be as follows:

Factory Overhead	239.27	
FICA Tax Payable		147.24
Federal Unemployment Tax Payable		18.41*
State Unemployment Tax Payable		73.62**
Recognized payroll taxes.		

*$1,840.50 × 0.01
**$1,840.50 × 0.04

Illustration of Accounting for Labor Costs

Magnum Manufacturing Company pays employees every two weeks. Monday, May 1, is the beginning of a new payroll period. The company maintains the following records:

Payroll record

Employee earnings records

General journal

General ledger

Job cost ledger

Factory overhead ledger

Magnum uses the following general ledger accounts in accounting for labor costs:

Cash

Work in Process

Wages Payable

FICA Tax Payable

Employees Income Tax Payable

Federal Unemployment Tax Payable

State Unemployment Tax Payable

Health Insurance Premiums Payable

Payroll

Factory Overhead

Sales Salaries

Administrative Salaries

Payroll Tax Expense—Sales Salaries

Payroll Tax Expense—Administrative Salaries

Applicable withholding and payroll tax rates and wage bases follow:

	Rates		
	Employee Withholdings	**Employer Payroll Taxes**	**Annual Wages/ Salaries Subject to Tax**
Federal income tax	Graduated*		100%
FICA	8%	8%	$100,000
Federal unemployment		1%	$ 8,000
State unemployment		4%	$ 8,000

*Federal income tax withholdings are determined from tables. State and local income taxes are not shown in this example.

The following payroll summary is prepared by the payroll department and forwarded to accounting for recording:

Payroll Summary
For the Period May 1–14

	Factory Employees	**Sales and Administrative Employees**	**Total**
Gross earnings	$100,000	$30,000	$130,000
Withholdings and deductions:			
FICA tax	$ 8,000	$ 2,400	$ 10,400
Income tax	11,250	3,500	14,750
Health insurance premiums	2,100	700	2,800
Total	$ 21,350	$ 6,600	$ 27,950
Net earnings	$ 78,650	$23,400	$102,050

After the data are verified, a general journal entry records the payroll:

		Debit	Credit
(A)	Payroll	130,000	
	FICA Tax Payable		10,400
	Employees Income Tax Payable		14,750
	Health Insurance Premiums Payable		2,800
	Wages Payable		102,050
	Incurred payroll for period ended May 14		

To record the payment of the net earnings to employees, the following entry must be made:

		Debit	Credit
(B)	Wages Payable	102,050	
	Cash		102,050
	Paid payroll for period ended May 14		

The schedule of earnings and payroll taxes shown below provides the information necessary to distribute the total payroll of $130,000 to the appropriate accounts and to record the employer's payroll taxes for the period.

Schedule of Earnings and Payroll Taxes
For Payroll Period May 1–14

			Unemployment Taxes		
Nonfactory Employees	**Gross Earnings**	**FICA 8%**	**Federal 1%**	**State 4%**	**Total Payroll Taxes**
Sales	$20,000	$ 1,600	$200	$ 800	$2,600
Administrative	10,000	800	100	400	1,300
	$30,000	$ 2,400	$300	$1,200	$3,900
Factory Employees					
Direct labor:					
Regular	$ 85,000	$ 6,800	$ 850	$3,400	$11,050
Overtime premium	10,000	800	100	400	1,300
Indirect labor	5,000	400	50	200	650
	$100,000	$ 8,000	$1,000	$4,000	$13,000
Total	$130,000	$10,400	$1,300	$5,200	$16,900

The distribution of the payroll and the employer's payroll taxes are recorded as follows:

		Debit	Credit
(C)	Work in Process	85,000	
	Factory Overhead	15,000*	
	Sales Salaries	20,000	
	Administrative Salaries	10,000	
	Payroll		130,000
	Distributed payroll for period ended May 14		

*Overtime premium ($10,000) + Indirect factory labor ($5,000)

		Debit	Credit
(D)	Factory Overhead	13,000**	
	Payroll Tax Expense—Sales Salaries	2,600***	
	Payroll Tax Expense—Administrative Salaries	1,300****	
	FICA Tax Payable		10,400
	Federal Unemployment Tax Payable		1,300
	State Unemployment Tax Payable		5,200
	Recognized employer's payroll taxes for period ended May 14		

**FICA ($8,000) + FUTA ($1,000) + SUTA ($4,000)
***FICA ($1,600) + FUTA ($200) + SUTA ($800)
****FICA ($800) + FUTA ($100) + SUTA ($400)

The general ledger accounts that reflect the entries related to the May 1–14 payroll period follow, assuming a beginning cash balance of $250,000:

Cash

	Debit		Credit
May 1	250,000	(B)	102,050

Work in Process

	Debit		Credit
(C)	85,000		

Wages Payable

	Debit		Credit
(B)	102,050	(A)	102,050

FICA Tax Payable

	Debit		Credit
		(A)	10,400
		(D)	10,400

Employees Income Tax Payable

	Debit		Credit
		(A)	14,750

Federal Unemployment Tax Payable

	Debit		Credit
		(D)	1,300

State Unemployment Tax Payable

	Debit		Credit
		(D)	5,200

Health Insurance Premiums Payable

	Debit		Credit
		(A)	2,800

Payroll

	Debit		Credit
(A)	130,000	(C)	130,000

Factory Overhead

	Debit		Credit
(C)	15,000		
(D)	13,000		

Sales Salaries

	Debit		Credit
(C)	20,000		

Administrative Salaries

	Debit		Credit
(C)	10,000		

Payroll Tax Expense—Sales Salaries

	Debit		Credit
(D)	2,600		

Payroll Tax Expense—Admin. Salaries

	Debit		Credit
(D)	1,300		

The next payroll period is May 15 to May 28. At the end of the two-week period, the following schedule for payroll is prepared:

Payroll Summary
For the Period May 15–28

	Factory Employees	Sales and Administrative Employees	Total
Gross earnings	$120,000	$30,000	$150,000
Withholdings and deductions:			
FICA tax	$ 9,600	$ 2,400	$ 12,000
Income tax	13,000	3,500	16,500
Health insurance premiums	2,300	700	3,000
Total	$ 24,900	$ 6,600	$ 31,500
Net earnings	$ 95,100	$23,400	$118,500

The payroll data are verified, and a general journal entry is prepared as shown below.

(E) Payroll	150,000	
FICA Tax Payable		12,000
Employees Income Tax Payable		16,500
Health Insurance Premiums Payable		3,000
Wages Payable		118,500
Incurred payroll for period ending May 28		

The payment of the net earnings to employees requires the following entry:

(F) Wages Payable	118,500	
Cash		118,500
Paid payroll for period ended May 28		

The schedule of earnings and payroll taxes provides the information necessary to distribute the total payroll of $150,000 to the appropriate accounts and to record the employer's payroll taxes for the period.

Schedule of Earnings and Payroll Taxes
For Payroll Period May 15–28

			Unemployment Taxes		
Nonfactory Employees	**Gross Earnings**	**FICA 8%**	**Federal 1%**	**State 4%**	**Total Payroll Taxes**
Sales	$20,000	$1,600	$200	$ 800	$2,600
Administrative	10,000	800	100	400	1,300
	$30,000	$2,400	$300	$1,200	$3,900

Factory Employees					
Direct labor:					
Regular	$100,000	$ 8,000	$1,000	$4,000	$13,000
Overtime premium	12,000	960	120	480	1,560
Indirect labor	8,000	640	80	320	1,040
	$120,000	$ 9,600	$1,200	$4,800	$15,600
Total	$150,000	$12,000	$1,500	$6,000	$19,500

The distribution of the payroll and the employer's payroll taxes are recorded as follows:

		Debit	Credit
(G)	Work in Process	100,000	
	Factory Overhead	20,000*	
	Sales Salaries	20,000	
	Administrative Salaries	10,000	
	Payroll		150,000
	Distributed payroll for period ended May 28		

*Overtime premium ($12,000) + Indirect factory labor ($8,000)

		Debit	Credit
(H)	Factory Overhead	15,600	
	Payroll Tax Expense—Sales Salaries	2,600	
	Payroll Tax Expense—Administrative Salaries	1,300	
	FICA Tax Payable		12,000
	Federal Unemployment Tax Payable		1,500
	State Unemployment Tax Payable		6,000
	Recognized employer's payroll taxes for period ended May 28		

Payroll Accrual

LO4 Prepare accruals for payroll earnings and taxes.

When the financial statement date does not coincide with the ending date for a payroll period, an accrual for payroll earnings and payroll tax expense should be made. The accrual computations will not include the employees' withholdings because they do not affect the employer's income or total liabilities to be reported. However, the employer's payroll taxes are accrued to avoid understating the expenses and liabilities for the period.

The next two-week payroll period for Magnum Manufacturing Company begins on May 29 and ends June 11. However, the financial statements to be prepared for May require an accrual of payroll earnings and taxes for the period May 29–31. The employee earnings and the payroll taxes for the accrual period are shown here, followed by the journal entries to record and distribute the accrued payroll and to record the employer's payroll taxes.

Schedule of Earnings and Payroll Taxes
For Payroll Period May 29–31

			Unemployment Taxes		
Nonfactory Employees	**Gross Earnings**	**FICA 8%**	**Federal 1%**	**State 4%**	**Total Payroll Taxes**
Sales	$6,000	$480	$60	$240	$ 780
Administrative	3,000	240	30	120	390
	$9,000	$720	$90	$360	$1,170
Factory Employees					
Direct labor:					
Regular	$30,000	$2,400	$300	$1,200	$3,900
Overtime premium	4,000	320	40	160	520
Indirect labor	2,000	160	20	80	260
	$36,000	$2,880	$360	$1,440	$4,680
Total	$45,000	$3,600	$450	$1,800	$5,850

		Debit	Credit
(I)	Payroll	45,000	
	Wages Payable		45,000
	Incurred payroll for May 29–31		
(J)	Work in Process	30,000	
	Factory Overhead	6,000*	
	Sales Salaries	6,000	
	Administrative Salaries	3,000	
	Payroll		45,000
	Distributed payroll for period May 29–31		

*Overtime premium ($4,000) + Indirect labor ($2,000)

		Debit	Credit
(K)	Factory Overhead	4,680	
	Payroll Tax Expense—Sales Salaries	780	
	Payroll Tax Expense—Administrative Salaries	390	
	FICA Tax Payable		3,600
	Federal Unemployment Tax Payable		450
	State Unemployment Tax Payable		1,800
	Recognized employer's payroll taxes for period May 29–31		

Before June transactions are recorded, the entry for accruing payroll should be reversed:

		Debit	Credit
(L)	Wages Payable	45,000	
	Payroll		45,000
	Reversed May 31 adjusting entry for accrued payroll		

The amount earned by the employees during the May 29–31 period is a portion of the total costs and expenses for production, sales, and administration for the month of May. However, the employees will not be paid until June 11 for the payroll period from May 29 to June 11. The credit balance in the payroll account, created by the reversing entry, will assure that only the payroll costs accumulated during the June 1 to June 11 period will be included in the June production, sales, and administrative costs. The ledger accounts would appear, as follows, after posting all of the preceding entries:

Cash

May 1	250,000	(B)	102,050
		(F)	118,500
			220,550
29,450			

Work in Process

(C)	85,000		
(G)	100,000		
(J)	30,000		
	215,000		

Wages Payable

(B)	102,050	(A)	102,050
(F)	118,500	(E)	118,500
(L) (reversing)	45,000	(I)	45,000

FICA Tax Payable

		(A)	10,400
		(D)	10,400
		(E)	12,000
		(H)	12,000
		(K)	3,600
			48,400

Employees Income Tax Payable

		(A)	14,750
		(E)	16,500
			31,250

Federal Unemployment Tax Payable

		(D)	1,300
		(H)	1,500
		(K)	450
			3,250

State Unemployment Tax Payable

		(D)	5,200
		(H)	6,000
		(K)	1,800
			13,000

Health Insurance Premiums Payable

		(A)	2,800
		(E)	3,000
			5,800

Payroll

(A)	130,000	(C)	130,000
(E)	150,000	(G)	150,000
(I)	45,000	(J)	45,000
	325,000	(L) (reversing)	45,000
			370,000
			45,000

Factory Overhead

(C)	15,000		
(D)	13,000		
(G)	20,000		
(H)	15,600		
(J)	6,000		
(K)	4,680		
	74,280		

Sales Salaries

(C)	20,000	
(G)	20,000	
(J)	6,000	
	46,000	

Administrative Salaries

(C)	10,000	
(G)	10,000	
(J)	3,000	
	23,000	

Payroll Tax Expense—Sales Salaries

(D)	2,600	
(H)	2,600	
(K)	780	
	5,980	

Payroll Tax Expense—Administrative Salaries

(D)	1,300	
(H)	1,300	
(K)	390	
	2,990	

Recall and Review 2

The total wages and salaries earned by all employees of Dilbert Mfg. Co. during the month of April, as shown in the labor cost summary and the schedule of fixed administrative and sales salaries, are classified as follows:

Direct labor	$312,563
Indirect labor	81,060
Administrative salaries	70,100
Sales salaries	86,250
Total wages	$549,973

a. Prepare a journal entry to distribute the wages earned during April.

b. What is the total amount of payroll taxes that will be imposed on the employer, assuming that two administrative employees with combined earnings this period of $2,000 have exceeded $8,000 in earnings prior to the period?____________________

(After working this exercise, see page 149 for the solution.)

You should now be able to work the following:
Questions 9–16; Exercises 3-4 to 3-11; Problems 3-3 to 3-10; and Self-Study Problem 1.

Special Labor Cost Problems

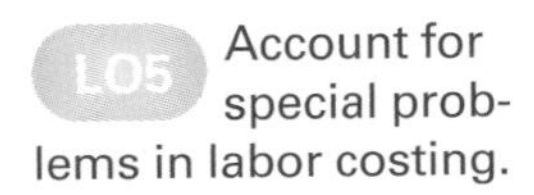
LO5 Account for special problems in labor costing.

An employer may be required to account for a variety of labor-related costs that do not fall into the normal routine of accounting for payroll costs. These special costs may include shift premiums, pensions (such as employer contributions to a 401k plan), bonuses, and vacation and holiday pay. If encountered, the employer should systematically record and recognize each of these costs related to manufacturing labor as costs of the production process. Some companies identify the fringe benefits of direct laborers with the specific job being worked on (Work in Process), while others allocate the fringe benefits to all jobs worked on during the period (Factory Overhead). It is theoretically more correct to trace the fringe benefit costs to the specific jobs because, if highly paid workers with their higher fringe benefits are required for a certain job, that job should also bear a greater amount of fringe benefit costs. In practice, however, fringe benefits more often than not are charged to Factory Overhead and spread over all jobs worked during the period.

Shift Premium

A **work shift** is defined as a regularly scheduled work period for a designated number of hours. If a company divides each workday into two or three 8-hour shifts, the employees working on shifts other than the regular daytime shift may receive additional pay, called a **shift premium**. For example, assume that a manufacturer operates three shifts: day shift, 8 A.M. to 4 P.M.; evening or "swing" shift, 4 P.M. to midnight; night or "graveyard" shift, midnight to 8 A.M. The company pays an additional $1.00 per hour to employees who work the "swing" shift and an additional $1.50 per hour to workers on the "graveyard" shift. The additional payroll costs for the shift premiums do not increase the productivity of the shifts, but are paid because of the social and other lifestyle adjustments required of the late-shift workers. The "other-than-normal" sleep and work schedules deprive the workers from participating in many established social activities and routines. The shift premiums are designed to attract workers to the later, less desirable shifts scheduled by a company. In reality, even though later shift workers are paid at higher rates, the productivity level of the day workers usually exceeds the productivity of the higher paid, late-shift employees due to the difficult adjustment to working other-than-normal daytime hours. To avoid a distortion in costing jobs depending on the time of day that they are worked on, shift premiums are usually charged to Factory Overhead and allocated to all jobs worked on during the period, regardless of the shift on which they happened to be produced.

Employee Pension Costs

Pension costs originate from an agreement between a company and its employee group, by which the company promises to provide income to employees after they retire. In what is called a **defined benefit plan**, the amount of pension benefits paid to a retired employee is commonly based on the employee's past level of earnings and length of service with the company. A **defined contribution plan** specifies the maximum amount of contributions that can be made to the plan by employer and employee, but the amount of the pension benefits is tied to the performance of the company stock or other investments. **Noncontributory plans** are completely funded (paid for) by the company. **Contributory plans,** which are more common in practice, require a partial contribution from the employee. When a pension plan is initiated, it is usually retroactive and recognizes the previous years of each employee's service with the company.

A 401(k) plan is an example of a defined contribution plan. Employees may contribute a prescribed percentage of their income to the plan (up to a maximum of $16,500 and $22,000 for employees under 50 years old and 50 years of age or greater, respectively, in 2009) for the purchase of company stock, mutual funds, or other investments. In most 401(k) plans, employers match a certain portion of the employee investment. Advantages of the plan, in addition to the employer matching contribution, include the tax-deferred features of the wages invested in the plan and the earnings on plan investments until withdrawals are made at retirement. Figure 3-7 illustrates the potential tax saving from investing in a 401(k).

A basic provision of all plans is to systematically accrue, over the period of active service, the total estimated pension cost from the beginning date of the pension plan to the employee's retirement date. If, for example, an employee works a 40-hour week and the company incurs a pension cost of $2 per hour, the amount of pension cost chargeable to the payroll period for this employee is $80. The pension costs related to the factory employees

Figure 3-7 **Annual tax saving from a 401(k) contribution**

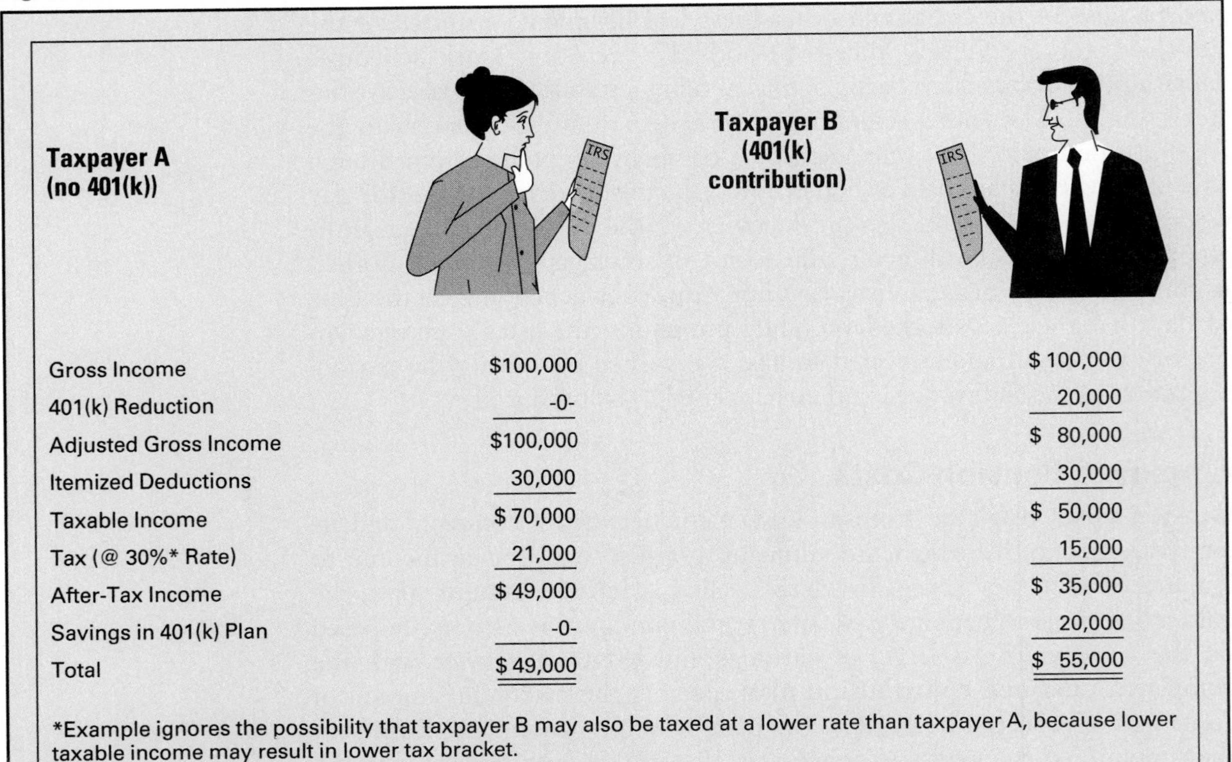

	Taxpayer A (no 401(k))	Taxpayer B (401(k) contribution)
Gross Income	$100,000	$ 100,000
401(k) Reduction	-0-	20,000
Adjusted Gross Income	$100,000	$ 80,000
Itemized Deductions	30,000	30,000
Taxable Income	$ 70,000	$ 50,000
Tax (@ 30%* Rate)	21,000	15,000
After-Tax Income	$ 49,000	$ 35,000
Savings in 401(k) Plan	-0-	20,000
Total	$ 49,000	$ 55,000

*Example ignores the possibility that taxpayer B may also be taxed at a lower rate than taxpayer A, because lower taxable income may result in lower tax bracket.

could be charged to general or administrative expenses under the premise that the existence of a pension plan is beneficial to the company as a whole. However, it is also considered appropriate to charge pension costs directly to the individual employee's department, such as to Factory Overhead for the pension costs of manufacturing employees.

Bonuses

Employees may receive **bonus pay** for a variety of reasons, such as higher-than-usual company profits, exceeding departmental quotas for selling or production, or for any other achievement that the company feels merits additional pay. Bonus plans may include some or all employees. The cost of bonuses is generally charged to the department in which the employee works. Therefore, factory workers' bonuses are charged to Factory Overhead, and sales and administrative employees' bonuses are charged to Selling and Administrative Expense.

Vacation and Holiday Pay

All permanent employees of a company expect a paid vacation each year. The **vacation pay** is earned by the employee for daily service on the job over the course of the year. Therefore, the vacation cost is accrued throughout the year and assigned to the employee's department. For example, assume that an employee earns $600 per week and is entitled to a four-week vacation. The total cost of the vacation to the company would be $2,400. For each of the 48 weeks that the employee works, the employee's department would be charged $50 [$2,400/(52 weeks – 4 weeks vacation)] for vacation pay expense.

Holiday pay is based on an agreement between management and company employees. The agreement stipulates that certain holidays during the year will be paid for by the company, but they are nonworking days for the employees.

Accounting for Bonuses, Vacations, and Holiday Pay

To illustrate accounting for bonuses, vacations, and holiday pay, assume that a factory worker, who is classified as direct labor, earns $700 each week. In addition, the worker will receive a $1,000 bonus at year-end, a 2-week paid vacation, and 10 paid holidays. The following entry records the weekly payroll and the costs and liabilities related to the bonus, vacation, and holiday pay as an expense of the 50 weeks (52 weeks – 2 weeks vacation) that the employee actually worked:

Account	Debit	Credit
Work in Process	700	
Factory Overhead (Bonus)*	20	
Factory Overhead (Vacation)**	28	
Factory Overhead (Holiday)***	28	
Payroll		700
Bonus Liability		20

Vacation Pay Liability		28
Holiday Pay Liability		28
Incurred payroll and bonus, vacation, and holiday pay		

*Bonus: $1,000/50 weeks = $20 per week.
**Vacation Pay: ($700 per week × 2 weeks)/50 weeks = $28 per week.
***Holiday Pay: ($700 per week ÷ 5 days) × 10 paid holidays = $1,400
$1,400/50 weeks = $28 per week.

Note in the previous example that Factory Overhead was debited for the cost of the bonus, vacation, and holiday pay earned by the direct laborers. If, instead, the workers' fringe benefits had been tracked to the individual jobs they had worked on, Work in Process would have been debited. If these fringe benefits had related to sales workers or general office workers, Sales Salaries and Administrative Salaries would have been debited, respectively.

Recall and Review 3

Larry Riester earns $1,000 per week for a five-day week, and he is entitled to 10 paid holidays and four weeks of paid vacation per year. What is the amount of the total holiday pay and how much of it should be expensed per week? $__________.

What is the total vacation pay and how much of it should be expensed per week? $______________.

(After working this exercise, see page 149 for the solution.)

You should now be able to work the following:
Questions 17–22; Exercises 3-12 to 3-14; Problems 3-11 and 3-12; Mini-Case 2; Internet Exercise; and Self-Study Problem 2.

KEY TERMS

ANSWERS TO RECALL AND REVIEW EXERCISES

R&R 1

Day	Hours	Units	Hourly Earnings	Piece-rate Earnings	Total Earnings
Monday	8	200	$ 160.00		$ 160.00
Tuesday	8	175	160.00		160.00
Wednesday	8	225	160.00	$ 12.50	172.50
Thursday	8	250	160.00	25.00	185.00
Friday	8	150	160.00		160.00
Total	40	1,000	$ 800.00	$ 37.50	$ 837.50

R&R 2

Work in Process	312,563	
Factory Overhead (Indirect Labor)	81,060	
Administrative Salaries	70,100	
Sales Salaries	86,250	
Payroll		549,973

Employer payroll taxes = 8.0% (FICA) + 1.0% (Federal Unemployment) + 4.0% (State Unemployment) = 13% of total wages for the period, reduced by 5% of portion of wages directed to employees whose calendar-year earnings prior to period have exceeded $8,000 (.13 × $549,973) − (.05 × $2,000) = $71,396.

R&R 3

Holiday pay: ($1,000 wk./5 days) × 10 paid holidays = $2,000
Expensed per wk.: $2,000/48 wks. worked = $41.67 per wk.
Vacation pay: $1,000 × 4 wks. = $4,000
Expensed per wk.: 4,000/48 wks. worked = $83.33 per wk.

SELF-STUDY PROBLEM 1

Payment and Distribution of Payroll

Bronx Company

The general ledger of the Bronx Company showed the following credit balances on March 15:

FICA Tax Payable	$1,550
Employees Income Tax Payable	975
FUTA Tax Payable	95
State Unemployment Tax Payable	380

Direct labor earnings amounted to $5,100, and indirect labor was $3,400 for the period from March 16 to March 31. The sales and administrative salaries for the same period amounted to $1,500.

Use the following tax rates and bases for this problem:

FICA: 8% on the first $100,000.
State unemployment: 4% on the first $8,000.
FUTA: 1% on the first $8,000.
Federal income tax: 10% of each employee's gross earnings.

Required:

1. Prepare the journal entries for the following:
   a. Recording the payroll.
   b. Paying the payroll.
   c. Recording the employer's payroll tax liability.
   d. Distributing the payroll for March 16 to 31.
2. Prepare the journal entries to record the payment of the amounts due for the month for FICA and income tax withholdings.

Suggestions:

Read the entire problem thoroughly, keeping in mind what you are required to do:

1. Journal entries to record the payroll, pay the payroll, record the employer's payroll taxes, and distribute the payroll.
2. Journal entries for the payment of FICA taxes and federal income tax withholdings.

   The specifics of the problem highlight the fact that there are three separate categories of labor: direct labor, indirect factory labor, and salespersons and administrators.

SOLUTION TO SELF-STUDY PROBLEM

1. a. Journal entry to record the payroll for the period March 16–31: To determine the amount of the debit to Payroll, the earnings of direct labor, indirect labor, and sales and administrative must be added together to obtain $10,000. The $800 of FICA to be withheld can be obtained by multiplying the $10,000 payroll (assuming that no employee's salary has already exceeded the $100,000 base for the year) by the 8% rate. The $1,000 withholding for income taxes is determined by multiplying the $10,000 payroll by the assumed withholding percentage of 10%. Lastly, the credit to Wages Payable for $8,200 represents the amount of net pay that is to appear on employees' paychecks.

Account	Debit	Credit
Payroll	10,000	
FICA Tax Payable		800
Employees Income Tax Payable		1,000
Wages Payable		8,200

   b. Journal entry to pay the payroll: A check drawn by the company for the total payroll net earnings is deposited in a separate payroll account at the bank, and individual checks are issued to the employees.

Wages Payable	8,200	
Cash		8,200

c. Journal entry to record the payroll tax liability: Payroll taxes consist of the employer's share of the FICA taxes and the federal and state unemployment insurance premiums. The employer pays an amount of FICA taxes that matches the employees' contributions and unemployment insurance premiums that are based on an experience rating related to the business's employment history. (In this example, $800 represents the employer's FICA contributions, $400 is the state unemployment insurance premium, and $100 is the federal unemployment insurance premium.) An important fact to note in the following journal entry is that the payroll taxes on factory labor, whether direct or indirect, are all charged to Factory Overhead, whereas the payroll taxes on the sales and administrative salaries are charged to Payroll Tax Expense (Sales and Administrative Salaries).

Factory Overhead	1,105*	
Payroll Tax Expense (Sales and Administrative Salaries)	195**	
FICA Tax Payable		800
Federal Unemployment Tax Payable		100
State Unemployment Tax Payable		400

*[0.08 ($5,100 + $3,400) + 0.01 ($8,500) +0.04 ($8,500)]
**[0.08 ($1,500) + 0.01 ($1,500) + 0.04 ($1,500)]

d. Journal entry to distribute the payroll: In distributing the payroll to the appropriate accounts, it is important to distinguish direct labor, which is charged to Work in Process, from indirect labor, which is debited to Factory Overhead.

Work in Process	5,100	
Factory Overhead	3,400	
Sales and Administrative Salaries	1,500	
Payroll		10,000

2. At appropriate times as designated by law, the employer payroll taxes and employee withholdings must be remitted to the proper authorities. In this example, FICA taxes and employee income taxes are remitted monthly. The entry would be as follows:

FICA Tax Payable	3,150*	
Employees Income Tax Payable	1,975**	
Cash		5,125

*$1,550 + $800 + $800
**$975 + $1,000

SELF-STUDY PROBLEM 2

Accounting for Bonus, Vacation Pay, and Holiday Pay

Glacier, Inc.

The factory payroll for the week is $100,000, consisting of $70,000 earned by 100 direct laborers and $30,000 earned by 30 indirect laborers. The total of factory bonuses to be received at year-end is estimated at $200,000. All factory workers receive a four-week paid vacation and 10 paid holidays.

Required:

1. Prepare the entry to distribute the weekly payroll.
2. Prepare the entry to record the cost and liabilities related to the bonus, vacation, and holiday pay, assuming that the fringe benefits of direct laborers are charged to Factory Overhead.

Suggestions:

Read the entire problem thoroughly, keeping in mind what you are required to do:

1. Prepare a journal entry to distribute the payroll to Work in Process and Factory Overhead depending on whether the wages are for direct or indirect labor.
2. Prepare a journal entry to record the expense and liability for the bonus pay, vacation pay, and holiday pay, keeping in mind that fringe benefits should be charged to all jobs (Factory Overhead) worked on during the period.

SOLUTION TO SELF-STUDY PROBLEM

1. The total payroll for the week of $100,000 needs to be distributed to Work in Process for the amount of the direct labor, $70,000, and to Factory Overhead for the amount of the indirect labor, $30,000. The entry would be:

Work in Process	70,000	
Factory Overhead	30,000	
Payroll		100,000

2. Computations must be performed for each of the fringe benefits before the journal entry can be made:

   Bonus—the estimated bonuses of $200,000 should be allocated equally to the 48 weeks that employees actually work: $200,000/48 weeks = $4,166.67 per week.

   Vacation—the total vacation pay is the $100,000 weekly payroll times the 4 weeks of vacation pay, allocated over the 48 weeks that employees work: ($100,000 × 4 weeks)/48 weeks = $8,333.33 per week.

   Holiday—the total holiday pay is the weekly pay of $100,000 times the 2 weeks of holiday pay (10 days), allocated over the 48 weeks that employees work: ($100,000 × 2 weeks)/48 weeks = $4,166.67 per week.

Because the fringe benefits are to be charged to all jobs, the debits in the entry to record the cost of the fringe benefits are to Factory Overhead and the credits are to the individual liability accounts:

Factory Overhead (Bonus Pay)	4,166.67	
Factory Overhead (Vacation Pay)	8,333.33	
Factory Overhead (Holiday Pay)	4,166.67	
Bonus Pay Liability		4,166.67
Vacation Pay Liability		8,333.33
Holiday Pay Liability		4,166.67

QUESTIONS

1. What is the difference between direct and indirect labor?
2. Briefly stated, what are the advantages and disadvantages of (a) the hourly rate wage plan and (b) the piece-rate wage plan?
3. What is a modified wage plan?
4. What is the concept of production work teams as it relates to incentive wage plans?
5. What is the function of the payroll department?
6. In a payroll system, what purpose is served by a labor time record? How is the information that is recorded on labor time records used?
7. What purpose do digital records and remote computer terminals serve in a payroll system?
8. Although payroll records may vary in design, what types of employee data would be found in the payroll records of most manufacturing companies?
9. What are the sources for posting direct labor cost to (a) individual jobs in the job cost ledger and (b) the work in process account in the general ledger?
10. What are the sources for posting indirect labor cost to the indirect labor account in the factory overhead ledger?
11. In accounting for labor costs, what is the distinction between the accounting treatment for regular pay and overtime premium pay?
12. Maintaining internal control over labor cost is necessary for a cost accounting system to function effectively. What are the internal control procedures regarding the charge to the work in process account and the credit to the payroll account in the general ledger?
13. What accounts are used to record employees' withholding taxes and the employer's payroll taxes?
14. What are the procedures involved in accounting for labor cost, and what supporting forms are used for each procedure?
15. What is the source of data used to:
    a. record the distribution of the payroll.
    b. record the employer's payroll taxes.
16. In what circumstance should an accrual for payroll earnings and payroll tax expense be made?
17. What is a shift premium, and how is it usually accounted for?
18. What is a basic requirement of all pension plans?

19. a. Distinguish between defined benefit pension plans and defined contribution pension plans.
    b. Distinguish between contributory and noncontributory pension plans.

20. In 2009, what was the maximum amount that an employee could contribute to a 401(k) plan?

21. What accounting treatments do factory bonuses, vacation pay, and holiday pay for factory employees have in common?

22. What are the two alternatives for accounting for the fringe benefits of direct laborers?

EXERCISES

Note: For the exercises and problems in this chapter, use the following tax rates:

FICA—Employer and employee, 8% of the first $100,000 of earnings per employee per calendar year.

State unemployment—4% of the first $8,000 of earnings per employee per calendar year.

Federal unemployment—1% of the first $8,000 of earnings per employee, per calendar year.

Federal income tax withholding—10% of each employee's gross earnings, unless otherwise stated.

E3-1 Computing payroll earnings and taxes

LO1 LO2

A. Jolly of Pittsburgh Manufacturing Company is paid at the rate of $20 an hour for an 8-hour day, with time-and-a-half for overtime and double-time for Sundays and holidays. Regular employment is on the basis of 40 hours a week, five days a week. At the end of a week, the labor time record shows the following:

Job or Indirect Labor	Su.	M	Tu.	W	Th.	F	Sa.	Total
007		5	5	3	5.0	6		24.0
009		3	3	5	6.5	5		22.5
Machine repair	4						6.5	10.5
Total	4	8	8	8	11.5	11	6.5	57.0

Because jobs are randomly scheduled for the overtime period, any overtime premium is charged to Factory Overhead.

a. Compute Jolly's total earnings for the week.
b. Present the journal entry to distribute Jolly's total earnings.

E3-2 Recording payroll

Using the earnings data developed in E3-1 and assuming that this was the first week of employment for A. Jolly with Pittsburgh Manufacturing Company, prepare the journal entries for the following:

a. The week's payroll.
b. Payment of the payroll.

(Note: *These single journal entries here and in E3-7 and E3-8 are for the purpose of illustrating the principle involved. Normally, the entries would be made for the total factory payroll plus the administrative and sales payroll.*)

E3-3 Modified wage plan

Marcia Young earns $25 per hour for up to 400 units of production per day. If she produces more than 400 units per day, she will receive an additional piece rate of $0.50 per unit. Assume that her hours worked and pieces finished for the week just ended were as follows:

Day	Hours Worked	Pieces Finished
Monday	8	400
Tuesday	8	380
Wednesday	8	440
Thursday	8	450
Friday	8	360

a. Determine Young's earnings for each day and for the week.
b. Prepare the journal entry to distribute the payroll, assuming that any make-up guarantees are charged to Factory Overhead.

E3-4 Overtime Allocation

Albert Machine Tool Company produces tools on a job order basis. During May, two jobs were completed, and the following costs were incurred:

	Job 401	Job 402
Direct materials	$28,000	$37,000
Direct labor: Regular	18,000	23,000
Overtime premium	—	6,000

Other factory costs for the month totaled $16,800. Factory overhead costs are allocated one-third to Job 401 and two-thirds to Job 402.

a. Describe two alternative methods for assigning the overtime premium cost to Jobs 401 and 402 and explain how the appropriate method would be determined.
b. Compute the cost of Job 401 and Job 402 under each of the two methods described in part a.

LO2 LO3

E3-5 Journal entries for payroll

A partial summary of the payroll data for Burrington Manufacturing Company for each week of June is as follows:

	June 7	June 14	June 21	June 28
Gross earnings	$ 36,500	$ 34,200	$ 37,300	$ 38,400
Deductions:				
FICA tax, 8%	$?	$?	$?	$?
Tax-sheltered annuity	1,825	1,780	1,855	1,870
Income tax	4,215	4,120	4,320	4,410
Health insurance	600	600	600	600
Total deductions	$?	$?	$?	$?
Net earnings	$?	$?	$?	$?

a. Compute the missing amounts in the summary, assuming that no employees have reached the $100,000 FICA maximum.

b. For each payroll period, prepare journal entries to (1) record the payroll and (2) record the payments to employees.

LO3

E3-6 Payroll taxes

Fontana Fabricating Company paid wages to its employees during the year as follows:

Burris	$ 15,400
Combs	16,700
Detrick	13,000
Edwards	23,300
Hobbs	33,200
McCormack	36,100
Otto	66,700
Sylvester	102,000

a. How much of the total payroll is exempt from the FICA rate of 8%?

b. How much of the total payroll is exempt from federal and state unemployment taxes?

c. How much of the total payroll is exempt from federal income tax withholding?

LO2 LO3

E3-7 Recording the payroll and payroll taxes

Using the earnings data developed in E3-1, and assuming that this was the eighth week of employment for Jolly and the previous earnings to date were $7,900, prepare the journal entries for the following:

a. The week's payroll.

b. Payment of the payroll.

c. The employer's payroll taxes.

E3-8 Recording the payroll and payroll taxes

LO2 LO3

Using the earnings data developed in E3-1, and assuming that this was the fiftieth week of employment for Jolly and the previous earnings to date were $99,800, prepare the journal entries for the following:

a. The week's payroll.
b. Payment of the payroll.
c. The employer's payroll taxes.

E3-9 Payroll distribution

LO3

The total wages and salaries earned by all employees of Cutler Manufacturing Company during the month of March, as shown in the labor cost summary and the schedule of fixed administrative and sales salaries, are classified as follows:

Direct labor	$ 625,125
Indirect labor	162,120
Administrative salaries	140,200
Sales salaries	172,500
Total wages earned	$1,099,945

a. Prepare a journal entry to distribute the wages earned during March.
b. What is the total amount of payroll taxes that will be imposed on the employer for the payroll, assuming that two administrative employees with combined earnings this period of $3,000 have exceeded $8,000 in earnings prior to the period?

E3-10 Employees' earnings and taxes

LO2 LO3

A weekly payroll summary made from labor time records shows the following data for Musketeer Manufacturing Company:

Employee	Classification	Hourly Rate	Hours Regular	Hours Overtime
Brown, D.	Direct	$12	40	2
Jackson, D.	Direct	12	40	3
Love, J.	Direct	15	40	4
Anderson, C.	Indirect	9	40	
Raymond, B.	Indirect	18	40	

Overtime is payable at one-and-a-half times the regular rate of pay for an employee and is distributed to all jobs worked on during the period.

a. Determine the net pay of each employee. The income taxes withheld for each employee amount to 15% of the gross wages.
b. Prepare journal entries for the following:
  1. Recording the payroll.
  2. Paying the payroll.

3. Distributing the payroll. (Assume that overtime premium will be charged to all jobs worked on during the period.)
4. The employer's payroll taxes. (Assume that none of the employees has achieved the maximum wage bases for FICA and unemployment taxes.)

E3-11 Employees' earnings using hourly and piece-rate methods

LO1 LO3

The payroll records of Torero Machining Company show the following information for the week ended April 17:

Employee	Classification	Hours Worked	Production (Units)	Rate	Income Tax W/held
Brown, D.	Direct	42		$18.00/hr	$ 80
Dorr, M.	Direct	48		$17.60/hr	84
Ginty, D.	Direct	39	2,000	$0.44/piece	110
Jackson, D.	Direct	40	1,800	$0.44/piece	100
Jones, R.	Indirect	40		$800/wk	100
Lewis, C.	Indirect	50		$1,600/wk	240
Pomare, G.	Indirect	40		$1,400/wk	120

Hourly workers are paid time-and-a-half for overtime.

a. Determine the net earnings of each employee.
b. Prepare the journal entries for the following:
   1. Recording the payroll.
   2. Paying the payroll.
   3. Distributing the payroll. (Assume that overtime premium will be distributed to all jobs worked on during the period.)
   4. Recording the employer's payroll taxes. (Assume that none of the employees has achieved the maximum wage bases for FICA and unemployment taxes.)

E3-12 Accounting for bonus and vacation pay

LO5

Beth Elkins, a factory worker, earns $1,000 each week. In addition, she will receive a $4,000 bonus at year-end and a four-week paid vacation. Prepare the entry to record the weekly payroll and the costs and liabilities related to the bonus and the vacation pay, assuming that Elkins is the only employee.

E3-13 Accounting for holiday and vacation pay

LO5

Clark Kent earns $800 per week for a five-day week, and he is entitled to 12 paid holidays and four weeks of paid vacation.

a. Over how many weeks should the holiday pay and vacation pay be expensed?
b. What is the amount of the total holiday pay, and how much of it should be expensed per week?
c. How much is the amount of the total vacation pay, and how much of it should be expensed per week?

PROBLEMS

P3-1 **Payroll computation with incentive bonus**

LO1

Fifteen workers are assigned to a group project. The production standard calls for 500 units to be completed each hour to meet a customer's set deadline for the products. If the required units can be delivered before the target date on the order, the customer will pay a substantial premium for early delivery. The company, wishing to encourage the workers to produce beyond the established standard, has offered an excess production bonus that will be added to each project employee's pay. The bonus is to be computed as follows:

a. $\frac{\text{Group's excess production over standard} \times 50\%}{\text{Standard units for week}} = \text{bonus percentage}$

b. Individual's hourly wage rate × bonus percentage = hourly bonus rate

c. Hourly wage rate + hourly bonus rate = new hourly rate for week

d. Total hours worked × new hourly rate = earnings for week

The average wage rate for the project workers is $15 per hour. The production record for the week shows the following:

	Hours Worked	Production (Units)
Monday	112	61,040
Tuesday	112	60,032
Wednesday	112	60,480
Thursday	112	65,632
Friday	108	57,344
Saturday	60	26,000
	616	330,528

Required:

1. Determine the hourly bonus rate and the total amount of the bonus for the week. (Round the bonus percentage to five decimal places and the bonus rate to the nearest whole cent.)
2. What are the total wages of B. Moxie, who worked 40 hours at a base rate of $15 per hour?
3. What are the total wages of C. Flood, who worked 35 hours at a base rate of $20 per hour?

P3-2 **Labor time record, direct vs. indirect labor**

Terri Whelan, SS# 036-47-2189, is a Grade 1 Machinist who earns $20 per hour. On Monday June 12 through Wednesday June 14, she worked four hours per day on each of Jobs 007 and 2525. On Thursday and Friday of the week, she worked six hours per day on Job 2525 and two hours per day on maintenance. Her supervisor is Tom Culver, who signs off on all labor time records on Saturday of the week just ended.

Required:

1. Prepare a labor time record (LTR 999) for Whelan for the week ended June 17, 2011.
2. Compute the amounts of direct labor costs, by job, and indirect labor costs created by Terri's work for the week.

P3-3 LO2 LO3 **Payroll calculation and distribution; overtime and idle time**

A rush order was accepted by San Diego Machine Conversions for five van conversions. The labor time records for the week ended January 27 show the following:

		Labor Time Records—Hour Distribution				
Employees	**Hours**	**Van #1**	**Van #2**	**Van #3**	**Van #4**	**Van #5**
Peavy (Supervisor)	42					
Bell	45	10	10	10	10	5
Gonzalez	48	24	24			
Hairston	48			24	24	
Headley	45	15	15	15		
Rodriguez	42	24	8			
Young	40	20	10			

All employees are paid $10.00 per hour, except Peavy, who receives $20 per hour. All overtime premium pay, except Peavy's, is chargeable to the job, and all employees, including Peavy, receive time-and-a-half for overtime hours.

Required:

1. Calculate the total payroll and total net earnings for the week. Assume that an 18% deduction for federal income tax is required in addition to FICA deductions. Assume that none of the employees has achieved the maximums for FICA and unemployment taxes. Hours not worked on vans are idle time and are not charged to the job.
2. Prepare the journal entries to record and pay the payroll.
3. Prepare the journal entry to distribute the payroll to the appropriate accounts.
4. Determine the dollar amount of labor that is chargeable to each van, assuming that the overtime costs are proportionate to the regular hours used on the vans. (First compute an average labor rate for each worker, including overtime premium, and then use that rate to charge all workers, hours to vans.)

P3-4 **Computing and journalizing employer's payroll taxes**

The following form is used by MoJo Manufacturing Company to compute payroll taxes incurred during the month of April:

Classification of Wages and Salaries	Earnings for Month	FICA Tax 8%	Unemployment Taxes: Federal Tax 1%	Unemployment Taxes: State Tax 4%	Total Payroll Taxes Imposed on Employer
Direct labor	$ 88,180				
Indirect labor	16,220				
Payroll taxes on factory wages	?				
Administrative salaries	12,000				
Sales salaries	11,500				
Total payroll taxes	?				

Required:

1. Using the above form, calculate the employer's payroll taxes for April. Assume that none of the employees has achieved the maximums for FICA and unemployment taxes.
2. Assuming that the employer payroll taxes on factory wages are treated as factory overhead, the taxes covering administrative salaries are an administrative expense, and the taxes covering sales salaries are a selling expense, prepare a general journal entry to record the employer's liability for the April payroll taxes.

P3-5 **Payroll for piece-rate wage system**

WTA Manufacturing Company operates on a modified wage plan. During one week's operation, the following direct labor costs were incurred:

Employee	Piece Rate per 100 Units	Units Completed: M	T	W	T	F
J. Jankovic	$1.20	6,800	7,100	6,500	8,000	4,800
M. Sharapova ..	1.10	6,300	6,400	2,900	2,800	7,000
S. Williams	1.30	6,200	6,100	7,100	6,000	2,800

The employees are machine operators. Piece rates vary with the kind of product being produced. A minimum of $70 per day is guaranteed each employee by union contract.

Required:

1. Compute the weekly earnings for Jankovic, Sharapova, and Williams.
2. Prepare journal entries to:
   a. Record the week's payroll, assuming that none of the employees has achieved the maximum base wage for FICA taxes.

b. Record payment of the payroll.
c. Record the employer's share of payroll taxes, assuming that none of the employees has achieved the maximum base wage for FICA or unemployment taxes.

P3-6 **Payment and distribution of payroll similar to Self-Study Problem 1**

LO3

The general ledger of Smokey Mountain Mfg., Inc., showed the following credit balances on January 15:

FICA Tax Payable	3,100.00
Employees Income Tax Payable	1,937.50
FUTA Tax Payable	193.75
State Unemployment Tax Payable	775.00

Direct labor earnings amounted to $10,500 from January 16 to 31. Indirect labor was $5,700, and sales and administrative salaries for the same period amounted to $3,800. All wages are subject to FICA, FUTA, state unemployment taxes, and 10% income tax withholding.

Required:

1. Prepare the journal entries for the following:
   a. Recording the payroll.
   b. Paying the payroll.
   c. Recording the employer's payroll tax liability.
   d. Distributing the payroll costs for January 16 to 31.
2. Prepare the journal entry to record the payment of the amounts due for the month for FICA and income tax withholdings.
3. Calculate the amount of total earnings for the period from January 1 to 15.

P3-7 **Payroll work sheet and journal entries**

LO2 LO3

The payroll records of XU Corporation for the week ending October 7, the fortieth week in the year, show the following:

Employee	Classification	Salary or Wage per 40-Hour Week	Hours Worked	Income Tax Withheld	Gross Earnings through Thirty-Ninth Week
Allen	President	$2,489	40	$488	$109,560
Devine	Vice President—Administration	2,238	40	402	99,500
Fiorelli	Supervisor—Production	700	40	180	27,300
O'Clock	Factory—Direct	500	48	150	19,820
O'Reilly	Factory—Direct	400	46	160	17,200
Pawlukiewicz	Factory—Direct	400	44	110	16,600
Surdick	Factory—Direct	380	42	120	15,200
Trebbi	Factory—Indirect	300	42	80	7,800
Webb	Factory—Indirect	300	42	60	6,600

Required:

1. Complete a work sheet with the following column headings:
   Employee
   3 columns for Earnings for Week:
   - Use one for Regular Pay.
   - Use one for Overtime Premium Pay. (The company pays time-and-a-half for overtime for all employees below the supervisory level.)
   - Use one for Total for Week.

   Total Earnings through Fortieth Week
   FICA Taxable Earnings
   FICA
   Income Tax Withheld
   Net Earnings
2. Prepare journal entries for the following:
   a. Payroll for the fortieth week.
   b. Payment of payroll for the week.
   c. Distribution of the payroll costs, assuming that overtime premium is charged to all jobs worked on during the period.
   d. Employer's payroll tax liability.
3. The company carries a disability insurance policy for the employees at a cost of $15 per week for each employee. Journalize the employer's cost of insurance premiums for the week.

P3-8 **Estimating labor costs for bids**

LO1 LO3

Pan-Am Manufacturing Company prepares cost estimates for projects on which it will bid. In order to anticipate the labor cost to be included in a request to bid on a contract for 1,200,000 units that will be delivered to the customer at the rate of 100,000 units per month, the company has compiled the following data related to labor:

a. The first 100,000 units will require 5 hours per unit.
b. The second 100,000 units will require less labor due to the skills learned on the first 100,000 units finished. It is expected that labor time will be reduced by 10% if an incentive bonus of one-half of the labor savings is paid to the employees.
c. For the remaining 1,000,000 units, it is expected that the labor time will be reduced 20% from the original estimate (the first 100,000 units) if the same incentive bonus (1/2 of the savings) is paid to the employees.
d. Overtime premiums are to be excluded when savings are computed.

The contract will require 2,250 employees at a base rate of $20.00 per hour, with time-and-a-half for overtime. The plant operates on a 5-day, 40-hour-per-week basis. Employees are paid for a two-week vacation in August and for eight holidays.

The scheduled production for the 50-week work year shows:

January—June: 26 weeks with 4 holidays
July—December: 24 weeks with 4 holidays

Required:
Prepare cost estimates for direct labor and labor-related costs for the contract, showing the following:

1. Wages paid at the regular rate.
2. Overtime premium payments. (Don't forget holidays in computing regular hours available.)
3. Incentive bonus payments.
4. Vacation and holiday pay.
5. Employer's payroll taxes (13% of total wages, assuming that no employee has exceeded the wage bases for FICA and the unemployment insurance taxes).

LO2

LO3

P3-9 Summary of payroll procedures

An analysis of the payroll for the month of November for Hollywood, Inc., reveals the information shown:

	Gross Earnings*—Week Ending			
Employee Name	**11/8**	**11/15**	**11/22**	**11/29**
R. Crowe	$ 300	$ 280	$ 290	$ 320
C. Eastwood	280	270	260	280
J. Carey	320	300	340	280
S. Penn	2,032	2,032	2,032	2,032
P. Giamatti	800	760	850	870

*All regular time

Crowe, Eastwood, and Carey are production workers, and Penn is the plant manager. Giamatti is in charge of the office.

Cumulative earnings paid (before deductions) in this calendar year prior to the payroll period ending November 8 were as follows: Crowe, $12,000; Eastwood, $7,800; Carey, $11,500; Penn, $89,400; and Giamatti, $32,800.

Required:
The solution to this problem requires the following forms, using the indicated column headings:

Employee Earnings Record	**Payroll Record**	**Labor Cost Summary**
Week Ending	Employee's Name	Week Ending
Weekly Gross Earnings	Gross Earnings	Dr. Work in Process (Direct Labor)
Accumulated Gross Earnings	Withholdings (2 columns): FICA Tax, Income Tax (10%)	Dr. Factory Overhead (Indirect Labor)
Weekly Earnings Subject to FICA	Net Amount Paid	Dr. Administrative Salaries (Office)
Withholding (2 columns):		Cr. Payroll (Total)
FICA Tax		
Income Tax (10%)		
Net Amount Paid		

1. Prepare an employee earnings record for each of the five employees.
2. Prepare a payroll record for each of the four weeks.
3. Prepare a labor cost summary for the month.
4. Prepare journal entries to record the following:
   a. The payroll for each of the four weeks.
   b. The payment of wages for each of the four payrolls.
   c. The distribution of the monthly labor costs per the labor cost summary.
   d. The company's payroll taxes covering the four payroll periods.

P3-10 Summary of payroll procedures

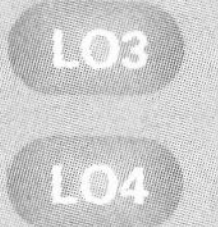

Giovanni Construction Company uses the job order cost system. In recording payroll transactions, the following accounts are used:

Cash	Administrative Salaries
Wages Payable	Miscellaneous Administrative Expense
FICA Tax Payable	Sales Salaries
Federal Unemployment Tax Payable	Miscellaneous Selling Expense
State Unemployment Tax Payable	Factory Overhead
Employees Income Tax Payable	Work in Process
Payroll	

Factory employees are paid weekly, while all other employees are paid semimonthly on the fifteenth and the last day of each month. All salaries and wages are subject to all taxes.

Following is a narrative of transactions completed during the month of January:

Jan. 7	Recorded total earnings of factory employees, amounting to $68,200, less deductions for employees' income taxes and FICA taxes.
7	Issued check for payment of the payroll.
14	Recorded total earnings of factory employees amounting to $66,300, less deductions for employees' income taxes and FICA taxes.
14	Issued check for payment of the payroll.
15	Recorded administrative salaries, $10,000, and sales salaries, $18,000, less deductions for employees' income taxes and FICA taxes.
15	Issued check for payment of the salaries.
21	Recorded total earnings of factory employees amounting to $72,500, less deductions for employees' income taxes and FICA taxes.
21	Issued check for payment of the payroll.
28	Recorded total earnings of factory employees amounting to $74,200, less deductions for employees' income taxes and FICA taxes.
28	Issued check for payment of the payroll.
31	Recorded administrative salaries, $10,000, and sales salaries, $18,000, less deductions for employees' income taxes and FICA taxes.
31	Issued check for payment of the salaries.
31	The following wages and salaries were earned or accrued during January:

Direct labor	$302,500
Indirect labor	22,500
Administrative salaries	20,000
Sales salaries	36,000
Total	$381,000

Giovanni Construction Company used the following form to compute the amount of payroll taxes incurred:

Items	Taxable Earnings	FICA Tax	Federal Unemployment Tax	State Unemployment Tax	Total Payroll Taxes
Factory wages					
Administrative salaries					
Sales salaries					
Total					

Required:

1. Complete the previous form to show the payroll taxes imposed on the employer for the month of January.
2. Prepare the journal entries to record the foregoing transactions, including the distribution of payroll costs and payroll taxes, assuming that the payroll taxes imposed on the employer for factory wages are to be charged to Factory Overhead, the taxes for administrative salaries are to be charged to Miscellaneous Administrative Expense, and the taxes for sales salaries are to be charged to Miscellaneous Selling Expense.
3. Assume that the factory employees worked on January 29, 30, and 31. What was the amount of accrued wages on January 31?

P3-11 **Accounting for bonus, vacation pay, and holiday pay similar to Self-Study Problem 2**

LO5

The factory payroll for the week is $200,000, consisting of $140,000 earned by 100 direct laborers and $60,000 earned by 30 indirect laborers. The total of factory bonuses to be received at year-end is estimated at $400,000. All factory workers receive a two-week paid vacation and five paid holidays.

Required:

Prepare the entries to distribute the weekly payroll and the costs and liabilities related to the bonus, vacation pay, and holiday pay, assuming that the fringe benefits of the direct laborers are charged to Factory Overhead.

P3-12 **Accounting for bonus, vacation pay, and holiday pay**

LO5

In P3-11 above, prepare the entries to distribute the weekly payroll and the costs and liabilities related to the bonus, vacation, and holiday pay, assuming that the fringe benefits of the direct laborers are charged to the individual jobs worked on during the period.

MINI-CASE 1

Incentive wage plan

LO1

Stacey Womack is considering the implementation of an incentive wage plan to increase productivity in her small manufacturing plant. The plant is nonunion, and employees have been compensated with only an hourly rate plan. Jane Moore, Vice President—Manufacturing, is concerned that the move to an incentive compensation plan will cause direct laborers to speed up production and, thus, compromise quality.

Required:

1. How might Womack accomplish her goals while alleviating Moore's concerns?
2. Does the compensation have to be all hourly rate or all incentive?
3. Can incentive compensation also apply to service businesses?

MINI-CASE 2

Allocating overtime premium and bonus costs

LO3 LO5

Elite Manufacturing Company uses a job order cost system to cost its products. It recently signed a new contract with the union that calls for time-and-a-half for all work over 40 hours a week and double-time for Saturday and Sunday. Also, a bonus of 1% of the employees' earnings for the year is to be paid to the employees at the end of the fiscal year. The controller, the plant manager, and the sales manager disagree as to how the overtime pay and the bonus should be allocated.

An examination of the first month's payroll under the new union contract provisions shows the following:

Direct labor:		
Regular—40,200 hours @ $10		$402,000
Overtime:		
Weekdays—1,700 hours @ $15	$25,500	
Saturdays—400 hours @ $20	8,000	
Sundays—300 hours @ $20	6,000	39,500
Indirect labor		14,800
		$456,300

Analysis of the payroll supporting documents revealed the following:

a. More production was scheduled each day than could be handled in a regular workday, resulting in the need for overtime.
b. The Saturday and Sunday hours resulted from rush orders with special contract arrangements with the customers.

The controller believes that the overtime premiums and the bonus should be charged to factory overhead and spread over all production of the accounting period, regardless of when the jobs were completed.

The plant manager favors charging the overtime premiums directly to the jobs worked on during overtime hours and the bonus to administrative expense.

The sales manager states that the overtime premiums and bonus are not factory costs chargeable to regular production but are costs created from administrative policies and, therefore, should be charged only to administrative expense.

Required:

1. Evaluate each position—the controller's, the plant manager's, and the sales manager's. If you disagree with all of the positions taken, present your view of the appropriate allocation.
2. Prepare the journal entries to illustrate the position you support, including the accrual for the bonus.

INTERNET EXERCISE

401(k) Plans

Go to the Vanguard Investments' Web site https://retirementplans.vanguard.com/VGApp/pe/PubHome for retirement information that is linked to the text Web site at www.cengage.com/accounting/vanderbeck. Enter "401(k) plans" in the search area and find the answers to the following questions:

Required:

1. Why have IRAs become the largest pool of retirement assets in the United States?
2. Which assets should you tap first in retirement? Why?
3. What is a "bear market"? On average, how often can one be expected to occur?

Chapter 4

Accounting for Factory Overhead

Learning Objectives

After studying this chapter, you should be able to:

- LO1 Identify cost behavior patterns.
- LO2 Separate semivariable costs into variable and fixed components.
- LO3 Prepare a budget for factory overhead costs.
- LO4 Account for actual factory overhead.
- LO5 Distribute service department factory overhead costs to production departments.
- LO6 Apply factory overhead using predetermined rates.
- LO7 Account for actual and applied factory overhead.

Sherwin-Williams offered the following advice to its painting contractors at the company Web site:

"Overhead costs are a very big deal costing companies, large and small, thousands of dollars each year ... Cost estimation isn't just about labor expenses and material costs. It's about making a profit, a profit that's built into every job bid. It begins with identifying and accounting for all costs—labor, materials, taxes, scaffolding, permits, lights, gas, office supplies, rent and everything else associated with operating your business."[1]

This advice is equally important for manufacturers, whose overhead costs are often in the millions, in costing the jobs that they produce. This chapter covers accounting for factory overhead that must be allocated in a rational way to all the jobs produced during the period, so that each job contributes to the company's "bottom line."

All costs incurred in the factory that are not chargeable directly to the finished product are called **factory overhead**. These operating costs of the factory cannot be traced specifically to a unit of production. A variety of other terms have been used to describe this type of cost, such as indirect expenses, indirect manufacturing costs, or factory burden. These costs are also referred to simply as "overhead" or "burden."

1 "Don't Underestimate Overhead Costs," http://www.sherwin-williams.com (visited 3/18/2009).

One method of determining whether a factory expenditure is an overhead item is to compare it to the classification standards established for direct materials and direct labor costs. If the expenditure cannot be charged to either of these two categories, it is classified as factory overhead. Thus, all indirect factory expenditures are factory overhead items. Factory overhead includes (1) indirect materials consumed in the factory, such as glue and nails in the production of wooden furniture and oil used for maintaining factory equipment; (2) indirect factory labor, such as wages of janitors, forklift operators, and supervisors and overtime premiums paid to all factory workers; and (3) all other indirect manufacturing expenses, such as insurance, property taxes, and depreciation on the factory building and equipment.

Accounting for factory overhead involves the following procedures:

1. Identifying cost behavior patterns.
2. Budgeting factory overhead costs.
3. Accumulating actual overhead costs.
4. Applying factory overhead estimates to production.
5. Calculating and analyzing differences between actual and applied factory overhead.

LO1 Identify cost behavior patterns.

Identifying Cost Behavior Patterns

Direct materials and direct labor are classified as variable costs. **Variable costs** are costs that vary in direct proportion to volume changes. In contrast are those costs that remain the same, in total, when production levels increase or decrease. These unchanging costs are referred to as **fixed costs**. **Semivariable costs,** also called **mixed costs,** have characteristics of both variable and fixed costs.

Whether a particular cost, such as labor, is classified as variable or fixed depends on how it reacts to changes in business activity. For example, workers at fast-food restaurants, such as **Taco Bell,** are only guaranteed a few hours per shift. If business is slow, they are sent home. This is an example of labor as a variable cost because the amount of labor used is tied to business activity. By comparison, the restaurant manager's salary would be a fixed cost because the restaurant needs a manager whether business activity is busy or slow. Recent studies indicate that companies in various countries classify costs differently. For example, 82% of U.S. companies surveyed classified materials-handling labor as either variable or semivariable, whereas 61% of Japanese companies classified it as fixed.[2]

2 NAA Tokyo Affiliate, "Management Accounting in Advanced Manufacturing."

Factory overhead expenses include costs that may be classified as variable, fixed, or mixed. Therefore, factory overhead creates a difficult problem for most companies because they must predict costs that will be incurred at various levels of production. The factory overhead costs, such as supplies, that behave in the same pattern as direct materials costs and direct labor costs are considered variable costs and are readily forecasted because they move up or down proportionately with production volume changes. The factory overhead charges deemed fixed costs, such as the plant manager's salary, remain unchanged when production varies; therefore, they are also quite predictable. The factory overhead costs that are semivariable, such as the cost of utilities, have to be first broken into their variable and fixed components before they can be predicted at different volume levels. In many companies, semivariable costs constitute a substantial portion of the factory overhead charges, and the method used to forecast these costs must be carefully selected.

Figure 4-1 shows the basic patterns of factory overhead costs as volume changes are encountered.

Examples of variable, fixed, and semivariable factory overhead costs include the following:

Variable: Electricity used to power the machines; depreciation expense computed on the units-of-production basis; supplies and small tools expense.

Fixed: Electricity used to heat and light the factory; factory property taxes; depreciation of equipment computed on a straight-line basis; plant manager's salary; insurance on factory building and equipment.

Semivariable:

Type A: Changes as various levels of production are reached. This type of cost, also known as a **step-variable cost**, will remain constant over a range of production, then abruptly change. The increases are not continuous, and costs will plateau before another cost change occurs. Examples are inspection and handling costs, and other indirect labor costs where up to a certain level of production a fixed number of employees can handle the task, but beyond this level new hires need to be made to handle the increased volume. If the steps are especially wide before moving up to the next level of costs, the item is known as a **step-fixed cost**. The

Figure 4-1 Cost Behavior Patterns

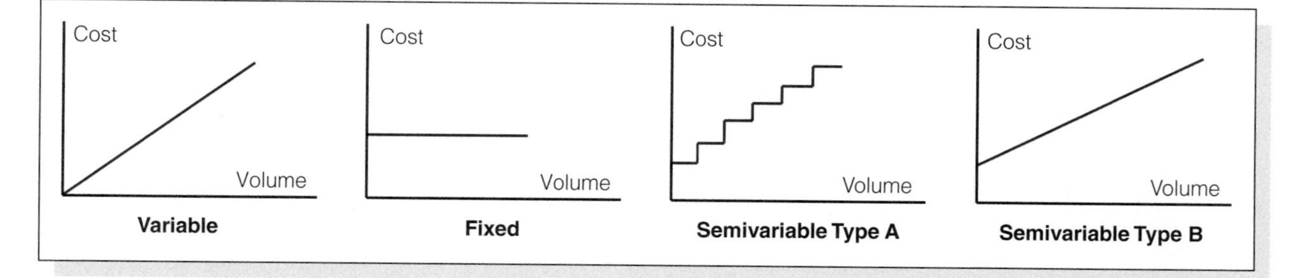

salaries of factory supervisors, which would stay the same in total over a wide range of production, would be a good example of this type of cost.

Type B: Varies continuously, but not in direct proportion to volume changes. Examples include utility costs and maintenance of factory equipment. For example, the electricity used to power the machines would vary in direct proportion to the level of production, whereas electricity used to light and heat the factory would not vary with the number of units produced.

The composition of the different semivariable factory overhead costs makes the prediction of a specific amount of overhead cost for a given level of production very challenging. Before a good approximation of overhead costs at various levels of production can be made, these semivariable costs need to be separated into their fixed and variable components. Mathematical techniques can be used to determine these fixed and variable components that comprise semivariable costs.

Analyzing Semivariable Factory Overhead Costs

LO2 Separate semivariable costs into variable and fixed components.

Many different techniques and theories exist regarding the prediction of future events. Most mathematical techniques attempt to establish a pattern from the historic evidence available, and then use the pattern as a model for predicting future outcomes. If history repeats itself, the model will satisfactorily simulate the future events, and the predictions will be beneficial to the decision-making process.

The statistical techniques to be discussed in this chapter use the relationships of historical costs to past activity levels to isolate variable and fixed costs. The nonmathematical (observation) method relies on personal experience and managerial judgment.

Observation Method

The **observation method**, also called the **account analysis method**, relies heavily on the ability of an observer to detect a pattern of cost behavior by reviewing past cost and volume data. The reaction of an expense to past changes in production is observed, and a decision is made to treat the expense as either a variable cost or a fixed cost, depending on which type of cost behavior it more closely resembles. The analyzed overhead item would thereafter be treated as either a variable or fixed cost, ignoring the fact that many overhead costs are semivariable. For example, electricity expense would be classified as a variable cost if the majority of the kilowatt hours used were for powering the machines rather than for heating and lighting the factory. Companies that use the observation method believe that the discrepancy between the actual costs and the forecast costs will be insignificant and will not affect management strategies or operations.

Some companies still use the observation method. Due to an increasing emphasis on quantifying business data and the availability of information technology to ease the task, however, mathematical methods have increased in popularity. Three of these methods are discussed in the following sections: (1) the high-low method, (2) the statistical scattergraph method, and (3) the least squares regression method. These methods isolate an element of a semivariable cost, then suggest that the remainder of the cost is the other element.

High-Low Method

The **high-low method** compares a high production volume and its related cost to a low production volume with its related cost. The difference in volume between the two points being compared is linear and will fall along a straight line.

To illustrate, assume that the following overhead costs were incurred at two different levels of production:

	1,000 Units	2,000 Units
Depreciation (fixed)	$2,000	$2,000
Electricity costs (semivariable)	3,000	5,000
Factory supplies (variable)	1,000	2,000
Total cost	$6,000	$9,000

Straight-line depreciation is a fixed cost and remained unchanged in total as production doubled. Factory supplies is a variable cost of $1 per unit, and it doubled in total when production volume doubled. Electricity expense, however, was neither entirely fixed, nor did it change proportionately with volume. It had an element of variable cost—the cost to run the machines that produce the product—and a fixed cost element—the cost to light and heat the plant. By using the high-low technique, part of the electricity cost will be determined to be variable and the remaining part fixed. The variable rate is determined by comparing the amount of volume change when moving from the lowest to the highest points in a data set to the amount of change in costs between those two points. In the following example only the high and low points are given, not the entire data set from which they were determined:

Variable cost:

	Units Produced	Electricity Costs
High volume	2,000	$5,000
Low volume	1,000	3,000
Change	1,000	$2,000

Variable cost per unit = Change in costs/Change in units

Variable cost per unit ($2,000/1,000 units) = $2

The amount of fixed cost, which will be the same for either level of volume, is computed by subtracting total variable cost from total cost at each volume level:

Fixed cost:

	1,000 Units	2,000 Units
Total cost	$3,000	$5,000
Variable cost @ $2 per unit	2,000	4,000
Fixed cost (remainder)	$1,000	$1,000

Electricity costs at various levels of production can now be estimated using the following formula:

$$\text{Electricity costs} = \text{Fixed costs} + \text{Variable costs}$$
$$\text{Electricity costs} = \$1,000 + (\$2 \times \text{number of units produced})$$

Assume that management wishes to estimate total factory overhead costs for one month at a production level of 4,000 units. Using the previous data and the formula for the semivariable cost, projected factory overhead costs for the month would be $15,000, computed as follows:

Depreciation (fixed)	$ 2,000
Electricity costs [semivariable, $1,000 + $2 (4,000)]	9,000
Factory supplies (variable, $1 × 4,000)	4,000
Total estimated factory overhead at 4,000 units	$15,000
Cost per unit	$ 3.75

Note that the cost per unit is $3.75 if 4,000 units are produced. If only 1,000 units are produced, the cost per unit is $6 ($6,000/1,000), as was shown earlier. This difference exists because the fixed costs remain the same in total as the number of units increases, thus lowering the unit cost as more units are produced.

Scattergraph Method

The **scattergraph method** estimates a straight line along which the semivariable costs will fall. The cost being analyzed is plotted on the *y*-axis of the graph, and the activity level, such as the number of units produced, is plotted on the *x*-axis. After the past observations of cost and production data are plotted on graph paper, such as shown in Figure 4-2, a line is drawn by visual inspection representing the trend shown by most of the data points. Usually an equal number of data points fall above and below the line. The point where the straight line intersects the *y*-axis represents the total fixed costs. The variable cost per unit is computed by subtracting fixed costs from total costs at any point on the graph and then dividing by the activity level for that point read from the *x*-axis.

Figure 4-2 **Scattergraph Method**

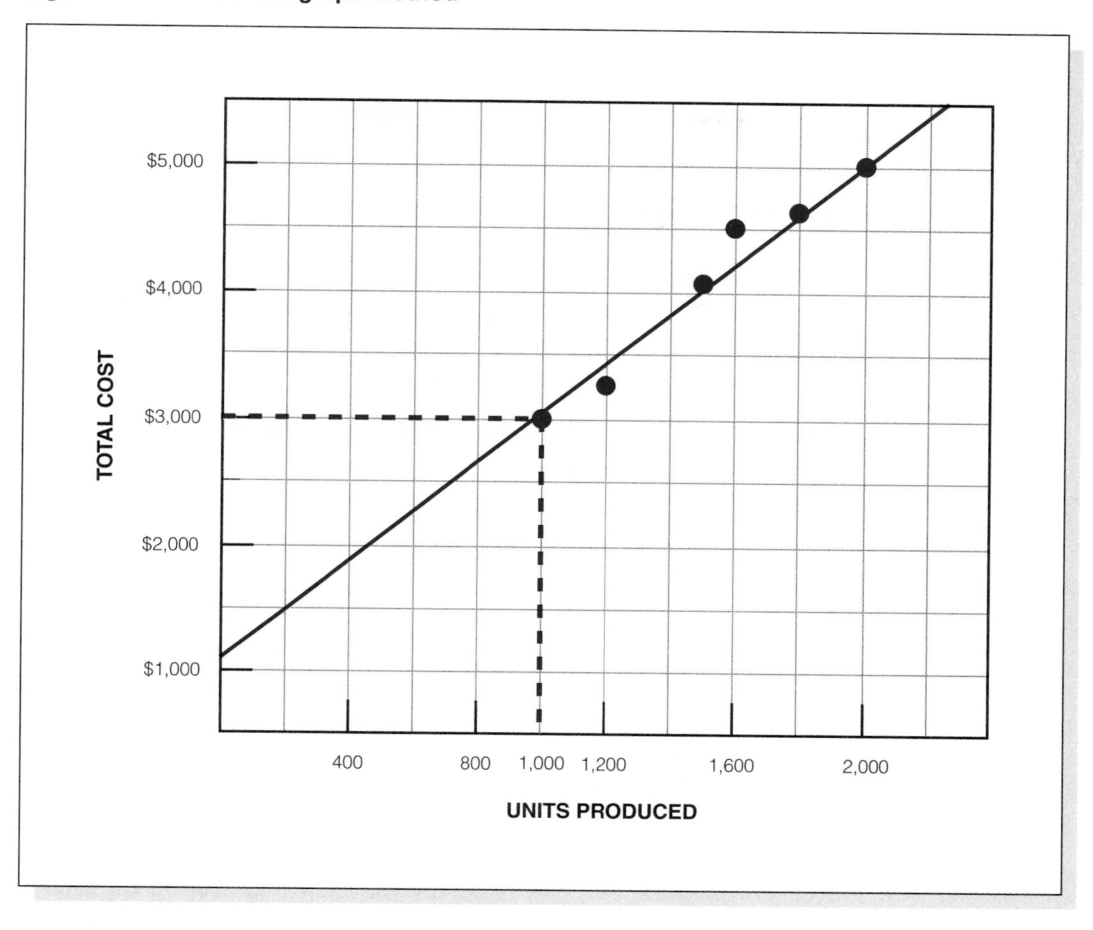

The following data will be used to illustrate the determination of the fixed and variable components of electricity cost, using cost and production data for the past six months:

Month	Electricity Cost for Month	Units Produced
July	$ 4,500	1,600
August	3,000	1,000
September	4,600	1,800
October	5,000	2,000
November	4,050	1,500
December	3,350	1,200
Total	$24,500	9,100

Figure 4-2 shows the scattergraph of these data. A line is visually fit to these data by positioning a ruler so that it is on or near all the data points, with an equal number of data points above and below the line. (The fact that more than one such line might be drawn, depending on who is doing the drawing, is among the limitations explained in the following section.) The cost line in Figure 4-2 intersects the *y*-axis at $1,100. This is the estimate of the fixed cost portion of the mixed cost for electricity. Subtract the fixed cost from the total cost at any volume level to determine the total variable cost at that level. For example, the total cost at a volume level of 1,000 units is $3,000, as indicated by the broken lines in Figure 4-2. The total variable cost would then be $3,000 (total cost) – $1,100 (fixed cost) = $1,900. The variable cost per unit would then be $1.90 ($1,900/1,000 units).

Note that because of the imprecision of the high-low and scattergraph methods, the difference in fixed costs between methods is $100 ($1,100 – $1,000), and the difference in variable costs per unit is $0.10 ($2.00 – $1.90).

Limitations of High-Low and Statistical Scattergraph Methods

The high-low and statistical scattergraph methods both use historical cost patterns to predict future costs and are, therefore, subject to the limitations that apply to all forecasting techniques. The use of mathematical techniques does not ensure accurate forecasts. To a great extent, the accuracy of a forecast depends on the validity of the data used with the chosen method.

Cost analysis is more useful for decision making when all costs are segregated into two categories: variable and fixed. Therefore, the semivariable costs should be analyzed and subdivided into the two categories. The high-low method bases its solution on two observations and assumes that all other unanalyzed relationships will fall along a straight line between these selected observations. Such an assumption may prove to be highly unrealistic because the two observations used may not be representative of the group from which the data were selected. The method may be considered reliable, however, if additional pairs of data are analyzed and the results approximate those obtained from the first observations.

The scattergraph method is an improvement over the high-low method because it uses all of the available data. Also, visual inspection of the graph enables nonrepresentative data points, called **outliers**, to be identified. The major disadvantage of the scattergraph method is that the cost line is drawn through the data points based on visual inspection rather than mathematical techniques. For example, two persons drawing a trend line through the same data set could end up with somewhat different results. Both the high-low and scattergraph methods stress the importance of the relationship of cost factors to volume of activity, such as units of production or direct labor hours worked; however, many other factors may affect cost behavior and should not be ignored. For example, consideration should also be given to price changes, and changes in the technology used to manufacture the products. Also, management policies directly influence the behavior of most costs.

Least-Squares Regression Method

More sophisticated techniques, using statistical software packages and usually covered in statistics courses, can be used to determine mathematically a line of best fit through a set of plotted points. These techniques, such as the **least-squares regression method**, use all of the data to separate a semivariable cost into its fixed and variable elements based on the equation for a straight line: Y = a + bX, where:

X = the activity level,
Y = the total semivariable cost,
a = the total fixed cost, and
b = the variable cost per unit

Spreadsheet applications such as Microsoft Excel, as illustrated in Figures 4-3 and 4-4, can also be used to perform regression analysis. In Figure 4-3, the units produced are entered in cells B4 through B9, and the electricity costs are entered in cells C4 through C9. The total fixed costs, variable cost per unit, and R^2 are then computed using the Excel functions and formulas: INTERCEPT (C4:C9,B4:B9), SLOPE (C4:C9,B4:B9), and RSQ (C4:C9,B4:B9), respectively, and the graph of the relationship between units of production and electricity costs in Figure 4-4 is plotted by choosing the range of values to be included, B4:C9, and using Chart Wizard on the toolbar.

Using the least-squares regression method, note that the more precise figures for total fixed cost and variable cost per unit are $961.86 (slightly below the $1,000 point on the *y*-axis in Figure 4-4) and $2.06, respectively. **RSQ,** in Figure 4-3, indicates the percentage of the variation in the dependent variable (electricity cost) that is explained by variation in the independent variable (units of production). The electricity cost is known as the **dependent variable** because the amount of cost incurred for the period is dependent upon the level of activity for the period. The level of activity is the **independent variable** because the number of units produced cause the variation in electricity cost. $R^2 = .974$ means that 97.4% of the variation in electricity cost is explained by the variation in the number of units produced.

Figure 4-3 Least-Squares Regression Worksheet

	A	B	C	D
1		**Units Produced**	**Electricity Costs**	
2	**Month**	**X**	**Y**	
3				
4	July	1,600	$4,500	
5	August	1,000	$3,000	
6	September	1,800	$4,600	
7	October	2,000	$5,000	
8	November	1,500	$4,050	
9	December	1,200	$3,350	
10				
11	Intercept	$961.86		
12	Slope	$2.06		
13	RSQ	0.974		
14				
15				

Figure 4-4 **Regression Analysis Using Microsoft Excel**

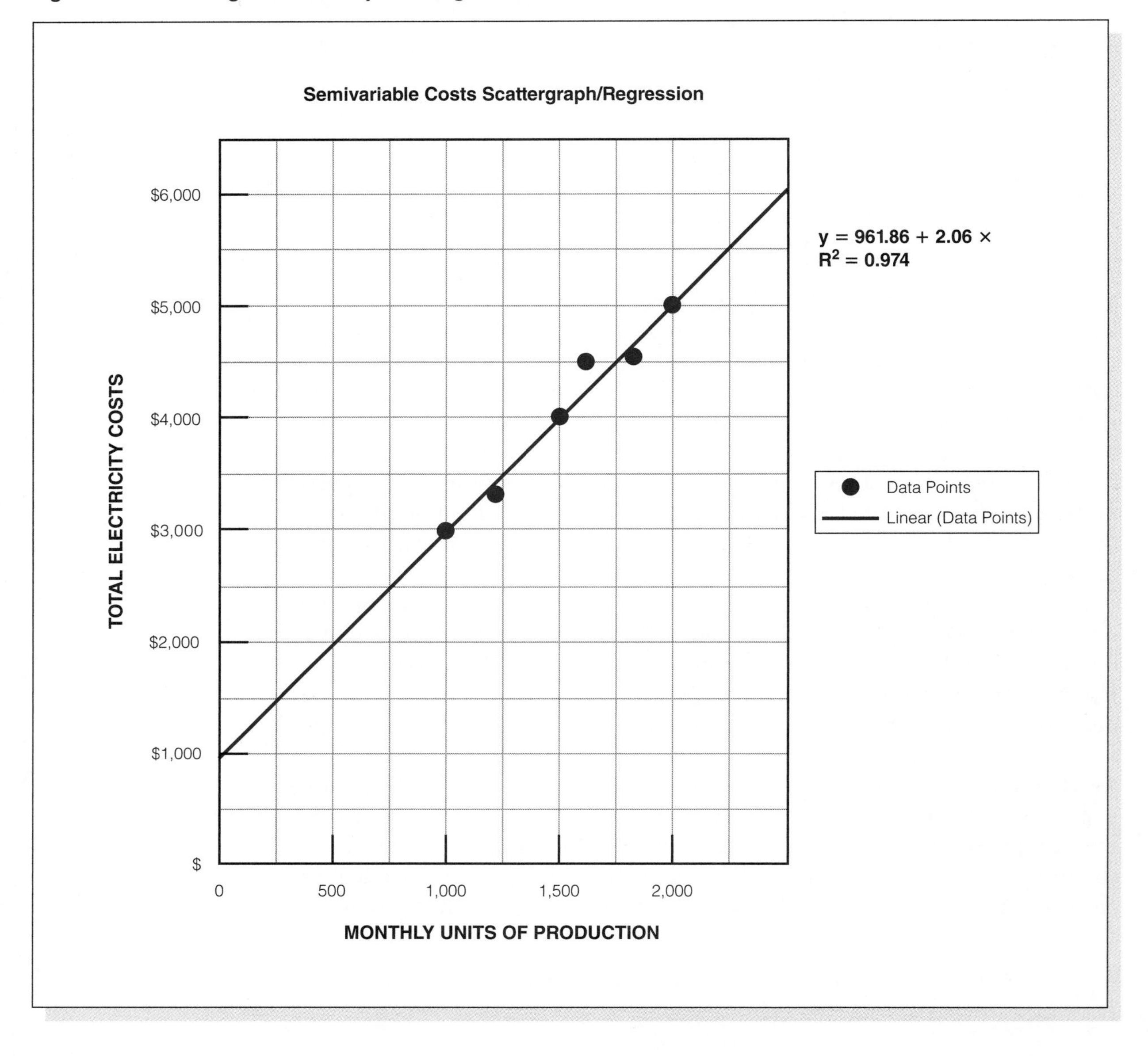

This is very high, and it is an indication that units of production are a good variable to use in explaining changes in electricity cost.

Note that the formula derived from using the scattergraph method ($1,100 + $1.90 per unit) is substantially less correct than the formula obtained by using the high-low method ($1,000 + $2 per unit) when compared to the least-squares regression formula ($961.86 + $2.06 per unit). The reason for this is that the scattergraph method is subject to preparer error in setting the trend line by inspection, and, in this instance, neither the high point nor the low point was an outlier. In other instances, the scattergraph method may more closely depict the regression line.

Recall and Review 1

Valley View Company has accumulated the following data over a four-month period:

Month	Machine Hours	Electricity Expense
September	10,000	$4,500
October	12,000	5,200
November	14,000	6,100
December	9,000	4,100

Using the high-low method, the variable cost per machine hour would be $__________ and the total fixed cost would be $__________.

(After working this exercise, see page 209 for the solution.)

You should now be able to work the following:
Questions 1–10; Exercises 4-1 to 4-4; and Problems 4-1 to 4-4.

Budgeting Factory Overhead Costs

LO3 Prepare a budget for factory overhead costs.

Budgets are management's operating plans expressed in quantitative terms, such as units of production and related costs. After factory overhead costs have been classified as either fixed or variable, budgets can be prepared for expected levels of production. The segregation of fixed and variable cost components permits the company to prepare a **flexible budget**. A flexible budget is a budget that shows estimated costs at different production volumes.

Assume that management desires to budget factory overhead costs at three levels of production—10,000, 20,000, and 40,000 units. The variable factory overhead cost is $5 per unit, and fixed overhead costs total $50,000. The budgeted costs at these volumes are as follows:

	10,000 units	20,000 units	40,000 units
Variable cost @ $5 per unit	$ 50,000	$100,000	$200,000
Fixed cost	50,000	50,000	50,000
Total factory overhead	$100,000	$150,000	$250,000
Factory overhead per unit	$ 10.00	$ 7.50	$ 6.25

As the volume of production increases, the factory overhead cost per unit decreases because the total fixed cost, $50,000, is spread over a larger number of units. For example, the fixed cost per unit will add $5 to the per-unit cost ($50,000/10,000 units) at the 10,000-unit level but only $1.25 ($50,000/40,000 units) when 40,000 units are produced. The variable cost remains constant at $5 per unit for the entire range of production.

Budgeting is a valuable management tool for planning and controlling costs. A flexible budget aids management in establishing realistic production goals and in comparing actual costs with budgeted costs.

Accounting for Actual Factory Overhead

Account for actual factory overhead.

Cost accounting systems are designed to accumulate, classify, and summarize the factory overhead costs actually incurred. The specific procedures used to account for actual factory overhead costs depend on the nature and organization of the manufacturing firm.

In a small manufacturing company that has only one production department, factory overhead may be accounted for in much the same manner as selling and administrative expenses. All of the factory overhead accounts, such as for indirect materials, indirect labor, and each of the other indirect manufacturing expenses, may be kept in the general ledger.

Indirect materials and indirect labor costs are recorded first in the general journal. These entries are made from the summary of materials issued and returned and from the labor cost summary. Other factory overhead expenses also are recorded in the general journal, from which they are posted to the appropriate accounts in the general ledger. The invoices that have been received are the sources for these entries. Schedules of fixed costs should be prepared and used as the source for general journal adjusting entries to record the amount of taxes, depreciation, insurance, and other similar expenses for the period.

A substantial modification must be made in the accounting system when the number of factory overhead accounts becomes sizable. A factory overhead subsidiary ledger should be created and maintained, along with a control account in the general ledger. The subsidiary ledger is known as the **factory overhead ledger**, and the control account is entitled "Factory Overhead" or "Manufacturing Overhead." At the end of each accounting period, the balance of the factory overhead control account is proved by comparing its balance to the total of the account balances in the subsidiary factory overhead ledger as shown in Figure 4-5.

Accounts in the factory overhead ledger should have titles clearly descriptive of the nature of the expenditure. Examples of typical factory overhead accounts include the following:

Defective Work	Overtime Premium
Depreciation—Machinery	Plant Security
Employee Fringe Benefits	Power
Fuel	Property Tax
Heat and Light	Rent
Indirect Labor	Repairs
Indirect Materials	Small Tools
Insurance	Spoilage
Janitorial Service	Supplies
Lubricants	Telephone/Fax
Maintenance	Water
Materials Handling	Workers' Compensation Insurance

Figure 4-5 **Relationship of Control Account to Factory Overhead Ledger**

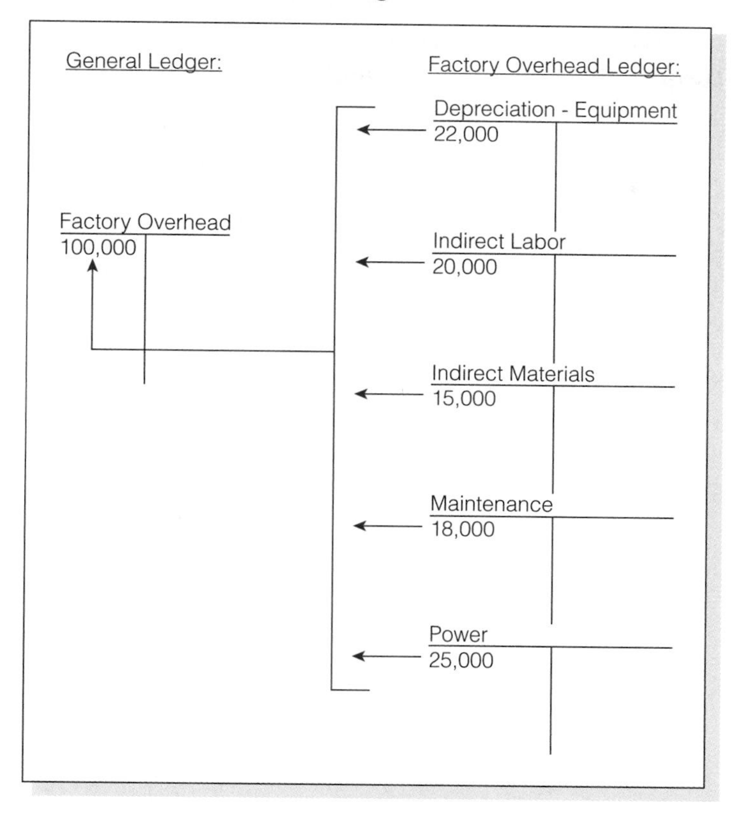

In manufacturing companies with several departments, the accounting system is designed to accumulate costs by department. Separate budgets are prepared for each department and then combined into a master budget for the company. The actual costs incurred can be readily compared with budgeted costs for each department.

Factory overhead expenses must be carefully analyzed before the expenses are assigned to departments. For example, total factory depreciation would be analyzed to determine the distribution of depreciation charges among the departments, using an allocation base such as the square footage of factory floor space. The accounting system should be designed to provide the necessary data promptly and accurately.

Factory Overhead Analysis Spreadsheets

Instead of expanding the factory overhead ledger to include a separate account for each department's share of different expenses, **factory overhead analysis spreadsheets** may be used to keep a subsidiary record of factory overhead expenses. A separate analysis spreadsheet may be used to record each type of expense, with individual columns for the departmental classification of the expense. Alternatively, a separate analysis spreadsheet can be used for each department, with individual columns for the expense classification.

Figure 4-6 shows an example of a factory overhead analysis spreadsheet used to keep individual records for each kind of factory overhead expense. The **expense-type analysis spreadsheet** provides a separate amount column for each department, making it possible to distribute charges among departments as expenses are recorded. Each column represents a department; therefore, each analysis spreadsheet replaces as many separate accounts as there are departments in the factory. In Figure 4-6, which illustrates the distribution of one month's depreciation to departments, the depreciation cost assignable to the various departments was determined by multiplying the cost basis of the equipment in each department (A: \$36,000; B: \$24,000; C: \$18,000; D: \$60,000) by the annual rate of depreciation (10%) applicable to the machinery. The estimated monthly depreciation (1/12 of the annual depreciation) was recorded in the general journal and became the source of posting to the analysis spreadsheet. For example, the depreciation expense allocated to Department A would have been computed as follows: $\$36,000 \times 10\% \times 1/12 = \$300$.

Figure 4-6 Factory Overhead Analysis Spreadsheet—Expense Type

	A	B	C	D	E	F	G	H	I	J
1					Distribution Base: Cost Basis					
2	Account No. 3113									
3	Account Depreciation Expense—Machinery									
4		DEPARTMENTAL ANALYSIS								
5							Post.			
6	Dept. A	Dept. B	Dept. C	Dept. D	Date	Description	Ref.	Debit	Credit	Balance
7	300.00	200.00	150.00	500.00	Jan. 31	Depreciation for January	GJ	1,150.00		1,150.00

The **department-type analysis spreadsheet** in Figure 4-7 provides a separate amount column for each kind of expense. This makes it possible to distribute expenses on a departmental basis as they are recorded. Each column represents a different expense. Therefore, each analysis spreadsheet replaces as many separate accounts as there are types of overhead expenses in the factory. Figure 4-7 shows all expenses incurred for Department A during January. Only the totals are entered. Expenses are posted from the

Figure 4-7 Factory Overhead Analysis Spreadsheet—Department Type

	A	B	C	D	E	F	G
1			FACTORY OVERHEAD—DEPARTMENT A				
2				Depreciation			General
3	Indirect	Indirect		Expense—	Factory		Factory
4	Materials	Labor	Power	Machinery	Property Tax	Insurance	Expenses
5	No. 3110	No. 3111	No. 3112	No. 3113	No. 3114	No. 3115	No. 3116
6	300.00	200.00	150.00	300.00	280.00	392.00	150.00

	H	I	J	K	L	M	N	O
4	Misc. Factory Expenses				Post.			
5	No.	Amount	Date	Description	Ref.	Debit	Credit	Balance
6			Jan. 31	Total expenses-January		1,772.00		1,772.00

books of original entry either in total or as of the date incurred. The fixed expenses are posted from the general journal at the end of the month.

Factory overhead analysis spreadsheets, both expense and department type, serve as subsidiary ledgers and are controlled by the factory overhead account in the general ledger. The advantage of using an expense-type analysis spreadsheet is that it provides only as many amount columns as there are departments within the factory (see Figure 4-6). However, a summary should be prepared at the end of an accounting period to determine the total expenses incurred for each department.

The advantage of using a department-type analysis spreadsheet is that fewer sheets are required and the preparation of a separate summary is not required at the end of an accounting period, because the total overhead charged to a department appears all in one place (see Figure 4-7). When a factory is departmentalized, the factory overhead must be recorded departmentally to determine the total cost of operating each department. Spreadsheet software facilitates the distribution of departmental factory overhead.

Schedule of Fixed Costs

Fixed costs are assumed not to vary in amount from month to month. Some fixed costs, such as insurance and property taxes, are either prepaid expenses or accrued expenses. Because these costs are considered to be very predictable, schedules for the periodic amount of fixed costs to be allocated to the various departments can be prepared in advance. A **schedule of fixed costs** similar to Figure 4-8 can be prepared for several periods. By referring to the schedule at the end of the period, a journal entry can be prepared to record the total for each of the fixed costs. The schedule also can be used as the source from which fixed costs can be posted to the departmental factory overhead analysis spreadsheets.

In Figure 4-8, the schedule of fixed costs shows that for the month of January, the total depreciation expense for machinery, $1,150, is allocated to the departments, based on the total cost of the equipment in each department, as follows: A, $300; B, $200; C, $150; D, $500. Figure 4-8 also shows the monthly departmental fixed costs for property tax and insurance on the factory building that were distributed on the basis of the square footage of space occupied by each department. For example, if Department A occupies 2,800 square feet of space in a building with a total of 10,000 square feet, its allocation for the monthly property tax of $1,000 would be computed as [(2,800/10,000) × $1,000], or $280. At the end of the month, the accountant would post the amounts from the schedule of fixed costs to each department's analysis spreadsheet.

General Factory Overhead Expenses

All factory overhead expenses are recorded in a regular, systematic manner so that at the end of an accounting period, all expenses chargeable to the period have already been distributed to the factory departments. The allocation of overhead to departments would have been made in proportion

Figure 4-8 **Schedule of Fixed Costs**

Schedule of Fixed Costs

Item of Cost	January	February	March	April	May	June
Depreciation—machinery						
Dept. A	$ 300.00	$ 300.00	$ 300.00	$ 300.00	$ 300.00	$ 300.00
Dept. B	200.00	200.00	200.00	200.00	200.00	200.00
Dept. C	150.00	150.00	150.00	150.00	150.00	150.00
Dept. D	500.00	500.00	500.00	500.00	500.00	500.00
Total	$ 1,150.00	$1,150.00	$1,150.00	$1,150.00	$1,150.00	$1,150.00
Property tax:						
Dept. A	$ 280.00	$ 280.00	$ 280.00	$ 280.00	$ 280.00	$ 280.00
Dept. B	270.00	270.00	270.00	270.00	270.00	270.00
Dept. C	250.00	250.00	250.00	250.00	250.00	250.00
Dept. D	200.00	200.00	200.00	200.00	200.00	200.00
Total	$ 1,000.00	$1,000.00	$1,000.00	$1,000.00	$1,000.00	$1,000.00
Insurance:						
Dept. A	$ 392.00	$ 392.00	$ 392.00	$ 392.00	$ 392.00	$ 392.00
Dept. B	378.00	378.00	378.00	378.00	378.00	378.00
Dept. C	350.00	350.00	350.00	350.00	350.00	350.00
Dept. D	280.00	280.00	280.00	280.00	280.00	280.00
Total	$ 1,400.00	$1,400.00	$1,400.00	$1,400.00	$1,400.00	$1,400.00
Total fixed cost .	$ 3,550.00	$3,550.00	$3,550.00	$3,550.00	$3,550.00	$3,550.00

to the measurable benefits received from such expenses. However, for some items of factory overhead, it is difficult to measure the benefits departmentally. Instead, the factory as a whole is the beneficiary. An example is the salary of the plant manager, who has the responsibility to oversee all factory operations. Another example would be the wages of the company security guards.

General factory overhead expenses not identified with a specific department are charged to departments by a process of allocation. This allocation is usually made on a logical basis, such as allocating heating costs to departments based on the factory space devoted to each department or distributing the plant manager's salary based on the estimated amount of time the manager devoted to each department. The allocation may be made for each item of expense as incurred and recorded, or expenses may be accumulated as incurred and the allocation of the total expenses made at the end of the accounting period. If the allocation is made at the end of the period, each kind of general factory overhead expense incurred during the period is recorded on a separate analysis spreadsheet. At the end of the period, the total is allocated and recorded on the departmental analysis spreadsheets.

Figure 4-9 **Summary of Factory Overhead**

Summary of Factory Overhead
For the Month Ended January 31, 2011

Expenses	Departmental Classification				
	Dept. A	Dept. B	Dept. C	Dept. D	Total
Indirect materials	$ 300	$ 50	$ 40	$ 30	$ 420
Indirect labor	200	150	140	160	650
Power	150	140	120	100	510
Depreciation	300	200	150	500	1,150
Factory property tax	280	270	250	200	1,000
Insurance	392	378	350	280	1,400
General factory expenses	150	350	200	300	1,000
Total	$1,772	$1,485	$1,200	$1,715	$6,172

Summary of Factory Overhead

All factory overhead expenses incurred during the accounting period, both variable and fixed, are recorded on factory overhead analysis spreadsheets and in the factory overhead control account in the general ledger. At the end of the accounting period, the balance of the factory overhead control account is proved by preparing a **summary of factory overhead** from the analysis spreadsheets (see Figure 4-9). This summary shows the items of expense by department and in total.

Distributing Service Department Expenses

LO5 Distribute service department factory overhead costs to production departments.

All job order and process cost systems are designed to accumulate the total cost of each job or product. To include factory overhead as part of the total cost, the amount of factory overhead incurred by each production department must be determined.

In a factory, the manufacturing process consists of a series of operations performed in departments or cost centers. Departments are divided into two classes: service departments and production departments. A **service department** is an essential part of the organization, but it does not work directly on the product. The function of a service department is to serve the needs of the production departments and other service departments. The product indirectly receives the benefit of the work performed by the service department. Examples of service departments include a department that generates power for the factory, a building maintenance department that is responsible for maintaining the buildings, or the cost accounting department that maintains the factory accounting records.

A **production department** performs the actual manufacturing operations that physically change the units being processed. Because the production departments receive the benefit of the work performed by the service departments, the total cost of production must include not only the costs incurred directly in the production departments but also a portion of the costs of operating the service departments. Therefore, the total product costs should include a share of service department costs.

The distribution of the service department costs to production departments requires an analysis of the service department's relationship to the other departments before an apportionment can be made. The cost of operating each service department should be distributed in proportion to the benefits received by the various other departments. The apportionment of service department costs is complicated because some service departments render service to other service departments as well as to the production departments. For example, the human resources department may provide personnel services to the maintenance department, and the maintenance department may clean the human resources offices. For a distribution to be equitable, the cost of operating a service department should be divided among all departments that it serves, service and production alike.

The first requirement of the distribution process is to determine how a particular service department divides its services among the other departments. In some cases, the services performed for another department may be determined precisely. More often, however, the distribution must be based on approximations. For example, the power department may be furnishing power for the operation of the machines and for lighting the building and the surrounding grounds. If the power used in each department is metered, the meters can be read at the end of the period and the departments charged for the exact amount of power used. This type of charge to a department would be termed a **direct charge**.

On the other hand, a department such as building maintenance, which keeps the building clean and in repair, cannot measure exactly the benefits it provides to the other departments that it serves. The cost of operating the building maintenance department is therefore distributed to the other departments on some equitable basis, such as square footage of floor space occupied by each department.

Common bases for distributing service department costs include the following:

Service Departments	Basis for Distribution
Building Maintenance	Floor space occupied by other departments
Inspection and Packing	Production volume
Machine Shop	Value of machinery and equipment
Human Resources	Number of workers in departments served
Purchasing	Number of purchase orders
Shipping	Quantity and weight of items shipped
Store Room	Units of materials requisitioned
Tool Room	Total direct labor hours in departments served

After the bases for distribution have been selected for the service departments, the next step is to distribute the total cost of each service department to the other departments. To illustrate the distribution process, assume the following conditions:

1. The maintenance department services the power plant building.
2. The power plant furnishes power to the maintenance department to run its maintenance equipment.
3. The power department and the maintenance department service the human resources department facilities.
4. The human resources department services the power and maintenance departments through its functions of hiring personnel and maintaining the departments' personnel records.

The first step is to compute the total cost of any one of these overlapping departments. Three different methods are available for use:

1. The **direct distribution method** distributes service department costs only to production departments, even though the service departments perform services for other service departments.
2. The **sequential distribution** or **step-down method** distributes service department costs regressively to other service departments and then to production departments. There are many ways to determine the order in which to allocate service department costs. Two of the more common methods are:
   a. The number of other departments served.
   b. The magnitude of total costs in each service department.
3. The **algebraic distribution method** takes into consideration that some service departments not only may provide service to, but also may receive service from, other service departments. Companies that use this method have software, based on a series of simultaneous equations, which performs the intricate calculations.

The direct distribution method makes no attempt to determine the extent to which one service department renders its services to another service department. Instead, the service department's costs are allocated directly and only to the production departments. For example, in Figure 4-10, Human Resources and Maintenance are ignored in the distribution of Power costs, even though the Power Department provides energy to them. This method has the advantage of simplicity, but it may produce less accurate results than the other methods. Use of the direct method is justified if the costs allocated to the production departments do not differ materially from the costs that would be allocated using another, more precise method.

Figure 4-10 **Method 1—Spreadsheet for Direct Distribution of Service Department Costs to Production Departments**

	A	B	C	D	E	F	G	H	I
1			Human	Main-	Dept.	Dept.	Dept.	Dept.	
2		Power	Resources	tenance	A	B	C	D	Total
3									
4	Total from factory overhead								
5	analysis spreadsheets........................	$30,000.00	$10,000.00	$20,000.00	$50,000.00	$40,000.00	$60,000.00	$90,000.00	$300,000.00
6									
7	Power distribution—								
8	(kw hours)	(30,000.00)							
9	A— 12,000 @ $0.30*............				3,600.00				
10	B— 18,000 @ 0.30............					5,400.00			
11	C— 20,000 @ 0.30............						6,000.00		
12	D— 50,000 @ 0.30............							15,000.00	
13	100,000 kilowatt hours								
14									
15	Human Resources								
16	distribution—(number								
17	of employees served)		(10,000.00)						
18	A— 30 @ $100**......................				3,000.00				
19	B— 10 @ 100........................					1,000.00			
20	C— 20 @ 100........................						2,000.00		
21	D— 40 @ 100........................							4,000.00	
22	100 employees								
23									
24	Maintenance distribution—								
25	(square feet)			(20,000.00)					
26	A— 5,000 @ $1.00***............				5,000.00				
27	B— 6,000 @ 1.00................					6,000.00			
28	C— 4,000 @ 1.00................						4,000.00		
29	D— 5,000 @ 1.00................							5,000.00	
30	20,000 sq ft	$0	$0	$0	$61,600.00	$52,400.00	$72,000.00	$114,000.00	$300,000.00
31									
32	*$30,000 ÷ 100,000 (kilowatt hours) = $0.30 per kilowatt hour								
33	**$10,000 ÷ 100 (number of employees served) = $100 per employee								
34	***$20,000 ÷ 20,000 (square feet) = $1.00 per square foot								

The sequential distribution method recognizes the interrelationships of the service departments. The power department costs are divided among the human resources, maintenance, and production departments. After the power department cost distribution, the human resources department's total costs—which now include a portion of the power department costs—will be allocated to the maintenance and the production departments. Finally, the maintenance department's costs will be distributed to the production departments. Note in Figure 4-11, that even though Maintenance and Human Resources provide service to Power, once Power has been fully allocated no reciprocal services are allocated back to it.

The distribution sequence for allocating service department costs is a high-priority decision when the sequential distribution method is used. The sequential procedure should first distribute the costs of the service department that services the greatest number of other departments. It should continue until all service department costs have been distributed to the production departments. The sequential distribution method can be long and laborious if software is not used to perform the allocations, but it has the advantage of being more accurate if the sequence established is based on a sound analysis of services rendered to the various departments. If each service department services the same number of other departments, the service department with the largest total overhead cost should be distributed first. This order of distribution is based on the assumption that the departments render services in direct proportion to the amount of expense they incur.

Figure 4-10 shows the direct distribution of service department costs to production departments, whereas Figure 4-11 shows the sequential distribution to service departments and production departments based on the magnitude of the total costs in each of the service departments. (Note that the magnitude of costs in each service department is used as the criterion for determining the order of distribution because each service department services the same number of other departments.) The organizational and operational structure of a company determines which distribution method should be selected and used. If the variation from one method to another is insignificant, the direct distribution method will be suitable because it saves time and effort.

The completed distribution work sheets are the basis for a series of general journal entries. The following entries are based on the distributions shown in Figure 4-11.

	Debit	Credit
Factory Overhead—Power Department	30,000	
Factory Overhead—Maintenance Department	20,000	
Factory Overhead—Human Resources Department	10,000	
Factory Overhead—Department A	50,000	
Factory Overhead—Department B	40,000	
Factory Overhead—Department C	60,000	
Factory Overhead—Department D	90,000	
Factory Overhead		300,000
Closed factory overhead expenses to service and production departments.		

Figure 4-11 **Method 2—Spreadsheet for Sequential Distribution of Service Department Costs Based on Magnitude of Total Costs in Service Departments**

	A	B	C	D	E	F	G	H	I
1			Main-	Human	Dept.	Dept.	Dept.	Dept.	
2		Power	tenance	Resources	A	B	C	D	Total
3	Total from factory overhead								
4	analysis spreadsheets..................	$30,000.00	$20,000.00	$10,000.00	$50,000.00	$40,000.00	$60,000.00	$90,000.00	$300,000.00
5									
6	Power distribution—								
7	(kw hours)	(30,000.00)							
8	Maintenance—								
9	10,000 @ $0.25*		2,500.00						
10	Human Resources—								
11	10,000 @ $0.25			2,500.00					
12	A— 12,000 @ 0.25*				3,000.00				
13	B— 18,000 @ 0.25					4,500.00			
14	C— 20,000 @ 0.25						5,000.00		
15	D— 50,000 @ 0.25							12,500.00	
16	120,000		$22,500.00						
17									
18	Maintenance distribution—								
19	(square feet)		(22,500.00)						
20	Human Resources—								
21	5,000 @ $0.90**......			4,500.00					
22	A— 5,000 @ 0.90**......				4,500.00				
23	B— 6,000 @ 0.90					5,400.00			
24	C— 4,000 @ 0.90						3,600.00		
25	D— 5,000 @ 0.90.........							4,500.00	
26	25,000			$17,000.00					
27									
28	Human Resources								
29	distribution—(number of								
30	employees served)			(17,000.00)					
31	A— 30 @ $170***.....				5,100.00				
32	B— 10 @ 170.........					1,700.00			
33	C— 20 @ 170.........						3,400.00		
34	D— 40 @ 170.........							6,800.00	
35	100	$0	$0	$0	$62,600.00	$51,600.00	$72,000.00	$113,800.00	$300,000.00
36									
37	*$30,000 ÷ 120,000 (kilowatt hours) = $0.25 per kilowatt hour								
38	**$22,500 ÷ 25,000 (square feet) = $0.90 per square foot								
39	***$17,000 ÷ 100 (number of employees served) = $170 per employee								

The allocation of service department costs would be journalized as follows:

Factory Overhead—Maintenance Department	2,500	
Factory Overhead—Human Resources Department	2,500	
Factory Overhead—Department A	3,000	
Factory Overhead—Department B	4,500	
Factory Overhead—Department C	5,000	
Factory Overhead—Department D	12,500	
Factory Overhead—Power Department		30,000
Closed factory overhead expenses of power department to service and production departments.		

Factory Overhead—Human Resources Department	4,500	
Factory Overhead—Department A	4,500	
Factory Overhead—Department B	5,400	
Factory Overhead—Department C	3,600	
Factory Overhead—Department D	4,500	
Factory Overhead—Maintenance Department		22,500
Closed factory overhead expenses of maintenance department to service and production departments.		

Factory Overhead—Department A	5,100	
Factory Overhead—Department B	1,700	
Factory Overhead—Department C	3,400	
Factory Overhead—Department D	6,800	
Factory Overhead—Human Resources Department		17,000
Closed factory overhead expenses of human resources department to production departments.		

An accounting system can be designed to reduce the number of factory overhead accounts to be maintained for the service departments. In such a system, after the distribution work sheet in Figure 4-11 has been completed, a journal entry can be made to close the factory overhead control account. The charges are made directly to the production departments as follows:

Factory Overhead—Department A	62,600	
Factory Overhead—Department B	51,600	
Factory Overhead—Department C	72,000	
Factory Overhead—Department D	113,800	
Factory Overhead		300,000
Closed factory overhead to production departments. (The departmental totals include the apportioned costs of the service departments.)		

After posting the journal entries to the general ledger, the total balances of the departmental factory overhead accounts will equal the balance of the factory overhead control account before it was closed. The journal entries have not affected the total of the factory overhead expenses. However, the general ledger now shows the amount of factory overhead expense being allocated to each of the production departments. This is as it should be, because overhead is only applied to products as they move through producing departments. That is why the service department costs need to end up in the producing departments, so that the products can be assigned their fair share of all the factory costs.

Recall and Review 2

Posh Perfumes, Inc., budgeted for 6,000 bottles of "Monique" during the month of June. Its unit cost was $10, consisting of direct materials, $3.00; direct labor, $4.50; fixed factory overhead, $1.50; and variable factory overhead, $1.00. The unit cost of "Monique" would be $__________ if 5,000 bottles were manufactured and $__________ if 7,500 bottles were manufactured.

(After working this exercise, see page 210 for the solution.)

You should now be able to work the following:
Questions 11–16; Exercises 4-5 to 4-7; Problems 4-5 to 4-7; and Self-Study Problem 1.

Applying Factory Overhead to Production

LO6 Apply factory overhead using predetermined rates.

Home Entertainment, Inc., manufactures two types of DVD players: standard and deluxe. It attempts to set selling prices based on a 50% markup on manufacturing costs to cover selling and administrative expenses and to earn an acceptable return for shareholders. Tom Sales, Vice President–Marketing, is confused because the numbers provided by Anne Cash, Controller, indicate that standard DVD players should be priced at $150 per unit and deluxe DVD players at $300 per unit. The competition is selling comparable models for $145 and $525, respectively.

Sales informs Cash that there must be something wrong with the job costing system. He had recently attended a seminar where the speaker stated that "All production costs are not a function of how many units are produced, or of how many labor hours, labor dollars, or machine hours are expended." He knows that the company uses direct labor dollars as its only cost allocation base. Tom thinks that, perhaps, this explains why the product costs and, therefore selling prices, are so different from the competitors.

This part of the chapter describes a more sophisticated costing system than the one that Home Entertainment is using. The Mini-Case at the end of the chapter is a continuation of the Home Entertainment saga.

In previous discussions, companies avoided estimating and applying factory overhead to production by charging the actual factory overhead costs to the work in process account. These procedures were used to emphasize the flow of costs and the basic cost accounting techniques without unduly complicating the fundamentals. However, factory overhead includes many different costs, some of which will not be known until the end of the accounting period. Because it is desirable to know the approximate cost of a job or product soon after its completion, some method must be established for estimating the amount of factory overhead that should be applied to the finished product. Through the estimating procedure, a job or product will be charged an estimated amount of factory overhead expense as it is worked on. At the end of a period, the actual factory overhead costs can be compared to the estimated factory overhead applied to jobs. If the company encounters a difference, it can determine the reasons for the variance and distribute it to the appropriate accounts.

The advantages of estimating and charging factory overhead on a current basis include timely billing of customers and more accurate bidding on new contracts. Many jobs are priced on the basis of cost plus a markup to cover selling and administrative expenses and to earn a profit. If it were not possible to bill a customer for a job until a month or more after its completion because all factory overhead costs were not known, the extension of time in collecting such accounts would negatively affect the company's cash flow. Also, many companies rely heavily on a bidding process to obtain new jobs. If a company cannot include a fairly accurate estimate of factory overhead in the cost of a bid, the financial health of the enterprise can be adversely affected.

The flexible budget, which includes the expected departmental factory overhead costs at given levels of production, is used to establish **predetermined factory overhead rates**. The rates are computed by dividing the budgeted factory overhead cost by the budgeted production. The budgeted production may be expressed in such terms as machine hours, direct labor hours, direct labor cost, and units produced; the first three of which are illustrated in the following sections. The accuracy of the rate depends on the accuracy of the cost projections and the production estimates included in the flexible budget. In budget projections, the fixed and variable cost components, historical cost behavior patterns, and possible future economic and operational differences must be carefully considered. Specifically, these factors include the anticipated volume of production, the variability of expenses, the fixed costs relevant to the production levels, the activity of the industry as forecast, and the possible price changes that may occur. Because of the many unknowns, absolute accuracy cannot be expected. Nevertheless, management should give a high priority to attaining the most accurate rate possible.

In a departmentalized company, factory overhead should be budgeted for each department. The procedures for distributing the budgeted departmental expenses are identical to those used to allocate the actual factory overhead expenses. The departmental overhead budgets should also include an allotment of budgeted fixed expenses, such as depreciation and a portion of the budgeted service department expenses.

Upon completing the factory overhead expense budget, the company must choose a method to use when allocating the estimated expenses to the departments. The usual allocation methods require that data from the period's production budgets be obtained. The production budgets will provide information such as the estimated direct labor cost, direct labor hours, or machine hours.

From the production estimates for the plant or for each department, the company can select a method that will charge the product with its fair share of the estimated factory overhead. The departmental composition of human labor versus machines will influence the method chosen for applying factory overhead to the product. A department with little automation will usually apply overhead using either the estimate of direct labor cost or direct labor hours for the coming period. A highly automated production department will normally use an estimate of machine hours to be worked in applying overhead to products. The point is to use as a cost allocation base an item that causes overhead costs to occur.

Direct Labor Cost Method

The **direct labor cost method** uses the amount of direct labor cost that has been charged to the job as the basis for applying factory overhead. The overhead rate to be used for the coming period is predetermined by dividing the estimated (budgeted) factory overhead cost by the estimated (budgeted) direct labor cost. The relationship of the overhead to the direct labor cost is expressed as a percentage of direct labor cost.

For example, assume that the budgeted factory overhead cost for Department A amounts to $100,000, and the estimated direct labor cost is expected to be $200,000. The predetermined overhead rate would be 50% of direct labor dollars ($100,000/$200,000). Also, assume that during the first month of operations, Job 100 incurred $1,000 for direct materials and $3,000 for direct labor, and that the job is completed by the end of the month. Using the predetermined rate to estimate factory overhead, the total job cost is computed as follows:

Job 100

Direct materials	$1,000
Direct labor	3,000
Factory overhead (50% of direct labor $)	1,500
Total cost of completed job	$5,500

The direct labor cost method is appropriate in departments that require mostly human labor and in which the direct labor cost charges are relatively stable from one job to another. If a labor force generates direct labor cost that varies widely due to the hourly rate range of the employees, another method should be used. For example, assume that a lower-paid hourly employee is replaced on a job by a higher-paid hourly employee. The higher-paid employee would increase the direct labor cost and thereby increase the amount of factory overhead charged to the job. Such increases in factory overhead charges to a department are usually unwarranted because the higher-paid employee would not necessarily increase the actual factory overhead expense incurred. Any fluctuation in the direct labor cost, not accompanied by a proportional increase in actual factory overhead expenses, will cause a distortion in a job's total cost. This can be detrimental to the company's ability to control costs and to make good production and marketing decisions.

Direct Labor Hour Method

The **direct labor hour method** overcomes the problem of varying wage rates by applying factory overhead using the number of direct labor hours worked on a job or process. The predetermined rate is computed by dividing the budgeted factory overhead cost for the upcoming period by the estimated direct labor hours to be worked. For example, assume that the budgeted factory overhead cost for the coming period is $100,000 and that production is expected to require 25,000 direct labor hours. The predetermined overhead rate would be $4 per direct labor hour ($100,000/25,000 hours).

If factory overhead is applied to Job 100 using the direct labor hour method, the records must include the number of direct labor hours worked on each job. Assuming that it took 500 direct labor hours to complete Job 100, and that the direct materials and direct labor costs were $1,000 and $3,000, respectively, the cost of Job 100 is as follows:

Job 100

Direct materials	$1,000
Direct labor (500 hours)	3,000
Factory overhead (500 hours @ $4)	2,000
Total cost of completed job	$6,000

An advantage of the direct labor hour method is that the amount of overhead applied to production is not affected by the mix of labor rates, as it is in the direct labor cost method. However, if factory overhead consists primarily of items that are more closely tied to employees' wages, such as fringe benefits, the direct labor hour method may not be as accurate as the direct labor cost method.

Machine Hour Method

A highly automated department is normally best served by the **machine hour method**. In such a department, the factory overhead cost should be more proportionate to the machine hours generated by the equipment than the direct labor hours or costs incurred by the employees operating the machinery. It is common in automated departments for one employee to operate more than one piece of equipment. Therefore, one direct labor hour may generate, possibly, five machine hours.

The machine hour method requires substantial preliminary study before installation, and an additional quantity of records needs to be maintained. However, the advantages to be gained by a more dependable factory overhead application rate may far outweigh the additional effort and costs involved. The machine hour rate is determined by dividing the budgeted factory overhead cost by the estimated machine hours to be used by production during the period.

For example, assume that the factory overhead budget is $100,000, consisting mostly of machine-related costs, and it is expected that 10,000 machine hours will be required to meet production. The predetermined rate would be $10 per machine hour ($100,000/10,000 hours). Assuming that Job 100, now completed, used $1,000 for direct materials, $3,000 for direct labor, and required 300 machine hours, its cost is as follows:

Job 100

Direct materials	$1,000
Direct labor	3,000
Factory overhead (300 machine hours @ $10)	3,000
Total cost of completed job	$7,000

Activity-based Costing Method

The preceding methods of applying overhead to products assumed that all overhead costs incurred were related to volume. This means that all of the overhead costs incurred were a function of how many direct labor hours or machine hours, **volume-related activities**, were worked. In a modern factory that produces many products, a substantial portion of the overhead may be more a function of the complexity of the product being made than the number of units produced, labor hours worked, or machine hours used. **Activity-based costing (ABC)** considers these **non-volume-related activities** that create overhead costs, such as the number of machine setups or product design changes required of a particular product line.

A product that is difficult to make may also be produced in small numbers, perhaps owing to its unusual nature and to the resulting limited demand. If overhead were applied to products strictly on the basis of the number of units produced, the direct labor hours worked, or the machine hours used, very little overhead would be charged to such a product due to its low production volume. Its complexity to produce, however, may have created a lot of additional overhead costs in the form of machine setups and design changes, even though the number of units in the production run was small.

To successfully employ an ABC system, a company must first identify non-volume-related factory activities that create costs. Examples of such activities would include design changes, inspections, materials movements, material requisitions, and machine setups. The cost of performing each of these activities in the coming period must then be estimated. The next step is to decide on the **cost driver**, or the basis used to allocate each of the activity cost pools. For example, for machine setup costs, the cost driver may be the total estimated setup time for the coming period or, more simply, the estimated number of setups to be performed. Lastly, the estimated cost in each activity pool would be divided by the estimated number of cost driver units, such as number of machine setups, related to that pool. This results in an overhead or activity rate that is used to charge each product or job based on its consumption of the resources required to sustain each activity.

For example, assume that the factory overhead budget is $100,000. The allocation bases, expected levels of activity for each cost pool, and overhead rates follow:

Factory Overhead Cost Pool	**Expected Amount**	**Expected Level of Allocation Base**	**Overhead Rate**
Direct labor usage			
(such as the wages of the supervisors and maintenance staff that support the direct laborers)	$ 30,000	10,000 direct labor hours	$3/direct labor hour
Machine usage:			
(such as electricity expense to run the machines)	40,000	5,000 machine hours	$8/machine hour
Machine setups:			
(cost of wages and technology needed to reconfigure production line)	20,000	100 setups	$200/setup
Design changes:			
(engineering salaries and computer-assisted design software)	10,000	25 design changes	$400/design change
	$100,000		

Assume that Job 100, now completed, required $1,000 for direct materials, $3,000 for direct labor, 500 direct labor hours, 75 machine hours, two setups, and two design changes. The cost of the job would be computed as follows:

Job 100

Direct materials	$1,000
Direct labor (500 hours)	3,000
Factory overhead related to:	
Direct labor usage (500 hours × $3/direct labor hour)	1,500
Machine usage (75 hours × $8/machine hour)	600
Machine setups (2 setups × $200/setup)	400
Design changes (2 changes × $400/design change)	800
Total cost of complete job	$7,300

Note that the overhead charged to this job using activity-based costing is greater than it was under any of the other methods of charging overhead.

In this instance, activity-based costing better reflects the additional costs of producing a job that requires two design changes and two setups. The use of activity-based costing is not limited to manufacturers. A recent survey of Irish hospitals indicated that hospitals changed to activity-based costing for the following reasons: more accurate cost information (78%), better use of hospital resources (50%), improved cost control (44.5%), more accurate performance measures for evaluating personnel (40%), and better insight into what causes costs to occur (37.5%).[3] **Activity-based management (ABM)** is the use of activity-based costing information to improve business performance by reducing costs and improving processes.

Recall and Review 3

If the ABC Company uses the machine hour method to apply factory overhead and the predetermined overhead rate is $20 per hour, $_________ is the amount that should be charged to Job 2525 for factory overhead and $_________ would be the total cost of the job. Assume that direct materials used totaled $3,000; direct labor was $2,200; direct labor hours were 150; and machine hours were 175.

(After working this exercise, see page 210 for the solution.)

You should now be able to work the following:
Questions 17–25; Exercises 4-8 to 4-10; Problems 4-8 to 4-10; Mini-Case; and Internet Exercise.

Accounting for Actual and Applied Factory Overhead

LO7 Account for actual and applied factory overhead.

After selecting the overhead application method and computing the predetermined rate to be used, all jobs or processes should be charged with the estimated overhead cost rather than the actual factory overhead costs being incurred. The estimated factory overhead is applied to production by a debit to Work in Process and a credit to an account entitled **Applied Factory Overhead**. Use of the separate applied factory overhead account rather than the credit side of the factory overhead control account avoids confusing the actual factory overhead charges, which are debited to the factory overhead control account, with the estimated charges that are debited to work in process. At the end of a period, the debit balance in Factory Overhead is compared to the credit balance in Applied Factory Overhead to determine the accuracy of the predetermined rates.

3 "An Empirical Survey of Adoption/Non-Adoption of Activity-Based Costing in Hospitals in Ireland," Working Paper, Doyle, Duffy, and McCahey, August 2002.

Factory Overhead

Debited for actual overhead incurred	

Applied Factory Overhead

Debited when closed to Factory Overhead	Credited for estimated overhead applied to jobs

To illustrate the use of a predetermined overhead rate, assume that a company has estimated a rate of $5 per direct labor hour and that production jobs actually required 1,000 direct labor hours to complete. Using the direct labor hour method, we see that $5,000 of estimated factory overhead cost would be applied to all jobs worked on during the period as follows:

(a) Work in Process	5,000	
Applied Factory Overhead		5,000
Applied factory overhead to jobs (1,000 hours @ $5).		

Also assume that the actual factory overhead for the period was $5,500, recorded as follows:

(b) Factory Overhead	5,500	
Accounts Payable		5,500

At the end of the period, the applied factory overhead account is closed to the factory overhead control account:

(c) Applied Factory Overhead	5,000	
Factory Overhead		5,000
Closed applied factory overhead account to control account.		

After the previous entries are posted, if a balance (debit or credit) remains in the factory overhead control account, it indicates that the actual factory overhead incurred did not equal the estimated factory overhead applied to jobs:

Factory Overhead

(b)	5,500	(c)	5,000
Bal. *500*		*(d)*	*500*

Applied Factory Overhead

(c)	*5,000*	*(a)*	*5,000*

The remaining debit balance of $500 in Factory Overhead indicates that a smaller amount of overhead was applied to production than was actually incurred during the period. The debit balance indicates that the factory overhead costs were **underapplied** or **underabsorbed**. In other words, the work in process account and the individual jobs worked on were undercharged for the costs of factory overhead incurred in the accounting period. Probable causes for the underapplication could include: (1) a lower level of operating capacity was achieved than was budgeted for when the predetermined rate was established or (2) the actual factory overhead expenses were more than budgeted for the operating level achieved. If, on the other hand, a credit balance remains in Factory Overhead after the applied factory overhead account is closed to the control account, the credit balance would represent **overapplied or overabsorbed factory overhead.** This means that more overhead was applied to production than was actually incurred in the period. To begin each new month with a zero balance in Factory Overhead, the debit or credit balance in the account is usually transferred to an account entitled **Under- and Overapplied Factory Overhead**, as follows:

(d) Under- and Overapplied Factory Overhead	500	
Factory Overhead		500
Closed debit balance (underapplied) in factory overhead control account.		

The special account, Under- and Overapplied Factory Overhead, will accumulate the month-to-month differences. At the end of the year, the balance of the under- and overapplied account will be closed to Cost of Goods Sold, as illustrated in Figure 4-12, or allocated on a pro rata basis to Work in Process, Finished Goods, and Cost of Goods Sold. The balance should be prorated if it will materially distort net income to charge the entire amount to Cost of Goods Sold.

The following table illustrates how under- and overapplied factory overhead costs typically offset each other over a given period of time as seasonal demands and production levels change:

Under- and Overapplied Factory Overhead

Month	Dr Underapplied	Cr Overapplied	Dr (Cr) Balance
January	$1,200		$ 1,200
February	800		2,000
March		$3,500	(1,500)
April		2,000	(3,500)
May		1,000	(4,500)
June		500	(5,000)
July	700		(4,300)
August	1,100		(3,200)
September	2,500		(700)
October	1,000		300
November	500		800
December		600	200
	$7,800	$7,600	

Figure 4-12 **Effects of Underapplied and Overapplied Overhead**

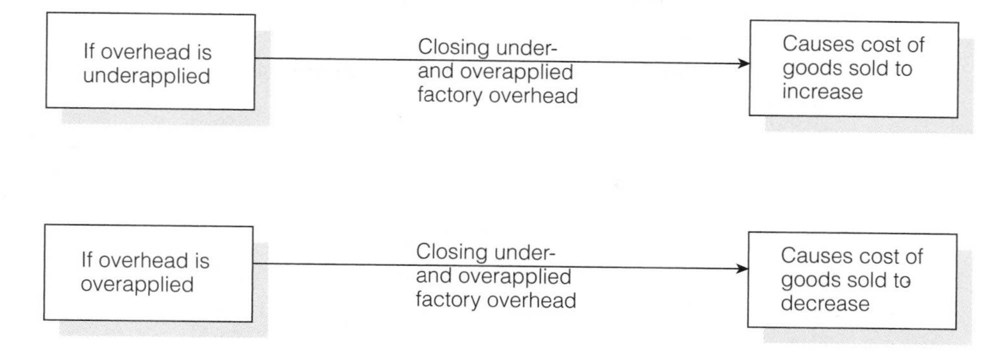

If a small balance, such as the $200 in the preceding example, remains in Under- and Overapplied Factory Overhead at year-end, it may be closed directly to Cost of Goods Sold because it will not materially misstate net income:

Cost of Goods Sold	200	
Under- and Overapplied Factory Overhead		200
Closed debit balance in Under- and Overapplied Factory Overhead.		

A large remaining balance, however, could distort the year's net income if it were closed entirely to Cost of Goods Sold when the company had material amounts of ending work in process and finished goods inventories that also would contain applied factory overhead. Therefore, an adjustment is required to restate the balances of the Work in Process, Finished Goods, and Cost of Goods Sold accounts.

To illustrate the proration procedure, assume that a debit balance of $10,000 (underapplied factory overhead) remained in the under- and overapplied factory overhead account at the end of the period. The year-end balances, before adjustment, of the following accounts were as follows:

		Percent of Total
Work in Process	$ 10,000	10%
Finished Goods	30,000	30
Cost of Goods Sold	60,000	60
Total	$100,000	100%

The pro rata amount of the $10,000 underapplied factory overhead that would be added to each account is computed as follows:

Work in Process ($10,000 × 10%)	$ 1,000
Finished Goods ($10,000 × 30%)	3,000
Cost of Goods Sold ($10,000 × 60%)	6,000
	$10,000

The journal entry to close the debit balance in Under- and Overapplied Factory Overhead would be as follows:

Work in Process	1,000	
Finished Goods	3,000	
Cost of Goods Sold	6,000	
Under- and Overapplied Factory Overhead		10,000
Closed debit balance in Under- and Overapplied Factory Overhead.		

The amount allocated to Cost of Goods Sold becomes a **period cost** that directly reduces net income for the current period. The amounts allocated to Work in Process and Finished Goods become part of the **product cost** of the inventories and will be deferred, along with the other inventory costs, to the next period when the inventories are completed and sold.

The preceding sections of this chapter have presented and illustrated the various aspects of accounting for factory overhead, including departmentalizing factory overhead costs, distributing service department costs, applying factory overhead to production using predetermined rates, and accounting for differences between actual and applied factory overhead. Figures 4-13 through 4-19 tie together these various aspects and show the flow of factory overhead costs through the accounting system.

Figure 4-13 Actual Factory Overhead Expenses

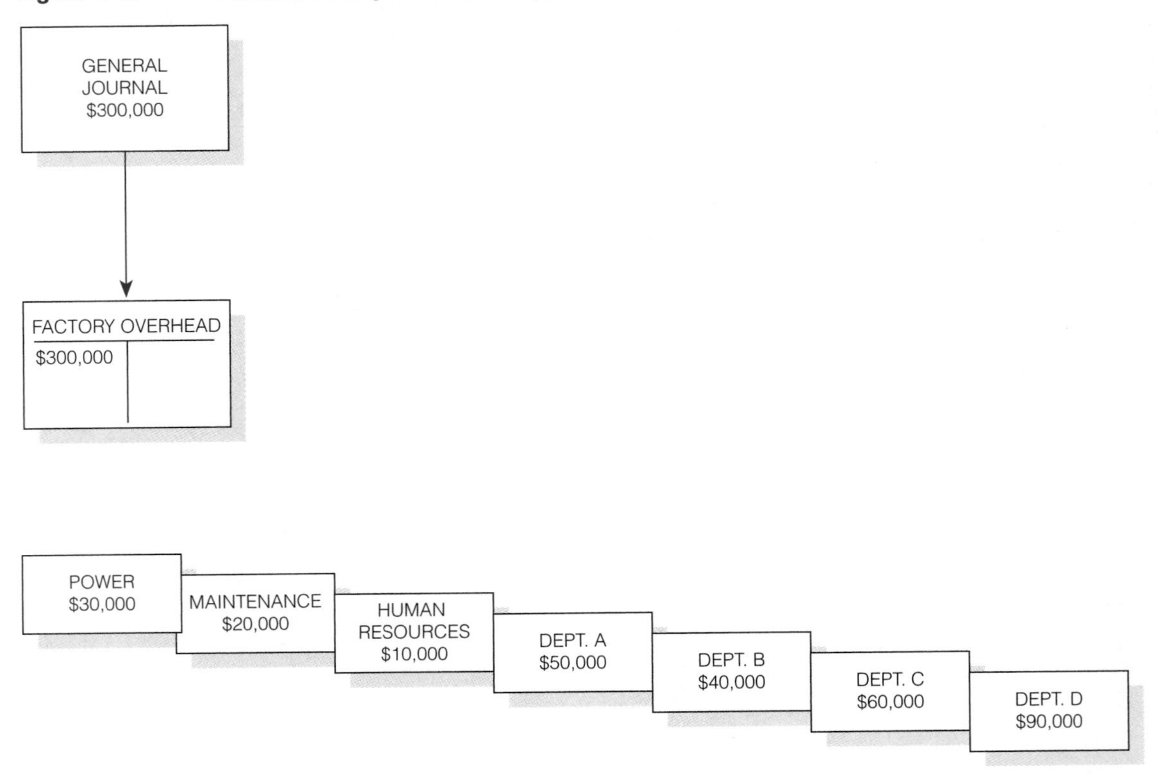

Figure 4-13 shows the flow of actual factory overhead expenses through the accounting records. The example assumes that the amounts posted to the factory overhead control account were originally recorded in the general journal. The total charge to the control account of $300,000 equals the sum of the actual factory overhead expenses incurred by the individual departments and recorded on the factory overhead analysis spreadsheets.

Figure 4-14 is a spreadsheet for actual factory overhead costs accumulated during the month and distributed at the end of the month, using the same data and sequential distribution method presented in Figure 4-11. Factory overhead was applied to the production departments as jobs were worked on throughout the month, as follows:

Department A	$ 66,000
Department B	56,000
Department C	70,000
Department D	110,000

Figure 4-14 also shows the under- or overapplied factory overhead, by department and in total, as follows:

	Actual Costs	**Applied**	**Under/(Over)**
Department A	$ 62,600	$ 66,000	$(3,400)
Department B	51,600	56,000	(4,400)
Department C	72,000	70,000	2,000
Department D	113,800	110,000	3,800
Total	$300,000	$302,000	$(2,000)

In Figure 4-15, the $300,000 balance in the factory overhead control account is transferred to the factory overhead accounts for both the service and production departments. The factory overhead analysis spreadsheets provide the data necessary for the distribution.

Figure 4-16 shows the distribution of the service department's costs to the production department's factory overhead accounts, using the sequential distribution method of service department costs, with the service department with the greatest total cost being distributed first. Figure 4-17 shows the application of factory overhead, based on predetermined rates, to the individual production departments. In Figure 4-18, the applied factory overhead accounts are closed to the departmental factory overhead accounts. Finally, as shown in Figure 4-19, the balances in the departmental factory overhead accounts are closed to

Figure 4-14 **Spreadsheet Summary of Actual and Applied Factory Overhead**

	A	B	C	D	E	F	G	H	I
1			Main-	Human	Dept.	Dept.	Dept.	Dept.	
2		Power	tenance	Resources	A	B	C	D	Total
3	Total actual expenses from factory								
4	overhead analysis spreadsheets	$30,000.00	$20,000.00	$10,000.00	$50,000.00	$40,000.00	$60,000.00	$90,000.00	$300,000.00
5									
6	Power distribution—								
7	(kw. hours)								
8	Maintenance—								
9	10,000 @ $0.25............		2,500.00						
10	Human Resources—								
11	10,000 @ 0.25............			2,500.00					
12	A— 12,000 @ 0.25............				3,000.00				
13	B— 18,000 @ 0.25............					4,500.00			
14	C— 20,000 @ 0.25............						5,000.00		
15	D— 50,000 @ 0.25............							12,500.00	
16	120,000		$22,500.00						
17									
18	Maintenance distribution—								
19	(square feet)								
20	Human Resources—								
21	5,000 @ $0.90............			4,500.00					
22	A— 5,000 @ 0.90............				4,500.00				
23	B— 6,000 @ 0.90............					5,400.00			
24	C— 4,000 @ 0.90............						3,600.00		
25	D— 5,000 @ 0.90............							4,500.00	
26	25,000			$17,000.00					
27									
28	Human Resources distribution—								
29	(number of employees served)								
30	A— 30 @ $170.................				5,100.00				
31	B— 10 @ 170.................					1,700.00			
32	C— 20 @ 170.................						3,400.00		
33	D— 40 @ 170.................							6,800.00	
34	100				$62,600.00	$51,600.00	$72,000.00	$113,800.00	$300,000.00
35									
36	Applied factory overhead				$66,000.00	$56,000.00	$70,000.00	$110,000.00	$302,000.00
37									
38	(Over-) or underapplied								
39	factory overhead				($3,400.00)	($4,400.00)	$2,000.00	$3,800.00	($2,000.00)
40									

Figure 4-15 **Distribution of Actual Factory Overhead to Service and Production Departments**

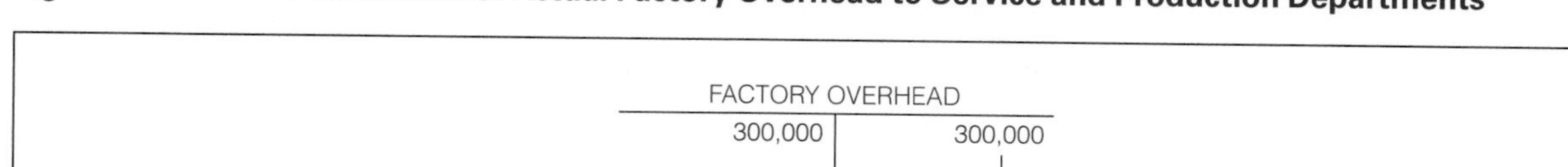

Figure 4-16 **Distribution of Service Department Costs**

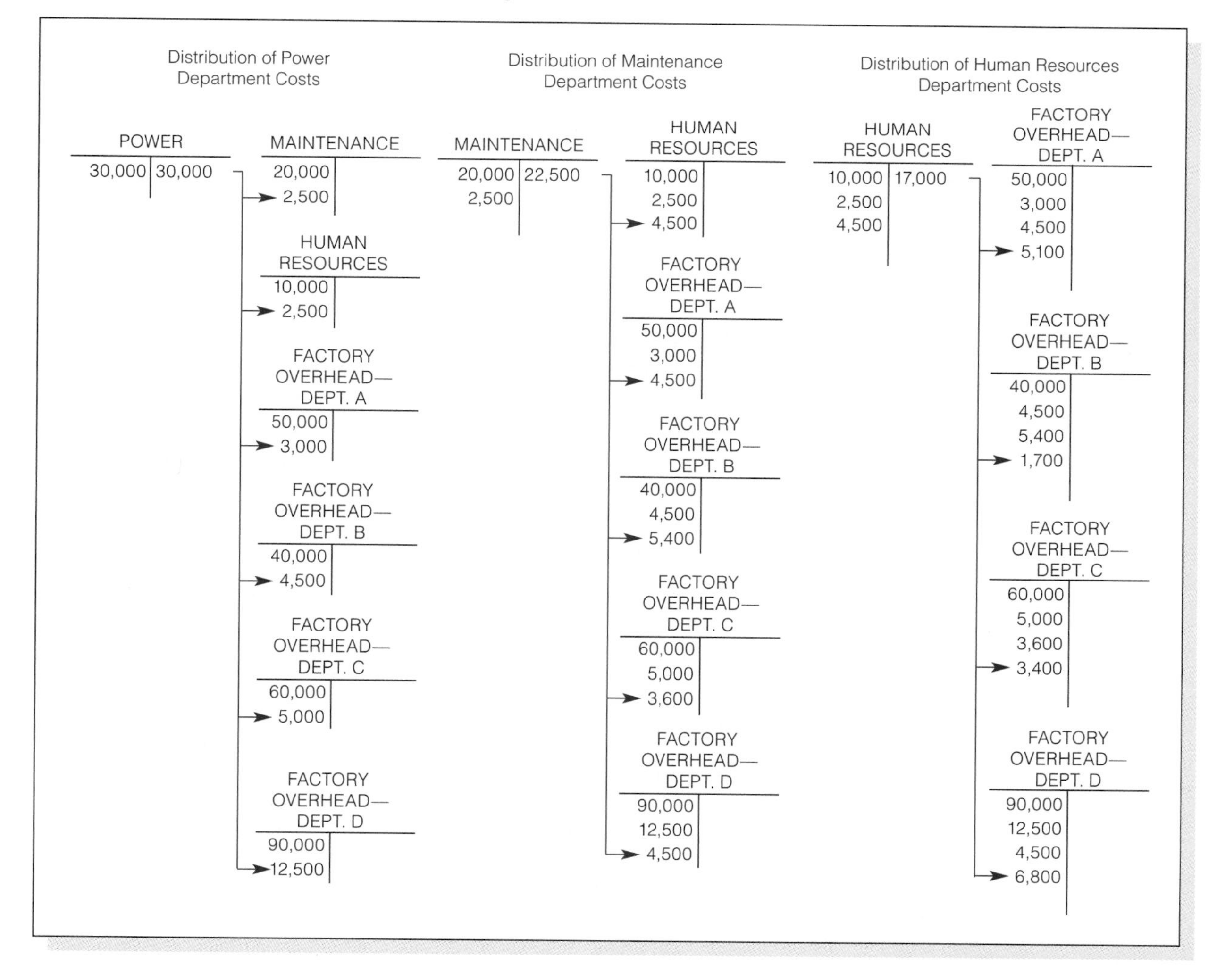

Figure 4-17 **Departmental Applied Factory Overhead**

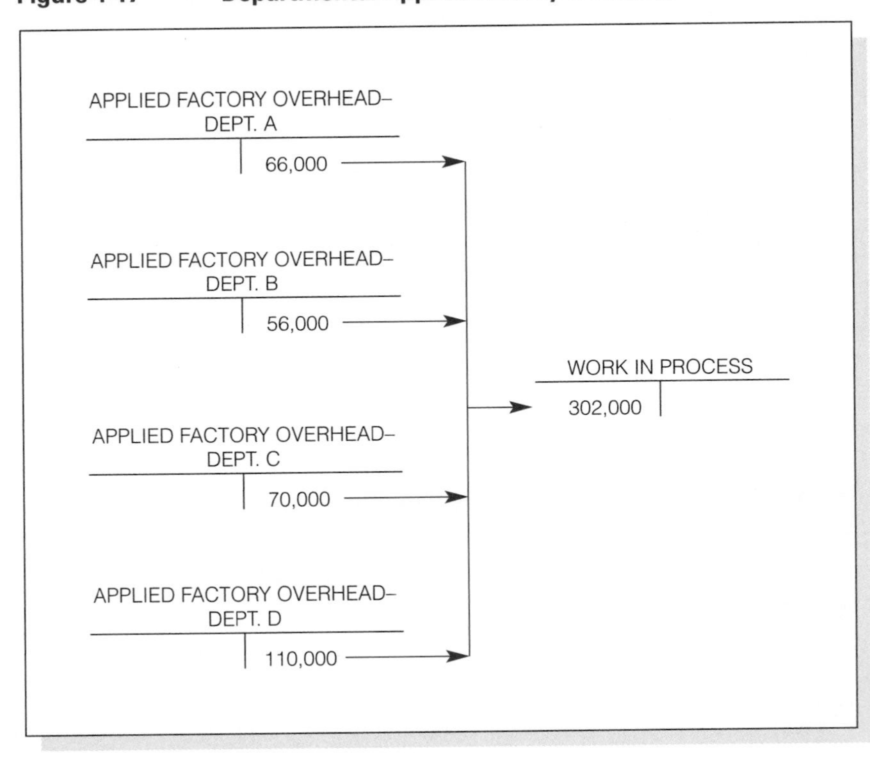

Figure 4-18 **Closing Applied Factory Overhead Accounts to Departmental Factory Overhead Accounts**

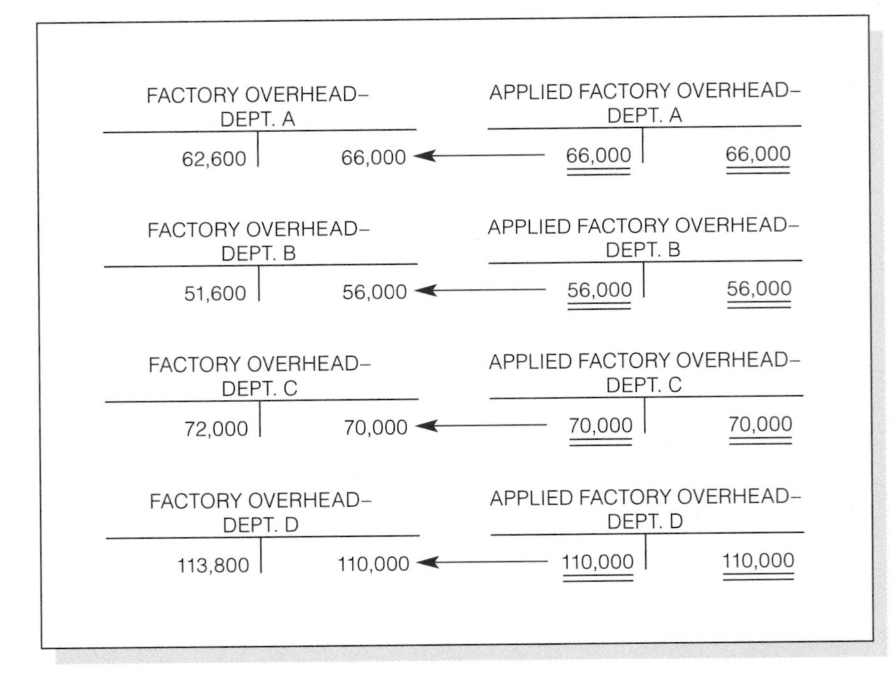

Figure 4-19 **Closing Balances in Departmental Factory Overhead Accounts**

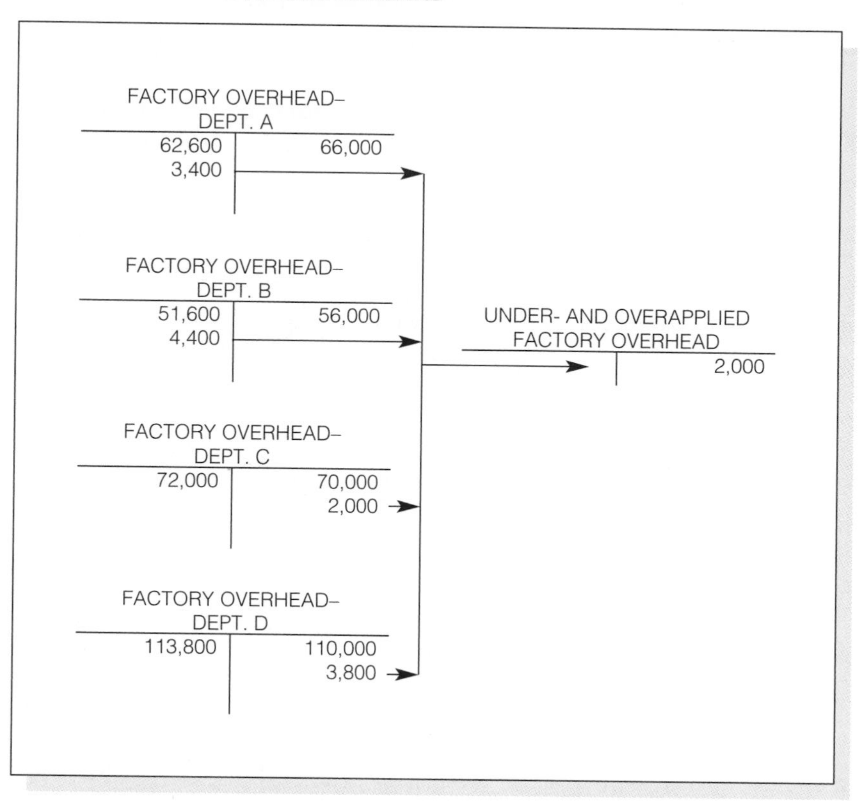

Under- and Overapplied Factory Overhead. The net amount of overapplied factory overhead, $2,000, is relatively small and most probably would be deducted from Cost of Goods Sold rather than prorated among Cost of Goods Sold and the inventory accounts. Figure 4-20 shows in summary form the transactions involved in accounting for factory overhead.

Figure 4-20 Summary of Factory Overhead Transactions

	A	B	C	D	E
1		**ACCOUNTING FOR FACTORY OVERHEAD**			
2		**Source**	**Book of**		**Subsidiary**
3		**of**	**Original**		**Cost**
4	**Transaction**	**Data**	**Entry**	**General Journal Entry**	**Records**
5	Indirect materials	Materials issued summary	General Journal or	Factory Overhead	Factory overhead
6	requisitioned from		Materials Requisition	Materials	analysis sheets
7	storeroom for factory use		Journal		Materials ledger cards
9					
10	Indirect labor employed	Labor cost summary	General Journal	Factory Overhead	Factory overhead
11	in factory			Payroll	analysis sheets
12					
13	Payroll taxes imposed	Payroll record	General Journal	Factory Overhead	Factory overhead
14	on the employer			FICA Tax Payable	analysis sheets
15				FUTA Tax Payable	
16				State Unemployment	
17				Tax Payable	
18					
19	Incurred factory overhead	Invoices	General Journal	Factory Overhead	Factory overhead
20	such as rent, power, and			Accounts Payable	analysis sheets
21	repairs				
22					
23	Adjustments for factory	Schedule of fixed costs	General Journal	Factory Overhead	Factory overhead
24	overhead such as expired			Prepaid Insurance	analysis sheets
25	insurance, accrued			Accrued Property	
26	property tax, and			Tax Payable	
27	depreciation			Accumulated	
28				Depreciation	
29					
30	Distribution of factory	Summary of factory	General Journal	Departmental Factory	None
31	overhead to service and	overhead		Overhead Accounts	
32	production departments			Factory Overhead	
33					
34	Distribution of service	Schedules	General Journal	Production Department	Factory overhead
35	department expenses to			Factory O/H Accts.	analysis sheets
36	production department			Service Department	
37	expense accounts			Expense Accounts	
38					
39	Application of factory	Schedule of predetermined	General Journal	Work in Process	Job cost sheets
40	overhead to jobs	departmental application		Applied Factory	
41		rates		Overhead	
42				Accounts	
43					
44	Close applied factory	Applied factory overhead	General Journal	Applied Factory Overhead	None
45	overhead accounts to	accounts		Accounts	
46	factory overhead control			Factory Overhead	
47					
48	Close factory overhead	Factory overhead control	General Journal	Under- and Overapplied	None
49	control balances to under-	accounts		Factory Overhead	
50	and overapplied factory			Factory Overhead	
51	overhead accounts			(if underapplied)	
52				Factory Overhead	
53				Under- and	
54				Overapplied Factory	
55				Overhead	
56				(if overapplied)	
57					

Recall and Review 4

RDI Co. had a year-end remaining debit balance of $15,000 in its under-and overapplied factory overhead account. The balance was considered to be large and, therefore, should be closed to Work in Process, Finished Goods, and Cost of Goods Sold. The year-end balance of these accounts, before adjustment, showed the following: Work in Process, $35,000; Finished Goods, $65,000; and Cost of Goods Sold, $100,000. The prorated amount of the underapplied factory overhead that is chargeable to each of the accounts would be Work in Process, $__________, Finished Goods, $__________, and Cost of Goods Sold, $__________.

(After working this exercise, see page 210 for the solution.)

You should now be able to work the following:
Questions 26 and 27; Exercises 4-11 to 4-14; Problems 4-11 to 4-16; Problem 4-17R, the Review Problem for Chapters 1–4; and Self-Study Problem 2.

KEY TERMS

Account analysis method, 172
Activity-based costing (ABC), 196
Activity-based management (ABM), 198
Algebraic distribution method, 187
Applied Factory Overhead, 198
Budgets, 179
Cost driver, 196
Department-type analysis spreadsheet, 182
Dependent variable, 177
Direct charge, 186
Direct distribution method, 187
Direct labor cost method, 194
Direct labor hour method, 195
Expense-type analysis spreadsheet, 182
Factory overhead, 169
Factory overhead analysis spreadsheets, 181
Factory overhead ledger, 180
Fixed costs, 170
Flexible budget, 179
General factory overhead expenses, 184
High-low method, 173
Independent variable, 177
Least-squares regression method, 177
Machine hour method, 195
Mixed costs, 170
Non-volume-related activities, 196
Observation method, 172
Outliers, 176
Overapplied or overabsorbed factory overhead, 200
Period cost, 202
Predetermined factory overhead rates, 193
Product cost, 202
Production department, 185
Scattergraph method, 174
Schedule of fixed costs, 183
Semivariable costs, 170
Sequential distribution or step-down method, 187
Service department, 185
Step-fixed cost, 171
Step-variable cost, 171
Summary of factory overhead, 185
Under- and Overapplied Factory Overhead, 200
Underapplied or underabsorbed, 199
Variable costs, 170
Volume-related activities, 196

ANSWERS TO RECALL AND REVIEW EXERCISES

R&R 1

	Hours	Expense
High volume	14,000	$6,100
Low volume	9,000	4,100
Difference	5,000	$2,000

Variable cost per hour = $2,000/5,000 hrs = $.40

	9,000 hours	14,000 hours
Total cost	$4,100	$6,100
Variable cost @ $.40 per hour	3,600	5,600
Fixed cost	$ 500	$ 500

R&R 2

	5,000 units	7,500 units
Direct materials	$ 3.00	$3.00
Direct labor	4.50	4.50
Fixed overhead	1.80*	1.20**
Variable overhead	1.00	1.00
Unit cost	$10.30	$9.70

*(6,000 units × $1.50)/5,000
**(6,000 units × $1.50)/7,500

R&R 3

$20 × 175 machine hours = $3,500.

Total cost of job = $3,000 + $2,200 + $3,500 = $8,700

R&R 4

	Year-End Balances	% of Total
Work in Process	$ 35,000	17.5 %
Finished Goods	65,000	32.5
Cost of Goods Sold	100,000	50.0
Total	$200,000	100.0 %

Work in Process	$15,000 × 17.5% = $2,625
Finished Goods	$15,000 × 32.5% = $4,875
Cost of Goods Sold	$15,000 × 50.0% = $7,500

SELF-STUDY PROBLEM 1

Distributing Service Department Expenses

Silicon Valley Manufacturing, Inc.

Silicon Valley Manufacturing, Inc., is divided into five departments that consist of three producing departments (Machining, Assembly, and Finishing) and two service departments (Building Maintenance and Storeroom). During September, the following factory overhead was incurred for the various departments:

Machining	$125,000
Assembly	155,000
Finishing	85,000
Building Maintenance	60,000
Storeroom	45,000

The bases for distributing service department expenses to the other departments were as follows:

Bldg. Maintenance—on the basis of square feet of floor space occupied: Machining, 5,000 sq ft; Assembly, 10,000 sq ft; Finishing, 3,000 sq ft; Storeroom, 2,000 sq ft.

Storeroom—on the basis of the number of materials requisitions processed: Machining, 400; Assembly, 250; Finishing, 100.

Required:
Rounding off allocated amounts to the nearest whole cent, prepare schedules showing the distribution of the service departments' expenses using:
1. The direct distribution method.
2. The sequential distribution method.

Suggestions:
1. When using the direct distribution method, you must realize that one service department's use of another service department is ignored in performing the distribution.
2. When using the sequential distribution method, you must first determine the order in which service departments will be distributed.

SOLUTION TO SELF-STUDY PROBLEM 1

Performing the Direct Distribution Method:
1. Observe that the distribution of Building Maintenance ignores the fact that the maintenance workers also clean and repair the 2,000-sq-ft

Storeroom. The denominator used in doing the allocations only includes the combined 18,000 sq ft for Machining, Assembly, and Finishing.

2. Note that when distributing the Storeroom, the amount of the denominator is not an issue because the Storeroom does not provide any services to Building Maintenance.

Performing the Sequential Distribution Method:

1. Since the number of departments served is the most common criterion for determining what service department to allocate first, Building Maintenance will be allocated first because it services four other departments, whereas Storeroom only services three other departments.
2. Note that the denominator used in doing the Building Maintenance distribution includes all 20,000 sq ft of factory floor space.
3. Note that the Storeroom amount distributed includes costs that originated in its department, as well as its share of the Building Maintenance costs.
4. Note that once a department's costs have been distributed, its share of other service departments' costs is not allocated back to it. (Note that it is not an issue here, because Building Maintenance is not serviced by the Storeroom.)

DIRECT DISTRIBUTION METHOD:

	A	B	C	D	E	F
1	**Dept.**	**Bldg. Maint.**	**Storeroom**	**Machining**	**Assembly**	**Finishing**
2	Total from factory overhead					
3	analysis spreadsheets..........................	$60,000	$45,000	$125,000	$155,000	$85,000
4						
5	Building Maintenance distribution—					
6	(sq ft):					
7	Machining (5,000 sq ft @ $3.33*).........			$16,650		
8						
9	Assembly (10,000 sq ft @ $3.33).........				$33,330	
10						
11	Finishing (3,000 sq ft @ $3.33).............					$9,990
12						
13	Storeroom distribution—	$(60,000)				
14	(# of requisitions):					
15						
16	Machining (400 reqs. @ $60**).............			$24,000		
17						
18	Assembly (250 reqs. @ $60).................				$15,000	
19						
20	Finishing (100 reqs. @ $60)..................					$6,000
21						
22	Total		$(45,000)	$165,650	$203,330	$100,990
23						
24	*$60,000/18,000 sq ft					
25	**$45,000/750 requisitions					

SEQUENTIAL DISTRIBUTION METHOD

	A	B	C	D	E	F
1						
2	**Dept.**	**Bldg. Maint.**	**Storeroom**	**Machining**	**Assembly**	**Finishing**
3	Total from factory overhead					
4	analysis spreadsheets:........................	$60,000	$45,000	$125,000	$155,000	$85,000
5	Building Maintenance					
6	distribution— (sq ft)............................	$(60,000)				
7						
8	Storeroom (2,000 @ $3*).....................		6,000			
9						
10	Machining (5,000 @ $3)......................			15,000		
11						
12	Assembly (10,000 @ $3)				30,000	
13						
14	Finishing (3,000 @ $3)..................					9,000
15			$51,000			
16						
18	Storeroom distribution—		$(51,000)			
19	(# of reqs.)..					
20						
21	Machining (400 @ $68**).....................			27,200		
22						
23	Assembly (250 @ $68).........................				17,000	
24						
25	Finishing (100 @ $68)					6,800
26						
27	Total	$0	$0	$167,200	$202,000	$100,800
28						
29	*$60,000/20,000 sq ft					
30	**$51,000/750 requisitions					
31						
32						

SELF-STUDY PROBLEM 2

Job Cost Sheets, Journal Entries

Water Wonders, Inc.

Water Wonders, Inc., makers of custom-made Jet Skis, completed Job 500 on March 31, and there were no jobs in process in the plant. Prior to April 1, the predetermined overhead application rate for April was computed from the following data, based on an estimate of 40,000 direct labor hours:

Estimated variable factory overhead	$100,000
Estimated fixed factory overhead	200,000
Total estimated factory overhead	$300,000
Estimated variable factory overhead per hour	$ 2.50
Estimated fixed factory overhead per hour	5.00
Predetermined overhead rate per direct labor hour	$ 7.50

The factory has one production department, and the direct labor hour method is used to apply factory overhead.

Three jobs are started during the month, and postings are made daily to the job cost sheets from the materials requisitions and labor-time records. The following schedule shows the jobs and the amounts posted to the job cost sheets:

Job	Date Started	Direct Materials	Direct Labor	Direct Labor Hours
401	April 1	$100,000	$120,000	12,000
402	April 12	200,000	250,000	18,000
403	April 15	80,000	75,000	8,000
		$380,000	$445,000	38,000

The factory overhead control account was debited during the month for actual factory overhead expenses of $325,000. On April 11, Job 401 was completed and delivered to the customer at a markup of 25% on manufacturing cost. On April 24, Job 402 was completed and transferred to Finished Goods. On April 30, Job 403 was still in process.

Required:

1. Prepare job cost sheets for Jobs 401, 402, and 403, including factory overhead applied when the job was completed or at the end of the month for partially completed jobs.
2. Prepare journal entries as of April 30 for the following:
   a. Applying factory overhead to production.
   b. Closing the applied factory overhead account.
   c. Closing the factory overhead account.
   d. Transferring the cost of the completed jobs to Finished Goods.
   e. Recording the cost of the sale and the sale of Job 401.

Suggestions:

1. When completing the job cost sheets, you must first determine how much overhead should be applied to each job.
2. When closing the factory overhead account, the balance will represent the under- or overapplied factory overhead.

SOLUTION TO SELF-STUDY PROBLEM 2

Preparing the Job Cost Sheets:

1. On April 11, Job 401 was completed and factory overhead was applied as follows:

Job 401

Direct materials	$100,000
Direct labor	120,000
Applied factory overhead (12,000 hours × $7.50)	90,000
Total cost	$310,000

On April 24, Job 402 was completed and factory overhead was applied as follows:

Job 402

Direct materials	$200,000
Direct labor	250,000
Applied factory overhead (18,000 hours × $7.50)	135,000
Total cost	$585,000

On April 30, Job 403 is not completed; however, factory overhead is applied to the partially completed job to estimate the total cost incurred during the month of April, as follows:

Job 403

Direct materials	$ 80,000
Direct labor	75,000
Applied factory overhead (8,000 hours × $7.50)	60,000
Total cost (for month of April)	$215,000

Preparing the Journal Entries:

2. **a.** The total factory overhead applied to the three jobs during April was $285,000. The general journal entry made on April 30 to apply factory overhead to production follows:

April 30	Work in Process	285,000	
	Applied Factory Overhead		285,000

The applied factory overhead of $285,000 has already been recorded on the job cost sheets. The preceding general journal entry brings the work in process control account into agreement with the subsidiary job cost ledger.

b. and **c.** The next procedure is to close the applied factory overhead account to Factory Overhead. Then, transfer any remaining balance to the under- and overapplied factory overhead account.

April 30	Applied Factory Overhead	285,000	
	Factory Overhead		285,000
April 30	Under- and Overapplied Factory Overhead	40,000	
	Factory Overhead		40,000
	Closed factory overhead ($325,000 actual – $285,000 applied).		

d. and **e.** During April, the following entries were made to transfer the cost of completed Jobs 401 and 402 to Finished Goods, and to record the cost of the sale and the sale of Job 401:

Finished Goods	895,000	
Work in Process		895,000
Completed Jobs 401 ($310,000) and 402 ($585,000) and transferred to finished goods.		
Accounts Receivable	387,500	
Sales		387,500
Delivered Job 401 to customer and billed at 25% markup ($310,000 × 125%).		
Cost of Goods Sold	310,000	
Finished Goods		310,000
Recorded cost of Job 401 delivered to customer.		

QUESTIONS

1. What are factory overhead expenses, and what distinguishes them from other manufacturing costs? What other terms are used to describe factory overhead expenses?
2. What are three categories of factory overhead expenses? Give examples of each.
3. What are the distinguishing characteristics of variable, fixed, and semivariable factory overhead costs?
4. When a product's cost is composed of both fixed and variable costs, what effect does the increase or decrease in production have on per unit cost?
5. What effect does a change in volume have on total variable, fixed, and semivariable costs?
6. Distinguish between a step-variable cost and a step-fixed cost.
7. What is the basic premise underlying the high-low method of analyzing semivariable costs?
8. What are the advantages and disadvantages of the scattergraph method as compared to the high-low method?
9. Differentiate between an independent variable and a dependent variable and give an example of each.
10. What does R^2 measure, and how would it be useful?
11. How does accounting for factory overhead differ in small enterprises versus large enterprises?
12. What is the function and use of each of the two types of factory overhead analysis spreadsheets?
13. What are two types of departments found in a factory? What is the function or purpose of each?
14. What are the two most frequently used methods of distributing service department costs to production departments?
15. When using the step-down method of distributing service department costs, if a service department receives services from other service departments, will those costs be allocated back to it even though it was the first service department distributed?
16. When using the step-down method of distributing service department costs, if each of two service departments services the same number of other departments, how is it determined as to which service department to allocate first?
17. What are the shortcomings of waiting until the actual factory overhead expenses are known before recording such costs on the job cost sheets?
18. What are the two types of budget data needed to compute predetermined overhead rates?
19. What are three methods traditionally used for applying factory overhead to jobs? Discuss the allocation base used in each method.
20. What factory operating conditions and data are required for each of the traditionally used methods for applying factory overhead to products? Discuss the strengths and weaknesses of each method.
21. Under what conditions would it be desirable for a company to use more than one method to apply factory overhead to jobs or products?
22. How does activity-based costing differ from traditional methods of applying overhead to products?
23. What steps must a company take to successfully employ activity-based costing?
24. What is the relationship between activity-based costing and activity-based management?

25. Distinguish between volume-related and non-volume-related overhead costs.

26. If the factory overhead control account has a debit balance of $1,000 at the end of the first month of the fiscal year, has the overhead been under- or overapplied for the month? What are some probable causes for the debit balance?

27. What are two ways that an under- or overapplied factory overhead balance can be disposed of at the end of a fiscal period? How can one decide which method to choose?

EXERCISES

E4-1 **Classifying fixed and variable costs** LO1

Classify each of the following items of factory overhead as either a fixed or a variable cost. (Include any costs that you consider to be semivariable within the variable category. Remember that variable costs change in total as the volume of production changes.)

a. Indirect labor
b. Indirect materials
c. Insurance on building
d. Overtime premium pay
e. Depreciation on building (straight-line)
f. Polishing compounds
g. Depreciation on machinery (based on machine hours used)
h. Employer's payroll taxes
i. Property taxes
j. Machine lubricants
k. Employees' hospital insurance (paid by employer)
l. Labor for machine repairs
m. Vacation pay
n. Janitor's wages
o. Rent
p. Small tools
q. Plant manager's salary
r. Factory electricity
s. Product inspector's wages

E4-2 **High-low methods** LO2

Copper Mountain Company has accumulated the following data over a six-month period:

	Indirect Labor Hours	Indirect Labor Costs
January	400	$ 6,000
February	500	7,000
March	600	8,000
April	700	9,000
May	800	10,000
June	900	11,000
	3,900	$51,000

Separate the indirect labor into its fixed and variable components, using the high-low method.

LO2

E4-3 Scattergraph method
Using the data in E4-2 and a piece of graph paper:

1. Plot the data points on the graph and draw a line by visual inspection, indicating the trend shown by the data points.
2. Determine the variable cost per unit and the total fixed cost from the information on the graph.

LO2

E4-4 Least-squares regression method
Using the data in E4-2 and Microsoft Excel, determine:

1. The variable cost per unit, the total fixed cost, and R^2.
2. The plotted data points using Chart Wizard.
3. Compare the results to your solutions in E4-2 and E4-3.

LO3

E4-5 Computing unit costs at different levels of production
Scentsation, Inc., budgeted for 12,000 bottles of perfume Oui during the month of May. The unit cost of Oui was $20, consisting of direct materials, $7; direct labor, $8; and factory overhead, $5 (fixed, $2; variable, $3).

a. What would be the unit cost if 10,000 bottles were manufactured? (*Hint:* You must first determine the total fixed costs.)
b. What would be the unit cost if 20,000 bottles were manufactured?
c. Explain why a difference occurs in the unit costs.

LO5

E4-6 Identifying basis for distribution of service department costs
What would be the appropriate basis for distributing the costs of each of the following service departments to the user departments?

a. Building maintenance
b. Inspection and packing
c. Machine repair
d. Human resources
e. Purchasing
f. Shipping
g. Raw materials storeroom

LO5

E4-7 Direct method and sequential method of distributing service department costs
A manufacturing company has two service and two production departments. Building Maintenance and Factory Office are the service departments. The production departments are Assembly and Machining.

The following data have been estimated for next year's operations:

Direct labor hours:	Assembly, 80,000; Machining, 40,000
Floor space occupied:	Factory Office, 10%; Assembly, 40%; Machining, 50%

The direct charges identified with each of the departments are as follows:

Building maintenance	$ 90,000
Factory office	171,000
Assembly	378,000
Machining	328,000

The building maintenance department services all departments of the company, and its costs are allocated using floor space occupied, while factory office costs are allocable to Assembly and Machining on the basis of direct labor hours.

1. Distribute the service department costs, using the direct method.
2. Distribute the service department costs, using the sequential distribution method, with the department servicing the greatest number of other departments distributed first.

E4-8 Determining job cost, using direct labor cost, direct labor hour, and machine hour methods

a. If the direct labor cost method is used in applying factory overhead and the predetermined rate is 100%, what amount should be charged to Job 2010 for factory overhead? Assume that direct materials used totaled $5,000 and that the direct labor cost totaled $3,200.

b. If the direct labor hour method is used in applying factory overhead and the predetermined rate is $10 an hour, what amount should be charged to 2010 for factory overhead? Assume that the direct materials used totaled $5,000, the direct labor cost totaled $3,200, and the number of direct labor hours totaled 250.

c. If the machine hour method is used in applying factory overhead and the predetermined rate is $12.50 an hour, what amount should be charged to 2010 for factory overhead? Assume that the direct materials used totaled $5,000, the direct labor cost totaled $3,200, the direct labor hours were 250 hours, and the machine hours were 295 hours.

E4-9 Determining job costs, using ABC method

LO6

Job 401k required $5,000 for direct materials, $2,000 for direct labor, 200 direct labor hours, 100 machine hours, two setups, and three design changes. The cost pools and overhead rates for each pool follow:

Cost Pool	Overhead Rate
Assembly support	$5/direct labor hour
Machining support	$10/machine hour
Machine setups	$250/setup
Design changes	$500/design change

Determine the cost of Job 401k.

E4-10 **ABC matching of cost pools and cost allocation bases**

Match each of the following cost pools with the most appropriate cost allocation base and determine the overhead rates:

Cost Pool	Amount
Assembly support	$50,000
Machining support	80,000
Machine setups	25,000
Design changes	15,000

Allocation Base	
Number of setups	200
Machine hours	2,000
Design hours	500
Direct labor cost	$ 75,000

LO6 LO7

E4-11 **Determining actual factory overhead**

The books of Prestige Products Company revealed that the following general journal entry had been made at the end of the current accounting period:

Factory Overhead	2,000	
Under- and Overapplied Factory Overhead		2,000
Closed credit balance in factory overhead control account.		

The total direct materials cost for the period was $40,000. The total direct labor cost, at an average rate of $10 per hour for direct labor, was one and one-half times the direct materials cost. Factory overhead was applied on the basis of $4 per direct labor hour. What was the total actual factory overhead incurred for the period? (*Hint:* First solve for direct labor cost and then for direct labor hours.)

LO6 LO7

E4-12 **Determining labor and factory overhead costs**

The general ledger of Stephens Products, Inc. contains the following control account:

Work in Process

Materials	15,000	Finished goods	40,000
Labor	16,000		
Factory overhead	16,000		

If the materials charged to the one uncompleted job still in process amounted to $3,400, what amount of labor and factory overhead must have been charged to the job if the factory overhead rate is 100% of direct labor cost? (*Hint:* First determine the balance in Work in Process.)

E4-13 **General ledger account analysis**

LO7

The following form represents an account taken from the general ledger of Brodsky Costumes Company:

Indirect materials	500	Work in Process	8,000
Supervisor's salary	1,200	(50% of $16,000 direct labor)	
Power	5,000		
Building expenses	1,000		
Miscellaneous overhead	1,400		
Bal. *1,100*	*9,100*		

Answer the following questions:

a. What is the title of the account?
b. Is this a departmentalized factory?
c. What does the balance of $1,100 represent?
d. How was the 50% rate determined? (Explain without numbers.)
e. What disposition should be made of the balance, assuming that this is the end of the fiscal year?

E4-14 **Computing under- and overapplied overhead**

LO7

ETA Company had a remaining credit balance of $20,000 in its under- and overapplied factory overhead account at year-end. The balance was deemed to be large and, therefore, should be closed to Work in Process, Finished Goods, and Cost of Goods Sold. The year-end balances of these accounts, before adjustment, showed the following:

Work in Process	$ 75,000
Finished Goods	25,000
Cost of Goods Sold	100,000
Total	$200,000

a. Determine the prorated amount of the overapplied factory overhead that is chargeable to each of the accounts.
b. Prepare the journal entry to close the credit balance in Under- and Overapplied Factory Overhead.

PROBLEMS

P4-1 **Variable and fixed cost pattern analysis**

LO1

The cost behavior patterns on page 222 are lettered A through H. The vertical axes of the graphs represent total dollars of expense, and the horizontal axes represent production in units, machine hours, or direct labor hours. In each case, the zero point is at the intersection of the two axes. Each graph may be used no more than once.

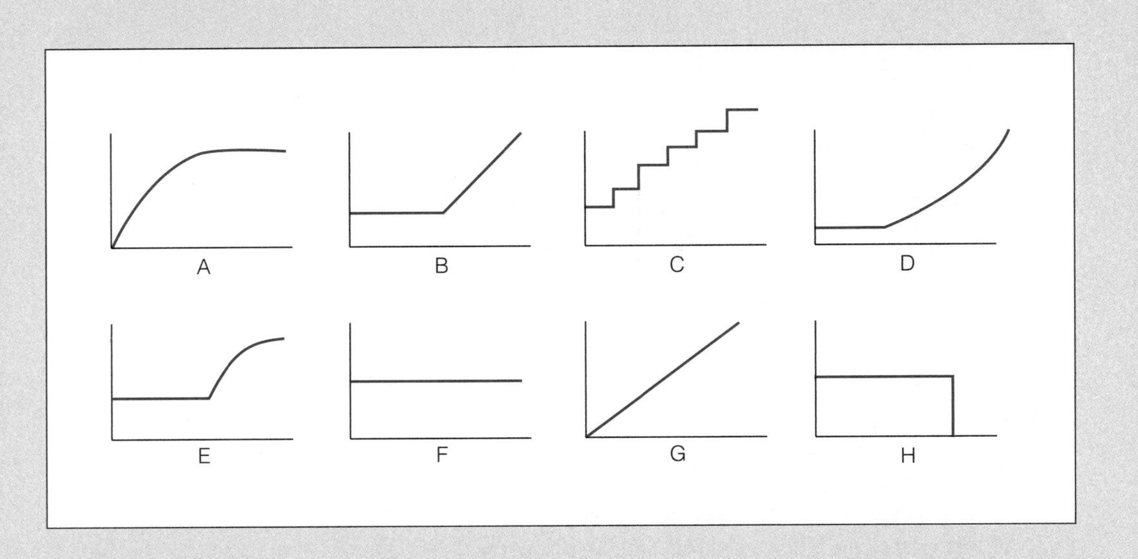

Required:

Select the graph that matches the lettered cost described here.

a. Depreciation of equipment—the amount of depreciation charged is computed based on the number of machine hours that the equipment was operated.

b. Electricity bill—flat fixed charge, plus a variable cost after a certain number of kilowatt hours are used.

c. City water bill—computed as follows:

First 1,000,000 gallons or less	$1,000 flat fee
Next 10,000 gallons	0.003 per gallon used
Next 10,000 gallons	0.006 per gallon used
Next 10,000 gallons	0.009 per gallon used

d. Depreciation of equipment—the amount is computed by the straight-line method.

e. Rent on a factory building donated by the city—the agreement calls for a fixed fee payment, unless 200,000 labor hours are worked, in which case no rent need be paid.

f. Salaries of repair workers—one repair worker is needed for every 1,000 machine hours or less (i.e., 0 to 1,000 hours requires one repair worker, 1,001 to 2,000 hours requires two repair workers, etc.).

P4-2 **Variable and fixed cost analysis; high-low method**

LO2

Fahrenheit Company manufactures a product that requires the use of a considerable amount of natural gas to heat it to a desired temperature. The process requires a constant level of heat, so the furnaces are maintained at a set temperature for 24 hours a day. Although units are not continuously processed, management desires that the variable cost be charged directly to the product and the fixed cost to the factory overhead. The following data have been collected for the year:

	Units	Cost		Units	Cost
January	2,400	$4,400	July	2,200	$4,400
February	2,300	4,300	August	2,100	4,100
March	2,200	4,200	September	2,000	3,800
April	2,000	4,000	October	1,400	3,400
May	1,800	3,800	November	1,900	3,700
June	1,900	3,900	December	1,800	4,050

Required:

1. Separate the variable and fixed elements, using the high-low method.
2. Determine the cost to be charged to the product for the year. (*Hint:* First determine the number of annual units produced.)
3. Determine the cost to be charged to factory overhead for the year.

P4-3 **Scattergraph method**

Using the data in P4-2 and a piece of graph paper:

1. Plot the data points on the graph and draw a line by visual inspection, indicating the trend shown by the data points.
2. Determine the variable cost per unit and the total fixed cost from the information on the graph.
3. Determine the cost to be charged to the product for the year.
4. Determine the cost to be charged to factory overhead for the year.
5. Do these answers agree with the answers to P4-2? Why or why not?

P4-4 **Least-squares regression method**

Using the data in P4-2 and Microsoft Excel:

LO2

1. Separate the variable and fixed elements.
2. Determine the cost to be charged to the product for the year.
3. Determine the cost to be charged to factory overhead for the year.
4. Determine the plotted data points using Chart Wizard.
5. How do these solutions compare to the solutions in P4-2 and P4-3?

P4-5 **Budgeted factory overhead costs**

Listed below are the budgeted factory overhead costs for 2011 for Muncie Manufacturing, Inc., at a projected level of 2,000 units:

LO3

Expenses:	
Indirect materials	$ 10,000
Indirect labor	20,000
Power	15,000
Straight-line depreciation	30,000
Factory property tax	28,000
Factory insurance	22,000
Total	$125,000

Required:
Prepare flexible budgets for factory overhead at the 1,000, 2,000, and 4,000 unit levels. (*Hint:* You must first decide which of the listed costs should be considered variable and which should be fixed.)

P4-6 Distribution of service department costs to production departments using the direct method similar to Self-Study Problem 1

Bakery Products, Inc., is divided into five departments, Mixing, Blending, Finishing, Factory Office, and Building Maintenance. The first three departments are engaged in production work. Factory Office and Building Maintenance are service departments. During the month of June, the following factory overhead was incurred for the various departments:

Mixing	$21,000	Factory Office	$9,000
Blending	18,000	Building Maintenance	6,400
Finishing	25,000		

The bases for distributing service department expenses to the other departments follow:

> Building Maintenance—On the basis of floor space occupied by the other departments as follows: Mixing, 10,000 sq ft; Blending, 4,500 sq ft; Finishing, 10,500 sq ft; and Factory Office, 7,000 sq ft.
>
> Factory Office—On the basis of number of employees as follows: Mixing, 30; Blending, 20; and Finishing, 50.

Required:
Prepare a schedule showing the distribution of the service departments' expenses using the direct distribution method.

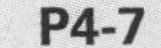

P4-7 Distribution of service department costs to production departments using the sequential distribution method similar to Self-Study Problem 1

Required:
Using the information in P4-6 above, prepare a schedule showing the distribution of the service departments' expenses using the sequential distribution method in the order of number of other departments served. (*Hint:* First distribute the service department that services the greater number of other departments.)

P4-8 Determining total job costs, using predetermined overhead rate

Barbara-Lee Manufacturing Company uses the job order cost system of accounting. The following is a list of the jobs completed during the month of March, showing the charges for materials requisitioned and for direct labor.

Job	Materials Requisitioned	Direct Labor
18AX	$ 300.00	$ 600.00
19BT	1,080.00	940.00
20CD	720.00	1,400.00
21FB	4,200.00	5,120.00

Assume that factory overhead is applied on the basis of direct labor costs and that the predetermined rate is 200%.

Required:

1. Compute the amount of overhead to be added to the cost of each job completed during the month.
2. Compute the total cost of each job completed during the month.
3. Compute the total cost of producing all the jobs finished during the month.

P4-9 **Determining job cost—calculation of predetermined rate for applying overhead by direct labor cost and direct labor hour methods**

LO6

Lexus Products, Inc., has its factory divided into three departments, with individual factory overhead rates for each department. In each department, all the operations are sufficiently alike for the department to be regarded as a cost center. The estimated monthly factory overhead for the departments is as follows: Forming, $64,000; Shaping, $36,000; and Finishing, $10,080. The estimated production data include the following:

	Forming	Shaping	Finishing
Materials used	$20,000	$10,000	$10,000
Direct labor cost	$16,000	$15,000	$ 8,400
Direct labor hours	800	500	350

The job cost ledger shows the following data for GS300, which was completed during the month:

	Forming	Shaping	Finishing
Materials used	$120	$140	$120
Direct labor cost	$220	$270	$240
Direct labor hours	12	10	8

Required:

Determine the cost of GS300. Assume that the factory overhead is applied to production orders, based on the following:

1. Direct labor cost
2. Direct labor hours

(*Hint:* You must first determine overhead rates for each department, rounding rates to the nearest cent.)

P4-10 Determining job costs, using activity-based costing

Julio Manufacturing Company uses activity-based costing. The factory overhead budget for the coming period is $500,000, consisting of the following:

Cost Pool	Budgeted Amount
Direct labor support	$150,000
Machine support	200,000
Machine setups	100,000
Design changes	50,000
Total	$500,000

The potential allocation bases and their estimated amounts were as follows:

Cost Pool	Budgeted Amount
Number of design changes	50
Number of setups	200
Machine hours	10,000
Direct labor hours	20,000

Required:

1. Determine the overhead rate for each cost pool, using the most appropriate allocation base for each pool.
2. Job 2525 required $25,000 for direct materials, $10,000 for direct labor, 500 direct labor hours, 1,000 machine hours, five setups, and three design changes. Determine the cost of Job 2525.

P4-11 General journal entries for factory overhead

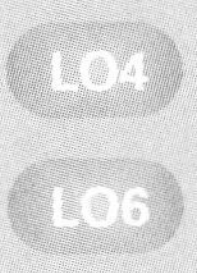

GGT Products, Inc., uses a job order cost system. Selected transactions dealing with factory items for the month follow:

a. Requisitioned indirect materials from storeroom, $3,200.
b. Purchased, on account, factory supplies for future needs, $4,400.
c. Purchased parts, on account, for repairing a machine, $1,400.
d. Requisitioned factory supplies from storeroom, $900.
e. Returned other defective factory supplies to vendor, $700.
f. Factory rent accrued for the month, $2,400.
g. Returned previously requisitioned factory supplies to storeroom, $350.
h. Depreciation of machinery and equipment, $2,800.
i. Payroll taxes liability for month, $3,200.
j. Heat, light, and power charges payable for the month, $6,400.
k. Expired insurance on inventories, $1,350.
l. Factory overhead applied to production, $34,600.

m. Indirect labor for the month, $2,600.
n. Goods completed and transferred to finished goods: materials, $14,400; labor, $40,400; factory overhead, $30,400.

Required:
Record the previous transactions. Assume that the records include a control account and a subsidiary ledger for factory overhead, to which the entries will be posted at some later date.

P4-12 Determining overhead rates, using direct labor cost, direct labor hour, and machine hour methods; determining job cost; computing underapplied and overapplied overhead

LO6 LO7

Lubbock Manufacturing Company is studying the results of applying factory overhead to production. The following data have been used: estimated factory overhead, $60,000; estimated materials costs, $50,000; estimated direct labor costs, $60,000; estimated direct labor hours, 10,000; estimated machine hours, 20,000; work in process at the beginning of the month, none.

The actual factory overhead incurred for the month of November was $80,000, and the production statistics on November 30 are as follows:

Job	Materials Costs	Direct Labor Costs	Direct Labor Hours	Machine Hours	Date Jobs Completed
101	$ 5,000	$ 6,000	1,000	3,000	Nov. 10
102	7,000	12,000	2,000	3,200	Nov. 14
103	8,000	13,500	2,500	4,000	Nov. 20
104	9,000	15,600	2,600	3,400	In process
105	10,000	29,000	4,500	6,500	Nov. 26
106	11,000	2,400	400	1,500	In process
Total	$50,000	$78,500	13,000	21,600	

Required:
1. Compute the predetermined rate, based on the following:
   a. Direct labor cost
   b. Direct labor hours
   c. Machine hours
2. Using each of the methods, compute the estimated total cost of each job at the end of the month.
3. Determine the under- or overapplied factory overhead, in total, at the end of the month under each of the methods.
4. Which method would you recommend? Why?

P4-13 Determining overhead rate, using direct labor cost, direct labor hour, and machine hour methods

LO6

LO7

The following information, taken from the books of Nicholas Company, represents the operations for the month of January:

	Bronzing	Casting	Finishing
Materials used	$20,000	$10,000	$10,000
Direct labor cost	$ 8,000	$ 5,000	$ 9,000
Direct labor hours	1,000	500	1,620
Machine hours	4,000	5,000	2,025
Factory overhead	$20,000	$10,000	$16,200

The job cost system is used, and the February cost sheet for Job M45 shows the following:

	Bronzing	Casting	Finishing
Materials	$20.00	$40.00	$20.00
Direct labor	$64.00	$60.00	$54.00
Direct labor hours	8	6	6
Machine hours	2	3	1

The following actual information was accumulated during February:

	Bronzing	Casting	Finishing
Direct labor hours	15,000	9,800	20,000
Factory overhead	$350,000	$220,000	$325,000

Required:

1. Using the January data, ascertain the factory overhead application rates to be used during February, based on the following:
   a. Direct labor cost
   b. Direct labor hours
   c. Machine hours
2. Prepare a schedule showing the total production cost of Job M45 under each method of applying factory overhead.
3. Prepare the entries to record the following for February operations:
   a. The liability for total factory overhead.
   b. Distribution of factory overhead to the departments.
   c. Application of factory overhead to the work in process, using direct labor hours. (Use the predetermined rate calculated in 1. and separate applied overhead accounts for each department.)
   d. Closing of the applied factory overhead accounts.
   e. Recording under- and overapplied factory overhead and closing the actual factory overhead accounts.

P4-14 **Determining the under- and overapplied overhead**

Ko-Be Corporation has four departmental accounts: Building Maintenance, General Factory Overhead, Machining, and Assembly. The direct labor hour method is used to apply factory overhead to the jobs being worked on in Machining and Assembly. The company expects each production department to use 30,000 direct labor hours during the year. The estimated overhead rates for the year include the following:

	Machining	Assembly
Variable cost per hour	$1.30	$1.50
Fixed cost per hour	2.70	3.00
	$4.00	$4.50

During the year, both Machining and Assembly used 28,000 direct labor hours. Factory overhead costs incurred during the year follow:

Building maintenance	$30,000
General factory overhead	75,400
Machining	45,800
Assembly	68,800

In determining application rates at the beginning of the year, cost allocations were made as follows, using the sequential distribution method:

> Building Maintenance to General Factory Overhead, 10%; to Machining, 50%; to Assembly, 40%.

General factory overhead was distributed according to direct labor hours.

Required:
Determine the under- or overapplied overhead for each production department. (*Hint:* First you must distribute the service department costs.)

P4-15 **Job cost sheets, journal entries similar to Self-Study Problem 2**

LO6
LO7

Planet Products, Inc., completed Job 2525 on May 31, and there were no jobs in process in the plant. Prior to June 1, the predetermined overhead application rate for June was computed from the following data, based on an estimate of 5,000 direct labor hours:

Estimated variable factory overhead	$20,000
Estimated fixed factory overhead	10,000
Total estimated factory overhead	$30,000

Estimated variable factory overhead per hour	$4
Estimated fixed factory overhead per hour	2
Predetermined overhead rate per direct labor hour	$6

The factory has one production department and uses the direct labor hour method to apply factory overhead.

Three jobs are started during the month, and postings are made daily to the job cost sheets from the materials requisitions and labor-time records. The following schedule shows the jobs and amounts posted to the job cost sheets:

Job	Date Started	Direct Materials	Direct Labor	Direct Labor Hours
2526	June 1	$ 5,000	$10,000	1,600
2527	June 12	10,000	15,000	1,900
2528	June 15	4,000	7,000	1,300
		$19,000	$32,000	4,800

The factory overhead control account was debited during the month for actual factory overhead expenses of $27,000. On June 11, Job 2526 was completed and delivered to the customer at a markup of 50% on manufacturing cost. On June 24, Job 2527 was completed and transferred to Finished Goods. On June 30, Job 2528 was still in process.

Required:

1. Prepare job cost sheets for Jobs 2526, 2527, and 2528, including factory overhead applied when the job was completed or at the end of the month for partially completed jobs.
2. Prepare journal entries as of June 30 for the following:
   a. Applying factory overhead to production.
   b. Closing the applied factory overhead account.
   c. Closing the factory overhead account.
   d. Transferring the cost of the completed jobs to finished goods.
   e. Recording the cost of the sale and the sale of Job 2526.

P4-16 LO7 **Closing under- and overapplied overhead at year-end**

Plano Products, Inc., had a remaining credit balance of $10,000 in its under- and overapplied factory overhead account at year-end. It also had year-end balances in the following accounts:

Work in Process	$ 25,000
Finished Goods	15,000
Cost of Goods Sold	85,000
Total	$125,000

Required:

1. Prepare the closing entry for the $10,000 of overapplied overhead, assuming that the balance is not considered to be material.
2. Prepare the closing entry for the $10,000 of overapplied overhead, assuming that the balance is considered to be material.

P4-17R **Review Problem for Chapters 1–4**

Chrome-It, Inc., manufactures special chromed parts made to the order and specifications of the customer. It has two production departments, stamping and plating, and two service departments, power and maintenance. In any production department, the job in process is wholly completed before the next job is started.

The company operates on a fiscal year, which ends September 30. Following is the post-closing trial balance as of September 30:

Chrome-It, Inc.
Post-Closing Trial Balance
September 30, 2011

Cash	$ 22,500	
Accounts Receivable	21,700	
Finished Goods	8,750	
Work in Process	3,600	
Materials	15,000	
Prepaid Insurance	4,320	
Factory Building	64,000	
Accum. Depr.—Factory Building		$ 22,500
Machinery and Equipment	38,000	
Accum. Depr.—Machinery and Equipment		16,000
Office Equipment	10,500	
Accum. Depr.—Office Equipment		7,500
Accounts Payable		2,500
FICA Tax Payable		3,120
Federal Unemployment Tax Payable		364
State Unemployment Tax Payable		1,404
Employees Income Tax Payable		5,200
Capital Stock		75,000
Retained Earnings		54,782
	$188,370	$188,370

Additional information:

1. The balance of the materials account represents the following:

Materials	**Units**	**Unit Cost**	**Total**
A	120	$25	$ 3,000
B	320	15	4,800
C	180	30	5,400
Factory Supplies			1,800
			$15,000

The company uses the FIFO method of accounting for all inventories. Material A is used in the stamping department, and materials B and C are used in the plating department.

2. The balance of the work in process account represents the following costs that are applicable to Job 905. (The customer's order is for 1,000 units of the finished product.)

Direct materials	$1,500
Direct labor	1,200
Factory overhead	900
	$3,600

3. The finished goods account reflects the cost of Job 803, which was finished at the end of the preceding month and is awaiting delivery orders from the customer.
4. At the beginning of the year, factory overhead application rates were based on the following data:

	Stamping Dept.	Plating Dept.
Estimated factory overhead for the year	$145,000	$115,000
Estimated direct labor hours for the year	29,000	6,000

In October, the following transactions were recorded:

a. Purchased the following materials and supplies on account:

Material A	1,100 units @ $26
Material B	900 units @ $17
Material C	800 units @ $28
Factory Supplies	$3,200

b. The following materials were issued to the factory:

	Job 905	Job 1001	Job 1002
Material A		600 units	400 units
Material B		400 units	200 units
Material C	200 units	400 units	

Factory Supplies—$2,450

Customers' orders covered by Jobs 1001 and 1002 are for 1,000 and 500 units of finished product, respectively.

c. Factory wages and office, sales, and administrative salaries are paid at the end of each month. The following data, provided from an analysis of labor-time records and salary schedules, will be sufficient for the preparation of the entries to record the payroll. (Assume FICA and federal income tax rates of 8% and 10%, respectively.) Record the company's liability for state and federal unemployment taxes. (Assume rates of 4% and 1%, respectively.) Record the payroll distribution for the month of October.

	Stamping Dept.	Plating Dept.
Job 905	100 hr @ $9	300 hr @ $11
Job 1001	1,200 hr @ $9	300 hr @ $11
Job 1002	800 hr @ $9	

Wages of the supervisors, custodial personnel, etc., totaled $9,500; administrative salaries were $18,300.

d. Miscellaneous factory overhead incurred during October totaled $4,230. Miscellaneous selling and administrative expenses were $1,500. These items as well as the FICA tax and federal income tax withheld for September were paid. (See account balances on the post-closing trial balance for September 30.)

e. Annual depreciation on plant assets is calculated using the following rates:

Factory buildings—5%

Machinery and equipment—20%

Office equipment—20%

f. The balance of the prepaid insurance account represents a three-year premium for a fire insurance policy covering the factory building and machinery. It was paid on the last day of the preceding month and became effective on October 1.

g. The summary of factory overhead prepared from the factory overhead ledger is reproduced here:

Summary of Factory Overhead for October

Transaction	Account	Stamping	Plating	Power	Maintenance	Total
a.	Factory supplies	$ 940.00	$ 750.00	$ 260.00	$ 500.00	$ 2,450.00
b.	Indirect labor	3,780.00	2,860.00	970.00	1,890.00	9,500.00
c.	Payroll taxes	2,948.40	1,229.80	126.10	245.70	4,550.00
d.	Miscellaneous	1,692.00	1,410.00	752.00	376.00	4,230.00
e.	Depreciation	360.00	270.00	90.00	180.00	900.00
f.	Insurance	48.00	40.00	16.00	16.00	120.00
	Total	$9,768.40	$6,559.80	$2,214.10	$3,207.70	$21,750.00

h. The total expenses of the maintenance department are distributed on the basis of floor space occupied by the power department (8,820 sq ft), stamping department (19,500 sq ft), and plating department (7,875 sq ft). The power department expenses are then allocated equally to the stamping and plating departments.

i. After the actual factory overhead expenses have been distributed to the departmental accounts and the applied factory overhead has been recorded and posted, any balances in the departmental accounts are transferred to Under- and Overapplied Overhead.

j. Jobs 905 and 1001 were finished during the month. Job 1002 is still in process at the end of the month.
k. During the month, Jobs 803 and 905 were sold at a markup of 50% on cost.
l. Received $55,500 from customers in payment of their accounts.
m. Checks were issued in the amount of $43,706 for payment of the payroll.

Required:
1. Set up the beginning trial balance in T-accounts.
2. Prepare materials inventory ledger cards and enter October 1 balances.
3. Set up job cost sheets as needed.
4. Record all transactions and related entries for the month of October and post to T-accounts.
5. Prepare a service department expense distribution work sheet for October.
6. At the end of the month:
   a. Analyze the balance in the materials account, the work in process account, and the finished goods account.
   b. Prepare the statement of cost of goods manufactured, income statement, and balance sheet for October 31.

MINI-CASE

LO6

Activity-based Costing

Home Entertainment, Inc., manufactures two types of DVD players: standard and deluxe. It attempts to set selling prices based on a 50% markup on manufacturing costs to cover selling and administrative expenses and to earn an acceptable return for shareholders. Tom Sales, Vice President–Marketing, is confused because the numbers provided by Anne Cash, Controller, indicate that standard DVD players should be priced at $150 per unit and deluxe DVD players at $300 per unit. The competition is selling comparable models for $145 and $525, respectively.

Sales informs Cash that there must be something wrong with the job costing system. He had recently attended a seminar where the speaker stated that "All production costs are not a function of how many units are produced, or of how many labor hours, labor dollars, or machine hours are expended." He knows that the company uses direct labor dollars as its only cost allocation base. Tom thinks that perhaps this explains why the product costs and, therefore selling prices, are so different from those of the competitors.

Currently, the costs per unit are determined as follows:

	Standard	Deluxe
Direct materials	$ 30.00	$ 50.00
Direct labor	17.50	37.50
Factory overhead (300% of direct labor $)	52.50	112.50
Manufacturing cost per unit	$100.00	$200.00

Factory overhead is currently applied using a plantwide rate based on direct labor cost. This year's rate was computed as follows:

Budgeted factory overhead:	
Direct labor support	$ 300,000
Machine support	400,000
Setup costs	200,000
Design costs	100,000
Total	$1,000,000

Budgeted direct labor cost is $333,333.

Budgeted factory overhead rate = $1,000,000/$333,333 = 300% of direct labor dollars

Cash, knowing that you had recently studied activity-based costing in your cost accounting course, employs you as a consultant to determine what effect its usage would have on the product costs. You first gathered the following data:

	Standard	Deluxe	Total
Units produced	10,000	2,000	12,000
Direct labor hours	60,000	40,000	100,000
Machine hours	30,000	20,000	50,000
Machine setups	200	800	1,000
Design changes	50	200	250

Required:

1. From the data that you gathered, determine the best allocation base for each of the four components of factory overhead.
2. Compute an overhead rate for each of the four components.
3. Determine the new unit cost for standard and deluxe models using activity-based costing.
4. Why are the product costs so dramatically different when activity-based costing is used?
5. Would Home Entertainment's selling prices be closer to those of the competition if activity-based costing were used?

INTERNET EXERCISE

Activity-based Costing

Go to the companion Web site at www.cengage.com/accounting/vanderbeck and click on the link to **Activity-based costing** from Economist.com.[4]

LO6

0 "Activity-based costing," www.economist.com (viewed 7/12/2009).

Required:

Answer the following questions based on the article:

1. If two activities use the same amount of direct costs, will they also consume approximately the same amount of overhead costs? Explain with an example.
2. As new technologies make it easier for firms to customize products, will activity-based costing become more or less important?
3. Name four activities that "purchasing" could be subdivided into for the purpose of allocating costs in an activity-based costing system.
4. Has activity-based costing been consistently popular since its introduction in the 1980s?
5. What did Kaplan say were the only two questions that needed to be answered in applying time-driven activity-based costing?

CHAPTER 5

Process Cost Accounting—General Procedures

Learning Objectives

After studying this chapter, you should be able to:

LO1 Recognize the differences between job order and process cost accounting systems.

LO2 Compute unit costs in a process cost system.

LO3 Assign costs to inventories, using equivalent units of production with the average cost method.

LO4 Prepare a cost of production summary and journal entries for one department with no beginning inventory.

LO5 Prepare a cost of production summary and journal entries for one department with beginning inventory.

LO6 Prepare a cost of production summary and journal entries for multiple departments with no beginning inventory.

LO7 Prepare a cost of production summary and journal entries for multiple departments with beginning inventory.

LO8 Prepare a cost of production summary with a change in the prior department's unit transfer cost.

Fenway Cola, Inc., manufactures 2-liter bottles of a carbonated beverage in a continuous production manufacturing process. Fenway's only in-house financial person is Michael Lowell, a bookkeeper with limited formal accounting education. To determine the unit cost per bottle for inventory costing purposes, Michael adds all of the materials, labor, and overhead costs for the period, and then divides that total by the number of filled and unfilled bottles produced.

Davida Ortiz, Vice President–Marketing, uses the unit cost figures to determine a selling price, and based on her perceptions, the cost figures are lower than would be expected, even with the current efficient manufacturing operations.

Why might the unit cost figures actually be higher than Michael's calculations? The answer lies in the computation of the number of bottles of cola manufactured. The unfilled bottles should not be given the same weight as the finished bottles in computing the number of units of production. This chapter introduces the concept of "equivalent units of production," an understanding of which would enable Michael to obtain a more accurate unit cost per bottle. The Ethics Mini-Case at the end of this chapter indicates how an incorrect computation of equivalent units of production can affect employee compensation.

Cost accounting provides management with accurate information about the cost of manufacturing a product. The type of cost accounting system a business uses depends on the nature of its manufacturing operations. The preceding chapters focused on the job order cost system. Chapters 5 and 6 focus on procedures applicable to a process cost system.

Comparison of Basic Cost Systems

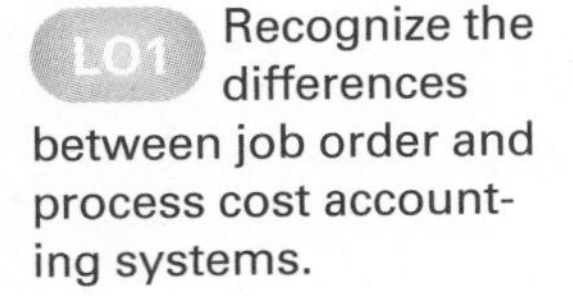

Recognize the differences between job order and process cost accounting systems.

As explained in Chapter 1, a **job order cost system** is appropriate when differentiated products or services are provided on a special-order basis. A **process cost system** is used when goods or services of a similar nature are provided.

The focal point of a job order cost system is the *job*. The costs of materials, labor, and overhead are accumulated for each job and are divided by the number of units produced to determine the cost per unit. The primary objective of job order costing is to determine the cost of producing each job completed during the period and the cost that has been incurred to date on each unfinished job. Management uses this information for inventory valuation as well as for planning and controlling operations. The focus of a process cost system is the **cost center** to which costs are assigned. It is usually a department, but it could be a process or an operation. Costs accumulated by a cost center are divided by the number of units produced in that cost center to compute the cost per unit. The primary objectives, like that of the job order cost system, are to compute the unit cost of the products completed and the cost to be assigned to the ending work in process inventory.

Many of the procedures utilized for job order cost accounting also apply to process cost accounting. The main difference in the two methods is the manner in which costs are accumulated. Examples of industries and companies within industries that would use process costing include: Clothing (**Levi Strauss**); Beverages (**Coca-Cola**); Food (**General Mills**); Petroleum (**ExxonMobil**); and Pharmaceuticals (**Merck & Co.**). The more homogeneous the products that a firm produces, the more apt it is to use process costing. For example, most firms in the food industry and the textile industry use process costing, whereas furniture and fixtures producers, as well as makers of computers and machinery, use job order costing because of their diversified product lines.

Note that service firms may also use process costing. For example, if **Southwest Airlines** wants to know its cost per passenger mile—the cost to move one passenger one mile—it would use process costing and divide its systemwide costs by the total number of passenger miles.

Materials and Labor Costs

Under a job order cost system, the costs of materials and labor, as determined from the summaries of materials requisitions and labor-time records, are charged to specific jobs or orders. Under a process cost system, the costs of materials and labor are charged directly to the departments in which they are incurred. Indirect materials, however, such as custodial supplies for the factory, and indirect labor, such as the salary of the plant manager, that cannot be directly associated with a particular department are charged to Factory Overhead.

A process cost system requires less clerical effort than a job order cost system, because costs are charged to a few departments rather than to many jobs. For example, in a process cost system, detailed labor-time records for an employee who only works in one department are not needed because the **cost object** (the item that you want to know the cost of) is the individual department where that employee works. By contrast, in a job order cost system, if a direct laborer works on several different jobs, the total hours worked must be traced to the individual jobs worked.

Other than these limited differences, the procedures for acquiring, controlling, accounting for, and paying for materials and labor are similar in both systems. At the end of each month, the materials requisitions summary provides the data for the journal entry debiting Work in Process for direct materials, debiting Factory Overhead for indirect materials, and crediting Materials. Similarly, the labor cost summary provides the data for the journal entry debiting Work in Process for direct labor, debiting Factory Overhead for indirect labor, and crediting Payroll.

Factory Overhead Costs

In a process cost system, overhead costs are accumulated from the various journals in the same manner as in a job order cost system. The actual costs for the period are collected in a general ledger control account to which postings are made from the appropriate journals. The control account is supported by a subsidiary ledger, which consists of factory overhead analysis sheets that show the detailed allocation of costs to the departments. At the end of the month, based on the data reflected in the analysis sheets, the total actual factory overhead is distributed to the departmentalized overhead accounts.

Application of Factory Overhead. In a job order cost system, overhead is applied to the jobs through predetermined rates. The use of predetermined rates is also common in a process cost system, but overhead is applied to departments rather than to jobs. As in the job order cost system, the amount of overhead applied is calculated by multiplying the predetermined rate by the selected allocation base. The base may be direct labor cost, direct labor hours, machine hours, or any other method that will equitably distribute overhead to the departments in proportion to the benefit received. Any under- or overapplied overhead at the end of the period is treated in the same manner as discussed in Chapter 4.

Product Cost in a Process Cost System

A basic principle established in comparing the two cost systems is that in a process cost system, all costs of manufacturing are charged to production departments, either directly or indirectly. The unit cost in each department

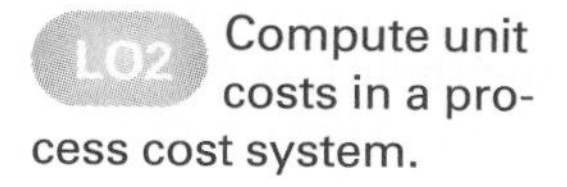

Compute unit costs in a process cost system.

is calculated by dividing the total cost charged to the department by the number of units produced during the period. The total cost of each unit finished equals the combined unit costs of all departments used in the manufacture of the product.

Nondepartmentalized Factory

When the factory is operated as a single department producing a single product in a continuous output, the process cost system is relatively simple. The costs of operating the factory are summarized at the end of each accounting period. Then the total costs incurred are divided by the quantity of units produced to calculate the cost of each unit manufactured during the period.

The following cost of production summary illustrates this procedure:

Materials	$ 50,000
Labor	75,000
Factory overhead	35,000
Total cost of production	$160,000
Unit output for the period	40,000 units
Unit cost for the period	$ 4.00*

*$160,000 ÷ 40,000 units = $4

Departmentalized Factory

Generally, a company has several production and service departments. Products accumulate costs as they pass through each successive production department. Departments record costs according to the following procedure: (1) the costs of materials, labor, and factory overhead directly identifiable with a department, are charged to the department; (2) the costs of the factory service departments, such as maintenance and human resources, are allocated to the production departments; and (3) the costs added by prior production departments are carried over to successive production departments. The unit cost within a department is calculated by dividing the total costs by the number of units produced during the period. Figure 5-1 illustrates the accumulation of production costs in two departments for Fenway Cola, a company that makes and bottles a carbonated beverage.

Work in Process Inventories

LO3 Assign costs to inventories, using equivalent units of production with the average cost method.

If there is no work in process at the end of an accounting period, calculating the unit cost using a process cost system is a simple procedure: merely divide the total production cost incurred for the period by the number of units produced. Departments, however, often have ending work in process. The calculation of the degree of completion of unfinished work in process presents one of the biggest challenges in process costing.

Figure 5-1 Production Process and Cost Flows

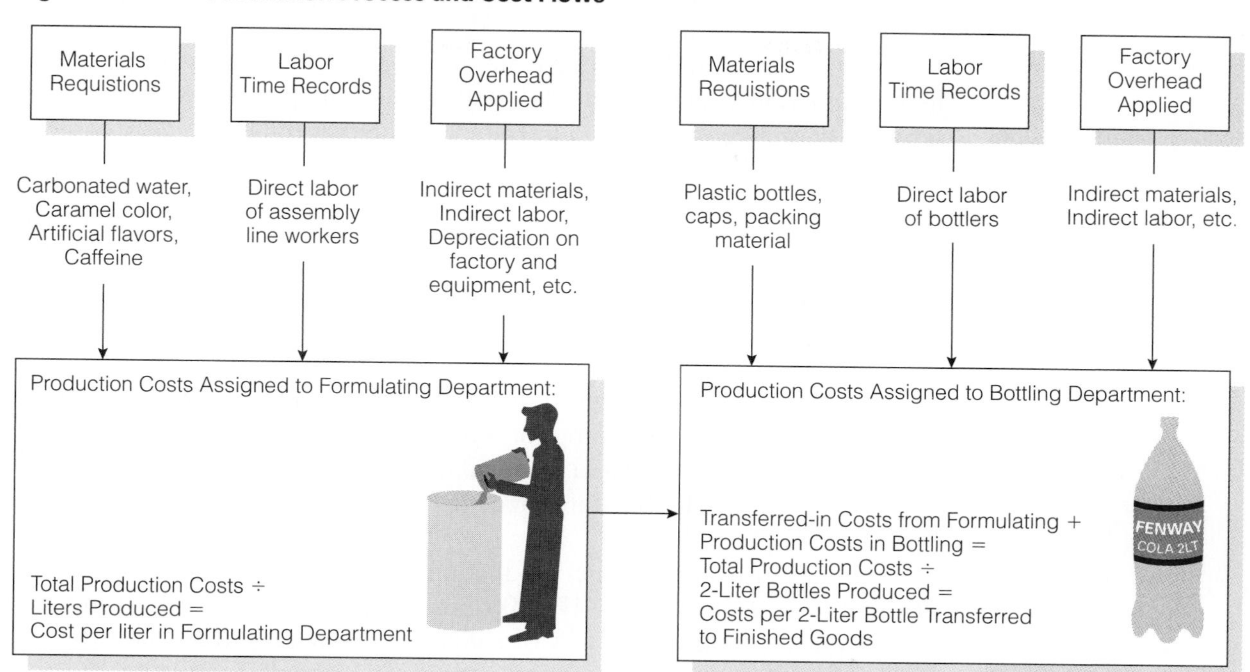

Normally, a factory will have units in varying stages of completion such as:

1. Units started in a prior period and completed during the current period.
2. Units started and finished during the current period.
3. Units started during the current period but not finished by the end of the period.

Because some materials, labor, and overhead may have been applied to each of the unfinished units, such charges cannot be ignored in computing the unit costs. Consideration must be given not only to the number of items finished during the period but also the units in process at the beginning and at the end of the period. The primary task is allocating total cost between (1) units finished during the period and (2) units still in process at the end of the period.

Two procedures are commonly used for assigning costs to the inventories: the **average cost method** and the **first-in, first-out (FIFO) method**. The average cost method is discussed and illustrated in the remainder of this chapter. Chapter 6 explains the first-in, first-out method.

Under the average cost method, the cost of the work in process at the beginning of the period is added to the production costs incurred in the current period. Average unit cost for the period is then calculated by dividing the total costs (costs in beginning inventory plus costs added this period) by the total equivalent production. **Equivalent production** represents the number of whole units that could have been completed during a period, given the amount of work that was performed. For example, if 1,000 units were 50% completed, that would represent the equivalent amount of work to fully complete 500 units. Therefore, calculating equivalent production requires that the ending work in process be restated in terms of completed units. To illustrate, assume that the production costs of a department during a given period are as follows:

Materials	$12,000
Labor	18,000
Factory overhead	6,000
Total cost of production	$36,000

If 18,000 units are produced during the period and no work in process exists either at the beginning or end of the period, the unit cost of production is easily calculated to be $2 ($36,000 ÷ 18,000), and $36,000 of inventory cost would be transferred to Finished Goods from Work in Process.

Assume, instead, that the production report for the period shows no beginning work in process, 17,000 units that were completed during the period, and an ending inventory of 2,000 units. The production cost for the period, $36,000, must be allocated between the goods completed and the goods still in process at the end of the period. What portion of the total production cost should be charged to the 17,000 units that were completed during the period and to the 2,000 units in ending work in process?

If the 2,000 units are almost finished, more cost should be assigned to them than if they had just been started in process. To make an accurate measurement, the stage of completion of the units still in process must be considered. **Stage of completion** represents the fraction or percentage of materials, labor, and overhead costs of a completed unit that has been applied to goods that have not been completed by the end of the month. The department manager estimates the stage of completion. The possibility of error is minimized because the manager usually has the expertise to make reliable estimates. In the event that the product is of a highly technical nature, the engineering staff can assist in determining the percentage of completion.

At the end of the month, the department manager submits a **production report** showing the following:

1. Number of units in the beginning work in process.
2. Number of units completed.
3. Number of units in the ending work in process and their estimated stage of completion.

Assume that the 2,000 units in the ending work in process inventory are one-half complete. If materials, labor, and overhead are applied evenly throughout the process, one-half of the total cost for completing 2,000 units can be applied to these units. Expressed in another way, the cost to

Figure 5-2 **Calculation of Equivalent Units**

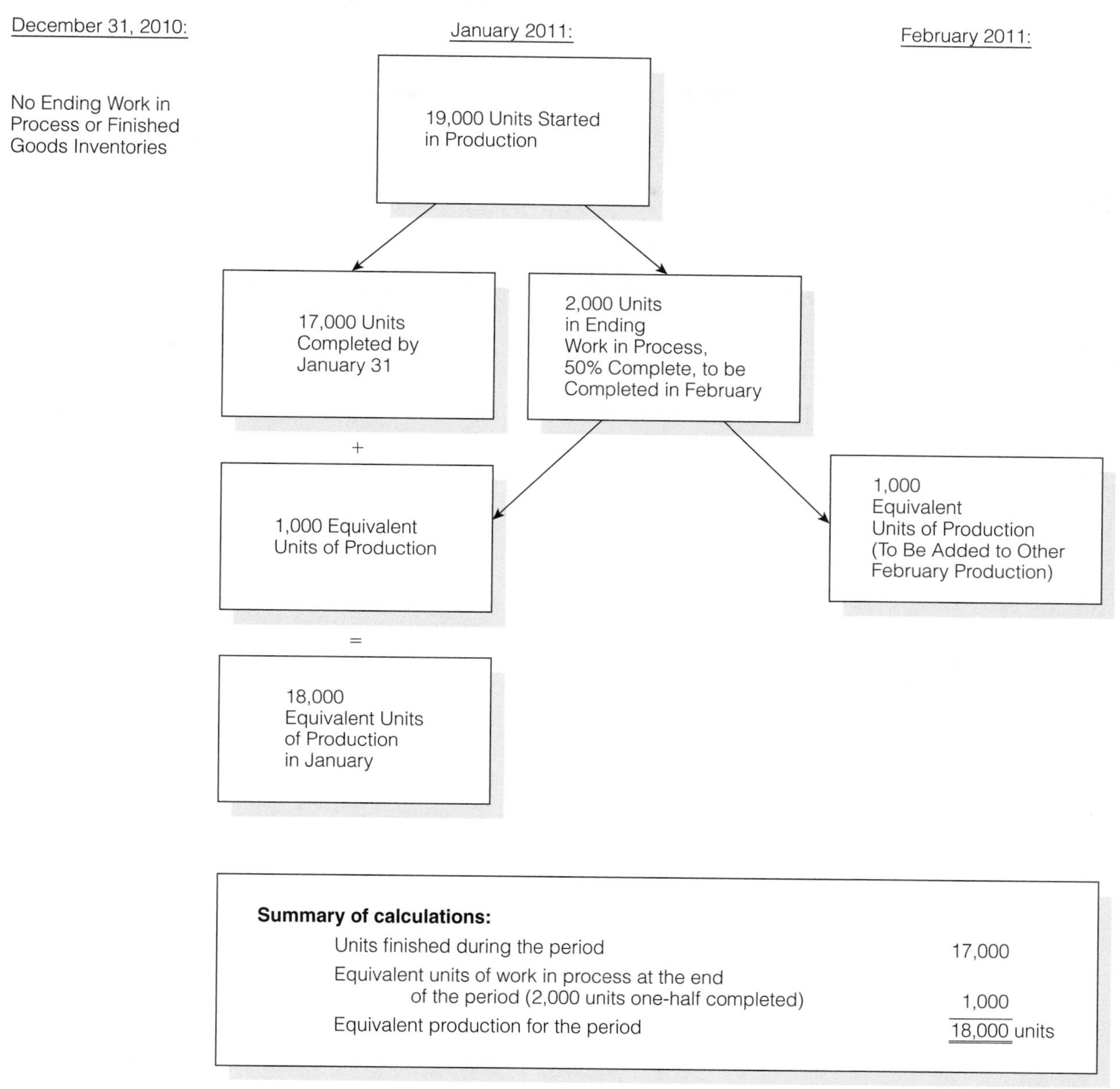

bring these 2,000 units to the halfway point of completion is equivalent to the cost of fully completing 1,000 units. Therefore, in terms of equivalent production, 2,000 units 50% complete equal 1,000 units fully completed. The calculation of equivalent units for the situation described above is illustrated in Figure 5-2.

The cost per equivalent unit, in the previous example, is calculated by dividing the total cost of production by the equivalent units, as shown below.

$$\$36,000 \div 18,000 = \$2 \text{ per equivalent unit}$$

The inventory cost at the end of the month can now be calculated as follows:

Transferred to finished goods (17,000 units at $2)	$34,000
Work in process (2,000 units × 1/2 × $2)	2,000
Total production costs accounted for	$36,000

Cost of Production Summary—One Department, No Beginning Inventory

LO4 Prepare a cost of production summary and journal entries for one department with no beginning inventory.

In a process cost system, the reporting of production and related costs in each department involves the following:

1. Accumulating costs for which the department is accountable.
2. Calculating equivalent production for the period.
3. Computing the unit cost for the period.
4. Summarizing the disposition of the production costs.

These data are reported on a **cost of production summary** that presents the necessary information for inventory valuation and serves as a source for summary journal entries that are posted to the work in process account for each department, as illustrated in Figure 5-3. To illustrate a cost of production summary, assume that Cleveland Can Company manufactures

Figure 5-3 **Relationship of Cost of Production Summaries to Cost Flows**

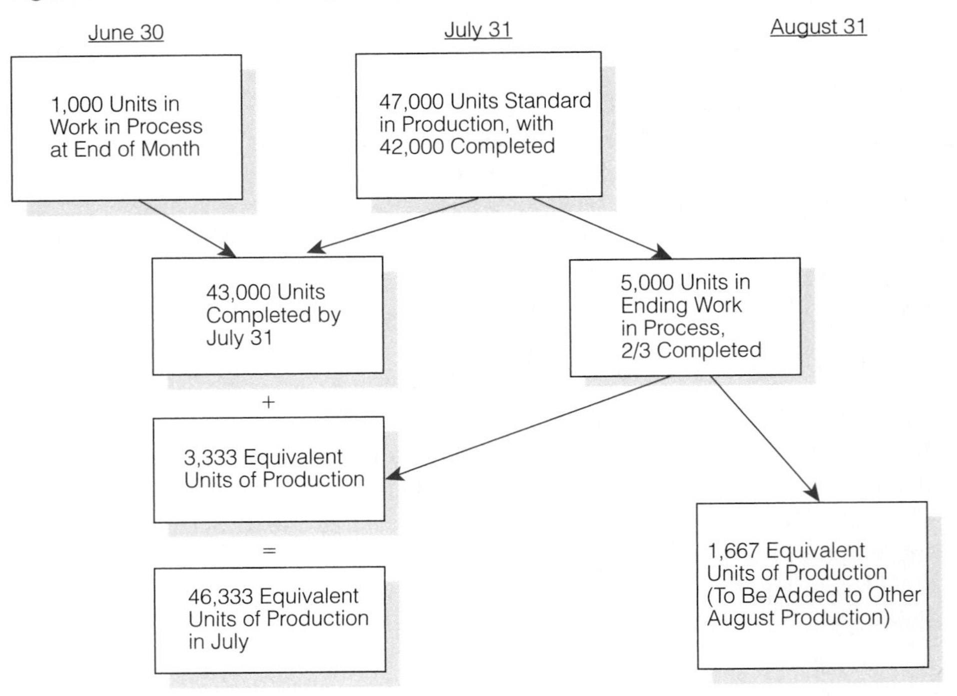

Figure 5-4 **Production Report, January 31**

PRODUCTION REPORT

For Month Ending January 31, 2011

In process, beginning of month none
Finished during the month 49,000 units
In process, end of month 2,000 units
Estimated stage of completion of work in process, end of month 1/2

Remarks

R.L.B.
Supervisor

aluminum cans on a continuous basis in a single department. The small factory, which had no inventory on January 1, places finished goods in stock to be withdrawn as orders are received. At the end of January, the first month of operation for the company, the factory supervisor submits the January production report that appears in Figure 5-4. The estimate of the stage of completion indicates that the cans in process at the end of the month were, on average, one-half completed.

After receiving the production report, the accountant begins the preparation of the following cost of production summary by collecting the period's production costs from summaries of materials requisitions, payroll, and factory overhead analysis sheets. The units in process are then converted to equivalent units. The estimate that the 2,000 cans in process are one-half completed means that one-half the total cost of the materials, labor, and factory overhead needed to produce 2,000 units has been incurred. The equivalent of 2,000 units in process, one-half completed, is 1,000 completed units. Therefore, the cost incurred to partially complete 2,000 units is considered to be equivalent to the total cost of fully producing 1,000 units. The work required producing 49,000 fully completed units and 2,000 units one-half completed is equivalent to the work required to produce 50,000 fully completed units, as illustrated in the following cost of production summary:

Cleveland Can Company
Cost of Production Summary
For the Month Ended January 31, 2011

Cost of production for month:	
Materials	$ 50,000
Labor	30,000
Factory overhead	20,000
Total costs to be accounted for	**$100,000**

Unit output for month:		
Finished during month		49,000
Equivalent units of work in process, end of month (2,000 units, one-half completed)		1,000
Total equivalent production		50,000
Unit cost for month:		
Materials ($50,000 ÷ 50,000 units)		$ 1.00
Labor ($30,000 ÷ 50,000 units)		0.60
Factory overhead ($20,000 ÷ 50,000 units)		0.40
Total		$ 2.00
Inventory costs:		
Cost of goods finished during month (49,000 × $2)		$ 98,000
Cost of work in process, end of month:		
Materials (2,000 × 1/2 × $1)	$1,000	
Labor (2,000 × 1/2 × $0.60)	600	
Factory overhead (2,000 × 1/2 × $0.40)	400	2,000
Total production costs accounted for		**$100,000**

At the end of the month, the following journal entries record the factory operations for January:

Jan. 31	Work in Process	50,000	
	Materials		50,000
	Issued direct materials into production.		
	Work in Process	30,000	
	Payroll		30,000
	Direct labor used in production.		
	Work in Process	20,000	
	Factory Overhead		20,000
	Applied factory overhead to production.		
	Factory Overhead	20,000	
	Various Accounts (Accumulated Depreciation, Prepaid Insurance, Accrued Taxes, Accounts Payable)		20,000
	Recorded actual factory overhead for the period. (Note that, for the ease of illustration, there is no under- or overapplied overhead and a single account, Factory Overhead, is used to record both actual [debit] and applied [credit] overhead.)		

After preparing the cost of production summary, the accountant can make the following entry for the cost of the goods completed during the period:

Jan. 31	Finished Goods	98,000	
	Work in Process		98,000

After posting these entries, the work in process account has a debit balance of $2,000, representing the cost of the work in process on January 31, shown as follows:

Work in Process

Jan. 31	50,000	Jan. 31	98,000
	30,000		
	20,000		
	100,000		
2,000			

The January statement of the cost of goods manufactured can now be prepared as follows:

Cleveland Can Company
Statement of Cost of Goods Manufactured
For the Month Ended January 31, 2011

Materials	$ 50,000
Labor	30,000
Factory overhead	20,000
Total	$100,000
Less work in process inventory, January 31	2,000
Cost of goods manufactured during the month	$ 98,000

Cost of Production Summary—One Department, Beginning Inventory

LO5 Prepare a cost of production summary and journal entries for one department with beginning inventory.

At the end of February, the second month of operations for Cleveland Can Company, the factory supervisor submits the February production report shown in Figure 5-5. The cost of production summary for February, assuming materials, labor, and factory overhead costs of $70,000, $42,000, and $28,000 respectively, is prepared as follows:

Cleveland Can Company
Cost of Production Summary
For the Month Ended February 28, 2011

Cost of work in process, beginning of month:*		
Materials	$ 1,000	
Labor	600	
Factory overhead	400	$ 2,000
Cost of production for month:		
Materials	$70,000	
Labor	42,000	
Factory overhead	28,000	140,000
Total costs to be accounted for		**$142,000**
Unit output for month:		
Finished during month		69,000
Equivalent units of work in process, end of month (6,000 units, one-third completed)		2,000
Total equivalent production		71,000

Figure 5-5 **Production Report, February 28**

PRODUCTION REPORT
For Month Ending February 28, 2011

In process, beginning of month	2,000 units
Finished during the month	69,000 units
In process, end of month	6,000 units
Estimated stage of completion of work in process, end of month	1/3

Unit cost for month:		
Materials [($1,000 + $70,000) ÷ 71,000]		$ 1.00
Labor [($600 + $42,000) ÷ 71,000]		0.60
Factory overhead [($400 + $28,000) ÷ 71,000]		0.40
Total		$ 2.00
Inventory costs:		
Cost of goods finished during month (69,000 × $2)		$138,000
Cost of work in process, end of month:		
Materials (6,000 × 1/3 × $1)	$ 2,000	
Labor (6,000 × 1/3 × $0.60)	1,200	
Factory overhead (6,000 × 1/3 × $0.40)	800	4,000
Total production costs accounted for		**$142,000**

*The beginning inventory in February was the ending work in process inventory for the month of January.

All costs incurred or assigned must be accounted for. Therefore, the cost of the ending work in process in January, which is the beginning inventory in February, is added to the total costs incurred during the month of February. The calculation of unit output for the month includes the units finished during the month and the equivalent units in process at the end of the current month. The calculation of equivalent units is illustrated in Figure 5-6. The fact that one-half of the work had been completed on 2,000 units in the prior month does not have to be considered separately in this calculation because the dollar cost of that work is added to the current month's costs for the purpose of calculating unit costs. This procedure is the identifying characteristic of the average costing method for process costing.

From the data developed on the cost of production summary, the following entry can now be made for the cost of the goods completed during the period:

Work in Process

Jan. 31	50,000	Jan. 31	98,000
	30,000		
	20,000		
	100,000		
2,000			

Work in Process

Feb. 28	70,000	Feb. 28	138,000
	42,000		
	28,000		
	240,000		*236,000*
4,000			

Figure 5-6 **Calculation of Equivalent Units with Beginning Work in Process**

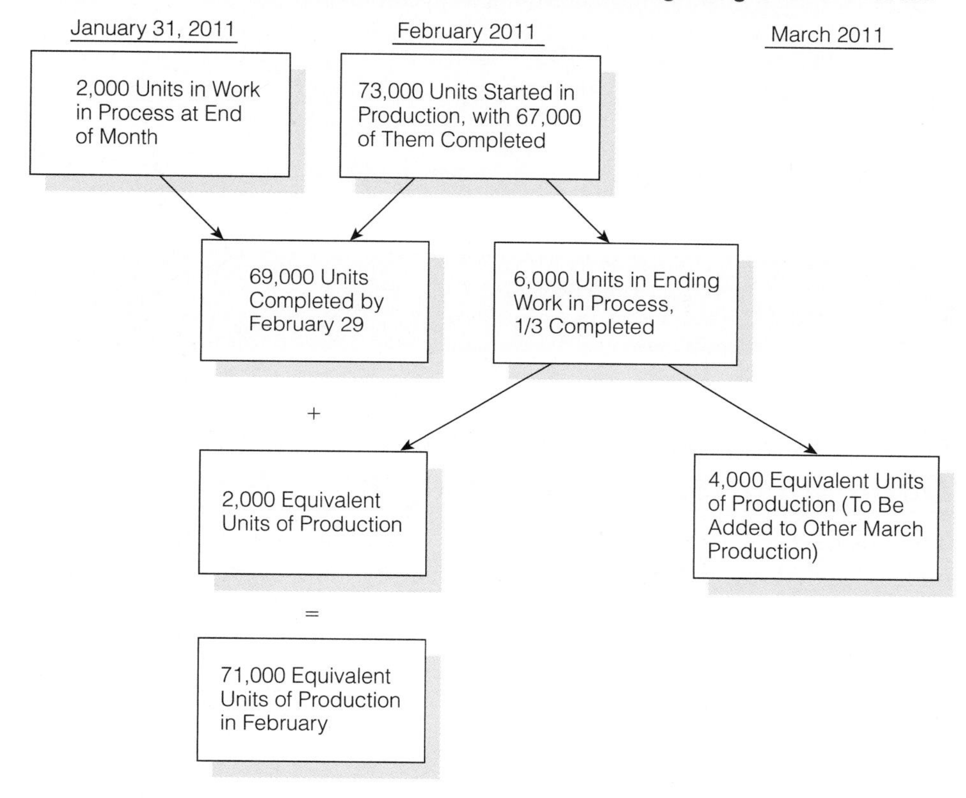

After posting this entry and the entries for the month's production costs, the work in process account has a debit balance of $4,000, as shown:

Feb. 28	Finished Goods	138,000	
	Work in Process		138,000

The following statement of the cost of goods manufactured can now be prepared:

Cleveland Can Company
Statement of Cost of Goods Manufactured
For the Month Ended February 28, 2011

Materials	$ 70,000
Labor	42,000
Factory overhead	28,000

Total	$140,000
Add work in process inventory, February 1	2,000
Total	$142,000
Less work in process inventory, February 28	4,000
Cost of goods manufactured during the month	$138,000

Recall and Review 1

Xanadu Company had 400 units in Work in Process at the beginning of the month. During the month, 14,600 units were started in production, 13,400 of which, along with the beginning work in process, were completed by the end of the month. The uncompleted units were in ending inventory, one-fourth complete. The equivalent units of production for the month were ________.

(After working this exercise, see page 269 for the solution.)

You should now be able to work the following:
Questions 1–11; Exercises 5-1 to 5-6; Problems 5-1 to 5-3; Self-Study Problem 1; and the Mini-Case (Ethics).

Cost of Production Summary—Multiple Departments, No Beginning Inventory

LO0 Prepare a cost of production summary and journal entries for multiple departments with no beginning inventory.

The business of Cleveland Can Company continued to grow until management decided to departmentalize the factory and reorganize the cost records. Accordingly, on January 1 of the following year, the factory was divided into three departments as follows:

Blanking

Forming

Finishing

Materials are placed into production in the Blanking Department, where direct labor and factory overhead are added before transfer to the Forming Department. More materials are added in Forming, and additional processing costs are incurred before transfer to Finishing. In the Finishing Department, coatings are added to the cans before they emerge as finished goods.

Separate control accounts are maintained in the general ledger to record the costs of operating each department. Departmental expense analysis sheets are used to record the manufacturing expenses incurred. Production reports are prepared for each department for January. There are no beginning inventories of work in process in any department. The production report for Blanking is shown in Figure 5-7.

After receiving the production report from the manager of Blanking, the accountant prepares the following cost of production summary. Journal

Figure 5-7 Production Report, Blanking

PRODUCTION REPORT	
For Month Ending	January 31, 2012
Dept.	Blanking
In process, beginning of period	none
Stage of completion	
Placed in process during period	37,000 units
Received from dept. ______ during period	
Transferred to dept. Forming during period	27,000 units
Transferred to stockroom during period	none
In process, end of period	10,000 units
Stage of completion	1/2

entries are then made from the cost of production summary to record the operations of the department and to transfer costs to Forming.

Cleveland Can Company
Cost of Production Summary—Blanking
For the Month Ended January 31, 2012

Cost of production for month:		
Materials		$160,000
Labor		86,400
Factory overhead		73,600
Total costs to be accounted for		**$320,000**
Unit output for month:		
Finished and transferred to Forming during month		27,000
Equivalent units of work in process, end of month (10,000 units, one-half completed)		5,000
Total equivalent production		32,000
Unit cost for month:		
Materials ($160,000 ÷ 32,000 units)		$ 5.00
Labor ($86,400 ÷ 32,000 units)		2.70
Factory overhead ($73,600 ÷ 32,000 units)		2.30
Total		$ 10.00
Inventory costs:		
Cost of goods finished and transferred to Forming during month (27,000 × $10.00)		$270,000
Cost of work in process, end of month:		
Materials (10,000 × 1/2 × $5.00)	$25,000	
Labor (10,000 × 1/2 × $2.70)	13,500	
Factory overhead (10,000 × 1/2 × $2.30)	11,500	50,000
Total production costs accounted for		**$320,000**

Note that the costs accumulated in the department are transferred to the next department along with the units completed during the period. Thus, costs follow the flow of goods through the process.

After posting the usual end-of-month entries, the work in process account for Blanking has a debit balance of $50,000, as shown below. The balance represents the cost of the partially completed ending inventory of 10,000 units.

Work in Process—Blanking

Jan. 31	160,000	Jan. 31	270,000
	86,400		
	73,600		
50,000	*320,000*		

The only difference in procedure between this example and the one for a single-department factory is that the goods completed in Blanking are transferred to Forming for further processing rather than being transferred to the stockroom as finished goods.

The production report for Forming is shown in Figure 5-8. Note that as the goods flow through the manufacturing process, the units transferred to Forming and their related costs are treated as completed products in Blanking, but they are considered to be raw materials that will be added at the beginning of the processing operation in Forming. The transferred cost of the units includes the costs of materials, labor, and factory overhead incurred in Blanking. The individual cost elements, however, are combined and transferred in total to Forming.

In reviewing the cost of production summary for Forming, note that the calculation of unit cost for the month in Forming takes into consideration only those costs incurred for materials, labor, and factory overhead

Figure 5-8 Production Report, Forming

PRODUCTION REPORT

For Month Ending January 31, 2012

Dept. Forming

In process, beginning of period		none
Stage of completion		
Placed in process during period		none
Received from dept. Blanking	during period	27,000 units
Transferred to dept. Finishing	during period	22,000 units
Transferred to stockroom during period		none
In process, end of period		5,000 units
Stage of completion		2/5

during the month and the equivalent units produced in the department. The transferred-in costs and units from the prior department are not included in the computations. In determining the cost transferred to Finishing, however, the prior department costs, along with Forming's production costs, must be considered. Also, in calculating the ending work in process valuation, the full cost of $10 per unit from Blanking is attached to the 5,000 units still in process in Forming. The transferred-in units have been fully completed by Blanking, while only a fraction of the cost of additional work performed by Forming, based on the stage of completion, is considered.

Cleveland Can Company
Cost of Production Summary—Forming
For the Month Ended January 31, 2012

Cost of goods received from Blanking during month (27,000 units × $10.00)			$270,000
Cost of production for month—Forming:			
Materials		$ 12,000	
Labor		30,000	
Factory overhead		18,000	60,000
Total costs to be accounted for			**$330,000**
Unit output for month:			
Finished and transferred to Finishing during month			22,000
Equivalent units of work in process, end of month (5,000 units, two-fifths completed)			2,000
Total equivalent production			24,000
Unit cost for month—Forming:			
Materials ($12,000 ÷ 24,000 units)			$ 0.50
Labor ($30,000 ÷ 24,000 units)			1.25
Factory overhead ($18,000 ÷ 24,000 units)			0.75
Total			$ 2.50
Inventory costs:			
Cost of goods finished and transferred to Finishing during month:			
Cost in Blanking (22,000 × $10.00)		$220,000	
Cost in Forming (22,000 × 2.50)		55,000	275,000
Cost of work in process, end of month:			
Cost in Blanking (5,000 × $10.00)		$ 50,000	
Cost in Forming:			
Materials (5,000 × 2/5 × $0.50)	$1,000		
Labor (5,000 × 2/5 × $1.25)	2,500		
Factory overhead (5,000 × 2/5 × $0.75)	1,500	5,000	55,000
Total production costs accounted for			**$330,000**

After posting the end-of-month entries, the work in process account for Forming has a debit balance of $55,000, as shown on the following page.

Work in Process—Forming

Jan. 31	12,000	Jan. 31	275,000
	30,000		
	18,000		
	270,000		
55,000	*330,000*		

Figure 5-9 Production Report, Finishing

PRODUCTION REPORT

For Month Ending January 31, 2011

Dept. Finishing

In process, beginning of period	none
Stage of completion	
Placed in process during period	none
Received from dept. Forming during period	22,000 units
Transferred to dept. during period	
Transferred to stockroom during period	20,000 units
In process, end of period	2,000 units
Stage of completion	1/2

The production report for Finishing is shown in Figure 5-9. The cost of production summary for Finishing, shown below, is prepared in a manner similar to the Forming summary. Note that the inventory costs section of the report shows the *cost of goods finished and transferred to finished goods during the month*. The $16.50 unit cost of goods finished and transferred represents the total unit cost of the goods through all of the departments. The detailed unit cost of completed goods, department by department, shows the accumulation of the total unit cost.

Cleveland Can Company
Cost of Production Summary—Finishing
For the Month Ended January 31, 2012

Cost of goods received from Forming during month (22,000 units × $12.50)		$275,000
Cost of production for month—Finishing:		
Materials	$31,500	
Labor	23,100	
Factory overhead	29,400	84,000
Total costs to be accounted for		**$359,000**
Unit output for month:		
Finished and transferred to finished goods during month		20,000
Equivalent units of work in process, end of month (2,000 units, one-half completed)		1,000
Total equivalent production		21,000

Unit cost for month—Finishing:			
Materials ($31,500 ÷ 21,000 units)			$ 1.50
Labor ($23,100 ÷ 21,000 units)			1.10
Factory overhead ($29,400 ÷ 21,000 units)			1.40
Total			$ 4.00
Inventory costs:			
Cost of goods finished and transferred to finished goods during month:			
Cost in Blanking (20,000 × $10.00)			$200,000
Cost in Forming (20,000 × $2.50)			50,000
Cost in Finishing (20,000 × $4.00)			80,000
(20,000 × $16.50)			$330,000
Cost of work in process, end of month:			
Cost in Blanking (2,000 × $10.00)		$20,000	
Cost in Forming (2,000 × $2.50)		5,000	
Cost in Finishing:			
Materials (2,000 × 1/2 × $1.50)	$1,500		
Labor (2,000 × 1/2 × $1.10)	1,100		
Factory overhead (2,000 × 1/2 × $1.40)	1,400	4,000	29,000
Total production costs accounted for			$359,000

After posting the end-of-month entries, the work in process account for Finishing has a debit balance of $29,000.

Work in Process—Finishing

Jan. 31	31,500	Jan. 31	330,000
	23,100		
	29,400		
	275,000		
	359,000		
29,000			

As a means of classifying and summarizing the factory operations for January, the "Summary" portion of the work sheet in Figure 5-10 provides the information for the following statement of cost of goods manufactured:

Cleveland Can Company
Statement of Cost of Goods Manufactured
For the Month Ended January 31, 2012

Materials	$203,500
Labor	139,500
Factory overhead	121,000
Total	$464,000
Less work in process inventories, January 31	134,000
Cost of goods manufactured during the month	$330,000

Figure 5-10 **Work Sheet, January 31**

	A	B	C	D	E	F
1	**Cleveland Can Company**					
2	**Departmental Cost Work Sheet**					
3	**For the Month Ended January 31, 2012**					
4						
5		**Cost**	**Units**	**Units**	**Amount**	**Amount**
6		**per unit**	**received in**	**transferred**	**charged to**	**credited to**
7	**Analysis**	**transferred**	**department**	**or on hand**	**department**	**department**
8						
9	Blanking:					
10	Started in process		37,000			
11	Costs for month:					
12	Materials				$160,000	
13	Labor				86,400	
14	Factory overhead				73,600	
15	Finished and transferred to Forming	$10.00		27,000		$270,000
16	Closing work in process			10,000		50,000
17	Total		37,000	37,000	$320,000	$320,000
18						
19	Forming:					
20	Received during month from Blanking		27,000		$270,000	
21	Costs added during month:					
22	Materials	0.50			12,000	
23	Labor	1.25			30,000	
24	Factory overhead	0.75			18,000	
25	Finished and transferred to Finishing	$12.50		22,000		$275,000
26	Closing work in process			5,000		55,000
27	Total		27,000	27,000	$330,000	$330,000
28						
29	Finishing:					
30	Received during month from Forming		22,000		$275,000	
31	Costs added during month:					
32	Materials	1.50			31,500	
33	Labor	1.10			23,100	
34	Factory overhead	1.40			29,400	
35	Finished and transferred to stock	$16.50		20,000		$330,000
36	Closing work in process			2,000		29,000
37	Total		22,000	22,000	$359,000	$359,000
38					**Amount**	**Total**
39	Summary:					
40	Materials:					
41	Blanking				$160,000	
42	Forming				12,000	
43	Finishing				31,500	$203,500
44	Labor:					
45	Blanking				$86,400	
46	Forming				30,000	
47	Finishing				23,100	139,500
48	Factory overhead:					
49	Blanking				$73,600	
50	Forming				18,000	
51	Finishing				29,400	121,000
52	Total production costs for January					$464,000
53	Deduct work in process inventory, end of month:					
54	Blanking				$50,000	
55	Forming				55,000	
56	Finishing				29,000	134,000
57						
58	Costs of production, goods fully					
59	manufactured during January					$330,000
60						

At the end of the month, the following journal entries are made:

Jan. 31	Work in Process—Blanking	160,000	
	Work in Process—Forming	12,000	
	Work in Process—Finishing	31,500	
	Factory Overhead*	10,000	
	Materials		213,500

*The amount charged to Factory Overhead for the actual amount of indirect materials is an arbitrary amount chosen for this example to illustrate how the costs are collected and distributed. This amount represents the cost of various supplies issued that could not be charged directly to a department as direct materials.

Jan. 31	Work in Process—Blanking	86,400	
	Work in Process—Forming	30,000	
	Work in Process—Finishing	23,100	
	Factory Overhead**	15,000	
	Payroll		154,500

**Again, the amount charged to the factory overhead control account is an arbitrary amount chosen to illustrate payroll costs, such as the plant manager's salary, that could not be charged directly to any given department as direct labor.

Jan. 31	Work in Process—Blanking	73,600	
	Work in Process—Forming	18,000	
	Work in Process—Finishing	29,400	
	Factory Overhead—Blanking		73,600
	Factory Overhead—Forming		18,000
	Factory Overhead—Finishing		29,400

Note that for ease of illustration, a single factory overhead account is used for each department, with applied overhead recorded as a credit and actual overhead as a debit.

The previous entry charges the applied factory overhead appearing on the cost of production summaries to the work in process control accounts. The amounts are calculated by multiplying a predetermined overhead application rate by the base used for applying overhead to each department, such as labor hours or machine hours. A different base might be used for different departments, so that overhead would be equitably applied according to the benefit each department has received.

Jan. 31	Factory Overhead	90,000	
	Various Accounts (Accumulated Depreciation, Prepaid Insurance, Payroll Taxes)		90,000

The previous entry summarizes several entries made in the general journal to reflect the actual amount of the current month's provision for depreciation, insurance, payroll taxes, and other factory overhead expenses.

Jan. 31	Factory Overhead—Blanking	66,000	
	Factory Overhead—Forming	21,000	
	Factory Overhead—Finishing	28,000	
	Factory Overhead		115,000

The previous entry distributes the actual overhead for the period to the departments. The basis for this entry would be the *factory overhead analysis sheets*, which show in detail the allocation or apportionment of the actual expenses to the various departments based on usage. Note that these actual amounts do not appear on the cost of production summaries, which contain the estimated amounts of factory overhead applied to production. Also note that the credit to Factory Overhead (see previous page) consists of the previously mentioned $10,000 of indirect materials and $15,000 of indirect labor, as well as the other factory overhead of $90,000.

The cost of production summary is used to develop the entries to record the transfer of costs from one department to another and to Finished Goods, as follows:

Jan. 31	Work in Process—Forming	270,000	
	Work in Process—Blanking		270,000
31	Work in Process—Finishing	275,000	
	Work in Process—Forming		275,000
31	Finished Goods	330,000	
	Work in Process—Finishing		330,000

These journal entries are reflected in the following T-accounts. The balances remaining in the work in process accounts are reflected in total on the statement of cost of goods manufactured. The balances in the departmental factory overhead accounts represent under- or overapplied overhead and would usually be carried forward to future months. However, these balances can be transferred to an under- and overapplied factory overhead account. As discussed in previous chapters, these amounts of under- and overapplied overhead would be analyzed to determine whether they are expected normal seasonal variances, or whether they represent inefficiencies that should be corrected.

Work in Process—Blanking

Jan. 31	160,000	Jan. 31	270,000
	86,400		
	73,600		
	320,000		
50,000			

Work in Process—Forming

Jan. 31	12,000	Jan. 31	275,000
	30,000		
	18,000		
	270,000		
	330,000		
55,000			

Work in Process—Finishing

Jan. 31	31,500	Jan. 31	330,000
	23,100		
	29,400		
	275,000		
	359,000		
29,000			

Finished Goods

Jan. 31	330,000		

Factory Overhead

Jan. 31	10,000	Jan. 31	115,000
	15,000		
	90,000		
	115,000		

Materials

	xxx	Jan. 31	213,500

Payroll

	xxx	Jan. 31	154,500

Factory Overhead—Blanking

Jan. 31	66,000	Jan. 31	73,600
		7,600	

Factory Overhead—Forming

Jan. 31	21,000	Jan. 31	18,000
3,000			

Factory Overhead—Finishing

Jan. 31	28,000	Jan. 31	29,400
		1,400	

Recall and Review 2

Without dollar amounts, list the account(s) debited and credited for each of the following types of transactions:

1. Issuance of raw materials and supplies to the factory.________
2. Incurrence of direct and indirect factory labor costs.________
3. Distribution of actual factory overhead costs to individual departments.________
4. Application of factory overhead to individual departments.________

(After working this exercise, see page 269 for the solution.)

You should now be able to work the following:
Questions 12–14; Exercises 5-7 to 5-9; and Problems 5-4 to 5-6.

Cost of Production Summary—Multiple Departments, Beginning Inventory

LO6 Prepare a cost of production summary and journal entries for multiple departments with beginning inventory.

The February production reports submitted by the department supervisors for Cleveland Can Company differ from the January production reports. There are now inventories for work in process in each department at the beginning of the month. After receiving the production reports for February, the accountant prepares a cost of production summary for each department and makes entries to record the operations of each department in the general ledger accounts.

The February production report for Blanking is shown in Figure 5-11. Note that the number of units in process at the beginning of the period *plus* the units placed in process or received from another department during the

Figure 5-11 **Production Report, Blanking, February 28**

PRODUCTION REPORT

For Month Ending February 28, 2012

Dept. Blanking

In process, beginning of period	10,000 units
Stage of completion	1/2
Placed in process during period	34,000 units
Received from dept. ______ during period	none
Transferred to dept. Forming during period	39,000 units
Transferred to stockroom during period	none
In process, end of period	5,000 units
Stage of completion	4/5

period equal the *total number of units* to be accounted for by the department.

In the following cost of production summary for Blanking, the unit cost is determined by adding the cost of beginning work in process from the prior month to the total costs incurred during the current month and dividing by the equivalent units. The prior month's cost of materials is added to the current month's cost of materials, and the total materials cost is divided by the equivalent production for materials. The same procedure is followed for labor and factory overhead. The calculation of unit output for the month takes into consideration all units finished during the month, including those in process at the beginning of the month, plus those units that are still in process at the end of the period.

Cleveland Can Company
Cost of Production Summary—Blanking
For the Month Ended February 28, 2012

Cost of work in process, beginning of month:		
Materials	$ 25,000	
Labor	13,500	
Factory overhead	11,500	$ 50,000
Cost of production for month:		
Materials	$190,000	
Labor	102,600	
Factory overhead	87,400	380,000
Total costs to be accounted for		**$430,000**
Unit output for month:		
Finished and transferred to Forming during month		39,000
Equivalent units of work in process, end of month (5,000 units, four-fifths completed)		4,000
Total equivalent production		43,000

Unit cost for month:		
Materials [($25,000 + $190,000) ÷ 43,000]		$ 5.00
Labor [($13,500 + $102,600) ÷ 43,000]		2.70
Factory overhead [($11,500 + $87,400) ÷ 43,000]		2.30
Total		$ 10.00
Inventory costs:		
Cost of goods finished and transferred to Forming during month (39,000 × $10.00)		$390,000
Cost of work in process, end of month:		
Materials (5,000 × 4/5 × $5.00)	$ 20,000	
Labor (5,000 × 4/5 × $2.70)	10,800	
Factory overhead (5,000 × 4/5 × $2.30)	9,200	40,000
Total production costs accounted for		**$430,000**

At this time, the following journal entry can be made:

Feb. 28	Work in Process—Forming	390,000	
	Work in Process—Blanking		390,000

The work in process account for Blanking now appears as follows:

Work in Process—Blanking

Jan. 31	160,000	Jan. 31	270,000
	86,400		
	73,600		
	320,000		
50,000			
Feb. 28	190,000	Feb. 28	390,000
	102,600		
	87,400		
	700,000		660,000
40,000			

The February production report for Forming is shown in Figure 5-12.

Figure 5-12 Production Report, Forming, February 28

PRODUCTION REPORT

For Month Ending February 28, 2012

Dept. Forming

In process, beginning of period	5,000 units
Stage of completion	2/5
Placed in process during period	none
Received from dept. Blanking during period	39,000 units
Transferred to dept. Finishing during period	41,000 units
Transferred to stockroom during period	none
In process, end of period	3,000 units
Stage of completion	1/3

The February cost of production summary for Forming is shown on the following page. In calculating the unit cost in Forming at the end of February, the amounts considered include (a) the production costs incurred by the department during the month, *plus* (b) the departmental cost of work in process at the beginning of the month. The costs from Blanking included in the beginning work in process valuation ($50,000) and in the goods received during the month ($390,000) are not used in this unit cost calculation because they are a *prior department's costs.*

Cleveland Can Company
Cost of Production Summary—Forming
For the Month Ended February 28, 2012

Cost of work in process, beginning of month—Forming:			
Cost in Blanking		$ 50,000*	
Cost in Forming:			
Materials	$1,000		
Labor	2,500		
Factory overhead	1,500	5,000	$ 55,000
Cost of goods received from Blanking during month			390,000*
Cost of production for month—Forming:			
Materials		$ 16,640	
Labor		50,000	
Factory overhead		33,360	100,000
Total costs to be accounted for			**$545,000**
Unit output for month:			
Finished and transferred to Finishing during month			41,000
Equivalent units of work in process, end of month (3,000 units, one-third completed)			1,000
Total equivalent production			42,000
Unit cost for month—Forming:			
Materials [($1,000 + $16,640) ÷ 42,000]			$ 0.42
Labor [($2,500 + $50,000) ÷ 42,000]			1.25
Factory overhead [($1,500 + $33,360) ÷ 42,000]			0.83
Total			$ 2.50
Inventory costs:			
Costs of goods finished and transferred to Finishing during month:			
Cost in Blanking (41,000 × $10.00)		$410,000	
Cost in Forming (41,000 × $2.50)		102,500	
(41,000 × $12.50)			$512,500

Cost of work in process, end of month:			
Cost in Blanking (3,000 × $10.00)		$ 30,000	
Cost in Forming:			
Materials (3,000 × 1/3 × $0.42)	$ 420		
Labor (3,000 × 1/3 × $1.25)	1,250		
Factory overhead (3,000 × 1/3 × $0.83)	830	2,500	32,500
Total production costs accounted for			**$545,000**

*Not to be considered in calculating February unit cost in Forming.

The following journal entry can now be made.

Feb. 28	Work in Process—Finishing	512,500	
	Work in Process—Forming		512,500

The general ledger account for work in process in Forming appears as follows:

Work in Process—Forming

	Debit		Credit
Jan. 31	12,000	Jan. 31	275,000
	30,000		
	18,000		
	270,000		
	330,000		
55,000			
Feb. 28	16,640	Feb. 28	512,500
	50,000		
	33,360		
	390,000		
	820,000		*787,500*
32,500			

The February production report for Finishing is shown in Figure 5-13.

Figure 5-13 Production Report, Finishing, February 28

PRODUCTION REPORT

For Month Ending February 28, 2012

Dept. Finishing

In process, beginning of period	2,000 units
Stage of completion	1/2
Placed in process during period	none
Received from dept. Forming during period	41,000 units
Transferred to dept. during period	
Transferred to stockroom during period	39,000 units
In process, end of period	4,000 units
Stage of completion	1/2

The February cost of production summary for Finishing is shown below.

Cleveland Can Company
Cost of Production Summary—Finishing
For the Month Ended February 28, 2012

Cost of work in process, beginning of month:			
Cost in Blanking		$ 20,000*	
Cost in Forming		5,000*	
Cost in Finishing:			
Materials	$1,500		
Labor	1,100		
Factory overhead	1,400	4,000	$ 29,000
Cost of goods received from Forming during month			512,500*
Cost of production for month—Finishing:			
Materials		$ 57,130	
Labor		45,640	
Factory overhead		57,230	160,000
Total costs to be accounted for			**$701,500**
Unit output for month:			
Finished and transferred to finished goods during month			39,000
Equivalent units of work in process, end of month (4,000 units, one-half completed)			2,000
Total equivalent production			41,000
Unit cost for month—Finishing:			
Materials [($1,500 + $57,130) ÷ 41,000]			$ 1.43
Labor [($1,100 + $45,640) ÷ 41,000]			1.14
Factory overhead [($1,400 + $57,230) ÷ 41,000]			1.43
Total			$ 4.00
Inventory costs:			
Cost of goods finished and transferred to finished goods during month:			
Cost in Blanking (39,000 × $10.00)		$ 390,000	
Cost in Forming (39,000 × $2.50)		97,500	
Cost in Finishing (39,000 × $4.00)		156,000	
(39,000 × $16.50)		$ 643,500	
Cost of work in process, end of month:			
Cost in Blanking 4,000 × $10.00)		$ 40,000	
Cost in Forming (4,000 × $2.50)		10,000	
Cost in Finishing:			
Materials (4,000 × 1/2 × $1.43)	$2,860		
Labor (4,000 × 1/2 × $1.14)	2,280		
Factory overhead (4,000 × 1/2 × $1.43)	2,860	8,000	58,000
Total production costs accounted for			**$701,500**

*Not to be considered in calculating February unit cost in Finishing.

The following journal entry can now be made:

Feb. 28	Finished Goods	643,500	
	Work in Process—Finishing		643,500

The general ledger account for work in process in Finishing appears as follows:

Work in Process—Finishing

Jan. 31	31,500	Jan. 31	330,000
	23,100		
	29,400		
	275,000		
	359,000		
29,000			
Feb. 28	57,130	Feb. 28	643,500
	45,640		
	57,230		
	512,500		
	1,031,500		*973,500*
58,000			

The work sheet in Figure 5-14 can now be prepared. It summarizes the factory operations for February and provides the data needed for preparing the following statement of cost of goods manufactured:

Cleveland Can Company
Statement of Cost of Goods Manufactured
For the Month Ended February 28, 2012

Materials	$263,770
Labor	198,240
Factory overhead	177,990
Total	$640,000
Add work in process inventories, February 1	134,000
	$774,000
Less work in process inventories, February 28	130,500
Cost of goods manufactured during the month	$643,500

Occasionally, finished goods in a department at the end of the month may not be transferred to the next department until the following month. Because these units are still on hand in the department at the end of the month, they cannot be considered transferred. They are accounted for as "goods completed and on hand," and their cost is shown at the full unit price. They are considered work in process for financial statement purposes. Although the goods are finished in the department, they are considered in process until they are officially transferred to finished goods.

Figure 5-14 **Work Sheet, February 28**

	A	B	C	D	E	F
1	**Cleveland Can Company**					
2	**Departmental Cost Work Sheet**					
3	**For the Month Ended February 28, 2012**					
4						
5		**Cost**	**Units**	**Units**	**Amount**	**Amount**
6		**per unit**	**received in**	**transferred**	**charged to**	**credited to**
7	**Analysis**	**transferred**	**department**	**or on hand**	**department**	**department**
8						
9	Blanking:					
10	Opening inventory in process		10,000		$50,000	
11	Started in process		34,000			
12	Costs for month:					
13	Materials				190,000	
14	Labor				102,600	
15	Factory overhead				87,400	
16	Finished and transferred to Forming	$10.00		39,000		$390,000
17	Closing work in process			5,000		40,000
18	Total		44,000	44,000	$430,000	$430,000
19						
20	Forming:					
21	Opening inventory in process		5,000		$55,000	
22	Received during month from Blanking		39,000		390,000	
23	Costs added during month:					
24	Materials	0.42			16,640	
25	Labor	1.25			50,000	
26	Factory overhead	0.83			33,360	
27	Finished and transferred to Finishing	$12.50		41,000		$512,500
28	Closing work in process			3,000		32,500
29	Total		44,400	44,000	$545,000	$545,000
30						
31	Finishing:					
32	Opening inventory in process		2,000		$29,000	
33	Received during month from Forming		41,000		512,500	
34	Costs added during month:					
35	Materials	1.43			57,130	
36	Labor	1.14			45,640	
37	Factory overhead	1.43			57,230	
38	Finished and transferred to stock	$16.50		39,000		$643,500
39	Closing work in process			4,000		58,000
40	Total		43,000	43,000	$701,500	$701,500

Changes in Prior Department's Unit Transfer Costs

LO7 Prepare a cost of production summary with a change in the prior department's unit transfer cost.

In the preceding illustrations, it was assumed that this month's unit cost from prior departments was the same transferred-in unit cost as that of last month. This assumption permitted the prior department's unit cost to be used without determining a *new average unit cost* for the goods transferred in, even though the transfers came from two different periods of production. However, the prior department's transfers from

Figure 5-14 **(Continued)**

	A	B	C	D	E	F
41					**Amount**	**Total**
42	Summary:					
43	Materials:					
44	Blanking				$190,000	
45	Forming				16,640	
46	Finishing				57,130	$263,770
47	Labor:					
48	Blanking				$102,600	
49	Forming				50,000	
50	Finishing				45,640	198,240
51	Factory overhead:					
52	Blanking				$87,400	
53	Forming				33,360	
54	Finishing				57,230	177,990
55	Total production costs for February					$640,000
56	Add work in process, begining of month:					
57	Blanking				$50,000	
58	Forming				55,000	
59	Finishing				29,000	134,000
60	Total					$774,000
61	Deduct work in process, end of month:					
62	Blanking				$40,000	
63	Forming				32,500	
64	Finishing				58,000	130,500
65	Costs of production, goods fully					
66	manufactured during February					$643,500

two different periods will often have different unit costs each month. Therefore, these previous department costs must be *averaged as a separate grouping* so that these transferred-in costs can be properly allocated to the products being produced in the department. The method resembles that used for the cost of materials, labor, and factory overhead in the department when the cost of these elements represents two different periods of time.

To illustrate, assume that 20,000 units are in process in Forming at the beginning of the month with a transferred cost of $106,000 from Blanking. During the month, 100,000 units with a total cost of $500,000 are received from Blanking; 110,000 units are finished and transferred to Finishing; and 10,000 units are in process in Forming at the end of the month, one-half completed. Processing costs in Forming for the month are $230,000 ($20,000 + $210,000) for materials, $161,000 ($14,000 + $147,000) for labor, and $115,000 ($10,000 + $105,000) for overhead. By using these data, the unit costs are calculated in the cost of production summary for Forming on page 268. Note the portion of the report where the unit cost from the prior department is adjusted to $5.05.

Cleveland Can Company
Cost of Production Summary—Forming
For the Month Ended February 28, 2012

Cost of work in process, beginning of month:			
Cost in Blanking		$106,000	
Cost in Forming:			
Materials	$20,000		
Labor	14,000		
Overhead	10,000	44,000	$ 150,000
Cost of goods received from Blanking			500,000
Cost in Forming:			
Materials		$210,000	
Labor		147,000	
Overhead		105,000	462,000
Total costs to be accounted for			**$1,112,000**
Unit output for month:			
Finished and transferred to Finishing			110,000
Equivalent production of work in process (10,000 units, one-half completed)			5,000
Total equivalent production			115,000
Unit cost for month:			
Cost from prior department:			
Beginning inventory (20,000 units)		$106,000	
Transferred in this month (100,000 units)		500,000	
Average cost per unit (120,000 units)		$606,000	$ 5.05
Cost in Forming:			
Materials [($20,000 + $210,000) ÷ 115,000]			$ 2.00
Labor [($14,000 + $147,000) ÷ 115,000]			1.40
Overhead [($10,000 + $105,000) ÷ 115,000]			1.00
			$ 4.40
Inventory costs:			
Cost of goods finished and transferred:			
Cost in Blanking (110,000 × $5.05)		$555,500	
Cost in Forming (110,000 × $4.40)		484,000	
Total finished and transferred (110,000 × $9.45)			$1,039,500
Cost of work in process, end of month:			
Cost in Blanking (10,000 × $5.05)		$ 50,500	
Materials (10,000 × 1/2 × $2.00)	$10,000		
Labor (10,000 × 1/2 × $1.40)	7,000		
Overhead (10,000 × 1/2 × $1.00)	5,000	22,000	72,500
Total production costs accounted for			**$1,112,000**

Recall and Review 3

Gurry Company has 2,000 units in process in Blending at the beginning of the month that have a transferred-in cost of $10,000 from Mixing. During the month, an additional 15,000 units are received from Mixing with a transferred-in cost of $77,000. Fourteen thousand units are completed and transferred to Finishing during the month, with the remaining units two-thirds complete at the end of the month. The adjusted unit cost from the prior department that should appear on the Blending cost of production summary is $______________. (Round unit cost to three decimal places.)

(After working this exercise, see page 270 for the solution.)

You should now be able to work the following:
Questions 15 and 16; Exercises 5-10 to 5-12; Problems 5-7 to 5-11; Self-Study Problem 2; and the Internet Exercise.

KEY TERMS

Average cost method, 241
Cost center, 238
Cost object, 239
Cost of production summary, 244
Equivalent production, 241
First-in, first-out (FIFO) method, 241
Job order cost system, 238
Process cost system, 238
Production report, 242
Stage of completion, 242

ANSWERS TO RECALL AND REVIEW EXERCISES

R&R 1

Units completed from beginning work in process	400	
Units started and completed this month	13,400	
Equivalent units in ending work in process	300	[(14,600 – 13,400) × .25]
Total equivalent units of production	14,100	

R&R 2

	Debit	Credit:
1.	Work in Process, Factory Overhead	Materials
2.	Work in Process, Factory Overhead	Payroll
3.	Factory Overhead (each department)	Factory Overhead
4.	Work in Process (each department)	Factory Overhead (each department)

R&R 3

	Units	Cost
Beginning inventory	2,000	$10,000
Transferred-in during month	15,000	77,000
Total	17,000	$87,000

Average cost per unit = $87,000 / 17,000 = $5.118

SELF-STUDY PROBLEM 1

Cost of Production Summary, One Department; Beginning Work in Process

Michaels, Inc.

Michaels, Inc., uses the process cost system. The following data, taken from the organization's books, reflect the results of manufacturing operations during the month of June in its only department, Machining:

Production Costs		
Work in process, beginning of period:		
Materials	$ 5,200	
Labor	4,600	
Factory Overhead	2,000	$11,800
Costs during the month:		
Materials	$20,000	
Labor	15,000	
Factory overhead	12,000	$47,000
Total		$58,800

Production Report	**Units**
Finished and transferred to stockroom during month	19,000
Work in process, end of period, 4,000 units, one-fourth completed	

Required:
Prepare a cost of production summary for June.

SOLUTION TO SELF-STUDY PROBLEM

Suggestions:
Read the entire problem carefully, keeping in mind what you are required to do: *Prepare a cost of production summary for a single department.* The specifics of the problem highlight the following facts:

1. There is a single department: Machining
2. To prepare a cost of production summary:
   a. Determine the total cost to be accounted for.
   b. Calculate the equivalent units of production.
   c. Using the beginning inventory costs and the costs incurred during the period, determine the total costs of material, labor, and factory overhead.
   d. Divide the total costs in each of the three categories by the equivalent units of production to obtain the individual unit costs for materials, labor, and factory overhead.
   e. Using the unit costs for materials, labor, and factory overhead, determine the following:
      1. The cost of goods completed and transferred to finished goods.
      2. The cost of the ending work in process inventory.

Prepare the cost of production summary for the Machining Department:

Michaels, Inc.
Cost of Production Summary—Machining
For the Month Ended June 30, 2011

First: Account for the total cost charged to the Machining Department.

Cost of work in process, beginning of month:		
Materials	$ 5,200	
Labor	4,600	
Factory overhead	2,000	$ 11,800
Costs of production for the month:		
Materials	$ 20,000	
Labor	15,000	
Factory overhead	12,000	47,000
Total cost to be accounted for		$ 58,800

Second: Determine the equivalent units of production for the month. Materials, labor, and factory overhead are added uniformly throughout the process. The average cost method of process costing is used.

Units of output for month:	
Finished and transferred to finished goods	19,000
Equivalent units of work in process, end of month: 4,000 units, one-fourth completed	1,000
Total equivalent production	20,000

Third: Determine unit costs for each element of manufacturing cost for the month. The average cost method requires that the beginning inventory cost be added to the current month's cost for each cost element. The total cost for each cost element is then divided by the equivalent units of production to obtain the unit cost for each cost element.

Unit cost for month:	
Materials ($5,200 + $20,000) ÷ 20,000	$ 1.26
Labor ($4,600 + $15,000) ÷ 20,000	0.98
Factory overhead ($2,000 + $12,000) ÷ 20,000	0.70
Total	$ 2.94

Fourth: Using the units costs computed on the previous page determine the cost of goods transferred to finished goods and the cost of the ending work in process inventory.

Inventory Costs:		
Cost of goods finished and transferred to finished goods (19,000 × $2.94)		$55,860
Cost of work in process, end of month:		
Materials (4,000 × 1/4 × $1.26)	$ 1,260	
Labor (4,000 × 1/4 × .98)	980	
Factory overhead (4,000 1/4 × .70)	700	2,940
Total production costs accounted for		$58,800

SELF-STUDY PROBLEM 2

Cost of Production, Two Departments; Beginning Inventory

Shiloh Chemicals, Inc.

Shiloh Chemicals, Inc., which manufactures products on a continuous basis, had 800 units in process in Dept. 1, one-half completed, at the beginning of May. The costs in April for processing these units were as follows: materials, $1,200; labor, $900; and factory overhead, $1,000. During May, Dept. 1 finished and transferred 10,000 units to Dept. 2 and had 400 units in process at the end of May, one-half completed.

Dept. 2 had 200 units in process at the beginning of the month, one-half completed. April costs for these units were as follows: cost transferred from Dept. 1, $1,550; materials, $200; labor, $175; and factory overhead, $225. During May, Dept. 2 completed 9,000 units and had 1,200 units in process at the end of the period, two-thirds completed.

Production costs incurred by the two departments during May were as follows:

	Dept. 1	Dept. 2
Materials	$29,400	$19,400
Labor	22,050	16,975
Factory overhead	24,500	21,825

Required:
Prepare a cost of production summary for each department.

SOLUTION TO SELF-STUDY PROBLEM

Suggestions:
Read the entire problem thoroughly, keeping in mind what you are required to do: *Prepare a cost of production summary for each department.*

The Specifics in the Problem Highlight the Following Facts:

1. There are two departments: Dept. 1 and Dept. 2.
2. Dept. 1 had 800 units in process, one-half completed, at the beginning of May. This statement indicates that materials, labor, and factory overhead are being added uniformly to production.
3. To prepare a cost of production summary:
   a. Determine the total cost to be accounted for in the department.
   b. Calculate the equivalent production.
   c. Using the beginning inventory costs and the costs incurred during the period, determine the total cost of materials, the total cost of labor, and the total cost of factory overhead. Then divide the total cost of materials by the equivalent production of materials to calculate the unit cost of materials for the period. Also, divide the total cost of labor and factory overhead by the equivalent production determined for them.
   d. Using the calculated unit costs for materials, labor, and factory overhead, determine the following:
      1. The cost of goods finished and transferred.
      2. The cost of the ending work in process inventory.

Prepare the Cost of Production Summary for Dept. 1:

Shiloh Chemicals, Inc.
Cost of Production Summary—Dept. 1
For the Month Ended May 31, 2011

First: Account for the total cost charged to Dept. 1.

Cost of work in process, beginning of month:		
Materials	$ 1,200	
Labor	900	
Factory overhead	1,000	$3,100
Cost of production for month:		
Materials	$29,400	
Labor	22,050	
Factory overhead	24,500	75,950
Total costs to be accounted for		$79,050

Second: Determine equivalent production for the month. (Materials, labor, and factory overhead are added uniformly. Method of costing—average cost.)

Units of output for month:	
Finished and transferred to Dept. 2	10,000
Equivalent units of work in process, end of month:	
400 units, one-half completed	200
Total equivalent production	10,200

Third: Determine unit cost, by elements, for the month. The average cost method requires that the beginning inventory's element cost be added to the current month's element cost. The total cost for each element is then divided by the equivalent production for that element.

Unit cost for month:		
Materials ($1,200 + $29,400) ÷ 10,200		$3.00
Labor ($900 + $22,050) ÷ 10,200		2.25
Factory overhead ($1,000 + $24,500) ÷ 10,200		2.50
Total		$7.75

Fourth: Using the unit costs, calculate the cost of goods transferred and the cost of the ending work in process.

Inventory costs:		
Cost of goods finished and transferred to Dept. 2 during the month (10,000 × $7.75)		$77,500
Cost of work in process, end of month:		
Materials (400 × 1/2 × $3.00)	$ 600	
Labor (400 × 1/2 × $2.25)	450	
Factory overhead (400 × 1/2 × $2.50)	500	1,550
Total production costs accounted for		$79,050

Prepare the Cost of Production Summary for Dept. 2:

Shiloh Chemicals, Inc.
Cost of Production Summary—Dept. 2
For the Month Ended May 31, 2011

First: Account for all costs charged to Dept. 2.

Cost of work in process, beginning of month:			
Cost in Dept. 1 (preceding department)		$ 1,550	
Cost in Dept. 2:			
Materials	$ 200		
Labor	175		
Factory overhead	225	600	$2,150
Cost of goods received from Dept. 1 during month			77,500
Cost of production for month:			
Materials		$19,400	
Labor		16,975	
Factory overhead		21,825	58,200
Total costs to be accounted for			$137,850

Second: Determine the equivalent production.

Finished and transferred to finished goods during month	9,000
Equivalent units of work in process, end of month (1,200 units, two-thirds completed)	800
Total equivalent production	9,800

Third: Determine unit cost by element. Add beginning inventory element cost to current month element cost and divide total by the equivalent production for that element.

Unit cost for month:	
Materials ($200 + $19,400) ÷ 9,800	$2.00
Labor ($175 + $16,975) ÷ 9,800	1.75
Factory overhead ($225 + $21,825) ÷ 9,800	2.25
Total unit cost for Dept. 2	$6.00

Fourth: Using the unit costs from Dept. 1 and Dept. 2, calculate the cost of goods transferred and the cost of the ending work in process.

Inventory costs:			
Cost of goods finished and transferred to finished goods during month:			
Cost in Dept. 1 (9,000 × $7.75)		$69,750	
Cost in Dept. 2 (9,000 × $6.00)		54,000	
Total (9,000 × $13.75)			$123,750
Cost of work in process, end of month:			
Cost in Dept. 1 (1,200 × $7.75)		$ 9,300	
Cost in Dept. 2:			
Materials (1,200 × 2/3 × $2.00)	$1,600		
Labor (1,200 × 2/3 × $1.75)	1,400		
Overhead (1,200 × 2/3 × $2.25)	1,800	4,800	14,100
Total production costs accounted for			$137,850

Note that, in the above ending work in process inventory, the unit cost from Dept. 1 is multiplied by the full 1,200 units because all of those units are complete as to Dept. 1 processing.

QUESTIONS

1. What are the two basic systems of cost accounting, and under what conditions may each be used advantageously?
2. Following is a list of manufactured products. For each product, would a job order or a process cost system be used to account for the costs of production?
   a. lumber
   b. buildings
   c. airplanes
   d. gasoline
   e. cereal
   f. textbooks
   g. paint
   h. jeans
3. What is the primary difference between the two cost accounting systems regarding the accumulation of costs and the calculation of unit costs?
4. What is the difference between the term *unit cost* as commonly used in a process cost system and the term *job cost* as commonly used in a job order system of cost accounting?
5. How do the two cost accounting systems differ in accounting for each of the following items?
   a. materials
   b. labor
   c. factory overhead
6. What is the primary objective in accumulating costs by departments?
7. What is meant by the term *equivalent production* as used in the process cost system?
8. Why is it necessary to estimate the stage or degree of completion of work in process at the end of the accounting period under the process cost system?
9. What would be the effect on the unit cost of finished goods if an estimate of the stage of completion of work in process was too high?
10. What information is reflected on a production report?
11. What are the four main sections of a cost of production summary?
12. What is the major difference between the disposition of units transferred out of a first department in a single-department factory versus a multiple-department factory?

13. Does the calculation of unit cost in a department subsequent to the first department take into consideration the costs transferred in from the previous departments?

14. In determining the costs transferred to a third department from a second department, are the costs from a first department considered? Are they considered in the computation of the ending work in process in the second department?

15. If finished goods are still on hand in a department at the end of the month, how are they reported on the cost of production summary and on the balance sheet?

16. If the prior department's transfers from two different periods have different unit costs each month, how are they treated for purposes of the cost of production summary for the department to which they were transferred?

EXERCISES

LO3

E5-1 Computing equivalent production

Compute the equivalent production (unit output) for the month for each of the following situations:

	Units Completed During Month	Units in Process, End of Month	Stage of Completion
a.	10,000	5,000	1/2
b.	22,000	4,000	3/4
c.	8,000	1,000	1/4
		500	2/5
d.	25,000	5,000	1/2
		5,000	3/4
e.	48,000	1,500	4/5
		4,000	1/4

LO3

E5-2 Computing units in process, units completed, and equivalent production

Using the following data, determine which figures should be inserted in the blank spaces.

	Beginning Units in Process	Units Started in Production	Units Transferred to Finished Goods	Ending Units in Process	Equivalent Units
a.	600	8,000	8,600	—	—
b.	900	6,500	—	400—1/2 completed	—
c.	1,500	—	12,900	1,200—1/4 completed	—
d.	—	7,250	7,200	150—1/2 completed	—
e.	—	8,400	8,200	200—1/2 completed	—
f.	400	6,200	6,200	—	6,300

E5-3 **Computing unit cost**

LO4

During the month, a company with no departmentalization incurred costs of $45,000 for materials, $36,000 for labor, and $22,500 for factory overhead. There were no units in process at the beginning or at the end of the month, and 20,000 units were completed. Determine the unit cost for the month for materials, labor, and factory overhead.

E5-4 **Computing unit cost**

LO4

Chavez Chemical Co. recorded costs for the month of $18,900 for materials, $44,100 for labor, and $26,250 for factory overhead. There was no beginning work in process, 8,000 units were finished, and 3,000 units were in process at the end of the period, two-thirds completed. Compute the month's unit cost for each element of manufacturing cost and the total per unit cost. (Round unit costs to three decimal places.)

E5-5 **Computing unit cost**

LO5

The records of Reuben, Inc., reflect the following data:

> Work in process, beginning of month—2,000 units one-half completed at a cost of $1,250 for materials, $675 for labor, and $950 for overhead.
>
> Production costs for the month—materials, $99,150; labor, $54,925; factory overhead, $75,050.
>
> Units completed and transferred to stock—38,500.
>
> Work in process, end of month—3,000 units, one-half completed.

Calculate the unit cost for the month for materials, labor, and factory overhead.

E5-6 **Computing unit cost**

LO5

Jason Manufacturing Co. had 500 units, three-fifths completed, in process at the beginning of the month. During the month, 2,000 units were started in process and finished. There was no work in process at the end of the month. Unit cost of production for the month was $1.20. Costs for materials, labor, and factory overhead incurred in the current month totaled $2,655. Calculate the unit cost for the *prior* month. (*Hint:* You must first determine what the dollar balance in work in process must have been at the beginning of the month.)

E5-7 **Computing unit cost for department and for completed units**

LO6

North Arlington Company has two production departments. The nature of the process is such that no units remain in process in Finishing at the end of the period. During the period, 10,000 units with a cost of $30,000 were transferred from Assembly to Finishing. Finishing incurred costs of $8,800 for materials, $7,200 for labor, and $8,800 for factory overhead, and finished 10,000 units during the month.

a. Determine the unit cost for the month in Finishing.
b. Determine the unit cost of the products transferred to finished goods.

LO6

E5-8 **In E5-7 above, prepare a statement of cost of goods manufactured for the period.**

LO6

E5-9 **Identifying cost flows in process cost system**

List in columnar form the transactions and the accounts debited and credited to reflect the flow of costs through a process cost accounting system for the:

1. purchase of materials and supplies, on account
2. issuance of materials and supplies to the factory
3. factory labor costs incurred
4. other factory costs incurred
5. distribution of actual factory overhead to the individual departments
6. application of factory overhead to the departments
7. transfer of units from one department to another
8. completion of units
9. sale of units

LO7

E5-10 **Computing unit cost for department and for completed units with beginning inventory**

U.S. Grant Company has two production departments. Blending had 1,000 units in process at the beginning of the period, two-fifths complete. During the period 7,800 units were received from Mixing, 8,200 units were transferred to Finished Goods, and 600 units were in process at the end of the period, 1/3 complete. The cost of the beginning work in process was:

Cost in Mixing	$10,000
Cost in Blending:	
Materials	200
Labor	500
Factory overhead	300

The costs during the month were:

Cost of goods received from Mixing	$78,000
Cost in Blending:	
Materials	3,328
Labor	10,000
Factory overhead	6,672

a. Determine the unit cost for the month in Blending.
b. Determine the total cost of the products transferred to finished goods.
c. Determine the total cost of the ending work in process inventory.

E5-11 **Cost of production summary and journal entries**

LO7

1. For E5-10, prepare a cost of production summary for the month for Blending.
2. Prepare a journal entry to transfer the completed units from Blending to Finished Goods.

E5-12 **Adjusted unit cost computation**

LO8

Colbert Company has 1,000 units in process in Forming at the beginning of the month with a transferred cost of $21,200 from Blanking. During the month, 5,000 units with a total cost of $100,000 are received from Blanking; 4,000 units are finished and transferred to Finishing; and 2,000 units are in process in Forming at the end of the month, one-half completed.

Required:
Compute the adjusted unit cost from the prior department in the Forming Department.
(Round the unit cost to three decimal places.)

PROBLEMS

P5-1 **Cost of production summary, one department; no beginning work in process**

LO5

Hugo Products Co. produces a latex paint and uses the process cost system. Materials, labor, and overhead are added evenly throughout the process. The following information was obtained from the company's accounts at the end of February.

Production Costs

Costs incurred during month:		
Materials	$30,000	
Labor	20,000	
Factory overhead	40,000	$90,000

Production Report	**Units**
Finished and transferred to stockroom during month	60,000
Work in process, end of period, one-fourth completed	10,000

Required:
Prepare a cost of production summary for February.

P5-2 **Cost of production summary, one department; beginning work in process**
similar to Self-Study Problem 1

LO5

Andrews Company uses the process cost system. The following data, taken from the organization's books, reflect the results of manufacturing operations during the month of October:

Production Costs

Work in process, beginning of period:		
Materials	$ 2,600	
Labor	2,300	
Factory overhead	1,000	$ 5,900
Costs incurred during month:		
Materials	$10,000	
Labor	7,500	
Factory overhead	6,000	23,500
Total		$29,400

Production Report	**Units**
Finished and transferred to stockroom during month	13,000
Work in process, end of period, one-half completed	2,000

Required:
Prepare a cost of production summary for October.

P5-3 Cost of production summary, one department; beginning inventory

LO5

Greene Company provides the following information regarding its units of production:

1,000 units in ending work in process, one-third complete, on June 30.

47,000 units started in production during July, with 42,000 completed in addition to the beginning work in process, by the end of July.

The ending work in process inventory was two-thirds complete at the end of July.

Required:
Map the calculation of the equivalent units of production for July, using the format in Figure 5-6 of the chapter.

P5-4 Cost of production summary, multiple departments; no beginning inventory

LO6

Department-Bravo, the second department in a three-department production process for Military, Inc., received 10,000 units with a total cost of $25,000 from Department-Alpha during the month of May. Production costs in Bravo during the month were: materials, $6,000; labor, $3,000; and factory overhead, $9,000. Of the 10,000 units transferred in, 8,000 were completed and transferred to Department-Charlie during the month and 2,000 remained in work in process at the end of the month, one-fourth complete.

Required:
Prepare a cost of production summary for Department-Bravo for the month ended May 31.

P5-5 **Departmental cost work sheet analysis; cost of production summary, three departments, no beginning inventories**

Cubbies Manufacturing Co. has three departments and uses the process cost system of accounting. A portion of the departmental cost work sheet prepared by the cost accountant at the end of July is reproduced below.

LO6

Cubbies Manufacturing Co.
Departmental Cost Work Sheet
For the Month Ended July 31, 2011

Analysis	Cost per unit transferred	Units received in department	Units transferred or on hand	Amount charged to department	Amount credited to department
Cutting:					
Started in process		6,600			
Costs for month:					
Materials				$30,000	
Labor				16,000	
Factory overhead				14,000	
Completed and transferred to Shaping	$10.00		5,400		$54,000
Closing inventory in process (1/2 completed)			1,200		6,000
Total		6,600	6,600	$60,000	$60,000
Shaping:					
Received during month from Cutting		5,400		$54,000	
Costs added during month:					
Materials	0.25			1,200	
Labor	1.25			6,000	
Factory overhead	1.00			4,800	
Completed and transferred to Finishing	$12.50		4,400		$55,000
Closing inventory in process (2/5 completed)			1,000		11,000
Total		5,400	5,400	$66,000	$66,000
Finishing:					
Received during month from Shaping		4,400		$55,000	
Costs added during month:					
Materials	1.50			6,300	
Labor	1.00			4,200	
Factory overhead	1.50			6,300	
Completed and transferred to stock	$16.50		4,000		$66,000
Closing inventory in process (1/2 completed)			400		5,800
Total		4,400	4,400	$71,800	$71,800

Required:

Prepare a cost of production summary for each department. (Round unit costs to three decimal places.)

P5-6 LO6 **Journal entries and cost of goods manufactured statement**

Required:

Using the data in P5-5:

1. Draft the necessary entries to record the manufacturing costs incurred during the month of July.
2. Prepare a statement of cost of goods manufactured for the month ended July 31.

P5-7 LO7 **Change in unit cost from prior department and valuation of inventory**

Gomez Products Co. has two departments: Mixing and Cooking. At the beginning of the month, Cooking had 4,000 units in process with costs of $8,600 from Mixing, and its own departmental costs of $500 for materials, $1,000 for labor, and $2,500 for factory overhead. During the month, 10,000 units were received from Mixing with a cost of $25,000. Cooking incurred costs of $4,250 for materials, $8,500 for labor, and $21,250 for factory overhead, and finished 12,000 units. At the end of the month, there were 2,000 units in process, one-half completed.

Required:

1. Determine the unit cost for the month in Cooking.
2. Determine the new average unit cost for all units received from Mixing.
3. Determine the unit cost of goods finished.
4. Determine the accumulated cost of the goods finished and of the ending work in process.

(Round unit costs to three decimal places.)

P5-8 LO7 **Cost of production summary, two departments; beginning inventory**
similar to Self-Study Problem 2

Roberts Corporation uses a process cost system. The records for the month of May show the following information:

Production Report	**Cutting**	**Grinding**
Units in process, May 1	5,000	10,000
Started during the month	20,000	—
Received from prior department	—	15,000
Finished and transferred	15,000	10,000
Finished and on hand	5,000	—
Units in process, May 31	5,000	15,000
Stage of completion	1/5	1/3
Production Costs		
Work in process, May 1:		
Costs in Cutting:		$50,000
Materials	$5,000	
Labor	6,450	
Factory overhead	3,550	

Production Costs		
Cost in Grinding:		
Materials	5,000	
Labor	5,500	
Factory overhead	3,500	
Costs incurred during the month:		
Materials	37,000	40,000
Labor	45,000	44,000
Factory overhead	50,000	37,000
Total	$147,000	$185,000

Required:
Prepare a cost of production summary for each department.

P5-9 **Ledger account analysis; cost of production summary**

LO7

Analyze the information presented in the following general ledger account of Mantle Manufacturing Co., which has three departments: Shaping, Forming, and Finishing:

Work in Process—Forming

Mar. 1	10,250	Mar. 31	50,000
31 Materials	4,000		
31 Labor	8,000		
31 Factory overhead	6,000		
31 Shaping	36,000		

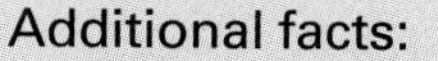

Additional facts:

a. 2,000 units were in process at the beginning of the month, one-half completed.
b. 10,000 units were received from Shaping during the month.
c. 8,000 units were transferred to Finishing during the month.
d. Unit costs in Shaping and Forming were the same for March as for the prior month.
e. The ratio of materials, labor, and factory overhead costs for Forming in the beginning and ending balances of Work in Process was in the same ratio as the costs incurred in Forming during the current month.

Required:
Prepare a cost of production summary for March.

P5-10 **Journal entries**

LO7

Required:
Using the data in P5-9, determine:

1. The cost of goods received from Shaping during the month.
2. The production costs incurred in Forming during the month.
3. The cost of goods completed and transferred to Finishing during the month.

P5-11 Cost of production summary, three departments; change in unit cost from prior department; departmental cost work sheet; journal entries; manufacturing statement

LO7 LO8

Ichiro Manufacturing Co. uses the process cost system. The following information for the month of December was obtained from the company's books and from the production reports submitted by the department heads:

Production Report	Mixing	Blending	Bottling
Units in process, beginning of period	2,500	1,500	3,000
Started in process during month	12,500	—	—
Received from prior department	—	13,000	10,000
Finished and transferred	13,000	10,000	11,000
Finished and on hand	—	500	—
Units in process, end of period	2,000	4,000	2,000
Stage of completion	1/4	4/5	1/2

Production Costs

	Mixing	Blending	Bottling
Work in process, beginning of period:			
Cost in Mixing		$3,075	$6,150
Materials	$1,470		
Labor	650		
Factory overhead	565		
Cost in Blending			3,660
Materials		240	
Labor		905	
Factory overhead		750	
Cost in Bottling			
Materials			900
Labor			3,100
Factory overhead			3,080
Costs incurred during month:			
Materials	15,000	2,500	1,500
Labor	4,750	8,000	6,500
Factory overhead	5,240	6,100	7,000
Total	$27,675	$21,570	$31,890

Required:

1. Prepare cost of production summaries for the Mixing, Blending, and Bottling departments.
2. Prepare a departmental cost work sheet.
3. Draft the journal entries required to record the month's operations.
4. Prepare a statement of cost of goods manufactured for December.

MINI-CASE

LO2

Ethics; Equivalent units of production

New York Beverages, Inc., has three plants that make and bottle cola, lemon-lime, and miscellaneous flavored beverages, respectively. The raw materials, labor costs, and automated technology are comparable among the three plants. Top management has initiated an incentive compensation plan whereby the workers and managers of the plant with the lowest unit cost per bottle will receive a year-end bonus. The results, approved by the plant manager and reported by the plant controllers at each location, were as follows:

(Note: tabular presentation not necessary in final draft.)

Item	Bronx	Brooklyn	Queens
Materials	$200,000	$450,000	$325,000
Labor	170,000	375,000	250,000
Overhead	340,000	750,000	500,000
Total	$710,000	$1,575,000	$1,075, 000
Equivalent units of production:			
Completed	3,500,000	6,200,000	6,450,000
Ending work in process	100,000 (50% complete)	400,000 (25% complete)	
Equivalent units	3,550,000	6,300,000	6,450,000
Unit cost	$0.20	$0.25	$0.167

Required:

1. When provided copies of the results as a justification for distributing the bonus to the Queens employees, the plant controllers at Bronx and Brooklyn accused Queens of manipulating the inventory figures. Reviewing the above schedule, what do you think is the nature of the accusation and how would such action affect the unit cost computation?
2. Is there anything in the Institute of Management Accountants (IMA) Code of Professional Ethics that the Queens plant controller should be aware of in this situation?
3. Assume that the Queens plant controller revises the unit cost to more accurately reflect reality. What should she do if the plant manager insists that the unit cost computation remain as is?

INTERNET EXERCISE

LO1 LO3

Process Costing

General Mills is a company that uses process costing extensively. Go to the companion Web site at www.cengage.com/accounting/vanderbeck and click on the file for General Mills.

Required:

Answer the following questions while navigating General Mills's "A Champion's Code of Conduct":

1. What guidance are supervisors given on how to handle a request from an outsider, claiming to be working as a General Mills consultant, for information on employees' start dates, titles, and base salaries?
2. What guidance is given to an employee who was planning to make a General Mills stock trade prior to becoming aware of material non-public information?
3. What advice is given to an employee working in Europe who received an expensive gift from a supplier in recognition of a new contract?
4. What advice is given to an employee who was told that she had to pay a gratuity to a minor official to clear General Mills's products through customs?

Chapter 6

Process Cost Accounting—Additional Procedures; Accounting for Joint Products and By-Products

Learning Objectives

After studying this chapter, you should be able to:

- LO1 Compute unit costs when materials are not added uniformly throughout the process.
- LO2 Account for units lost in the production process.
- LO3 Account for units gained in the production process.
- LO4 Assign costs to inventories, using the first-in, first-out method.
- LO5 Identify the methods used to apportion joint costs to joint products and account for by-products.

An article, "PepsiCo offers to buy 2 bottlers for $6 billion," in the April 21, 2009 *San Diego Union Tribune* reported that PepsiCo, a company whose manufacturing process is ideal for process costing because its major brands (Pepsi-Cola, Frito-Lay, Tropicana, Quaker, and Gatorade) are produced in a continuous flow of identical bottles of soda, bags of chips, and the like, is attempting to acquire its two largest bottlers. If successful, "the company will handle about 80% of its total North American beverage volume." This is a competitive move taken "in an effort to update the way it delivers its products." In 1999 PepsiCo spun off Pepsi Bottling Group, but since then soft drink sales have fallen as the sales of noncarbonated beverages have soared. To learn more about PepsiCo and its brands visit www.pepsico.com.

The illustrative problems presented in Chapter 5 are based on the assumption that materials, labor, and factory overhead were uniformly applied during the processing period. When the work in process at the end of the accounting period was considered to be one-half completed, it was assumed that one-half of the materials cost, one-half of the labor cost, and one-half of the factory overhead cost had been added. Chapter 6 illustrates process cost accounting when materials, labor, and overhead are not applied uniformly during the period. Additional topics covered in this chapter include accounting for units lost and gained during production, assigning costs to inventories using the first-in, first-out method, and accounting for joint products and by-products.

Equivalent Production—Materials Not Uniformly Applied

LO1 Compute unit costs when materials are not added uniformly throughout the process.

In industries that use continuous production systems, materials may be put into production in varying quantities and at different points in the processing cycle. Before any manufacturing process can begin, some material must be introduced in the first production department. For example, in the production of chemicals, various ingredients may be mixed, blended, and then packaged by direct laborers using machinery and other factory overhead items. In this example, all of the ingredients are added at the beginning of processing in the first department, Mixing. Then, labor and factory overhead are used to convert the raw material into a finished product. The stage of completion of the partially completed units in ending work in process is 100% as to materials because all materials will have been added at the very beginning of production. Some labor and overhead costs will need to be applied to the ending work in process during the next period to complete it.

In the second production department, Blending, the chemical ingredients are processed further through another labor operation. At the end of the process in the second department, several new ingredients are added. The ending work in process inventory in the second department, therefore, would have had a part of the departmental labor and overhead costs applied to them, but no materials cost would have been added because the extra ingredients are added at the very end of the process.

In the third department, Packaging, other materials, such as coloring, may be added to the units at the start of production. Then, the finished chemicals are placed in plastic containers, which are yet another type of raw material. In this department, the units in ending work in process will have had some new materials (coloring) and some labor and overhead added, while the packaging materials (plastic containers) will not have been added until the completion stage. This is an example of a single cost item (materials) requiring two equivalent unit computations because the coloring additive and the packaging materials are added at different times in the same department.

To illustrate the problems involved in calculating unit costs under these conditions, this chapter presents three problems using the average cost method. In these examples, materials are added at different stages in the process. Labor and factory overhead are assumed to be applied evenly throughout the process. This assumption is reasonable in a manufacturing process where direct labor is significant, because the application of overhead is usually so closely related to the incurrence of labor costs that overhead is generally thought of as being incurred or applied in the same ratio as labor expense.

Illustrative Problem No. 1

Computing the unit cost in the Mixing Department where all the materials are added at the beginning of processing—average cost method. The production report for the month submitted by the department head, presented in Figure 6-1, resembles those studied in the previous chapter. This

Figure 6-1 **Production Report, Mixing**

PRODUCTION REPORT	
For Month Ending	January 31, 2011
Dept.	Mixing
In process, beginning of period	500 units
Stage of completion	2/5
Placed in process during period	2,500 units
Received from dept. ______ during period	
Transferred to dept. Blending during period	2,600 units
Transferred to stockroom during period	
In process, end of period	400 units
Stage of completion	All materials; 3/4 labor and overhead

illustration is for the Newark Chemical Company, which has the following departments: Mixing, Blending, and Packaging.

The cost of production summary, Figure 6-2, is similar to the summaries previously discussed, but it has the added highlighted feature of determining equivalent units of production for materials separately from those for labor and factory overhead.

In Mixing, because all materials are added at the start of processing, it is easy to determine the equivalent units for materials. The production report from the factory indicates that 500 units were in process at the beginning of the month with all materials added, and enough materials were issued to production during the month to make another 2,500 units. Therefore, the equivalent production for materials is 3,000 units. Another way to calculate the figure by the method used in this chapter is as follows: the 2,600 units finished during the month plus the 400 units in process at the end of the month have all of the materials added. Thus, the total equivalent production for materials is 3,000 units (2,600 + 400).

The equivalent production for labor and factory overhead is calculated as shown in the preceding chapter: 2,600 completed units, plus the equivalent of 300 completed units (400 units in ending work in process, three-fourths completed), for a total of 2,900.

With the equivalent production figures calculated for materials, labor, and overhead, the unit cost for the month can now be calculated. The cost of each element in the beginning work in process is added to the cost for that element incurred in the current month. The total cost for the element is then divided by the appropriate equivalent production figure to determine the unit cost for each element. In this example, the unit costs are: materials, $3.00; labor, $1.25; and overhead, $0.75; for a total unit cost of $5.00.

The 2,600 units transferred to Blending are costed at $5.00, amounting to a total cost of $13,000. In costing the ending work in process, the stage of completion and the point at which materials were added must be

Figure 6-2 Cost of Production Summary, Mixing

Newark Chemical Company
Cost of Production Summary—Mixing Department
For the Month Ended January, 31, 2011

Cost of work in process, beginning of month:		
Materials	$1,500	
Labor	250	
Factory overhead	150	$ 1,900
Cost of production for month:		
Materials	$7,500	
Labor	3,375	
Factory overhead	2,025	12,900
Total costs to be accounted for		$14,800
Unit output for month:		
Materials:		
Finished and transferred to Blending during month		**2,600**
Equivalent units of work in process, end of month (400 units, all materials)		**400**
Total equivalent production		**3,000**
Labor and factory overhead:		
Finished and transferred to Blending during month		**2,600**
Equivalent units of work in process, end of month (400 units, three-fourths completed)		**300**
Total equivalent production		**2,900**
Unit cost for month:		
Materials [($1,500 + $7,500) ÷ 3,000]		$3.00
Labor [($250 + $3,375) ÷ 2,900]		1.25
Factory overhead [($150 + $2,025) ÷ 2,900]		0.75
Total		$ 5.00
Inventory costs:		
Cost of goods finished and transferred to Blending during month (2,600 × $5)		$13,000
Cost of work in process, end of month:		
Materials (400 × $3)	$1,200	
Labor (400 × 3/4 × $1.25)	375	
Factory overhead (400 × 3/4 × $0.75)	225	1,800
Total production costs accounted for		$14,800

considered. In this instance, because materials were put into production at the beginning of the manufacturing cycle, the 400 units in process at the end of the period have had all materials added and are, therefore, costed at the full unit cost of $3.00 for materials. Because the goods are only three-fourths completed as to labor and factory overhead, the 400 partially completed units have the equivalent amount of labor and overhead added that would be needed to complete 300 whole units (400 × 3/4).

Illustrative Problem No. 2

Computing the unit cost in the Blending Department where all the materials are added at the close of processing—average cost method. Figure 6-3 shows the production report for Blending. Because the materials are added at the end of the process in Blending, those costs will be applied only to those units finished and transferred out of Blending. Therefore, the equivalent production for the month for materials in Blending is the same as the number of units completed and transferred out, 2,500. The equivalent unit computation for labor and factory overhead adds the 2,500 finished units to the equivalent production of the ending work in process, 350 units two-fifths completed, or 140 (350 × 2/5), for a total of 2,640. The cost of production summary for Blending, with the equivalent unit computations highlighted, is illustrated in Figure 6-4.

As was done for Mixing, the unit cost for each element is determined by adding the cost in the beginning work in process to the cost for that element incurred during the month and then dividing the total by the equivalent units of production. For Blending, these unit costs for materials, labor, and factory overhead are $4, $4, and $2, respectively, for a total cost of $10.

The units finished and transferred to the Packaging Department are valued at the full unit cost of $5 from Mixing, plus the unit cost of $10 added in Forming, for a total cost transferred of $37,500 (2,500 units × $15).

The cost of the units in process at the end of the period in Blending includes the full cost of $5 from Mixing. There is no Blending Department materials cost in the ending work in process inventory for that department, because materials are added only at the end of the process. Because the units are two-fifths completed as to labor and factory overhead in Blending, the

Figure 6-3 Production Report, Blending

PRODUCTION REPORT

For Month Ending January 31, 2011

Dept. Blending

In process, beginning of period		250 units
Stage of completion		1/2
Placed in process during period		
Received from dept. Mixing	during period	2,600 units
Transferred to dept. Packaging	during period	2,500 units
Transferred to stockroom during period		
In process, end of period		350 units
Stage of completion	No materials; 2/5 labor and overhead	

Figure 6-4 **Cost of Production Summary, Blending**

Newark Chemical Company
Cost of Production Summary—Blending Department
For the Month Ended January 31, 2011

Cost of work in process, beginning of month—Blending:			
Cost in Mixing		$ 1,250	
Cost in Blending:			
Materials	-0-		
Labor	$1,560		
Factory overhead	780	750	$ 2,000
Cost of goods received from Mixing during month			13,000
Cost of production for month:			
Materials		$10,000	
Labor		9,000	
Factory overhead		4,500	25,090
Total costs to be accounted for			$40,090
Unit output for month:			
Materials:			
Finished and transferred to Packaging during month			**2,500**
Equivalent units of work in process, end of month			**-0-**
Total equivalent production			**2,500**
Labor and factory overhead:			
Finished and transferred to Packaging during month			**2,500**
Equivalent units of work in process, end of month (350 units, two-fifths completed)			**140**
Total equivalent production			**2,640**
Unit cost for month—Blending:			
Materials ($10,000 ÷ 2,500)			$ 4.00
Labor [($1,560 + $9,000) ÷ 2,640]			4.00
Factory overhead [($780 + $4,500) ÷ 2,640]			2.00
Total			$ 10.00
Inventory costs:			
Cost of goods finished and transferred to Packaging during month:			
Cost in Mixing (2,500 × $ 5)			$12,500
Cost in Blending (2,500 × $10)			25,000
(2,500 × $15)			$37,500
Cost of work in process, end of month:			
Cost in Mixing (350 × $5)		$ 1,750	
Cost in Blending:			
Materials	-0-		
Labor (350 × 2/5 × $4)	$ 560		
Factory overhead (350 × 2/5 × $2)	280	840	2,590
Total production costs accounted for			$40,090

350 partially completed units in ending work in process have the equivalent amount of labor and overhead added that would be needed to complete 140 (350 × 2/5) whole units. The combination of these items results in a cost of $2,590 for the ending work in process, as shown in Figure 6-4.

Illustrative Problem No. 3

Computing the unit cost in the Packaging Department, where 60% of the materials cost is added to production at the beginning of processing and 40% of the materials are added when the processing is one-half completed—average cost method. In Packaging, the calculation of equivalent production is more difficult because materials are added at different points throughout the process. The stage of completion of units in process cannot be averaged but must be reported in separate groups of units at various points in the manufacturing operation as indicated in the production report, shown in Figure 6-5. In calculating the units of output for the period, as highlighted in the cost of production summary for Packaging (Figure 6-6), the stage of completion for each type of material must be computed separately.

The equivalent production for materials for the month is calculated as follows: 2,400 units were finished, which included all of the materials; 200 units in ending work in process are one-fourth completed—because they are not yet at the halfway point of the production process, only 60% of the materials and the color additives, but no packaging materials, have been added to these uncompleted units, which is an equivalent of 120 units (200 × 60%); and 400 units in ending work in process are three-fourths completed. Since these 400 units have passed the halfway stage, both the coloring and packaging materials have been added to these units, representing a total of 400 equivalent units. Combining these figures—2,400, 120, and 400—results in equivalent production for materials of 2,920 units.

Figure 6-5 Production Report, Packaging

PRODUCTION REPORT

For Month Ending January 31, 2011

Packaging

In process, beginning of period 500 units
Stage of completion 200 units 3/4 completed; 300 units 1/3 completed
Placed in process during period
Received from dept. Blending during period 2,500 units
Transferred to dept. during period
Transferred to stockroom during period 2,400 units
In process, end of period 600 units
Stage of completion 400 units 100% completed and 200 units 60% completed as to materials; 200 units 1/4 completed and 400 units 3/4 completed as to labor and overhead

Figure 6-6 **Cost of Production Summary, Packaging**

Newark Chemical Company
Cost of Production Summary—Packaging Department
For the Month Ended January 31, 2011

Cost of work in process, beginning of month—Packaging:			
Cost in Mixing		$ 2,500	
Cost in Blending		5,000	
Cost in Packaging			
Materials	$665		
Labor	300		
Factory overhead	150	1,115	$ 8,615
Cost of goods received from Blending during month			37,500
Cost of production for month:			
Materials		$ 4,445	
Labor		3,000	
Factory overhead		1,500	8,945
Total costs to be accounted for			$55,060
Unit output for month:			
Materials:			
Finished and transferred to finished goods during month			**2,400**
Equivalent units of work in process, end of month:			
200 units, one-fourth completed (60% of materials)			**120**
400 units, three-fourths completed (all materials)			**400**
Total equivalent production			**2,920**
Labor and overhead:			
Finished and transferred to finished goods during month			**2,400**
Equivalent units of work in process, end of month:			
200 units, one-fourth completed			**50**
400 units, three-fourths completed			**300**
Total equivalent production			**2,750**
Unit cost for month—Packaging:			
Materials [($665 + $4,445) ÷ 2,920]			$ 1.75
Labor [($300 + $3,000) ÷ 2,750]			1.20
Factory overhead [($150 + $1,500) ÷ 2,750]			0.60
Total			$ 3.55
Inventory costs:			
Cost of goods finished and transferred to finished goods during month:			
Cost in Mixing (2,400 × $ 5.00)		$12,000	
Cost in Blending (2,400 × $10.00)		24,000	
Cost in Packaging (2,400 × $ 3.55)		8,520	
(2,400 × $18.55)			$44,520

(Continued)

Figure 6.6 (*Continued*)

Cost of work in process, end of month:			
200 units, one-fourth completed:			
Cost in Mixing (200 × $5)		$ 1,000	
Cost in Blending (200 × $10)		2,000	
Cost in Packaging:			
Materials (200 × 60% × $1.75)	$210		
Labor (200 × 25% × $1.20)	60		
Factory overhead (200 × 25% × $0.60) ...	30	300	
400 units, three-fourths completed:			
Cost in Mixing (400 × $5)		2,000	
Cost in Blending (400 × $10)		4,000	
Cost in Packaging:			
Materials (400 × $1.75)	$700		
Labor (400 × 75% × $1.20)	360		
Factory overhead (400 × 75% × $0.60) ...	180	1,240	10,540
Total production costs accounted for			$55,060

It is simpler to calculate the equivalent units for labor and factory overhead: 2,400 completed units, plus the equivalent of 50 completed units (200 × ¼), plus the equivalent of 300 completed units (400 units × ¾) totals 2,750 units of equivalent production for labor and overhead.

The unit costs for the month are calculated as previously illustrated and are $1.75, $1.20, and $0.60 for materials, labor, and factory overhead, respectively, for a total unit cost of $3.55 in Packaging. The cost of the units finished and transferred to the finished goods storeroom includes the unit costs from Mixing of $5, from Blending of $10, and from Packaging of $3.55, for a total cost of $18.55.

In calculating the cost to be assigned to the ending work in process, the stage of completion must be considered. The 200 units that are one-fourth completed will have all the costs from Mixing and Blending assigned to them because they would not have been transferred on had they not been complete as to those departments. The costs in Packaging are determined as follows: 60% of the materials cost has been added to the 200 units, an equivalent of 120 units. The cost of the materials will be as follows: 200 units × 60% × $1.75 = $210. The costs allocated for labor and overhead are one-fourth of this month's unit cost for each, or 200 units × 25% × $1.20 = $60 for labor and 200 units × 25% × $0.60 = $30 for overhead.

The 400 units that are three-fourths completed are again assigned all of the unit costs from Blanking ($5) and Forming ($10). Although these units are still in process, all materials required by Packaging have been added. Therefore, they are charged for the full cost of materials in Packaging, $700 (400 units × $1.75). Three-fourths of the cost for labor and factory overhead would also be included in the cost of these units: $360 for labor

(400 units × 75% × \$1.20), and \$180 for overhead (400 units × 75% × \$0.60).

After the cost of production summaries have been prepared for each department, the journal entries can be made as illustrated in Chapter 5. Entries would be made to transfer costs from one department to the next department and so on, ending at Finished Goods. The actual costs incurred during the month for materials, labor, and factory overhead would be recorded in the journals and ledgers. After all entries have been made, the work in process accounts in the general ledger should have balances that equal the cost assigned to work in process on the cost of production summaries. If desired, a departmental cost work sheet can be prepared as was illustrated in Chapter 5.

Recall and Review 1

Beginning inventory was 4,000 units, one-fourth complete as to labor and factory overhead. During the period, 30,000 units were started in process and 28,000 units were finished. There were 6,000 units in ending work in process, one-half complete as to labor and factory overhead. Assuming that the average costing method is used and that all materials are put into production at the beginning of the process, while labor and overhead are applied evenly throughout production, the equivalent units of production for direct materials and for direct labor and factory overhead would be ________ and ________, respectively.

(After working this exercise, see page 315 for the solution.)

You should now be able to work the following:
Questions 1–5; Exercises 6-1 to 6-6; Problems 6-1 to 6-4; and Internet Exercise.

Units Lost in Production

LO2 Account for units lost in the production process.

In many industries that have a process manufacturing operation, the production process is of a nature that some units will always be lost due to evaporation, shrinkage, spillage, or other factors. The effect of such losses is that when the number of units completed in a given period is added to the number of units still in process at the end of the period, the total units calculated will be less than the number of units that were initially placed into production.

These **normal losses** are expected in the manufacturing process and cannot be avoided. They represent a necessary cost of producing the good units. These normal losses are treated as **product costs**; that is, the cost of the lost units is included as a part of the cost of all units finished or still in process because the good units could not have been produced without this normal spoilage. In other words, the good units absorb the cost of the units lost. The effect is that the unit cost of the remaining units is greater than if no losses had occurred, because the production costs for the period are spread over a smaller number of good units. In many industries, costing the waste or spoilage is more than just spreading the production costs over the remaining good units. For example, in the chemical industry additional costs may include the costs of disposing of or treating the chemical waste in accordance with environmental regulations and the cost of any cleaning fluids needed to cleanse the plant and equipment contaminated by the waste.

The following example illustrates the concept of normal lost units. Assume that materials, labor, and factory overhead are applied evenly throughout the process; units are lost throughout the process, but inspection does not occur until the end of the process. The monthly production report for the Refining Department of Texas Oil Corporation reports the following data:

Units started in process		12,000
Units finished and transferred to the next department	9,000	
Units still in process, one-half completed (materials, labor, and overhead)	2,000	11,000
Units lost in production		1,000

This report is significant to factory managers, who review these figures to determine whether they represent normal unavoidable losses or abnormal losses that will require a different type of action. From the production statistics and costs of production data for the month, a cost of production summary as shown in Figure 6-7 can be prepared.

The cost of production summary shows that the lost units have not been considered. They have been ignored in the highlighted calculation of equivalent production and in the determination of inventory costs. If the 1,000 units had not been spoiled but instead had been completed according to specifications, equivalent production would have been 11,000 units (10,000 finished units + 1,000 equivalent units in ending work in process), and the unit costs for materials, labor, and factory overhead would have been lower. In the case illustrated, there is a loss of units that have already incurred some costs, which will be absorbed by the good units produced during the month.

The preceding discussion has considered only normal losses such as those that result from the inability to achieve perfection in the production process, with the cost of lost units being treated as product cost—that is, charged to the remaining good units and, therefore, increasing the cost per unit. But **abnormal losses**, such as those caused by machine breakdowns due to inadequate maintenance and machine operator errors, may also occur. Such losses are not expected in the manufacturing process and should not happen under normal, efficient operating conditions. These abnormal losses are not included as part of the cost of transferred or finished goods, but are treated as a period cost—that is, they are charged to a separate account, such as Loss from Abnormal Spoilage, and are shown as a separate item of expense on the current income statement. These losses do not become a part of the manufacturing costs transferred to subsequent departments, finished goods, and cost of goods sold.

Figure 6-7 **Texas Oil Cost of Production Summary, Refining Dept.**

Texas Oil Corporation
Cost of Production Summary—Refining Department
For the Month Ended July 31, 2011

Cost of production for month:		
Materials		$20,000
Labor		10,000
Factory overhead		5,000
Total costs to be accounted for		$35,000
Unit output for month:		
Finished and transferred to Transportation Dept. during month		**9,000**
Equivalent units of work in process, end of month (2,000 units, one-half completed as to materials, labor, and factory overhead)		**1,000**
Total equivalent production		**10,000**
Unit cost for month:		
Materials ($20,000 ÷ 10,000)		$ 2.00
Labor ($10,000 ÷ 10,000)		1.00
Factory overhead ($5,000 ÷ 10,000)		0.50
Total		$ 3.50
Inventory costs:		
Cost of goods finished and transferred to Transportation Dept. during month (9,000 × $3.50)		$31,500
Cost of work in process, end of month:		
Materials (2,000 × 1/2 × $2)	$2,000	
Labor (2,000 × 1/2 × $1)	1,000	
Factory overhead (2,000 × 1/2 × $0.50)	500	3,500
Total production costs accounted for		$35,000

Units Gained in Production

Account for units gained in the production process.

For some products, the addition of materials in any department after the first department may increase the number of units being processed. For example, assume that a liquid product is being produced. In the first department, 1,000 gallons of various materials are put into production. In the next department, an additional 500 gallons of a different material are added, increasing the number of gallons being manufactured to 1,500. This increase in units has the opposite effect on unit costs than did lost units, and it requires an adjustment to the unit cost. The calculation of this adjusted unit cost is similar to that made when units are lost, except that the total cost for the original units are now spread over a greater number of units in the subsequent department, thereby reducing the cost per unit.

Figure 6-8 **Genie Cost of Production Summary, Blending**

G & P Manufacturing Company
Cost of Production Summary for Genie—Blending Department
For the Month Ended May 31, 2011

Cost of goods received from Mixing Dept. during month (10,000 gallons × $1.50)			$15,000
Cost of production for month:			
Materials		$15,400	
Labor		3,500	
Factory overhead		2,800	21,700
Total costs to be accounted for			$36,700
Unit output for month:			
Finished and transferred to finished goods			13,000
Equivalent units of work in process, end of month (2,000 gallons, one-half completed as to materials, labor, and factory overhead)			1,000
Total equivalent production			14,000
Unit cost for month:			
Materials ($15,400 ÷ 14,000)			$ 1.10
Labor ($3,500 ÷ 14,000)			0.25
Factory overhead ($2,800 ÷ 14,000)			0.20
Total			$ 1.55
Inventory costs:			
Cost of goods finished and transferred to finished goods:			
Cost in Mixing (13,000 × $1.00*, adjusted unit cost)		**$13,000**	
Cost in Blending (13,000 × $1.55)		20,150	
(13,000 × $2.55)			$33,150
Cost of work in process, end of month:			
Cost in Mixing Dept. (2,000 × $1.00*, adjusted unit cost)		**$ 2,000**	
Cost in Blending Dept.:			
Materials (2,000 × 1/2 × $1.10)	$1,100		
Labor (2,000 × 1/2 × $0.25)	250		
Factory overhead (2,000 × 1/2 × $0.20)	200	1,550	3,550
Total production costs accounted for			$36,700

**$15,000 ÷ 15,000 gal = $1 per gal*

To illustrate, assume that a concentrated detergent, Genie, is manufactured. During the month, 10,000 gallons of the partially processed product are transferred to the Blending Department at a cost of $15,000, and a unit cost of $1.50 ($15,000/10,000 gal). In the Blending Department, 5,000 gallons of additional materials are added to these units in process. As these materials are added, the mixing and refining of the liquid involves the equal application of materials, labor, and overhead. A production report shows that 13,000 gallons were completed and transferred to finished goods, leaving 2,000 gallons in process, one-half completed. The cost of production summary, Figure 6-8, shows that the cost transferred from the Mixing Department for the production of 10,000 gallons was $15,000, or $1.50 per unit. The addition of 5,000 gallons in the Blending Department increased the liquid in process to 15,000 gallons. The $15,000 cost from the Mixing Department must now be spread over these 15,000 gallons, resulting in an adjusted unit cost of $1.00 per gallon in the previous department, as highlighted in the cost of production summary.

Equivalent Production: First-In, First-Out Method

LO4 Assign costs to inventories, using the first-in, first-out method.

The previous discussion and illustrations have used the average costing method. As mentioned in Chapter 5, another method commonly used is the **first-in, first-out (FIFO) method**. This procedure assumes that the unit costs calculated for the current period are used for a variety of reasons: first, to complete the beginning units of work in process; second, to start and fully complete an additional number of units; and finally, to start other units that will remain unfinished at the end of the period.

The two problems that follow illustrate the FIFO method and compare it to the average costing method for Robotics Manufacturing, Inc., which has the following two departments: Department 1—Machining and Department 2—Assembly. When studying these examples, note that FIFO costing differs from average costing only if there are units in process at the start of the period. If no beginning work in process exists, both methods will produce the same results.

Whether using the FIFO or the average cost method, the first step in preparing the cost of production summary is to list the costs that must be accounted for: the beginning balance of work in process, the current period's production costs, and the cost of units transferred from a prior department, if any. With the FIFO method, it is not necessary to break down the cost of the beginning work in process into its cost elements as the average cost method requires.

The second step under the FIFO method, as with the average cost procedure, is to determine the unit output for the month. If there were units in process at the start of the period, the total equivalent production figures for the FIFO method will differ from those for the average cost method because the unit output required to complete the beginning work in process must be calculated under FIFO. A comparison of the computation of equivalent units of production using average costing and FIFO costing, with the amounts in the following Illustrative Problem No. 1, is presented in Figure 6-9.

Figure 6-9 **Comparison of Equivalent Units Computation in Department 1 by Using Average Costing and FIFO Costing**

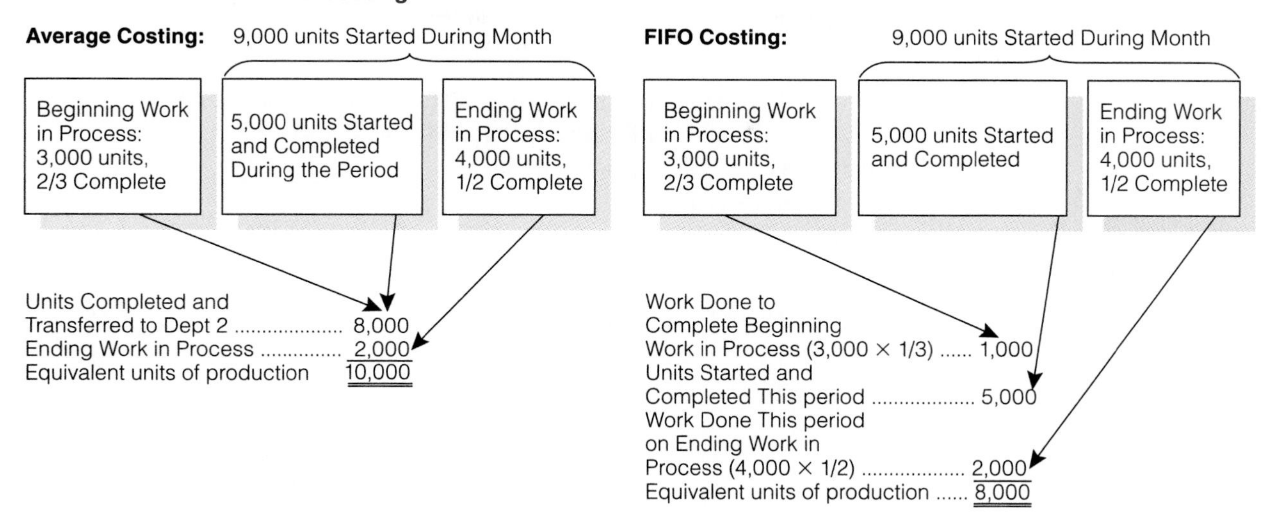

Illustrative Problem No. 1

FIFO cost method compared with average cost method—materials added at start of process. Assume that in Department 1 (Machining), materials are added at the start of processing. Labor and factory overhead are applied evenly throughout the process. The production report for March reflects the following data:

Units in process, beginning of month, two-thirds completed as to labor and factory overhead	3,000
Units started in process	9,000
Units finished and transferred to Dept. 2 (Assembly)	8,000
Units in process, end of month, one-half completed as to labor and factory overhead	4,000
Cost data are as follows:	
Beginning work in process, prior month's cost:	
Materials	$ 9,600
Labor	3,600
Factory overhead	2,800
Total	$16,000
Current month's production costs:	
Materials	$27,000
Labor	16,000
Factory overhead	8,000
Total	$51,000

A cost of production summary using the FIFO method is presented in Figure 6-10 with the unit output section highlighted. For comparative purposes, Figure 6-11 shows a cost of production summary using the average cost method with the same data.

Figure 6-10 **Cost of Production Summary, Dept. 1, FIFO Method**

FIFO METHOD
Robotics Manufacturing, Inc.
Cost of Production Summary—Department 1 (Machining)
For the Month Ended March 31, 2011

Cost of work in process, beginning of month		$ 16,000
Cost of production for month:		
Materials	$ 27,000	
Labor	16,000	
Factory overhead	8,000	51,000
Total costs to be accounted for		$ 67,000

Unit output for month:

	Materials	**Labor and Factory Overhead**
To complete beginning units in process (no materials, 1/3 labor and overhead)*	**-0-**	**1,000**
Units started and finished during month (9,000 started – 4,000 in ending WIP)	**5,000**	**5,000**
Ending units in process (all materials, 1/2 labor and overhead)**	**4,000**	**2,000**
Total equivalent production	**9,000**	**8,000**

Unit cost for month:		
Materials ($27,000 ÷ 9,000)		$ 3.00
Labor ($16,000 ÷ 8,000)		2.00
Factory overhead ($8,000 ÷ 8,000)		1.00
Total		$ 6.00
Inventory costs:		
Cost of goods finished and transferred to Dept. 2 (Assembly) during month:		
Beginning units in process:		
Prior month's cost	$ 16,000	
Current cost to complete:		
Materials	-0-	
Labor (3,000 × 1/3 × $2)	2,000	
Factory overhead (3,000 × 1/3 × $1)	1,000	$ 19,000
Units started and finished during month (5,000 × $6.00)		30,000
Total cost transferred (8,000 × $6.125***)		$ 49,000
Cost of work in process, end of month:		
Materials (4,000 × $3)	$ 12,000	
Labor (4,000 ×1/2 × $2)	4,000	
Factory overhead (4,000 × 1/2 × $1)	2,000	18,000
Total production costs accounted for		$ 67,000

*indicates what is needed to complete these units
**indicates what has already been added
***$49,000 ÷ 8,000 = $6.125

Figure 6-11 **Cost of Production Summary, Dept. 1, Average Cost Method**

AVERAGE COST METHOD
Robotics Manufacturing, Inc.
Cost of Production Summary—Department 1 (Machining)
For the Month Ended March 31, 2011

Cost of work in process, beginning of month:		
Materials	$ 9,600	
Labor	3,600	
Factory overhead	2,800	$16,000
Cost of production for month:		
Materials	$27,000	
Labor	16,000	
Factory overhead	8,000	51,000
Total costs to be accounted for		$67,000
Unit output for month:		
Materials:		
Finished and transferred to Dept. 2 (Assembly) during month		**8,000**
Work in process, end of month (4,000 units, 100% complete)		**4,000**
Total equivalent production		**12,000**
Labor and factory overhead:		
Finished and transferred to Dept. 2 (Assembly) during month		**8,000**
Work in process, end of month (4,000 units, 1/2 completed)		**2,000**
Total equivalent production		**10,000**
Unit cost for month:		
Materials [($9,600 + $27,000) ÷ 12,000]		$ 3.05
Labor [($3,600 + $16,000) ÷ 10,000]		1.96
Factory overhead [($2,800 + $8,000) ÷ 10,000]		1.08
Total		$ 6.09
Inventory costs:		
Cost of goods finished and transferred to Dept. 2 (Assembly) during month (8,000 × $6.09)		$48,720
Cost of work in process, end of month:		
Materials (4,000 × $3.05)	$12,200	
Labor (4,000 × 1/2 × $1.96)	3,920	
Factory overhead (4,000 × 1/2 × $1.08)	2,160	18,280
Total production costs accounted for		$67,000

There were 3,000 units in process at the beginning of the month. These units were complete as to materials and two-thirds complete as to labor and factory overhead.

In the current month, no materials had to be added to the beginning inventory. However, the equivalent of 1,000 units (3,000 × 1/3) of labor and overhead had to be applied to finish the units in Department 1 (Machining).

Of the 8,000 units finished and transferred to Department 2 (Assembly) during the month, 3,000 were from the beginning units in process. Therefore, 5,000 units were started and fully completed during the month. Under the FIFO cost method, the beginning units in process and their costs, $16,000, *are not merged* with the units started and finished during the month.

The calculation of equivalent production for the *ending work in process* is the *same* under FIFO and average costing. These 4,000 units in ending inventory have had all materials added and only one-half of the labor and overhead. Thus, the ending inventory equivalent production for materials is 4,000 units and for labor and overhead, 2,000 units (4,000 × 1/2).

The calculation of unit costs with the FIFO method takes into consideration only the current period's cost data. The total cost of each element—materials, labor, and factory overhead—is divided by the equivalent production for the period to determine the unit cost for each element. The cost elements of the beginning work in process are not merged with current cost elements under the FIFO method, as they are under average costing. Whereas the average costing method computes a single average cost per unit for the beginning inventory plus the current period production, the FIFO method separates beginning inventory from current production so that a separate unit cost can be computed for the current month.

When assigning costs to the units finished and transferred, the average cost approach charges the 8,000 units transferred with the total unit cost of $6.09. Under the FIFO method, however, two calculations are necessary to determine the cost assigned to units transferred. First, the 3,000 units in process at the beginning of the month were previously completed as to materials; therefore, no cost for materials is added. However, the units had been only two-thirds completed as to labor and overhead during the previous month and must be one-third completed this month. Thus, one-third of the current period's unit cost for labor and overhead is assigned to each of the 3,000 units. The cost to complete the beginning inventory then is added to the $16,000 beginning inventory cost carried over from the prior period to arrive at a completed cost for the beginning inventory of $19,000.

Second, the 5,000 units started and fully manufactured during the month are priced at the unit cost of $6 for the current period. The total accumulated cost of the 3,000 units in process at the beginning of the month ($19,000) plus the cost of the 5,000 units started and finished during the month ($30,000) is then transferred to Department 2 ($49,000). Note that when making this transfer of cost, the cost and unit cost related to the beginning inventory units lose their identity because they are merged with the cost of units started and finished during the current period. Thus, the $49,000 of the total cost transferred to Department 2 is divided by the 8,000 units transferred to Department 2 to arrive at a single unit cost of $6.125 as computed in the footnote to Figure 6-10. The costs assigned to the ending work in process inventory are determined in the same manner under the FIFO method as they are using average costing. The 4,000 units are complete as to materials and are charged with the full cost of materials. They are one-half complete as to labor and overhead and are allocated one-half of the labor and overhead cost. Although the method of calculation is the same, the total costs charged to the ending units in process differ between FIFO ($18,000) and average costing ($18,280) because of the difference in unit costs determined by the two methods.

Illustrative Problem No. 2

FIFO cost method compared with average cost method—materials added at end of process. Assume that in Department 2 (Assembly), materials are added at the end of the process and labor and factory overhead are applied evenly throughout the process. The production for March reflects the following information:

Units in process, beginning of month, three-fourths completed	2,000
Units received from Dept. 1 (Machining)	8,000
Units finished	8,000
Units in process, end of month, one-half completed as to labor and factory overhead	2,000
Cost data are as follows:	
Beginning work in process, prior month's cost:	
Prior department cost	$12,000
Materials	-0-
Labor	4,160
Factory overhead	3,000
Total	$19,160
Cost of units received from Dept. 1 (Machining) during month	$49,000
Current month's production costs:	
Materials	$16,000
Labor	21,000
Factory overhead	13,875
Total	$50,875

Figure 6-12 shows the cost of production summary for Department 2 (Assembly), using the FIFO method, and Figure 6-13 shows the summary using the average cost method with the unit output sections highlighted.

In the cost of production summary using the FIFO method, the costs to be accounted for are listed, and then the unit output for the period is determined. In this department, materials are added at the end of the process. Therefore, in order to finish the 2,000 units in process at the beginning of the period, all materials have to be added—a total of 2,000 units. Three-fourths of the labor and factory overhead were applied to these beginning inventory units in the previous period, so one-fourth of the labor and overhead need to be applied in the current month to finish the 2,000 units—an equivalent of 500 units.

Figure 6-12 **Cost of Production Summary, Dept. 2, FIFO Method**

FIFO METHOD

Robotics Manufacturing, Inc.

Cost of Production Summary—Department 2 (Assembly)

For the Month Ended March 31, 2011

Cost of work in process, beginning of month		$ 19,160
Cost of goods received from Dept. 1 (Machining) during month		49,000
Cost of production for month:		
Materials	$16,000	
Labor	21,000	
Factory overhead	13,875	50,875
Total costs to be accounted for		$119,035

Unit output for month:

	Materials	**Labor and Factory Overhead**
To complete beginning units in process (all materials, 1/4 labor and overhead)	**2,000**	**500**
Units started and finished during month (8,000 started–2,000 in ending WIP)	**6,000**	**6,000**
Ending units in process (no materials, 1/2 labor and overhead)	**-0-**	**1,000**
Total equivalent production	**8,000**	**7,500**

Unit cost for month:		
Materials ($16,000 ÷ 8,000)		$ 2.00
Labor ($21,000 ÷ 7,500)		2.80
Factory overhead ($13,875 ÷ 7,500)		1.85
Total		$ 6.65
Inventory costs:		
Cost of goods finished:		
Beginning units in process:		
Prior month's cost	$19,160	
Current cost to complete:		
Materials (2,000 × $2)	4,000	
Labor (2,000 × 1/4 × $2.80)	1,400	
Factory overhead (2,000 × 1/4 × $1.85)	925	$ 25,485
Units started and finished during month:		
Cost in Dept. 1 (6,000 × $6.125)	$36,750	
Cost in Dept. 2 (6,000 × $6.65)	39,900	76,650
Total costs transferred to finished goods [(2,000 units + 6,000 units) × $12.7669]*		$102,135
Cost of work in process, end of month:		
Cost in Dept. 1 (2,000 × $6.125)	$12,250	
Cost in Dept. 2:		
Materials	-0-	
Labor (2,000 × 1/2 × $2.80)	2,800	
Factory overhead (2,000 × 1/2 × $1.85)	1,850	16,900
Total production costs accounted for		$119,035

**$102,135 ÷ 8,000 units = $12.7669*

Figure 6-13 **Cost of Production Summary, Dept. 2, Average Cost Method**

AVERAGE COST METHOD
Robotics Manufacturing, Inc.
Cost of Production Summary—Department 2 (Assembly)
For the Month Ended March 31, 2011

Cost of work in process, beginning of month:			
Cost in Dept. 1 (Machining)		$12,000	
Cost in Dept. 2 (Assembly):			
Materials	-0-		
Labor	$4,160		
Factory overhead	3,000	7,160	$ 19,160
Cost of goods received from Dept. 1 (Machining) during month			49,000
Cost of production for month:			
Materials		$16,000	
Labor		21,000	
Factory overhead		13,875	50,875
Total costs to be accounted for			$119,035
Unit output for month:			
Materials finished during month			**8,000**
Labor and overhead:			
Finished during month		**8,000**	
Work in process, end of month		**1,000**	**9,000**
Unit cost for month:			
Materials ($16,000 ÷ 8,000)			$ 2.0000
Labor [($4,160 + $21,000) ÷ 9,000]			2.7956
Factory overhead [($3,000 + $13,875) ÷ 9,000]			1.8750
Total			$ 6.6706
Inventory costs:			
Cost of goods finished:			
Cost in Dept. 1 (8,000 × $ 6.1000)		$48,800	
Cost in Dept. 2 (8,000 × $ 6.6706)		53,365	
(8,000 × $12.7706)			$102,165
Cost of work in process, end of month:			
Cost in Dept. 1 (2,000 × $6.10)		$12,200	
Cost in Dept. 2:			
Materials		-0-	
Labor (2,000 × 1/2 × $2.7956)		2,795	
Factory overhead (2,000 × 1/2 × $1.8750)		1,875	16,870
Total production costs accounted for			$119,035

Of the 8,000 units completed during the period, 2,000 were from the beginning inventory; therefore, 6,000 new units were started and fully manufactured during the current month. The 2,000 units in process at the end of the month have had no materials added, but are one-half complete as to labor and overhead—an equivalent of 1,000 units.

As in Department 1, unit cost for FIFO is calculated by dividing the current period's cost of each element by the equivalent production for that element. Under the average cost method, unit cost is calculated by dividing the combined costs of the current period and the beginning work in process by the equivalent production for each element.

In FIFO, to calculate the total completed cost of the beginning inventory, the total cost balance of the beginning work in process from the previous period is added to the costs incurred to complete these units in the current period. The 2,000 units are charged for the full cost of materials and for one-fourth of the current costs for labor and overhead. The average cost method does not require a separate computation to complete the beginning inventory.

Under the FIFO method, the cost transferred from Department 1 during the period, $49,000, is divided by the 8,000 units transferred, which results in an adjusted unit cost of $6.125 for the goods received from Department 1. The 6,000 units started and finished during the month are charged with the $6.125 adjusted unit cost from the prior department *plus* the $6.65 current unit cost generated by Department 2.

Under the average cost method, all of the units from Department 1, whether this month's or last month's, must be considered in determining the unit cost. The 2,000 units in process at the beginning of the period and the 8,000 units received during the month are included in the calculation. The prior department cost of $12,000, carried over from the previous month, is added to the current month's cost of $49,000 transferred from Department 1. The total prior department cost of $61,000 is then divided by 10,000 units to produce a unit cost of $6.10. The 8,000 units completed during the period have a total unit cost for the period of $12.7706, which consists of the transferred-in cost of $6.10 plus the cost added in Department 2 operations of $6.6706.

The costs to be charged to the units in process at the end of the month differ slightly between FIFO ($16,900) and average costing ($16,870), although both FIFO and average costing use the same mathematical methods. The values of the ending work in process differ because of the procedures used to derive the prior department and current-month unit costs.

In comparing FIFO and average costing, FIFO provides that units started within the current period are valued at the current period's costs and are not distorted by the merging of the current costs with costs from the preceding period, which could be considerably different. The units and costs in the beginning inventory in a processing department maintain their separate identity. This helps to identify trends and control costs by having purely current unit costs each month to make month-to-month cost comparisons. Use of the FIFO method, however, means that the units in the beginning inventory are valued when completed at a cost that represents neither the prior period's cost nor the current period's cost, but a combination of the two. Also, the identity of the beginning units in process is not maintained when these units are transferred to the next department or to finished goods. At the time of transfer, the cost of these units is usually combined with the cost of units fully manufactured during the month.

The average cost method has an advantage when compared to FIFO in that all units completed during the period will be assigned the same unit cost. This cost assignment procedure makes average costing a simpler method to use. In the final analysis, however, a manufacturer should choose the method that not only minimizes the clerical cost of application but also most accurately gauges its cost of production so that its products can successfully compete in the marketplace.

Recall and Review 2

Beginning inventory was 4,000 units, one-fourth complete as to labor and factory overhead. During the period, 30,000 units were started in process and 28,000 units were finished. There were 6,000 units in ending work in process, one-half complete as to labor and factory overhead. Assuming that the FIFO costing method is used and that all materials are put into production at the beginning of the process, while labor and overhead are applied evenly throughout production, the equivalent units of production for direct materials and for direct labor and factory overhead would be __________ and __________, respectively.

(After working this exercise, see page 315 for the solution.)

You should now be able to work the following:
Questions 6–13; Exercises 6-7 to 6-10; Problems 6-5 to 6-9 and Self-Study Problem 1.

Joint Products and By-Products

LO5 Identify the methods used to apportion joint costs to joint products and account for by-products.

Sioux City Meatpackers, Inc., processes hogs into bacon, ham, pork roast, and spare ribs. The materials, labor, and overhead processing costs to get the products to the point where they can be separately identified total $10,000,000 per year. Not having adequate in-house accounting expertise, Jamie Hyland asks you, a current cost accounting student, if it is acceptable to merely charge the $10,000,000 of costs equally to each of the four products. You inform Jamie that these costs and products are referred to as joint costs and joint products, respectively. You further inform her that there is a more equitable way to allocate the joint costs. The joint costing coverage that follows describes this more sophisticated method of allocating joint costs, and Self-Study Problem 2 at the end of the chapter continues with the Sioux City Meatpackers, Inc., example.

In many industries, the manufacturing process originates with one or more raw materials started in process, from which two or more distinct products are derived. Examples of these industries are petroleum refineries, lumber mills, and meatpacking plants. Petroleum yields gasoline, heating oils, and lubricants. Lumber mills produce various grades of lumber and salable sawdust.

Figure 6-14 The Output of a Joint Process

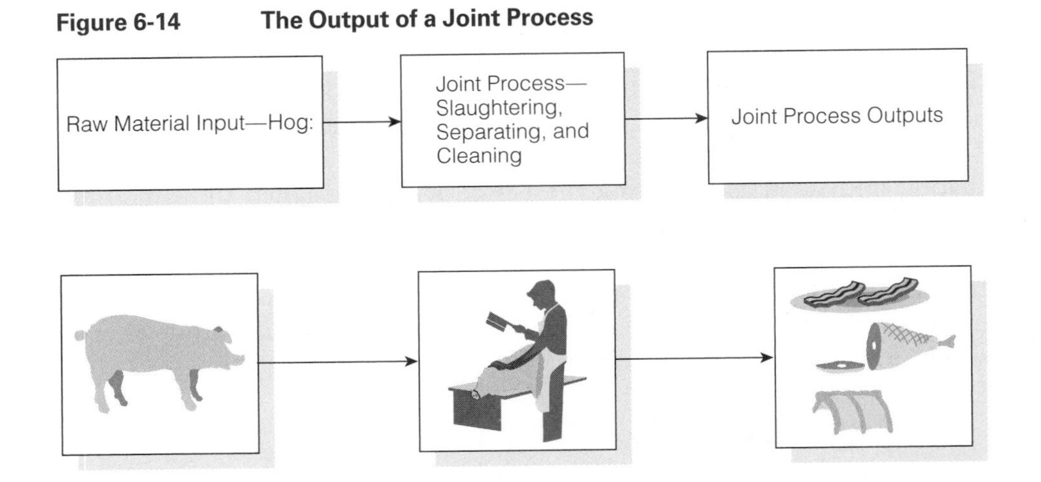

Meatpacking processes result in a variety of different cuts of meat and other products as illustrated in Figure 6-14. The several items obtained from a common process are divided into two categories: those that are the primary objectives of the process, called **joint products** (e.g., lumber), and secondary products with relatively little value, called **by-products** (e.g., sawdust).

Accounting for Joint Products

How does a milk producer decide on the allocation of the costs of producing raw milk? This is a concern because the raw milk will be further processed into whole milk, 2% milk, skim milk, and heavy and light cream. The costs of materials, labor, and overhead incurred during such a joint production process are called **joint costs**. The point where these joint products become separately identifiable is known as the **split-off point**. The manufacturing costs incurred in processing the raw milk up to the point where the milk products can be separately identified cannot be specifically identified with any one of the individual products. Some method, however, must be adopted to equitably allocate the joint costs to each identifiable product. If further processing of any of the products is required after the split-off point, these additional costs can be identified directly with the specific products.

Typical bases for apportionment of joint costs to joint products follow:

1. Relative (or adjusted) sales value of each product.
2. A physical unit of measure such as volume, weight, size, or grade.
3. Chemical, engineering, or other types of analyses.

The assignment of costs in proportion to the **relative sales value** of each product is most commonly used and is the only method that will be illustrated here. This method assumes a direct relationship between selling prices and joint costs. It follows the logic that the greatest share of joint cost should be assigned to the product that has the highest sales value.

To illustrate, assume that Clean It, Inc., produces two liquid products from one process. In the manufacturing process, various materials are mixed in a huge vat and allowed to settle, so that a light liquid rises to the top and a heavier liquid settles to the bottom of the vat. The products,

Figure 6-15 Joint Costs and Joint Products

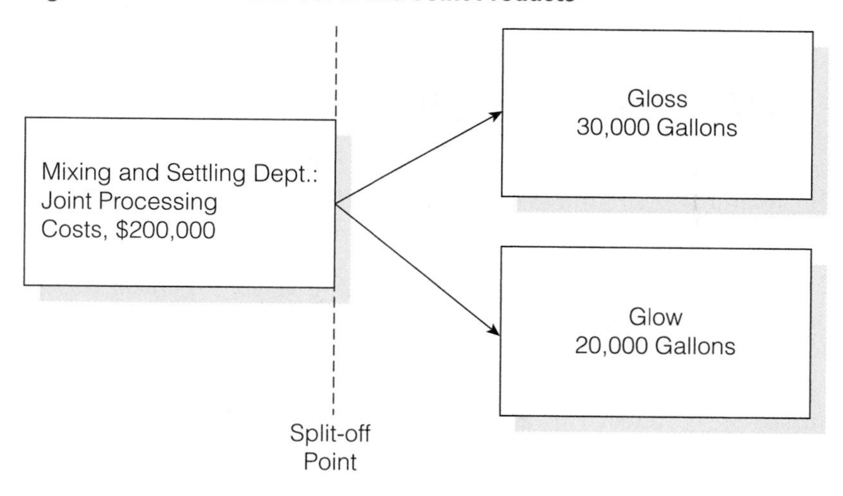

Gloss and Glow, are drawn off separately and piped directly into tank cars for shipment. The joint processing costs of materials, labor, and overhead total $200,000, producing 30,000 gallons of Gloss and 20,000 gallons of Glow. A diagram of these relationships appears in Figure 6-15.

Gloss sells for $10.00 a gallon and Glow for $25.00 a gallon. Using the relative sales value method, we would allocate the joint costs of $200,000 as follows:

Product	Gallons Produced		Selling Price/ Gallon		Total Sales Value	Percent of Sales Value	Assignment of Joint Costs
Gloss	30,000	×	$10.00	=	$300,000	37.5%	$ 75,000
Glow	20,000	×	25.00	=	500,000	62.5%	125,000
Total	50,000				$800,000	100.0%	$200,000

The amounts in the final column of the above table were determined as follows:

$$\text{Gloss: } \$200,000 \times .375 = \$75,000$$
$$\text{Glow: } \$200,000 \times .625 = \$125,000$$

Some companies further refine this method by subtracting each product's estimated selling expenses from its sales value to determine the net realizable value of the product. If a product is to be processed further after the point of separation, costs should not be assigned on the basis of ultimate sales value because the additional processing adds value to the product. In a case such as this, an **adjusted sales value** is used that takes into consideration the cost of the processing after split-off.

Assume that Clean It's market researchers determine that Glow would have a better market if it were sold in powder form in individual packages. (Two gallons of liquid are needed for one pound of powder.) After studying this proposition, the company decides to pipe Glow into ovens to dehydrate it. The resulting powder is divided into one-pound packages that will sell for $80 each.

During the month of October, when the new process began, the joint costs of materials, labor, and factory overhead in the Mixing and Settling Department were again $200,000, and 30,000 gallons of Gloss were transferred to tank cars. In the Baking Department, costs totaled $100,000 for baking and packaging the 20,000 gallons of Glow received from Mixing and Settling, and 10,000 one-pound packages were produced.

The assignment of joint costs of $200,000 in Mixing and Settling, using the adjusted sales value method, follows:

Units Produced		Unit Selling Price		Ultimate Sales Value	Less Cost after Split Off	Sales Value at Split-Off	Percent Sales Value	Assignment of Joint Costs
Gloss—30,000 gal	×	$10.00	=	$ 300,000	-0-	$ 300,000	30%	$ 60,000
Glow—10,000 lb*	×	80.00	=	800,000	$100,000	700,000	70	140,000
Total				$1,100,000	$100,000	$1,000,000	100%	$200,000

*20,000 gallons of liquid is further processed into 10,000 lb of powder.

The following journal entries illustrate the allocated cost of Gloss being transferred to a finished goods inventory account and the assigned cost of Glow being transferred to a work in process account to which the additional costs of processing after split-off are charged as follows:

Account	Debit	Credit
Work in Process—Baking	140,000	
Finished Goods (Gloss)	60,000	
Work in Process—Mixing and Settling		200,000
Allocation of split-off costs to the two products		
Work in Process—Baking	100,000	
Materials, Wages Payable, Applied Factory Overhead		100,000
Processing costs after split-off charged to Glow		
Finished Goods (Glow)	240,000	
Work in Process—Baking		240,000
Completed cost of Glow ($140,000 + $100,000) charged to finished goods		

Accounting for By-Products

In accounting for by-products, the common practice is to make no allocation of the processing costs up to the split-off point. Costs incurred up to that point are chargeable to the main products. If no further processing is required to make the by-products marketable, they may be accounted for by debiting an inventory account, By-Products, and crediting Work in Process for the estimated sales value of the by-products recovered. Under this procedure, the estimated sales value of the by-products reduces the cost of the main products that is accumulated in the work in process account. The reduction in costs, due to the by-product, is shown in the inventory costs section of the cost of production summary. If the by-products are sold for more or less than the estimated sales value, the difference may be credited or debited to Gain and Loss on Sales of By-Products. The journal entries to reflect the above, with amounts assumed, are as follows:

By-Product Inventory	200	
Work in Process		200
to reduce cost of main products by estimated by-product sales value.		
Accounts Receivable	300	
Gain or Loss on Sale of By-Product		100
By-Product Inventory		200
to record the sale of by-product at a gain.		

Assume that the production management of Clean It finds that nonusable residue at the bottom of the vat can be sold for $10,000 without further processing. Also assume that other data for the month of November are the same as for October. The cost of production summary in Figure 6-16

Figure 6-16 **Cost of Production Summary, Joint Products and By-Products**

Clean It, Inc.
Cost of Production Summary—Mixing and Settling Department
For the Month Ended November 30, 2011

Cost of production for month:	
Materials	$127,500
Labor	42,500
Factory overhead	30,000
Total costs to be accounted for	$200,000
Unit output for month:	
Finished and transferred to finished goods (Gloss)	30,000
Finished and transferred to Baking Department (Glow)	20,000
Total	50,000
Unit cost for month:	
Materials ($127,500 ÷ 50,000)	$ 2.55
Labor ($42,500 ÷ 50,000)	0.85
Factory overhead ($30,000 ÷ 50,000)	0.60
Total	$ 4.00
Total costs to split-off point	$200,000
Less market value of by-product	10,000
Total cost to be assigned to joint products finished and transferred	$190,000
Inventory costs:	
Cost of goods finished (Gloss) and transferred to finished goods (30%* × $190,000)	$ 57,000
Cost of goods finished (Glow) and transferred to Baking Department (70% × $190,000)	133,000
Market value of by-product finished and transferred to by-product inventory account	10,000
Total production costs accounted for	$200,000

**Using adjusted sales values from the table on page 312.* (marked *) reflects the assignment of joint costs under the adjusted sales value method and uses the by-product sales value as a reduction in the cost of the joint products and as the cost assigned to the by-product.

In some instances, an unstable market will make the sales value of the by-product so insignificant or so uncertain that the cost of the main products will not be reduced. In this case, no entry for the by-product is made at the point of separation. When the by-product is sold, the transaction is recorded by debiting Cash or Accounts Receivable and crediting By-Product Sales or Miscellaneous Income. The revenue account will usually be treated as "other income" on the income statement. If the amount is significant, however, some companies may show this revenue under the main category "Sales," as a deduction from the cost of the main products sold, or as a reduction in the total cost of the main products manufactured.

If further processing is required to make the by-product salable, an account entitled By-Products in Process may be opened, and all subsequent processing costs are charged to that account. As with other products, when the processing is completed, an entry is made to transfer the costs from the in-process account to a finished goods inventory account.

Recall and Review 3

Fraternity Row, Inc., makes one main product, Gamma, and a by-product, Sigma. The estimated sales value of the units of Sigma produced during the month is $5,000. Assuming that the value of the by-product is treated as a reduction in cost of the main product, prepare the journal entries to record the placing of Sigma in stock and the subsequent sale of Sigma for $4,000, on account.

(After working this exercise, see page 315 for the solution.)

You should now be able to work the following:
Questions 14–17; Exercises 6-11 to 6-14; Problems 6-10 and 6-11; Mini-Case; and Self-Study Problem 2.

KEY TERMS

ANSWERS TO RECALL AND REVIEW EXERCISES

R&R 1

Equivalent units of production for direct material:	
Units finished and transferred out	28,000
Units in ending inventory, 100% complete	6,000
Equivalent units of production	34,000
Equivalent units of production for direct labor and factory overhead:	
Units finished and transferred out	28,000
Units in ending inventory, 6,000 × 50%	3,000
Equivalent units of production	31,000

R&R 2

Equivalent units of production for direct materials:	
To complete beginning work in process	-0-
Added to units started and finished during month	24,000*
Units in ending inventory, 100% complete	6,000
Equivalent units of production	30,000

*28,000 finished – 4,000 from beginning inventory

Equivalent units of production for direct labor and factory overhead:	
To complete beginning work in process, 4,000 × 75%	3,000
Added to units started and finished during month	24,000
Units in ending inventory, 6,000 × 50%	3,000
Equivalent units of production	30,000

R&R 3

(1) By-Product Inventory	5,000	
Work in Process		5,000
(2) Accounts Receivable	4,000	
Gain and Loss on Sale of By-Product	1,000	
By-Product Inventory		5,000

SELF-STUDY PROBLEM 1

Average and FIFO Cost Methods; Losses at the Beginning and End of Processing

Coronado Manufacturing Company

Coronado Manufacturing Company uses a process cost system. Its manufacturing operation is carried on in two departments: Machining and Finishing. The Machining Department uses the average cost method, and the Finishing Department uses the FIFO cost method. Materials are added in both departments at the beginning of operations, and the added materials do not increase the number of units being processed. Units are lost in the Machining Department throughout the production process, and inspection occurs at the end of the process. The lost units have no scrap value and are considered to be a normal loss.

Production statistics for May show the following data:

	Machining	Finishing
Units in process, May 1 (all material, 20% of labor and overhead)	10,000	
Units in process, May 1 (all material, 60% of labor and overhead)		20,000
Units started in production	70,000	
Units completed and transferred	50,000	
Units transferred from Machining		50,000
Units completed and transferred to finished goods		50,000
Units in process, May 31 (all material, 40% of labor and overhead)	20,000	
Units in process, May 31 (all material, 20% of labor and overhead)		20,000
Units lost in production	10,000	

Production Costs	**Machining**	**Finishing**
Work in process, May 1:		
Materials	$ 20,000	$ 55,000
Labor	12,000	30,000
Factory overhead	4,000	20,000
Costs in machining department		120,000
Costs incurred during month:		
Materials	139,600	120,000
Labor	89,500	80,220
Factory overhead	30,220	39,900

Required:

Prepare a cost of production summary for each department.

SOLUTION TO SELF-STUDY PROBLEM

Suggestions:

Read the entire problem thoroughly, keeping in mind that you will *prepare a cost of production summary for each department.*

Highlight the following facts:

1. The company has two departments.
2. The Machining Department uses the average cost method, while the Finishing Department uses the FIFO cost method.
3. Units are lost throughout the process in Machining, but inspection doesn't occur until the end of the process.
4. The lost units have no scrap value, and the losses are considered normal.
5. The materials are added at the beginning of operations in both departments, but the labor and overhead are added evenly. Therefore, the equivalent production for materials will differ from the labor and overhead equivalent production in each department.

Prepare a Cost of Production Summary for the Machining Department:

1. Account for the total cost charged to the department.
2. Calculate the equivalent production, using the average cost procedures for (a) materials and (b) labor and factory overhead.
3. Calculate the unit costs for materials, labor, and overhead. (Note that the good units that make it to the end of the production process will bear all of the production costs, including the costs incurred up until the time the units were lost.)
4. Using the calculated unit costs, determine the following:
   a. Cost of goods finished and transferred.
   b. The cost of the ending work in process.

Coronado Manufacturing Company
Cost of Production Summary—Machining Department
For the Month Ended May 31, 2011

First: Account for the total cost charged to the department.		
Cost in work in process, beginning of month:		
Materials	$ 20,000	
Labor	12,000	
Factory overhead	4,000	$ 36,000
Cost of production for month:		
Materials	$139,600	
Labor	89,500	
Factory overhead	30,220	259,320
Total costs to be accounted for		**$295,320**
Second: Calculate the unit output (equivalent production).		
Unit output for month:		
Materials:		
Finished and transferred during month		50,000
Equivalent units of work in process, end of month (20,000, 100% completed)		20,000
Total equivalent production		70,000

Labor and factory overhead:		
Finished and transferred during month		50,000
Equivalent units of work in process, end of month (20,000, 40% completed)		8,000
Total equivalent production		58,000
Third: Calculate unit costs.		
Materials [($20,000 + $139,600) ÷ 70,000]		$ 2.28
Labor [($12,000 + $89,500) ÷ 58,000]		1.75
Factory overhead [($4,000 + $30,220) ÷ 58,000]		0.59
Total		$ 4.62
Fourth: Determine inventory costs using calculated unit costs.		
Inventory costs:		
Cost of goods finished and transferred (50,000 × $4.62)		$231,000
Cost of work in process, end of month:		
Materials (20,000 × $2.28)	$ 45,600	
Labor (20,000 × 40% × $1.75)	14,000	
Factory overhead (20,000 × 40% × $0.59)	4,720	64,320
Total production costs accounted for		**$295,320**

Prepare a Cost of Production Summary for the Finishing Department:
Note: Use the same sequence of instructions as were given for the Machining Department.

Coronado Valley Manufacturing Company
Cost of Production Summary—Finishing Department
For the Month Ended May 31, 2011

Cost of work in process, beginning of month:			
Cost in Machining Department		$120,000	
Cost in Finishing Department:			
Materials	$55,000		
Labor	30,000		
Factory overhead	20,000	105,000	$225,000
Cost of goods received from Machining during month			231,000
Cost of production for month:			
Materials		$120,000	
Labor		80,220	
Factory overhead		39,900	240,120
Total costs to be accounted for			**$696,120**
Unit output for month:			
Materials:			
To complete beginning units in process			-0-
Units started and fully manufactured during month (50,000 – 20,000)			30,000
Ending units in process (20,000, all materials)			20,000
Total equivalent production			50,000

Labor and factory overhead:		
To complete beginning units in process (20,000, 40% to complete)		8,000
Units started and fully manufactured during month		30,000
Ending units in process (20,000, 20% completed)		4,000
Total equivalent production		42,000
Unit cost for month:		
Materials ($120,000 ÷ 50,000)		$ 2.40
Labor ($80,220 ÷ 42,000)		1.91
Factory overhead ($39,900 ÷ 42,000)		0.95
Total		$ 5.26
Inventory costs:		
Cost of goods finished and transferred to finished goods during month:		
Beginning units in process:		
Prior month's cost	$225,000	
Current cost to complete:		
Labor (20,000 × 40% × $1.91)	15,280	
Overhead (20,000 × 40% × $0.95)	7,600	$247,880
Units started and finished during month:		
Cost in prior dept. (30,000 × $4.62)	$138,600	
Cost in Finishing Dept. (30,000 × $5.26)	157,800	
Total cost transferred (30,000 × $9.88)		296,400
Cost of work in process, end of month:		
Cost in prior dept. (20,000 units × $4.62)	$ 92,400	
Materials (20,000 units × $2.40)	48,000	
Labor (20,000 units × 20% × $1.91)	7,640	
Factory overhead (20,000 units × 20% × $0.95)	3,800	151,840
Total production costs accounted for		**$696,120**

SELF-STUDY PROBLEM 2

Joint Products and By-Products Costing

Sioux City Meatpackers, Inc.

Sioux City Meatpackers, Inc., processes hogs into bacon, ham, pork roast, and spare ribs. The materials, labor, and overhead processing costs to get the products to the point where they can be separately identified total $10,000,000. Additional information includes:

Product	Lb Produced	Cost after Split-Off	Selling Price per Lb
Bacon	1,000,000	$200,000	$2
Ham	2,500,000	500,000	4
Pork roast	2,000,000	425,000	3
Spare ribs	500,000	350,000	5

A by-product, animal fat, was sold for a total of $1,000,000 at the split-off point.

Required:
Determine the allocation of joint costs, using the relative sales value method.

SOLUTION TO SELF-STUDY PROBLEM

Suggestions:
Read the entire problem carefully, keeping in mind that you are to *allocate the joint processing costs to the four joint products*.
Highlight the following facts:

1. There are four joint products.
2. Each product incurs separable costs after the split-off point.
3. The joint products are sold only after further processing.
4. By-product revenue is also present.

Steps in Performing the Allocations:

1. Reduce the amount of the joint cost to be allocated by the amount of the by-product revenue:

Joint processing costs...	$10,000,000
Less: By-product revenue	1,000,000
Joint costs to be allocated	$ 9,000,000

2. Determine the ultimate sales value of the four products:

Product	Lb.	Price per lb	Ultimate Sales Value
Bacon	1,000,000	$2	$ 2,000,000
Ham	2,500,000	4	10,000,000
Pork roast	2,000,000	3	6,000,000
Spare ribs	500,000	5	2,500,000

3. Deduct the costs after split-off to determine the adjusted sales value at split-off:

Product	Ultimate Sales Value	Costs after Split-Off	Sales Value at Split-Off
Bacon	$ 2,000,000	$200,000	$1,800,000
Ham	10,000,000	500,000	9,500,000
Pork roast	6,000,000	425,000	5,575,000
Spare ribs	2,500,000	350,000	2,150,000

4. Using the adjusted sales value at split-off, compute the relative sales value percentages and assign the joint costs:

Product	Sales Value at Split-Off	Sales Value Percentage	Joint Costs Assigned
Bacon	$ 1,800,000	9.46%	$ 851,400
Ham	9,500,000	49.94	4,494,600
Pork roast	5,575,000	29.30	2,637,000
Spare ribs	2,150,000	11.30	1,017,000
Total	$19,025,000	100.00%	$9,000,000

QUESTIONS

1. Under what conditions may the unit costs of materials, labor, and overhead be computed by using only one equivalent production figure?
2. When is it necessary to use separate equivalent production figures in computing the unit costs of materials, labor, and overhead?
3. Why is it usually reasonable to assume that labor and factory overhead are added evenly throughout the production process?
4. If materials are not put into process uniformly, what must be considered when determining the cost of the ending work in process?
5. In what way does the cost of production summary, Figure 6-2, differ from the cost of production summaries presented in Chapter 5? What is the reason for this difference in treatment?
6. Why might the total number of units completed during a month plus the number of units in process at the end of a month be less than the total number of units in process at the beginning of the month plus the number of units placed in process during the month?
7. What is the usual method of handling the cost of losses that occur normally during processing?
8. If some units are normally lost during the manufacturing process and all units absorb the cost, what effect does this have on the unit cost of goods finished during the period and the cost of the work in process at the end of the period?
9. How is the cost of units normally lost in manufacturing absorbed by the unit cost for the period?
10. How would you describe the method used to treat the cost of abnormal processing losses?
11. What computations must be made if materials added in a department increase the number of units being processed in that department?
12. What is the difference between the average cost method and the first-in, first-out (FIFO) cost method?
13. What advantage does the FIFO cost method have over the average cost method relative to providing information for cost control?
14. How would you define each of the following?
    a. joint products
    b. by-products
    c. joint costs
    d. split-off point
15. What are three methods of allocating joint costs?
16. How would you describe accounting for by-products for which no further processing is required?
17. Explain the refinement that some companies make to the relative sales value method of accounting for joint products.

EXERCISES

E6-1 Computing equivalent units of production for materials, labor, and overhead

LO1

Using the data given for Cases 1–3 below, and assuming the use of the average cost method, compute the separate equivalent units of production—one for materials and one for labor and overhead—under each of the following assumptions (labor and factory overhead are applied evenly during the process in each assumption):

a. All materials go into production at the beginning of the process.

b. All materials go into production at the end of the process. (Note that this would have to be a department subsequent to the first department for all materials to be added at the end of the process.)

c. At the beginning of the process, 75% of the materials go into production and 25% go into production when the process is one-half completed.

Note that you will have three solutions for each of the following cases:

Case 1—Started in process 5,000 units; finished 3,000 units; work in process, end of period 2,000 units, three-fourths completed.

Case 2—Opening inventory 5,000 units, three-fifths completed; started in process 40,000 units; finished 39,000 units; work in process, end of period 6,000 units, one-fourth completed.

Case 3—Opening inventory 1,000 units, one-half completed, and 8,000 units, one-fourth completed; started in process 30,000 units; finished 29,000 units; closing inventory work in process 5,000 units, one-fourth completed, and 5,000 units, one-half completed.

E6-2 Computing equivalent production, unit costs, and costs for completed units and ending inventory

LO1

Swedish Navy Company manufactures wristwatches on an assembly line. The work in process inventory as of March 1 consisted of 1,000 watches that were complete as to materials and 75% complete as to labor and overhead. The March 1 work in process costs were as follows:

Materials	$ 5,000
Labor	5,000
Overhead	8,000
Total	$18,000

During the month, 10,000 units were started and 9,500 units were completed. The 1,500 units of ending inventory were complete as to materials and 25% were complete as to labor and overhead.

The costs for March were as follows:

Materials	$ 61,000
Labor	20,000
Overhead	48,000
Total	$129,000

Calculate:

a. Equivalent units for material, labor, and overhead, using the average cost method
b. Unit costs for materials, labor, and overhead
c. Cost of the units completed and transferred
d. Detailed cost of the ending inventory
e. Total of all costs accounted for

E6-3 **Computing unit costs; cost of units finished; cost of units in process**

LO1

The following data appeared in the accounting records of Royale Manufacturing Company, which uses an average cost production system:

Started in process	12,000 units
Finished and transferred	10,500 units
Work in process, end of month	1,500 units (2/5 completed)
Materials	$36,000
Labor	$44,400
Factory overhead	$22,200

Case 1—All materials are added at the beginning of the process, and labor and factory overhead are added evenly throughout the process.

Case 2—One-half of the materials are added at the start of the manufacturing process, and the balance of the materials is added when the units are one-half completed. Labor and factory overhead are applied evenly during the process.

Make the following computations for each case:

a. Unit cost of materials, labor, and factory overhead for the month
b. Cost of the units finished during the month
c. Cost of the units in process at the end of the month

E6-4 **Calculating equivalent units**

LO1

Camacho Chemical Company uses an average cost processing system. All materials are added at the start of the production process. Labor and overhead are added evenly at the same rate throughout the process. Camacho's records indicate the following data for May:

Beginning work in process, May 1 (50% completed)	1,000 units
Started in May	5,000 units
Completed and transferred	4,000 units

Ending work in process, May 31, is 75% completed as to labor and factory overhead. Make the following calculations:

a. Equivalent units for direct materials
b. Equivalent units for labor and overhead

E6-5 Computing costs and units

LO1

Assuming that all materials are added at the beginning of the process and the labor and factory overhead are applied evenly during the process, compute the figures to be inserted in the blank spaces of the following data, using the average cost method.

	Case 1	Case 2	Case 3
Units in process, beginning of period	300	None	—
Materials cost in process, beginning of period	$ 915	None	$568
Labor cost in process, beginning of period	$ 351	None	$200
Overhead cost in process, beginning of period	$ 300	None	$188
Units started in process	—	—	19,200
Units transferred	1,300	8,000	—
Units in process, end of period	200	—	1,400
Stage of completion	1/4	—	1/5
Equivalent units—materials	—	—	—
Equivalent units—labor and factory overhead	—	—	18,440
Materials cost, current month	$3,660	$13,120	$—
Labor and factory overhead cost, current month	$5,100	$16,200	$—
Materials unit cost for period	$—	$1.60	$0.30
Labor and factory overhead unit cost for period	$—	$2.00	$0.20

E6-6 Computing average unit costs

LO1

Foamy, Inc., manufactures shaving cream and uses an average cost system. In November, production is 14,800 equivalent units for materials and 13,300 units for labor and overhead. During the month, materials, labor, and overhead costs were as follows:

Materials	$73,000
Labor	68,134
Overhead	77,200

Beginning work in process for November had a cost of $11,360 for materials, $11,666 for labor, and $9,250 for overhead.

Compute the following:

a. Average cost per unit for materials
b. Average cost per unit for labor
c. Average cost per unit for overhead
d. Total unit cost for the month

E6-7 Calculating unit costs; units lost in production

LO2

Seymour Brothers Products, Inc., manufactures a liquid product in one department. Due to the nature of the product and the process, units are regularly lost at the beginning of production. Materials and conversion costs are added evenly throughout the process. The following summaries were prepared for the month of January:

Production Summary	**Units**
Started in process	10,000
Finished and transferred to the stockroom	8,000
In process, end of the month	1,000
Stage of completion	1/2
Lost in process	1,000
Cost Summary	
Materials	$132,000
Labor	33,000
Factory overhead	20,625

Calculate the unit cost for materials, labor, and factory overhead for January and show the costs of units transferred and in process.

E6-8 Calculating unit costs; units gained in production

LO3

A company manufactures a liquid product called Glitter. The basic ingredients are put into process in Department 1. In Department 2, other materials are added that increase the number of units being processed by 50%. The factory has only two departments.

	Units	
Production Summary	**Dept. 1**	**Dept. 2**
Started in process	18,000	
Received from prior department		14,000
Added to units in process		7,000
Finished and transferred	14,000	15,000
In process, end of month	4,000	6,000
Stage of completion—materials, labor, and factory overhead	1/4	1/2
Cost Summary		
Materials	$90,000	$36,000
Labor	30,000	13,500
Factory overhead	15,000	4,500

Calculate the following for each department: (a) unit cost for the month for materials, labor, and factory overhead, (b) cost of the units transferred, and (c) cost of the work in process.

E6-9 Computing equivalent units, FIFO method

LO4

Using the data given for Cases 1–3 and the FIFO cost method, compute the separate equivalent units of production, one for materials and one for labor and overhead, under each of the following assumptions (labor and factory overhead are applied evenly during the process in each assumption):

a. All materials go into production at the beginning of the process.

b. All materials go into production at the end of the process. (Note that this would have to be a department subsequent to the first department for all materials to be added at the end of the process.)

c. At the beginning of the process, 75% of the materials go into production and 25% go into production when the process is one-half completed.

Note that you will have three solutions for each of the following cases:

Case 1—Started in process 5,000 units; finished 3,000 units; work in process, end of period 2,000 units, three-fourths completed.

Case 2—Opening inventory 5,000 units, three-fifths completed; started in process 40,000 units; finished 39,000 units; work in process, end of period 6,000 units, one-fourth completed.

Case 3—Opening inventory 1,000 units, one-half completed, and 8,000 units, one-fourth completed; started in process 30,000 units; finished 29,000 units; closing inventory work in process 5,000 units, one-fourth completed, and 5,000 units, one-half completed.

Compare your answers with those from E6-1 on the average cost basis.

E6-10 **Computing equivalent units, FIFO and average cost methods**

Assume each of the following conditions concerning the data given:

1. All materials are added at the beginning of the process.
2. All materials are added at the end of the process. (Note that this would have to be a department subsequent to the first department for all materials to be added at the end of the process.)
3. Half of the materials are added at the beginning of the process, and the balance of the materials is added when the units are three-fourths completed.

In all cases, labor and factory overhead are added evenly throughout the process.

	Units		
Production Summary	**Dept. 1**	**Dept. 2**	**Dept. 3**
Work in process, beginning of month	3,000	1,500	1,200
Stage of completion	1/2	3/5	4/5
Started in process	18,000	16,000	21,000
Finished and transferred	19,000	15,500	21,000
Work in process, end of month	2,000	2,000	1,200
Stage of completion	3/4	1/2	1/4

Compute separate equivalent units of production, one for materials and one for labor and factory overhead, for each of the conditions listed, using (a) the average cost method and (b) the FIFO cost method.

E6-11 Making a journal entry—joint products

LO5

Lexington Lumber Co. processes rough timber to obtain three grades of finished lumber, A, B, and C. The company allocates costs to the joint products on the basis of market value. During the month of May, Lexington incurred total production costs of $300,000 in producing the following:

Grade	Thousand Board Feet	Selling Price per 1,000 Board Feet
A	200	$200
B	300	100
C	500	150

Make the journal entry to transfer the finished lumber to separate inventory accounts for each product.

E6-12 Computing joint costs—relative sales value method

LO5

Cooper Company's joint cost of producing 1,000 units of Product A, 500 units of Product B, and 500 units of Product C is $200,000. The unit sales values of the three products at the split-off point are Product A—$20, Product B—$200, and Product C—$160. Ending inventories include 100 units of Product A, 200 units of Product B, and 300 units of Product C.

a. Compute the amount of joint cost that would be included in the ending inventory valuation of the three products on the basis of their relative sales values.

b. Assume that Product C can be sold for $200 a unit if it is processed after split-off at a cost of $25 a unit. Compute the amount of joint cost that would be included in the ending inventory valuation of the three products on the basis of their adjusted sales values.

E6-13 Making a journal entry—by-product

Orlando Metals manufactures tin. During the process, a by-product—scrap metal—is obtained and placed in stock. The estimated sales value of the scrap metal produced during the month of April is $2,000. Assume that the value of the by-product is treated as a reduction in production cost.

Make the journal entry for April to record the following:

a. Placing of the scrap metal in stock

b. Sale of one-half of the scrap metal for $850, on account

E6-14 Making journal entries—by-product

LO5

Alphabet Manufacturing Co. makes one main product, X, and a by-product, Z, which splits off from the main product when the work is three-fourths completed. Product Z is sold without further processing and without being placed in stock. During June, $1,200 is realized from the sale of the by-product.

Make the entries to record the recovery and sale of the by-product, on account, on the assumption that the recovery is treated as one of the following:

a. A reduction in the cost of the main product
b. Other income

PROBLEMS

P6-1 **Cost of production summaries, one department, two months; journal entries**

LO1

Manufacturing data for the months of January and February in the Mixing Department of Cappy Cleaning Products follow:

	January	February
Materials used	$20,000	$28,400
Labor	$15,200	$23,000
Factory overhead	$11,400	$19,800
Finished and transferred to Blending Dept.	3,600	3,200
Work in process, end of month	400	600
Stage of completion	3/4	1/4

All materials are added at the start of the process. Labor and factory overhead are added evenly throughout the process. No units were in process at the beginning of January. Goods finished in Mixing are transferred to Blending for further processing.

Required:

1. From an analysis of this information, prepare a cost of production summary for each month, using the average cost method.
2. Make the journal entries necessary to record each month's transactions. (*Hint:* See Chapter 5 to review.)

P6-2 **Journal entries for a manufacturer**

LO1

On December 1, Lake George Production Company had a work in process inventory of 1,200 units that were complete as to materials and 50% complete as to labor and overhead. December 1 costs follow:

Materials	$6,000
Labor	2,000
Overhead	2,000

During December the following transactions occurred:

a. Purchased materials costing $50,000 on account.
b. Placed direct materials costing $49,000 into production.
c. Incurred production wages totaling $50,500.

d. Incurred overhead costs for December:

Depreciation	$20,000
Utilities	28,000 (Cash payment)
Salaries	11,000 (Cash payment)
Supplies	2,000 (From inventory)

e. Applied overhead to work in process at a predetermined rate of 125% of direct labor cost.

f. Completed and transferred 10,000 units to Finished Goods. (*Hint:* You should first compute equivalent units and unit costs.)

Lake George uses an average cost system. The ending inventory of work in process consisted of 1,000 units that were completed as to materials and 25% complete as to labor and overhead.

Required:
Prepare the journal entries to record the above information for the month of December.

P6-3 **Cost of production summaries, three departments; departmental cost work sheet; journal entries; statement of cost of goods manufactured**

LO1

Akron Manufacturing Company manufactures a cement sealing compound called Ultra-Seal. The process requires that the product pass through three departments. In Dept. 1, all materials are put into production at the beginning of the process; in Dept. 2, materials are put into production evenly throughout the process; and in Dept. 3, all materials are put into production at the end of the process. In each department, it is assumed that the labor and factory overhead are applied evenly throughout the process.

At the end of January, the production reports for the month show the following:

	Dept. 1	Dept. 2	Dept. 3
Started in process	50,000	—	—
Received from prior department	—	40,000	30,000
Finished and transferred	40,000	30,000	28,000
Finished and on hand	—	5,000	—
Work in process, end of month	10,000	5,000	2,000
Stage of completion	1/2	1/4	3/4

The cost summary for January shows the following:

	Dept. 1	Dept. 2	Dept. 3
Materials	$22,500	$23,200	$19,600
Labor	7,200	14,500	11,800
Factory overhead	10,800	14,500	8,850
	$40,500	$52,200	$40,250

Required:

1. Prepare a cost of production summary for each department for January, using the average cost method.
2. Prepare a departmental cost work sheet for January. (*Hint:* See Chapter 5 to review.)
3. Make the required journal entries to record the January operations.
4. Prepare a statement of cost of goods manufactured for the month ended January 31.

P6-4 Cost of completed units and ending inventory

Gold Giant Products, Inc., cans peas and uses an average cost system. For the month of November, the company showed the following:

Peas completed and canned	245,000 pounds
Peas in process at the end of November: 100% complete as to peas, 50% complete as to labor and overhead, 0% complete as to cans	16,500 pounds
Cost data:	
Peas	$0.10 per equivalent pound
Labor	$0.25 per equivalent pound
Overhead	$0.15 per equivalent pound
Cans	$0.07 per can

Each can contains 16 oz, or 1 lb, of peas.

Required:

1. Calculate the cost of the completed production for November.
2. Show the detailed cost of the ending inventory for November.

P6-5 Lost units; cost of production summaries

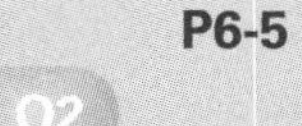

Sinaloa Products Co. uses the process cost system. A record of the factory operations for the month of October follows:

Production Summary	**Units**
Started in process	12,500
Finished and transferred to stockroom	9,500
In process, end of month, one-half completed as to materials, labor, and overhead	1,000
Cost Summary	
Materials	$30,000
Labor	12,000
Factory overhead	18,000

Required:

Prepare a cost of production summary, assuming that the cost of lost units is absorbed by the good units completed.

P6-6 **Units gained; cost of production summaries similar to Self-Study Problem 1**

Cancun Chemicals, Inc., which uses the process cost system, has two departments: A and B. In both departments, all of the materials are put into production at the beginning of the process. The materials added in Dept. B increase the number of units being processed by 25%. Labor and factory overhead are incurred uniformly throughout the process in all departments.

A record of the factory operations for May follows:

Cost Summary	**Dept. A**	**Dept. B**
Materials	$25,000	$ 7,500
Labor	10,800	10,140
Factory overhead	8,100	7,215

Production Summary	**Units**	
	Dept. A	**Dept. B**
Started in process	10,000	
Received from prior department		8,500
Added to units in process		1,500
Finished and transferred	8,500	9,500
Units in process, end of month	1,500	500
Stage of completion	1/3	1/2

Required:

Prepare a cost of production summary for each department for the month of May.

P6-7 **FIFO cost method; cost of production summary**

Boise Beverages, Inc., uses the FIFO cost method and adds all materials, labor, and factory overhead evenly to production. A record of the factory operations for the month of October follows:

Production Summary	**Units**
Work in process, beginning of month, one-fourth completed	5,000
Started in process	13,000
Finished and transferred to stockroom	11,000
Work in process, end of month, three-fourths completed	7,000
Cost Summary	
Work in process, beginning of month	$10,000
Materials	45,000
Labor	30,000
Factory overhead	15,000

Required:

Prepare a cost of production summary for the month.

P6-8 **Cost of units completed and ending inventory; FIFO method**

Columbus Candy Company had a cost per equivalent pound for the month of $4.56 for materials, $1.75 for labor, and $1.00 for overhead. During the month, 10,250 pounds were completed and transferred to finished goods. The 3,200 pounds in ending work in process were 100% complete as to materials and 60% complete as to labor and overhead. At the beginning of the month, 1,500 pounds were in process, 100% complete as to materials and 50% complete as to labor and overhead. The beginning inventory had a cost of $8,775. Columbus uses FIFO costing.

Required:

1. Calculate the cost of the pounds completed and transferred.
2. Calculate the cost of ending work in process.

P6-9 **Average and FIFO cost methods; losses at the beginning and end of processing**
similar to Self-Study Problem 1

Mt. Repose Manufacturing Company uses a process cost system. Its manufacturing operation is carried on in two departments: Machining and Finishing. The Machining Department uses the average cost method, and the Finishing Department uses the FIFO cost method. Materials are added in both departments at the beginning of operations, but the added materials do not increase the number of units being processed. Units are lost in the Machining Department throughout the production process, and inspection occurs at the end of the process. The lost units have no scrap value and are considered to be a normal loss.

Production statistics for July show the following data:

	Machining	Finishing
Units in process, July 1 (all material, 40% of labor and overhead)	20,000	
Units in process, July 1 (all material, 80% of labor and overhead)		40,000
Units started in production	140,000	
Units completed and transferred	100,000	
Units transferred from Machining		100,000
Units completed and transferred to finished goods		100,000
Units in process, July 31 (all material, 60% of labor and overhead)	40,000	
Units in process, July 31 (all material, 40% of labor and overhead)		40,000
Units lost in production	20,000	

Production Costs	**Machining**	**Finishing**
Work in process, July 1:		
Materials	$ 40,000	$110,000
Labor	24,000	60,000
Factory overhead	8,000	40,000
Costs in Machining Department		240,000

Production Costs	**Machining**	**Finishing**
Costs incurred during month:		
Materials	$280,000	$240,000
Labor	180,000	160,000
Factory overhead	60,000	80,000

Required:

Prepare a cost of production summary for each department. (Round to three decimal places.)

P6-10 Joint cost allocations

LO5

Chikin, Inc., specializes in chicken farming. Chickens are raised, packaged, and sold mostly to grocery chains. Chickens are accounted for in batches of 50,000. At the end of each growing period, the chickens are separated and sold by grades. Grades AA and A are sold to large grocery chains, and B and C are sold to other buyers. For costing purposes, Chikin treats each batch of chicks as a joint product. The cost data for a batch of 50,000 chicks follows:

Grade	Number of Chickens	Average Pounds per Chicken	Selling Price per Pound
AA	25,000	5	$1.00
A	15,000	4	0.75
B	6,000	2	0.50
C	4,000	1	0.25

Total joint costs for the batch were $125,000.

Required:

Compute the cost allocations for each product, using the relative sales value method.

P6-11 Joint cost allocation with costs after split-off and by-product revenue
similar to Self-Study Problem 2

Boone Oil Company transports crude oil to its refinery where it is processed into main products gasoline, kerosene, and diesel fuel, and by-product base oil. The base oil is sold at the split-off point for $500,000 of annual revenue, and the joint processing costs to get the crude oil to split-off are $5,000,000. Additional information includes:

Product	Barrels Produced	Cost After Split-Off	Selling Price Per Barrel
Gasoline	500,000	$2,000,000	$25
Kerosene	100,000	500,000	30
Diesel fuel	250,000	1,000,000	20

Required:

Determine the allocation of joint costs, using the adjusted sales value method. (*Hint:* Reduce the amount of the joint costs to be allocated by the amount of the by-product revenue.)

MINI-CASE

Allocation of joint costs
Clark Kent, Inc., buys crypton for $0.80 a gallon. At the end of processing in Dept. 1, crypton splits off into products A, B, and C. Product A is sold at the split-off point with no further processing. Products B and C require further processing before they can be sold. Product B is processed in Dept. 2, and Product C is processed in Dept. 3. Following is a summary of costs and other related data for the year ended December 31:

	Dept. 1	Dept. 2	Dept. 3
Cost of crypton	$ 76,000	—	—
Direct labor	14,000	$51,000	$ 65,000
Factory overhead	10,000	26,500	49,000
Total	$100,000	$77,500	$114,000

	Product A	Product B	Product C
Gallons sold	20,000	30,000	45,000
Gallons on hand at December 31	10,000	—	15,000
Sales in dollars	$30,000	$96,000	$141,750

No inventories were on hand at the beginning of the year, and no crypton was on hand at the end of the year. All gallons on hand at the end of the year were complete as to processing. Kent uses the relative sales value method of allocating joint costs.

Required:

1. Calculate the allocation of joint costs.
2. Calculate the total cost per unit for each product.
3. In examining the product cost reports, Lois Lane, Vice President—Marketing, notes that the per-unit cost of Product B is greater than the selling price of $3.20 that can be received in the competitive marketplace. Lane wonders if they should stop selling Product B. How did Lane determine that the product was being sold at a loss? What per-unit cost should be used in determining whether Product B should be sold?

INTERNET EXERCISE

Process Costing
The Coca-Cola Company's manufacturing operations are ideal for process costing because it and its bottlers produce long runs of identical beverages in a continuous flow production process. Go to the companion

Web site at www.cengage.com/accounting/vanderbeck and visit the link for Coca-Cola to answer the following questions:

1. Where is Coca-Cola headquartered, and how many employees does it have worldwide?
2. What functions does the Coca-Cola Company perform?
3. Who are Coca-Cola's bottlers?
4. What functions do the bottlers perform?
5. Where does Coca-Cola rank in the sales of various types of beverages?

CHAPTER 7

The Master Budget and Flexible Budgeting

Learning Objectives

After studying this chapter, you should be able to:

LO1 Explain the general principles involved in the budgeting process.

LO2 Identify and prepare the components of the master budget.

LO3 Identify and prepare components of the flexible budget.

LO4 Explain the procedures to determine standard amounts of factory overhead at different levels of production

"Prediction is very difficult, especially about the future."
Niels Bohr

This humorous but wise quotation is relevant to the major topic of this chapter—financial planning via the budgeting process. Budgets aren't just for making sure that your household expenditures don't exceed your income. Many businesses do the "lion's share" of their planning as part of their annual budgeting exercise. This chapter examines, in depth, two types of budgets that are commonly used in practice: the **master budget** prepared prior to the beginning of the period that is based on the company's planned accomplishments; and the **flexible budget** prepared after the fact to compare the actual operating results to what should have occurred, given the level of operations achieved for the period.

Most successful companies today use operating budgets to help them in their constant effort to analyze and control operations, keep costs in line, and reduce expenses. A **budget** is a planning device that helps a company set goals and that serves as a gauge against which actual results can be measured. Many heads of households are familiar with the basic aspects of budgeting whereby they estimate their income for the following year, determine what their living expenses will be, and then, depending on the figures, reduce unnecessary spending, set up a savings plan, or possibly determine additional ways to supplement their income. During the year, they compare their budget with their actual income and expenditures to be sure that expenses do not exceed income and cause financial difficulties.

Budgeting in business and industry is a formal method of detailed financial planning. It encompasses the coordination and control of every significant item in the balance sheet and income statement. Budgeting is used to help the company reach its long-term and short-term objectives. If the principles of budgeting are carried out in a proper manner, the company can be more assured that it will efficiently use all of its resources and achieve the most favorable results possible in the long run.

Principles of Budgeting

LO1 Explain the general principles involved in the budgeting process.

A primary objective of any for-profit organization is to maximize its income by attaining the highest volume of sales at the lowest possible cost. Planning and control are absolutely essential in achieving this goal, and budgeting produces the framework by which the organization can reach this objective. The budget then becomes a road map that guides managers along the way and lets them know when the company is straying from its planned route. It is a chart of the course of operations. In addition to forecasting costs and profits as a means of cost control, the budget requires those in authority in all areas of the business to carefully analyze all aspects of their responsibility for costs as well as to analyze company strengths and weaknesses.

The general principles of budgeting have several requirements:

1. Management must clearly define its objectives.
2. Goals must be realistic and possible to attain.
3. The budget must carefully consider economic developments, the general business climate, and the condition of the industry, along with changes and trends that may influence sales and costs, because the budgeting process involves looking to the future. Historical data should be used only as a stepping-off point for projections into the future.
4. There must be a plan, which is consistently followed, to constantly analyze the actual results as compared with the budget.
5. The budget must be flexible enough so that it can be modified in the light of changing conditions; it must not be so restrictive that changes cannot be made where more favorable results are foreseeable.
6. Responsibility for forecasting costs must be clearly defined, and accountability for actual results must be enforced. This principle encourages careful analysis and precise evaluation.

Preparing the Master Budget

Identify and prepare the components of the master budget.

The **master** or **static budget** is prepared for a single level of volume based on management's best estimate of the level of production and sales for the coming period. The master budget is usually prepared one year in advance, corresponding with the company's fiscal year. It is often divided into the

Figure 7-1 **Components of the Master Budget**

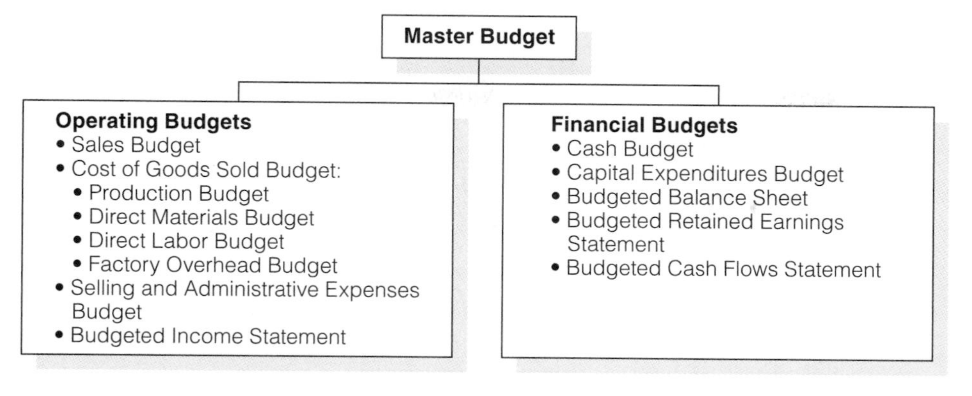

four calendar quarters of the year, with the upcoming quarter broken down further into months. Many companies prepare a **continuous** or **rolling budget** that "rolls forward" so that as one month or quarter is completed a new month or quarter is added at the end of the budget, resulting in a budget that is always one year in advance. Advocates of continuous budgeting argue that it causes managers to have a more long-term perspective, rather than just concentrating on the next month or quarter.

The master budget includes operating budgets and financial budgets as illustrated in Figure 7-1. **Operating budgets** include components of the **pro-forma (projected) financial statements**, such as the sales and production budgets that are part of the budgeted income statement. Operating budgets are stated in both units and dollars. **Financial budgets** include the budget balance sheet, budgeted retained earnings statement, and budgeted cash flows statement, as well as the cash and capital expenditures budgets. Details from the operating budgets are incorporated into the financial budgets to determine the organization's generation and use of funds for the period.

The various components of the operating budget for a manufacturer will be emphasized in this chapter. The budgeting process for a manufacturer is much more complex than that for a merchandising or service business. Manufacturers have to budget for the acquisition of raw materials and labor, as well as for the incurrence of a significant amount of manufacturing overhead costs. In contrast, merchandisers purchase products in their final form, and service businesses provide a service rather than a product, thus simplifying the budgeting process. Although this example is for a manufacturing business, budgeting is equally important for merchandising and service businesses, as illustrated in Chapter 9.

Sales Budget

In preparing operating budgets, management must consider all the items of revenue and expense. The usual starting point in the budgeting process is a sales budget, followed by a determination of inventory policy, a production budget, budgets for direct materials, direct labor, factory overhead, and

Figure 7-2 Operating Budgets Resulting in Budgeted Income Statement

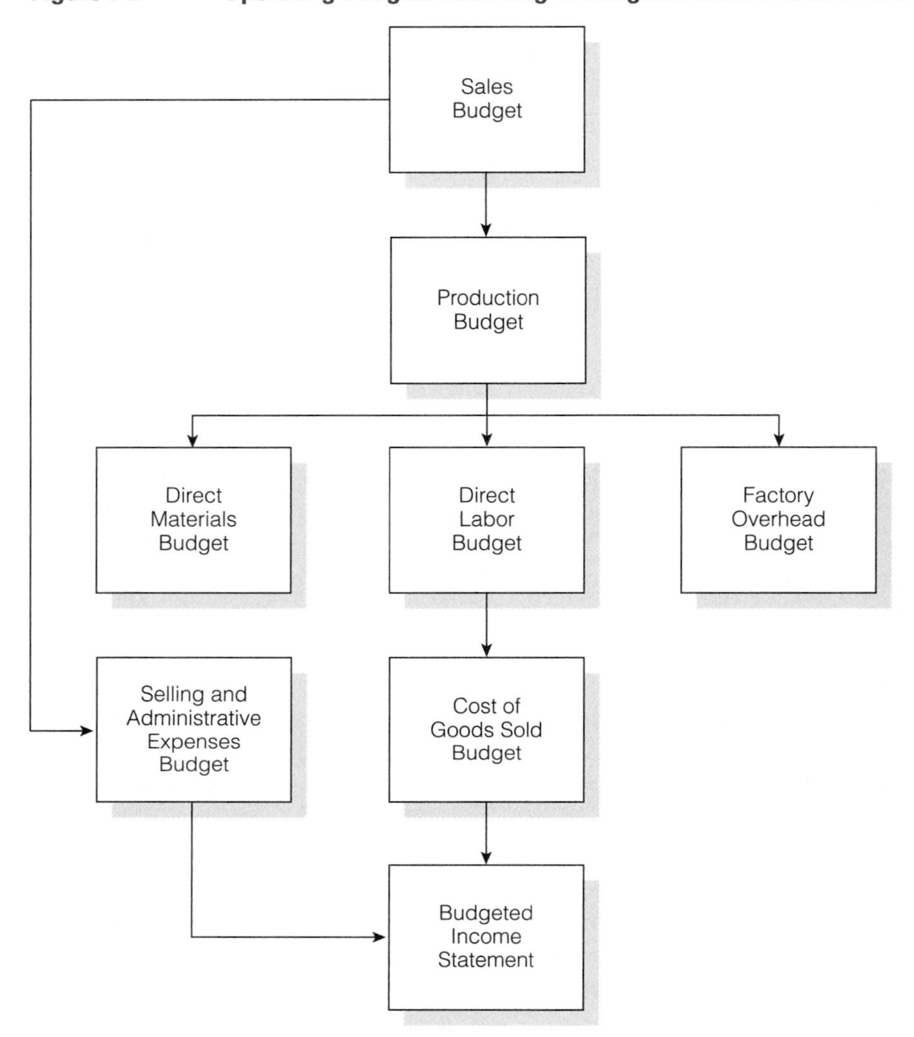

then cost of goods sold, plus budgeted selling and administrative expenses, all culminating in a budgeted income statement. A flow diagram of the operating budgets appears in Figure 7-2.

Although all of the aforementioned budgets are important, the sales budget is especially significant, because management must use this information as a basis for preparing all other budgets. The **sales budget** projects the volume of sales in both units and dollars. In estimating the sales for the coming year, the sales department must take into consideration present and future economic situations. It should research and carefully analyze market prospects for its products and give consideration to the development of new products and the discontinuance of old products. It should make these analyses by territory, by type of product, and possibly by type of customer. Marketing researchers should also carefully survey and evaluate consumer demand. A new aid in budgeting for sales is

demand software that takes numerous variables into consideration when forecasting sales, such as projected economic conditions in the industry and in the economy as a whole, population trends, and predicted weather patterns.

It is important for front-line managers, who are responsible for generating revenue or controlling costs, to initiate the budgeting process for their areas because they are the ones closest to the individual sales territory or production department situation. This is known as **participative budgeting** or **"bottom up" budgeting**, where the managers closest to the situation make projections that are then reviewed by their superiors. Research has shown that managers are more apt to meet or beat their budget projections in companies that practice participative budgeting. Their motivation is higher because they are the ones who set the budget numbers and there is no one else to blame for imposing unrealistic standards. Companies that practice participative budgeting should still have the individual budgets reviewed by the manager's immediate supervisor. This will preclude excessive **budget slack** where a manager sets unrealistically low goals in an effort to make only average performance look good.

After the above considerations, the mix of the products to be sold as well as the projected unit volume and selling price of each can be determined. Figure 7-3 is the sales budget for California Casuals, Inc., the manufacturer of one type of patio table and chair.

Figure 7-3 **Sales Budget**

	A	B	C	D
1	California Casuals, Inc.			
2	Schedule 1—Sales Budget			
3	For the Year Ended December 31, 2011			
4				
5		Unit	Unit	
6		Sales	Selling	
7	**Product and Region**	**Volume**	**Price**	**Total Sales**
8	Table:			
9	Southwest	12,000	$150	$1,800,000
10	West	18,000	150	$2,700,000
11	Total	30,000		$4,500,000
12				
13	Chair:			
14	Southwest	40,000	$50	$2,000,000
15	West	60,000	50	$3,000,000
16	Total	100,000		$5,000,000
17	Total Revenue			$9,500,000

Production Budget

After the sales forecast and desired inventory levels have been determined, management can determine production requirements. Assume the sales forecast for chairs in Figure 7-3, stable production throughout the year, a beginning inventory of 2,500 units, and a desired ending inventory 2,000 units greater than the beginning inventory. The number of chairs to be produced can be set forth in a **production budget** as follows:

Units to be sold	100,000
Ending inventory required	4,500
Total	104,500
Beginning inventory	2,500
Units to be manufactured	102,000
Units per month (102,000/12)	8,500

In actual practice, this computation may be more complex than the above example. Management must try to achieve a satisfactory balance between production, inventory, and the timely availability of goods to be sold. For example, if the company's sales are seasonal rather than evenly distributed throughout the year, stable production might produce the following situation:

	Number of Units		
	Produced	Sold	On Hand
Beginning balance			2,500
January	8,500	1,000	10,000
February	8,500	2,000	16,500
March	8,500	3,000	22,000
April	8,500	10,000	20,500
May	8,500	15,000	14,000
June	8,500	15,000	7,500
July	8,500	12,000	4,000
August	8,500	9,000	3,500
September	8,500	9,000	3,000
October	8,500	8,000	3,500
November	8,500	8,000	4,000
December	8,500	8,000	4,500
Total	102,000	100,000	

The "On Hand" column in the above table indicates that the company must have enough storage facility to handle as many as the 22,000 units in inventory at the end of March. However, most of this space would be unused during several months of the year, such as July through December. This would result in overinvestment in inventory and excess inventory carrying costs for storage space, insurance, and taxes. In this situation, a manufacturing concern might lease some storage facilities during the peak months, thereby requiring a much smaller company-owned facility. However, leasing may present problems of inconvenience, expense, and unavailability of the facilities at the right time and in the right place. In addition, during months such as March and April, the company would have a considerable amount of capital tied up in finished goods that could be threatened by obsolescence.

Another solution is for management to schedule different levels of production each month based on estimated monthly sales, in order to maintain a relatively stable inventory and to minimize the number of units stored. The following table shows this approach:

	Number of Units		
	Produced	**Sold**	**On Hand**
Beginning balance			2,500
January	1,500	1,000	3,000
February	2,500	2,000	3,500
March	3,000	3,000	3,500
April	10,000	10,000	3,500
May	15,000	15,000	3,500
June	15,000	15,000	3,500
July	12,000	12,000	3,500
August	9,500	9,000	4,000
September	9,500	9,000	4,500
October	8,000	8,000	4,500
November	8,000	8,000	4,500
December	8,000	8,000	4,500
Total	102,000	100,000	

This alternative requires minimum storage space and related expenses, but it creates a new problem. The factory must have enough capacity to handle the peak production of 15,000 units in May and June, but these facilities would be from 50 to 90% idle during some months. A possible solution is to maintain a smaller facility and to engage two or three shifts of employees during the busier months. Although the capital investment problem would be reduced, a bigger problem would be created because the workforce could vary by as much as 1,000% from the slowest period, January, to the most active periods, May and June. Fine tuning the workforce would require hiring new employees in the earlier months as production climbed, with the resulting high cost of recruiting and training, as well as the potential quality problem resulting from the use of new, inexperienced employees. In the later months, as production dropped, many workers would have to be laid off, resulting in additional expense for unemployment compensation premiums as well as potential severance pay, and a feeling of ill-will toward the company in the community.

Companies with good management will carefully analyze the above alternatives and arrive at a plan that represents a reasonable compromise between the two alternatives. Note that the utilization of a just-in-time purchasing and manufacturing system would minimize the above problems.

The production budget for California Casuals, Inc., appears in Figure 7-4.

Figure 7-4 Production Budget

	A	B	C
1	**California Casuals, Inc.**		
2	**Schedule 2—Production Budget**		
3	**For the Year Ended December 31, 2011**		
4			
5		**Units**	
6		**Tables**	**Chairs**
7	Sales..	30,000	100,000
8	Plus desired ending inventory, Dec. 31.....	1,500	$4,500
9	Total..	31,500	104,500
10	Less estimated beginning inventory, Jan. 1	1,000	$2,500
11	Total Production	30,500	102,000

Direct Materials Budget

Following the preparation of the production budget, the direct materials budget, direct labor budget, and factory overhead budget can be prepared. The format of the **direct materials budget** is similar to the production budget. The desired ending inventory for each material is added to the quantity needed to meet production needs, and then that total is reduced by the estimated beginning inventory to determine the amount of material to be purchased. Multiplying the quantity of material to be purchased by the budgeted, or standard, unit cost results in the total materials purchase cost. (Recall that standard costs are costs that would be incurred under efficient operating conditions and are forecast before the budget is prepared.) The direct materials budget for California Casuals, Inc., appears in Figure 7-5.

In the direct materials budget, the standard quantity and price of material to be used for each unit of product is as follows:

Table	**Chair**
Lumber: 10 board feet per unit @ $2 per board foot	5 board feet per unit
Paint: 0.2 gallons per unit @ $20 per gallon	0.1 gallons per unit

The desired beginning and ending inventories for raw materials in the direct materials budget are as follows:

	Lumber (Board Feet)	**Paint (Gallons)**
Beginning inventory	30,000	1,000
Ending inventory	40,000	800

There should be close coordination between the purchasing and production functions, so that materials are purchased as closely as possible to the time that they will be placed into production, thus minimizing inventory carrying costs while guarding against stockouts.

Figure 7-5 **Direct Materials Budget**

	A	B	C	D
1	**California Casuals, Inc.**			
2	**Schedule 3—Direct Materials Budget**			
3	**For the Year Ended December 31, 2011**			
4				
5		**Direct Materials**		**Total**
6		**Lumber**	**Paint**	
7	**Product and Region**	**(Board Feet)**	**(Gallons)**	
8	Quantities required for production:			
9	Tables (Note A)	305,000	6,100	
10	Chairs (Note B)	510,000	10,200	
11	Plus desired ending inventory, Dec. 31	40,000	800	
12	Total	855,000	17,100	
13	Less estimated beginning inventory, Jan. 1	30,000	1,000	
14	Total quantity to be purchased	825,000	16,100	
15	Unit price	$2	$20	
16	Total direct materials purchases	$1,650,000	$322,000	$1,972,000
17	Note A: 30,500 units x 10 board feet/unit = 305,000 bd ft			
18	30,500 units x 0.2 gallons/unit = 6,100 gal			
19	Note B: 102,000 units x 5 board feet/unit = 510,000 bd ft			
20	102,000 units x 0.1 gallon/unit = 10,200 gal			

Direct Labor Budget

The production requirements from the production budget are used for preparation of the **direct labor budget**. The standard labor time allowed per unit for each factory operation is multiplied by the number of required units to obtain the total direct manufacturing labor hours allowed. The total hours required for each operation are then multiplied by the hourly rate for that operation to obtain the budgeted direct labor cost. The direct labor budget for California Casuals, Inc., appears in Figure 7-6.

In the direct labor budget, the standard quantity and price of labor allowed for each unit of product is as follows:

	Table	**Chair**
Cutting Department	0.25 hours per unit @ $15 per hour	0.10 hours per unit
Assembly Department	0.20 hours per unit @ $12 per hour	0.15 hours per unit
Painting Department	0.15 hours per unit @ $10 per hour	0.10 hours per unit

Just as there was a need for close coordination between purchasing and production functions, interaction between the human resources and production departments is equally important to ensure that enough of the right kind of labor is available to meet production. The Japanese concept of *kaizen* is relevant to the topic of setting standards such as the labor times listed above. **Kaizen** means continuous improvement, and **kaizen budgeting** is the practice of building continuous improvement into the budget numbers. For example, although the standard labor time was .25 hours per unit in the Cutting Department for 2011, it may be adjusted to .20 hours per unit in 2012 because the employees should now be more proficient at

Figure 7-6 **Direct Labor Budget**

	A	B	C	D	
1	**California Casuals, Inc.**				
2	**Schedule 4—Direct Labor Budget**				
3	**For the Year Ended December 31, 2011**				
4					
5		**Cutting**	**Assembly**	**Painting**	**Total**
6	Hours required for production:				
7	Tables (Note A)	7,625	6,100	4,575	
8	Chairs (Note B)	10,200	15,300	10,200	
9	Total	17,825	21,400	14,775	
10	Hourly rate	$15	$12	$10	
11	Total direct labor cost	$267,375	$256,800	$147,750	$671,925
12	Note A: Cutting	30,500 units × 0.25 hours per unit = 7,625 hours			
13	Assembly	30,500 units × 0.20 hours per unit = 6,100 hours			
14	Painting	30,500 units × 0.15 hours per unit = 4,575 hours			
15	Note B: Cutting	102,000 units × 0.10 hours per unit = 10,200 hours			
16	Assembly	102,000 units × 0.15 hours per unit = 15,300 hours			
17	Painting	102,000 units × 0.10 hours per unit = 10,200 hours			

completing the task. Often the standards are changed monthly or quarterly to capture the more immediate effect of learning how to perform the task more proficiently.

Factory Overhead Budget

The **factory overhead budget** consists of the estimated individual factory overhead items needed to meet production requirements. The factory overhead budget for California Casuals, Inc., based on production estimates of 30,500 tables and 102,000 chairs, appears in Figure 7-7.

Cost of Goods Sold Budget

The **cost of goods sold budget** is prepared upon completion of the direct materials, direct labor, and factory overhead budgets. The estimated beginning inventories, as well as the desired ending inventories, of work in

Figure 7-7 **Factory Overhead Budget**

	A	B
1	**California Casuals, Inc.**	
2	**Schedule 5—Factory Overhead Budget**	
3	**For the Year Ended December 31, 2011**	
4	Indirect materials	$225,000
5	Indirect labor	375,250
6	Depreciation of building	85,000
7	Depreciation of machinery and equipment	67,500
8	Insurance and property taxes	48,750
9	Power and light	29,800
10	Total factory overhead cost	$831,300
11		

Figure 7-8 **Cost of Goods Sold Budget**

	A	B	C	D
1	**California Casuals, Inc.**			
2	**Schedule 6—Cost of Goods Sold Budget**			
3	**For the Year Ended December 31, 2011**			
4				
5	Finished goods inventory, Jan. 1			$72,400
6	Work in process inventory, Jan. 1		$22,600	
7	Direct materials inventory, Jan. 1 (Note A)	$80,000		
8	Direct materials purchases (Schedule 3)	1,972,000		
9	Direct materials available for use	$2,052,000		
10	Less direct materials inventory, Dec. 31 (Note B)	96,000		
11	Cost of direct materials used	$1,956,000		
12	Direct labor (Schedule 4)	671,925		
13	Factory overhead (Schedule 5)	831,300		
14	Total manufacturing costs		3,459,225	
15	Total work in process during year		$3,481,825	
16	Less work in process inventory, Dec. 31		18,000	
17	Cost of goods manufactured			3,463,825
18	Cost of goods available for sale			$3,536,225
19	Less finished goods inventory, Dec. 31			120,825
20	Cost of goods sold			$3,415,400
21	Note A: Lumber 30,000 bd ft × $2 per bd ft	= $60,000		
22	Paint 1,000 gal × $20 per gal	= 20,000		
23	Direct materials inventory, Jan. 1	$80,000		
24	Note B: Lumber 40,000 bd ft × $2 per bd ft	= $80,000		
25	Paint 800 gal × $20 per gal	= 16,000		
26	Direct materials inventory, Dec. 31	$96,000		

process and finished goods must be included in the computation of cost of goods sold. California Casual's projections for beginning and ending inventories in dollars are as follows:

Estimated beginning inventories on January 1:	
Finished Goods	$ 72,400
Work in Process	22,600
Desired ending inventories on December 31:	
Finished Goods	$120,825
Work in Process	18,000

The cost of goods sold budget for California Casuals, Inc., appears in Figure 7-8.

Selling and Administrative Expenses Budget

Once the sales forecast has been made, a **selling and administrative expenses budget** can be prepared. The sales forecast will affect the planned expenditure level for such items as sales commissions, advertising, and travel. The budget has separate sections for selling and for administrative expenses, with line item expenses within each category. A selling and administrative expenses budget appears in Figure 7-9.

Figure 7-9 Selling and Administrative Expenses Budget

	A	B	C
1	California Casuals, Inc.		
2	Schedule 7—Selling and Administrative Expenses Budget		
3	For the Year Ended December 31, 2011		
4			
5	Selling expenses:		
6	Advertising expense	$730,300	
7	Sales salaries expense	688,500	
8	Travel expense	398,000	
9	Total selling expenses		$1,816,800
10	Administrative expenses:		
11	Officers' salaries expense	$655,000	
12	Office salaries expense	511,500	
13	Office rent expense	65,000	
14	Office supplies expense	32,500	
15	Telephone, fax, and copier expense	14,500	
16	Total administrative expenses		1,278,500
17	Total selling and administrative expenses		$3,095,300

Budgeted Income Statement

Upon completion of the preceding budgets, a **budgeted income statement** can be prepared. The budgeted income statement summarizes the data from all of the other operating budgets and enables management to determine the impact of all of these budget estimates on operating income. If the budgeted profit does not meet expectations, top management may revisit the individual budget estimates with the appropriate managers, for the purpose of determining what changes, if any, can be made to improve profitability.

Note that, although spreadsheets were utilized throughout this section, many companies are now using **Web-based budgeting,** where each employee can input the data for which they are responsible at the budget Web site. This precludes them from having to prepare individual spreadsheets for their area of responsibility, which then have to uploaded and coordinated. A budgeted income statement for California Casuals, Inc., assuming a 40% income tax rate, appears in Figure 7-10.

Other Budgets

Although not illustrated here, the company could now prepare its financial budgets, including the budgeted financial statements. The **cash budget** shows the anticipated flow of cash and the timing of receipts and disbursements based on projected revenues, the production schedule, and expenses. Using this budget, management can plan for necessary financing or for temporary investment of surplus funds.

The company also may prepare a **capital expenditures budget**, which is a plan for timing acquisitions of buildings, equipment, or other significant assets. This plan ties in with the sales and production plans and may influence the cash budget for expenditures, to the extent that additional financing may be necessary. A capital expenditures budget is typically prepared for a three- to five-year time horizon. A budgeting time horizon is

Figure 7-10 Budgeted Income Statement

	A	B
1	**California Casuals, Inc.**	
2	**Budgeted Income Statement**	
3	**For the Year Ended December 31, 2011**	
4	Net sales (Schedule 1)	$9,500,000
5	Cost of goods sold (Schedule 6)	3,415,400
6	Gross profit	$6,084,600
7	Selling and administrative expenses (Schedule 7)	3,095,300
8	Income from operations	$2,989,300
9	Income tax	1,195,720
10	Net income	$1,793,580

often a function of the nature of the business and its industry. For example, long-established businesses, such as **Coca Cola** and **Kellogg's**, in relatively stable industries, such as beverages and food products, would typically have a longer time horizon than an Internet startup company.

Evaluating Budget Performance

If budgeting is to be used successfully as a management tool for controlling operations, the actual results should be periodically compared with the budgeted amounts, and the reasons for any significant variances should be explained, as will be discussed in the next chapter. Without this follow-up, the benefits of budgeting would not be fully utilized. If material differences are found to exist between budgeted and actual amounts, management must determine who in the organization can best explain the reasons for the variances. Figure 7-11 illustrates the above process.

Performance reports comparing budgeted to actual amounts should be distributed to the managers responsible for a particular operation or department. For example, individual salespersons would receive in-depth reports of budgeted and actual sales by customer and product in their territories. The regional sales manager would receive a summarized report of budgeted and actual sales for all salespersons in that region. The national sales manager would receive a summarized report of budgeted and actual sales for each region.

Recall and Review 1

The sales department of Big Papi Manufacturing has forecast sales in May to be 35,000 units. Beginning finished goods inventory on May 1 is 6,000 units, and the finished goods inventory required on May 31 is 2,000 units. Two pounds of Material X, at a cost of $10 per pound, is required to produce each unit. The May 1 inventory of Material X is 3,000 lb and the desired May 31 inventory is 4,000 lb. The required production of units in May is ______________ and the direct materials purchases, in dollars, should be $______________________.

(After working this exercise, see page 361 for the solution.)

You should now be able to work the following:
Questions 1–14; Exercises 7-1 to 7-5; Problems 7-1 through 7-3; Self-Study Problem 1; and the Internet Exercise.

Figure 7-11 **Comparison of Budgeted to Actual Performance**

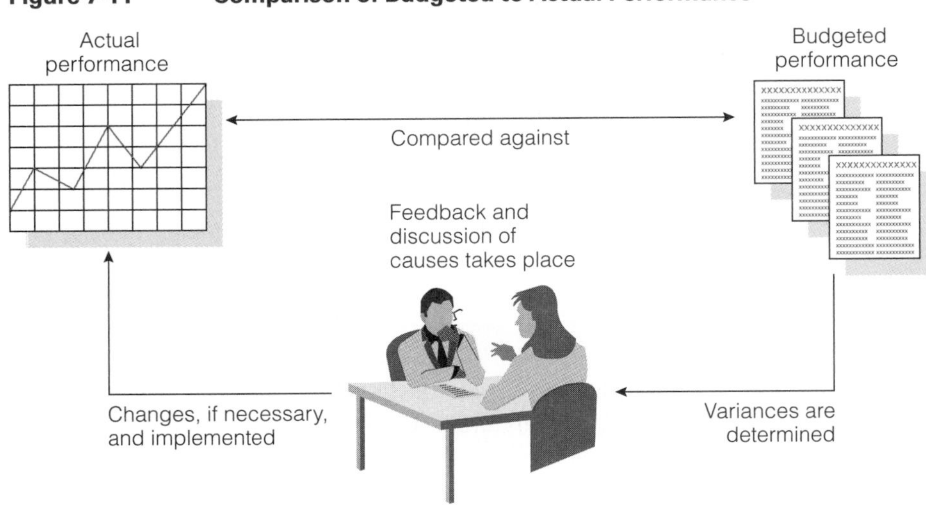

Flexible Budgeting

LO3 Identify and prepare components of the flexible budget.

Branson Manufacturing, Inc., produces a single type of small motor. The bookkeeper, who does not have an in-depth understanding of accounting principles, prepared the following report with the help of the production manager:

	A	B	C	D	E
1		Branson Manufacturing, Inc.			
2		Performance Report			
3		May, 2011			
4					
5		Flexible Budget	Actual Results	Master Budget	Variance
6		Per Unit	(45,000 units)	(50,000 units)	
7	**Sales**	**$25.00**	**$1,125,000**	**$1,250,000**	**$125,000U**
8	Less variable expenses:				
9	Direct materials	4.50	$212,500	$225,000	$12,500 F
10	Direct labor	3.75	175,750	187,500	11,750 F
11	Variable factory overhead	2.25	110,250	112,500	2,250 F
12	Variable selling and administrative expense	1.50	70,500	75,000	4,500 F
13	Total variable expense	$12.00	$569,000	$600,000	$31,000 F
14	Contribution margin	$13.00	$556,000	$650,000	$94,000 U
15	Less fixed expenses:				
16	Fixed factory overhead expense	$100,000	$95,000	$100,000	$5,000 F
17	Fixed selling and administrative expense	150,000	160,000	150,000	10,000 U
18	Total fixed expense	$250,000	$255,000	$250,000	$5,000 U
19	Income from operations		$301,000	$400,000	$99,000 U

In a conversation with the sales manager, the production manager was overheard saying, "You sales guys really messed up our May performance, and it is only because production did such a great job controlling costs that we aren't in even worse shape." Do you agree

with the production manager? The use of flexible budgeting in comparing actual results to budgeted expectations is the focus of this section of the chapter. The mini-case at the end of the chapter is a continuation of the Branson Manufacturing situation.

The comparison of actual results with the budget to see if the planned objectives are being met leads to the use of a **flexible budget**. Whereas the master budget is prepared for a single level of activity, the flexible budget is prepared for a range of activities within which the firm may operate. To implement a flexible budget, a company must decide how it will respond to varying sets of conditions—for example, the sale of 10,000 units per month rather than 9,000; the production of 15,000 units per month rather than 17,000; the addition or replacement of a machine in a department; and the development of new products or the discontinuance of old products.

A company should plan in advance what the effect will be on revenue, expense, and profit if sales or production differ from the master budget. To illustrate, if budgeted sales for a month are $100,000 and the budgeted selling expense is $25,000, it is reasonable to assume that if actual sales are only $80,000, the actual selling expense would be less than $25,000, because certain selling expenses, such as sales commissions, vary with sales volume. Also, if production volume is 10,000 units rather than the budgeted 9,000 units, the actual production costs should logically be greater than the amount budgeted for 9,000 units because certain manufacturing expenses, such as direct materials, vary with the volume of units produced.

The flexible budget is influenced by the presence of fixed and variable costs as discussed in Chapter 4. Recall that **fixed costs** are those costs that do not change as production changes over a given range of activity. These expenses are a function of time, and generally they will be incurred regardless of the level of production. For example, such expenses as straight-line depreciation, insurance, property taxes, and supervisory salaries will remain the same in dollar total, except in the extreme case of a major change in production that requires more or fewer machines, facilities, and supervisory personnel.

Variable costs vary in total dollar amount in proportion to any change in production or sales volume. These costs may include such items as direct materials, direct labor, factory overhead expenses such as supplies, the electricity to run the machines, and repair costs, and selling and administrative expenses such as sales commissions and copying charges. It is because of these variable items that the total cost or revenue will differ from amounts in the master budget, when the actual level of production or sales volume is different from the master budget level. For example, if a manufacturer has budgeted direct materials cost of $50,000 based on budgeted production of 5,000 units for the month, but the actual production is 6,000 units, there will be little value in comparing the actual direct materials cost incurred with the $50,000 in the master budget. One would expect that if the actual units produced were greater than 5,000, then the direct materials cost would be greater than $50,000. A flexible budget, however, would be useful because it would indicate the budgeted direct materials cost for the 6,000 units of production achieved. This would enable management to determine how well direct materials costs were controlled, given the actual level of production attained.

Preparing the Flexible Budget

Assume that California Casuals' sales budget for tables in Figure 7-3 was not met; actual sales of tables were 28,000, not the 30,000 units appearing in the master budget; and dollar sales were $4,250,000, not the budgeted sales of $4,500,000. If California's management wanted to know how good of a job it did generating revenue, given the number of units that were actually sold, the master budget numbers would not be helpful. For an "apples to apples" comparison of budgeted and actual sales revenue at the same unit volume, the accountant would need to prepare a flexible budget that was useful within a relevant range of activity. The flexible budget in Figure 7-12 assumes that the relevant range within which the master budget cost and revenue relationships would hold is between 28,000 and 32,000 tables per year, and it only includes sales revenue, direct materials, and direct labor broken out in detail, using the budgeted selling price and unit costs for California Casuals presented earlier in the chapter. To reduce the level of detail in the example, the factory overhead and selling and administrative expenses in the California Casuals illustration are listed in total as variable and fixed, assuming that approximately half of each type of expense is variable, and half is fixed at the 30,000-unit master budget level. (Budgeting for factory overhead is covered in depth in the next section of this chapter.)

Figure 7-12 **Flexible Budget for Production and Sale of Tables**

	A	B	C	D
1	**Item**	**28,000 units**	**30,000 units**	**32,000 units**
2	Sales ($150 per unit)	$4,200,000	$4,500,000	$4,800,000
3	Direct materials:			
4	Lumber ($20 per unit)	560,000	600,000	640,000
5	Paint ($4 per unit)	112,000	120,000	128,000
6	Direct labor:			
7	Cutting ($3.75 per unit)	105,000	112,500	120,000
8	Assembly ($2.40 per unit)	67,200	72,000	76,800
9	Painting ($1.50 per unit)	42,000	45,000	48,000
10	Variable factory overhead ($6.93 per unit)	194,040	207,900	221,760
11	Variable selling and administrative expense	722,120	773,700	825,280
12	($25.79 per unit)			
13	Contribution margin	$2,397,640	$2,568,900	$2,740,160
14	Fixed factory overhead	207,825	207,825	207,825
15	Fixed selling and administrative expense	773,825	773,825	773,825
16	Operating income	$1,415,990	$1,587,250	$1,758,510

Note that the three levels of production and sales were chosen merely for illustrative purposes, and that a flexible budget could be prepared for any volume level within the relevant range of 28,000 to 32,000 units. Also note that the per-unit amounts for the variable costs came from the standard amounts per unit given in the master budget section of the chapter. For example, the $20 per-unit cost for lumber was obtained by multiplying the standard quantity of 10 board feet per table by the standard cost of $2 per board foot.

Preparing a Performance Report Based on Flexible Budgeting

In preparing the performance report for the production and sale of tables in Figure 7-13, the actual revenue and expense amounts are assumed. (Note that for ease of illustration, unlike the master budget illustration, it is assumed that the number of units produced equals the number of units sold so that there are no complications related to inventory level changes.) The budgeted revenue and expense amounts were taken from the flexible budget at the 28,000-unit level in Figure 7-12.

Note that the variance for the sale revenue was $50,000 favorable. Since the comparison of budgeted and actual revenue is at the same 28,000-unit level, the actual selling price per unit must have been greater than the budgeted selling price of $150 per table. In fact, the actual average selling price was $151.80 ($4,250,000/28,000). So, given the number of units sold, California Casuals obtained favorable selling prices. Recall that the master budget, however, planned for the sale of 30,000 units and $4,500,000 in revenue. Therefore, the company was unsuccessful in generating enough unit volume to meet master budget revenue projections—maybe, in part, because it raised the selling price per unit.

The same type of flexible budget analysis may be made for the expense items. For example, the flexible budget indicates that there was an unfavorable $25,000 variance for lumber. For the production of 28,000 tables, $560,000 (28,000 × 10 bd ft × $2 per bd ft) should have been spent for lumber. The actual amount spent was $585,000. Given the amounts budgeted, the company did a poor job controlling the purchase cost of lumber and/or

Figure 7-13 **Performance Report for Production and Sale of Tables**

	A	B	C	D
1		**Budget**	**Actual**	**Variance**
2	**Item**	(28,000 units)	(28,000 units)	
3	Sales	$4,200,000	$4,250,000	$50,000 F
4	Direct materials:			
5	Lumber	560,000	585,000	25,000 U
6	Paint	112,000	108,000	4,000 F
7	Direct labor:			
8	Cutting	105,000	120,000	15,000 U
9	Assembly	67,200	72,000	4,800 U
10	Painting	42,000	40,000	2,000 F
11	Variable factory overhead	194,040	206,823	12,783 U
12	Variable selling and administrative expense	722,120	719,456	2,664 F
13	Contribution margin	$2,397,640	$2,398,721	$1,081 F
14	Fixed factory overhead	207,825	211,765	3,940 U
15	Fixed selling and administrative expense	773,825	770,550	3,275 F
16	Operating income	$1,415,990	$1,416,406	$416 F

the quantity of lumber used in the production process. Chapter 8 will illustrate the breakout of a materials variance into these two components.

Direct labor variances can also be analyzed. For example, $15,000 more was spent for Cutting labor than the $105,000 (28,000 × .25 hr per unit × $15 per hr) flexible budget amount for the production of 28,000 tables. This could have been caused by paying a higher wage than the $15 per hour standard called for and/or spending more time per unit than the .25 hours per table budgeted. Again, Chapter 8 will decompose the labor variance into these components.

Other items that deserve a brief explanation include overhead expenses, selling and administrative expenses, and operating income. Note that the amount of variable factory overhead spent was $12,783 greater than budgeted for the 28,000-unit level. That is not surprising, since the direct labor variances were mostly unfavorable. The excess hours that the direct laborers probably worked to complete production would have resulted in additional variable factory overhead costs such as supplies, electricity expense, and indirect labor. The variable selling and administrative expense had a favorable $2,664 variance, indicating that expenditures for items such as travel and office supplies were adequately controlled.

Fixed factory overhead and fixed selling and administrative expenses were slightly unfavorable and favorable, respectively, meaning that budgeted fixed expenditures were overspent or underspent, respectively. For example, less may have been spent on an advertising campaign than planned, perhaps contributing to the lack of sales volume. Note that the operating income variance was $416 favorable at the 28,000-unit level. This means that, given the number of units that California Casuals produced and sold, revenue generation and cost control were acceptable. However, the master budget called for the production and sale of 30,000 units, which if achieved should have resulted in budgeted operating income of $1,587,250 as illustrated in Figure 7-12—$170,844 more than the actual operating income. This indicates that the company has forgone a significant amount of profit by operating 2,000 units below the master budget volume level.

Recall and Review 2

Dilbert Co. has the following items and amounts as part of its master budget at the 20,000-unit level of sales and production: sales revenue, $150,000; direct materials, $36,000; direct labor, $20,000; variable factory overhead, $16,000; fixed factory overhead, $40,000. Determine the total dollars amounts for each of the above items that would appear in a flexible budget at the 22,000-unit level.

(After working this exercise, see pages 361 and 362 for the solution.)

You should now be able to work the following:
Questions 15–19; Exercises 7-6 to 7-8; Problems 7-4 to 7-6; and Mini-Case.

Preparing the Flexible Budget for Factory Overhead

LO4 Explain the procedures to determine standard amounts of factory overhead at different levels of production.

The complexities of budgeting for factory overhead require more explanation than appears in the preceding section. Determining the standard overhead cost per unit and preparing the flexible budget for factory overhead follow the basic principles suggested for establishing standards for materials and labor costs. All costs that might be incurred should be carefully considered. Prior costs, as adjusted, must be studied as well as the effect of new costs, future economic conditions, changes in processes, and trends. As with other standards, the individuals responsible for setting factory overhead standards should have considerable experience and familiarity with manufacturing operations.

Because costs are affected by the level of production, the first step is to determine what should be the standard volume of production. **Standard production** is the volume on which the initial calculation of costs is based. Several approaches may be used to determine this figure based on a choice of several definitions of manufacturing capacity. These types of capacity include the following:

1. **Theoretical capacity** represents the maximum number of units that can be produced with the completely efficient use of all available facilities and personnel. Generally, this production level is impossible to attain. It represents a rigid standard for the factory because it requires maximum production, with no allowance for inefficiencies of any kind.

2. **Practical capacity** is the level of production that provides complete utilization of all facilities and personnel, but allows for some idle capacity due to operating interruptions, such as machinery breakdowns, idle time, and other inescapable inefficiencies.

3. **Normal capacity** is the level of production that will meet the normal requirements of ordinary sales demand over a period of years. Although it conceivably can be equal to or greater than practical capacity, normal capacity usually does not involve a plan for maximum usage of manufacturing facilities but allows for some unavoidable idle capacity and some inefficiencies in operations. Most manufacturing firms use this level of capacity for budget development because it represents a logical balance between maximum production capacity and the capacity demanded by actual sales volume. The following discussion will assume the use of normal capacity for planning purposes.

To illustrate the flexible budget, the following figures were determined to be the factory overhead costs at the normal capacity of 1,000 units. (To simplify the illustration, only a few overhead classifications are used. In actual practice, many types of expenses would be broken down into fixed and variable categories.)

Standard production—1,000 units

Standard direct labor hours—2,000

Fixed cost:		
Depreciation of building and equipment	$4,000	
Property tax and insurance	1,000	
Supervisory salaries	4,000	
Total fixed cost		$ 9,000
Variable cost:		
Maintenance	$2,000	
Supplies	1,000	
Total variable cost		3,000
Total factory overhead cost		$12,000

Standard factory overhead application rate per direct labor hour:	
Fixed cost ($9,000 ÷ 2,000 hours)	$ 4.50
Variable cost ($3,000 ÷ 2,000 hours)	1.50
Total factory overhead rate ($12,000 ÷ 2,000 hours)	$ 6.00
Standard overhead cost per unit ($12,000 ÷ 1,000 units)	$ 12.00

As discussed in Chapter 4, factory overhead can be applied to work in process using different bases, such as direct labor hours, direct labor cost, or machine hours. One of the most commonly used bases—direct labor hours—applies overhead in relation to the standard number of direct labor hours allowed for the current actual production.

In the preceding schedule, both standard units and standard hours are given because production may be expressed in terms of output (units) or input (the standard number of direct labor hours allowed for the actual production). Whichever base for measuring production is chosen, the results are not affected. Based on the preceding budget, if 900 units are manufactured, Work in Process would be charged with $10,800 (900 units × $12 standard overhead cost per unit) for factory overhead. If production is expressed in terms of standard direct labor hours of 1,800 (900 units × 2 standard direct labor hours per unit), Work in Process would still be charged with $10,800 (1,800 hours × $6 per direct labor hour).

Figure 7-14 shows the flexible budget for this illustration. The individuals responsible for the work have determined what the fixed and variable costs will be at various levels of production. Notice that the factory overhead per direct labor hour decreases as volume increases, because the fixed factory overhead, which does not change in total within the relevant range, is being spread over more production. Also, notice that the standard volume of production is expressed as being 100% of capacity. This production level is not necessarily the maximum capacity of the manufacturing facility. It represents, considering sales demand, the most efficient use of the present facilities under normal operating conditions, with some allowance for operating interruptions. A factory can always produce more than

Figure 7-14 **Factory Overhead Cost Budget**

	A	B	C	D	E	F
1	**Percent of Normal Capacity**	**80%**	**90%**	**100%**	**110%**	**120%**
2	Number of units	800	900	1,000	1,100	1,200
3	Number of standard direct labor hours	1,600	1,800	2,000	2,200	2,400
4	Budgeted factory overhead:					
5	Fixed cost:					
6	Depreciation of building and equipment	$4,000	$4,000	$4,000	$4,000	$4,000
7	Property taxes and insurance	1,000	1,000	1,000	1,000	1,000
8	Supervisory salaries	4,000	4,000	4,000	4,000	4,000
9	Total fixed cost	$9,000	$9,000	$9,000	$9,000	$9,000
10	Variable cost:					
11	Maintenance	$1,600	$1,800	$2,000	$2,200	$2,400
12	Supplies	800	900	1,000	1,100	1,200
13	Total variable cost	$2,400	$2,700	$3,000	$3,300	$3,600
14	Total factory overhead cost	$11,400	$11,700	$12,000	$12,300	$12,600
15	Factory overhead per direct labor hour	$7.125	$6.50	$6.00	$5.59	$5.25

the normal volume by working overtime, adding a shift, or squeezing in more machinery and workers; but these conditions are not normal. Because it is not uncommon to operate above or below normal, the flexible budget shows the budgeted expense amounts for production above and below the normal capacity of 100%, as illustrated in Figure 7-14.

Using the Flexible Budget

If, for example, actual production for a given period is 1,000 units, a comparison of factory overhead costs incurred with these budgeted figures can be made and variances determined as follows:

Factory Overhead Cost Variances

Normal production .... 1,000 units (or 2,000 direct labor hours)
Actual production .... 1,000 units (or 2,000 direct labor hours)

	Budget	**Actual**	**Variances Favorable (Unfavorable)**
Fixed cost:			
Depreciation of building and equipment	$ 4,000	$ 4,000	
Property taxes and insurance	1,000	1,000	
Supervisory salaries	4,000	4,000	
Total fixed cost	$ 9,000	$ 9,000	
Variable cost:			
Maintenance	$ 2,000	$ 2,500	$(500)
Supplies	1,000	900	100
Total variable cost	$ 3,000	$ 3,400	$(400)
Total factory overhead cost	$12,000	$12,400	$(400)

Usually, factory activity will not be exactly at the normal capacity level as it was in the previous example. The volume of production invariably fluctuates to a certain extent from the standard production level because it is affected by such factors as vacations, holidays, employee absenteeism, work interruptions, and equipment breakdowns. If a seasonal factor is involved, the fluctuation from one month to the next could be significant. Under these circumstances, the flexible budget provides the budgeted figures for the actual levels of production rather than the established normal level.

Upon receiving the report on actual volume for the period, the factory overhead costs that should have been incurred at that volume can be compared with the actual costs to determine variances. If the volume of production falls between two of the amounts shown in the budget, an approximation of budgeted cost can be interpolated as follows:

Actual production 850 units (85%):	
Budgeted cost at 90% in Figure 7-14	$11,700
Budgeted cost at 80% in Figure 7-14	11,400
Difference	$ 300
Range between volume levels	10%

Dividing the difference of $300 by 10 determines an additional cost of $30 for each percentage point increase above the lower of the two volume levels.

Next lower budgeted volume	80%
Costs at 80% volume	$11,400
Additional costs at 85% volume (5 percentage points × $30)	150
Budgeted costs at 85% volume	$11,550

Rather than doing the somewhat laborious calculations above, by preparing budget formulas in an Excel spreadsheet for each of the line items, you only need to input the actual number of units produced to obtain the allowable budgeted expenditures for that level of production.

Semifixed and Semivariable Costs

Unit production different from that given in the budget is satisfactory if the overhead increases evenly throughout each range of activity, as would be the case if all costs were either fixed or variable. However, if significant semifixed or semivariable costs exist, then this method would not always be accurate enough for a meaningful evaluation.

Semifixed costs, or **step costs**, are those costs that tend to remain the same in dollar amount through a wide range of activity, but increase when production exceeds certain limits. For example, the salary of a department head is generally considered a fixed cost because no other department head will be employed through a given range of activity, and the salary cost will not change as the volume fluctuates. But if the production level exceeds a given number of units, an assistant department head might have to be employed to aid in supervising the greater number of workers that would be necessary. In this case, at 120% of normal capacity, the fixed expense for supervisory personnel would increase with the addition of an assistant department head, as illustrated with the assumed numbers in the following table.

Percent of Normal Capacity	80%	90%	100%	110%	120%	130%
Fixed cost	$20,000	$20,000	$20,000	$20,000	**$28,000**	**$28,000**
Variable cost	24,000	27,000	30,000	33,000	36,000	39,000
Total factory overhead	$44,000	$47,000	$50,000	$53,000	$64,000	$67,000

Semivariable costs are those costs that may change with production but not necessarily in direct proportion. For example, if a company incurs expense to train new employees before they go into the factory, this expense will increase as production increases and new employees are hired. But if the volume of production decreases and no new employees are hired, no training expense will be incurred.

The existence of semifixed or semivariable costs indicates an even greater need for careful analysis and evaluation of the costs at each level of production. The approach in this chapter, however, assumes that fixed costs remain constant and variable costs vary evenly throughout the ranges of activity given, unless stated otherwise.

Service Department Budgets and Variances

Preparing a budget for a service department, such as Maintenance or Factory Office, requires the same procedures as those used for production departments, such as Assembly and Finishing. Expenses at different levels of production are estimated, and a standard rate for application of service department expenses to production departments is determined based on the type of service provided and the estimated usage of that service by the production departments. The production departments will take these allocated service department expenses into consideration in setting up their budgets.

During the period, the production departments are charged with service department expenses at the standard rate based on their usage of the activity base, such as kilowatt hours or hours of maintenance labor. At the end of the period, the service department's actual expenses are compared with the amount charged to the production departments to determine any service department variances.

Figure 7-15 **Determination of Production Requirements and Standard Product Cost**

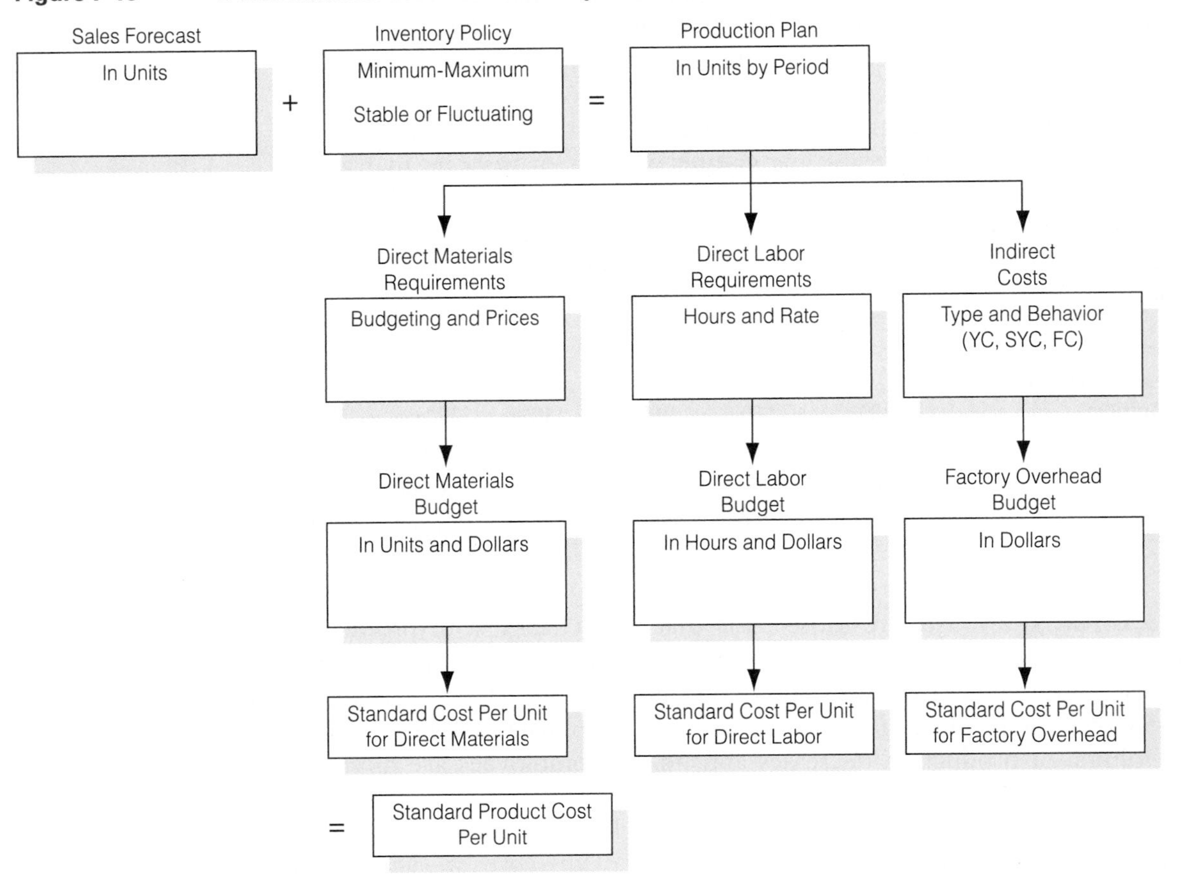

Summary of the Budgeting Process

Figure 7-15 summarizes the determination of factory production requirements and standard product cost.

Recall and Review 3

The normal capacity of a manufacturing plant is 10,000 units per month. Fixed overhead at this volume level is $5,000, and variable overhead is $10,000. If actual production for the month is 12,000 units, the budgeted factory overhead would be $__________ variable and $__________ fixed, and the overhead application rate per unit would be $__________ (carried to two decimal places).

(After working this exercise, see page 362 for the solution.)

You should now be able to work the following:
Questions 20–23; Exercises 7-9 and 7-10; Problems 7-7 to 7-9; and Self-Study Problem 2.

KEY TERMS

"Bottom up" budgeting, 341
Budget, 337
Budget slack, 341
Budgeted income statement, 348
Capital expenditures budget, 348
Cash budget, 348
Continuous budget, 339
Cost of goods sold budget, 346
Demand software, 341
Direct labor budget, 345
Direct materials budget, 344
Factory overhead budget, 346
Financial budgets, 339
Fixed costs, 351
Flexible budget, 351
Kaizen, 345
Kaizen budgeting, 345
Liabilities budget, 338
Master budget, 338
Normal capacity, 355
Operating budgets, 339
Participative budgeting, 341
Practical capacity, 355
Pro-forma (projected) financial statements, 339
Production budget, 342
Rolling budget, 339
Sales budget, 340
Selling and administrative expenses budget, 347
Semifixed costs, 358
Semivariable costs, 359
Standard production, 355
Static budget, 338
Step costs, 358
Theoretical capacity, 355
Variable costs, 351
Web-based budgeting, 348

ANSWERS TO RECALL AND REVIEW EXERCISES

R&R 1

Units to be sold	35,000
Desired ending inventory	2,000
Total	37,000
Less estimated beginning inventory	6,000
Units to be produced in May	31,000
Quantity required for production	62,000*
Desired ending inventory	4,000
Total	66,000
Less estimated beginning inventory	3,000
Total quantity to be purchased	63,000
Price per pound	×$10
Total direct materials purchases	$630,000

*31,000 × 2 lb.

R&R 2

Sales (22,000 × $7.50*)	$165,000
Direct materials (22,000 × $1.80**)	39,600
Direct labor (22,000 × $1.00***)	22,000
Variable factory overhead (22,000 × $0.80****)	17,600
Fixed factory overhead (unchanged)	40,000

*$150,000 / 20,000 = $7.50
**$36,000 / 20,000 = $1.80
***$20,000 / 20,000 = $1.00
****$16,000 / 20,000 = $0.80

R&R 3

	10,000 units	12,000 units
Fixed costs	$ 5,000	$ 5,000
Variable costs	10,000	12,000
Total factory overhead	$15,000	$17,000

SELF-STUDY PROBLEM 1

Sales, production, direct materials, direct labor, and factory overhead budgets

YOTO Tire Company

Yoto Tire Company's budgeted unit sales for the year 2011 were:

Passenger car tires	60,000
Truck tires	12,500

The budgeted selling price for truck tires was $300 per tire, and that for passenger car tires was $90 per tire. The beginning finished goods inventories were expected to be 2,500 truck tires and 6,000 passenger tires, for a total cost of $400,510, with desired ending inventories at 2,000 and 5,000, respectively, and a total cost of $326,478. There was no anticipated beginning or ending work in process inventory for either type of tire.

The standard materials quantities for each type of tire were as follows:

	Truck	Passenger Car
Rubber	35 lb	15 lb
Steel belts	4.5 lb	2.0 lb

The purchase prices of rubber and steel were $3 and $2 per pound, respectively. The desired ending inventories for rubber and steel were 60,000 and 6,000 pounds, respectively. The estimated beginning inventories for rubber and steel were 75,000 and 7,500 pounds, respectively. The direct labor hours required for each type of tire were as follows:

	Molding Department	Finishing Department
Truck tire	0.20	0.10
Passenger car tire	0.10	0.05

The direct labor rate for each department is as follows:

Molding Department	$13 per hour
Finishing Department	$15 per hour

Budgeted factory overhead costs for 2011 were as follows:

Indirect materials	$170,560
Indirect labor	158,800
Depreciation of building and equipment	98,320
Power and light	126,000
Total	$553,680

Required:
Prepare each of the following budgets for Yoto for the year ended 2011:

1. Sales budget
2. Production budget
3. Direct material budget
4. Direct labor budget
5. Factory overhead budget
6. Cost of goods sold budget

SOLUTION TO SELF-STUDY PROBLEM

1. Prepare the Sales Budget

In preparing the sales budget, the forecasted unit sales must be multiplied by the budgeted selling price to obtain the sales volume in dollars.

Yoto Tire Company Sales Budget For the Year Ended December 31, 2011

Product	Unit Sales Volume	Unit Selling Price	Total Sales
Passenger car tires	60,000	$ 90	$5,400,000
Truck tires	12,500	$300	3,750,000
Total	72,500		$ 9,150,00

2. Prepare the Production Budget

In preparing the production budget, the forecasted unit sales from the sales budget are added to the desired ending inventory to determine the total units needed; then the estimated beginning inventory is deducted from that total to determine the unit production needed.

Yoto Tire Company
Production Budget
For the Year Ended December 31, 2011

	Units	
	Passenger Car Tires	Truck Tires
Sales (from sales budget)	60,000	12,500
Plus desired ending inventory, Dec. 31	5000	2,000
Total	65,000	14,500
Less estimated beginning inventory, Jan. 1	6,000	2,500
Total production	59,000	12,000

3. Prepare the Direct Materials Budget

In preparing the direct materials budget, the quantities of materials needed for production must be added to the desired ending inventory of materials to determine the materials needed. Then, the estimated beginning inventory must be subtracted from this total to determine the quantity of materials to be purchased.

Yoto Tire Company
Direct Materials Budget
For the Year Ended December 31, 2011

	Direct Materials		Total
	Rubber (lbs.)	Steel Belts (lbs.)	
Quantities required for production:			
Passenger car tires:			
59,000 × 15 lb	885,000		
59,000 × 2.0 lb		118,500	
Truck tires:			
12,000 × 35 lb	420,000		
12,000 × 4.5 lb		54,000	
Plus desired ending inventory, Dec. 31	60,000	6,000	
Total	1,365,000	178,000	
Less estimated beginning inventory, Jan. 1	75,000	7,500	
Total quantity to be purchased	1,290,000	170,500	
Unit price	$ 3	$ 2	
Total direct materials purchases	$3,870,000	$341,000	$4,211,000

4. Prepare the Direct Labor Budget

In preparing the direct labor budget, the total direct labor hours that should be worked on all products must be determined for each department and then multiplied by the wage rate for that department.

Yoto Tire Company
Direct Labor Budget
For the Year Ended December 31, 2011

	Department		Total
	Molding	**Finishing**	
Hours required for production:			
Passenger car tires:			
59,000 × .10	5,900		
59,000 × .05		2,950	
Truck tires:			
12,000 × .20	2,400		
12,000 × .10		1,200	
Total	8,300	4,150	
Hourly rate	$ 13	$ 15	
Total direct labor cost	$107,900	$62,250	$170,150

5. Prepare the Factory Overhead Budget

In this problem, the budgeted costs for each factory overhead item are given. In practice, the challenge is to determine the variable and fixed components of semivariable factory overhead costs.

Yoto Tire Company Factory
Overhead Budget
For the Year Ended December 31, 2011

Indirect materials	$170,560
Indirect labor	158,800
Depreciation of building and equipment	98,320
Power and light	126,000
Total factory overhead cost	$553,680

6. Prepare the Cost of Goods Sold Budget

The information from the direct materials, direct labor, and factory overhead budgets, in addition to data on desired beginning and ending inventories, is used to prepare the cost of goods sold budget.

Yoto Tire Company
Cost of Goods Sold Budget
For the Year Ended December 31, 2011

Finished goods inventory, Jan. 1		$ 400,510
Direct materials inventory, Jan. 1*	$ 240,000	
Direct materials purchases	4,211,000	
Total direct materials available	$ 4,451,000	
Less direct materials inventory, Dec. 31**	192,500	
Cost of direct materials used	$ 4,259,500	
Direct labor	170,150	
Factory overhead	553,680	

Cost of goods manufactured		4,982,830
Cost of goods available for sale		$ 5,383,340
Less finished goods inventory, Dec. 31		326,478
Cost of goods sold		$ 5,056,862

*Rubber	75,000 lb × $3	$225,000
Steel belts	7,500 lb × $2	15,000
		$240,000
**Rubber	60000 lb × $3	$180,000
Steel belts	6,000 lb × $2	12,000
		$192,000

SELF-STUDY PROBLEM 2

Huggins Manufacturing Company

Huggins Manufacturing Company uses a job order cost system and standard costs. It manufactures one product, whose standard cost follows:

Materials, 10 yards @ $2.00 per yard	$ 20
Direct labor, 4 hours @ $12.00 per hour	48
Total factory overhead per unit (the ratio of variable costs to fixed costs is 2 to 1)	42
Total unit cost	$110

The standards are based on normal capacity of 3,600 direct labor hours. Actual activity for October follows:

Materials purchased, 20,000 yards @ $1.95 per yard	$39,000
(Materials used, 19,500 yards)	
Direct labor, 3,500 hours @ 12.10 per hour	19,215
Total factory overhead, 900 units actually produced	37,500

Required:

1. Compute the variable and fixed factory overhead rates per unit.
2. Compute the variable and fixed overhead rates per direct labor hour.
3. Determine the total fixed factory overhead based on normal capacity.

SOLUTION TO SELF-STUDY PROBLEM

1. Compute the variable and fixed factory overhead rates per unit:
   We know that the total factory overhead cost per unit is $42 and the variable rate is twice the fixed rate; therefore:

Let X = the fixed factory overhead rate, and
$2X$ = the variable factory overhead rate, then

$$2X + X = \$42$$
$$3X = \$42$$
$$X = \$14 \text{ fixed factory overhead rate per unit}$$
$$2X = \$28 \text{ variable factory overhead rate per unit}$$

2. Compute the variable and fixed overhead rates per direct labor hour:
In (1), we determined that the variable factory overhead rate was $28 per unit and the fixed factory overhead rate was $14 per unit. The problem indicates that the standard number of direct labor hours to make a unit is four. Therefore:

Variable factory overhead rate per direct labor hour = $28/4 direct labor hours = $7
Fixed factory overhead rate per direct labor hour = $14/4 direct labor hours = $ 3.50

3. Determine the total fixed factory overhead based on normal capacity.
We know from above that the fixed factory overhead rate computed at normal capacity is $3.50 per direct labor hour. The problem indicated that the standards were based on a normal capacity of 3,600 direct labor hours. Therefore:

Total fixed factory overhead
$= \$3.50 \times 3,600$ direct labor hours at normal capacity $= \$12,600$

(Note that the fixed factory overhead stays the same in total but varies per unit within a relevant range of activity. At any capacity level other than 3,600 hours, the rate will be something other than $3.50, but the budgeted total will still be $12,600.)

QUESTIONS

1. What is a budget?
2. What are the advantages of using budgets in a business setting?
3. What are six principles of good budgeting?
4. What is a continuous budget, and why is it useful?
5. Give three examples each of operating budgets and financial budgets.
6. Which budget must be prepared before the others? Why?
7. What is "demand software," and where in the budgeting process is it useful?
8. Why is it important to have front-line managers participate in the budgeting process?
9. If the sales forecast estimates that 50,000 units of product will be sold during the following year, should the factory plan on manufacturing 50,000 units in the coming year? Explain.
10. What are the advantages and disadvantages of each of the following for a company that has greatly fluctuating sales during the year?
    a. A stable production policy
    b. A stable inventory policy
11. What three manufacturing budgets can be prepared subsequent to preparation of the production budget?
12. What does the Japanese term *kaizen* mean, and how is it used in the budgeting process?
13. What are the three budgets that are needed in order to prepare the budgeted income statement?
14. Why might Web-based budgeting be more useful than using spreadsheets to budget?
15. What is a flexible budget?
16. Why is a flexible budget better than a master budget for comparing actual results to budgeted expectations?
17. Why is it important to distinguish between variable costs and fixed costs for budgeting purposes?

18. Why is the concept of relevant range important when preparing a flexible budget?

19. In comparing actual sales revenue to flexible budget sales revenue, would it be possible to have a favorable variance and still not have met revenue expectations?

20. How would you define the following?
    a. Theoretical capacity
    b. Practical capacity
    c. Normal capacity

21. Is it possible for a factory to operate at more than 100% of normal capacity?

22. If a factory operates at 100% of capacity one month, 90% of capacity the next month, and 105% of capacity the next month, will a different cost per unit be charged to Work in Process each month for factory overhead assuming that a predetermined annual overhead rate is used?

23. How is the standard cost per unit for factory overhead determined?

EXERCISES

E7-1 LO2 **Preparing sales budget and production budget**

The sales department of S. Miller Manufacturing Company has forecast sales for its single product to be 20,000 units for the month of June, with three-quarters of the sales expected in the East region and one-fourth in the West region. The budgeted selling price is $25 per unit. The desired ending inventory on June 30 is 2,000 units, and the expected beginning inventory on June 1 is 3,000 units.

Prepare the following:

a. A sales budget for June.

b. A production budget for June.

E7-2 LO2 **Preparing production budget and direct materials budget**

The sales department of P. Gillen Manufacturing Company has forecast sales in March to be 20,000 units. Additional information follows:

Finished goods inventory, March 1	3,000 units
Finished goods inventory required, March 31	1,000 units

Materials used in production:

	Inventory March 1	Required Inventory March 31	Standard Cost
A (one gallon per unit)	500 gal	1,000 gal	$2 per gal
B (one pound per unit)	1,000 lb	1,000 lb	$1 per lb

Prepare the following:

a. A production budget for March (in units).

b. A direct materials budget for the month (in units and dollars).

E7-3 LO2 **Preparing production budget and direct labor budget**

S. Prosser Manufacturing Company forecast October sales to be 45,000 units. Additional information follows:

Finished goods inventory, October 1	5,000 units
Finished goods inventory desired, October 31	4,000 units

Direct labor hours required in production:

Department	Hours per Unit
Cutting	0.25
Assembly	0.50

Direct laborers earn: Cutting, $14 per hour; Assembly, $12 per hour.

Prepare the following:

a. A production budget for October.

b. A direct labor budget for October.

E7-4 **Preparing cost of goods sold budget**

LO2

Prepare a cost of goods sold budget for the Summit Manufacturing Company for the year ended December 31, 2011, from the following estimates.

Inventories of production units:

	Work in Process	Finished Goods
January 1, 2011	$28,500	$19,300
December 31, 2011	23,700	22,400

Direct materials purchased during the year, $854,000; beginning inventory of direct materials, $31,000; and ending inventory of direct materials, $26,000.

Totals from other budgets included:

Direct labor cost	$539,500
Total factory overhead costs	818,000

E7-5 **Preparing budgeted income statement**

Gyro Company has the following totals from its operating budgets:

Selling and administrative expenses budget	$ 244,500
Cost of goods sold budget	727,300
Sales budget	1,222,700

Prepare a budgeted income statement for the year ended December 31, 2011, assuming that income from operations is taxed at a rate of 30%.

E7-6 **Determining flexible budget amounts**

Solar Panels, Inc., has the following items and amounts as part of its master budget at the 10,000-unit level of sales and production:

Sales revenue	$100,000
Direct materials	20,000
Direct labor	15,000
Variable factory overhead	10,000
Fixed factory overhead	25,000

Determine the total dollar amounts for the above items that would appear in a flexible budget at the following volume levels, assuming that both levels are within the relevant range:

a. 8,000-unit level of sales and production

b. 12,000-unit level of sales and production

(*Hint:* You must first determine the unit selling price and certain unit costs.)

LO3

E7-7 Preparing a flexible budget

Using the following per-unit and total amounts, prepare a flexible budget at the 14,000-, 15,000-, and 16,000-unit levels of production and sales for Celestial Products, Inc.:

Selling price per unit	$ 75.00
Direct materials per unit	$ 24.00
Direct labor per unit	$ 7.50
Variable factory overhead per unit	$ 15.00
Fixed factory overhead	$ 75,000
Variable selling and administrative expense per unit	$ 12.00
Fixed selling and administrative expense	$ 80,000

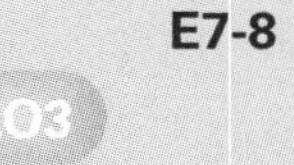

E7-8 Preparing a performance report

Strand Manufacturing, Inc., has the following flexible budget formulas and amounts:

Sales	$	25 per unit
Direct materials		5 per unit
Direct labor		3 per unit
Variable factory overhead		4 per unit
Variable selling and administrative expense		1 per unit
Fixed factory overhead		$25,000 per month
Fixed selling and administrative expense		$20,000 per month

Actual results for the month of May for the production and sale of 5,000 units were as follows:

Sales	$120,000
Direct materials	26,000
Direct labor	14,000
Variable factory overhead	25,500
Variable selling and admin.	5,500
Fixed factory overhead	26,750
Fixed selling and admin.	19,800

Prepare a performance report for the month of May that includes the identification of the favorable and unfavorable variances.

E7-9 **Calculating factory overhead**

LO4

The normal capacity of a manufacturing plant is 5,000 units per month. Fixed overhead at this volume is $2,500, and variable overhead is $7,500. Additional data follow:

	Month 1	Month 2
Actual production (units)	5,200	4,500
Actual factory overhead	$10,100	$9,200

a. Calculate the amount of factory overhead allowed for the actual levels of production.
b. Compute the overhead application rate per unit at the various levels of production. (Round to the nearest whole cent.)

E7-10 **Calculating factory overhead**

LO4

The normal capacity of a factory is 8,000 units per month. Cost and production data follow:

Standard application rate for fixed overhead	$0.50 per unit
Standard application rate for variable overhead	$1.50 per unit
Production—Month 1	7,200 units
Production—Month 2	8,400 units
Actual factory overhead—Month 1	$ 14,700
Actual factory overhead—Month 2	$ 17,400

Calculate the amount of factory overhead allowed for the actual volume of production each month and the variance between budgeted and actual overhead for each month.

PROBLEMS

P7-1 **Production, direct materials, and direct labor budget**

LO2

The sales department of Optimo Company has forecast sales for May 2011 to be 40,000 units. Additional information follows:

Finished goods inventory, May 1	2,000 units
Finished goods inventory, May 31	

Materials used in production:

	Required Inventory May 1	Required Inventory May 31	Standard Cost
X (one gallon per unit)	1,000 gal	2,000 gal	$4 per gal
Y (one pound per unit)	2,000 lb	2,000 lb	$ 2 per lb

Direct labor hours required in production:

Department	Hours per Unit	Standard Cost
Forming	0.50	$18 per hour
Finishing	1.00	$15 per hour

Prepare the following:

a. A production budget for May.
b. A direct materials budget for May.
c. A direct labor budget for May.

P7-2 Sales, production, direct materials, direct labor, and factory overhead budgets
similar to Self Problem1

Cruise Tire Company's budgeted unit sales for the year 2011 were:

Passenger car tires	120,000
Truck tires	25,000

The budgeted selling price for truck tires was $200 per tire, and that for passenger car tires was $65 per tire. The beginning finished goods inventories were expected to be 2,000 truck tires and 5,000 passenger tires, for a total cost of $326,478, with desired ending inventories at 2,500 and 6,000, respectively, with a total cost of $400,510. There was no anticipated beginning or ending work in process inventory for either type of tire.
The standard materials quantities for each type of tire were as follows:

	Truck	Passenger Car
Rubber	30 lb	10 lb
Steel belts	4 lb	1.5 lb

The purchase prices of rubber and steel were $2 and $3 per pound, respectively. The desired ending inventories for rubber and steel were 60,000 and 6,000 pounds, respectively. The estimated beginning inventories for rubber and steel were 75,000 and 7,000 pounds, respectively. The direct labor hours required for each type of tire were as follows:

	Molding Department	Finishing Department
Truck tire	0.25	0.15
Passenger car tire	0.10	0.05

The direct labor rate for each department is as follows:

Molding Department	$15 per hour
Finishing Department	$13 per hour

Budgeted factory overhead costs for 2011 were as follows:

Indirect materials	$198,500
Indirect labor	213,200
Depreciation of building and equipment	157,500
Power and light	122,900
Total	$692,100

Required:
Prepare each of the following budgets for Cruise for the year ended 2011:

1. Sales budget.
2. Production budget.
3. Direct material budget.
4. Direct labor budget.
5. Factory overhead budget.
6. Cost of goods sold budget.

P7-3 Selling and administrative expenses budget and budgeted income statement

LO2

Budgeted selling and administrative expenses for Cruise Tire Company in P7-2 for the year ended December 31, 2011, were as follows:

Advertising expense	$942,000
Office rent expense	125,000
Office salaries expense	821,000
Office supplies expense	45,500
Officers' salaries expense	661,000
Sales salaries expense	868,000
Telephone and fax expense	33,500
Travel expense	443,000

Required:

1. Prepare a selling and administrative expenses budget, in good form, for the year 2011.
2. Using the information above and the budgets prepared in P7-2, prepare a budgeted income statement for the year 2011, assuming an income tax rate of 40%.

P7-4 Preparing a flexible budget

LO3

Use the information in Figure 7-12 of the chapter.

Required:
Prepare flexible budgets for the production and sale of 29,000 units and 31,000, respectively.

P7-5 Preparing a performance report

LO3

Use the flexible budget prepared in P7-4 for the 31,000-unit level and the actual operating results listed below for the 31,000-unit level.

Required:

1. Prepare a performance report.
2. List the major reason why the actual operating income at 31,000 units differs from the master budget operating income at 30,000 units in Figure 7-12.
3. Given the level that the company operated at, how was its cost control?

Item	
Sales	$4,800,000
Direct materials:	
Lumber	633,000
Paint	127,500
Direct labor:	
Cutting	115,200
Assembly	75,300
Painting	47,100
Variable factory overhead	222,905
Variable selling and administrative expense	777,400
Fixed factory overhead	210,500
Fixed selling and administrative expense	765,800

P7-6 LO3

Preparing a performance report

Use the flexible budget prepared in P7-4 for the 29,000-unit level of activity and the actual operating results below for the 29,000-unit level.

Required:

1. Prepare a performance report.
2. List the major reason why the actual operating income at 29,000 units differs from the master budget operating income at 30,000 units in Figure 7-12.
3. Given the level that the company operated at, how was its cost control?

Item	
Sales	$4,200,000
Direct materials:	
Lumber	565,000
Paint	121,000
Direct labor:	
Cutting	110,000
Assembly	71,200
Painting	44,600
Variable factory overhead	202,000
Variable selling and administrative expense	741,300
Fixed factory overhead	210,000
Fixed selling and administrative expense	770,200

P7-7 **Flexible budget for factory overhead**

LO4

Presented below are the monthly factory overhead cost budget (at normal capacity of 5,000 units or 20,000 direct labor hours) and the production and cost data for a month. The predetermined overhead rate is based on normal capacity.

Factory Overhead Cost Budget

Fixed cost:		
Depreciation on building and machinery	$1,200	
Taxes on building and machinery	500	
Insurance on building and machinery	500	
Superintendent's salary	1,500	
Supervisors' salaries	2,300	
Maintenance wages	1,000	$7,000
Variable cost:		
Repairs	$ 400	
Maintenance supplies	300	
Other supplies	200	
Payroll taxes	800	
Small tools	300	2,000
Total standard factory overhead		$9,000

Required:

1. Assuming that variable costs will vary in direct proportion to the change in volume, prepare a flexible budget for production levels of 80%, 90%, and 110% of normal capacity. Also determine the rate for application of factory overhead to work in process at each level of volume in both units and direct labor hours.
2. Prepare a flexible budget for production levels of 80%, 90%, and 110%, assuming that variable costs will vary in direct proportion to the change in volume, but with the following exceptions. (*Hint:* Set up a third category for semifixed expenses.)
   a. At 110% of capacity, an assistant department head will be needed at a salary of $10,500 annually.
   b. At 80% of capacity, the repairs expense will drop to one-half of the amount at 100% capacity. (At other levels it is perfectly variable.)
   c. Maintenance supplies expense will remain constant at all levels of production.
   d. At 80% of capacity, one part-time maintenance worker, earning $6,000 a year, will be laid off.
   e. At 110% of capacity, a machine not normally in use and on which no depreciation is normally recorded will be used in production. Its cost was $12,000, it has a ten-year life, and straight-line depreciation will be taken.

P7-8 Flexible budget formulas and interpolation

LO4

Required:

1. Using the facts and the flexible budget prepared in Part (1) of P7-7 above, determine the budgeted cost at 96% of capacity, using interpolation.
2. Using the flexible budget prepared in Part (1) of P7-7 above, determine the budgeted cost at 104% of capacity, using a method other than interpolation.

P7-9 Overhead application rate similar to Self-Study Problem 2

LO4

Mountaineer Manufacturing Company uses a job order cost system and standard costs. It manufactures one product, whose standard cost follows:

Materials, 20 yards @ $0.90 per yard	$18
Direct labor, 4 hours @ $9.00 per hour	36
Total factory overhead per unit (the ratio of variable costs to fixed costs is 3 to 1)	32
Total unit cost	$86

The standards are based on normal capacity of 2,400 direct labor hours. Actual activity for October follows:

Materials purchased, 18,000 yards @ $0.92 per yard	$16,560
Materials used, 9,500 yards	
Direct labor, 2,100 hours @ $9.15 per hour	19,215
Total factory overhead, 500 units actually produced	17,760

Required:

1. Compute the variable and fixed factory overhead rates per unit.
2. Compute the variable and fixed overhead rates per direct labor hour.
3. Determine the total fixed factory overhead based on normal capacity.

MINI-CASE

Flexible budgeting, performance measurement, and ethics

LO3

Branson Manufacturing, Inc., produces a single type of small motor. The bookkeeper who does not have an in-depth understanding of accounting principles prepared the following performance report with the help of the production manager.

In a conversation with the sales manager, the production manager was overheard saying, "You sales guys really messed up our May

	A	B	C	D	E
1		**Branson Manufacturing, Inc.**			
2		**Performance Report**			
3		**May, 2011**			
4					
5		**Flexible Budget**	**Actual Results**	**Master Budget**	**Variance**
6		**Per Unit**	**(45,000 units)**	**(50,000 units)**	
7	**Sales**	**$25.00**	**$1,125,000**	**$1,250,000**	**$125,000U**
8	Less variable expenses:				
9	Direct materials	4.50	$212,500	$225,000	$12,500 F
10	Direct labor	3.75	175,750	187,500	11,750 F
11	Variable factory overhead	2.25	110,250	112,500	2,250 F
12	Variable selling and administrative expense	1.50	70,500	75,000	4,500 F
13	Total variable expense	$12.00	$569,000	$600,000	$31,000 F
14	Contribution margin	$13.00	$556,000	$650,000	$94,000U
15	Less fixed expenses:				
16	Fixed factory overhead expense	$100,000	$95,000	$100,000	$5,000 F
17	Fixed selling and administrative expense	150,000	160,000	150,000	10,000U
18	Total fixed expense	$250,000	$255,000	$250,000	$5,000U
19	Income from operations		$301,000	$400,000	$99,000U

performance, and it is only because production did such a great job controlling costs that we aren't in even worse shape."

Required:

1. Do you agree with the production manager that the manufacturing area did a good job of controlling costs?
2. Prepare a flexible budget for Branson Manufacturing's expenses at the following activity levels: 45,000 units, 50,000 units, and 55,000 units.
3. Prepare a revised performance report, using the most appropriate flexible budget from (2) above.
4. Now what is your response to the production manager's claim?
5. Assume that you have just been hired as the new accountant. You observe that the production manager is about to receive a large bonus based on the favorable materials, labor, and factory overhead variances indicated in the flexible budget prepared by the bookkeeper. Using the IMA Statement of Ethical Professional Practice as your guide, what standards, if any, apply to your responsibilities in this matter?

INTERNET EXERCISE

Kaizen

Go to the text Web site at www.cengage.com/accounting/vanderbeck and click on the link to "kaizen," from Wikipedia, the free encyclopedia. After reading the entry, answer the following questions:

LO2

1. What is the meaning of kaizen?
2. What is the goal of kaizen?

3. What was the basis of the "kaizen revolution" that took place in Japan in the 1950s?
4. How does kaizen differ from the "command and control" improvement programs of the mid-twentieth century?
5. How does the Toyota Production System apply kaizen to its production operations?

CHAPTER 8

Standard Cost Accounting—Materials, Labor, and Factory Overhead

Learning Objectives

After studying this chapter, you should be able to:

LO1 Describe the different standards used in determining standard costs.

LO2 Determine procedures for recording standard costs.

LO3 Compute and analyze variances.

LO4 Prepare journal entries to record variances.

LO5 Examine and interpret variances.

LO6 Recognize the features of a standard cost system.

LO7 Account for standard costs in a departmentalized factory.

LO8 Distinguish between actual and applied factory overhead.

LO9 Compute variances using the two-variance method.

LO10 Compute variances using the four-variance method.

LO11 Compute variances using the three-variance method.

For both individuals and businesses, performance is measured as the difference between actual performance and standard, or best practices, performance. On a par 66 golf course, your performance is evaluated in relation to that number, as is illustrated in Figure 8-1. In selecting new members to the Baseball Hall of Fame in Cooperstown, New York, a batter's career statistics are compared to such benchmarks as a .300 batting average, 300 or more home runs, and 1,500 or more runs batted in.

This same type of performance measurement may be applied to employees. For example, a Taco Bell work crew's performance may be measured against standards such as: how long it should take to service a customer at the drive-through window; how many pounds of ground beef should be used to make a certain number of burritos; and the cleanliness of the restaurant as compared to predetermined company standards.

This chapter examines how to measure how well the three elements of manufacturing cost—materials, labor, and overhead—are utilized relative to predetermined standards, and how to use this information to improve the efficiency and effectiveness of operations.

The discussions of cost control in previous chapters emphasized the comparison of current costs with historical costs—costs of yesterday, last week, last month, or last year. When current costs differed unfavorably from earlier costs, it was suggested that management immediately investigate the cause of the deviation and try to eliminate it before the change became too costly. Management was also advised not

Figure 8-1 **Illustration of Performance vs. Standard in Golf**

Blue	369	153	271	432	354	142	358	177	362	2618	245	290	149	351	368	320	156	142	324	2345	4963		
White	355	131	265	388	333	136	338	171	288	2405	242	249	132	331	334	290	150	136	318	2182	4587		
Gold	246	127	260	235	319	138	328	133	270	2218	230	240	105	305	309	253	147	123	290	2016	4234		
Lynne	5	4	5	4	(3)	4	5	4	(3)	37	5	4	4	4	5	4	3	4	5	38	75		
Matt	6	5	5	5	4	3	(3)	4	5	40	4	6	3	5	5	4	4	3	5	39	79		
Linda	4	4	6	5	5	3	5	4	4	40	6	(3)	4	5	4	5	3	4	4	38	78		
ED	5	3	5	6	5	4	4	3	4	39	5	4	4	(3)	5	(3)	4	4	(3)	35	74		
Hole Number	**1**	**2**	**3**	**4**	**5**	**6**	**7**	**8**	**9**	**Out**	**10**	**11**	**12**	**13**	**14**	**15**	**16**	**17**	**18**	**In**	**Total**	**Hcp**	**Net**
+/−																							
Par	**4**	**3**	**4**	**4**	**4**	**3**	**4**	**3**	**4**	**33**	**4**	**4**	**3**	**4**	**4**	**4**	**3**	**3**	**4**	**33**	**66**		
Handicap	5/1	17/15	11/11	1/7	9/5	13/13	7/3	15/7	3/9		12/10	10/11	10/26	4/6	2/2	8/8	16/14	18/16	6/4				

Date: 8/7/09 **Scorer:** Ed

only to watch for these fluctuations and to attempt to correct them, but also to consider all possible ways to control costs.

Although these previous methods of cost control are useful, management may tend to become complacent if the costs of manufacturing do not differ significantly from period to period. Managers may feel that the manufacturing operation is efficient because unit and overall costs have stabilized at a certain level. But stability of costs does not necessarily indicate efficiency when the earlier costs, with which current costs are being compared, may have built-in inefficiencies. Also, it may be possible to utilize current costs more effectively.

The purpose of **standard cost accounting** is to control costs and promote efficiency. This system is not another accounting method for accumulating manufacturing costs, but it is used in conjunction with such methods as job order, process, or backflush costing. Standard costing is based on a predetermination of what it should cost to manufacture a product, and the inventory accounts are debited for these standard costs. A comparison is then made between these standard costs and the actual costs that were incurred. Any deviation from the standards can be quickly detected and responsibility pinpointed so that the company can take appropriate action to eliminate inefficiencies or take advantage of efficiencies. This is known as **management by exception**, where both significant unfavorable and favorable differences from standard are the focal point of management attention. Surveys have indicated that 76% of U.S. manufacturers and 90% of Japanese manufacturers use standard costing.[1] Even service businesses such as **McDonald's** and **Sears** have standards for tasks,

---

1 Ernst and Young, "2003 Survey of Management Accounting"; Hema Wijewardena and Anura DeZoysa, "A Comparative Analysis of Management Accounting Practices in Australia and Japan: An Empirical Investigation," *International Journal of Accounting*, Volume 34 (1999), pp. 49–70.

such as how long it should take to service a customer in the drive-through line or how long it should take to replace a muffler, respectively.

Standard costs are usually determined for a period of one year and should be revised annually. However, if cost analyses during the year indicate that a standard is incorrect, or if a significant change has occurred in the costs to acquire materials or labor or in the production process, then management should not hesitate to adjust the standard to better reflect the current reality.

Types of Standards

LO1 Describe the different standards used in determining standard costs.

A **standard** is a norm against which the actual performance can be measured. The objective of setting standards is to measure efficiency and to monitor costs by assigning responsibility for deviations from the standards. Also, a standard can motivate employees by providing a goal for achievement. But a question that often arises is, "What is the proper standard to use?" A company can estimate materials, labor, and factory overhead usage and costs, but what about the unforeseen costs, such as spoilage, lost time, and equipment breakdowns? Should these items be considered in determining the standard cost to manufacture a product?

Some companies set their standards at the maximum degree of efficiency. Using such an **ideal standard**, they determine costs by considering estimated materials, labor, and overhead costs; the condition of the factory and machinery; and time for rest periods, holidays, and vacations—but make no allowances for inefficient conditions such as lost time, waste, or spoilage. This ideal standard can be achieved only under the most efficient operating conditions; therefore, it is practically unattainable, generally giving rise to unfavorable variances. Companies using this type of standard feel that it provides a maximum objective for which to strive in the attempt to improve efficiency. There is, however, a psychological disadvantage—factory personnel may become discouraged and lose their incentive to meet standards that are usually impossible to attain except under perfect operating conditions.

Recognizing this potential problem, most companies set **attainable standards** that include such factors as lost time and normal waste and spoilage. These companies realize that some inefficiencies cannot be completely eliminated, so they design standards that can be met or even bettered in efficient production situations. The primary concern of the manufacturer should be to set standards that are high enough to provide motivation and promote efficiency, yet not so high that they are unattainable and, thus, bad for worker morale.

Standard Cost Procedures

LO2 Determine procedures for recording standard costs.

Standard cost accounting is based on the following procedures:

1. Standard costs are determined for the three elements of cost: direct materials, direct labor, and factory overhead.

2. The standard costs, the actual costs, and the variances between the actual and standard costs are recorded in appropriate accounts.
3. Significant variances are analyzed and investigated and then appropriate action is taken.

Determination of Standard Costs for Materials and Labor

The first step, the determination of standard costs for a product, is a complex task that requires considerable experience and familiarity with manufacturing operations as well as the cooperation of the departmental employees. The accounting department is often consulted to help determine historical costs, to point out cost trends, and to assist in establishing the standards. A **materials cost standard** is based on estimates of the *quantity of materials required* for a unit of product and the *unit cost to purchase* the materials used. In setting a materials cost standard, management may consult the production engineering department to determine the amounts and types of materials needed, and the purchasing agent should provide information regarding suppliers' prices.

A **labor cost standard** is based on estimates of the *labor hours required* to produce a unit of product and the *cost of labor per unit*. In establishing a labor cost standard, the heads of various departments contribute their knowledge of the processing operations. The manufacturer may use the services of time-study engineers to establish the time necessary to perform each operation, and the human resources manager should be consulted regarding prevailing wage rates for the various types of labor needed.

Historical costs and processes are studied to gain familiarity with these items, but the individuals who set the standards should also consider prevailing trends that may cause changes to the prices and quantities of materials and labor required. In setting standards for materials and labor, a variety of factors should be considered:

1. the trend of prices for raw materials
2. the use of different types of materials due to new production processes or market developments
3. the effect of negotiations with labor unions on labor rates; and
4. the possible saving of labor time due to the use of more modern machinery and equipment or the **learning effect**, which occurs when employees become more proficient at complex production processes the more often they perform the task

Figure 8-2 illustrates a **standard cost card** for the production of a premium-quality skateboard. This standard cost card summarizes the standard quantities and costs to assemble, test, and package one skateboard.

Figure 8-2 **Standard Cost Card for a Skateboard**

Product: Premium Skateboard
Product Number: 0078

	Direct Materials		
Component Stock #	**Quantity**	**Unit Cost**	**Total Cost**
GT-05	1	$1.00	$ 1.00
D-02	1	7.50	7.50
TB-12	8	.10	.80
RP-11	2	.25	.50
T-01	2	1.50	3.00
B-08	8	.15	1.20
W-14	4	1.25	5.00
Total			$ 19.00

			Direct Labor			
Operation TD #	**Wage Rate**	**Total Hours**	**Assembling**	**Testing**	**Packaging**	**Total Cost**
006	$15	.25	$3.75			$3.75
010	18	.20		$3.60		3.60
015	12	.10			$1.20	1.20
Total		55	$3.75	$3.60	$1.20	$8.55

Manufacturing Overhead	
Variable Overhead ($10 per D.L.HR × $.55)	$ 5.50
Fixed Overhead ($5 per Skateboard @Normal Capacity)	5.00
Total Overhead	$ 10.50
Total Standard Cost per Unit	$ 38.05

Recording Standard Costs for Materials and Labor

Once the standard cost for manufacturing a product has been determined, the standard costs, the actual costs, and the variances are recorded in journals and transferred to the general ledger. The journalizing and posting may occur monthly or more frequently, depending on the needs of management for current information and the capabilities of the accounting information system.

Determination of Variances

 Compute and analyze variances.

A **variance** represents the difference between the actual and the standard costs of materials, labor, and overhead. Variances measure efficiencies or inefficiencies in **usage** (quantity of materials used or number of labor hours worked) and **price** (cost of materials and wage rates). Note that although the variances computed here are for a manufacturer, they could just as well be computed for a service business, such as food cost and labor cost variances for a **Wendy's** restaurant. Also, a manufacturer can compute variances for nonmanufacturing items such as marketing costs that would explain, for example, why delivery employees' actual wages differ from budgeted wages.

The variances illustrated in this chapter are examples of financial performance measures because they are expressed in dollars. Companies also use **nonfinancial performance measures** to evaluate operations, such as the percentage of defective blouses produced by a garment manufacturer, the percentage of lost baggage by an airline, and the average compared to standard wait time at a fast-food drive-through window. This is consistent with the **balanced scorecard** approach to measuring a business's success by considering both financial and nonfinancial performance measures. The balanced scorecard will be further explained in Chapter 9.

Assume that the production report of Charlie's Products, Inc., whose standard cost summary is shown below, indicates that equivalent production for the month, calculated as discussed in previous chapters, was 10,000 units. The standard cost per unit and for the 10,000 units is computed as follows:

Charlie's Products, Inc.
Standard Cost Summary
Product X

Materials—(1 lb @ $4 per lb)	$ 4.00
Labor—(1/2 hr @ $10 per hr)	5.00
Factory overhead—40% of direct labor cost	2.00
Standard cost per unit	$ 11.00
Standard materials cost (10,000 units × $4.00)	$ 40,000
Standard labor cost (10,000 units × $5.00)	50,000
Standard factory overhead cost (10,000 units × $2.00)	20,000
Total standard cost of manufacturing 10,000 units	$110,000

Assume that the materials requisitions, the labor time records, and the factory overhead records indicate the following actual costs to manufacture 10,000 units:

Cost of direct materials used (11,000 lb @ $3.80)	$ 41,800
Cost of direct labor (4,500 hr @ $11.00)	49,500
Factory overhead	20,000
Total actual cost of manufacturing 10,000 units	$111,300

The standards can now be compared to the actual costs to determine whether any variances exist. This analysis is performed as follows and is illustrated in Figure 8-3:

	Standard Cost	Actual Cost	Net Variances—Favorable (Unfavorable)
Materials	$ 40,000	$ 41,800	$(1,800)
Labor	50,000	49,500	500
Factory Overhead	20,000	20,000	–
Total	$110,000	$111,300	$(1,300)

Figure 8-3 **Breakout of Difference between Actual and Budgeted Manufacturing Costs**

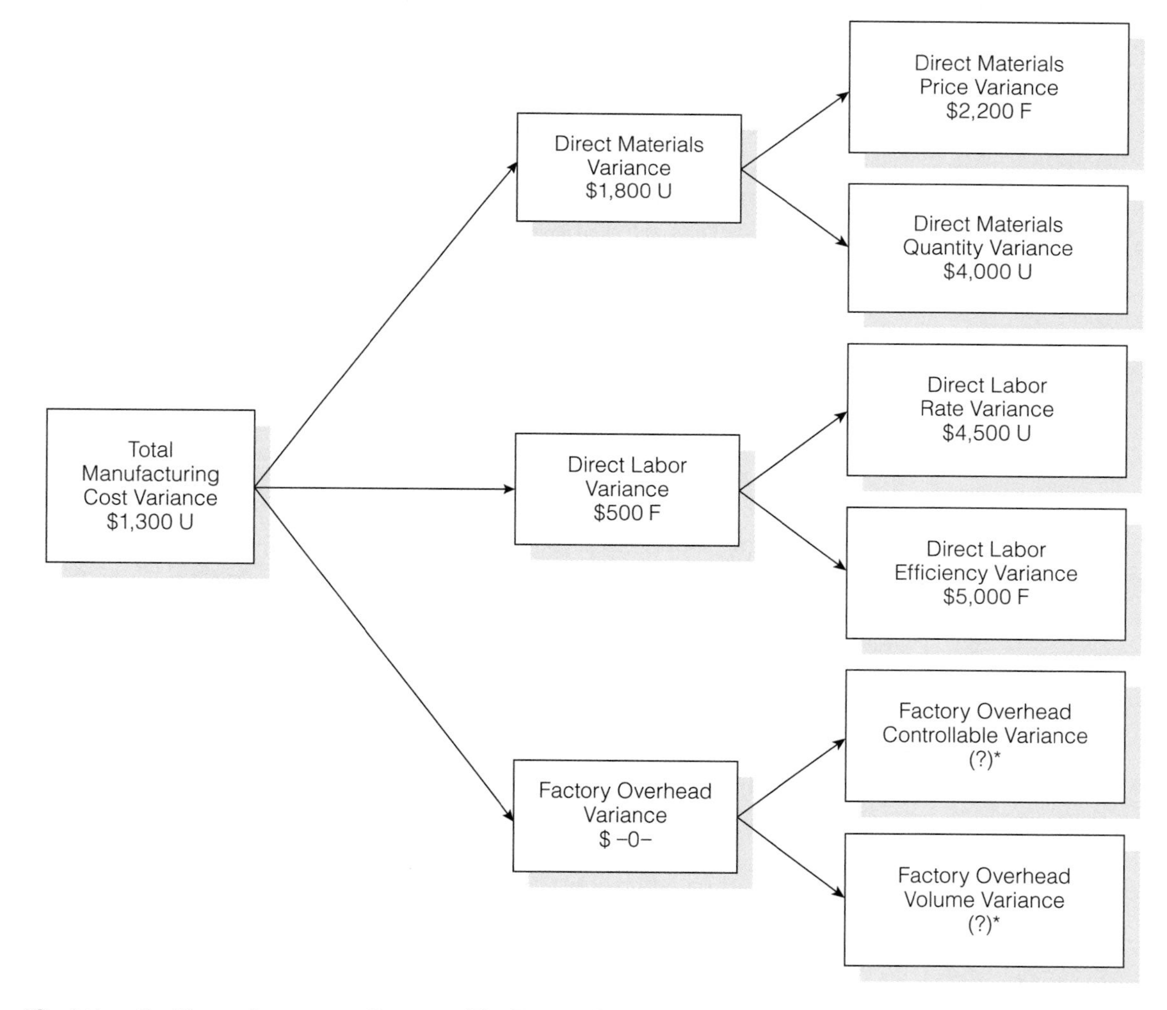

*Could be offsetting variances equaling zero. (The Factory Overhead Variances will be explained later in this chapter.)

The information presented by these comparative figures is significant because it shows that the total actual manufacturing costs have exceeded the standards previously established. The variances indicate that the cost of materials was $1,800 higher than it should have been and that the cost of labor was $500 less than expected, resulting in an overall unfavorable variance of $1,300. These figures can be of more value to cost control, however, if a further breakdown of the variances is made. The formulas used to segregate the materials and labor variances into price and usage components, along with the calculation of the variances based on the preceding data, are as follows:

1. **Materials price variance** reflects the actual unit price of materials above or below the standard unit price, multiplied by the actual quantity of materials used.

   (Actual unit price of materials – standard unit price of materials)
   × actual quantity of materials used = Materials Price Variance
   ($3.80 – $4.00) × 11,000 lb = $2,200 F*

   * F = favorable; U = unfavorable

2. **Materials quantity (usage) variance** represents the actual quantity of direct materials used above or below the standard quantity allowed for the actual level of production, at standard price.

   (Actual quantity of materials used – standard quantity of materials allowed)
   × standard unit price of material = Materials Quantity Variance
   [11,000 lb – (10,000 units × 1 lb/unit)] × $4.00 = $4,000 U

3. **Labor rate (price) variance** represents the actual hourly rates paid above or below the standard hourly rates, multiplied by the actual number of hours worked.

   (Actual labor rate per hour – standard labor rate per hour)
   × actual number of labor hours worked = Labor Rate Variance
   ($11 – $10) × 4,500 hr = $4,500 U

4. **Labor efficiency (usage) variance** indicates the number of actual direct labor hours worked above or below the standard hours allowed for the actual level of production, at the standard labor rate.

   (Actual number of labor hours worked – standard number of labor hours allowed)
   × standard labor rate per hour = Labor Efficiency Variance
   [4,500 hr – (10,000 units × 0.5 hr/unit)] × $10 = $5,000 F

A *debit balance* in a variance account indicates an **unfavorable variance**; that is, actual costs have exceeded the established standard cost. A *credit balance* reflects a **favorable variance**, indicating that actual costs were less than the standard cost. In management terminology, an unfavorable variance means that a charge (debit) has been added that increases the cost beyond the standard established, thereby reducing the expected profitability of the product. A favorable variance (credit) would add to a product's anticipated profitability because it reduces the cost set for the product below the standard established. When a company uses a standard cost system, it usually considers the product's standard cost to be the cost for setting its selling price. Therefore, any movement of cost above or below the standard will have a direct effect on profitability.

Figure 8-4 shows an alternative format, sometimes referred to as the "goalpost diagram," for calculating the materials and labor variances, using the data previously presented for materials and labor.

Whichever format you choose, this analysis shows the specific variances as quantity and price deviations from the established standards. The required manufacturing effort exceeded the established materials standard for 10,000 units; this, given a standard price of $4.00 per pound, created an unfavorable materials quantity variance of $4,000 (1,000 pounds used in excess of standard allowed × $4.00). The variance was partially offset by the fact that the 11,000 pounds of materials used were obtained at a below-standard cost of $3.80 per pound, thereby creating a favorable price variance of $2,200 (11,000 pounds used at a saving of $0.20 per pound). Note that the combined effect of the two variances is the unfavorable net materials variance of $1,800. It can also be obtained by subtracting the $40,000 standard cost in the right post of the "goalpost" diagram from the $41,800 actual cost shown in the left post.

The calculation of labor variances indicates a favorable labor efficiency variance of $5,000, because the 4,500 actual hours worked was 500 hours below the standard hours allowed for the production of 10,000 units. During the period, however, the company paid an actual labor rate of $11 per hour, which was higher than the standard labor rate of $10 per hour, creating an unfavorable rate variance of $4,500. Note that the combined effect of the two variances is a favorable net labor variance of $500. It can also be obtained by subtracting the $49,500 actual cost shown in the left post of the "goalpost" diagram from the $50,000 standard cost shown in the right post.

It is important to understand that the terms *favorable* and *unfavorable* indicate only a deviation of the actual cost below or above standard. Further analysis and investigation may indicate that the unfavorable variance does not necessarily reflect an inefficiency; nor does the favorable variance always indicate a desirable situation. An apparently unfavorable condition may be more than offset by a favorable situation. For example, a favorable materials price variance that results from buying less expensive materials than called for by the standards may more than offset an unfavorable materials quantity variance that results from additional spoilage due to the use of cheaper materials. In any event, all significant variances, favorable or unfavorable, should be analyzed to determine the cause for and the effect of the deviations. Appropriate action should then be taken to improve the problem areas.

Figure 8-4 Calculating Variances

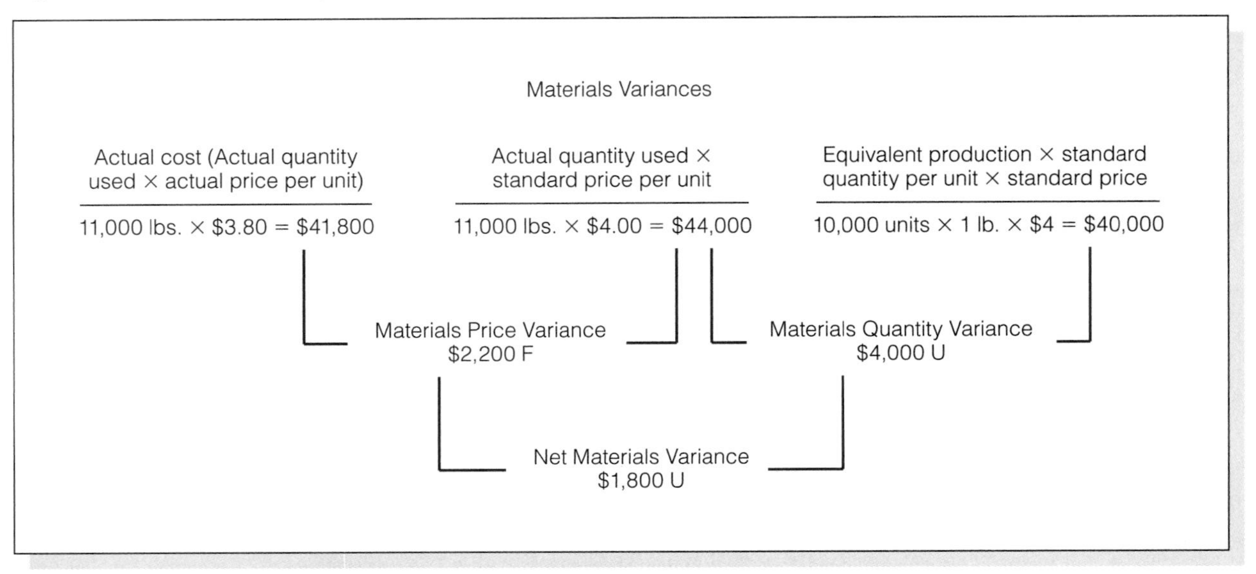

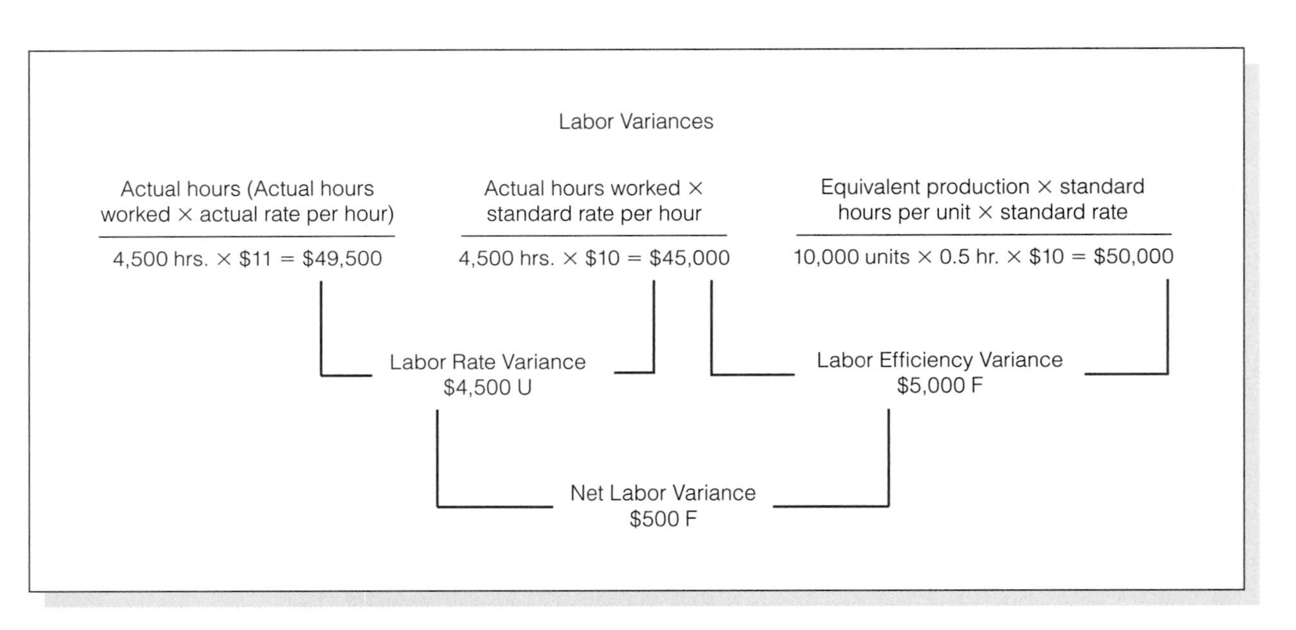

Alternative Method of Recording Materials Cost

Some companies recognize materials price variances at the time materials are purchased, rather than waiting until they are used, by recording a **materials purchase price variance**. This variance represents the deviation of the actual purchase price from the standard purchase price on all the materials purchased, whether or not they were used in production during the period. The rationale for recording this variance at the time of purchase is that the difference between actual and standard cost is known at this time, so there is no reason for delaying the recognition of this variance until the materials are used. A further reason for recording the variance at the time of purchase is that the purchasing agent should be responsible for the price of all materials purchased, whether or not they were used in production during the period.

Using the previous unit price figures and assuming that 12,000 pounds are purchased and 11,000 pounds are used, the materials purchase price variance would be computed as follows:

Actual unit cost of materials – Standard unit cost of materials
$\times$ Actual quantity purchased
($3.80 – $4.00) $\times$ 12,000 = 2,400 F

Recall and Review 1

The standard operating capacity of Vermont Manufacturing, Inc., is 2,000 units. It should take three hours of direct labor time to produce one unit of product, at a standard rate of $15 per hour. It actually took 6,500 direct labor hours to produce the 2,000 units, at an actual wage rate of $16 per hour. Based on the information above, the labor rate variance is $__________, the labor efficiency variance is $__________, and the net labor variance is $__________. (Be sure to designate each variance as favorable or unfavorable.)

(After working this exercise, see page 417 for the solution.)

You should now be able to work the following:
Questions 1–10; Exercises—8-1 to 8-5, Parts a. and b.; Exercises 8-6 to 8-9; Problems 8-1 to 8-6; and the Internet Exercise.

Accounting for Variances

LO4 Prepare journal entries to record variances.

The work in process account is always debited with the standard cost (standard quantity $\times$ standard price) determined for the period's equivalent production. The materials inventory account is credited for the actual cost of materials issued to the factory as indicated by materials requisitions and inventory ledger cards. The payroll account is credited with the actual cost of labor incurred for the period. The differences between the debits (at standard costs) and the credits (at actual costs) are debited (unfavorable variances) or credited (favorable variances) to the variance accounts. The standard cost of units finished is transferred from Work in Process to Finished Goods.

To illustrate, use the figures previously presented for materials and labor costs in Figure 8-4:

1. to record the entry for direct materials cost:

Work in Process (10,000 lb @ $4.00)	40,000	
Materials Quantity Variance	4,000	
Materials Price Variance		2,200
Materials (11,000 lb @ $3.80)		41,800

2. to record the entry for direct labor cost:

Work in Process (5,000 hr @ $10)	50,000	
Labor Rate Variance	4,500	
Labor Efficiency Variance		5,000
Payroll (4,500 hr @ $11)		49,500

3. to record the entry applying factory overhead to work in process (assuming no overhead variances):

Work in Process (10,000 units @ $2)	20,000	
Applied Factory Overhead		20,000

4. to record the entry for finished goods at standard cost (assuming no beginning or ending inventory of work in process and 10,000 units at a standard cost of $11.00 per unit from the standard cost summary on page 384):

Finished Goods (50,000 units @ $11)	110,000	
Work in Process		110,000

The balance sheet of Charlie's Products, Inc., using a standard cost system, would reflect inventories for work in process and finished goods at standard cost, while the materials inventory account would be shown at actual cost. The materials inventory account, however, may also be shown at standard cost, as explained in the following section.

Alternative Method of Recording Materials Cost

Using the previous unit price figures and assuming that 12,000 pounds are purchased while only 11,000 pounds are used, the entry to record the materials at standard cost and the materials purchase price variance at the time of purchase would be:

Materials (12,000 lb @ $4.00 standard price)	48,000	
Materials Purchase Price Variance		2,400
Accounts Payable (12,000 lb @ $3.80 actual price)		45,600

Note that the materials inventory account on the balance sheet would be reflected at standard cost. A benefit of using the purchase price variance method is that the individual materials inventory accounts are maintained at standard cost. This saves recordkeeping expense because it is only necessary to keep track of the quantities purchased, issued, and on hand. It is not necessary to post individual materials costs or to continuously calculate dollar amounts in the inventory ledger files. Because the materials inventory account is kept at standard cost, the balance, in dollars, can be determined at any time by multiplying the standard price per unit by the quantity on hand.

At the time the materials are used, there would be no materials price variance to record, and the materials quantity variance would be recorded as follows:

Work in Process (10,000 lb* @ $4.00 standard price)	40,000	
Materials Quantity Variance	4,000	
Materials (11,000 lb @ $4.00)		44,000

*10,000 units / standard quantity of 1 lb per unit

Disposition of Standard Cost Variances

At the end of the accounting period, the variances of actual cost from standard must be reflected in some appropriate manner on the financial statements. There are several different approaches for handling these items:

1. Some companies prorate these variances to Cost of Goods Sold, Work in Process, and Finished Goods. With the increased affordability of computer hardware and software, this method is gaining in popularity. The net effect of this method is that these accounts are adjusted to actual or historical cost. The rationale is that standard costs are important for management's evaluation of operations but are not appropriate for external financial reports. Hence, the variances, as a part of actual manufacturing cost, should be included in inventory costs. When this method is followed, the allocation of materials, labor, and overhead variances will be in proportion to the standard materials, labor, and overhead costs included in Cost of Goods Sold, Work in Process, and Finished Goods.

2. A more common approach is to show an unfavorable net variance as an addition to the cost of goods sold for the period and a favorable net variance as a deduction from cost of goods sold. This approach is based on the fact that these variances result from unfavorable or favorable conditions or inefficiencies during the period and should therefore be charged or credited to the current period. Also, for most manufacturers, the vast majority of items produced during the period are sold by the end of the period. This means that most of the production costs have flowed to Cost of Goods Sold, making it the right account to adjust. The worksheet that follows shows this approach using the figures from the Charlie's Products, Inc., example. The cost of goods sold at actual, $111,300, is the amount that would appear on the income statement prepared for the use of external parties, since external users are not interested in the level of detail included in the following worksheet.

Worksheet to Convert Standard Cost of Goods Sold to Actual

	A	B	C
1	Cost of goods sold (standard cost)......		$110,000
2	Add unfavorable variance:		
3	Materials quantity variance	$4,000	
4	Direct labor rate variance	4,500	8,500
5			$118,500
6	Less favorable variances:		
7	Materials price variance	$2,200	
8	Labor efficiency variance	5,000	7,200
9	Cost of goods sold (actual cost).....		$111,300

3. If charging or crediting the entire amount of the variances to Cost of Goods Sold would materially misstate the financial statements, the variances should be allocated to Work in Process, Finished Goods, and Cost of Goods Sold.
4. If production is seasonal, with extreme peaks and valleys during the year, then variances should be shown as deferred charges or credits on interim balance sheets, using the logic that they would be mostly offset in future periods. At the end of the year, however, some disposition of these variances, as described previously, must be made and the variance accounts closed.
5. If the variances are due to abnormal or unusual circumstances—such as strikes, fires, storms, or floods—then there is justification for charging off these items as extraordinary losses on the income statement.

This text will, unless indicated otherwise, use the more common approach of reflecting the materials and labor variances as adjustments to the standard cost of goods sold, as illustrated in Item 2 above. Variances for factory overhead costs, to be discussed later in this chapter, would also be reflected in the statements in a similar manner. Figure 8-5 provides an aid to understanding cost flow through a standard cost system.

Interpreting Variances

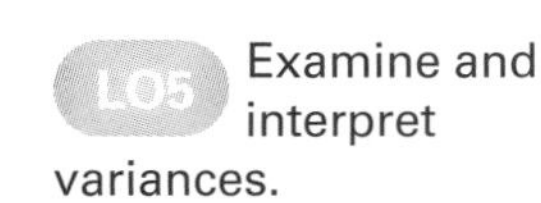

Examine and interpret variances.

In analyzing materials and labor variances, two components are investigated: usage (quantity) and price. The analyst looks closely at the quantity of materials used, the cost per unit of each type of material, the number of direct labor hours worked, and the cost of each labor hour. When the usage and/or price differ from the established standards, the analyst examines the reasons for the variances and considers what actions, if any, can be taken.

In analyzing the materials cost variance, the usage of materials may be above, below, or at standard, and the price per unit paid for the materials might be above, below, or at standard. Management needs this information to take corrective measures, if necessary. Consider the three possibilities (on pages 394 through 395) in the manufacture of 10,000 units.

Figure 8-5 Cost Flow through a Standard Cost System

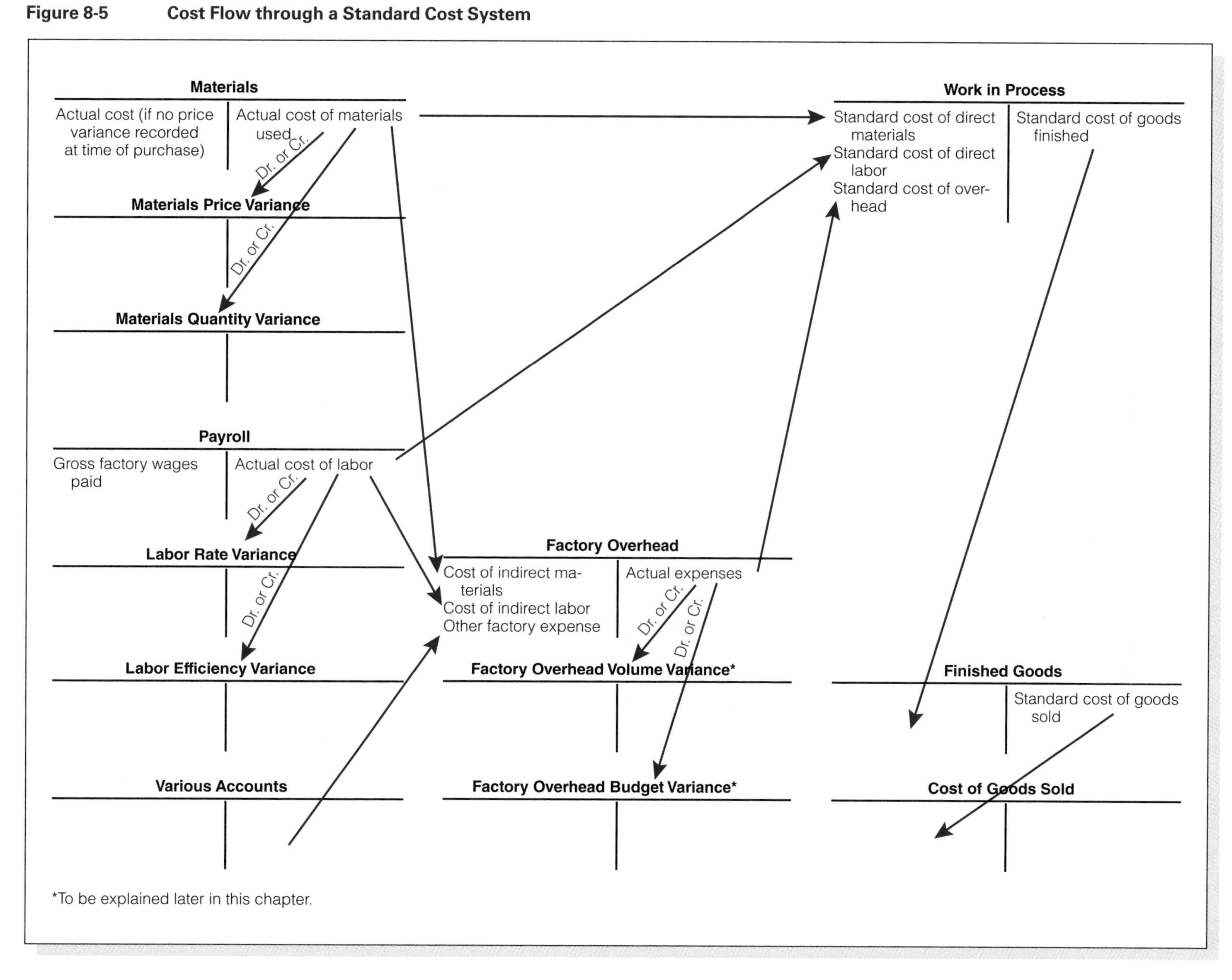

*To be explained later in this chapter.

Example 1:

Actual cost, 10,000 lb of materials @ $4.18	$41,800
Standard cost, 10,000 lb of materials @ $4.00	40,000
Unfavorable materials price variance (10,000 × $0.18)	$ 1,800

This analysis shows that the factory usage of materials is at standard, but the standard price for the materials has been exceeded. The variance is caused by the fact that the company used materials costing $0.18 more than the standard price. With 10,000 standard pounds used, this $0.18 per unit variance resulted in an unfavorable variance of $1,800.

Management now has the data with which to investigate why the materials cost per unit is higher than the standard of $4.00 per pound. Several possibilities exist, including:

1. inefficient purchasing methods;
2. use of a different material than the standard called for; and
3. increase in market price.

Inefficient purchasing can be corrected by better planning and by more careful selection of suppliers. If different, higher-priced material than the standard called for is selected, the standard cost per unit of materials will have to be increased if this is more than a one-time experiment. The standard cost would also have to be increased if there is an increase in market price that is considered to be permanent.

The example illustrates the principle that management should carefully investigate any significant variance, favorable or unfavorable, so that corrective action can be taken. Such a decision may involve eliminating inefficiencies or changing the standard cost of the product.

Example 2:

Actual cost, 10,450 lb of materials @ $4.00	$41,800
Standard cost, 10,000 lb of materials @ $4.00	40,000
Unfavorable materials quantity variance (450 × $4.00)	$ 1,800

In this instance, the price paid for the materials is at standard but the materials usage is excessive. The manufacturing operation used 450 pounds of materials more than called for by the standard in order to make 10,000 units. This additional 450 pounds (at a cost of $4.00 per pound) created the unfavorable quantity variance of $1,800.

As with the previous example, management must now determine why the extra materials were used. Again, various circumstances might have created this situation:

1. Materials were spoiled or wasted. This loss could have been due to a different type of material being used than the standard called for, or by careless workers and lax supervisory personnel. If possible, the cause of the loss should be eliminated.

2. More materials were deliberately used per manufactured unit as an experiment to determine whether the product's quality could be increased. If management decides to continue this increased usage, the standard quantity per unit must be changed.

Example 3:

Actual cost, 11,000 lb of materials @ $3.80	$41,800
Standard cost, 10,000 lb of materials @ $4.00	40,000
Unfavorable net materials variance	$ 1,800

In this example, a combination of usage and price variances causes the overall unfavorable variance. The factory has used 1,000 pounds of materials over standard but has purchased these materials at a cost that is $0.20 per pound below standard. Once again, management should know why the additional materials were used and why a cost per pound lower than standard was paid:

1. It is important to recognize that the price variance of $0.20 will also require investigation. That this variance is favorable—below standard cost—is no reason for production personnel to be complacent and ignore it. This "better" price may have been created by more efficient buying techniques, a bargain purchase, or a general price reduction. On the other hand, materials of a lesser quality might have been purchased, thereby reducing the quality of the product and creating an unfavorable product image.
2. It is also possible that the greater usage of materials, and the resulting unfavorable materials quantity variance, may be related to the lower price. Waste and spoilage might be created by (1) use of cheaper materials or (2) production workers' unfamiliarity with use of a different material. Further investigation may reveal that the standard was not properly determined and should be revised. (If the standard cost is changed, the units in inventory are often revalued at the new figure.)

The three examples that had identical net unfavorable variances of $1,800 illustrate the following important points:

1. The total variance between standard and actual cost must be broken down by usage and price.
2. The variances in usage and price, whether unfavorable or favorable, must be analyzed with regard to cause and effect. Variances may be stated in dollar amounts or in terms of units such as pounds or hours. The method chosen should be one that provides the greatest benefit in determining the cause of the variances.
3. Appropriate action must be taken. This action may include a change in methods of manufacturing, supervision, or purchasing, or an adjustment to the standard cost of the product. If the variances are favorable, it may involve noting the "best practices" that resulted in efficient purchasing and production.

The same principles of analysis apply to the labor cost variances. Three similar examples are presented below.

Example 1:

Actual cost, 5,000 hr @ \$9.90 per hr	\$49,500
Standard cost, 5,000 hr @ \$10.00 per hr	50,000
Favorable labor rate variance (5,000 × \$0.10)	\$ 500

Example 2:

Actual cost, 4,950 hr @ \$10 per hr	\$49,500
Standard cost, 5,000 hr @ \$10 per hr	50,000
Favorable labor efficiency variance (50 × \$10)	\$ 500

Example 3:

Actual cost, 4,500 hr @ \$11 per hr	\$49,500
Standard cost, 5,000 hr @ \$10 per hr	50,000
Favorable net labor variance	\$ 500

In the first example, it is apparent that the number of actual labor hours was at standard, but the wage paid per hour was lower than the standard of \$10.00. Although this result appears to be favorable, the reason and the possible effect should still be determined. It may be that the human resources department is doing a more efficient job of hiring qualified employees and should be commended; or it may be that less-than-qualified workers are being hired at a lower rate, possibly reducing the quality of the work on the product. This second condition would not be acceptable.

The second example indicates that the labor rate is at standard, but the production time required was 50 hours below standard. The manufacturing and/or supervisory functions may have become more efficient so that more work was done well in less time. It is also possible that the speed of production has been increased, and the employees are working too fast to do top-quality work. This situation could have an adverse effect on future sales.

In the third example, a saving of 500 hours has been achieved, but there has been a wage rate per hour of \$1.00 in excess of standard. These two factors could be related. The hiring of more highly skilled and higher-paid personnel quite often results in a reduction in the number of hours needed to complete the work. But, as with the other examples, management should investigate to determine the cause and the potential long-term effect of the variances in usage and price. In instances where the labor efficiency variance is unfavorable, it may have been caused by the use of unskilled workers, by time lost because of machine breakdowns or improper production scheduling, or by an inefficient flow of materials to the production line.

The analyses of materials and labor variances are not isolated from each other. It is quite possible that a difference above or below the standard for one of them is directly related to a variance for the other. For example, the hiring of more highly skilled personnel at a higher labor rate does not always reduce the number of hours worked, but it may reduce the amount of materials lost through waste. Conversely, the use of less skilled workers at a lower rate may cause greater materials loss. In examining any variance, management should not look at each individual variance in a vacuum but rather at the relationship of that variance to other variances.

Features of Standard Cost Accounting

LO6 Recognize the features of a standard cost system.

This is a good place to summarize some features of standard cost accounting:

1. The company does not determine the actual per-unit cost of manufacturing a product for input into the accounting system.
2. The fact that standards are based on estimates does not make them unreliable. A close examination of variances will quickly gauge the efficiency of the manufacturing operation and the reasonableness of the standards.
3. Standards will change as conditions change. Permanent changes in prices and processes may indicate the need for the standards to be adjusted.
4. The purpose of using a standard cost accounting system is to provide continual incentive for factory personnel to keep costs and performance in line with predetermined management objectives. As mentioned earlier in the chapter, comparisons between actual costs and predetermined standards are much more effective than comparisons between current actual costs and actual costs of prior periods.
5. A standard cost system, through the recording and analysis of manufacturing cost variances, helps focus management's attention on the following questions and their causes:
   a. Were materials purchased at prices above or below standard?
   b. Were materials used in quantities above or below standard?
   c. Is labor being paid at rates above or below standard?
   d. Is labor being used in amounts above or below standard?
6. Although the discussion in this text suggests that variances are determined at the end of the month, most manufacturing companies calculate variances on a weekly (or even daily) basis to allow for more timely action in correcting inefficiencies or taking advantage of efficiencies. The variances for the month, however, are still recorded in the accounts at the end of the month.

Illustration of Standard Cost in a Departmentalized Factory

LO7 Account for standard costs in a departmentalized factory.

The following example demonstrates standard cost accounting procedures in a factory having two departments.

Standard Cost Summary

	Machining	Assembly	Total
Materials: 5 lb @ $1lb	$ 5		
1 lb @ $2 lb		$ 2	$ 7
Labor: 1 hr @ $8	8		
2 hr @ $10		20	28
Factory overhead:			
Per unit	1	2	3
Standard costs per unit	$14	$24	$38

Production Report for the Month

	Machining	Assembly
Beginning units in process	None	None
Units finished and transferred	2,200	1,800
Ending units in process	None	400
Stage of completion		1/2

Units pass through Machining to Assembly. In both departments, materials, labor, and overhead are added evenly throughout the process. Actual costs for the month—as determined from materials requisitions, payroll records, and factory overhead records—are as follows:

	Machining		Assembly		Total
Direct materials:					
12,000 lb @ $0.95		$11,400			
1,900 lb @ $2.10				$ 3,990	$15,390
Direct labor:					
2,000 hr @ $8.10		16,200			
4,100 hr @ $9.90				40,590	56,790
Factory overhead:					
Indirect materials	$1,400		$2,500		
Indirect labor	800	2,200	1,500	4,000	6,200
		$29,800		$48,580	$78,380

From the data given on the standard cost summary, the standard costs of production can be determined. To facilitate the comparison of these figures with actual costs and the determination of variances, a form similar to Figure 8-6 can be used.

Figure 8-6 **Calculation of Variances**

	A	B	C	D	E	F	G	H	I	J
1		Machining Equivalent Production of 2,200 Units			Assembly Equivalent Production of 2,000* Units				Total	
5		Standard Cost	Actual Cost	Net Favorable (Unfavorable) Variance	Standard Cost	Actual Cost	Net Favorable (Unfavorable) Variance	Standard Cost	Actual Cost	Net Favorable (Unfavorable) Variance
7	Materials:									
8	11,000 lb @ $1.00	$11,000								
9	12,000 lb @ $0.95		$11,400	$(400)						
10	2,000 lb @ $2.00				$4,000					
11	1,900 lb @ $2.10					$3,990	$10	$15,000	$15,390	$(390)
12	Labor:									
13	2,200 hr @ $8.00	17,600								
14	2,000 hr @ $8.10		16,200	1,400						
15	4,000 hr @ $10.00				40,000					
16	4,100 hr @ $9.90					40,590	(590)	57,600	56,790	810
17	Factory overhead:									
18	Standard cost per									
19	unit, $1.00	2,200								
20	Actual cost		2,200	—						
21	Standard cost per									
22	unit, $2.00				4,000					
23	Actual cost					4,000	—	6,200	6,200	—
24	Total	$30,800	$29,800	$1,000	$48,000	$48,580	$(580)	$78,800	$78,380	$ 420
25	* 1,800 units finished and transferred + (400 × 1/2) equivalent production in ending inventory.									

Using the data given in Figure 8-6 on page 399, we can compute the specific variances for materials using either of the following two formats.

Materials – Machining:

Materials price variance = (Actual unit price – Standard unit price) × Actual quantity
= ($0.95 – $1.00) × 12,000 lb = $600 F

Materials quantity variance = (Actual quantity – Standard quantity) × Standard price
= [12,000 lb – (2,200 units × 5 lb/unit)] × $1 = $1,000 U

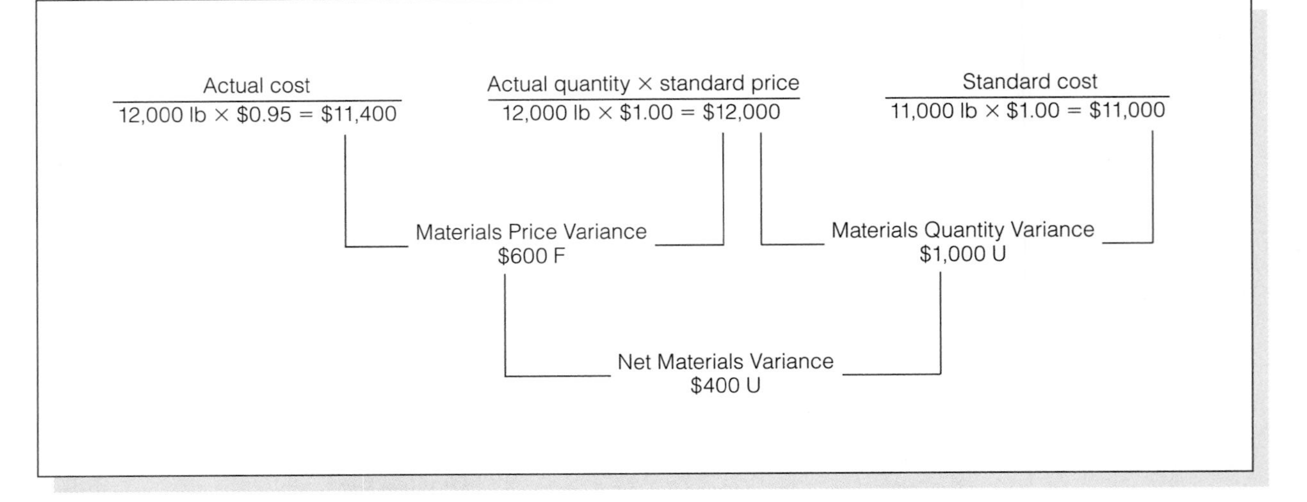

Materials – Assembly:

Materials price variance = ($2.10 – $2.00) × 1,900 lb = $190 U

Materials quantity variance = [1,900 lb – (2,000 units × 1 lb/unit)] × $2 = $200 F

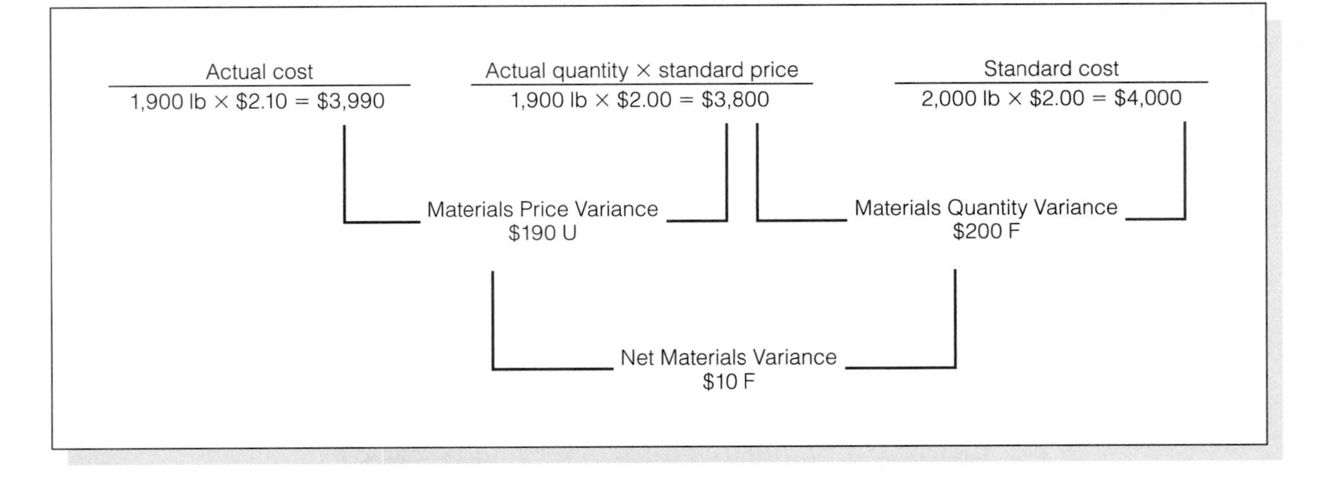

One thousand pounds of materials in excess of standard were used in Machining, which, at the standard price of $1.00, caused an unfavorable quantity variance of $1,000. If prices had not changed, there would have been no other variances. But price did change—12,000 pounds of materials at a cost of $0.05 below standard resulted in a favorable price variance of $600. The combined variances resulted in a net unfavorable materials cost variance of $400 in Machining.

Assembly used 100 pounds of materials less than standard. At a standard price of $2.00 per pound, the favorable quantity variance was $200. But this variance was partially offset by the unfavorable price variance created by the increase of $.10 in the cost per unit of the materials. With 1,900 pounds being used, the price variance was $190 above standard. The two variances resulted in a net favorable materials variance of $10 in Assembly.

The journal entries for the issuance of direct and indirect materials into production and to record the materials variances are as follows:

Account	Debit	Credit
Work in Process—Machining (11,000 lb @ $1)	11,000	
Materials Quantity Variance—Machining	1,000	
Materials Price Variance—Machining		600
Materials (12,000 lb @ $.95)		11,400
Work in Process—Assembly (2,000 lb @ $2)	4,000	
Materials Price Variance—Assembly	190	
Materials Quantity Variance—Assembly		200
Materials (1,900 lb @ $2.10)		3,990
Factory Overhead (Indirect Materials)	3,900	
Materials		3,900

Note that the accounts for work in process are charged for the standard cost of direct materials; the factory overhead account is debited for the actual cost of indirect materials used; the materials account is credited at actual cost for all direct and indirect materials used; and the variance accounts are debited if the variance is unfavorable and credited if it is favorable. (If this company followed the practice of recording the materials price variance at the time of purchase, no price variances would be recorded at this time because the materials purchase price variance would have been recorded when the goods were received.)

Based on the data in Figure 8-6, the specific variances for labor can be computed using either of the following formats.

Labor – Machining:

$$\begin{aligned}\text{Labor rate variance} &= (\text{Actual labor rate} - \text{Standard labor rate}) \\ &\quad \times \text{Actual hours} \\ &= (\$8.10 - \$8.00) \times 2{,}000 \text{ hr} = \$200 \text{ U} \\ \text{Labor efficiency variance} &= (\text{Actual labor hours} - \text{Standard labor hours}) \\ &\quad \times \text{Standard labor rate} \\ &= [2{,}000 \text{ hr} - (2{,}200 \text{ units} \times 1 \text{ hr/unit})] \\ &\quad \times \$8 = \$1{,}600 \text{ F}\end{aligned}$$

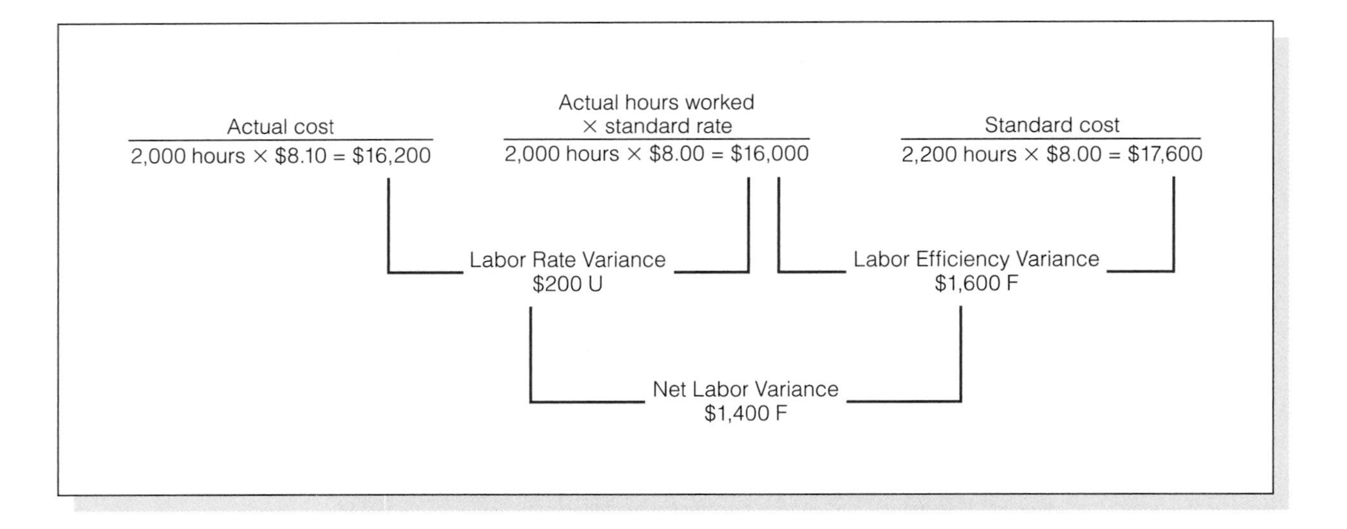

Labor – Assembly:

$$\text{Labor rate variance} = (\$9.90 - \$10.00) \times 4{,}100 \text{ hr} = \$410 \text{ F}$$

$$\text{Labor efficiency variance} = [4{,}100 \text{ hr} - (2{,}000 \text{ units} \times 2 \text{ hr/unit})] \times \$10 = \$1{,}000 \text{ U}$$

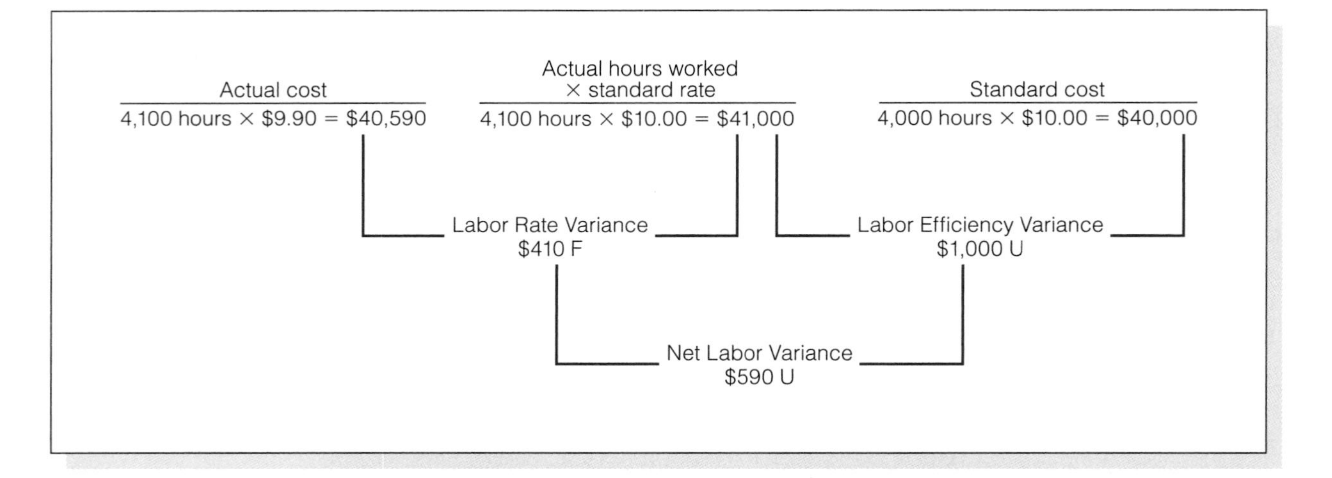

During the month, Machining saved 200 hours by working fewer hours than the standard for the number of units produced. At a standard cost of $8.00 per hour, a favorable efficiency variance of $1,600 was realized. The average hourly rate of pay, however, was $0.10 above standard, and so there was also an unfavorable rate variance. The company paid $0.10 more per hour than the standard rate for the 2,000 hours actually worked, a total of $200.

Assembly used 100 hours more than the standard. Therefore, at the standard rate of $10.00, it had an unfavorable efficiency variance of $1,000. Because the actual rate was $0.10 below standard, a favorable rate variance of $410 resulted, which is determined by multiplying the 4,100 hours worked by the $0.10 rate differential. The journal entry to record the direct and indirect labor used in production and the labor variances is as follows:

Account	Debit	Credit
Work in Process—Machining (2,200 hr @ $8.00)	17,600	
Labor Rate Variance—Machining	200	
Labor Efficiency Variance—Machining		1,600
Payroll (2,000 hr @ $8.10)		16,200
Work in Process—Assembly (4,000 hr @ $10.00)	40,000	
Labor Efficiency Variance—Assembly	1,000	
Labor Rate Variance—Assembly		410
Payroll (4,100 hr @ $9.90)		40,590
Factory Overhead (Indirect Labor)	2,300	
Payroll		2,300

As with materials, only standard costs for direct labor are charged to Work in Process. The factory overhead account is debited for the actual cost of the indirect labor used, the payroll account is credited for the actual cost of direct and indirect labor during the month, and the variances are debited or credited to the appropriate accounts.

Factory overhead would be applied to Work in Process by the following entry, using the predetermined overhead rates of $1 per unit in Machining and $2 per unit in Assembly:

Account	Debit	Credit
Work in Process—Machining (2,200 units × $1)	2,200	
Work in Process—Assembly (2,000 units × $2)	4,000	
Applied Factory Overhead		6,200

The entries are then made to transfer the standard cost of units finished in Machining to Assembly and from Assembly to Finished Goods.

Account	Debit	Credit
Work in Process—Machining	30,800	
Work in Process—Assembly		30,800
(2,200 units @ $14)		
Finished Goods	68,400	
Work in Process—Assembly		68,400
(1,800 units @ $38)		

After these entries have been posted, the general ledger accounts would reflect the data, as shown, in T-account form. (Note that the postings assume that entries were previously made for the purchase of materials and to record the payroll.)

Materials

Debit	Credit
19,290	11,400
	3,990
	3,900
	19,290

Work in Process—Machining

Debit	Credit
11,000	30,800
17,600	
2,200	
30,800	

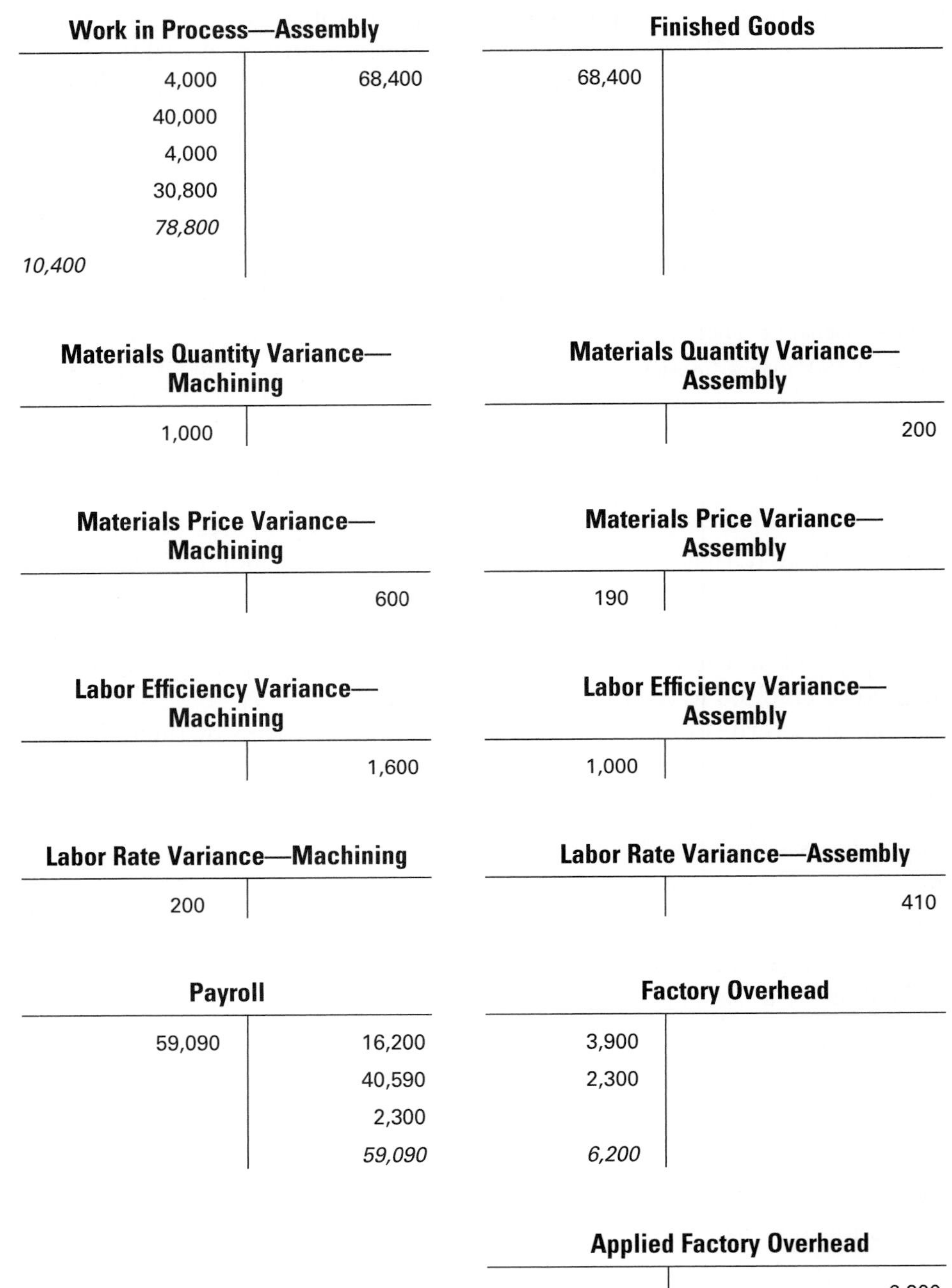

Work in Process—Assembly

Debit	Credit
4,000	68,400
40,000	
4,000	
30,800	
78,800	
10,400	

Finished Goods

Debit	Credit
68,400	

Materials Quantity Variance—Machining

Debit	Credit
1,000	

Materials Quantity Variance—Assembly

Debit	Credit
	200

Materials Price Variance—Machining

Debit	Credit
	600

Materials Price Variance—Assembly

Debit	Credit
190	

Labor Efficiency Variance—Machining

Debit	Credit
	1,600

Labor Efficiency Variance—Assembly

Debit	Credit
1,000	

Labor Rate Variance—Machining

Debit	Credit
200	

Labor Rate Variance—Assembly

Debit	Credit
	410

Payroll

Debit	Credit
59,090	16,200
	40,590
	2,300
	59,090

Factory Overhead

Debit	Credit
3,900	
2,300	
6,200	

Applied Factory Overhead

Debit	Credit
	6,200

The work in process account for Machining has no balance because all work has been completed and transferred to Assembly. The work in process account for Assembly has a balance of $10,400, accounted for as follows:

Cost in Machining—400 units @ $14	$ 5,600
Cost in Assembly—(400 units, 1/2 completed) @ $24	4,800
	$10,400

Recall and Review 2

The normal capacity of Hillary Company is 30,000 direct labor hours allowed for the production of 15,000 units of Brite per month. A finished unit requires 5 pounds of material at a standard cost of $4 per pound. The standard cost of direct labor is $15 per hour. The plant accountant estimates that overhead for the month should be $450,000 at normal capacity. Based on the above information, the standard unit cost should be $__________.

(After working this exercise, see page 418 for the solution.)

You should now be able to work the following:
Questions 11–19; Exercises 8-2 to 8-5, Parts c. and d.; Exercises 8-10 to 8-13; Problems 8-7 to 8-9; Mini-Case; and Self-Study Problem 1.

Analysis of Factory Overhead Standard Cost Variances

LO8 Distinguish between actual and applied factory overhead.

Determining the standard unit cost for factory overhead involves estimating factory overhead cost at the standard, or normal, level of production while considering historical data (adjusted for distorting items in the past such as strikes or fire losses) and forecasting future changes and trends. The estimated factory overhead cost is divided by the standard number of labor or machine hours expected for the planned units to be produced. For example, assume that the budgeted production is 1,000 units, which will require 2,000 direct labor hours. At this level of activity, the budgeted factory overhead is determined, as follows:

Depreciation on building and machinery	$ 4,000
Taxes and insurance on building and machinery	1,000
Supervisory salaries	4,000
Maintenance costs	2,000
Supplies	1,000
Total standard factory overhead	$12,000

Dividing the budgeted factory overhead cost of $12,000 by the 2,000 budgeted direct labor hours results in a standard cost of $6 per direct labor hour, and because each unit requires two direct labor hours, the standard cost per unit produced is $12. If equivalent production during the period is exactly 1,000 units, requiring a standard 2,000 direct labor hours, then Work in Process will be charged with $12,000 of estimated factory overhead (1,000 units × 2 hours per unit × $6 per hour). As illustrated in the following journal entry and T-accounts, if the actual factory overhead is also $12,000, then all of this cost would be applied to the work in process account, and no over- or underapplied factory overhead would exist.

Work in Process (2,000 hr @ $6)	12,000	
Factory Overhead		12,000

Work in Process	
12,000	

Factory Overhead	
12,000 (actual cost from various journals)	12,000 (standard cost applied to Work in Process)

If the actual factory overhead is greater than $12,000, then the factory overhead account will have a debit balance after $12,000 of standard cost has been applied to Work in Process. This balance would reflect the amount of actual factory overhead cost not charged to the goods produced. This underapplied amount represents the amount of overhead incurred over and above the standard cost allowed for the attained level of production. The debit balance in the account would be considered an unfavorable variance. Conversely, if the actual factory overhead is less than $12,000, then the factory overhead account will have a credit balance after $12,000 of standard cost is applied to Work in Process. This overapplied cost represents the amount of overhead incurred below the standard cost allowed for the attained level of production. The credit balance in the account would be considered a favorable variance.

The next section of this chapter (and the appendix that follows) analyzes, in detail, the factors that could cause an overhead variance. Although many companies favor the two-variance method of factory overhead analysis, the three-variance and four-variance methods illustrated in the appendix are also used.

Two-Variance Method of Analysis

LO9 Compute variances using the two-variance method.

The method a company chooses to analyze factory overhead variances depends on the benefits the company derives from the detailed analysis. The cost incurred in applying the standard factory overhead to production, maintaining the necessary accounts, and analyzing the results also plays a part in the process of selecting a method. The **two-variance method** is the least complex approach; it divides the total variance into a controllable variance and a volume variance.

The **controllable variance** measures the amount by which the actual factory overhead costs differ from the standard overhead costs for the level of production attained. The difference results from the behavior of the fixed and variable cost items. As discussed previously, fixed cost items tend to remain the same in total dollars despite normal fluctuations in production volume, while total variable costs tend to vary proportionately with changes in production. In the previous example, depreciation, taxes, insurance, and supervisory salaries are typical items of fixed expense, while maintenance costs and supplies are usually listed in the category of variable cost.

Assume that the actual level of production achieved in the previous example was 900 units—or 90% of the planned production of 1,000 units—and the 900 units are allowed 1,800 standard direct labor hours (900 units × 2 hours per unit) to complete. The actual amount of factory overhead for this period is then:

Depreciation on building and machinery (fixed)	$ 4,000
Taxes and insurance on the above (fixed)	1,000
Supervisory salaries (fixed)	4,000
Maintenance costs (variable)	1,800
Supplies (variable)	1,000
	$11,800

The fixed costs remain the same as budgeted at 1,000 units of production, but the variable costs should be lower. Because 900 units were produced and each unit is allowed two direct labor hours at $6 of standard overhead per hour, Work in Process was debited and Factory Overhead credited for $10,800. Factory Overhead shows a $1,000 underapplied (debit) balance as follows:

Factory Overhead

Debit	Credit
11,800 (actual cost)	10,800 (applied 900 units × 2 standard hours per unit × $6)
(*1,000* underapplied)	

Using the variable and fixed cost rates per unit, from the data on page 357, of $1.50 ($3,000 variable costs / 2,000 direct labor hours) for variable cost and $4.50 ($9,000 fixed costs / 2,000 direct labor hours) for fixed cost, the calculation of the controllable variance is as follows:

Standard factory overhead budgeted for *actual* level of production:	
Variable cost:	
900 units × 2 hours per unit × $1.50	$ 2,700
Fixed cost:	
As budgeted (total from budget)	9,000
Flexible budget at *actual* production level	$11,700
Actual factory overhead incurred	11,800
Controllable variance (unfavorable)	$ 100

Note that the controllable variance is unfavorable by $100 because the variable expense for supplies should have been $900 (900 units × $1), whereas it was actually $1,000 per the list of expenses above.

The **volume variance** measures the difference between the budgeted fixed overhead and the fixed overhead applied to work in process. It is the result of operating at a level of production different from the standard level. Its calculation uses the same flexible budget amount as determined in the previous calculation ($11,700) and compares the budget amount to the overhead applied to the production for the period.

Flexible budget at *actual* production level	$11,700
Factory overhead applied:	
900 units × 2 hours per unit × $6 per hour	10,800
Volume variance (unfavorable)	$ 900

In summary, the controllable and volume variances explain the underapplied $1,000 in the factory overhead account as follows:

Controllable variance (unfavorable)	$ 100
Volume variance (unfavorable)	900
Underapplied factory overhead	$1,000

The budget for the year anticipated that the fixed cost of $9,000 would be spread over 2,000 direct labor hours and would be used to produce 1,000 units of product. Because only 900 units were produced, only $8,100 of fixed cost (1,800 standard direct labor hours × $4.50 fixed cost per hour) was applied to units produced. The result was an unfavorable variance of $900. The following illustration shows this effect:

Actual Level of Production—900 units

	Applied	Budget for 900 Units	Volume Variance
Fixed cost applied:			
900 units × 2 hours × $4.50	$ 8,100	$ 9,000	$900 U
Variable cost applied:			
900 units × 2 hours × $1.50	2,700	2,700	-0- U
Total applied (900 × 2 hours × $6)	$10,800	$11,700	$800 U

The volume variance is a significant factor because it indicates the degree that production was below the established standard. If management feels that 1,000 units should have been produced during the period, then it will be concerned that only 900 units were produced and will investigate to determine the cause. The reduced production may have resulted from inefficiencies in labor or supervision, from machine breakdowns due to faulty maintenance, or from any number of other unfavorable conditions. On the other hand, this level of production may indicate a normal seasonal fluctuation that will be offset by higher than normal production in other periods. If the reduction in production is not seasonal, then it may have occurred because sales were not as high as predicted, in which case the marketing department could then be held accountable.

Whatever the circumstances, a factory that is producing below its normal capacity has idle and possibly wasted excess capacity. It has committed to a greater level of fixed costs than are being efficiently utilized by current operations. By spreading the fixed costs over a fewer number of units than budgeted for, the per-unit manufacturing cost is more expensive than planned. Such situations should be scrutinized by management, which is ultimately responsible for planning and implementing the most efficient production methods and schedules.

The factory overhead account in the preceding example would have a debit balance of $1,000, as shown in the following T-account. The debit balance represents a net unfavorable variance.

Factory Overhead

11,800 (actual costs recorded from various journals)	10,800 (standard cost applied to Work in Process)
Balance *1,000*	

This means that the volume variance is responsible for $900 of the net unfavorable factory overhead variance of $1,000. The amount of overhead applied to production is $900 less than the factory overhead calculated in the flexible budget for the actual level of production. This variance is unfavorable because the fixed overhead budgeted at the beginning of the period was not completely charged to production owing to an insufficient number of units produced. It is referred to as a *volume variance* because it is created by the excess or (as in this case) lack of actual units produced compared to the planned production quantity.

The *controllable variance* accounts for the other $100 of the net variance because the actual factory overhead for the period exceeded the amount of overhead allowed for the level of production. This is a result of the previously mentioned overspending on supplies. The controllable variance is favorable when the actual expenditures are less than the flexible dollar amount calculated for the attained level of production. It is unfavorable when the actual factory overhead costs exceed the calculated budget.

The formula for calculating factory overhead variances using the two-variance method is illustrated in the following example:

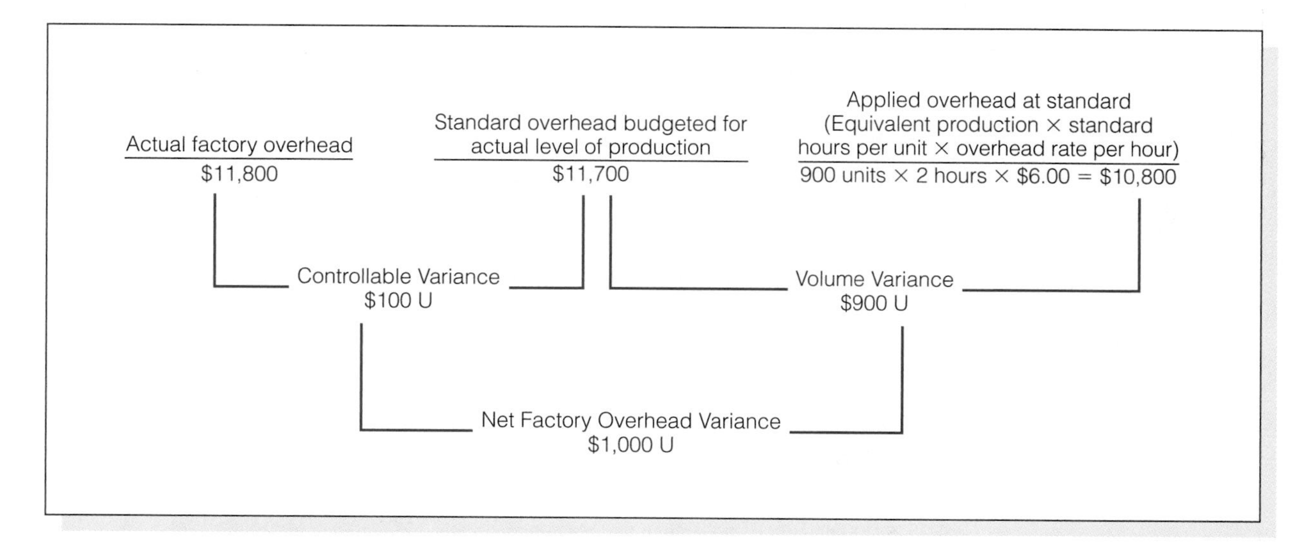

After the variance analysis, the following journal entry can be made. This entry closes out the account for factory overhead on page 409 and records the variances in individual accounts.

Factory Overhead—Volume Variance	900	
Factory Overhead—Controllable Variance	100	
Factory Overhead		1,000

Alternatively, the journal entries to apply overhead to Work in Process, to close Factory Overhead, and to record the variances may be combined in the following single end-of-period entry:

Work in Process (1,800 hr @ $6)	10,800	
Factory Overhead—Volume Variance	900	
Factory Overhead—Controllable Variance	100	
Factory Overhead		11,800

Production below the standard number of units will always cause an unfavorable volume variance. Conversely, production greater than the standard number of units will always produce a favorable volume variance. Assume the following facts for the period:

Standard overhead cost per unit (2 direct labor hours × $6)	$ 12
Number of units actually produced	1,200
Number of units expected to be produced (budgeted)	1,000
Actual factory overhead	$14,000
Standard factory overhead budgeted for actual level of production:	
Fixed costs (as budgeted):	$ 9,000
Variable costs:	
1,200 units × 2 hours per unit × $1.50	3,600
Flexible budget for actual production level	$12,600
Actual factory overhead incurred	14,000
Controllable variance (unfavorable)	$ 1,400

The volume variance would be calculated as follows:

Flexible budget for actual production level	$ 12,600
Factory overhead applied: 1,200 units × 2 hours per unit × $6	14,400
Volumevariance (favorable)	$ 1,800

Under these circumstances, the work in process account would be charged with $14,400 applied factory overhead (1,200 units × 2 hours per unit × $6). The factory overhead account, as shown in the following T-account, would have a credit balance of $400. The credit balance represents a favorable net variance.

Factory Overhead

14,000	14,400
(actual cost)	(applied 1,200 units × 2 std. hr per unit × $6)
	Balance (400 overapplied)

The breakdown of the net variance shows a favorable volume variance of $1,800 because factory overhead was overapplied due to the actual volume of production being higher than the established standard. The unfavorable controllable variance of $1,400 indicates that the actual overhead costs exceeded the amount allowed for the actual level of production achieved.

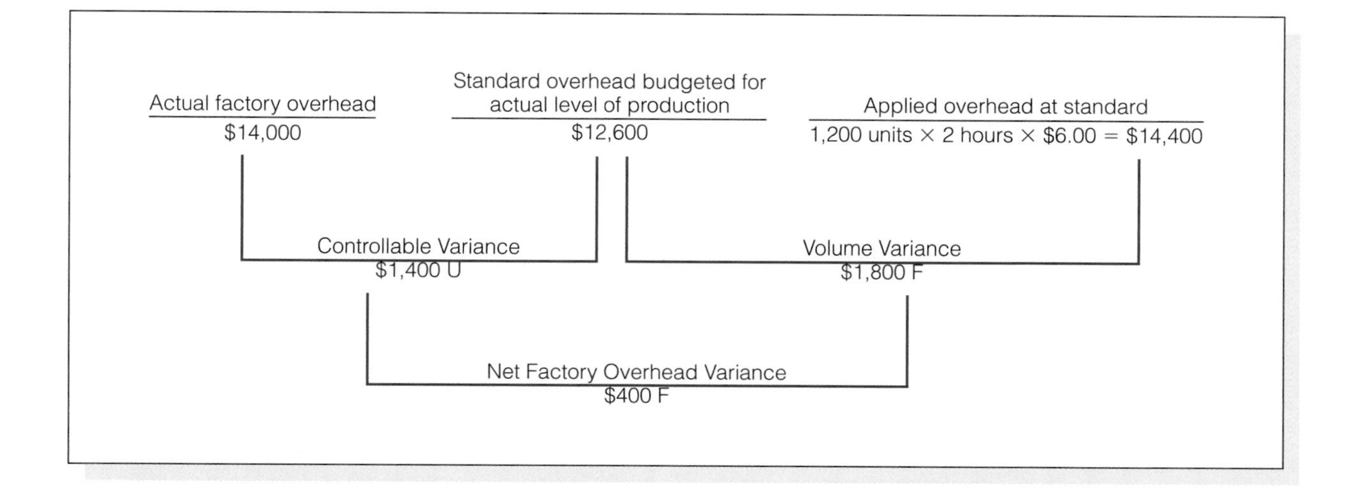

Both variances should be investigated for cause and effect. The *favorable volume variance* may be due to an anticipated seasonal fluctuation, and it may offset all or part of the previous unfavorable volume variances that arose during periods of low production. However, this level of production may have occurred because the company received more orders for goods than it had anticipated. From the standpoint of increased profits, this factor is favorable. However, if the factory worked beyond an established efficient capacity of production then the quality of the product may have suffered.

The *unfavorable controllable variance* should be examined to determine why the costs were higher than expected, where the responsibility for this condition lies, and what steps can be taken to keep these costs under control in the future. This variance could result from several factors, such as laxity in purchasing, inefficiency in supervision, or weak control of expenditures. However, some portion of the controllable variance may result from additional machine maintenance and repair costs, which are attributable to the increased use of facilities at the higher level of production.

Recall and Review 3

The overhead application rate for a company is $5 per unit, made up of $3 per unit for fixed overhead and $2 per unit for variable overhead. Normal capacity is 5,000 units. In one month there was an unfavorable controllable variance of $500. Actual overhead for the month was $30,000. The amount of the budgeted overhead for the actual level of production must have been $________________.

(After working this exercise, see page 418 for the solution.)

You should now be able to work the following:
Questions 20–25; Exercises 8-14 to 8-17; Problems 8-10 to 8-14; Review Problem 8-20R part 4 (a); and Self-Study Problem 2 part 4 (a).

Appendix

Four-Variance and Three-Variance Methods of Analysis

Four-Variance Method of Analysis

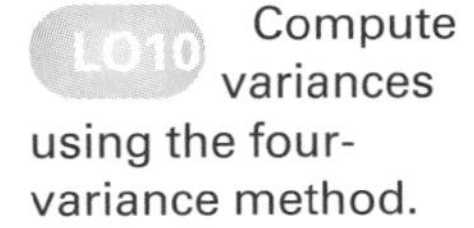

Compute variances using the four-variance method.

A refined management view of the two-variance method isolates the fixed and variable components that comprise the factory overhead cost and calculates separate variances for the variable costs and the fixed costs. The **four-variance method** recognizes *two* variable cost variances and *two* fixed cost variances. The cost variances are identified as a *variable overhead spending variance*, a *variable overhead efficiency variance*, a *fixed overhead budget variance*, and a *fixed overhead volume variance*.

The **variable overhead spending variance** measures the effect of differences in the actual variable overhead rate and the standard variable overhead rate. The **variable overhead efficiency variance** measures the change in the variable overhead consumption that occurs because of efficient or inefficient use of the cost allocation base, such as direct labor hours. The **fixed overhead budget variance** measures the difference between the actual fixed overhead and the budgeted fixed overhead. The **fixed overhead volume variance** is the difference between budgeted fixed overhead and applied fixed overhead.

The four-variance method has two important aspects: (1) separate actual factory overhead accounts must be maintained for variable costs and fixed costs; and (2) actual direct labor hours worked must be known. When we use the same data for factory overhead as shown in the previous illustration (except recognizing that the actual factory overhead of $14,000 was composed of $6,000 of variable overhead costs and $8,000 of fixed overhead costs and that 3,000 direct labor hours were used in production), we see that the four-variance calculations would be as follows:

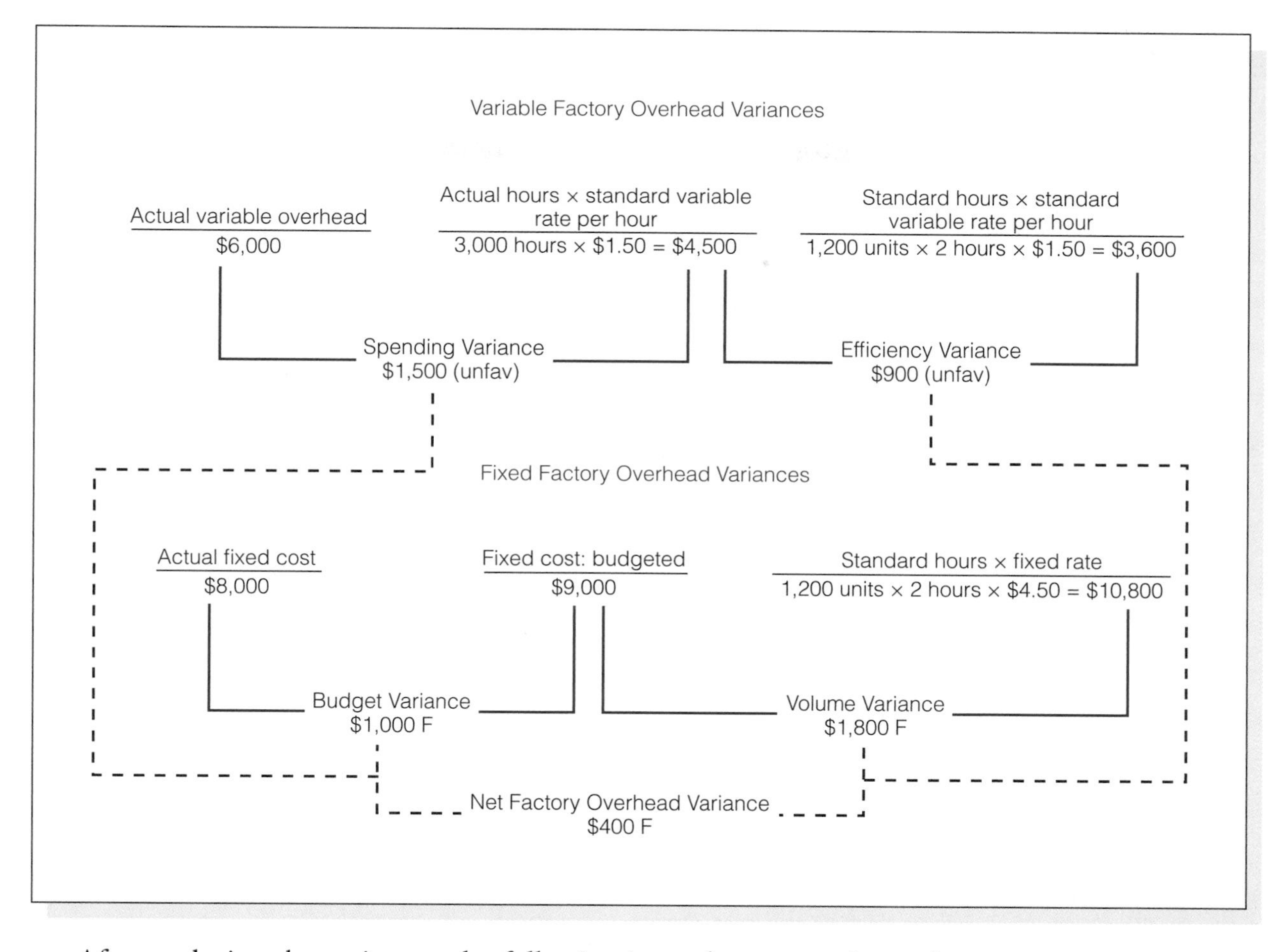

After analyzing the variances, the following journal entry can be made to record the variances and to close the factory overhead account:

Factory Overhead—Spending Variance	1,500	
Factory Overhead—Efficiency Variance	900	
Factory Overhead	400	
Factory Overhead—Budget Variance		1,000
Factory Overhead—Volume Variance		1,800
To close the factory overhead account and record variances.		

The four-variance method and the two-variance method result in the same net factory overhead variance—$400 favorable—which can be shown as follows:

Four-Variance Method		**Two-Variance Method**	
Variable cost:			
Spending variance—	$1,500 U	Controllable variance—	$1,400 U
Efficiency variance—	900 U		
Fixed cost:			
Budget variance—	1,000 F		
Volume variance—	1,800 F	Volume variance—	1,800 F
Net variance	$ 400 F		$ 400 F

Although the four-variance method identifies the fixed cost budget variance as originating from the differences between actual fixed cost expenditures and the amount of fixed cost budgeted, the controllable variance (two-variance method) considers the budget variance to be a variable cost and includes it as part of the total controllable variance. The controllable variance encompasses the spending, efficiency, and budget variances in one total variance. The volume variance amount is shown as a single, separate item by both methods.

Historically, most companies have used the two-variance method of analysis for factory overhead and have applied the factory overhead to production using a single rate that combines both the fixed and variable components. These companies consider it too costly from a clerical standpoint to apply separate fixed and variable rates to completed products while also maintaining separate factory overhead accounts for fixed and variable elements. The most valuable use of the four-variance method, however, is that it demonstrates the cost behavior patterns of fixed and variable costs when production volumes fluctuate. It is an excellent exercise in the study of cost behavior because it demonstrates the behavior patterns important in making management cost decisions that affect profitability. For companies that consider this additional information important, the computer age has made this type of data analysis much more cost effective.

Three-Variance Method of Analysis

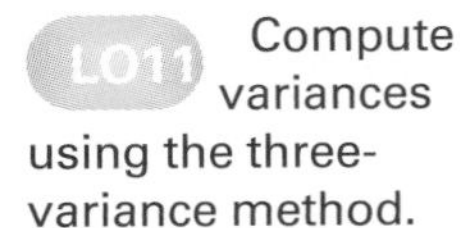

Compute variances using the three-variance method.

The **three-variance method** of factory overhead analysis, though not as common as the two-variance method, is frequently used by manufacturers. This method separates actual and applied overhead into three variances: (1) budget (spending), (2) capacity, and (3) efficiency.

The **budget variance**, or **spending variance**, reflects the difference between the actual costs of overhead and the budgeted amount calculated for the actual hours worked. The saving or overspending is chargeable to the manager or departmental supervisor responsible for the costs.

These budget variances should not be confused with those for the two-variance method. The calculations are different and result in a sharper distinction in variances. The primary difference between the two methods of variance analysis is that the three-variance method determines the budget allowances based on actual hours worked rather than on the standard number of hours allowed for the units produced.

The **capacity variance** indicates that the volume of production was either more or less than normal. It reflects an under- or overapplication of fixed costs and measures the difference between actual hours worked (multiplied by the standard overhead rate) and the budget allowance based on actual hours worked. This variance is considered the responsibility of management and can be due to expected seasonal variations or changes in the volume of production (caused by poor scheduling, improper use of labor, strikes, or other factors).

The **efficiency variance** measures the difference between the overhead applied (standard hours at the standard rate) and the actual hours worked multiplied by the standard rate. It shows the effect on fixed and variable overhead costs when the actual hours worked are either more or less than standard hours allowed for the production volume. Unfavorable variances may be caused by inefficiencies in the use of labor or by an excessive use of labor hours. Favorable efficiency variances indicate a more effective use of labor than was anticipated by the standards.

Many accountants feel that the budget allowance for overhead is more appropriate when the base used reflects actual labor hours rather than standard labor hours. They believe that a more definitive relationship exists between actual hours worked and factory expense involved and that the three-variance method provides a more precise analysis of overhead costs.

In the illustration that follows, the budget variance is unfavorable because the actual overhead exceeded the budget allowance. Again, the amount differs from the two-variance method because actual (rather than standard) hours are used to determine the budget amount. Note that a budget variance is calculated for the four-variance method, but it is specifically used to compare the fixed costs actually incurred for the period to the previously budgeted fixed costs. It is unfortunate that these variances have similar designations. The designations were not changed because both are widely accepted by accountants. These terms are rarely confused because they refer to different types of factory overhead analyses.

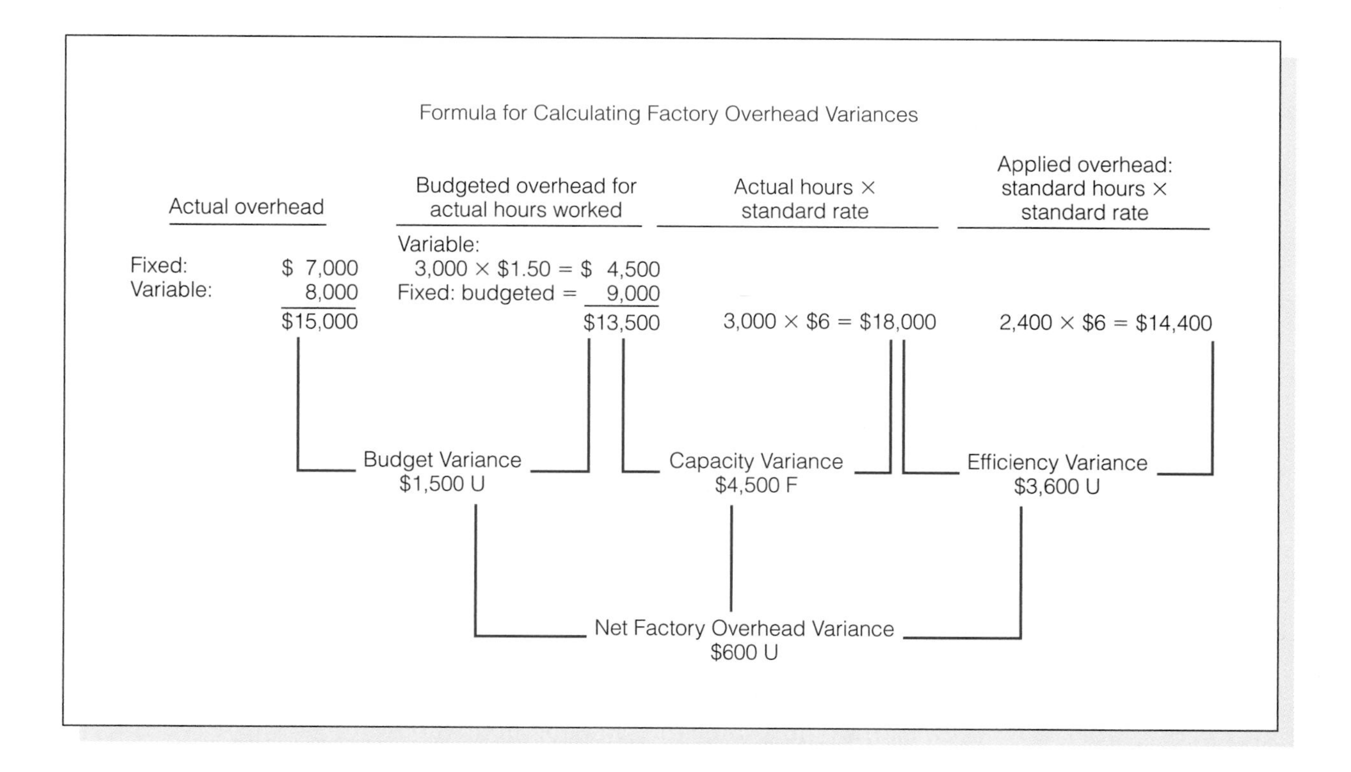

The efficiency variance, as illustrated, is unfavorable because the labor hours worked were more than the standard hours allowed for the level of production. In this case, the excess 600 hours multiplied by the standard overhead application rate of \$6 equals the variance of \$3,600 and reflects the underapplication of fixed and variable costs.

The new budget for overhead, based on the actual hours worked, is calculated by multiplying the actual hours worked by the variable rate for overhead (3,000 hours × \$1.50 per hour), amounting to \$4,500, and adding the expected fixed cost of \$9,000 for the period. The new budget for hours worked totals \$13,500. The capacity variance theoretically reflects the cost of unused plant facilities and involves mostly fixed costs. At 3,000 actual labor hours worked, \$13,500 (3,000 × \$4.50) of fixed cost was absorbed in Work in Process, \$4,500 more than the \$9,000 budgeted for fixed costs. This variance is similar to the volume variance under the two-variance method, but the amount differs because it is based on actual hours worked rather than on the standard hours allowed for 1,200 units.

For comparison purposes, the two-variance method would produce the following results:

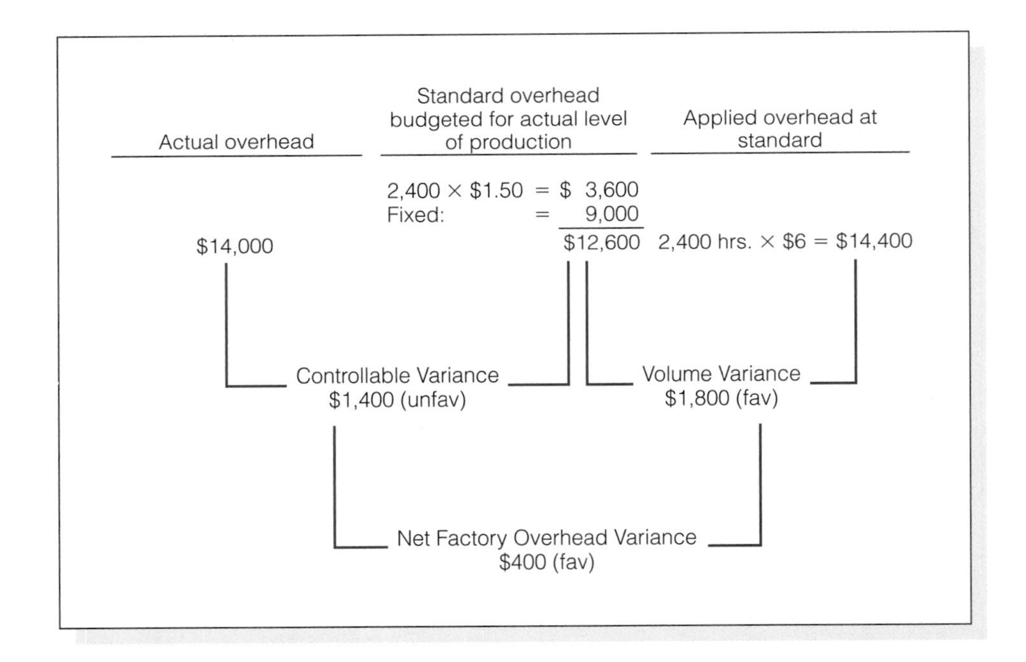

Whether the two-, three-, or four-variance method is used, the overhead applied to production is the same because the application is based on the standard number of labor hours allowed (for the actual production) multiplied by the standard rates established for overhead. Also, the actual overhead incurred would be the same in all cases. Therefore, the calculated net factory overhead variance (actual factory overhead − applied factory overhead) would also be the same for all methods.

Recall and Review 4

Calipari Plastics, Inc., budgets 16,000 direct labor hours for the year. The total overhead budget is expected to amount to $40,000. The standard cost for a unit of the company's product estimates the variable factory overhead as 3 hours @ $2 per direct labor hour, or $12 per unit. The actual data for the period is: actual completed units, 5,000; actual direct labor hours, 15,500; actual variable overhead, $32,000; and actual fixed overhead, $8,200. Using the four-variance method, we see that the spending variance is $__________, the efficiency variance is $__________, the budget variance is $__________, and the volume variance is $__________.

(After working this exercise, see page 418 for the solution.)

You should now be able to work the following:
Questions 26 and 27; Exercises 8-18 and 8-19; Problems 8-15 to 8-19; Review Problem 8-20R parts 4 (b) and (c); and Self-Study Problem 2 parts 4 (b) and (c).

KEY TERMS

Attainable standards, 381
Balanced scorecard, 384
Budget variance, 414
Capacity variance, 414
Controllable variance, 406
Efficiency variance, 415
Favorable variance, 386
Fixed overhead budget variance, 412
Fixed overhead volume variance, 412
Four-variance method, 412
Ideal standard, 381
Labor cost standard, 382
Labor efficiency (usage) variance, 386
Labor rate (price) variance, 386
Learning effect, 382
Management by exception, 380
Materials cost standard, 382
Materials price variance, 386
Materials purchase price variance, 388
Materials quantity (usage) variance, 386
Nonfinancial performance measures, 384
Price, 384
Spending variance, 414
Standard, 381
Standard cost accounting, 380
Three-variance method, 414
Two-variance method, 406
Unfavorable variance, 386
Usage, 384
Variable overhead efficiency variance, 412
Variable overhead spending variance, 412
Variance, 384
Volume variance, 407

ANSWERS TO RECALL AND REVIEW EXERCISES

R&R 1

Labor rate variance = 6,500 ($16 – $15) = $6,500 U

Labor efficiency variance = $15 [6,500 – (2,000 × 3)] = $7,500 U

Net labor variance = $6,500 U + $7,500 U = $14,000 U

R&R 2

Materials (5 lb per unit × $4 per lb)	$20.00
Labor (2 hrs per unit × $15 per hr)	30.00
Factory overhead ($450,000 / 15,000 units)	30.00
Standard cost per unit	$80.00

R&R 3

Actual overhead for the month	$30,000
Less unfavorable controllable variance	500
Budgeted overhead for actual production	$29,500

R&R 4

Computation of budgeted fixed overhead:

Total budgeted overhead	$40,000
Variable overhead (16,000 × $2)	32,000
Budgeted fixed overhead	$ 8,000

Variable overhead spending variance:

Actual variable overhead – (Actual hours × standard rate)
= $32,000 – (15,500 × $2)
= $1,000 favorable

Variable overhead efficiency variance:

= (Actual hours × Standard rate) – (Standard hours × Standard rate)
= (15,500 × $2) – (5,000 units × 3 hrs × $2)
= $1,000 unfavorable

Fixed overhead budget variance:

Actual fixed overhead – Budgeted fixed overhead
$8,200 – $8,000 = $200 unfavorable

Fixed overhead volume variance:

Budgeted fixed overhead – (Actual units × standard hrs × standard rate)
= $8,000 – (5,000 × 3 hrs × $.50*)
= $500 unfavorable

*$8,000/16,000 hrs = $.50 per direct labor hour

SELF-STUDY PROBLEM 1

Materials and Labor Variance Analyses

Cabrera Chemical Company

Cabrera Chemical Company manufactures one product and uses a standard cost system. The established standards for materials and labor follow:

Material A: 3 lb @ $6 per lb	$18
Labor: 4 hr @ $7.50 per hr	$30

The operating data for the month of May follow:

Work in process, May 1: 200 units, all materials, 20% complete as to labor.

Work in process, May 31: 600 units, all materials, 80% complete as to labor.

Completed during the month: 6,400 units.

All materials are added at the beginning of processing in the department.

20,900 pounds of materials were used in production during the month, at a total cost of $123,310. Direct labor amounted to $208,670, which was at a rate of $7.70 per hour.

Required:
Using the FIFO method of costing, calculate the following variances:
1. Materials quantity variance.
2. Materials price variance.
3. Labor efficiency variance.
4. Labor rate variance.

SOLUTION TO SELF-STUDY PROBLEM 1

The Specifics in the Problem Highlight the Following Facts:
In addition to the usual procedures used to solve standard cost problems, equivalent production (FIFO) must be calculated. The equivalent production determined by the FIFO method will be used to calculate the standard materials and standard labor allowed. Two variances (price and quantity) must be determined for materials, and two variances (rate and efficiency) must be determined for labor.

Calculating Equivalent Production for Materials and Labor by the FIFO Method:

	Units
Materials:	
Work in process, May 1: 200 units (all materials added last period)	-0-
Units started and finished during May (6,400 – 200)	6,200
Work in process, May 31: 600 units (all materials added)	600
Total equivalent production—materials	6,800

	Units
Labor:	
Work in process, May 1: 200 units (80% of labor required)	160
Units started and finished during May	6,200
Work in process, May 31: 600 units (80% labor added)	480
Total equivalent production—labor	6,840

Determining the Materials and Labor Variances:
Materials Variances

$$\text{Materials price variance} = (\text{Actual price} - \text{Standard price}) \times \text{Actual quantity}$$
$$= (\$5.90^{*} - \$6.00) \times 20{,}900 = \$2{,}090\ \text{F}$$
$$\text{Materials quantity variance} = (\text{Actual quantity} - \text{Standard quantity}) \times \text{Standard price}$$
$$= [20{,}900 - (6{,}800 \times 3)] \times \$6 = \$3{,}000\ \text{U}$$

*$123,310/$20,900 = $5.90 per pound

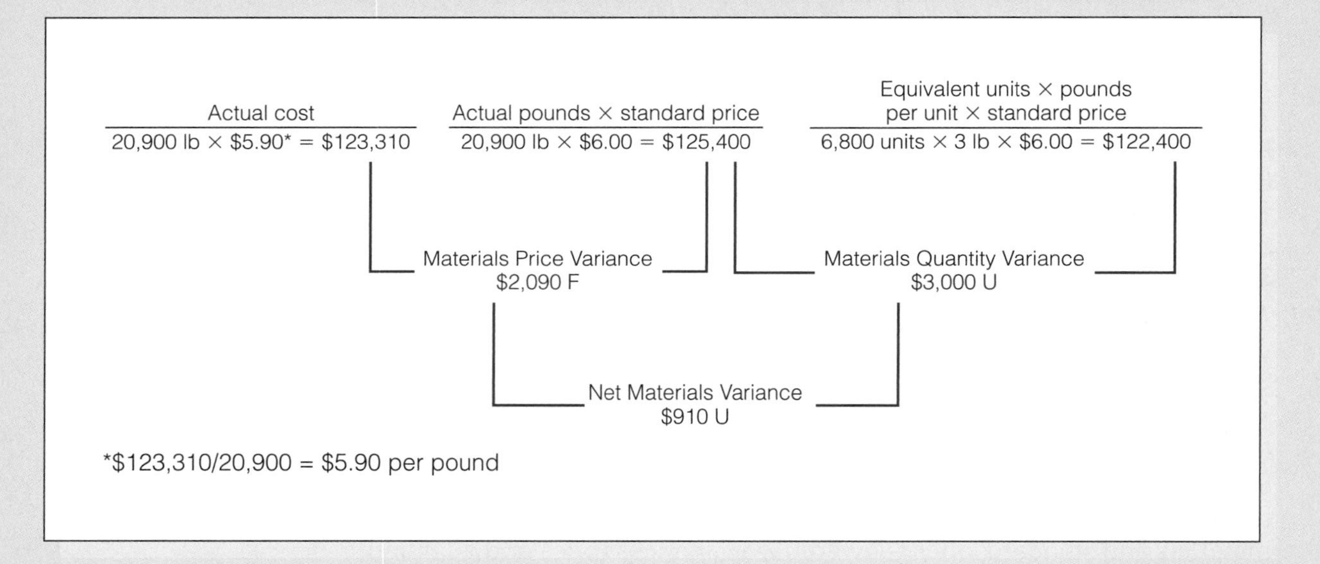

Labor Variances

$$\text{Labor rate variance} = (\text{Actual rate} - \text{Standard rate}) \times \text{Actual hours}$$
$$= (\$7.70 - \$7.50) \times 27{,}100^{*} = \$5{,}420\ \text{U}$$
$$\text{Labor efficiency variance} = (\text{Actual hours} - \text{Standard hours}) \times \text{Standard rate}$$
$$= [27{,}100 - (6{,}840 \times 4)] \times \$7.50 = \$1{,}950\ \text{F}$$

*$208,670/$7.70 = 27,100 hours

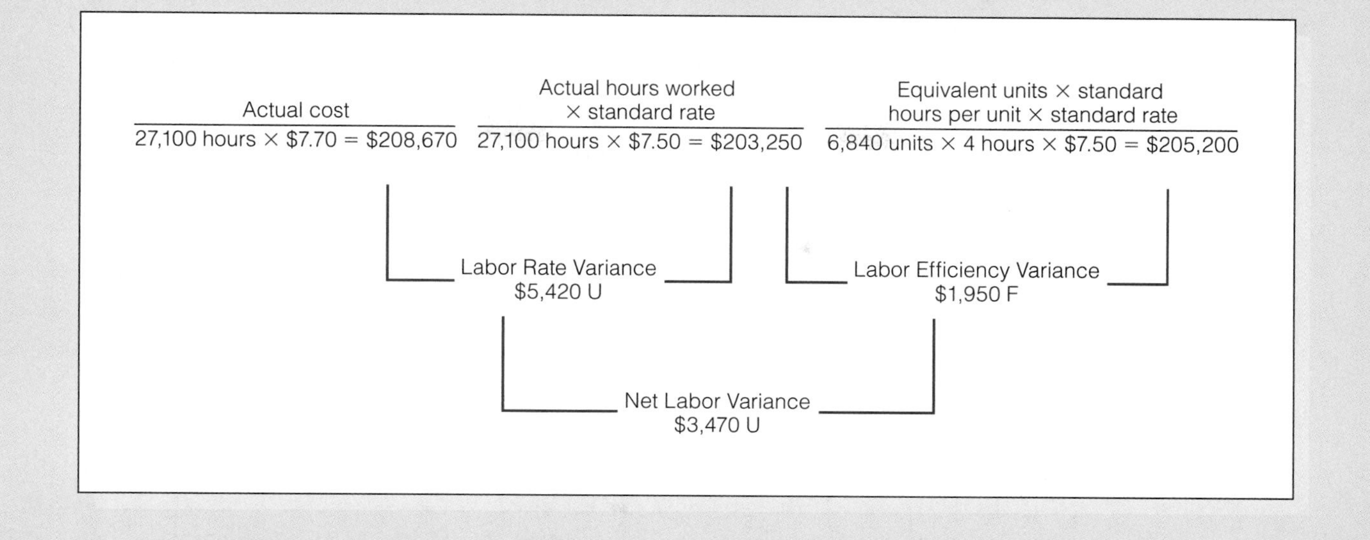

SELF-STUDY PROBLEM 2

Flexible Budgets; Two-, Three-, and Four-Variance Methods of Factory Overhead Analysis

Baton Rouge Manufacturing, Inc.

Baton Rouge manufactures a single product and uses a standard cost system. The factory overhead is applied on the basis of direct labor hours. A condensed version of the company's flexible budget follows:

Direct labor hours	20,000	25,000	40,000
Factory overhead costs:			
Variable costs	$ 40,000	$ 50,000	$ 80,000
Fixed costs	200,000	200,000	200,000
Total	$240,000	$250,000	$280,000

The product requires 3 pounds of materials at a standard cost per pound of $7 and 2 hours of direct labor at a standard cost of $6 per hour.

For the current year, the company planned to operate at 25,000 direct labor hours and to produce 12,500 units of product. Actual production and costs for the year follow:

Number of units produced	14,000
Actual direct labor hours worked	30,000
Actual variable overhead costs incurred	$ 52,000
Actual fixed overhead costs incurred	$208,000

Required:

1. Compute the factory overhead rate that will be used for production for the current year. Show the variable and fixed components that make up the total predetermined rate to be used.
2. Prepare a standard cost card for the product. Show the individual elements of the overhead rate as well as the total rate.
3. Compute (a) standard hours allowed for production and (b) under- or overapplied factory overhead for the year.
4. Determine the reason for any under- or overapplied factory overhead for the year by computing all variances, using each of the following methods:
   a. Two-variance method
   b. Three-variance method (appendix)
   c. Four-variance method (appendix)

SOLUTION TO SELF-STUDY PROBLEM 2

Compute the Factory Overhead Rate by Variable and Fixed Elements:

1. Show the total predetermined rate that will be used during the current year.

				Per DLH
Variable rate:				
Variable costs		$ 50,000	=	$ 2.00
Direct labor hours		25,000		
Fixed rate:				
Fixed costs		$200,000	=	8.00
Direct labor hours		25,000		
Total rate:				
Variable costs	$ 50,000			
Fixed costs	200,000			
Total costs		$250,000	=	$10.00
Direct labor hours		25,000		

2. Prepare a standard cost card for each unit of product.

Direct materials: 3 lb @ $7 per lb		$21.00
Direct labor: 2 hr @ $6 per hr		12.00
Factory overhead:		
Variable cost: 2 hr @ $2	$ 4.00	
Fixed cost: 2 hr @ $8	16.00	20.00
Standard cost per unit		$53.00

3. a. Compute the standard hours allowed for production for the year.

Actual units produced	14,000
Number of hours allowed by standard established for each unit of product ×	2
Total standard hours allowed	28,000

b. **Compute the under- or overapplied factory overhead for the year.**

Actual factory overhead incurred:	
Variable costs	$ 52,000
Fixed costs	208,000
Total actual overhead costs	$260,000
Factory overhead costs applied:	
Standard hours allowed × standard rate:	
28,000 hours × $10.00	280,000
Overapplied factory overhead	$ 20,000

4. Calculate the reason for the overapplied factory overhead by:

a. Two-variance method:

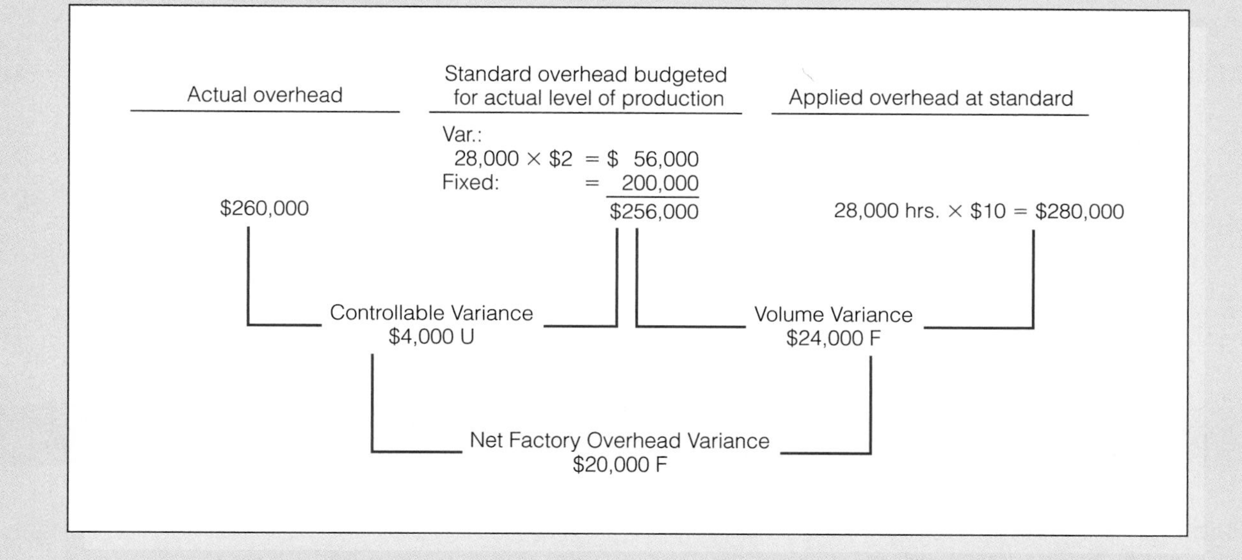

b. Three-variance method (appendix):

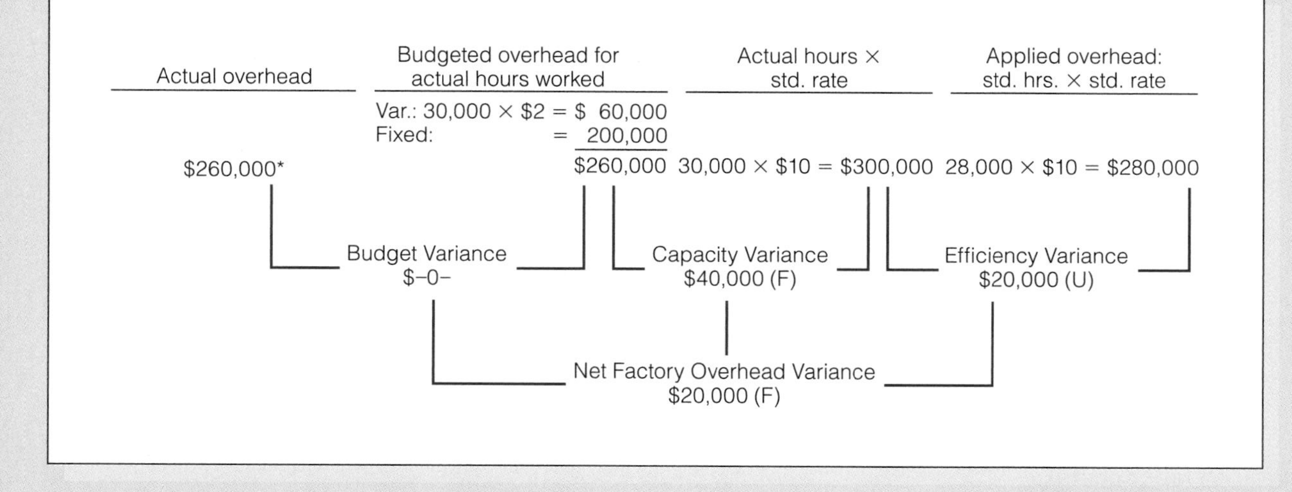

c. Four-variance method (appendix):

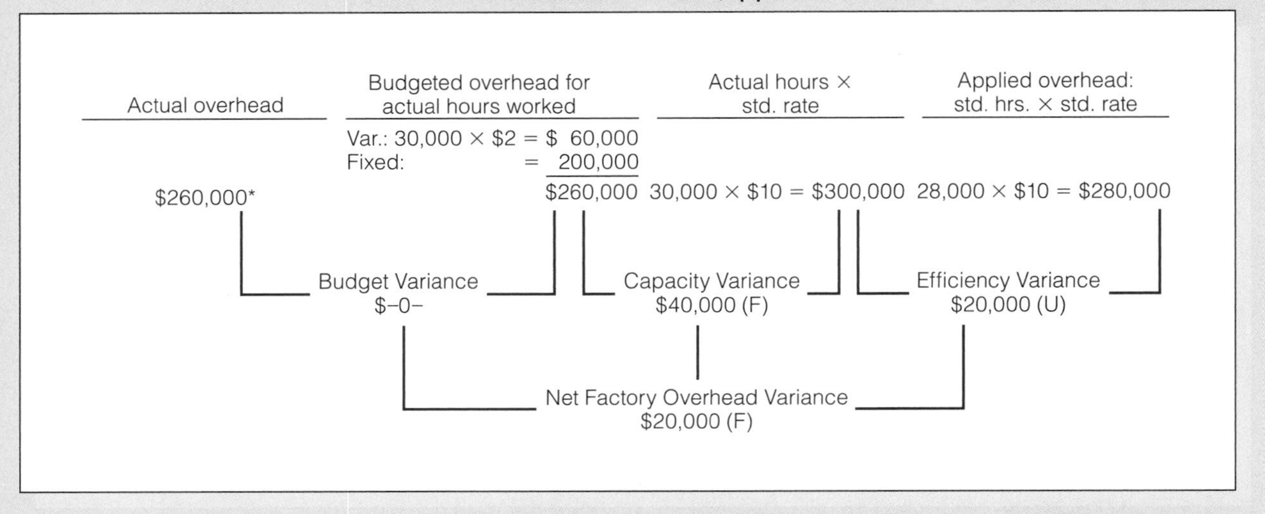

***** *These total costs represent actual hours × actual rates per hour. When the total cost is given, it is not necessary to determine the specific components that make up the total cost unless you do it to understand the formulas being used.*

QUESTIONS

1. How does a standard cost accounting system work, and why is it valuable to management?
2. What is the difference between the standard cost and the actual cost of production?
3. What is a "standard"? Give some examples such as those appearing in the chapter introduction.
4. What are the specific procedures on which a standard cost accounting system is based?
5. How are standards for materials and labor costs determined?
6. What is a variance?
7. How do price and quantity variances relate to materials costs?
8. How do rate and efficiency variances relate to labor costs?
9. Is a favorable variance "good" and an unfavorable variance "bad"? Explain.
10. How does a materials purchase price variance differ from a materials price variance.
11. When are variances usually recorded in the journals?
12. Are actual costs or standard costs charged to Work in Process?
13. When a company uses a standard cost system, are the inventory accounts—Finished Goods, Work in Process, and Materials—valued at actual cost or standard cost?
14. What two factors must be considered when breaking down a variance into its components? Explain.
15. What might cause the following materials variances?

a. An unfavorable materials price variance.
b. A favorable materials price variance.
c. An unfavorable materials quantity variance.
d. A favorable materials quantity variance.

16. What might cause the following labor variances?

a. An unfavorable labor rate variance.
b. A favorable labor rate variance.
c. An unfavorable labor efficiency variance.
d. A favorable labor efficiency variance.

17. Is it possible that a variance of one type might be partially or fully offset by another variance? Explain.

18. If, in a given period, the total actual cost of all materials used is exactly the same as the standard cost so that no net variance results, should the data be further analyzed? Explain.

19. At what amount is the entry made to transfer the cost of finished goods from the first department to a subsequent department in a standard cost system?

20. What is a controllable variance?

21. Why is it important to determine controllable variances?

22. What is a volume variance?

23. What is the significance of a volume variance?

24. If production is more or less than the standard volume, is it possible that no controllable or volume variances would exist? Explain.

25. At the end of the current fiscal year, the trial balance of Flatbush Corporation revealed the following debit (unfavorable) balances:

Controllable Variance—$2,000
Volume Variance—$75,000

What conclusions can be drawn from these two variances?

26. What variances from the four-variance method are included in the controllable variance from the two-variance method? (appendix)

27. What is the primary difference between the two-variance and three-variance methods of calculation? (appendix)

EXERCISES

In all of the exercises involving variances, use "F" and "U" to designate favorable and unfavorable variances, respectively.

E8-1 through E8-5 use the following data:
The standard operating capacity of Tecate Manufacturing Co. is 1,000 units. A detailed study of the manufacturing data relating to the standard production cost of one product revealed the following:

1. Two pounds of materials are needed to produce one unit.
2. Standard unit cost of materials is $8 per pound.
3. It takes one hour of labor to produce one unit.
4. Standard labor rate is $10 per hour.
5. Standard overhead for this volume is $4,000.

Each case in E8-1 through E8-5 requires the following:
a. Set up a standard cost summary showing the standard unit cost.
b. Analyze the variances for materials and labor.

c. Make journal entries to record the transfer to Work in Process of:
   1. Materials costs
   2. Labor costs
   3. Overhead costs

   When making these entries, include the variances.

d. Prepare the journal entry to record the transfer of costs to the finished goods account.

LO2 LO3 LO4

E8-1 Standard unit cost; variance analysis; journal entries

1,000 units were started and finished.

Case 1: All prices and quantities for the cost elements are standard, except for materials cost, which is $8.50 per pound.
Case 2: All prices and quantities for the cost elements are standard, except that 1,900 pounds of materials were used.

LO2 LO3 LO4

E8-2 Standard unit cost; variance analysis; journal entries

1,000 units were started and finished.

Case 1:.All prices and quantities are standard, except for the labor rate, which is $10.20 per hour.
Case 2: All prices and quantities are standard, except for labor hours, which totaled 900.

LO2 LO3 LO4

E8-3 Computing standard unit cost; variance analysis; journal entries

All of the deviations listed in E8-1 and E8-2 took place, and 1,000 units were started and finished. (Note that the quantities used will affect the rate variances for both materials and labor.)

LO2 LO3 LO4

E8-4 Standard unit cost; variance analysis; journal entries

All of the deviations listed in E8-1 and E8-2 took place, and 900 units were started and finished.

LO2 LO3 LO4

E8-5 Standard unit cost; variance analysis; journal entries

All of the deviations listed in E8-1 and E8-2 took place, and 1,100 units were started and finished.

LO3

E8-6 Computing materials variances

D-List Calendar Company specializes in manufacturing calendars that depict obscure comedians. The company uses a standard cost system to control its costs. During one month of operations, the direct materials costs and the quantities of paper used showed the following:

Actual purchase price	$0.175 per page
Standard quantity allowed for production	170,000 pages

Actual quantity purchased during month	200,000 pages
Actual quantity used during month	185,000 pages
Standard price per page	$0.17 per page

Calculate the following variances:

1. Total cost of purchases for the month
2. Materials price variance
3. Materials quantity variance
4. Net materials variance

LO3

E8-7 **Computing labor variances**

Overhead Doors, Inc., manufactures garage doors for homes. The standard quantity of direct labor to manufacture a door is 4.5 hours. The standard hourly wage in this department is $12.50 per hour. During August, 6,100 doors were produced. The payroll records indicate that 31,110 hours were worked at a total cost for payroll of $411,274.20.

Calculate the following, using the "goalpost" diagram format shown in Figure 8-4 to compute variances:

1. Labor rate variance.
2. Labor efficiency variance.
3. Net labor variance.

LO2

LO3

E8-8 **Standard cost summary; materials and labor cost variances**

AACSB Processors, Inc., produces an average of 10,000 units each month. The factory standards are 20,000 hours of direct labor and 10,000 pounds of materials for this volume. The standard cost of direct labor is $9.00 per hour, and the standard cost of materials is $4.00 per pound. The standard factory overhead at this level of production is $20,000.

During the current month the production and cost reports reflected the following information:

Beginning units in process	None
Units finished	9,500
Units in process, end of month	None
Direct labor hours worked	20,000
Pounds of material purchased	10,000
Pounds of materials used	9,400
Cost of direct labor	$178,000
Cost of materials purchased	$ 42,000

On the basis of this information:

1. Prepare a standard cost summary.
2. Calculate the materials (use the materials purchase price variance) and labor cost variances, and indicate whether they are favorable or unfavorable, using the formulas on page 386.

E8-9 Computing labor variances

Fill in the missing figures for each of the following independent cases:

	Case 1	Case 2
Units produced	1,200	?
Standard hours per unit	2	0.6
Standard hours allowed	?	1,200
Standard rate per hour	$ 5	?
Actual hours used	2,340	1,220
Actual labor cost	?	?
Labor rate variance	$725 U	$290 U
Labor efficiency variance	?	$ 40 U

(Round all rates to the nearest cent and all totals to the nearest dollar.)

E8-10 Preparing a standard cost summary and making journal entries

The normal capacity of Austin Adhesives, Inc., is 40,000 direct labor hours and 20,000 units per month. A finished unit requires 6 pounds of materials at an estimated cost of $2 per pound. The estimated cost of labor is $10.00 per hour. The plant estimates that overhead for a month will be $40,000.

During the month of March, the plant totaled 34,800 direct labor hours at an average rate of $9.50 an hour. The plant produced 18,000 units, using 105,000 pounds of materials at a cost of $2.04 per pound.

1. Prepare a standard cost summary showing the standard unit cost.
2. Make journal entries to charge materials and labor to Work in Process.

E8-11 Making journal entries

Assume that during the month of April the production report of Austin Adhesives, Inc., in E8-10 revealed the following information:

Units produced during the month	21,000
Direct labor hours for the month	41,000
Materials purchased (in pounds)	130,000
Materials used (in pounds)	125,000
Labor rate per hour	$10.04
Materials cost per pound	$ 1.98

Make journal entries to charge materials (use the materials purchase price variance) and labor to Work in Process. (Remember to retrieve the standard costs from E8-10 before solving this exercise.)

E8-12 **Using variance analysis and interpretation**

Last year, Tri-Rivers Corporation adopted a standard cost system. Labor standards were set on the basis of time studies and prevailing wage rates. Materials standards were determined from materials specifications and the prices then in effect.

On June 30, the end of the current fiscal year, a partial trial balance revealed the following:

	Debit	Credit
Materials Price Variance	25,000	
Materials Quantity Variance		9,000
Labor Rate Variance		30,000
Labor Efficiency Variance		7,500

Standards set at the beginning of the year have remained unchanged. All inventories are priced at standard cost. What conclusions can be drawn from each of the four variances shown in Tri-Rivers' trial balance?

E8-13 **Journalizing standard costs in two departments**

LO7

Marblehead Manufacturing, Inc., has two departments, Mixing and Blending. When goods are completed in Mixing, they are transferred to Blending and then to the finished goods storeroom. There was no beginning or ending work in process in either department. Listed below is information to be used in preparing journal entries at the end of October:

Standard cost of direct materials for actual production—Mixing	$ 185,000
Actual cost of direct materials used in production—Mixing	177,000
Materials price variance—Mixing	10,000 F
Materials quantity variance—Mixing	2,000 U
Standard cost of direct materials for actual production—Blending	130,000
Actual cost of direct materials used in production—Blending	136,000
Materials price variance—Blending	4,000 U
Materials quantity variance—Blending	2,000 U
Standard cost of direct labor for actual production—Mixing	110,000
Actual cost of direct labor used in production—Mixing	103,000
Labor rate variance—Mixing	10,000 F
Labor efficiency variance—Mixing	3,000 U
Standard cost of direct labor for actual production—Blending	95,000
Actual cost of direct labor used in production—Blending	110,000
Labor rate variance—Blending	8,000 U
Labor efficiency variance—Blending	7,000 U
Actual factory overhead	145,000
Factory overhead applied—Mixing	85,000
Factory overhead applied—Blending	70,000

Prepare journal entries for the following:

1. The issuance of direct materials into production and the recording of the materials variances.
2. The use of direct labor in production and the recording of the labor variances.
3. The entries to record the actual and applied factory overhead.
4. The entries to transfer the production costs from Mixing to Blending and from Blending to finished goods.

LO8

E8-14 Calculating factory overhead

The standard capacity of a factory is 8,000 units per month. Cost and production data follow:

Standard application rate for fixed overhead	$0.50 per unit
Standard application rate for variable overhead ...	$1.50 per unit
Production—Month 1	7,400 units
Production—Month 2	8,200 units
Actual factory overhead—Month 1	$15,100
Actual factory overhead—Month 2	$17,200

Calculate the amount of factory overhead allowed for the actual volume of production each month and the variance between budgeted and actual overhead for each month.

LO8 LO9

E8-15 Calculating factory overhead: two variances

Missoula Manufacturing Company normally produces 10,000 units of product X each month. Each unit requires 2 hours of direct labor, and factory overhead is applied on a direct labor hour basis. Fixed costs and variable costs in factory overhead at the normal capacity are $5 and $3 per unit, respectively. Cost and production data for May follow:

Production for the month	9,000 units
Direct labor hours used	18,500 hours
Factory overhead incurred for:	
Variable costs	$28,500
Fixed costs	$52,000

a. Calculate the controllable variance.
b. Calculate the volume variance.
c. Was the total factory overhead under- or overapplied? By what amount?

LO8 LO9

E8-16 Making journal entries for factory overhead and variances; analysis of variances

The normal capacity of a manufacturing plant is 30,000 direct labor hours or 20,000 units per month. Standard fixed costs are $6,000, and variable costs are $12,000. Data for two months follow:

	June	July
Units produced	18,000	21,000
Factory overhead incurred	$17,300	$20,800

For each month, make a single journal entry to charge overhead to Work in Process, to close Factory Overhead, and to record variances. Indicate the types of variances and state whether each is favorable or unfavorable. (*Hint:* You must first compute the controllable and volume variances.)

E8-17 **Calculating amount of factory overhead applied to work in process**
The overhead application rate for a company is $2.50 per unit, made up of $1.00 for fixed overhead and $1.50 for variable overhead. Normal capacity is 10,000 units. In one month, there was an unfavorable controllable variance of $200. Actual overhead for the month was $27,000. What was the amount of the budgeted overhead for the actual level of production?

LO8 LO9

E8-18 **(Appendix) Calculating factory overhead: four variances**
Georgia Gasket Company budgets 8,000 direct labor hours for the year. The total overhead budget is expected to amount to $20,000. The standard cost for a unit of the company's product estimates the variable overhead as follows:

LO10

Variable factory overhead (3 hours @ $2 per direct labor hour)	$6 per unit

The actual data for the period follow:

Actual completed units	2,500
Actual direct labor hours	7,640
Actual variable overhead	$16,100
Actual fixed overhead	3,920

Using the four-variance method, calculate the overhead variances. (*Hint:* First compute the budgeted fixed overhead rate.)

E8-19 **(Appendix) Calculating factory overhead: three variances**
Using the data shown in E8-15, calculate the following overhead variances:

LO11

a. Budget variance.
b. Capacity variance.
c. Efficiency variance.
d. Was the factory overhead under- or overapplied? By what amount?

PROBLEMS

In all problems involving variances, use "F" and "U" to indicate favorable and unfavorable variances, respectively.

P8-1 **Materials and labor variances**
Ichiro Inspections, Inc., specializes in determining whether a building or house's drain pipes are properly tied into the city's sewer system. The company pours colored chemical through the

LO3

pipes and collects an inspection sample from each outlet, which is then analyzed. Each job should take 15 hours for each of four inspectors, who are paid $18 per hour. Each job uses 5 gallons of Brite (a colored chemical), which should cost $25 per gallon. Data from the company's most recent job (a building) follow:

5 men worked a total of 80 hours and were paid $17.50 per hour ...	$1,400.00
5.5 gallons of Brite were used and cost $27.50 per gallon	151.25
Total cost of the job	$1,551.25

Required:

Compute the following variances, using the formulas on page 386:

1. Materials price and quantity variances.
2. Labor rate and efficiency variances.

P8-2 LO3 **Materials and labor variances**

Folsom Fabricators, Inc., uses a standard cost system to account for its single product. The standards established for the product include the following:

Materials	8 lb @ $0.50 per lb
Labor	6 hr @ $8.00 per hr

The following operating data came from the records for the month:

In process, beginning inventory, none.

In process, ending inventory, 800 units, 80% complete as to labor; material is issued at the beginning of processing.

Completed during the month, 5,600 units.

Materials issued to production were 51,680 pounds @ $0.55 per pound.

Direct labor was $304,000 at the rate of $7.60 per hour.

Required:

Calculate the following variances, using the diagram format in Figure 8-4.

1. Materials price.
2. Materials quantity.
3. Net materials variance.
4. Labor rate.
5. Labor efficiency.
6. Net labor variance.

(*Hint:* Before determining the standard quantity for materials and labor, you must first compute the equivalent units for materials and labor.)

P8-3 LO3 **Materials and labor variances analyses**

Accelerator, Inc., manufactures a fuel additive, Surge, that has a stable selling price of $44 per drum. The company has been producing and selling 80,000 drums per month.

In connection with your examination of Accelerator's financial statements for the year ended September 30, management has asked you to review some computations made by Accelerator's cost accountant. Your working papers disclose the following about the company's operations:

Standard costs per drum of product manufactured:

Materials:		
8 gallons of chemicals @ $2	$16	
1 empty drum	1	$17
Direct labor—1 hour		$ 8
Factory Overhead		$ 6

Costs and expenses during September:

Chemicals: 645,000 gallons purchased at a cost of $1,140,000; 600,000 gallons used.

Empty drums: 94,000 purchased at a cost of $94,000; 80,000 drums used.

Direct labor: 81,000 hours worked at a cost of $654,480.
Factory overhead: $768,000.

Required:
Calculate the following variances for September, using the formulas on page 386:

1. Materials quantity variance.
2. Materials purchase price variance.
3. Labor efficiency variance.
4. Labor rate variance.

P8-4 Calculation of materials and labor variances

LO3

Prado Corporation manufactures and sells a single product. The company uses a standard cost system. The standard cost per unit of product follows:

Materials—1 lb plastic @ $3.00	$ 3.00
Direct labor—1.6 hr @ $10.00	16.00
Factory overhead	4.45
Total	$23.45

The charges to the manufacturing department for November, when 5,000 units were produced, follow:

Materials—5,300 lb @ $3.00	$ 15,900
Direct labor—8,200 hr @ $9.80	80,360
Factory overhead	23,815
Total	$120,075

The purchasing department normally buys about the same quantity as is used in production during a month. In November, 5,500 pounds were purchased at a price of $2.90 per pound.

Required:
Calculate the following variances from standard costs for the data given, using the formulas on pages 386:
1. Materials quantity.
2. Materials purchase price (at time of purchase).
3. Labor efficiency.
4. Labor rate.

P8-5 LO3

Analysis of materials and labor variances
Stylized Products, Inc., uses a standard cost system in accounting for the cost of production of its only product, Suave. The standards for the production of one unit of Suave follow:

Direct materials: 10 feet of Class at $0.75 per foot and 3 feet of Chic at $1.00 per foot.
Direct labor: 4 hours at $8.00 per hour.
Factory overhead: applied at 150% of standard direct labor costs.

There was no beginning inventory on hand at July 1. Following is a summary of costs and related data for the production of Suave during the following year ended June 30:

100,000 feet of Class were purchased at $0.72 per foot.
30,000 feet of Chic were purchased at $1.05 per foot.
8,000 units of Suave were produced that required 78,000 feet of Class; 26,000 feet of Chic; and 31,000 hours of direct labor at $7.80 per hour.
6,000 units of product Suave were sold.

On June 30, there are 22,000 feet of Class, 4,000 feet of Chic, and 2,000 completed units of Suave on hand. All purchases and transfers are "charged in" at standard.

Required:
Calculate the following, using the formulas on page 386:
1. Materials quantity variance for Class.
2. Materials quantity variance for Chic.
3. Materials purchase price variance for Class.
4. Materials purchase price variance for Chic.
5. Labor efficiency variance.
6. Labor rate variance.

P8-6 LO3

Analysis of materials and labor variances
TBA Products Company manufactures a variety of products made of plastic and aluminum components. During the winter months, substantially all of the production capacity is devoted to the production of lawn sprinklers for the following spring and summer seasons. Other products are manufactured during the remainder of the year.

The company has developed standard costs for its several products. Standard costs for each year are set in the preceding October. The standard cost of a sprinkler for the current year is $3.70, computed as follows:

Direct materials:	
Aluminum—0.2 lb @ $0.40 per lb	$0.08
Plastic—1.0 lb @ $0.38 per lb	0.38

Production labor—0.3 hr @ $8.00 per hr	2.40
Factory overhead	0.84
Total	$3.70

During February, TBA Products manufactured 8,500 good sprinklers. The company incurred the following costs, which it charged to production:

Materials requisitioned for production:	
Aluminum—1,900 lb @ $0.40 per lb	$ 760
Plastic—Regular grade—6,000 lb @ $0.38 per lb	2,280
Low grade—3,500 lb @ $0.38 per lb	1,330
Production labor—2,700 hr @ $8.60 per hr	23,220
Factory overhead	7,140
Costs charged to production	$34,730

Materials price variations are not determined by usage but are charged to a materials price variation account at the time the invoice is entered. All materials are carried in inventory at standard prices. Materials purchases for February were as follows:

Aluminum—1,800 lb @ $0.48 per lb	$ 864
Plastic—Regular grade—3,000 lb @ $0.50 per lb	1,500
Low grade*—6,000 lb @ $0.29 per lb	1,740

*Due to plastic shortages, the company was forced to purchase lower grade plastic than called for in the standards. This increased the number of sprinklers rejected on inspection.

Required:

Calculate price and usage variances for each type of material and for labor, using the formulas on page 386.

P8-7 Materials and labor variance analyses similar to Self-Study Problem 1

LO3 LO5

The standard cost summary for the most popular product of Phase-Five Products Company is shown as follows, together with production and cost data for the period.

Standard Cost Summary

Materials:		
2 gallons of liquid lead @ $2.00	$4.00	
2 gallons of varnish @ $3.00	6.00	$10.00
Labor:		
1 hour @ $12.00		12.00
Factory overhead:		
$1.00 per direct labor hour		1.00
Total standard unit cost		$23.00

Production and Cost Summary

Units completed during the month	9,000
Ending units in process (one-fourth completed)	2,000
Gallons of liquid lead used	21,000
Gallons of varnish used	20,000
Direct labor hours worked	10,000
Cost of liquid lead used	$ 41,160
Cost of varnish used	$ 60,000
Cost of direct labor	$117,000

One gallon each of liquid lead and varnish are added at the start of processing. The balance of the materials is added when the process is two-thirds complete. Labor and overhead are added evenly throughout the process.

Required:

1. Calculate equivalent production. (Be sure to refer to the standard cost summary to help determine the percentage of materials in ending work in process.)
2. Calculate materials and labor variances and indicate whether they are favorable or unfavorable, using the diagram format shown in Figure 8-4.
3. Determine the cost of materials and labor in the work in process account at the end of the month.
4. Prove that all materials and labor costs have been accounted for. (*Hint:* Don't forget the net variances in reconciling the costs accounted for with the costs to be accounted for.)

P8-8 LO4 **Journal entries for materials and labor variances**

Suzy-Q Corporation has established the following standard cost per unit:

Materials—5.5 lb @ $2.20 per lb	$12.10
Labor—1.8 hr @ $6.25 per hr	11.25

Although 10,000 units were budgeted, only 8,800 units were produced.

The purchasing department bought 55,000 pounds of materials at a cost of $123,750. Actual pounds of materials used were 54,305. Direct labor cost was $127,400 for 18,200 hours worked.

Required:

1. Make journal entries to record the materials transactions, assuming that the materials price variance was recorded at the time of purchase.
2. Make journal entries to record the labor variances.

P8-9 LO4 LO5 **Allocation of variances**

Newport Beach Manufacturing Corporation uses a standard cost system that records raw materials at actual cost, records materials price variances at the time that raw materials are issued to work in process, and prorates all variances at year-end. Variances associated with direct materials are prorated based on the direct materials balances in the appropriate accounts, and variances associated with direct labor are prorated based on the direct labor balances in the appropriate accounts. The following information is available for Newport Beach for the year ended December 31:

Raw materials inventory at December 31	$ 65,000
Finished goods inventory at December 31:	
Direct materials	87,000
Direct labor	130,500
Applied factory overhead	104,400
Cost of goods sold for the year ended December 31:	
Direct materials	348,000
Direct labor	739,500
Applied factory overhead	591,600
Materials quantity variance (favorable)	15,000
Materials price variance (unfavorable)	10,000
Labor efficiency variance (favorable)	5,000
Labor rate variance (unfavorable)	20,000
Factory overhead applied	696,000

There were no beginning inventories and no ending work in process inventory.

Required:

Calculate the following:

1. Amount of materials price variance to be prorated to finished goods inventory at December 31. (*Hint:* You must first determine the ratio of direct materials cost in the ending finished goods inventory.)
2. Total amount of direct materials cost in the finished goods inventory at December 31, after all variances have been prorated.
3. Total amount of direct labor cost in the finished goods inventory at December 31, after all variances have been prorated.
4. Total cost of goods sold for the year ended December 31, after all variances have been prorated.

P8-10 Analyses; review of chapter

LO2 LO3 LO8

On May 1, Maximus Company began the manufacture of a new mechanical device known as Caesar. The company installed a standard cost system in accounting for manufacturing costs. The standard costs for a unit of Caesar follow:

Raw materials (5 lb @ $1 per lb)	$ 5
Direct labor (1 hr @ $8 per hr)	8
Overhead (50% of direct labor costs)	4
	$17

The following data came from Maximus's records for the month of May:

	Units
Actual production	4,000
Units sold	2,500

	Debit	Credit
Sales		$50,000
Purchases (22,000 pounds)	$23,300	
Materials price variance	1,300	
Materials quantity variance	1,000	
Direct labor rate variance	770	
Direct labor efficiency variance		1,200
Manufacturing overhead total variance	500	

The amount shown above for the materials price variance is applicable to raw materials purchased during May.

Required:
Compute each of the following items for Maximus for the month of May. Show computations in good form.

1. Standard quantity of raw materials allowed (in pounds) for actual production.
2. Actual quantity of raw materials used (in pounds). (*Hint:* Be sure to consider the materials quantity variance.)
3. Standard direct labor hours allowed.
4. Actual direct labor hours worked.
5. Actual direct labor rate. (*Hint:* Be sure to consider the direct labor rate variance.)
6. Actual total overhead.

P8-11 Two-variance overhead analysis

LO8 LO9

The standard specifications for an electric motor manufactured by B&B Electric Corporation follow:

Standard cost per unit:	
Materials (2 lb × $5 per lb)	$10.00
Labor (4 hr × $6 per hr)	24.00
Factory overhead (4 hr × $3.38* per hr)	13.52
Total standard cost	$47.52

*$1.00 variable + $2.38 fixed = $3.38

Factory overhead rates are based on a normal 70% capacity and use the following flexible budget:

	Normal 70%	85%	100%
Motors to be produced	2,100	2,550	3,000
Variable overhead	$ 8,400	$10,200	$12,000
Fixed overhead	$20,000	$20,000	$20,000

The actual production was 2,500 motors, and factory overhead costs totaled $29,750.

Required:
Calculate the factory overhead variances using the two-variance method.

P8-12 Journal entries; variance analysis; other analyses; review of chapter

Cost and production data for Gigante Products Company follow:

LO8 LO9

Standard Cost Sheet (Normal capacity—1,000 units)

			Mixing	Blending	Total
Materials:					
I—2 lb @ $2 per lb			$ 4		
II—2 lb @ $1 per lb				$ 2	$ 6
Labor:					
2 hr @ $5 per hr			10		
1 hr @ $6 per hr				6	16
Factory overhead (per standard labor hour):					
Fixed	Variable				
$2	$1	(2 hr per unit)	6		
1	3	(1 hr per unit)		4	10
Total			$20	$12	$32

Production Report

	Mixing	Blending
Beginning units in process	None	None
Units finished and transferred	1,000	900
Ending units in process	200	100
Stage of completion	1/2	1/2

Actual Cost Data

	Mixing		Blending	
Direct materials used:				
I—2,300 lb		$4,715		
II—1,850 lb				$1,813
Direct labor:				
2,150 hr		10,965		
1,000 hr				5,900
Factory overhead:				
Indirect materials	$1,000		$ 500	
Indirect labor	1,300		1,000	
Other (fixed costs)	4,400	6,700	2,250	3,750
Total		$22,380		$11,463

During the month, 850 units were sold at $60 each.
Note: Materials, labor, and overhead are added evenly throughout the process.

Required:

1. Make general journal entries to record all transactions and variances. Use the two-variance method for overhead variance analysis. (*Hint:* You must first compute equivalent units and the variances for materials, labor, and factory overhead.)
2. Prove the ending balances of Work in Process in both departments.
3. Prove that all costs have been accounted for. (*Hint:* Remember to include the variances in the "Costs accounted for" section.)

P8-13 **Variance analysis**

LO5 LO9

Poway Shirts, Inc., manufactures men's sport shirts for large stores. Folsom produces a single quality shirt in lots of a dozen according to each customer's order and attaches the store's label. The standard costs for a dozen shirts include the following:

Direct materials	24 yards @ $0.55	$13.20
Direct labor	3 hours @ $7.35	22.05
Factory overhead	3 hours @ $2.00	6.00
Standard cost per dozen		$41.25

During October, Poway worked on three orders for shirts. Job cost records for the month disclose the following:

Lot	Units in Lot	Materials Used	Hours Worked
30	1,000 dozen	24,100 yards	2,980
31	1,700 dozen	40,440 yards	5,130
32	1,200 dozen	28,825 yards	2,890

The following information is also available:

a. Poway purchased 95,000 yards of materials during October at a cost of $53,200. The materials price variance is recorded when goods are purchased, and all inventories are carried at standard cost.
b. Direct labor incurred amounted to $81,400 during October. According to payroll records, production employees were paid $7.40 per hour.
c. Overhead is applied on the basis of direct labor hours. Factory overhead totaling $22,800 was incurred during October.
d. A total of $288,000 was budgeted for overhead for the year, based on estimated production at the plant's normal capacity of 48,000 dozen shirts per year. Overhead is 60% fixed and 40% variable at this level of production.
e. There was no work in process at October 1. During October, Lots 30 and 31 were completed, and all materials were issued for Lot 32, which was 80% completed as to labor and overhead.

Required:

1. Prepare a schedule computing the October standard cost of Lots 30, 31, and 32.
2. Prepare a schedule computing the materials price variance for October and indicate whether it is favorable or unfavorable.
3. For each lot produced during October, prepare schedules computing the following (indicate whether favorable or unfavorable):
   a. Materials quantity variance in yards.
   b. Labor efficiency variance in hours. (*Hint:* Don't forget the percentage of completion.)
   c. Labor rate variance in dollars.
4. Prepare a schedule computing the total controllable and volume overhead variances for October and indicate whether they are favorable or unfavorable.

P8-14 Materials, labor, and overhead variances—two-variance method

LO8 LO9

Fargo Company manufactures products in batches of 100 units per batch. The company uses a standard cost system and prepares budgets that call for 500 of these batches per period. Fixed overhead is $60,000 per period. The standard costs per batch follow:

Material (80 gallons)	$ 32
Labor (60 hours)	480
Factory overhead	252
Standard cost per batch	$764

During the period, 503 batches were manufactured, and the following costs were incurred:

Materials used (40,743 gallons)	$ 15,482.34
Labor (29,677 hours at $8.65 per hour)	256,706.05
Actual variable overhead	67,080.00
Actual fixed overhead	60,500.00

Required:

Calculate the variances for materials, labor, and overhead. For overhead, use the two-variance method.

P8-15 (Appendix) All variances; four variances for factory overhead

LO10

Metropolis Manufacturing Company manufactures a small electric motor that is a replacement part for the more popular gas furnaces. The standard cost card shows the product requirements as follows:

Direct materials—2 lb @ $4 per lb	$ 8.00
Direct labor—5 hr @ $8 per hr	40.00
Factory overhead:	
Variable cost—5 hr @ $2 per hr	10.00
Fixed cost—5 hr @ $4 per hr	20.00
Total standard cost per unit	$78.00

Factory overhead rates are based on normal 100% capacity and the following flexible budgets:

	90%	Normal 100%	110%
Units produced	2,500	3,000	3,500
Factory overhead—variable	$25,000	$30,000	$35,000
Factory overhead—fixed	$60,000	$60,000	$60,000

The company produced 3,500 units, using 18,375 direct labor hours and incurring the following overhead costs:

Factory overhead—fixed	$61,950
Factory overhead—variable	$33,710

Required:

1. Calculate the factory overhead, spending, efficiency, budget, and volume variances.
2. Does the net variance represent under- or overapplied factory overhead?

P8-16 **(Appendix) Materials, labor, and overhead variances—four-variance method**

LO10

K-Rod Corporation uses a standard cost system and manufactures one product. The variable costs per product follow:

Materials (4 parts)	$ 2
Labor (2 hours)	6
Overhead	3
	$11

Budgeted fixed costs for the month are $4,000, and K-Rod expected to manufacture 2,000 units. Actual production, however, was only 1,800 units. Materials prices were 10% over standard, and labor rates were 5% over standard. Of the factory overhead expense, only 80% was used, and fixed overhead was $100 over the budgeted amount. The actual variable overhead cost was $4,800. In materials usage, 8% more parts were used than were allowed for actual production by the standard, and 6% more labor hours were used than were allowed.

Required:

1. Calculate the materials and labor variances.
2. Calculate the variances for overhead by the four-variance method.

P8-17 **(Appendix) Labor variances and four-variance overhead analysis**

Tech-Elec Manufacturing Company estimates the following labor and overhead costs for the period:

Variable overhead	$44,200
Fixed overhead	50,050
Total estimated overhead	$94,250
Estimated direct labor cost	$65,000

Standard direct labor rate per hour	$10
Each unit will require 26 hours of labor.	
Estimated production for the period	500 units
Production statistics for the period:	
Actual production	510 units
Actual direct labor hours used	13,015 hours
Actual direct labor cost	$133,400
Actual overhead costs:	
Variable costs	$45,009
Fixed costs	50,125

Required:
Use the four-variance method for overhead analysis. Calculate the variances for direct labor and overhead. Prove that the overhead variances equal over- or underapplied factory overhead for the period.

P8-18 **(Appendix) Three-variance overhead analysis**
Using the data provided in P8-12, calculate the overhead cost variances under the three-variance method.

LO11

P8-19 **(Appendix) Variance analysis using the three-variance method for overhead costs**
Wausau Furniture Company uses a standard cost system in accounting for its production costs. The standard cost of a unit of furniture follows:

LO11

Lumber, 100 ft @ $150 per 1,000 ft		$15.00
Direct labor, 4 hr @ $10 per hr		40.00
Factory overhead:		
Fixed (15% of direct labor)	$ 6.00	
Variable (30% of direct labor)	12.00	18.00
Total unit cost		$73.00

The following flexible monthly overhead budget applies:

Direct Labor Hours	Estimated Overhead
5,200	$21,600
4,800	20,400
4,400	19,200
4,000 (normal capacity)	18,000
3,600	16,800

The actual unit costs for the month of December follow:

Lumber used (110 ft @ $120 per 1,000 ft)		$13.20
Direct labor (4 1/4 hr @ $10.24 per hr)		43.52
Factory overhead:		
Variable costs	$7,400	
Fixed costs	13,720	
	$21,120 ÷ 1,200 units	17.60
Total actual unit cost		$74.32

Required:
Compute the variances for materials, labor, and factory overhead, using the three-variance method for overhead costs.

P8-20R Review Problem for Chapters 7 & 8
Flexible budgets; two-, three-, and four-variance methods of factory overhead analysis
similar to Self-Study Problem 2

LO9 LO10 LO11

Madden Manufacturing, Inc., manufactures a single product and uses a standard cost system. The factory overhead is applied on the basis of direct labor hours. A condensed version of the company's flexible budget follows:

Direct labor hours	5,000	6,250	10,000
Factory overhead costs:			
Variable costs	$10,000	$12,500	$20,000
Fixed costs	50,000	50,000	50,000
Total	$60,000	$62,500	$70,000

The product requires 3 pounds of materials at a standard cost of $5 per pound and 2 hours of direct labor at a standard cost of $10 per hour.

For the current year, the company planned to operate at the level of 6,250 direct labor hours and to produce 3,125 units of product. Actual production and costs for the year follow:

Number of units produced	3,500
Actual direct labor hours worked	7,000
Actual variable overhead costs incurred	$14,000
Actual fixed overhead costs incurred	$52,000

Required:

1. For the current year, compute the factory overhead rate that will be used for production. Show the variable and fixed components that make up the total predetermined rate to be used.
2. Prepare a standard cost card for the product. Show the individual elements of the overhead rate as well as the total rate.
3. Compute (a) standard hours allowed for production and (b) under- or overapplied factory overhead for the year.
4. Determine the reason for any under- or overapplied factory overhead for the year by computing all variances, using each of the following methods:
   a. Two-variance method
   b. Three-variance method (appendix)
   c. Four-variance method (appendix)

MINI-CASE

Biloxi Beverages, Inc.

Variance analysis; journal entries; other analyses for multiple departments

Cost and production data for Biloxi Beverages, Inc., are presented as follows.

Standard Cost Summary

	Mixing	Blending	Total
Materials:			
4 lb @ $0.50	$ 2		
1 gal @ $1.00		$ 1	$ 3
Labor:			
1 hr @ $8.00	8		
1 hr @ $10.00		10	18
Factory overhead:			
Per unit	1	2	3
	$11	$13	$24

Production Report

	Mixing	Blending
Beginning units in process	None	None
Units finished and transferred	6,000	5,000
Ending units in process	2,000	1,000
Stage of completion	1/2	1/2

Cost Data

	Mixing		Blending	
Direct materials:				
30,000 lb @ $0.52		$15,600		
5,500 gal @ $0.95				$ 5,225
Direct labor:				
6,800 hr @ $8.00		54,400		
5,600 hr @ $10.20				57,120
Factory overhead:				
Indirect materials	$ 500		$1,000	
Indirect labor	2,000		5,000	
Other	4,500	7,000	5,000	11,000
		$77,000		$ 73,345

Required:

1. Calculate net variances for materials, labor, and factory overhead.
2. a. Calculate specific materials and labor variances by department, using the diagram format in Figure 8-4.
   b. Comment on the possible causes for each of the variances that you computed.
3. Make all journal entries to record production costs in Work in Process and Finished Goods.
4. Prove balances of Work in Process for both departments.
5. Prove that all costs have been accounted for. *Note:* Assume that materials, labor, and overhead are added evenly throughout the process.
6. Assume that 4,000 units were sold at $40 each.
   a. Calculate the gross margin based on standard cost.
   b. Calculate the gross margin based on actual cost.
   c. Why does the gross margin at actual cost differ from the gross margin at standard cost.
7. As the plant controller, you present the variance report in Item 1 above to Pat Crowley, the plant manager. After reading it, Pat states: "If we present this performance report to corporate with that large unfavorable labor variance in Blending, nobody in the plant will receive a bonus. Those standard hours of 5,500 are way too tight for this production process. Fifty-eight hundred hours would be more reasonable, and that would result in a favorable labor efficiency variance that would more than offset the unfavorable labor rate variance. Please redo the variance calculations using 5,800 hours as the standard." You object, but Pat ends the conversation with "That is an order."
   a. What standards of ethical professional practice would be violated if you adhered to Pat's order?
   b. How would you attempt to resolve this ethical conflict?

INTERNET EXERCISE

McDonald's Corporation Uses a Standard Cost System

This includes standards for such items as food, labor, and paper products. Given the level of sales volume achieved, the actual costs incurred are compared to the standard costs that should have been achieved for each cost item. Go to the text Web site at www.cengage.com/accounting/vanderbeck and click on the link to McDonald's Web site. Then click on the 2008 Consolidated Statement of Income. Assuming that the 2007 operating results were used in setting standards for 2008, what cost items do you expect had favorable or unfavorable variances in 2008? (*Hint:* Compare "Food and paper," "Payroll and employee benefits," and "Occupancy and other operating expenses" to "Sales by Company-operated restaurants," and compare "Selling, general, and administrative expenses" to "Total revenues" for both 2007 and 2008 in making your determinations.)

CHAPTER 9

Cost Accounting for Service Businesses and the Balanced Scorecard

Learning Objectives

After studying this chapter, you should be able to:

LO1 Perform job order costing for service businesses.

LO2 Prepare budgets for service businesses.

LO3 Apply activity-based costing for a service firm.

LO4 Compare the results of cost allocations using simplified costing versus activity-based costing.

LO5 Prepare a balanced scorecard for various business entities.

"The long-term shift from goods-producing to service-producing employment is expected to continue. Service-producing industries are expected to account for approximately 15.7 million new wages and salary jobs generated over the 2006–2016 period, while goods-producing industries will see overall job loss."—*Tomorrow's Jobs*, Occupational Outlook Handbook, 2008–2009 Edition.

A **service** is an intangible benefit, such as consulting, designing, grooming, transporting, and entertaining. It does not have physical properties and is consumed at the time that it is provided. It cannot be saved or stored and, therefore, is not inventoried. Examples of service businesses include accounting firms, airlines, hair stylists, video game arcades, professional sports teams, and hotels. Note that some service businesses have an associated raw material or product. While a restaurant, for example, is in the business of *serving* food, the food itself has tangible properties.

The main features of service businesses are that they have little or no inventory and that labor costs represent a large percentage of total costs. Even a restaurant would not keep most food items for more than a day or two, and labor costs often comprise three-fourths or more of the total costs. Service businesses are important because, as of June 2009, they employed roughly 85% of U.S. nonfarm workers and, as explained in the chapter introduction, that percentage is expected to grow.[1] The lack of growth in

1 Bureau of Labor Statistics, Economic News Release, Table B-1, Employment in Nonfarm Payrolls by Industry Sector, www.bls.gov (visited 7/27/2009).

manufacturing employment is due primarily to inexpensive imports and to the automation of U.S. factories. Automated production processes have resulted in the manufacturing of many more goods with fewer workers, thus creating a need for more people to market, distribute, and service these additional products.

Historically, cost accountants spent most of their time developing product costs for manufactured goods and spent little time on costing services. Given the importance of services in our modern economy, the related cost issues can no longer be ignored. Knowing the cost of providing services is important to managers for such purposes as contract bidding and deciding what services to emphasize or deemphasize in their line of offerings. Be aware, however, that even services are being outsourced to other countries, such as India and China, that can provide them more cheaply. Information technology and customer service work are the most commonly outsourced service activities by U.S. companies.

Job Order Costing for Service Businesses

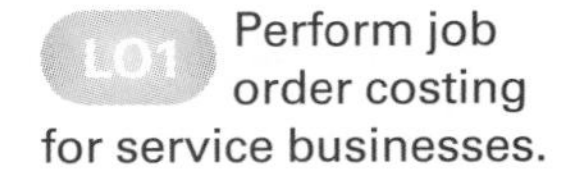

Perform job order costing for service businesses.

The amount and complexity of services provided can vary substantially from customer to customer. When this is the case, a service firm should use job order costing, just as the manufacturers of differentiated products use such a system. Examples of service firms using job order costing include accounting firms whose cost of an audit would depend on the size and complexity of a client's operations and auto repairers whose charges are based on the parts, supplies, and labor time needed on each job. For example, when the international accounting firm **Pricewaterhouse-Coopers (PwC)** wants to know how much it costs the firm to audit **ExxonMobil**, the hours worked by the accounting professionals can be traced directly to the ExxonMobil audit. Other expenses such as depreciation on the auditors' laptops, secretarial wages, and recruiting expenses incurred to hire new accountants are expenses incurred to service all clients, including ExxonMobil, but are not easily traceable to specific clients. PwC, therefore, must use an allocation base, such as direct labor hours or direct labor dollars, to allocate to each client its fair share of these indirect costs.

Job Cost Sheet for a Service Business

The basic document used to accumulate costs for a service business using job order costing is the job order cost sheet, which was also used in our manufacturing examples. Figure 9-1 is a job cost sheet used by an accounting firm for the audit of an automotive group with dealerships in a three-state area. Note that the cost per hour of partner, manager, and staff time includes both their compensation per hour and a share of the firm's overhead. Assume that a partner earns $100 per hour and it has been determined that for every $1 spent on direct labor (partner, manager, and staff time), the firm will spend $1.50 for overhead, such as secretarial support, fringe benefits, depreciation on computers, rent, and utilities. Because direct labor cost is the single largest cost to the firm and the need for these direct laborers

Figure 9-1 Job Cost Sheet for a Service Business

	A	B	C	D
1	O'Reilly and Stevens			
2	Summary of Engagement Account			
3				
4	**Client Name:** Mission Valley Automotive, Inc.			
5	**Engagement Type:** Audit			
6	**Engagement Number:** 727			
7	**Date Contracted:** 12/19/2010			
8	**Date Completed:** 2/22/2011			
9	**Supervising Partner:** Stevens			
10	**Partners' Time:**			
11	**Period ending**	**Hours**	**Rate**	**Amount**
12	1/31/2011	10	$250*	$2,500
13	2/28/2011	8	$250*	$2,000
14	Subtotals	18		$4,500
15	**Manager's Time:**			
16	**Period ending**	**Hours**	**Rate**	**Amount**
17	1/31/2011	45	$125*	$5,625
18	2/28/2011	25	$125*	3,125
19	Subtotals	70		$8,750
20	**Staff Time:**			
21	**Period ending**	**Hours**	**Rate**	**Amount**
22	1/31/2011	120	$75*	$9,000
23	2/28/2011	80	$75*	6,000
24	Subtotals	200		$15,000
25				
26	**Other Direct Costs:**	**Period ending**	**Period ending**	**Total**
27		**1/31/2011**	**2/28/2011**	**Other**
28	Travel	$2,970	$1,975	$4,945
29	Meals	1,430	795	2,225
30	Total Other	$4,400	$2,770	$7,170
31	**Total Engagement Costs**			$35,420
32	**Includes direct labor plus overhead based on direct labor cost*			

results in all the other costs the firm incurs, the amount of direct labor cost incurred on a job determines how much overhead will be charged to it. For example, the charge of $250 for each hour of partner time consists of the $100 per hour wage rate and $150 of overhead. Therefore, the overhead rate is 150% ($150/$100) of direct labor cost.

The 150% overhead rate is a predetermined annual rate computed as follows:

Budgeted Overhead for 2011

Secretarial support	$1,500,000
Fringe benefits	1,250,000
Lease expense	500,000
Depreciation—equipment	750,000
Utilities	300,000
Telephone and fax	150,000
Photocopying	50,000
Total	$4,500,000

Budgeted Direct Labor for 2011

Partners	$ 425,000
Managers	775,000
Staff	1,800,000
Total	$3,000,000

$$\begin{aligned}\text{Budgeted overhead rate} &= \text{Budgeted overhead/Budgeted direct labor}\\ &= \$4{,}500{,}000/\$3{,}000{,}000\\ &= 150\%\end{aligned}$$

Choosing the Cost Allocation Base

Note that the firm could have used direct labor hours instead of direct labor dollars to charge overhead to jobs. By choosing direct labor cost, the firm decided that its overhead was more related to the direct labor dollars charged to a job than to the direct labor hours worked on the job. This means that partners who earn higher wages than managers and staff accountants create more overhead costs. They have more secretarial help and nicer offices, and they order more computer studies than managers and staff accountants. If all three categories of direct labor consumed the same amount of overhead per hour worked on a job, then direct labor hours would be the more appropriate basis to use for charging overhead.

Tracing Direct Costs to the Job

There are costs other than direct labor that can be traced to a job. Note the travel and meal charges appearing in the "Other Direct Costs" category in Figure 9-1. These are expenses that can be specifically identified with a job and do not have to be allocated to the job using an overhead rate. For example, the accountants can keep a log of the travel and meal expenses incurred in servicing clients with out-of-town locations.

Cost Performance Report

Once the job is completed and all of the costs have been charged to it, management can use the information in a number of ways. It can compare the costs charged to the job with the bid price accepted by the client to determine the profitability of the job. For example, if the bid price were $48,000 for the job in Figure 9-1, the profit would be computed as follows:

Bid price		$48,000
Costs:		
Total labor and overhead	$28,250	
Total other direct costs	7,170	35,420
Profit		$12,580

The profit was approximately 26% ($12,580/$48,000) of the bid price, and labor and overhead costs were approximately 80% ($28,250/$35,420) of the total costs. The firm can use such information in bidding on the Mission Valley Automotive audit next year, in bidding on audits for similar businesses, and in comparing budgeted to actual costs on the audit for purposes of controlling future costs. Figure 9-2 illustrates a **cost performance report** for the Mission Valley Automotive job. It compares the budgeted costs for the job to the actual costs incurred and indicates the **variance**, or difference, for each item.

Figure 9-2 Cost Performance Report

	A	B	C	D
1	**Mission Valley Automotive, Inc.**			
2	**Cost Performance Report**			
3	**Audit of Year Ended 2011**			
4				
5		**Actual**		
6	**Item**	**Result**	**Budget**	**Variance**
7	Partners' salaries and overhead	$ 4,500	$ 3,900	$ 600 U
8	Managers' salaries and overhead	8,750	8,500	250 U
9	Staff accountants' salaries and overhead	15,000	13,500	1,500 U
10	Travel	4,945	4,695	250 U
11	Meals	2,225	2,060	165 U
12	Total	$35,420	$32,655	$2,765 U
13				
14	U = unfavorable			
15	F = favorable			

The actual costs of the job were $2,765 over budget. The partners will want to determine what caused the job to come in over budget. Was it poor budgeting that resulted in an unrealistically low cost estimate, or was it an inefficient use of resources on the job? If the budget had been met on the job, then the profit on the job would have been $15,345 instead of $12,580, and the profit as a percentage of bid price would have been 32% ($15,345 / $48,000) instead of 26%.

Budgeting for Service Businesses

LO2 Prepare budgets for service businesses.

The estimate of revenue and expenses from the Mission Valley Automotive job would be part of the budgeted figures appearing in the annual budget for O'Reilly and Stevens CPAs. The **revenue budget**, illustrated in Figure 9-3, is the starting point for the annual budget because the amount of client business must be projected before estimating the labor hours and overhead required. (Note that the billing rates differ from the rates appearing on the job cost sheet in Figure 9-1, because those cost rates did not include an element of profit.)

The Revenue Budget

The revenue budget in Figure 9-3 is developed around the three major services that the firm provides: audit, consulting, and tax. The professional labor hours to be worked in each area are budgeted based on the firm's knowledge of time spent on continuing clients in the past, expected new business, and the expected mix of audit, consulting, and tax work by professional

Figure 9-3 Revenue Budget

	A	B	C	D
1		**Schedule 1**		
2	**Revenue Budget for the Year Ended December 31, 2011**			
3		**Professional**	**Billing**	**Total**
4	**Item**	**Hours**	**Rate**	**Revenues**
5	Audit:			
6	Partners	2,000	$300	$ 600,000
7	Managers	8,000	175	1,400,000
8	Staff	30,000	100	3,000,000
9	Subtotal	40,000		$5,000,000
10	Consulting:			
11	Partners	750	$300	$ 225,000
12	Managers	2,500	175	437,500
13	Staff	10,000	100	1,000,000
14	Subtotal	13,250		$1,662,500
15	Tax:			
16	Partners	1,500	$300	$ 450,000
17	Managers	5,000	175	875,000
18	Staff	20,000	100	2,000,000
19	Subtotal	26,500		$3,325,000
20	Total	79,750		$9,987,500

labor category. The **billing rates** reflect the firm's best estimate of what it will charge clients for the various categories of professional labor in the coming year. The total revenue from all client services is budgeted at $9,987,500.

The Labor Budget

Once the amount of professional labor hours required to meet client services is budgeted, a **professional labor budget**, as in Figure 9-4, may be prepared. The budgeted hours required in each client service area are multiplied by the budgeted rate to obtain the wages expense for each category of professional labor.

The wage rates in Figure 9-4 differ from the rates appearing on the job cost sheet in Figure 9-1. This is because the job cost sheet includes labor and overhead in a single combined rate. For budgeting purposes, we want to budget separately for professional labor hours and for overhead.

Although we usually think of professional employees, such as accountants, as earning a salary rather than an hourly wage, it is important to develop an hourly rate for budgeting and billing purposes. For example, the $100 per hour wage rate for a partner was developed as follows:

$$\begin{aligned}\text{Hourly rate} &= \text{Annual salary/Annual billable hours}\\ &= \$200{,}000/2{,}000 \text{ hours}\\ &= \$100 \text{ per hour}\end{aligned}$$

It is very important to budget the professional labor hours needed with care. If the firm overestimates the number of hours needed, then it will be overstaffed and the additional labor costs will reduce profits. If the firm underestimates the number of labor hours needed, then it will be

Figure 9-4 **Professional Labor Budget**

	A	B	C	D
1		Schedule 2		
2	Professional Labor Budget for the Year Ended December 31, 2011			
3		Professional	Wage	Total
4	Item	Hours	Rate	Labor Dollars
5	Audit:			
6	Partners................	2,000	$100	$ 200,000
7	Managers.............	8,000	50	400,000
8	Staff......................	30,000	30	900,000
9	Subtotal................	40,000		$1,500,000
10	Consulting:			
11	Partners................	750	$100	$ 75,000
12	Managers.............	2,500	50	125,000
13	Staff......................	10,000	30	300,000
14	Subtotal................	13,250		$ 500,000
15	Tax:			
16	Partners................	1,500	$100	$ 150,000
17	Managers.............	5,000	50	250,000
18	Staff......................	20,000	30	600,000
19	Subtotal................	26,500		$1,000,000
20	Total..............	79,750		$3,000,000

understaffed and the lack of enough professionals will cause it to pass up jobs that would increase revenues and profits.

The Overhead Budget

The firm must next prepare an overhead budget that includes all of the expense items that cannot be traced directly to jobs and must instead be allocated to them by using an overhead rate. The overhead budget for O'Reilly and Stevens appears in Figure 9-5.

Do not confuse use of the term *overhead* here with its use in Chapter 4. Chapter 4 illustrated the accounting for manufacturing overhead, which consists only of the indirect expenses incurred in the factory. In this

Figure 9-5 **Overhead Budget**

Schedule 3 Overhead Budget for the Year Ended December 31, 2011	
Secretarial support	$1,500,000
Fringe benefits	1,250,000
Lease expense	500,000
Depreciation—equipment	750,000
Utilities	300,000
Telephone and fax	150,000
Photocopying	50,000
Total	$4,500,000

Figure 9-6 Other Direct Expenses

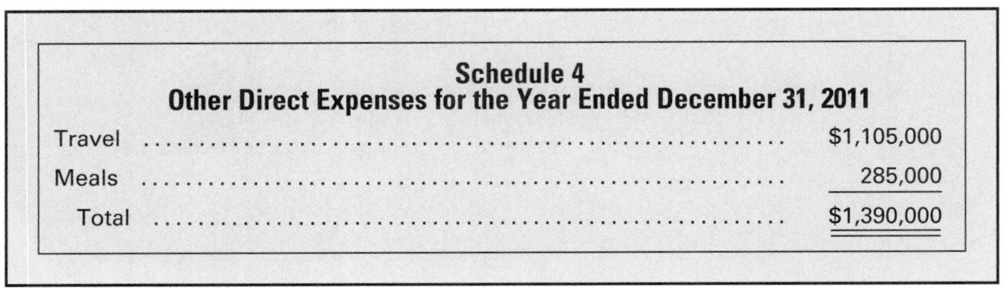

Schedule 4
Other Direct Expenses for the Year Ended December 31, 2011

Travel	$1,105,000
Meals	285,000
Total	$1,390,000

example, *the overhead consists of the indirect expenses incurred to support the activities of a professional services firm.* The totals from the professional labor budget (Figure 9-4) and the overhead budget (Figure 9-5) were used to compute the overhead rate of 150% ($4,500,000/$3,000,000) of direct labor dollars.

The Other Direct Expenses Budget

The last of the individual budgets for this firm would be the Other Direct Expenses budget, appearing in Figure 9-6, which consists of the direct expenses other than professional labor that can be traced to specific jobs. Recall that $7,170 of these types of expense, $4,945 of travel and $2,225 of meals, was traced to the Mission Valley Automotive job.

The Budgeted Income Statement

Once all of the individual budgets have been prepared, the information they contain can be used to prepare the budgeted income statement in Figure 9-7. Note the differences between this income statement and the income statements illustrated earlier for a manufacturer. There is no line item for cost of goods sold because the firm sells a service rather than a product. All of the operating expenses are charged against income in the period incurred because there are no inventory accounts to which they can be attached. In a manufacturing firm, any expense incurred in the factory would be allocated to the jobs produced during the period and remain as

Figure 9-7 Budgeted Income Statement

Budgeted Income Statement
O'Reilly and Stevens CPAs
For the Year Ended December 31, 2011

Revenues (Schedule 1)		$9,987,500
Operating costs:		
Professional labor (Schedule 2)	$3,000,000	
Overhead support (Schedule 3)	4,500,000	
Other expenses (Schedule 4)	1,390,000	8,890,000
Operating income		$1,097,500

part of the asset accounts (Work in Process and Finished Goods) until the jobs were completed and sold. At that time, they would be charged against income as cost of goods sold expense.

The income statement in Figure 9-7 also may be used for planning purposes in advance of the calendar year. For example, operating income is estimated to be 11% of revenue ($1,097,500/$9,987,500). If the partners expect operating income to be at least 15% of revenue, then they should return to the individual budgets and determine how to increase operating income by $400,625 [($9,987,500 × .15) – $1,097,500] through some combination of increasing budgeted revenues and/or decreasing budgeted costs. The income statement may also be used for control purposes during and at the end of the calendar year. By comparing budgeted to actual revenues and expenses, the partners can determine how well the firm is meeting expectations and take corrective action where necessary.

Recall and Review 1

Mantle and Maris own a professional services firm that has the following budgeted costs for the year: associates salaries, $500,000; fringe benefits, $300,000; lease expense, $450,000; partner salaries, $700,000; telephone and fax, $50,000. The budgeted overhead rate for the year, using direct labor dollars as the overhead allocation base would be $________________.

(After working this exercise, see page 468 for the solution.)

You should now be able to work the following:
Questions 1–11; Exercises 9-1 to 9-4; Problems 9-1 to 9-4; Self-Study Problem 1 (Part 1); and the Internet Exercise.

Activity-Based Costing in a Service Firm

Kaufman and D'Esti, a law firm, has two categories of professional labor—partner and associate. It also has two types of indirect costs—legal support and secretarial support. In charging professional labor to jobs, it averages the rates earned by partners and associates, and then multiplies the average rate by the number of professional hours worked on a job. Likewise, it divides the total of legal support and secretarial support by the total professional labor hours worked to determine the overhead charging rate. Lately, the partners have been frustrated because jobs that they thought were competitively bid were lost, and jobs that they overbid in times of peak activity were often won. As an example, a rather high bid to represent Binghamton Industries at an accounting fraud trial was accepted, whereas a relatively low bid to draft contracts for Johnson City Mfg. was rejected. Marc Kaufman, one of the partners, thinks that the strange results were related to the firm's simplified costing system and the fact that a lot of partner labor would be required on the litigation

work, whereas mostly lower-priced associate labor would be used in drafting the contracts. He also knows that only partners have the use of secretarial services, even though overhead costs are allocated using all professional labor hours. For the above reasons, Kaufman contracts with Ed Hickey, an activity-based costing consultant, to review the firm's job costing system. The mini-case study at the end of this chapter includes the results of Hickey's findings.

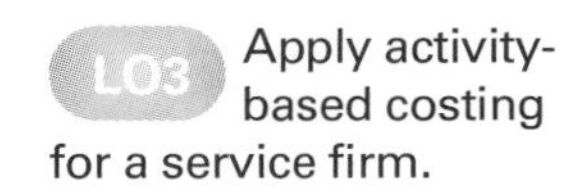
Apply activity-based costing for a service firm.

Recall that O'Reilly and Stevens CPAs had only two major categories of direct costs—professional labor, and meals and travel—and only a single overhead rate was used for indirect costs. In Chapter 4, we introduced the concept of activity-based costing for a manufacturing firm. In this chapter, those same principles will be applied to a service firm. Activity-based costing (ABC) is not the exclusive property of manufacturers. Examples of ABC pioneers in service industries include **Union Pacific** (railroads), **Charles Schwab** (stock brokerage), and the **U.S. Postal Service** (government).

Firms that use **activity-based costing** attempt to shift as many costs as possible out of the indirect cost pool that has to be allocated to jobs and into direct cost pools that can be specifically traced to the individual jobs that caused the costs to occur. The remaining costs that cannot be traced to individual jobs are separated into homogeneous cost pools and then allocated to individual jobs by using separate allocation bases for each cost pool. For example, if the amount of payroll department and human resources department costs is related to the number of persons employed, then they may be grouped in a single indirect cost pool and allocated to jobs on the basis of the number of employees.

Converting Indirect Costs to Direct Costs

Photocopying and telephone/fax charges are two overhead costs incurred by O'Reilly and Stevens CPAs that would be prime candidates to be traced directly to the individual jobs. A client code number can be entered prior to running each photocopying job to identify the client recipient of the job, and long-distance calls and faxes can be traced to individual clients via telephone bills or a log kept by the business. The increased sophistication and affordability of information processing technology enable such costs, which previously were classified as indirect and were included in the overhead rate, to be traced directly to specific jobs at minimal cost. For example, if telephone/fax and photocopying charges were traced directly to the Mission Valley Automotive, Inc., job, then the Other Direct Costs section of the cost sheet now would appear as follows:

Other	Period Ending 1/31/2011	Period Ending 2/28/2011	Total
Travel	$2,970	$1,975	$4,945
Meals	1,430	795	2,225
Photocopying	280	175	455
Telephone/fax	370	220	590
Total	$5,050	$3,165	$8,215

Note that the overhead rate of 150% used in Figure 9-1 should now be slightly lower because the overhead component of the rate no longer includes telephone/fax and photocopying charges. These items, which had previously been "spread like peanut butter" over all the jobs, can now be specifically identified with the jobs that caused these costs to occur. **Peanut-butter costing** refers to the practice of assigning costs evenly to jobs using an overhead rate, even though different jobs actually consume resources in different proportions.

Multiple Indirect Cost Pools

The other main ingredient of activity-based costing is to take overhead costs that were previously in a single indirect cost pool and then separate them into a number of homogeneous cost pools with a separate cost driver, or cost allocation base, for each pool. For example, the single overhead cost pool of $4,500,000 that previously was allocated to jobs on the basis of direct labor dollars could be separated into three cost pools with a different cost driver for each pool, as follows:

Cost Pool	Cost Allocation Base
Secretarial support	Partner labor hours
Fringe benefits	Professional labor dollars
Audit support	Professional labor hours

Using the budgeted numbers from Figure 9-5 and the budgeted labor hours from Figure 9-4, we find that the overhead rates, rounded to the nearest whole cent, for the individual cost pools would be computed as follows:

Cost Pool	Budgeted Costs	Budgeted Cost Drivers	Budgeted Rate
Secretarial support	$1,500,000	4,250 hours	$352.94/partner labor hour
Fringe benefits	$1,250,000	$ 3,000,000	$0.42/professional labor dollar
Audit support	$1,550,000	79,750 hours	$19.44/professional labor hour

Note that the $1,550,000 amount in the audit support cost pool was determined from the overhead budget in Figure 9-5 as follows:

Lease expense	$ 500,000
Depreciation—equipment	750,000
Utilities expense	300,000
	$1,550,000

The budgeted amounts for secretarial support ($1,500,000) and fringe benefits ($1,250,000) were separate line items in the overhead budget. If we use an activity-based costing system to charge overhead costs to the Mission

Valley Automotive, Inc., job, the amounts allocated, using the previous rates, would be as follows:

Cost Pool	Budgeted Rate	Number of Cost Driver Units Consumed	Amount
Secretarial support	$352.94/partner labor hour	18 hours	$ 6,353
Fringe benefits	$0.42/professional labor dollar	$11,300	4,746
Audit support	$19.44/professional labor hour	288 hours	5,599
Total			$16,698

The cost driver numbers came from Figure 9-1, where 18 partner hours, 288 total professional hours, and $11,300 professional labor dollars (not including overhead) were expended on the Mission Valley Automotive, Inc. job.

The professional labor dollars incurred on the job were computed as follows, using the hours worked from Figure 9-1 and the hourly rates from Figure 9-4:

Partners	18 hours @ $100	=	$ 1,800
Managers	70 hours @ $50	=	3,500
Staff	200 hours @ $30	=	6,000
Total			$11,300

Job Cost Sheet—Activity-Based Costing

Figure 9-8 diagrams the activity-based costing system used by O'Reilly and Stevens. The revised job cost sheet reflecting all charges to the Mission Valley Automotive, Inc. job appears as Figure 9-9:

Figure 9-8 Diagram of Activity-Based Costing System

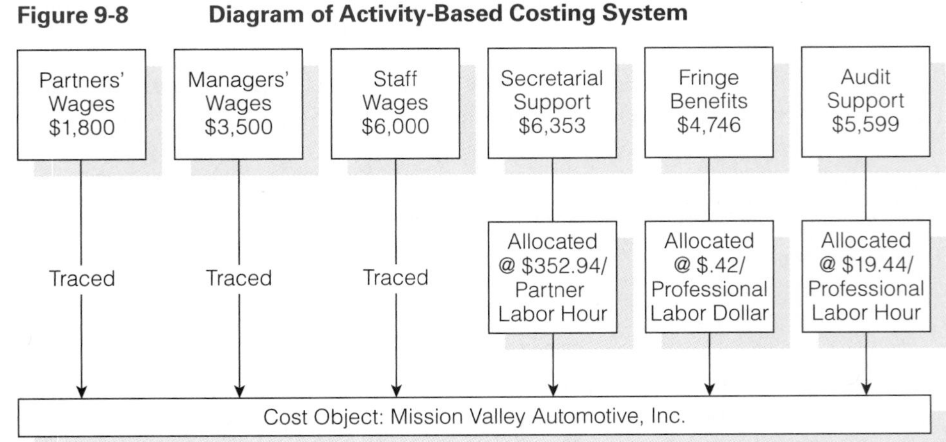

Figure 9-9 **Job Cost Sheet with Activity-Based Costing**

	A	B	C	D
1		**O'Reilly and Stevens CPAs**		
2		**Summary of Engagement Account**		
3	Client Name:	Mission Valley Automotive, Inc.		
4	Engagement Type:	Audit		
5	Engagement Number:	727		
6	Date Contracted:	12/19/2010		
7	Date Completed:	2/22/2011		
8	Supervising Partner:	Stevens		
9	**Partners' Time:**			
10	**Period ending**	**Hours**	**Rate**	**Amount**
11	1/31/2011	10	$100	$1,000
12	2/28/2011	8	$100	800
13	Subtotals	18		$1,800
14	**Managers' Time:**			
15	**Period ending**	**Hours**	**Rate**	**Amount**
16	1/31/2011	45	$50	$2,250
17	2/28/2011	25	$50	1,250
18	Subtotals	70		$3,500
19	**Staff Time:**			
20	**Period ending**	**Hours**	**Rate**	**Amount**
21	1/31/2011	120	$30	$3,600
22	2/28/2011	80	$30	2,400
23	Subtotals	200		$6,000
24	**Overhead:**		**Number of**	
25		**Budgeted**	**Cost Driver**	
26	**Cost Pool**	**Rate**	**Units**	**Amount**
27	Secretarial support	$352.94/partner labor hour	18 hours	$ 6,353
28	Fringe benefits	$0.42/professional labor dollar	$11,300	4,746
29	Audit support	$19.44/professional labor hour	288 hours	5,599
30	Subtotals			$16,698
31		**Period**	**Period**	
32	**Other Direct**	**Ending**	**Ending**	**Total**
33	**Cost:**	**1/31/2011**	**2/28/2011**	**Other**
34	Travel	$2,970	$1,975	$ 4,945
35	Meals	1,430	795	2,225
36	Photocopying	280	175	455
37	Telephone/fax	370	220	590
38	Subtotals	$5,050	$3,165	$ 8,215
39	**Total Engagement Costs**			$36,213

Allocations Using Simplified Costing Versus Activity-Based Costing

In the examples in Figures 9-1 and 9-9, the total costs charged to the job using a simplified costing system ($35,420) vary less than 3% from the total costs using activity-based costing ($36,213). Such small differences are not always the case, as illustrated by the following example. Assume that a law firm has two categories of professional labor—partner and associate. It also has two types of indirect costs—legal support and secretarial support. Budgeted information for the year is as follows:

LO4 Compare the results of cost allocations using simplified costing versus activity-based costing.

	Partner Labor	Associate Labor
Number of attorneys	10	40
Annual billable hours per attorney	2,000	2,000
Annual compensation per attorney	$200,000	$75,000

	Legal Support	Secretarial Support
Annual overhead estimate	$2,000,000	$500,000

The direct cost category includes all professional labor costs, which are traced to jobs on a per hour basis. The indirect cost category includes all overhead costs. These costs are included in a single indirect cost pool—professional support—and are allocated to jobs using professional labor hours as the allocation base. Using a simplified costing system with one direct cost category and one indirect cost category, we see that the jobs would be costed as shown in Figure 9-10 for two potential clients: Horne, who requires 50 hours of trial work, and Nguyen, who requires 75 hours of tax work.

The professional labor rate of $50 per hour was computed as follows:

$$\text{Professional labor rate} = \frac{\text{Annual professional labor dollars}}{\text{Annual professional labor hours}}$$

$$= \frac{(10 \times \$200{,}000) + (40 \times \$\ 75{,}000)}{(10 \times 2{,}000 \text{ hours}) + (40 \times 2{,}000 \text{ hours})}$$

$$= \frac{\$\ 5{,}000{,}000}{100{,}000 \text{ hours}}$$

$$= \$50 \text{ per hour}$$

Figure 9-10 Simplified Job Costing for a Law Firm

	Horne	Nguyen
Professional labor cost:		
50 hours × $50	$2,500	
75 hours × $50		$3,750
Professional support:		
50 hours × $25	1,250	
75 hours × $25		1,875
Total	$3,750	$5,625

The professional support indirect cost rate of \$25 per hour was computed as follows:

$$\text{Professional support rate} = \frac{\text{Annual support cost}}{\text{Annual professional labor hours}}$$

$$= \frac{\$2{,}000{,}000 + \$500{,}000}{100{,}000 \text{ hours}}$$

$$= \frac{\$2{,}500{,}000}{100{,}000 \text{ hours}}$$

$$= \$25 \text{ per hour}$$

Now, let's assume that the firm decides to implement a more sophisticated costing system because it feels that many bids, such as the Nguyen job, are being rejected as too high. The firm decides to have two direct cost categories—partner labor and associate labor—and two indirect cost categories—legal support and secretarial support. The cost allocation base for legal support is professional labor hours; for secretarial support it is partner labor hours because only partners have access to secretarial help. Using the data on page 460, the rates for each cost category would be as follows:

Category	**Rate**		
Partner labor	\$200,000/2,000 hours	=	\$100 per hour
Associate labor	\$75,000/2,000 hours	=	\$37.50 per hour
Legal support	\$2,000,000/100,000 professional hours	=	\$20 per hour
Secretarial support	\$500,000/20,000 partner hours	=	\$25 per hour

Further assume that the Horne job will require 40 partner hours and 10 associate hours whereas the Nguyen job will require 70 associate hours and five partner hours. Using an activity-based costing system with two direct cost categories and two indirect cost categories, the jobs would be costed as shown in Figure 9-11.

Figure 9-11 Activity-Based Costing for a Law Firm

	Horne	Nguyen
Partner labor cost:		
40 hours × \$100	\$4,000	
5 hours × \$100		\$ 500
Associate labor cost:		
10 hours × \$37.50	375	
70 hours × \$37.50		2,625
Legal support:		
50 professional hours × \$20	1,000	
75 professional hours × \$20		1,500
Secretarial support:		
40 partner hours × \$25	1,000	
5 partner hours × \$25		125
Total	\$6,375	\$4,750

The cost of the two jobs under the two costing systems is summarized as follows:

	Horne	Nguyen
Cost using simplified system	$ 3,750	$5,625
Cost using activity-based system	6,375	4,750
Difference (under)- or overcosted	$(2,625)	$ 875

Using the simplified costing system, the Horne job was undercosted by $2,625 (a difference of 70%), and the Nguyen job was overcosted by $875 (almost 16%). This helps explain why the firm lost the bid on the Nguyen job. Although it won the bid on the Horne job, it is conceivable that it may have done the job at a loss. If the firm added 50% to the cost estimate in bidding on the Horne job, the adjusted bid would be undercosted by $750 relative to the activity-based cost of the job. This amount is determined as follows:

Bid price using simplified cost system [$3,750 + (0.50 × $3,750)]	$5,625
Activity-based cost of job	6,375
Loss on job	$ (750)

To summarize, activity-based costing is worthwhile to implement when different jobs use resources in different proportions. In the preceding example, because of the nature of trial work, the Horne job predominately required partner time, which is more expensive and requires more support services. It should be a **cost/benefit decision** determining whether to implement a more sophisticated costing system. Namely, does the benefit received from the more refined information exceed the cost of implementing and maintaining the more sophisticated system?

Recall and Review 2

A law firm identifies the following two cost pools and budgeted amounts for the coming year: paralegal support, $250,000; and research support, $750,000. The best cost driver for paralegal support is partner labor hours, 6,000, and the driver for research support is professional labor hours, 40,000. The budgeted overhead rate for paralegal support is $__________, and for research support is $__________. (Round to two decimal places.)

(After working this exercise, see page 468 for the solution.)

You should now be able to work the following:
Questions 12–15; Exercises 9-5 to 9-7; Problems 9-5 to 9-7; Self-Study Problem 1 (Parts 2 and 3); Mini-Case; and the Internet Exercise.

The Balanced Scorecard

LO5 Prepare a balanced scorecard for various business entities.

The variances illustrated in Chapter 8 are examples of financial performance measures because they are expressed in dollars. Companies often use **nonfinancial performance measures** to evaluate operations, such as the percentage of defective polo shirts produced by **Ralph Lauren**, the percentage of baggage lost by **Delta Airlines**, and the average wait time compared to standard wait time at a **Burger King** drive-through window. This is consistent with the **balanced scorecard** approach to measuring a business's success by considering both financial and nonfinancial performance measures. Many major businesses use a balanced scorecard approach to performance measurement, including such well-known entities as **Apple Computer**, **AT&T**, **Verizon Communications**, and the Big Four accounting firm **KPMG**.

The Four Categories of a Balanced Scorecard

A balanced scorecard translates a company's strategy into performance measures that are used to implement the strategy and that employees can understand. These performance measures typically are divided into four categories, as illustrated in Figure 9-12. Note in the illustration that the arrows point upward to indicate, for example, that if a company has good

Figure 9-12 **The Four Categories of Balanced Scorecard Performance Measures**

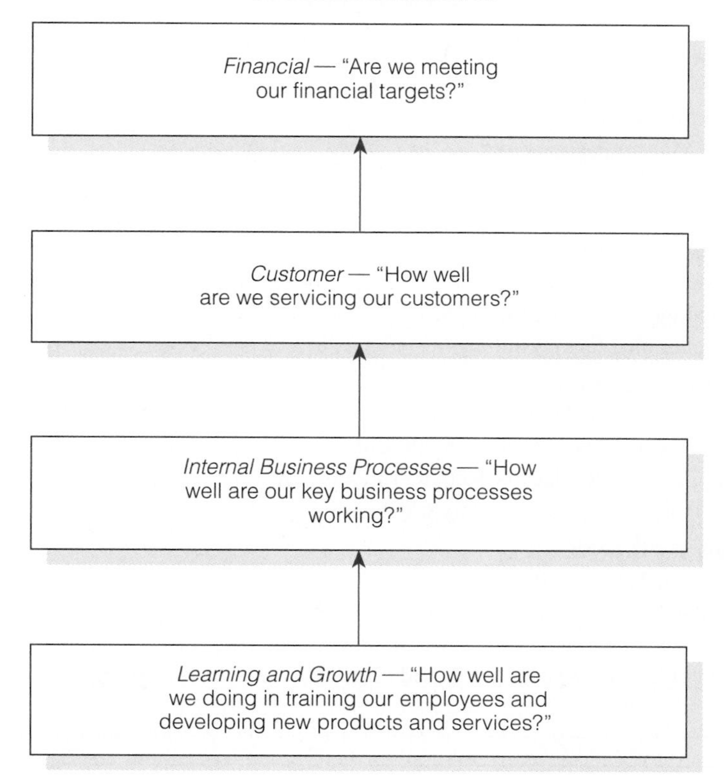

training programs (Learning and Growth), then its percentage of on-time deliveries should be high (Internal Business Processes), resulting in more satisfied customers (Customer Perspective) and greater sales dollars (Financial Perspective). Examples of balanced scorecard performance measures appear in Figure 9-13. Note that balanced scorecards are used by manufacturers, merchandisers, and service businesses.

One may ask, "Why bother with the other three categories (Customer, Internal Business Processes, and Learning and Growth) when the company is in business to earn enough profits to satisfy its owners (Financial)." The reason is that, without the balanced scorecard approach, a company might take actions to increase short-term profits that could be harmful to long-term profitability. For example, it could decrease spending on training programs; this would reduce expenses and increase profits in the short run, but it could result in increased product defect rates, dissatisfied customers, and a lower sales volume in the long run.

"Real-world" examples of balanced scorecard successes include the following:

In 2007 **U.S. Airways** was in last place among major airlines in on-time performance. In 2008 the airline "invested in new baggage-handling equipment, acquired more gates to reduce delays, built more buffer into its schedule and beefed up management at its Philadelphia hub to fix problems

Figure 9-13 Examples of Balanced Scorecard Performance Measures

Financial
- Return on Investment (ROI)
- Operating Income
- Gross Margin Percentage
- Revenue from New Products

Customer
- Number of New Customers
- Market Share
- Percentage of Product Returned
- Customer Satisfaction Surveys

Internal Business Processes
- Percentage of On-Time Deliveries
- Percentage of Defect-Free Units Produced
- Time Taken to Replace Defective Products
- Time from Receipt of Order to Shipment

Learning and Growth
- Employee Turnover Ratio
- Number of Employee Suggestions
- Percentage of Employees Trained in New Processes
- Percentage of Compensation Based on Employee/Team Performance

there." By June 2008, these improvements in its Internal Business Processes performance measures resulted in a second-best on-time performance, behind only **Southwest Airlines.**[2]

Many companies are basing a portion of executive bonuses on employee turnover, a Learning and Growth performance measure. **Penske Automotive Group, Inc.**, tied 8%, $240,000, of Chief Executive Roger Penske's 2007 bonus to "holding employee turnover below 31%. Mr. Penske earned his $240,000 reward. The company which owns 300 dealerships worldwide, posted 30.8% attrition in 2007, down from 31.2% a year earlier and 80% in 1999 when Penske Corp. acquired a controlling stake."[3]

Guidelines for a Good Balanced Scorecard

It is important to observe the following guidelines when choosing performance measures:

- To be effective, the performance measures must be consistent with the company strategy.
- There should not be too many performance measures.
- Employees should be able to understand and have control over the performance measures by which they are evaluated.

If a performance measure (say, the percentage of on-time deliveries) is being met but the company's strategy (say, increased dollar sales to current customers) is not attained, then this performance measure alone is not sufficient to accomplish the strategy. The company must further examine what their customers want—and what is not being provided—in order to accomplish its strategy. Relative to the second guideline above, if there are too many performance measures, then employees will have a difficult time choosing the measures on which to concentrate.

Lastly, if employee compensation and advancement within the firm are tied to achieving performance measures, then those measures should be understandable to and controllable by the employee.

The Balanced Scorecard Illustrated

Figure 9-14 illustrates a balanced scorecard for Tao Electronics, which manufactures television sets, DVD players, and other leisure-time electronic equipment. Because there are numerous manufacturers of these types of products, Tao's strategy is to increase profits by engendering customer loyalty through the production of defect-free products and the provision of

---

2 Scott McCartney, "Flying Was Supposed to Be Better This Summer. It's Not," *The Wall Street Journal*, July 8, 2008.

3 Cari Tuna, "In Some Offices Keeping Workers Earns a Bonus," *The Wall Street Journal*, June 30, 2008.

Figure 9-14 The Balanced Scorecard for Tao Electronics

Perspective	Measures	Target Performance	Actual Performance
Financial	• Increase Revenues from Existing Customers	10%	13%
	• Increase Operating Income through Cost Reduction	$120,000	$150,000
Customer	• Market Share in Industry	8%	10%
	• Customer Satisfaction Ratings	80% Give Top Rating	85% Give Top Rating
Internal Business Processes	• Percentage of Defect-Free Units Produced	92%	95%
	• Percentage of On-Time Deliveries	95%	94%
Learning and Growth	• Percentage of Employees Trained in New Processes	85%	91%
	• Number of Employees' Suggestions Implemented	50	63

on-time deliveries. The performance measures in Figure 9-14 indicate the success of this strategy. In general, Tao has done a good job of increasing profits through cost reduction and revenue growth from existing customers. Note that revenue from repeat customers increased by 13% as compared to a target increase of 10%. It was expected that operating income would increase by $120,000 through more efficient manufacturing processes, yet it actually increased by $150,000.

What measures help explain Tao's ability to increase revenues and profits? Starting with Learning and Growth, we see that more employees were trained in new production processes than targeted and that more employee suggestions were implemented than budgeted. These advances in the learning and growth category resulted in the percentage of defect-free units produced exceeding the targeted percentage. An unfavorable result in the Internal Business Processes category was that the percentage of on-time deliveries to customers was slightly less than targeted: 94% versus the expected 95%. Lastly, the performance measures in the Customer category help to explain the increase in revenues and profits. Tao's market share of the industry was 10%, as compared to a targeted share of 8%. Also, 85% of customers surveyed gave Tao the top rating for quality and service, which exceeded the target of 80%. All told, Tao did a good job of meeting or beating its target performance measures, and these measures appear to align well with the company strategy. The On-Time Deliveries category will require a closer look.

Recall and Review 3

From the following group of performance measures, label each one as either Financial (F), Customer (C), Internal Business Processes (IBP), or Learning and Growth (LG):

Percentage of employees trained in new processes__________.
Time taken to replace defective products______________.
Market share______________________.
Gross margin percentage___________________________________.
Return on investment______________________________________.
Percentage of products returned____________________________.
Time from receipt of order to shipment______________________.
Employee turnover ratio___________________________________.

(After working this exercise, see page 468 for the solution.)

You should now be able to work the following:
Questions 16–20; Exercises 9-8 and 9-9; and Problems 9-8 and 9-9.

KEY TERMS

Activity-based costing, 456
Balanced scorecard, 463
Billing rates, 452
Cost/benefit decision, 462
Cost performance report, 451
Nonfinancial performance measures, 463
Peanut-butter costing, 457
Professional labor budget, 452
Revenue budget, 451
Variance, 451

ANSWERS TO RECALL AND REVIEW EXERCISES

R&R 1

Budgeted overhead:	
Fringe benefits	$ 300,000
Lease expense	450,000
Telephone and fax	50,000
Total	$ 800,000
Budgeted direct labor dollars:	
Associate salaries	$ 500,000
Partner salaries	700,000
Total	$1,200,000

Budgeted overhead rate = $800,000 / $1,200,000 = 66.67% of direct labor $

R&R 2

Budgeted overhead rate for paralegal support = $250,000/6,000 = $41.67 per partner hour.

Budgeted overhead rate for research support = $750,000/40,000 = $18.75 per professional labor hour.

R&R 3

Percentage of employees trained in new processes, Learning and Growth; Time taken to replace defective products, Internal Business Processes; Market share, Customer; Gross margin percentage, Financial; Return on investment, Financial; Percentage of products returned, Customer; Time from receipt of order to shipment, Internal Business Processes; Employee turnover ratio, Learning and Growth.

SELF-STUDY PROBLEM 1

Allocations Using Simplified Costing Versus Activity-Based Costing

Carson and Peyton

Carson and Peyton, architects, have been using a simplified costing system in which all professional labor costs are included in a single direct cost category, professional labor; and all overhead costs are included in a single indirect cost category, professional support, and allocated to jobs by using professional labor hours as the allocation base. Consider two clients: Henry's Restaurant, which required 25 hours of design work for a new addition, and O. Cinco, who required plans for a new ultramodern home that took 40 hours to draw. The firm has two partners, who each earn a salary of $150,000 a year, and four associates, who each earn $60,000 per year. Each professional has 1,500 billable hours per year. The professional support is $1,080,000, which consists of $700,000 of design support and $380,000 of staff support. Henry's job required five hours of partner time and 20 hours of associate time. Cinco's job required 30 hours of partner time and 10 hours of associate time.

Required:

1. Prepare job cost sheets for Henry's Restaurant and O. Cinco, using a simplified costing system with one direct and one indirect cost pool.
2. Prepare job cost sheets for the two clients, using an activity-based costing system with two direct cost categories—partner labor and associate labor—and two indirect cost categories—design support and staff support. Use professional labor dollars as the cost allocation base for design support and professional labor hours for staff support. (Round rates to two decimal places.)
3. Determine the amount by which each job was under- or - overcosted, using the simplified costing system.

Suggestions:

1. When computing the overhead rate using the simplified costing system, be sure to use professional labor dollars as the cost allocation base.
2. When computing the job cost using activity-based costing, be sure to distinguish between partner labor hours and associate labor hours worked on each job.
3. When computing the job cost using activity-based costing, be sure to use professional labor dollars as the cost allocation base for design support and professional labor hours as the cost allocation base for staff support.

SOLUTION TO SELF-STUDY PROBLEM

1. Preparing the Job Cost Sheets Using a Simplified Costing System

You first must compute the average hourly wage rate for professional labor:

$$\text{Average professional wage rate} = \frac{\text{Professional salaries}}{\text{Billable hours}}$$

$$= \frac{(2 \times \$150{,}000) + (4 \times \$60{,}000)}{6 \times 1{,}500 \text{ hours}}$$

$$= \frac{\$540{,}000}{9{,}000 \text{ hours}}$$

$$= \$60 \text{ per hour}$$

Next you must compute the indirect cost rate:

$$\text{Indirect cost rate} = \frac{\text{Total indirect costs}}{\text{Professional labor hours}}$$

$$= \frac{\$1{,}080{,}000}{9{,}000 \text{ hours}}$$

$$= \$120 \text{ per hour}$$

Now you may prepare the cost sheets:

	Henry's Restaurant	**O. Cinco**
Professional labor cost:		
25 hours × $60	$1,500	
40 hours × $60		$2,400
Professional support:		
25 hours × $120	3,000	
40 hours × $120		4,800
Total	$4,500	$7,200

2. Preparing the Job Cost Sheet Using an Activity-Based Costing System
You must first compute the average hourly wage rate for each classification of professional labor:

$$\text{Partner wage rate} = \frac{\text{Partner salaries}}{\text{Partner billable hours}} = \frac{\$300{,}000}{3{,}000 \text{ hours}} = \$100 \text{ per hour}$$

$$\text{Associate wage rate} = \frac{\text{Associate salaries}}{\text{Associate billable hours}} = \frac{4 \times \$60{,}000}{4 \times 1{,}500 \text{ hours}} = \$40 \text{ per hour}$$

Next you must compute the indirect cost rates for design support and for staff support:

$$\text{Design support} = \frac{\text{Budgeted design costs}}{\text{Budgeted professional labor dollars}} = \frac{\$700{,}000}{\$540{,}000} = \$1.30 \text{ per professional labor dollar}$$

$$\text{Staff support} = \frac{\text{Budgeted staff costs}}{\text{Budgeted professional labor hours}} = \frac{\$380{,}000}{9{,}000 \text{ hours}} = \$42.22 \text{ per professional labor hour}$$

Now you may prepare the cost sheets:

	Henry's Restaurant	O. Cinco
Professional labor cost:		
5 hours × $100	$ 500	
30 hours × $100		$3,000
Associate labor cost:		
20 hours × $40	800	
10 hours × $40		400
Design support:		
$1.30 × $1,300	1,690	
$1.30 × $3,400		4,420
Staff support:		
25 hours × $42.22	1,056	
40 hours × $42.22		1,689
Total	$4,046	$9,509

3. Determining the Amount by Which Each Job Was Under- or Overcosted Using a Simplified Costing System

	Henry's Restaurant	O. Cinco
Cost using simplified system	$4,500	$ 7,200
Cost using activity-based system	4,046	9,509
Difference	$ 454	$(2,309)

The simplified costing system overcosted Henry's job by $454 (10%) and undercosted Cinco's job by $2,309 (32%).

SELF-STUDY PROBLEM 2

Designing a Balanced Scorecard

Varsity Jerseys

Varsity Jerseys manufactures athletic jerseys that are then sold to retailers. It is a very competitive industry where quality and price are important to gain space on retailers' racks. Varsity's strategy is to produce defect-free sports jerseys that can be sold at moderate prices.

Required:
Prepare a balanced scorecard, without numbers, for Varsity Jerseys that will help them to achieve their strategy and to maximize long-term shareholder value.

Suggestions:
1. Be sure to identify the company's strategy before attempting to design performance measures for a balanced scorecard.
2. Set up the four categories of balanced scorecard performances measures before including the individual performance measures.

SOLUTION TO SELF-STUDY PROBLEM
1. **Identifying the company's strategy**—Varsity's strategy is to produce high-quality jerseys at moderate prices.
2. **Identifying performance measures to meet Varsity's strategy, within the framework of the balanced scorecard:**

   Financial—Given the company's strategy, it must concentrate on increasing profits through cost reduction and expanded unit sales. (Charging premium prices is not an option given the competitiveness of the industry.) Performance measures might include:
   - Increase in operating income through cost reduction.
   - Increase in revenue through the sale of defect-free products.

Customer: Given its strategy, Varsity must appeal to cost-conscious customers who also appreciate quality. Performance measures might include:

- Number of new customers.
- Market share in the cost-conscious market.
- Percentage of jerseys returned due to customer dissatisfaction with quality and/or order filling.

Internal Business Processes: Given its strategy, Varsity must be certain that its manufacturing processes are producing high-quality jerseys in time to meet customer demand. Performance measures might include:

- Percentage of defect-free units produced.
- Number of manufacturing processes improved.
- Amount of time needed to replace defective jerseys.

Learning and growth: To achieve the high-quality production required, management must emphasize training programs and employee feedback in an effort to achieve continuous improvement. Performance measures might include:

- Percentage of employees trained in new business processes.
- Number of employee suggestions that are adopted.

QUESTIONS

1. Give at least five examples of service businesses.
2. Name two distinguishing features of service businesses.
3. What factors help to explain the growth of service businesses relative to manufacturing businesses in the United States in recent years?
4. What type of costing system do most service businesses use, and why do they use it?
5. What factors would you consider in deciding whether to use direct labor dollars or direct labor hours in charging overhead to jobs in a service firm?
6. Distinguish between a direct cost and an indirect cost when the cost object is the job.
7. What are the elements of a cost performance report?
8. Which of the various budgets is the starting point for preparing an annual budget?
9. Why is it important for professional labor hours to be budgeted with extreme care?
10. What is the difference between the accounting treatment of overhead for a service business and for a manufacturer?
11. Explain how a budgeted income statement for a service business may be used for both planning and control purposes.
12. What are the two main things that an activity-based costing system attempts to accomplish relative to direct and indirect costs?
13. Explain the concept of peanut-butter costing.
14. When is it generally worthwhile to implement an activity-based costing system?
15. Explain the concept of a cost/benefit decision and how it relates to job costing systems.
16. What is a balanced scorecard?
17. Give five examples of nonfinancial performance measures.

18. What is the relationship between a company's strategy and its choice of performance measures?

19. Name the four categories that performance measures are typically divided into, and give an example of a performance measure for each category.

20. Why should a company bother with a balanced scorecard approach to performance measurement when its primary goal is to earn a sufficient return on investment for its shareholders?

EXERCISES

E9-1 **Computing budgeted overhead rates**

LO1

Hayes and Manolis have a professional service firm that has the following budgeted costs for the current year:

Associates' salaries	$300,000
Depreciation—equipment	50,000
Fringe benefits	150,000
Lease expense	220,000
Partners' salaries	200,000
Telephone and fax	30,000

Compute the budgeted overhead rate for the coming year, using direct labor dollars as the overhead allocation base.

E9-2 **Computing profit or loss on a bid**

LO1

Brown and Stetham, plumbers, successfully bid $30,000 for the plumbing work on a new luxury home. Total direct labor cost on the job was $9,500, other direct costs were $2,500, and overhead is charged to jobs at 150% of direct labor cost.

1. Compute the profit or loss on the job in (a) dollars and (b) as a percentage of the bid price.
2. Express labor and overhead as a percentage of total costs.

E9-3 **Preparing a revenue budget**

LO2

Chiao and Piaker, CPAs, budgeted for the following professional labor hours for the coming year: partners, 1,500; managers, 5,000; and staff, 20,000. Budgeted billing rates are: partners, $250 per hour; managers, $120 per hour; and staff accountants, $80 per hour.

Prepare a revenue budget for the year ending December 31, 2011.

E9-4 Preparing a budgeted income statement

LO2

Jones and Wang, physicians, budgeted for the following revenue and expenses for the month of September:

Depreciation—equipment	$ 1,850
Fringe benefits	3,300
Lease expense	2,500
Nursing wages	4,500
Physicians' salaries	28,000
Patient revenue	58,500
Secretarial support	2,200
Utilities	650

Prepare a budgeted income statement for the month ending September 30, 2011.

E9-5 Computing activity-based costing rates

LO3

The partners of Harris and Whelan, attorneys-at-law, decide to implement an activity-based costing system for their firm. They identify the following three cost pools and budgeted amounts for each for the coming year: fringe benefits, $450,000; paralegal support, $250,000; and research support, $650,000. It is determined that the best cost driver for fringe benefits is professional labor dollars ($1,500,000); paralegal support is partner labor hours (4,000); and research support is professional labor hours (20,000).

Compute the budgeted overhead rates for each of the three cost pools.

E9-6 Job cost for a client (continuation of E9-5)

LO3

A client, Carolyn Goode, requires 10 partner labor hours and 25 professional associate hours from Harris and Whelan, the law firm in E9-5. Partners are paid $125 per hour, and associates make $60 per hour.

Compute the job cost of servicing Carolyn Goode.

E9-7 Comparisons of a simplified costing system with an activity-based system (continuation of E9-5 and E9-6)

LO4

Prior to instituting an activity-based costing system, Harris and Whelan, the attorneys in E9-5 and E9-6, utilized a simplified costing system with one direct cost category, professional labor, and one indirect cost category, professional support. The average wage rate for professional labor was $75 per hour, and the overhead rate for professional support was $67.50 per professional labor hour.

Compute the job cost for Carolyn Goode, the client in E9-6, using the simplified costing system, and determine the difference between it and the job cost using activity-based costing in E9-6 and discuss the reasons for the difference.

E9-8 **Categorizing balanced scorecard performance measures**

LO5

From the following list of performance measures, label each one as Financial, Customer, Internal Business Processes, or Learning and Growth:

Percentage of on-time deliveries
Employee turnover ratio
Revenue from new products
Number of new customers
Percentage of compensation based on team performance
Percentage of products returned
Operating income
Time taken to replace defective products

E9-9 **Evaluating the appropriateness of performance measures**

LO5

Hi-End, Inc., a chain of gasoline service stations, has a strategy of charging premium prices for its gasoline by providing excellent service such as attendants to pump gas, clean restrooms, and free air for tire inflation. Its balanced scorecard performance measures include: Increase in operating income through cost reduction (Financial); Market share in the overall gasoline market (Customer); Wait-time at the pump (Internal Business Processes); and Employee bonus based on number of customers served (Learning and Growth). Indicate whether or not each of these performance measures is appropriate, given Hi-End's strategy.

PROBLEMS

P9-1 **Job cost sheet for a service business**

LO1

Shank and Verst, attorneys-at-law, provided legal representation to Baldwin Equipment, Inc., in a product liability suit. Twenty partner hours and 65 associate hours were worked in defending the company. The cost of each partner hour is $325, which includes partner wages plus overhead based on direct labor cost. The cost of each associate hour is $145, which also includes both wages and overhead. Other costs that can be directly identified with the job are travel ($2,800) and telephone/fax/copying charges ($1,740). The date Baldwin contracted with Shank and Verst was May 8, 2011, and the defense was successfully completed on December 21, 2011. The engagement number is 525.

Required:

Prepare a job order cost sheet, in good form, for Baldwin Equipment, Inc.

P9-2 **Cost performance report and budgeted profit and actual profit for a service business**

LO1

The budget for the Baldwin Equipment, Inc. job in P9-1 consisted of the following amounts:

Partners' salary and overhead	$6,300
Associates' salary and overhead	9,175
Travel	4,150
Telephone/fax/copying	1,475

The successful bid price of the job was $30,000.

Required:

1. Prepare a cost performance report.
2. Compute the budgeted profit and the actual profit on the job.

P9-3 **Preparing a revenue budget and a labor budget for a service business**

Matthews and Thomas, partners in a systems consulting firm, budgeted the following professional labor hours for the year ended December 31, 2011:

Partners	4,000
Associates	14,000
Staff	22,000

Partners have a billing rate of $225 per hour and actually earn $110 per hour. Associates bill out at $140 per hour and earn $85 per hour. Staff bill out at a rate of $75 per hour and earn $35 per hour.

Required:

1. Prepare a revenue budget.
2. Prepare a professional labor budget.

P9-4 **Preparing an overhead budget, an other expenses budget, and a budgeted income statement**

LO2

Matthews and Thomas, the systems consultants in P9-3, budgeted overhead and other expenses as follows for the year ended December 31, 2011:

Overhead:	
Depreciation—equipment	$ 60,000
Depreciation—building	135,000
Fringe benefits	385,000
Photocopying	95,000
Secretarial support	465,000
Telephone/fax	115,000
Utilities	193,000
Other direct expenses:	
Travel	$123,000
Meals	37,000

Required:
1. Prepare an Overhead budget.
2. Prepare an Other Expenses budget.
3. Prepare a Budgeted Income Statement.

P9-5 Computing activity-based costing rates

LO3

The partners of Mayweather and Pacquiao, a security services firm, decide to implement an activity-based costing system. They identify the following three cost pools and budgeted amounts for each for the coming year: fringe benefits, $400,000; technology support, $20,000; and litigation support, $300,000. It is determined that the best cost driver for fringe benefits is professional labor dollars ($2,000,000); technology support is partner labor hours (2,000); and research support is professional labor hours (25,000).

Required:
Compute the budgeted overhead rate for each of the three cost pools.

P9-6 Allocations using simplified costing versus activity-based costing
similar to Self-Study Problem 1

LO4

Boyer and Kubek, architects, have been using a simplified costing system in which all professional labor costs are included in a single direct cost category, professional labor; and all overhead costs are included in a single indirect cost pool, professional support, and allocated to jobs using professional labor hours as the allocation base. Consider two clients: Young Products, which required 50 hours of design work for a new addition, and Doug's Markets, which required plans for a new store that took 20 hours to draw. The firm has two partners, who each earn a salary of $150,000 a year, and four associates, who each earn $60,000 per year. Each professional has 1,500 billable hours per year. The professional support is $360,000, which consists of $120,000 of design support and $240,000 of staff support. Young's job required 30 hours of partner time and 20 hours of associate time. Doug's job required 5 hours of partner time and 15 hours of associate time.

Required:
1. Prepare job cost sheets for Young Products and Doug's Markets, using a simplified costing system with one direct and one indirect cost pool.
2. Prepare job cost sheets for the two clients, using an activity-based costing system with two direct cost categories, partner labor and associate labor, and two indirect cost categories, design support and staff support. Use professional labor dollars as the cost allocation base for design support and professional labor hours for staff support. (Round rates to two decimal places.)

LO4

P9-7 Comparing the results of cost allocations, using simplified costing versus activity-based costing

Required:
Referring to P9-6, compare the results of the cost allocations to the Young Products and Doug's Markets jobs under the simplified costing system and the activity-based costing system. Label each difference as undercosted or overcosted relative to the simplified costing system.

LO5

P9-8 Designing a balanced scorecard similar to Self-Study Problem 2

Mercury Athletics manufactures sporting goods that are then sold to retailers. It is a very competitive industry where quality and price are important to gain space on retailers' shelves. Mercury's strategy is to produce defect-free athletic equipment that can be sold at moderate prices.

Required:
Prepare a balanced scorecard, without numbers, for Mercury Athletics that will help them to achieve their strategy and to maximize long-term shareholder value.

LO5

P9-9 Designing a balanced scorecard

Dayton Dairies is a vertically integrated company that has dairy farms, processing plants, and retail ice cream stores. Dayton's strategy is to maximize shareholder value by providing top-of-the-line ice cream products that are high in butter fat and for which consumers will pay premium prices.

Required:
Prepare a balanced scorecard for Dayton Dairies, without numbers, that will help them to achieve their strategy and to maximize long-term shareholder value.

MINI-CASE

LO4

Comparing the results of cost allocations, using simplified costing versus activity-based costing

Ed Hickey, the consultant introduced at the beginning of section two of the chapter (p. 456), has obtained the following data relative to the Kaufman and D'Esti consulting job:

	Partner Labor	Associate Labor
Number of attorneys	5	20
Annual billable hours per attorney	2,000	2,000
Annual compensation per attorney	$250,000	$100,000

	Legal Support	Secretarial Support
Annual overhead estimate	$2,500,000	$1,000,000

Assume that the Binghamton job will require 50 partner hours and 20 associate hours, while the Johnson City job will require 15 partner hours and 55 associate hours.

Required:

1. **a.** Using a simplified costing system with one direct cost category for professional labor and one indirect cost category for support costs with professional labor hours as the allocation base, compute the bid price for the Binghamton job and the Johnson City job, assuming a 25% markup on cost. (Round to the nearest whole dollar.)
   b. Do you think that your results seem reasonable?
2. Using an activity-based costing system with two direct cost categories for partner labor and associate labor and two indirect cost categories, one for legal support and one for secretarial support with cost allocation bases of professional labor hours and partner labor hours, respectively, compute the bid price for the Binghamton job and the Johnson City job assuming a markup of 25% on cost.
3. **a.** Compute the difference in bid price for each job between the simplified costing system and the activity-based costing system.
   b. Were the jobs undercosted, overcosted, or a combination of each? Which job had the greater differential, depending on which costing system was used, and why?

INTERNET EXERCISE

A service business that uses job order costing

One of the service businesses referred to in the chapter was the international accounting firm of PricewaterhouseCoopers (PwC). Go to the text Web site at www.cengage.com/accounting/vanderbeck and click on the link to PricewaterhouseCoopers' Web site. Then answer the following questions.

1. Explain PwC's "Connected Thinking" approach to work.
2. Approximately how many students per year does PwC hire for its internship program? What type of professional guidance do you receive as a PwC intern? Describe the training that takes place during the approximately first two weeks of a PwC internship?
3. Relative to PwC's Code of Conduct, list at least five examples that are given to define professional behavior.

Chapter 10

Cost Analysis for Management Decision Making

Learning Objectives

After studying this chapter, you should be able to:

- LO1 Compute net income under variable and absorption costing.
- LO2 Discuss the merits and limitations of variable costing.
- LO3 Define segment profitability and distinguish between direct and indirect costs.
- LO4 Compute the break-even point and the target volume needed to earn a certain profit.
- LO5 Calculate the contribution margin ratio and the margin of safety ratio.
- LO6 Discuss the impact of income tax on break-even computations.
- LO7 Use differential analysis to make special decisions.
- LO8 Identify techniques for analyzing and controlling distribution costs.

An article, "Steelmakers Weigh Cuts in Production," appearing in the October 8, 2008, *Wall Street Journal*, reported on a Washington meeting of steelmakers at which they discussed how far to cut output in an effort to preclude the selling price of steel falling below the break-even cost of making it:

"The price of the benchmark steel product, hot-rolled steel, is $780 a metric ton on global markets, says Peter Marcus, steel analyst for World Steel Dynamics. That is down from $1,000 a metric ton earlier this year but still above the $650 it costs for most steelmakers to make a metric ton of steel."[1]

The **break-even point** is the point at which sales revenue is adequate to cover all costs to manufacture and sell the product, but no profit is earned. Break-even analysis is one of the useful tools described in this chapter that help managers to make better business decisions.

Many studies that generate special reports for management use regularly accumulated cost data. Often, however, the accounting system's regularly compiled data must be altered and enhanced to create additional reports because of economic occurrences that were not predicted. These reports, which are prepared for internal use and are not distributed to external parties, require that the user understand terminology not commonly used in operational cost accounting systems.

1 Robert Guy Matthews, "Steelmakers Weigh Cuts in Production," *The Wall Street Journal*, October 8, 2008.

This chapter introduces and defines several new terms relating to the special-purpose reports for internal management decision making.

Variable Costing and Absorption Costing

 Compute net income under variable and absorption costing.

Under **variable costing**, the cost of a manufactured product includes only the costs that vary directly with volume: direct materials, direct labor, and variable factory overhead. This method is referred to as variable costing, sometimes called **direct costing**, because only variable manufacturing costs are assigned to the inventoried product cost, whereas fixed factory overhead is classified as a period cost and charged to expense in the period in which the fixed costs were incurred.

The alternative to variable costing is **absorption costing** or **full costing** (the method used in the preceding chapters and the only one accepted for external financial reporting). Under this method, both fixed and variable manufacturing costs are assigned to the product, and no particular attention is given to classifying the costs as either fixed or variable.

Product Costs Versus Period Costs

All costs, both manufacturing and nonmanufacturing, can be classified as either product costs or period costs. As discussed in previous chapters, **product costs** (or inventory costs) are assigned to Work in Process as production occurs and subsequently transferred to Finished Goods as products are completed. When inventory is sold, product costs are recognized as an expense (cost of goods sold) and matched with the related revenues from the sale of the products. In contrast, **period costs** are not assigned to the product but are recognized as expenses in the period incurred. All nonmanufacturing costs are period costs. These include selling expenses as well as general and administrative expenses.

The only difference between variable costing and absorption costing is the classification of fixed factory overhead. Under variable costing, fixed overhead costs are classified as period costs. Under absorption costing, they are treated as product costs. Selling and administrative expenses are period costs under both methods. Figure 10-1 compares the flow of costs under variable costing and absorption costing.

Illustration of Variable and Absorption Costing Methods

To illustrate the differences between variable costing and absorption costing, assume the following budgeted selling price and standard costs for a three-month period:

Selling price per unit	$ 11
Variable cost per unit:	
Direct materials	$ 2
Direct labor	2
Variable factory overhead	1
Variable cost per unit	$ 5

Figure 10-1 Comparison of Absorption Costing and Variable Costing

Absorption Costing:

Direct Material
Direct Labor
Variable Manufacturing Overhead
Fixed Manufacturing Overhead

Product Costs

Inventory Accounts on Balance Sheet → Cost of Goods Sold When Finished Goods Are Sold → Expense Accounts on Income Statement

Selling Costs
Administrative Costs

Period Costs

Variable Costing:

Direct Material
Direct Labor
Variable Manufacturing Overhead

Product Costs

Inventory Accounts on Balance Sheet → Cost of Goods Sold When Finished Goods Are Sold → Expense Accounts on Income Statement

Fixed Manufacturing Overhead
Selling Costs
Administrative Costs

Period Costs

Fixed cost per unit:

Fixed factory overhead for the year	$108,000
Normal production for the year in units	36,000
Fixed cost per unit ($108,000 ÷ 36,000)	$ 3

	Units Produced	Units Sold
January	3,000	1,500
February	500	2,000
March	4,000	2,000

January has no beginning inventories.

The comparative production report in Figure 10-2 shows the costs charged to the product under each costing method. Note that under absorption costing, the goods manufactured in January are charged with the standard costs of the direct materials, direct labor, and both variable and fixed factory overhead, totaling $8 ($2 + $2 + $1 + $3) per unit. Under variable costing, the fixed factory overhead is not charged to the product, resulting in a unit cost of $5.

Figure 10-2 **Comparison of Product Costs for Absorption Costing and Variable Costing**

Comparative Production Report

	January (3,000 units)		February (500 units)		March (4,000 units)	
	Absorption Costing	Variable Costing	Absorption Costing	Variable Costing	Absorption Costing	Variable Costing
Direct materials	$ 6,000	$ 6,000	$1,000	$1,000	$ 8,000	$ 8,000
Direct labor	6,000	6,000	1,000	1,000	8,000	8,000
Variable factory overhead	3,000	3,000	500	500	4,000	4,000
Fixed factory overhead	9,000	—	1,500	—	12,000	—
Total cost	$24,000	$15,000	$4,000	$2,500	$32,000	$20,000
Unit cost	$ 8	$ 5	$ 8	$ 5	$ 8	$ 5

Figure 10-3 uses absorption costing to compare the average fixed factory overhead of $9,000 ($108,000 ÷ 12) per month with the amount applied to units produced each month. In January, 3,000 units are manufactured, and the manufacturing costs under absorption costing include $9,000 ($3 × 3,000) in fixed factory overhead. February manufacturing costs covering the 500 units produced include fixed factory overhead of $1,500 ($3 × 500), and the manufacturing costs for March covering the 4,000 units produced include $12,000 ($3 × 4,000) of fixed factory overhead. As a result of the unevenness of production, $7,500 ($9,000 actual − $1,500 applied) of fixed expense in February is not included in manufacturing costs (underapplied), but in March, the fixed overhead is overapplied by $3,000 ($12,000 applied − $9,000 actual). These variances of underapplied and overapplied factory overhead are reflected in the income statements for February and March as (respectively) an addition to and a deduction from cost of goods sold. Under variable costing, no fixed factory overhead expenses are charged to production in any month. These fixed costs appear as an expense of $9,000 on each month's income statement, along with selling and administrative expenses.

Figure 10-4 compares the effects of variable costing and absorption costing on income. Each month, the cost of goods sold reflects a cost of $8 per unit under absorption costing, compared to $5 per unit under variable

Figure 10-3 **Schedule of Fixed Overhead Applied under Absorption Costing**

Fixed Overhead Applied—Absorption Costing

	January	February	March
Monthly fixed factory overhead	$9,000	$9,000	$ 9,000
Fixed factory overhead applied	9,000	1,500	12,000
Under (over)applied overhead	-0-	$7,500	$ (3,000)

Figure 10-4 **Comparison of Net Income for Absorption Costing and Variable Costing**

Comparative Income Statements
For Three Months Ended March 31, 2011

	January (3,000 units produced, 1,500 units sold)		February (500 units produced, 2,000 units sold)		March (4,000 units produced, 2,000 units sold)	
	Absorption Costing	Variable Costing	Absorption Costing	Variable Costing	Absorption Costing	Variable Costing
Sales	$ 16,500	$16,500	$ 22,000	$ 22,000	$ 22,000	$ 22,000
Cost of goods sold (see schedule below)	(12,000)	(7,500)	(16,000)	(10,000)	(16,000)	(10,000)
(Under-)/overapplied factory overhead	—	—	(7,500)	—	3,000	—
Gross margin (loss)	$ 4,500		$ (1,500)		$ 9,000	
Manufacturing margin		$ 9,000		$ 12,000		$ 12,000
Less:						
Fixed factory overhead		(9,000)		(9,000)		(9,000)
Selling and administrative expenses	(2,000)	(2,000)	(2,000)	(2,000)	(2,000)	(2,000)
Net income (loss)	$ 2,500	$ (2,000)	$ (3,500)	$ 1,000	$ 7,000	$ 1,000

Comparative Schedule of Cost of Goods Sold
For Three Months Ended March 31, 2011

Beginning finished goods inventory	—	—	$12,000	$ 7,500	—	—
Cost of goods manufactured	$24,000	$15,000	4,000	2,500	$32,000	$20,000
Goods available for sale	$24,000	$15,000	$16,000	$10,000	$32,000	$20,000
Less ending finished goods inventory	12,000	7,500	—	—	16,000	10,000
Cost of goods sold	$12,000	$ 7,500	$16,000	$10,000	$16,000	$10,000

costing. Under absorption costing, the difference between sales revenue and cost of goods sold is termed the **gross margin** or **gross profit** (Sales – Cost of Goods Sold). The term commonly used in variable costing to designate the difference between sales and cost of goods sold is **manufacturing margin** (Sales – Variable Cost of Goods Sold). Because cost of goods sold determined under absorption costing includes both fixed and variable overhead but includes only variable overhead under variable costing, it follows that the gross margin under absorption costing is always lower than the manufacturing margin under direct costing.

Under absorption costing, selling and administrative expenses are deducted from the gross margin to determine net income or loss. In the illustration, all of these costs are assumed to be fixed costs of $2,000 each month. Under variable costing, the total amount of monthly fixed overhead is deducted from the manufacturing margin, along with the fixed selling and administrative expenses. Thus, $9,000 ($108,000/12) of fixed overhead costs is charged against revenue each month regardless of the number of units produced or sold.

An examination of the comparative income statements in Figure 10-4 reveals the effect of fluctuating production on reported income under absorption costing. Although February sales revenue of $22,000 exceeded January sales revenue of $16,500, the net income decreased from $2,500 in January to a net loss of $3,500 in February (as a result of the decreased production that caused more of the fixed factory overhead to be released to cost of goods sold). This decrease is caused by adding $7,500 ($9,000 monthly fixed factory overhead – $1,500 overhead applied) of underapplied overhead at the end of February to the cost of goods sold.

March sales revenue of $22,000 is the same as February sales revenue, but reported net income under absorption costing increased from a $3,500 net loss in February to a $7,000 net income in March. This increase is due to the increased production that caused more of the fixed factory overhead to be applied to production in March than in February. In fact, overhead is overapplied in March, and this overapplication is shown as a decrease in cost of goods sold of $3,000 ($9,000 monthly fixed factory overhead – $12,000 overhead applied) because some of the fixed overhead costs are held back in inventory.

Figure 10-5 The Effect of Changes in Inventory Levels on Income under Absorption Costing and Variable Costing

Monthly Production vs. Sales	Inventory Effect 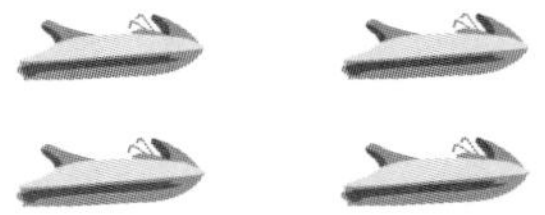	Absorption Costing vs. Variable Costing Operating Income
Production = Sales	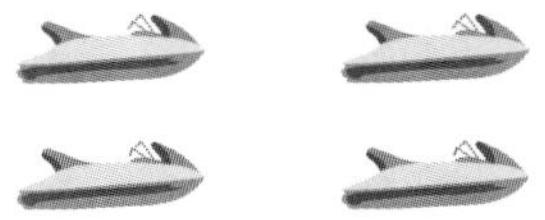	Absorption Costing Income Equals Variable Costing Income
Production > Sales		Absorption Costing Income Greater Than Variable Costing Income (Some Fixed Manufacturing Overhead Is Held Back in Inventory under Absorption Costing as Inventories Increase)
Sales > Production		Variable Costing Income Greater Than Absorption Costing Income (Some Fixed Manufacturing Overhead Is Released from Inventory and Charged to Cost of Goods Sold under Absorption Costing as Inventories Decrease)

A study of the income statements under variable costing shows that as sales increase in February, income also increases from a $2,000 loss to a $1,000 profit. When sales remain the same in March as they were in February, income remains at $1,000. Variable costing is often used for management decision making because of the intuition that profits should increase as sales increase. Under absorption costing, profits are affected by the dynamic of units produced versus units sold, with the fixed overhead either being held back in inventory (production exceeds sales) or released to cost of goods sold (sales exceed production). Figure 10-5 illustrates the effect that differences between the number of units produced and sold have on income as computed under absorption costing and under variable costing.

Inventories have a higher cost under absorption costing than under variable costing because fixed costs are included in the cost of inventory in absorption costing. This element of fixed cost will not be reported as a charge against revenue until the goods are sold. Under variable costing, fixed costs are not included in inventory; they are charged against revenue for the period in which they are incurred.

Merits and Limitations of Variable Costing

LO2 Discuss the merits and limitations of variable costing.

The merits of variable costing may be viewed in terms of the usefulness of the data provided by its application. Some company managers believe that variable costing furnishes more understandable data regarding costs, volumes, revenues, and profits to members of management who are not formally trained in the field of accounting. It presents cost data in a manner that highlights the relationship between sales and variable production costs, which move in the same direction as sales. Furthermore, they believe that variable costing helps management planning because it presents a clearer picture of how changes in production volume affect costs and income. From the variable costing portion of the production report in Figure 10-2, management can determine that units produced and sold above normal production of 3,000 units will cost only $5 each in out-of-pocket expenditures for variable costs because the fixed manufacturing costs of $9,000 have been completely covered by the expected normal production (3,000 units × $3 per unit). Therefore, the additional units will produce a marginal income of $6 ($11 selling price − $5 variable manufacturing costs) each. Assume that a plant's capacity is not fully utilized and management has the opportunity to fill a special order at a selling price of $7 each without incurring any additional selling and administrative expenses. If management incorrectly used the absorption cost of $8 per unit in Figure 10-2 to make this decision, then it would reject the special order. If management correctly compared the selling price of $7 per unit to the additional variable costs of $5, then it would accept the special order and earn additional income of $2 per unit because the fixed overhead cost of $3 per unit had already been absorbed by the normal production and thus should not be considered in making this decision. Only the additional variable costs are relevant to the decision concerning whether to make the sale at a reduced price.

Although variable costing may provide useful information for internal decision making, it is not a generally accepted method of inventory costing for external reporting purposes. The measurement of income, in traditional accounting theory, is based on the matching of revenues with all associated costs. Under absorption costing, product costs include all variable and fixed manufacturing costs. These costs are matched with the sales revenue in the period in which the goods are sold. Variable costing, however, matches only the variable manufacturing costs with revenue. Absorption costing must be used for income tax purposes as well as for external financial statements. Regulations of the Internal Revenue Service specifically prohibit variable costing in computing taxable income.

Variable costing is also criticized because no fixed factory overhead cost is included in work in process or finished goods inventories. In the opinion of variable costing opponents, both fixed and variable costs are incurred in manufacturing products. Because the inventory figures do not reflect the total cost of production, they do not present a realistic inventory cost valuation on the balance sheet.

Adjustments can be made to the inventory figures to reflect absorption cost on published financial reports while retaining the benefits of variable costing for internal decision-making purposes. In the example given, the unit cost was $5 under variable costing and $8 under absorption costing. Absorption costing is 160% ($8/$5) of variable costing, so inventories could be adjusted as follows:

	Ending Inventory Under Variable Costing	Absorption-Variable Cost Ratio	Ending Inventory Under Absorption Costing
January	$ 7,500	× 160%	$12,000
February	None		None
March	$10,000	× 160%	$16,000

Recall and Review 1

A company had income of $100,000 using variable costing for a given period. Beginning and ending inventories were 9,000 and 12,000 units, respectively. If the fixed overhead application rate was $4 per unit, then the income using absorption costing must have been $__________.

(After working this exercise, see page 508 for the solution.)

You should now be able to work the following:
Questions 1-4; Exercises 10-1 to 10-6; Problems 10-1 and 10-2; and Mini-Case 1.

Segment Reporting for Profitability Analysis

LO3 Define segment profitability and distinguish between direct and indirect costs.

Segment reporting provides data that management can use to evaluate the operations and profitability of individual segments within a company. A **segment** may be a division, a product line, a sales territory, or other identifiable organizational unit.

The validity of a segment profitability analysis may be questioned if it is based on absorption costing data. This is because the measure of each segment's profitability may be distorted by arbitrarily assigning indirect costs to the segments being examined. The contribution margin approach (as used in variable costing), which separates the fixed and variable elements that constitute cost, is often used to overcome these objections.

Segment profitability analysis requires that all costs be classified into one of two categories: direct or indirect. A **direct (traceable) cost** is a cost that can be traced to the segment being analyzed. Direct costs include both variable and fixed costs that are directly identifiable with a specific segment. An **indirect (nontraceable) cost** is a cost that cannot be identified directly with a specific segment; this cost is often referred to in segment analysis as a **common cost**. Under the contribution margin approach, only those costs directly traceable to a segment are assigned to the segment. The excess of segment revenue over variable direct costs—manufacturing as well as selling and administrative—is called **contribution margin**, and the remainder after direct fixed costs (also manufacturing and selling and administrative) are assigned to the segment is called the **segment margin**. Indirect costs are excluded from the computation of the segment margin.

Although indirect costs cannot be directly identified with a specific segment, they are identifiable as being common to all segments at a particular level of an organization. Often the differences between direct and indirect costs are not markedly distinctive; however, the costs that will disappear when the company eliminates the segment should be classified as direct costs. Costs that are difficult to classify should not be allocated to individual segments without a careful evaluation of the allocation method. For instance, if a company consists of two divisions, then each division manager's salary would be a direct fixed cost to the division. However, if each division manufactured two products, then each division's product segment report would classify the manager's salary as an indirect cost. Arbitrarily allocating the manager's salary to one of the products would distort the profitability shown for each product.

Figure 10-6 shows two segment reports, one listed by divisions and the other listed by products for one of the divisions. The company is divided into two divisions, and each division manufactures two products.

An analysis of the segment report by divisions reveals that the division segment margin was $75,000 for the total company. The Paper Division contributed $10,000 to the margin, and the Cosmetics Division contributed $65,000. The direct fixed costs chargeable to the divisions totaled $125,000, and the unallocated common fixed costs totaled $50,000.

When the Paper Division is isolated and analyzed to determine how each product contributed to the segment margin of $10,000, the direct fixed costs chargeable to the individual products amount to $35,000. Tissues are charged $20,000 and Towels, $15,000. The Paper Division has unallocated common fixed costs of $30,000, which are not directly chargeable to either product. For example, the $25,000 for Administration listed under common fixed costs in the segment report by product, may represent the monthly salary of

Figure 10-6 **Segment Report by Division and by Product**

	Segment Report by Division for the Month Ended March 31, 2011			Segment Report by Product for the Month Ended March 31, 2011—Paper Division		
	Total Company	Paper Division	Cosmetics Division	Total Paper Division	Product Tissues	Product Towels
Sales	$1,000,000	$750,000	$250,000	$750,000	$500,000	$250,000
Less variable costs	800,000	675,000	125,000	675,000	450,000	225,000
Contribution margin	$ 200,000	$ 75,000	$125,000	$ 75,000	$ 50,000	$ 25,000
Less direct fixed costs:						
Production	$ 50,000	$ 25,000	$ 25,000	$ 20,000	$ 10,000	$ 10,000
Administration	75,000	40,000	35,000	15,000	10,000	5,000
Total direct fixed costs	$ 125,000	$ 65,000	$ 60,000	$ 35,000	$ 20,000	$ 15,000
Segment margin	$ 75,000	$ 10,000	$ 65,000	$ 40,000	$ 30,000	$ 10,000
Less common fixed costs:						
Selling	$ 30,000					
Production				$ 5,000		
Administration	20,000			25,000		
Total common fixed costs	$ 50,000			$ 30,000		
Segment margin				$ 10,000		
Net income	$ 25,000					

the Senior Vice-President of the Paper Division who oversees both products. The $5,000 common fixed costs for Production may represent monthly depreciation on the plant where both tissues and towels are produced. These reports reveal how costs shift from one category to another depending on the segment under scrutiny. Each segment report prepared for a company isolates those costs, variable and fixed, that can be charged directly to the segment elements. As different segments are analyzed, these costs may be direct costs in one segment and indirect costs in another segment.

The divisions' contribution margins are determined by subtracting the variable costs from the sales. The contribution margin can be used as a guide in making management decisions regarding short-run opportunities, such as pricing special orders when there is excess capacity.

The direct fixed costs chargeable to each segment are subtracted from the contribution margin to determine the segment margin. The segment margin can be used as a guide indicating the segment's long-run profitability. In other words, it measures the ability of the division or product to recover not only its variable costs but also the direct fixed costs that must be recovered to keep the company solvent in the long run. In the short run, if a segment margin is positive, then the segment should be retained even if the company as a whole is operating at a loss. Because the common fixed costs will usually remain at the same level even if a segment is eliminated, deleting a segment with a positive segment margin can only increase the amount of the company's net loss. The segment margin remaining after direct variable and fixed costs have been deducted is the amount left over to help cover the unallocated common costs and to earn a profit. The segment margin analysis is particularly beneficial as an aid to making decisions that relate to a company's long-run requirements and performance: changing production capacities, product pricing policies, decisions to retain or eliminate specific segments, and analyses of segment managers' performance.

Cost-Volume-Profit Analysis

LO4 Compute the break-even point and the target volume needed to earn a certain profit.

A company's net income is a measure of management's success in attaining its goals. In planning, management must anticipate how selling prices, costs, expenses, and profits will react to changes in activity when the activity is measured in terms of capacity or volume. When the degree of variability in costs is known, the effect of volume changes can be predicted.

Cost-volume-profit (CVP) analysis is a technique that uses the degrees of cost variability to measure the effect of changes in volume on resulting profits. Such analysis assumes that the fixed costs of the firm will remain the same in total within a wide range of production volume within which the firm expects to operate, known as the **relevant range**. The publisher of this textbook incurred both variable and fixed costs. For example, the costs of typesetting to produce the book and advertising to sell the book are fixed because these costs are not much affected by whether a large or small number of textbooks are eventually sold. In comparison, printing and binding costs are variable because the greater the number of books that are sold, the greater the number that have to be printed and bound.

Break-even Analysis

The usual starting point in CVP analysis is the determination of a firm's break-even point. The **break-even point** is defined as the point at which sales revenue is adequate to cover all costs to manufacture and sell the product but not enough to generate any profit. Surveys indicate that more than 50% of companies worldwide use break-even analysis. Typical break-even points include 60% occupancy for the hotel industry and 70% capacity for the airline industry. Figure 10-7 illustrates the percentage of seats filled on international flights in 2006 through 2008 and in the first quarter of 2009.[2] The equation for the break-even point can be stated as follows:

Sales revenue (to break even) = Cost to manufacture
+ Selling and administrative costs

2 International Air Transport Association, www.iataonline.com, viewed August 13, 2009.

Figure 10-7 Airline Load Factors (percentage of seats filled)

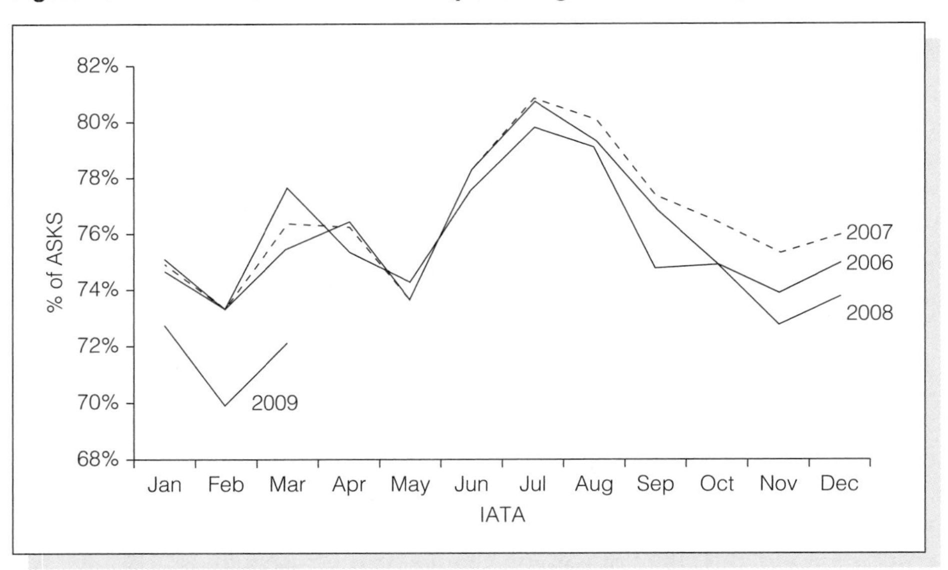

Break-even analysis relies on segregating costs according to whether they are "variable" (changing as the activity level changes) or "fixed" (not changing as the activity level changes) within a relevant range. The break-even equation may be rewritten as follows:

Sales revenue (to break even) = Fixed Manufacturing and Selling and Administrative Costs + Variable Manufacturing and Selling and Administrative Costs

Note that the variable and fixed costs may each consist of both manufacturing costs and selling and administrative costs. The annual income statement for Vortex Manufacturing, Inc., a new startup company, in condensed form follows. (**Net operating income** equals profit before interest expense and income tax expense.)

Vortex Manufacturing Company
Income Statement
For the Year Ended December 31, 2011

Net sales (10,000 units at $10)		$100,000
Cost of goods sold:		
Materials	$20,000	
Labor	25,000	
Factory overhead	15,000	60,000
Gross margin on sales		$ 40,000
Operating expenses:		
Selling expense	$15,000	
Administrative expense	10,000	25,000
Net operating income		$ 15,000

The costs and expenses of Vortex Manufacturing, Inc., were analyzed and classified as follows [The analysis shows that variable costs are 70% of net sales ($70,000/$100,000), meaning that $.70 of each sales dollar is consumed by variable costs. Fixed costs will remain at $15,000 within a wide range of production and sales volume]:

Items	Total	Variable Costs	Fixed Costs
Materials	$20,000	$20,000	
Labor	25,000	25,000	
Factory overhead	15,000	10,000	$ 5,000
Selling expense	15,000	10,000	5,000
Administrative expense	10,000	5,000	5,000
	$85,000	$70,000	$15,000

The break-even equation in mathematical terms is as follows:

$$\text{Break-even sales volume (dollars)} = \frac{\text{Total fixed costs}}{\text{Contribution margin ratio}}$$

The **contribution margin** is determined by subtracting variable costs from sales revenue; it represents the amount available to cover fixed costs and earn a profit. The **contribution margin ratio** expresses the relationship, in percentage terms, between contribution margin and sales. In the Vortex Manufacturing, Inc., example, if variable costs are $.70 of each sales dollar, then the contribution margin is $.30 of each sales dollar and the contribution margin ratio is 0.30 or 30%. The break-even point in sales revenue for Vortex Manufacturing, Inc., would be determined as follows (note that once the denominator is simplified, it becomes the contribution margin ratio of 30%):

$$\begin{aligned}\text{Break-even sales volume (dollars)} &= \frac{\text{Total fixed costs}}{1 - (\text{Variable costs/Sales revenue})}\\ &= \frac{\$15{,}000}{1 - (\$70{,}000/\$100{,}000)}\\ &= \frac{\$15{,}000}{1 - 0.70}\\ &= \frac{\$15{,}000}{0.30}\\ &= \$50{,}000\end{aligned}$$

This means that $50,000 in sales revenue must be generated to cover all costs. The break-even sales volume in dollars can be proved by preparing an income statement in contribution format:

Sales at break-even point	$50,000
Less variable costs at break-even point (70% × $50,000)	35,000
Contribution margin	$15,000
Less fixed costs	15,000
Net operating income (loss)	-0-

The break-even point can also be calculated in units by using the following equation:

$$\text{Break-even sales volume (units)} = \frac{\text{Total fixed cost}}{\text{Unit contribution margin}}$$

The unit contribution margin is merely the unit sales price minus the unit variable costs. Using this equation, we find that the break-even point for Vortex Manufacturing, Inc., would be as follows:

$$\text{Break-even sales volume} = \frac{\text{Total fixed cost}}{\text{Unit sales price} - \text{Unit variable costs}}$$

$$\text{Break-even sales volume} = \frac{\$15{,}000}{\$10 - (\$70{,}000 \text{ variable costs}/10{,}000 \text{ units})}$$

$$= \frac{\$15{,}000}{\$3}$$

$$= 5{,}000 \text{ units}$$

Note that 5,000 units multiplied by a selling price of $10 per unit equals the $50,000 break-even sales volume computed previously. Therefore, if you know one of the break-even figures in units or dollars, then you do not need the formula to determine the other.

Break-even Chart

The break-even point can also be graphically depicted by a break-even chart, as in Figure 10-8. The break-even chart for Vortex Manufacturing, Inc., can be constructed and interpreted as follows:

1. A horizontal line, the x-axis, is drawn and divided into equal distances to represent the sales volume in dollars.
2. A vertical line, the y-axis, is drawn and divided into equal parts representing costs and revenues in dollars.
3. A fixed cost line is drawn parallel to the x-axis at the $15,000 point on the y-axis.
4. A total cost line is drawn from the $15,000 fixed cost point on the y-axis to the $85,000 total cost point at the right of the graph.
5. A sales line is drawn from the intersection of the x-axis and y-axis to the $100,000 total sales point at the right of the graph.
6. The sales line intersects the total cost line at the break-even point, representing $50,000 of sales.
7. The shaded area to the left of the break-even point, where the total cost line is above the sales line, is the net loss area; the shaded area to the right of the break-even point, where the sales line is above the total cost line, is the net income area.

Figure 10-8 Break-even Chart in Dollars

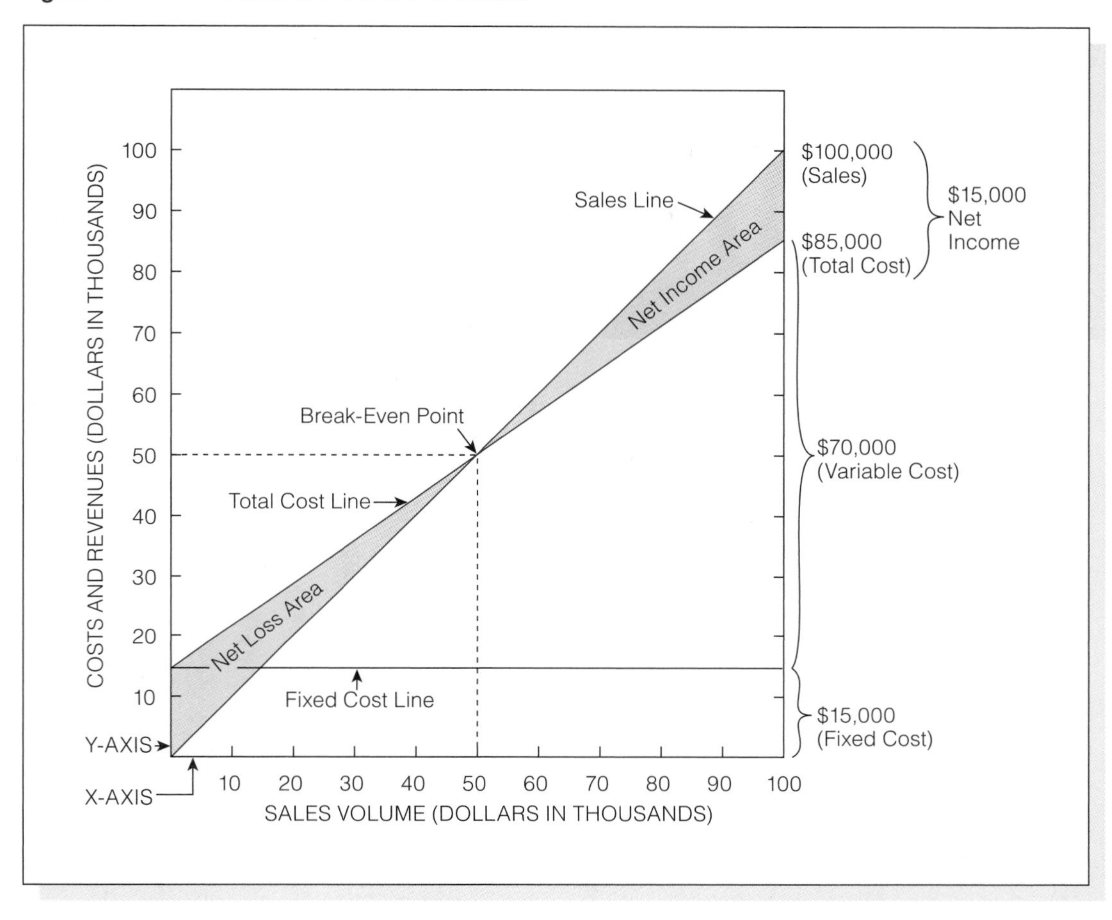

Note that a break-even chart may also be prepared graphically with the break-even point expressed in units, as in Figure 10-9.

Break-even Analysis for Management Decisions

Break-even analysis can be used to help management select an action when several alternatives exist. This analysis is based on the conditions that variable costs will vary in constant proportion to the sales volume and that fixed costs will be fixed over a prescribed or relevant range of activity. Therefore, if management wishes to test new proposals that will change the percentage of variable costs to sales volume, or the total amount of fixed costs, or a combination of these changes, then it can use the basic break-even equation to calculate the results.

Assume that Vortex Manufacturing, Inc., has established its break-even point in sales volume at $50,000 and now wishes to determine the amount of sales dollars needed to earn a net operating income of $18,000. The $18,000 net income is viewed as a nonvariable factor just as are the fixed costs. The **target volume** (the amount of sales volume needed, in units or

Figure 10-9 Break-even Chart in Units

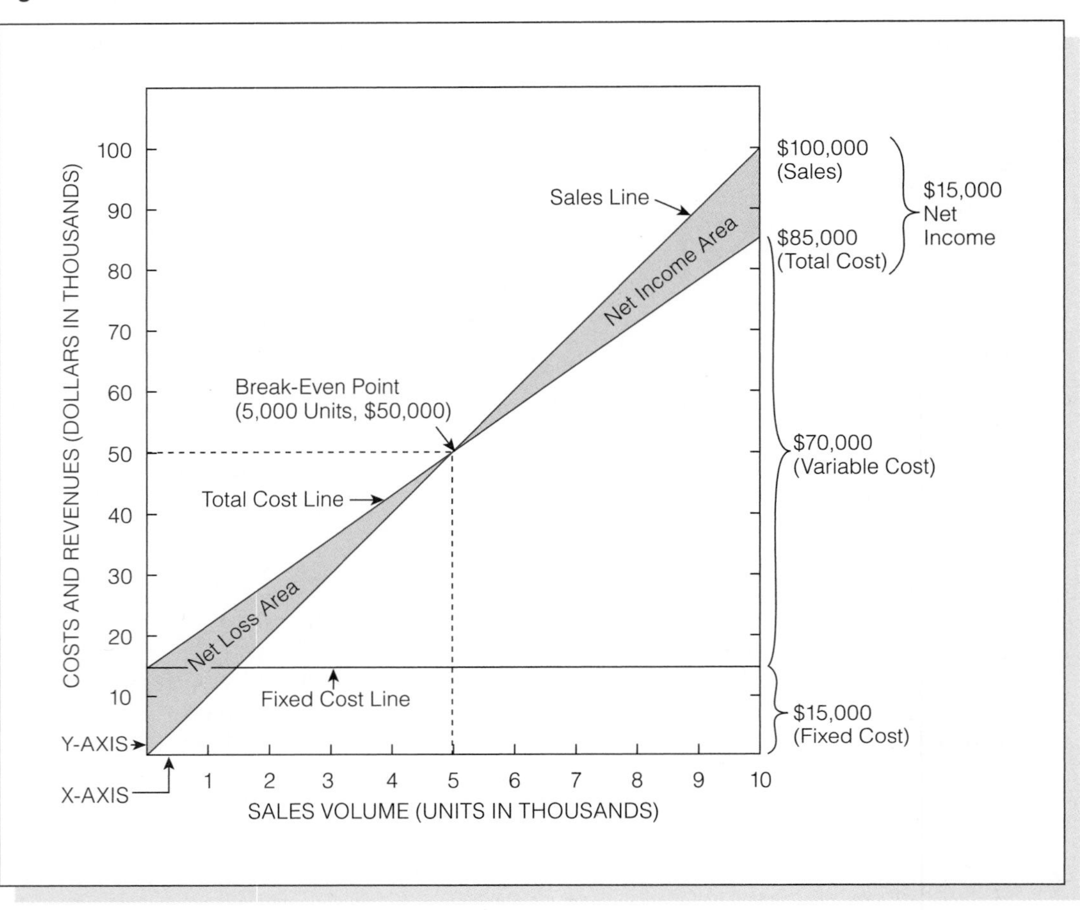

dollars, to cover all costs and earn a certain amount of profit) would be calculated via the following modified equation:

$$\text{Target volume (dollars)} = \frac{\text{Total fixed costs} + \text{Net income}}{1 - (\text{Total variable costs/Total sales volume})}$$

$$= \frac{\$15{,}000 + \$18{,}000}{1 - (\$70{,}000/\$100{,}000)}$$

$$= \frac{\$33{,}000}{1 - 0.70}$$

$$= \frac{\$33{,}000}{0.30}$$

$$= \$110{,}000$$

The new conditions can be checked, in income statement form, as follows:

Sales	$110,000
Less variable costs (70% × $110,000)	77,000
Contribution margin	$ 33,000
Less fixed costs	15,000
Net operating income	$ 18,000

Further assume that the management of Vortex Manufacturing, Inc.—fearing that changing economic conditions may make it difficult for the company to attain its present sales volume—wants to analyze the effect on the break-even point of increasing the percentage of variable costs to sales and lowering fixed costs. Management believes that fixed costs can be reduced to $5,000, with a corresponding increase in the percentage of variable costs to 80%. (For example, the base salaries of salespersons could be lowered, and their commission percentage could be raised.)

The break-even sales volume calculated with these conditions is as follows:

$$\text{Break-even sales volume} = \frac{\$5{,}000}{1 - 0.80}$$

$$= \frac{\$5{,}000}{0.20}$$

$$= \$25{,}000$$

If the proposed shift from fixed costs to variable costs is accomplished, then the break-even point would be reduced from $50,000 to $25,000. The higher the variable costs, the smaller the risk of not attaining the expected break-even point because the variable costs are incurred only if orders for the product are received. On the other hand, if the sales volume exceeds expectations, then a large portion of the sales revenue beyond break-even will be used to cover the variable costs; thus, a smaller net operating income must be anticipated than if costs were mostly fixed.

To illustrate, assume that Vortex Manufacturing, Inc., achieves a sales volume of $200,000. With a variable cost percentage of 70% and $15,000 of fixed costs, the net income would amount to $45,000. If the fixed costs were reduced to $5,000 and the variable cost percentage increased to 80%, the profit would be only $35,000—a reduction of $10,000 at the same sales volume:

	Variable Cost Rate	
	70%	**80%**
Sales	$200,000	$200,000
Variable costs	140,000	160,000
Contribution margin	$ 60,000	$ 40,000
Fixed costs	15,000	5,000
Net operating income	$ 45,000	$ 35,000

Effect of Sales Mix on Break-even Analysis

The examples so far have assumed a single product firm. Most manufacturers produce and sell numerous products. Often, each of these products has different unit sales prices, unit variable costs, and unit contribution margins. In such instances, the sales mix must be computed before a break-even point can be determined. The **sales mix** is the relative percentage of unit sales among the various products made by the firm.

For example, assume that Vortex Manufacturing, Inc., which had unit sales of 10,000 of a single product in the preceding example, now has a second product with sales of 6,000 units. The sales mix would be computed as follows:

Product	Unit Sales	Sales Mix Percentage
A	10,000	62.5%
B	6,000	37.5%
Total	16,000	100.0%

Assume that adding Product B results in no increase to Vortex's fixed costs of $15,000 and that the unit sales prices, unit variable costs, and unit contribution margins are as follows:

Product	Unit Sales Price	Unit Variable Cost	Unit Contribution Margin
A	$10	$ 7	$3
B	15	10	5

Vortex's break-even point depends on the sales mix and the unit contribution margins of the individual products. The first step in the break-even computation is determining the weighted-average contribution margin per unit:

$$\text{Weighted-average contribution margin per unit} = \frac{(\text{Product A unit contribution} \times \text{Product A units sold}) + (\text{Product B unit contribution} \times \text{Product B units sold})}{\text{Product A units sold} + \text{Product B units sold}}$$

$$= \frac{(\$3 \times 10{,}000) + (\$5 \times 6{,}000)}{10{,}000 + 6{,}000}$$

$$= \$3.75$$

After the weighted-average contribution margin is computed, the break-even point can be determined in the usual manner:

$$\text{Break-even sales volume (units)} = \frac{\text{Fixed cost}}{\text{Weighted-average unit contribution margin}}$$

$$= \frac{\$15{,}000}{\$3.75}$$

$$= 4{,}000 \text{ units}$$

Since the sales mix percentages for products A and B are 62.5% and 37.5% respectively, break-even units for the individual products are as follows:

$$\text{Product A: } 0.625 \times 4{,}000 = 2{,}500$$
$$\text{Product B: } 0.375 \times 4{,}000 = 1{,}500$$

Observe that the individual and composite number of break-even units will be different at any other level of sales mix. One easy way to determine the break-even point in sales dollars for the individual products, after the break-even units have been computed, is to multiply the break-even number of units per product by its unit sales price:

Product A: 2,500 units × $10 per unit =	$25,000
Product B: 1,500 units × $15 per unit =	22,500
Total break-even sales dollars	$47,500

Contribution Margin Ratio and Margin of Safety

LO5 Calculate the contribution margin ratio and the margin of safety ratio.

Two terms frequently used in cost-volume-profit relationships are *contribution margin* and *margin of safety*. The contribution margin, introduced in previous discussions, is the difference between sales revenue and variable costs. When an income statement depicts the contribution margin, management can use it as a tool for studying the effects of changes in sales volume on profits. The contribution margin ratio, also previously defined, is the relationship of contribution margin dollars to sales dollars.

The **margin of safety** indicates the amount that sales can decrease before the company will suffer a loss; it may be expressed as unit sales or dollar sales. The **margin of safety ratio** is a relationship computed by dividing margin of safety in dollars by the total sales revenue. To illustrate, assume the following income statement:

Sales (10,000 units @ $100)	$1,000,000	100%
Variable costs	600,000	60
Contribution margin	$ 400,000	40%
Fixed costs	300,000	30
Net operating income	$ 100,000	10%

In this income statement, the contribution margin is $400,000. The contribution margin ratio is calculated as follows:

$$\text{Contribution margin ratio} = \frac{\text{Contribution margin}}{\text{Sales}}$$
$$= \frac{\$400{,}000}{\$1{,}000{,}000}$$
$$= 40\%$$

Using the contribution margin ratio of 40%, the break-even point can be calculated as follows:

$$\text{Break-even sales volume (dollars)} = \frac{\text{Fixed costs}}{\text{Contribution margin ratio}}$$
$$= \frac{\$300{,}000}{0.40}$$
$$= \$750{,}000$$

The margin of safety is computed as follows:

$$\text{Margin of safety (dollars)} = \text{Sales revenue} - \text{Break-even sales revenue}$$
$$= \$1{,}000{,}000 - \$750{,}000$$
$$= \$250{,}000$$

The margin of safety ratio is calculated as follows:

$$\text{Margin of safety ratio} = \frac{\text{Margin of safety}}{\text{Sales}}$$
$$= \frac{\$250{,}000}{\$1{,}000{,}000}$$
$$= 25\%$$

If break-even sales equal $750,000 but the total expected sales are $1,000,000, then the margin of safety ratio shows that the $1,000,000 sales forecast can be off by as much as 25% before the firm reaches its break-even point. Because the margin of safety is directly related to net operating income, the margin of safety ratio can be used to calculate net operating income as a percentage of sales and vice versa. As the following examples illustrate, if two of the three variables are known, then the third can be determined:

$$\text{Net operating income percentage} = \text{Contribution margin ratio} \times \text{Margin of safety ratio}$$
$$= 40\% \times 25\%$$
$$= 10\%$$

(*Note*: This figure agrees with the net operating income as a percent of sales as shown in the income statement on page 499.)

$$\text{Margin of safety ratio} = \frac{\text{Net operating income percentage}}{\text{Contribution margin ratio}}$$
$$= \frac{0.10}{0.40}$$
$$= 25\%$$

Cost-volume-profit analysis assumes that the cost and profit will remain constant (unchanged) for a given period of time. It is unrealistic to assume that the established relationship between sales and production will remain as forecast, or even that the established sales mix will remain constant for any long period. Even price changes that have not been predicted can occur, and the CVP analysis outcome will be substantially affected. If a fairly stable set of relationships cannot be established, then a series of analyses should be prepared that recognizes the changing sets of circumstances and their related outcomes.

Effect of Income Tax on Break-even Point and Net Income

LO6 Discuss the impact of income tax on break-even computations.

Income tax has no effect on the number of units that must be sold to break even because the break-even point is where the total revenue exactly equals the total costs, resulting in zero profit and no income tax expense. However, the income tax rate does affect the number and dollar amount of units that must be sold to earn a certain amount of after-tax net income. For example, if a company is in the 40% tax bracket and wants to earn an after-tax income of $100,000, then it must have $166,667 of income before taxes (net operating income); this is computed as follows:

$$\begin{aligned}\text{Pretax income} &= \text{After-tax income}/1 - \text{Tax rate}\\ &= \$100{,}000/(1-0.40)\\ &= \$166{,}667\end{aligned}$$

Now assume that the fixed costs are $500,000, the unit sales price is $100, and the unit variable costs are $30. The number of units that must be sold to earn an after-tax income of $100,000 is computed as follows:

$$\begin{aligned}\text{Target volume (units)} &= \frac{\text{Fixed costs} + \dfrac{\text{Target after-tax income}}{1-\text{Tax rate}}}{\text{Unit contribution margin}}\\ &= \frac{\$500{,}000 + \dfrac{\$100{,}000}{1-0.40}}{\$100-\$30}\\ &= 9{,}524 \text{ units}\end{aligned}$$

Without income taxes, the number of units that must be sold to earn a profit of $100,000 would have been only 8,571 ($600,000/$70), approximately 1,000 fewer units than with the 40% tax rate. The dollar amount of revenue needed to earn the $100,000 after-tax income can be computed by multiplying the 9,524 unit volume by the unit sales price of $100 to obtain $952,400, or it can be computed directly by using the target volume formula as follows:

$$\begin{aligned}\text{Target volume (dollars)} &= \frac{\text{Fixed costs} + \dfrac{\text{Target after-tax income}}{1-\text{Tax rate}}}{\text{Contribution margin ratio}}\\ &= \frac{\$500{,}000 + \dfrac{\$100{,}000}{1-0.40}}{(\$100-\$30)/\$100}\\ &= \$952{,}381 \text{ (A rounding difference of \$19 when compared to \$952,400 calculated previously.)}\end{aligned}$$

Recall and Review 2

Terry Company sells its only product for $35 per unit. Fixed expenses total $550,000 per year. Variable expenses are $800,000 when 60,000 units are sold. The number of units that must be sold to earn an income of $50,000 is ____________.

(After working this exercise, see page 508 for the solution.)

You should now be able to work the following:
Questions 5–12; Exercises 10-7 to 10-14; Problems 10-3 to 10-10, Review Problem 10-12R; and Self-Study Problem 1.

Differential Analysis

Marcus Foster, Sales Manager for Aero Industries, has been asked by a potential foreign customer to sell 10,000 units of a certain gear for $10 per unit. Aero normally sells this item for $15 per unit, but it has had excess manufacturing capacity in recent months. It is anticipated that this would be a one-time-only order from this customer. The product unit cost report for this type of gear is as follows:

Direct materials	$ 3.00
Direct labor	2.50
Variable manufacturing overhead	1.25
Fixed manufacturing overhead	2.50
Variable selling and administrative expense	1.75
Fixed selling and administrative expense	2.25
Total per unit cost	$ 13.25

After looking at the product cost report, Foster informs the customer, "I may not be an accountant, but I am smart enough to know that I will lose $3.25 per unit if I make this sale. Therefore, I must refuse your offer." Do you agree with Foster's analysis? Differential analysis, which is a major topic in this chapter, addresses this type of situation. Self-Study Problem 2, at the end of this chapter, is a continuation of this scenario.

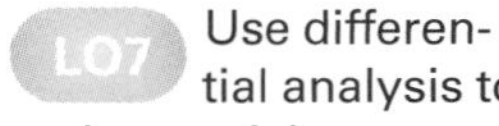
LO7 Use differential analysis to make special decisions.

Not all management requirements can be satisfied by one concept or combination of cost and revenue data. The designated purpose for which a cost or revenue measurement is required must determine what items should be included in the analysis. This study should then provide a series of alternative solutions based on comparison of the different sets of relevant cost and revenue data. A study that highlights the significant cost and revenue data alternatives is referred to as **differential analysis**. The difference in revenue between two alternatives—say to lease a warehouse that you own versus using it for storage—is called **differential revenue**. The difference in cost between two alternatives, such as to make a component part of your final product versus buying it from an outside supplier, is called **differential cost**. The amount of extra profit earned from choosing the better of the alternatives is known as **differential income**. There are a number of different types of these analyses, a few of which are illustrated next.

Accept or Reject a Special Order

Assume that a company, now operating at 80% capacity, has been asked by a one-time purchaser to sell additional units at less than its established sales price. The company would make a study to determine the difference in revenue and costs at the two volume levels.

The company produces 30,000 units at 80% of its total capacity. Its fixed factory overhead costs are $20,000, and it sells each unit for $10. A new customer wishes to purchase 7,500 units for $4 per unit. Should the company agree to the terms or reject the offer?

The variable production costs per unit are as follows:

Direct materials	$2.00
Direct labor	1.00
Variable overhead	0.75
Total variable cost per unit	$3.75

At the present level of operations, the total production cost per unit is $4.42 ([(30,000 units × $3.75 per unit variable costs) + $20,000 fixed costs]/ 30,000 units). If the additional units are produced, the total cost per unit would be $4.28 ([(37,500 units × $3.75) + $20,000 fixed overhead]/37,500 units). Because the new customer is offering only $4 per unit, the company apparently should not accept such an offer.

However, the total fixed factory overhead cost of $20,000 is not affected by producing the additional units; only the differential cost (in this case variable cost) will increase. Thus, each additional unit produced and then sold at $4 will increase the contribution margin by $0.25 ($4.00 selling price – $3.75 variable cost). If the company accepts the offer, its total increase in contribution margin would be $1,875 (7,500 units × $0.25). Because the fixed cost will not change, the operating income would also increase by $1,875; this is shown as follows:

	Accept Order	Reject Order
Sales:		
30,000 units @ $10	$ 300,000	$ 300,000
7,500 units @ $4	30,000	-0-
Total revenues	$ 330,000	$ 300,000
Variable costs	140,625*	112,500**
Contribution margin	$ 189,375	$ 187,500
Fixed overhead costs	20,000	20,000
Operating income	$ 169,375	$ 167,500

*37,500 units × $3.75 (variable cost)

**30,000 units × $3.75 (variable cost)

Another way of analyzing the situation is:

Differential revenue from special order (7,500 units × $4)	$ 30,000
Differential cost from special order (7,500 × $3.75)	28,125
Differential income from special order	$ 1,875

The differential analysis approach is applicable only when there is excess capacity that can be utilized at little or no increase in fixed cost. Also, in accepting additional orders at selling prices below the usual price levels, care should be exercised so that legislation barring sales to different customers at different prices is not violated or that regular customers will not expect the same price treatment for their purchases.

Many companies follow this practice of **contribution pricing**, which means that they accept a selling price if it exceeds variable cost, and thus generates a positive contribution margin in times of excess capacity. For example, **Delta Air Lines** usually offers a new list of deeply discounted Internet fares each week for travel on the upcoming weekend. The cities listed are on Delta routes where excess capacity exists. Since most of the costs of the flight (e.g., pilot and flight attendant salaries, ground crew at the arrival city, and depreciation and repairs on the plane) are fixed in relation to the number of passengers, the differential revenue generated by additional passengers exceeds the few differential costs that may exist—for example, snacks and beverages and a slight increase in jet fuel used due to the additional weight of the plane. Note that Delta offers these bargain fares to attract leisure passengers, who otherwise would not travel on the designated route, thus increasing its total contribution margin and differential income.

Make or Buy

To illustrate another analysis of differential costs, assume that a company currently purchases a finished part that could perhaps be more economically manufactured in its own plant. For example, assume that 40,000 parts are purchased each month at a unit price of $2.00 per part. All the tools and necessary skills required for manufacturing this part are available in the company's Machining Department.

The Machining Department has a total capacity of 30,000 direct labor hours per month. The present utilization is 24,000 direct labor hours, or 80% of plant capacity, and it would take 6,000 direct labor hours to make the parts. Analyses of the Machining Departments factory overhead costs include the following:

	Budgeted (80%) 24,000 Hours		Normal (100%) 30,000 Hours	
	Total Costs	Per Hour Costs	Total Costs	Per Hour Costs
Fixed overhead	$ 72,000	$3.00	$ 72,000	$2.40
Variable overhead	48,000	2.00	60,000	2.00
Total	$120,000	$5.00	$132,000	$4.40
Differential cost			$ 12,000	$0.60

The costs to manufacture the 40,000 parts in-house would be:

Materials	$ 2,000
Labor, 6,000 hours @ $8	48,000

Total	$50,000
Add differential variable overhead cost of 6,000 labor hours	12,000
Total cost to manufacture parts	$62,000
Cost per unit ($62,000 ÷ 40,000)	$1.55

Because the Machining Department is presently operating at 80% of its total capacity, the company can save $18,000 ($80,000 purchased cost – $62,000 cost to make), or $0.45 per part ($2.00 – $1.55), by making rather than buying the 40,000 parts. If the 80% capacity level in the Machining Department is a short-run condition, this factor must be considered before the final decision is made. The estimated savings may not be realized if the excess capacity of the department will soon be required for the company's regularly manufactured products.

Distribution Costs

LO8 Identify techniques for analyzing and controlling distribution costs.

Cost accounting is frequently thought of as a method of accounting only for the costs of manufacturing. However, "cost" as a general term covers more than merely manufacturing costs; it should include all of the costs of doing business. In other words, efficient control of all costs should cover distribution costs as well as production costs. **Distribution costs** include the costs incurred to sell and deliver the product.

In recent years, state and federal laws prohibiting discriminatory sale prices and the advent of increasing competition have forced accountants to devote more time to the study of distribution costs. An attempt is being made to determine, by means of activity-based costing, the answers to a variety of questions:

1. How much of the selling and administrative expense should be charged to each type of product sold?
2. How much of the selling and administrative expense is chargeable to each particular sales office?
3. How much of the selling and administrative expense is allocable to each salesperson?
4. How much of the selling and administrative expense should be charged to each order sold?

To illustrate some of the difficulties encountered, assume that a company selling bakery products also operates a fleet of delivery trucks for distributing the finished items. Each driver is a salesperson; therefore, each truck is a combination sales and delivery truck. At each stop, the driver takes an order from the store manager for bread, cakes, cookies, and other bakery products carried on the truck and then stocks the shelves. In one store, 15 minutes may be spent selling four dozen loaves of bread, two dozen breakfast rolls, and a dozen boxes of doughnuts. In another store, the salesperson may need 45 minutes to sell only a dozen loaves of bread.

Suppose that the daily costs of the operation are $75 for the salesperson-driver's salary, $30 for truck depreciation, $15 for gasoline and oil, and $5 for miscellaneous operating expenses. How much of the total truck expense is chargeable to each sale? Should it be allocated on the basis of the number of sales made? Should it be allocated on the basis of the time spent at each stop by the driver? What is the cost of selling a loaf of bread, a dozen doughnuts, or a package of breakfast rolls?

Businesses devote a considerable amount of time attempting to arrive at meaningful answers to such questions. The following example will show the usefulness of distribution cost studies.

Assume that a company is making three products, A, B, and C. The manufacturing cost per unit follows:

A	$10
B	15
C	5

During one month, 1,000 units of each product are sold at $15, $18, and $6 each, respectively, and the total production costs are $30,000. The gross margin for the month would be $9,000 ($39,000 revenue – $30,000 production costs). If the selling and administrative expense for the month is $4,850, then net income for the month would be $4,150, a result that management would probably regard as satisfactory. Now assume that an activity-based costing study indicates that the distribution cost per product is as follows.

Expense	**A**	**B**	**C**	**Total**
Selling expenses:				
Salaries	$ 618	$ 414	$ 618	$1,650
Commissions			500	500
Advertising	600	200	200	1,000
Telephone and fax	40		60	100
Sales manager's salary	133	133	134	400
Miscellaneous selling expense	127	17	56	200
Total selling expense	$1,518	$ 764	1,568	3,850
Administrative expense	300	350	350	1,000
Total	$1,818	$1,114	$1,918	$4,850
Number of units	÷1,000	÷1,000	÷1,000	
Cost per unit	$1.82	$1.11	$1.92	

To arrive at these figures, the company must identify the most appropriate cost driver for each expense and allocate these expenses to the products. For example, sales salaries might be allocated to the products on the basis of time reports showing the amount of time devoted to selling each product. Advertising might be allocated on the basis of the number of square inches of advertising space purchased for each product. The sales manager's salary might be allocated based on the sales manager's estimate of the amount of time devoted to each product. Miscellaneous selling expenses might be allocated on the basis of the number of orders received for each product.

Using the preceding cost and sales data, we see that a profit is actually being made only on Products A and B. Product C is being sold at a loss. The following table, based on the sales for the month, shows the extent of the gain and loss:

Product	Cost to Make	Cost to Sell	Total Cost	Selling Price	Profit (Loss)
A	$10,000	$1,818	$11,818	$15,000	$3,182
B	15,000	1,114	16,114	18,000	1,886
C	5,000	1,918	6,918	6,000	(918)
Total	$30,000	$4,850	$34,850	$39,000	$4,150

As a result of the analysis of distribution costs, management determines that the company might make more money by selling less. If the sale of Product C were discontinued, it appears that the overall company profit would be greater by the amount of the loss being sustained on C. However, a more intensive study may show that Products A and B could not sustain their profit margins if the inescapable costs charged to Product C, such as the sales manager's salary, were now charged only to A and B. Also, the benefits of carrying a full line of products must be considered. Frequently, those factors that are more difficult to quantify play a major role in determining whether one action or another is more justified. The perceived overall effect on the company usually determines such decisions.

Recall and Review 3

A company produces 25,000 units at 75% of its total capacity. Its fixed factory overhead is $50,000, variable costs are $7.50 per unit, and it sells each unit for $12. A foreign customer wishes to purchase 5,000 units at a one-time price of $8 per unit. Should the company agree to the terms or reject the offer?_________ How much additional contribution margin, if any, would the special order generate?_________

(After working this exercise, see page 508 for the solution.)

You should now be able to work the following:
Questions 13–18; Exercises 10-15 to 10-17; Problems 10-11 to 10-13; Self-Study Problem 2; Mini-Case 2; and the Internet Exercise.

KEY TERMS

Absorption costing, 482
Break-even point, 481
Break-even analysis, 492
Common cost, 489
Contribution margin, 489
Cost-volume-profit (CVP) analysis, 491
Contribution margin ratio, 493
Contribution pricing, 504
Direct costing, 482
Direct (traceable) cost, 489
Differential analysis, 502
Differential revenue, 502
Differential cost, 502
Differential income, 502
Distribution costs, 505
Full costing, 482
Gross margin, 485
Gross profit, 485
Indirect (nontraceable) cost, 489
Manufacturing margin, 485
Margin of safety, 499
Margin of safety ratio, 499
Net operating income, 492
Product costs, 482
Period costs, 482
Relevant range, 491
Segment, 488
Segment margin, 489
Sales mix, 498
Target volume, 495
Variable costing, 482

ANSWERS TO RECALL AND REVIEW EXERCISES

R&R 1

Change in inventory:	
Beginning inventory	9,000
Ending inventory	12,000
Increase in inventory	3,000 units
Fixed costs added to inventory under absorption costing: 3,000 units × $4 = $12,000	
Net income using variable costing	$ 100,000
Plus: fixed costs added to inventory	12,000
Net income under absorption costing	$ 112,000

R&R 2

Variable expenses = $800,000/60,000 units = $13.33 per unit

Selling price per unit	$35.00
Variable cost per unit	13.33
Contribution margin per unit	21.67

Target volume = $550,000 + $50,000/$21.67 = 27,688 units

R&R 3

Yes, the company should accept the special order. It has enough excess capacity: 25,000 units / .75 = 33,000 units total capacity – 25,000 units current usage = 8,333 excess capacity compared to 5,000 units in the special order. Also, the special order selling price of $8 per unit is greater than the variable cost of $7.50 per unit, resulting in additional contribution margin of $.50 per unit or $2,500 total. Fixed costs are irrelevant.

SELF-STUDY PROBLEM 1

Break-even Point; Absorption and Variable Costing

Lone Star Products Company

Lone Star Products Company has a maximum productive capacity of 100,000 units per year. Normal capacity is 90,000 units per year. Standard variable manufacturing costs are $20 per unit. Fixed factory overhead is $450,000 per year. Variable selling expense is $10 per unit, and fixed selling expense is $300,000 per year. The unit sales price is $50.

The operating results for the year are as follows: sales, 80,000 units; production, 85,000 units; and beginning inventory, 5,000 units. All variances are written off as additions to (or deductions from) the standard cost of goods sold.

Required:

1. What is the break-even point expressed in dollar sales?
2. How many units must be sold to earn a net income of $50,000 per year?
3. Prepare a formal income statement for the year ended December 31, 2011 under the following:
   a. Absorption costing. (*Hint:* Don't forget to compute the volume variance. You may want to review the discussion of this variance in Chapter 8.)
   b. Variable costing.

SOLUTION TO SELF-STUDY PROBLEM

1. To compute the break-even point in sales dollars, you must first identify the total fixed costs, the variable cost per unit, and the selling price per unit and put them into the following formula:

$$\text{Break-even sales volume} = \frac{\text{Fixed costs}}{1 - (\text{Variable costs/Sales})}$$

$$= \frac{\$450{,}000 + \$300{,}000}{1 - [(\$20 + \$10)/\$50]}$$

$$= \frac{\$750{,}000}{1 - 0.60}$$

$$= \frac{\$750{,}000}{0.40}$$

$$= \$1{,}875{,}000$$

2. To solve for the target volume in units, you must first identify the total fixed costs, the desired net income, the unit sales price, and the unit variable cost and put them into the following formula:

$$\text{Target volume in units} = \frac{\text{Fixed costs} + \text{Net income}}{\text{Unit sales price} - \text{Unit variable cost}}$$

$$= \frac{\$750{,}000 + \$50{,}000}{\$50 - \$30}$$

$$= 40{,}000 \text{ units}$$

3. a. Before preparing an income statement under absorption costing, you must:

1. Compute the standard production cost per unit:

$$\text{Standard production cost per unit} = \text{Variable cost} + \text{Fixed cost}$$
$$= \$20 + \frac{\$450{,}000}{90{,}000 \text{ units}^*}$$
$$= \$25$$

*Note that the fixed overhead per unit is based on normal capacity.

2. Compute the ending inventory:

Beginning inventory	5,000
Add production	85,000
Inventory available for sale	90,000
Less sales	80,000
Ending inventory	10,000

3. Determine the unfavorable volume variance:

Normal capacity	90,000
Actual production	85,000
Volume variance in units	5,000
Fixed overhead per unit	× $ 5
Unfavorable volume variance	$25,000

Lone Star Products Company
Absorption Costing Income Statement
For the Year Ended December 31, 2011

Sales (80,000 × $50)		$4,000,000
Less cost of goods sold:		
Beginning inventory (5,000 × $25)	$ 125,000	
Cost of goods manufactured (85,000 × $25)	2,125,000	
Goods available for sale	$2,250,000	
Ending inventory (10,000 × $25)	250,000	
Cost of goods sold at standard	$2,000,000	
Add unfavorable volume variance	25,000	
Cost of goods sold		2,025,000
Gross margin		$1,975,000
Selling expenses:		
Variable (80,000 × $10)	$ 800,000	
Fixed	300,000	1,100,000
Net income		$ 875,000

b. Before preparing an income statement under variable costing, you must:

1. Realize that the variable production cost per unit is only $20.
2. Use the contribution margin format for your income statement, where

Sales – Variable cost of goods sold = Manufacturing margin
Manufacturing margin – Variable selling and administrative = Contribution margin
Contribution margin – Fixed costs = Net income

Lone Star Products Company
Variable Costing Income Statement
For the Year Ended December 31, 2011

Sales		$ 4,000,000
Variable costs:		
Beginning inventory (5,000 × $20)	$ 100,000	
Cost of goods manufactured (85,000 × $20)	1,700,000	
Goods available for sale	$1,800,000	
Ending inventory (10,000 × $20)	200,000	
Variable cost of goods sold		$ 1,600,000
Manufacturing margin		$ 2,400,000
Variable selling expense (80,000 × $10)		800,000
Contribution margin		$ 1,600,000
Fixed costs:		
Fixed factory overhead	$ 450,000	
Fixed selling expense	300,000	750,000
Net income		$ 850,000

SELF-STUDY PROBLEM 2

Differential Analysis

Aero Industries

Marcus Foster, Sales Manager for Aero Industries, has been asked by a potential foreign customer to sell 10,000 units of a certain gear for $10 per unit. Aero normally sells this item for $15 per unit, but it has had some excess manufacturing capacity in recent months. It is anticipated that this would be a one-time-only order from this customer. The product unit cost report for this type gear is as follows:

Direct materials	$ 3.00
Direct labor	2.50
Variable manufacturing overhead	1.25
Fixed manufacturing overhead	2.50

Variable selling and administrative expense	1.75
Fixed selling and administrative expense	2.25
Total per unit cost	$ 13.25

After looking at the product cost report, Foster informs the customer, "I may not be an accountant, but I am smart enough to know that I will lose $3.25 per unit if I make this sale. Therefore, I must refuse your offer."

Required:

1. From the list of costs in the product cost report, which costs would be relevant to the decision to sell at the special price?
2. What will be the amount of the total relevant cost per unit in regard to this order?
3. What would be the differential income (loss) to Aero Industries if this order were accepted?
4. Are there any nonfinancial factors that you would consider in making this decision?

SOLUTION TO SELF-STUDY PROBLEM

1. The relevant costs in this case are the ones that will change if the special order is accepted. These include the variable costs which are:
   Direct materials
   Direct labor
   Variable manufacturing overhead
   Variable selling and administrative expense*

   *Some of the usual variable selling and administrative expenses may not be incurred if the special order is accepted, because the customer came to Foster unsolicited. For the remainder of this solution, the assumption is that all of this expense is relevant.

2. The additional costs that will be incurred per unit if the special order is accepted are as follows:

Direct materials	$3.00
Direct labor	2.50
Variable mfg. overhead	1.25
Variable S&A expense	1.75
Total per unit relevant cost	$8.50

3. To determine the differential profit (loss) to the company if the order is accepted, the differential (additional) revenue from the order must be compared to the differential (additional) costs that will be incurred if the order is accepted. The differential revenue is computed as follows:

   10,000 units × $10 per unit = $100,000

   The differential costs consist of the $8.50 of variable costs per unit that will be incurred only if the order is accepted:

   10,000 units ×$8.50 per unit = $85,000

To compute the differential income, the differential revenue must be compared to the differential costs:

Differential revenue	$100,000
Differential costs	85,000
Differential income	$ 15,000

4. Nonfinancial factors to be considered include whether:
   a. the excess capacity is sufficient to produce the 10,000 units without taking away from the manufacture of units that can be sold at full price.
   b. the selling price will become known to regular customers, who then will demand a similar price.
   c. it will be a one-time-only order or if this customer will be a source of future business, thus demanding the same price breaks on follow-up orders.

QUESTIONS

1. What is the difference between absorption costing and variable costing?
2. What effect will applying variable costing have on the income statement and the balance sheet?
3. What are the advantages and disadvantages of using variable costing?
4. How is it possible, under absorption costing, to increase net income by simply producing more goods?
5. Why are there objections to using absorption costing when segment reports of profitability are being prepared?
6. What are common costs?
7. How is a contribution margin determined, and why is it important to management?
8. What are considered direct costs in segment analysis?
9. What is cost-volume-profit analysis?
10. What is the break-even point?
11. What steps are required in constructing a break-even chart?
12. What is the difference between the contribution margin ratio and the margin of safety ratio?
13. Define differential analysis, differential revenue, differential cost, and differential income.
14. What is the importance of make-or-buy studies for a company?
15. How can an airline generate additional profit if it is charging last-minute passengers significantly less than full price?
16. What are distribution costs?
17. What is the purpose of the analysis of distribution costs?
18. In cost analysis, what governs which costs are to be included in the study?

EXERCISES

E10-1 **Computing unit cost and cost of inventory—variable and absorption costing**

LO2

Lynne Products Company uses a process cost system and applies actual factory overhead to work in process at the end of the month. The following data came from the records for the month of March:

Direct materials	$200,000
Direct labor	$100,000
Variable factory overhead	$ 80,000
Fixed factory overhead	$ 60,000
Selling and administrative expenses	$ 40,000
Units produced	25,000
Units sold	20,000
Selling price per unit	$ 25

There were no beginning inventories and no work in process at the end of the month.

From the information presented, compute the following:

1. Unit cost of production under absorption costing and variable costing.
2. Cost of the ending inventory under absorption costing and variable costing.

LO1

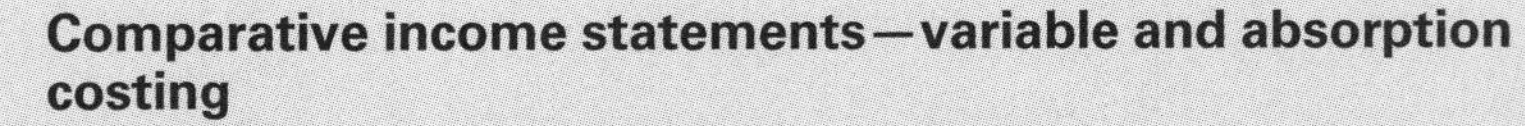

E10-2 **Comparative income statements—variable and absorption costing**

Using the information presented in E10-1, prepare comparative income statements for March (a) under absorption costing and (b) under variable costing.

E10-3 **Using variable costing and absorption costing**

LO1

The chief executive officer (CEO) of Button Corporation attended a conference in which one of the sessions was devoted to variable costing. The CEO was impressed by the presentation and has asked that the following data of Button Corporation be used to prepare comparative statements using variable costing and the company's absorption costing. The data follow:

Direct materials	$ 90,000
Direct labor	120,000
Variable factory overhead	60,000
Fixed factory overhead	150,000
Fixed marketing and administrative expense	180,000

The factory produced 80,000 units during the period, and 70,000 units were sold for $700,000.

1. Prepare an income statement using variable costing.
2. Prepare an income statement using absorption costing.

(Round unit costs to three decimal places.)

E10-4 **Using variable and absorption costing**

LO1

The following production data came from the records of LeShaq Athletic Enterprises for the year ended December 31, 2011:

Materials	$480,000
Labor	260,000
Variable factory overhead	44,000
Fixed factory overhead	36,800

During the year, 40,000 units were manufactured but only 35,000 units were sold.

Determine the effect on inventory valuation by computing the following:

1. Total inventoriable costs and the cost of the 35,000 units sold and of the 5,000 units in the ending inventory, using variable costing.
2. Total inventoriable costs and the cost of the 35,000 units sold and of the 5,000 units in the ending inventory, using absorption costing.

E10-5 **Determining income by absorption costing**

LO1 LO2

A company had income of $50,000, using variable costing for a given period. Beginning and ending inventories for the period were 18,000 units and 13,000 units, respectively. If the fixed overhead application rate was $2 per unit, what was the net income, using absorption costing?

E10-6 **Adjusting variable cost income to absorption net income**

The fixed overhead budgeted for Hamlet Company at an expected capacity of 500,000 units is $1,500,000. Variable costing is used internally, and the net income is adjusted to an absorption costing net income at year-end. Data collected over the last three years show the following:

	First Year	Second Year	Third Year
Units produced	502,000	498,000	495,000
Units sold	496,000	503,000	495,000
Net income—(variable cost)	$500,000	$521,000	$497,000

Determine the adjustment each year to convert the variable costing income to absorption costing net income. Compute the absorption costing net income for each year.

E10-7 **Segment reporting by division**

Grecian Products, Inc., has two divisions, Athens and Sparta. For the month ended March 31, Athens had sales and variable costs

of $500,000 and $225,000, respectively, and Sparta had sales and variable costs of $800,000 and $475,000, respectively. Athens had direct fixed production and administrative expenses of $60,000 and $35,000, respectively, and Sparta had direct fixed production and administrative expenses of $80,000 and $45,000, respectively. Fixed costs that were common to both divisions and couldn't be allocated to the divisions in any meaningful way were selling, $33,000, and administration, $27,000.

Prepare a segmented income statement by division for the month of March.

LO4

E10-8 Computing break-even

The sales price per unit is $13 for the Dakota Company's only product. The variable cost per unit is $5. In year 2011, the company sold 80,000 units, which was 10,000 units above the break-even point.

Compute the following:

1. Total fixed expenses. (*Hint:* First compute the contribution margin per unit.)
2. Total variable expense at the break-even volume.

LO4

E10-9 Computing break-even plus target volume

Jackson Company sells its only product for $50 per unit. Fixed expenses total $800,000 per year. Variable expenses are $1,000,000 when 40,000 units are sold.

How many units must be sold to earn a net operating income of $75,000?

LO4

E10-10 Using break-even analysis

A new product is expected to have sales of $100,000, variable costs of 60% of sales, and fixed costs of $20,000.

1. Using graph paper, construct a break-even chart and label the sales line, total cost line, fixed cost line, break-even point, and net income and net loss areas.
2. From the chart, identify the break-even point and the amount of income or loss if sales are $100,000.

LO4

E10-11 Sales mix and break-even analysis

Leisure Products, Inc., manufactures and sells two products, golf balls and tennis balls. Fixed costs are $100,000, and unit sales are 60,000 sheaths of golf balls and 40,000 cans of tennis balls. The unit sales prices and unit variable costs are as follows:

Product	Unit Sales Price	Unit Variable Cost
Golf balls	$6	$3.00
Tennis balls	4	1.50

1. Compute the sales mix percentages.
2. Compute the overall break-even unit sales.
3. Compute the unit sales of golf balls and tennis balls at the break-even point.

E10-12 **Using CVP analysis**

LO4 LO5

A company has sales of $1,000,000, variable costs of $250,000, and fixed costs of $600,000. Compute the following:

1. Contribution margin ratio.
2. Break-even sales volume.
3. Margin of safety ratio.
4. Net operating income as a percentage of sales.

E10-13 **Using break-even analysis**

LO4 LO7

A company has prepared the following statistics regarding its production and sales at different capacity levels.

Capacity level	**60%**	**80%**	**100%**
Units	60,000	80,000	100,000
Sales	$240,000	$320,000	$400,000
Total costs:			
Variable	$120,000	$160,000	$200,000
Fixed	150,000	150,000	150,000
Total costs	$270,000	$310,000	$350,000
Net operating income (loss)	$ (30,000)	$ 10,000	$ 50,000

1. At what point is break-even reached in sales dollars? In units?
2. If the company is operating at 60% capacity, should it accept an offer from a customer to buy 10,000 units at $3 per unit?

E10-14 **Effect of taxes on break-even and target volume**

LO6

Lewis Products, Inc., desires to earn an after-tax income of $150,000. It has fixed costs of $1,000,000, a unit sales price of $500, and unit variable costs of $200. The company is in the 30% tax bracket.

1. How many dollars of sales revenue must be earned to achieve the after-tax profit of $150,000?
2. How many dollars of revenue would have to be earned to achieve the $150,000 of profit, if there had been no income tax?

E10-15 **Using differential analysis—special customer order**

LO7

Dribble, Inc., manufactures basketballs. The company's forecasted income statement for the year, before any special orders, is as follows:

	Amount	Per Unit
Sales	$8,000,000	$10.00
Manufacturing cost of goods sold	6,400,000	8.00
Gross profit	$1,600,000	$ 2.00
Selling expenses	600,000	1.00
Net operating income	$1,000,000	$ 1.00

Fixed costs included in the forecasted income statement are $4,000,000 in manufacturing cost of goods sold and $400,000 in selling expenses.

A new client placed a special order with Dribble, offering to buy 100,000 basketballs for $6.00 each. The company will incur no additional selling expenses if it accepts the special order. Assuming that Dribble has sufficient capacity to manufacture 100,000 more basketballs, by what amount would differential income increase (decrease) as a result of accepting the special order? (*Hint:* First compute the variable cost per unit relevant to this decision.)

LO7

E10-16 Deciding to make or buy

Alpha Company needs 20,000 units of a certain part to use in its production cycle. The following information is available:

Cost to Alpha to make the part:	
Direct materials	$ 4
Direct labor	16
Variable factory overhead	12
Fixed factory overhead applied	6
Total	$38
Cost to buy the part from Bravo Company	$36

If Alpha buys the part from Bravo instead of making it, Alpha could not use the released facilities in another manufacturing activity. Eighty percent of the fixed factory overhead applied will continue regardless of what decision Alpha makes.

1. In deciding whether to make or buy the part, what are the total relevant costs per unit to make the part?
2. What decision should Alpha make?

LO3

LO8

E10-17 Using comparative net income analysis

Julian Manufacturing, Inc., wishes to determine the profitability of its products and asks the cost accountant to make a comparative analysis of sales, cost of sales, and distribution costs of each product for the year. The accountant gathers the following information, which will be useful in preparing the analysis:

	Product X	Product Y	Product Z
Number of units sold	30,000	20,000	20,000
Number of orders received	5,000	2,500	1,000
Selling price per unit	$ 50	$ 75	$ 100
Cost per unit	$ 30	$ 50	$ 75

Advertising expenses total $600,000 for the year, with an equal amount expended to advertise each product. The sales representative's commission is based on the selling price of each unit and is 10% for Product X, 14% for Product Y, and 18% for Product Z. The sales manager's salary of $75,000 per year is allocated evenly to each product. Other miscellaneous selling and administrative expenses are estimated to be $15 per order received.

Prepare an analysis for Julian Manufacturing, Inc., that will show in comparative form the income derived from the sale of each product for the year.

PROBLEMS

P10-1 **Absorption and variable costing income statements**

LO1

Spaulding Manufacturing Company has determined the cost of manufacturing a unit of product as follows, based on normal production of 100,000 units per year:

Direct materials	$ 5
Direct labor	4
Variable factory overhead	3
Fixed factory overhead	3
Total cost	$15

Operating statistics for the months of March and April include the following:

	March	April
Units produced	12,000	8,000
Units sold	8,000	12,000
Selling and administrative expenses (all fixed)	$12,000	$12,000

The selling price is $20 per unit. There were no inventories on March 1, and there is no work in process on April 30.

Required:
Prepare comparative income statements for each month under each of the following:
1. Absorption costing (include under- or overapplied fixed overhead).
2. Variable costing.

LO1

P10-2 Absorption costing versus direct costing
Marion Corporation has determined the following selling price and manufacturing cost per unit based on normal production of 72,000 units per year:

Selling price per unit	$	22
Variable cost per unit:		
Direct materials	$	4
Direct labor		4
Variable factory overhead		2
Variable cost per unit	$	10
Fixed cost per unit:		
Fixed factory overhead per year	$	360,000
Fixed selling and administrative expense per year		48,000
Normal unit production per year		72,000

Month	Units Produced	Units Sold
October	6,000	3,000
November	1,000	4,000
December	8,000	6,000

October has no beginning inventories.

Required:
Prepare comparative income statements, including a comparative schedule of cost of goods sold, for each of these three months in 2011 under each of the following:
1. Absorption costing (include under- or overapplied overhead).
2. Variable costing.

LO3

P10-3 Segmented income statement
Janitorial Products, Inc., manufactures two products, brooms and mops, which are sold in two territories designated by the company as East Territory and West Territory. The following income statement prepared for the company shows the product-line segments.

Janitorial Products, Inc.
Income Statement

	Total	Brooms		Mops	
Sales	$1,000,000	$600,000	100%	$400,000	100%
Less variable expenses	600,000	420,000	70	180,000	45
Contribution margin	$ 400,000	$180,000	30%	$220,000	55%
Less direct fixed costs	200,000	50,000		150,000	
Segment margin	$ 200,000	$130,000		$ 70,000	
Less common fixed costs	120,000				
Net income	$ 80,000				

The territorial product sales are as follows:

	East	West
Brooms	$400,000	$200,000
Mops	200,000	200,000
Total	$600,000	$400,000

The direct fixed costs of brooms ($50,000) and mops ($150,000) are not identifiable with either of the two territories. The common fixed costs are partially identifiable with East Territory, West Territory, and the general administration as follows:

East Territory	$ 54,000
West Territory	36,000
General administration	30,000
Total common fixed costs	$120,000

Required:

1. Prepare a segmented income statement by territories. The direct fixed costs of the product lines should be treated as common fixed costs on the segmented statement being prepared.
2. What is the significance of this analysis?

P10-4 **Segment reporting**

LO3

Digital Software, Inc., has two product lines. The income statement for the year ended December 31 shows the following:

Digital Software, Inc.
Product Line and Company Income Statement
For the Year Ended December 31, 2011

	Num 1	Num 2	Total
Sales	$400,000	$600,000	$1,000,000
Less variable expenses	160,000	240,000	400,000
Contribution margin	$240,000	$360,000	$ 600,000
Less direct fixed expenses	160,000	140,000	300,000
Product margin	$ 80,000	$220,000	$ 300,000
Less common fixed expenses			120,000
Net income			$ 180,000

The products, Num 1 and Num 2, are sold in two territories, North and South, as follows:

	North	South
Num 1	$240,000	$160,000
Num 2	180,000	420,000
Total sales	$420,000	$580,000

The common fixed expenses are traceable to each territory as follows:

North fixed expenses	$ 40,000
South fixed expenses	60,000
Home office administrative fixed expenses	20,000
Total common fixed expenses	$120,000

The direct expenses of Num 1, $160,000, and of Num 2, $140,000, are not identifiable with either of the two territories.

Required:

1. Prepare income statements for the year, segmented by territory and including a column for the entire company.
2. Why are direct expenses of one type of segment report not direct expenses of another type of segment report?

P10-5 **Segment reporting**

South-Central Publishing Company prepares income statements segmented by divisions, but the chief operating officer is not certain about how the company is actually performing. Financial data for the year follow:

	Segments		
	Textbook Division	**Electronic Division**	**Total Company**
Sales	$360,000	$840,000	$1,200,000
Less variable expenses:			
Manufacturing	$ 64,000	$422,000	$ 486,000
Selling and administrative	8,000	42,000	50,000
Total	$ 72,000	$464,000	$ 536,000
Contribution margin	$288,000	$376,000	$ 664,000
Less direct fixed expenses	30,000	440,000	470,000
Net income	$258,000	$ (64,000)	$ 194,000

The Electronic Publishing Division appears to be floundering, and the CEO believes a closer look should be taken concerning its operating effectiveness. Additional data regarding this division follow:

	Accounting	**Executive**	**Management**
Sales	$300,000	$280,000	$260,000
Variable manufacturing expenses as a percentage of sales	60%	40%	50%
Other variable expenses as a percentage of sales	5%	5%	5%
Direct fixed expenses	$100,000	$150,000	$100,000

The Electronic Division's accounting books are downloadable texts sold to auditors and controllers. The current data on these two markets follow:

	Sales Market	
	Auditors	**Controllers**
Sales	$80,000	$220,000
Variable manufacturing expenses as a percentage of sales	60%	60%
Other variable expenses as a percentage of sales	5%	5%
Direct fixed expenses	$30,000	$ 50,000

Required:

1. Prepare an income statement segmented by products of the Electronic Division, for the year ended 2011, including a column for the division as a whole. (*Hint:* To obtain the common fixed expenses, start with the total direct expenses in the Electronic Division.)
2. Prepare an income statement, segmented by markets, for the accounting books of the Electronic Division.
3. Evaluate the accounting books of the Electronic Division. Should all books be kept, or should some books be discontinued?

LO1 LO4

P10-6 Break-even analysis

The production of a new product required Mirage Manufacturing Company to lease additional plant facilities. Based on studies, the following data have been made available:
Estimated annual sales—24,000 units

	Amount	Per Unit
Estimated costs:		
Materials	$ 96,000	$4.00
Direct labor	14,400	0.60
Factory overhead	24,000	1.00
Administrative expense	28,800	1.20
Total	$163,200	$6.80

Selling expenses are expected to be 5% of sales, and net income is to amount to $2.00 per unit.

Required:

1. Calculate the selling price per unit. (*Hint*: Let "X" equal the selling price and express selling expense as a percent of "X".)
2. Prepare an absorption costing income statement for the year ended December 31, 2011.
3. Calculate the break-even point expressed in dollars and in units, assuming that administrative expense and factory overhead are all fixed but other costs are fully variable.

LO4

P10-7 Contribution margin and break-even analysis

Rancho Santa Fe Manufacturing, Inc., produces and sells a product with a price of $100 per unit. The following cost data have been prepared for its estimated upper and lower limits of activity:

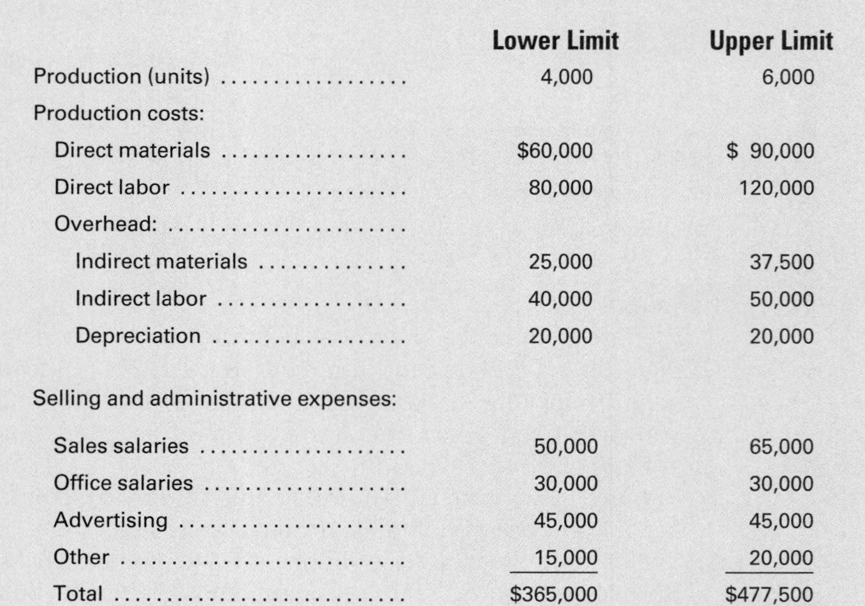

	Lower Limit	Upper Limit
Production (units)	4,000	6,000
Production costs:		
Direct materials	$60,000	$ 90,000
Direct labor	80,000	120,000
Overhead:		
Indirect materials	25,000	37,500
Indirect labor	40,000	50,000
Depreciation	20,000	20,000
Selling and administrative expenses:		
Sales salaries	50,000	65,000
Office salaries	30,000	30,000
Advertising	45,000	45,000
Other	15,000	20,000
Total	$365,000	$477,500

Required:

1. Classify each cost element as either variable, fixed, or semi-variable. (*Hint:* Recall that variable expenses must go up in direct proportion to changes in the volume of activity.)
2. Calculate the break-even point in units and dollars. (*Hint:* First use the high-low method illustrated in Chapter 4 to separate costs into their fixed and variable components.)
3. Prepare a break-even chart.
4. Prepare a contribution income statement, similar in format to the statement appearing at the top of page 497, assuming sales of 5,000 units.
5. Recompute the break-even point in units, assuming that variable costs increase by 20% and fixed costs are reduced by $50,000.

P10-8 Calculating sales mix, break-even point in units, and break-even point in dollars

LO4

The Nut House, Inc., sells three types of nuts: almonds, cashews, and walnuts. Ten thousand cans of nuts were sold in 2011, and the amount of walnuts sold were twice as much as the number of cans of cashews, whereas almond sales were one-half the amount of cashew sales. Fixed costs were $40,000, and the unit sales prices and unit variable costs were as follows:

Product	Unit Sales Price	Unit Variable Cost
Almonds	$ 8	$4
Cashews	10	5
Walnuts	6	4

Required:

1. Compute the number of cans of each kind of nut sold.
2. Compute the sales mix percentages.
3. Compute the weighted-average contribution margin per unit.
4. Compute the overall break-even unit sales.
5. Compute the unit sales of almonds, cashews, and walnuts at the break-even point.
6. Compute the break-even dollar sales of almonds, cashews, and walnuts.

P10-9 Calculating break-even point, contribution margin ratio, and margin of safety ratio

Limerick Enterprises, Inc., is considering building a manufacturing plant in Dublin. Predicting sales of 100,000 units, Limerick estimates the following expenses:

	Total Annual Expenses	Percent of Total Annual Expenses That Are Fixed
Materials	$19,000	10%
Labor	26,000	20%
Overhead	40,000	40%
Marketing and administration	14,000	60%
	$99,000	

An Irish firm that specializes in marketing will be engaged to sell the manufactured product and will receive a commission of 10% of the sales price. None of the U.S. home office expense will be allocated to the Irish facility.

Required:

1. If the unit sales price is $2, how many units must be sold to break even? (*Hint:* First compute the variable cost per unit.)
2. Calculate the margin of safety ratio.
3. Calculate the contribution margin ratio.

P10-10 Effect of taxes on break-even and target volume

LO6

Buscemi Products, Inc., desires an after-tax income of $500,000. It has fixed costs of $2,500,000, a unit sales price of $300, and unit variable costs of $150, and is in the 40% tax bracket.

Required:

1. What amount of pre-tax income is needed to earn an after-tax income of $500,000?
2. What target volume sales revenue must be reached to earn the $500,000 after-tax income?
3. Assuming that this is a single-product firm, how many units must be sold to earn the after-tax income of $500,000?
4. What target volume sales revenue would have been needed to achieve the $500,000 of income had no income tax existed?

P10-11 Make or buy

LO7

Eradicate, Inc., produces and sells a line of insect repellants that are sold primarily in the summer months. Recently, the chief operating officer has become interested in possibly manufacturing a repellant, "Halt" that can prevent a person from being attacked by use of a "pepper" repellant. The appeal of this product is that it would have year-round sales and would help stabilize the income of the company.

The product, however, must be sold in a specially designed spray can that will be safe from being discharged accidentally. The product will be sold in cartons that hold 24 cans of the repellant. The sales price will be $96 per carton. The plant is now operating at only 65% of its total capacity, so no additional fixed costs will be incurred. However, a $100,000 fixed overhead charge will be allocated to the new product from the company's present total of fixed costs.

Using the current estimates for 100,000 cartons of "Halt" as a standard volume, the following costs were developed for each carton, including the cost of the can:

Direct materials	$12
Direct labor	6
Overhead (includes allocated fixed charge)	4
Total cost per carton	$22

Eradicate, Inc., has requested a bid from a manufacturer of specialty dispensers for a purchase price of an empty can that could be used for the new product. The specialty company offered a price of $5 for a carton of cans. If the proposal is accepted, Eradicate, Inc., estimates that direct labor and variable overhead costs would be reduced by 10% and direct materials would be reduced by 20%.

Required:

1. Should Eradicate make or buy the special cans? (*Hint:* First compute the costs that could be saved by buying the cans.)
2. What would be the maximum purchase price acceptable to Eradicate for the cans?

P10-12R Comprehensive Review Problem: Break-even point; absorption and variable cost analysis
similar to Self-Study Problem 1

LO1 LO4

Mallory Manufacturing Company has a maximum productive capacity of 210,000 units per year. Normal capacity is 180,000 units per year. Standard variable manufacturing costs are $10 per unit. Fixed factory overhead is $360,000 per year. Variable selling expense is $5 per unit, and fixed selling expense is $252,000 per year. The unit sales price is $20.

The operating results for the year are as follows: sales, 150,000 units; production, 160,000 units; beginning inventory, 10,000 units. All variances are written off as additions to (or deductions from) the standard cost of sales.

Required:

1. What is the break-even point expressed in dollar sales?
2. How many units must be sold to earn a net operating income of $100,000 per year?
3. Prepare a formal income statement for the year ended December 31, 2011 under the following:
   a. Absorption costing. (*Hint:* Don't forget to compute the volume variance.)
   b. Variable costing.

MINI-CASE 1

Ethics, absorption costing

LO1

The board of directors of Garden City Gaskets, Inc., set the profit goal for the calendar year 2011 at $2,200,000. It also established a bonus plan in which the top five officers of the company will share $150,000 if the profit goal is met or exceeded. If the goal is not met, the bonus is zero. John Giamatti, the Chief Financial Officer and one of the top five executives, prepared the following budgeted income statement for 2011, based on the board's profit directive:

Garden City Gaskets, Inc.
Budgeted Income Statement
For the Year Ended Dec. 31, 2011

Sales (500,000 units)		$15,000,000
Cost of goods sold:		
Beginning inventory	$ -0-	
Cost of goods manufactured	8,000,000*	
Cost of goods available for sale	$8,000,000	
Ending inventory	-0-	8,000,000
Gross margin		$ 7,000,000
Selling and administrative expenses:		
Variable selling and administrative	$2,800,000	
Fixed selling and administrative	2,000,000	4,800,000
Net operating income		$ 2,200,000

*Variable manufacturing: 500,000 units × $5 per unit = $2,500,000; Fixed manufacturing: $5,500,000.

By late September, it became apparent that sales were running below forecast and that annual sales would approximate 450,000 units, for an estimated net income of $1,230,000 and no bonus. In an executive committee strategy meeting Bob Arnzen, Vice President of Manufacturing, suggested that the production capacity was available to produce the entire 500,000 units or more, even if that sales level could not be reached. He remembered a presenter, from a seminar that he recently attended, describing how net income could be increased by producing more than can be sold. He urged Giamatti to determine how many extra units they would need to produce to achieve the profit goal and, thus, earn the bonus.

Required:

1. If sales only reach 450,000 units for the year, how many additional units would have to be produced, given the current selling price and cost structure, to meet the budgeted profit of $2,200,000?
2. Prepare an absorption costing income statement to prove your answer above.
3. What ethical responsibility, if any, does Giamatti have in this situation?
4. What is there about the bonus plan that potentially encourages unethical behavior?

MINI-CASE 2

Differential analysis
similar to Self-Study Problem 2

LO7 LO8

Handyman Helper, Inc., manufactures household products such as windows, light fixtures, ladders, and work tables. During the year it produced 10,000 Model 10X windows but only sold 5,000 units at $40 each. The remaining units cannot be sold through normal channels. Cost for inventory purposes on December 31 included the following data on the unsold units:

Materials	$10.00
Labor	5.00
Variable overhead	3.00
Fixed overhead	2.00
Total cost per window	$20.00

Handyman Helper can sell the 5,000 windows at a liquidation price of $20.00 per window, but it will incur a packaging and shipping charge of $7.50 per window.

Required:

1. Identify the relevant costs and revenues for the liquidation sale alternative. Is Handyman Helper better off accepting the liquidation price rather than doing nothing?
2. Assume that Model 10X can be reprocessed to another size window, Model 20X, which will require the same amount of labor and overhead as was required to initially produce, but sells for only $33. Determine the most profitable course of action—liquidate or reprocess.

INTERNET EXERCISE

Accepting business at a special price.

LO7

Go to the Web site for Delta Air Lines, which is linked to the text Web site at www.cengage.com/accounting/vanderbeck. Click on "Specials," then "Web Fares" and do the following:

1. Find a fare departing from a city located closest to you with a destination furthest from you. What is the amount of this round-trip fare for the upcoming weekend? (Note that the fares usually are not posted until Wednesday of the week of travel.)
2. Now find the best fare for the same itinerary departing two weeks from now, with a Saturday night stay. How much is the difference between the two fares?
3. Do you think that Delta is generating any positive contribution margin on the weekend Web fare, or is it merely creating good customer relations?
4. Are most of Delta's costs variable or fixed in relation to an individual passenger? Give some examples of each.
5. If the cost object were a specific flight rather than an individual passenger, what would be some examples of variable costs?

GLOSSARY

A

Absorption (or full) costing. A method of accounting for manufacturing costs that charges both fixed and variable costs to the product.

Account analysis method. *See* Observation method.

Accounting information system. A set of procedures designed to provide the financial information needed within a business organization.

Activity-based costing (ABC). A method of applying overhead to products that considers non–volume-related activities that create overhead costs as well as volume related activities.

Activity-based management (ABM). The use of activity-based costing information to improve business performance by reducing costs and improving processes.

Adjusted sales value. A basis for allocating joint costs that takes into consideration the cost of processing after split-off.

Algebraic distribution method. A method for allocating service department costs to production departments using algebraic techniques. While this method may provide the most accurate distribution of costs, it is more complicated than the other methods and the results obtained may not justify the additional effort involved.

Applied factory overhead. The account credited when applying estimated overhead to production with the debit to Work in Process. Use of a separate "applied" account avoids confusion with actual overhead costs charged to Factory Overhead, the control account in the general ledger.

Attainable standard. A performance criterion that recognizes inefficiencies that are likely to result from such factors as lost time, spoilage, or waste.

Average cost method. A commonly used procedure for assigning costs to the ending inventories under a process cost accounting system. Under this method, ending inventories are valued using an average unit cost, computed as follows: (cost of beginning work in process + current period production costs) divided by the total equivalent production for the period.

B

Backflush costing. The name for the accounting system used with JIT manufacturing. Costs are not "flushed out" of the accounting system until goods are completed and sold.

Balanced scorecard. A set of performance measures, both financial and nonfinancial, that is used to evaluate an organization's or a segment of an organization's performance.

Billing rates. The hourly rates that a firm charges its clients for the various categories of professional labor worked on the job.

Bonus pay. An amount paid to employees in addition to regular earnings for a variety of reasons, such as outstanding performance, as a result of higher-than-usual company profits.

Break-even analysis. An analytical technique based on the determination of a break-even point expressed in terms of sales revenue or sales volume.

Break-even point. The point at which sales revenue adequately covers all costs to manufacture and sell the product, but no profit is earned.

Budget. Management's operating plan expressed in quantitative terms, such as units of production and related costs.

Budget variance (two-variance method). The difference between budgeted factory overhead at the capacity attained and the actual factory overhead incurred.

Budgeted income statement. A summary of anticipated revenues and expenses for the coming year based on budgets for sales, manufacturing costs, and nonmanufacturing expenses (selling, administrative, and other).

By-products. Secondary products with relatively little value that are obtained in the process of manufacturing the primary product.

C

Capacity variance. Reflects an under-or overabsorption of fixed costs by measuring the difference between actual hours worked, multiplied by the standard overhead rate, and the budget allowance based on actual hours worked.

Capital expenditures budget. A plan for the timing of acquisitions of buildings, equipment, and other operating assets during the year.

Carrying costs. The costs incurred as a result of maintaining (carrying) inventories. These costs generally include: materials storage and handling costs; interest, insurance, and taxes; losses from theft, deterioration, or obsolescence; and record keeping and supplies.

Cash budget. Budget showing the anticipated flow of cash and the timing of receipts and disbursements based on projected sales, production schedule, and other expenses.

Common cost (or indirect [nontraceable] cost). The term used in segment analysis to describe a cost that cannot be traced to, or specifically identified with, a particular business segment.

Contribution margin. The difference between sales revenue and variable costs.

Contribution margin ratio. The relationship of contribution margin to sales.

Contribution pricing. The method of pricing where any price greater than variable costs is accepted for the purpose of increasing contribution margin during periods of excess capacity.

Contributory plans. Pension plans that require a partial contribution from the employees.

Control. The process of monitoring the company's operations and determining whether the objectives identified in the planning process are being accomplished.

Controllable variance. The amount by which the actual factory overhead costs differ from the standard overhead costs for the attained level of production.

Conversion cost. The combined cost of direct labor and factory overhead, which is necessary to convert the direct materials into finished goods.

Cost accounting. Includes those parts of financial and management accounting that collect and analyze cost information.

Cost accounting system. A set of methods and procedures used by a manufacturing organization to accumulate detailed cost data relating to the manufacturing process.

Cost and production report. A summary of cost and production data for a particular cost center.

Cost–benefit decision. A decision as to whether the benefit received from pursuing a certain course of action exceeds the costs of that action.

Cost center. A unit of activity, such as a department, to which costs may be practically and equitably assigned.

Cost driver. The basis used to allocate each of the activities in activity-based costing such as number of setups and number of design changes.

Cost of goods manufactured. Determined by adding the cost of the beginning work in process to the manufacturing costs incurred during the period, and then subtracting the cost of the ending work in process.

Cost of goods sold budget. Consists of information from the direct materials, direct labor, and factory overhead budgets, as well as projections of beginning and ending work in process and finished goods inventories.

Cost of production summary. A report that summarizes production costs for a period for each department and provides the information necessary for inventory valuation.

Cost performance report. Compares the budgeted costs for a job with its actual costs and indicates the variance for each line item.

Cost–volume–profit (CVP) analysis. An analytical technique that uses the degrees of cost variability for measuring the effect of changes in volume on resulting profits.

Credit memorandum. A document used to notify the vendor that a larger quantity has been received than was ordered.

D

Debit memorandum. A document used to notify the vendor that less materials were received than were ordered.

Defective units. Units of product with imperfections that are considered correctable because the market value of the corrected unit will be greater than the total cost incurred for the unit.

Defined benefit plan. Pension benefits paid to a retired employee based on the employee's past level of earnings and length of service with the company.

Defined contribution plan. A plan showing the maximum amount of contributions that can be made by employer and employee.

Department-type analysis spreadsheet. One form of factory overhead analysis spreadsheet; a separate analysis spreadsheet is maintained for each department with individual amount columns for each type of overhead expense.

Differential analysis. A study that highlights the significant cost data of alternatives.

Differential cost. The difference in cost between two decision alternatives.

Differential income. The amount of extra profit earned from choosing the better of two alternatives.

Differential revenue. The difference in revenue between two decision alternatives.

Direct charge. A charge that can be exactly measured and charged to a specific department.

Direct (traceable) cost. The term used in segment analysis to describe a cost that can be traced to a specific business segment.

Direct costing. *See* Variable costing.

Direct distribution method. A method for allocating service department costs to production departments. No attempt is made to determine the extent to which service departments provide services to each other; instead, all service department costs are distributed directly to the production departments.

Direct labor. The cost of labor for employees who work directly on the product being manufactured.

Direct labor budget. A detailed plan of the labor requirements in both hours and dollars for a specific period of time.

Direct labor cost method. A method of applying factory overhead to production based on the amount of direct labor cost incurred for a job or process.

Direct labor hour method. A method of applying factory overhead to production based on the number of direct labor hours worked on a job or process.

Direct materials. Materials that become part of the product being manufactured and that can be readily identified with a certain product.

Direct materials budget. A detailed plan of the materials requirements in both units and dollars for a specific period of time.

Distribution costs. Costs incurred to sell and deliver a product.

E

Economic order quantity (EOQ). The optimal (most economical) quantity of materials that should be ordered at one time; represents the order size that minimizes total order and carrying costs.

Efficiency variance. The difference between overhead applied (standard hours at the standard rate) and the actual hours worked multiplied by the standard rate; indicates the effect on fixed and variable overhead costs when actual hours worked are more or less than standard hours allowed for the production volume.

Electronic data interchange (EDI). The process of business-to-business electronic communication for the purpose of expediting commerce and eliminating paperwork.

Employee earnings record. A form prepared for each employee showing the employee's earnings each pay period and cumulative earnings for each quarter and for the year.

Equivalent production. The number of units that could have been completed during a period using the total production costs for the period.

Expense-type analysis spreadsheet. One form of factory overhead analysis spreadsheet; a separate analysis spreadsheet is used for each type of overhead expense with individual amount columns for each department.

F

Factory overhead. All costs related to the manufacture of a product except direct materials and direct labor; these costs include indirect materials, indirect labor, and other manufacturing expenses, such as depreciation, supplies, utilities, maintenance, insurance, and taxes.

Factory overhead analysis spreadsheets. A subsidiary record of factory overhead expenses; replaces a subsidiary factory overhead ledger. Analysis spreadsheets are commonly used bylarger enterprises withseveraldepartments and manydifferent types of overheadexpenses.

Factory overhead budget. A budget consisting of the estimated individual factory overhead items needed to meet production requirements.

Factory overhead ledger. A subsidiary ledger containing the individual factory overhead accounts; the total of the individual account balances in the subsidiary ledger should equal the balance in the control account, Factory Overhead, in the general ledger.

Favorable variance. The difference when actual costs are less than standard costs.

Federal Insurance Contributions Act (FICA). Federal legislation requiring both employers and employees to pay social security taxes on wages and salaries.

Federal Unemployment Tax Act (FUTA). Federal legislation requiring employers to pay an established rate of tax on wages and salaries to provide for compensation to employees if they are laid off from their regular employment.

Financial accounting. The branch of accounting that focuses on the gathering of information to be used in the preparation of external financial statements, that is, balance sheet, income statement, and statement of cash flows.

Finished goods. The inventory account that represents the total cost incurred in manufacturing goods that are complete but still on hand at the end of the accounting period.

First-in, first-out (FIFO). An inventory costing method based on the assumption that materials issued are taken from the oldest materials in stock. Thus, materials issued are costed at the earliest prices paid for materials in stock, and ending inventories are costed at the most recent purchase prices.

Fixed costs. Manufacturing costs that remain constant when production levels increase or decrease; examples include straight-line depreciation, periodic rent payments, insurance, and salaries paid to production executives.

Fixed overhead budget variance. A measure of the difference between the actual fixed overhead and the budgeted fixed overhead.

Fixed overhead volume variance. A measure of the difference between budgeted fixed overhead and applied fixed overhead.

Flexible budget. A budget that shows expected costs at different production levels.

Flow of costs. The order in which unit costs are assigned to materials issued.

Flow of materials. The order in which materials are actually issued for use in the factory.

For-profit service businesses. These are businesses that sell services rather than products, such as airlines and accountants.

Four-variance method. The analysis of fixed and variable factory overhead costs based on the computation of a spending variance and an efficiency variance for variable costs and a budget variance and a volume variance for fixed costs.

Full costing. *See* Absorption costing.

G

General factory overhead expenses. Overhead expenses that cannot be identified with a specific department and must be charged to departments by a process of allocation.

Gross margin (or gross profit). The difference between sales revenue and cost of goods sold.

Gross profit. *See* Gross margin.

H

High-low method. A method used to isolate the fixed and variable elements of a semivariable cost; involves comparison of a high volume and its related cost with a low volume and its related cost to determine the variable amount per unit and the fixed element.

Holiday pay. An amount paid to employees for designated holidays on which the employee is not required to work.

Hourly rate plan. A wage plan under which an employee is paid an established rate per hour for each hour worked.

I

Ideal standard. A performance criterion that reflects maximum efficiency, with no allowance for lost time, waste, or spoilage.

Incentive wage plan. A wage plan modified to increase worker productivity by paying a bonus rate per hour when an employee meets or exceeds established production quotas.

Indirect (nontraceable) cost. *See* Common cost.

Indirect labor. The wages and salaries of employees who are required for the manufacturing process but who do not work directly on the units being produced; examples include department heads, inspectors, materials handlers, and maintenance personnel.

Indirect materials. Materials and supplies necessary for the manufacturing process that cannot be readily identified with any particular product manufactured or whose relative cost is too insignificant to measure.

Inventory report. A form prepared when making physical count of inventory on hand and used to reconcile differences between recorded inventory and the inventory quantities determined by physical count.

J

Job cost ledger. A subsidiary ledger that consists of the individual job cost sheets.

Job cost sheet. A form or computer file used to accumulate costs applicable to each job under a job order cost accounting system.

Job order cost system. A method or system of cost accounting that is appropriate for manufacturing operations that produce custom-made or special-order goods. Manufacturing costs are accumulated separately for each job and recorded on a job cost sheet.

Joint costs. The costs of materials, labor, and overhead incurred during the production of joint products.

Joint products. Two or more products that are obtained from the same manufacturing process and are the primary objectives of the process.

Just-in-time (JIT) inventory system. A system that significantly reduces inventory carrying costs by requiring that raw materials be delivered by suppliers to the factory at the exact time that they are needed for production.

K

Kanban. Card indicating a manufacturing cell's need for more raw materials or component parts.

Labor cost standard. A predetermined estimate of the direct labor cost required for a unit of product based on estimates of the labor hours required to produce a unit of product and the cost of labor per unit.

Labor cost summary. A form showing the allocation of total payroll to Work in Process and Factory Overhead.

Labor efficiency (usage) variance. The difference between the actual number of direct labor hours worked and the standard hours for the actual level of production at the standard labor rate.

Labor rate (price) variance. The difference between the average hourly direct labor rate actually paid and the standard hourly rate, multiplied by the number of hours worked.

Labor time record. A record (usually a computer file) that shows an employee's time spent on each job.

Last-in, first-out (LIFO). An inventory costing method based on the assumption that materials issued are the most recently purchased materials. Thus, materials issued are costed at the most recent purchase prices, and ending inventories are costed at the prices paid for the earliest purchases.

Lead time. The estimated time interval between the placement of an order and the receipt of materials.

Learning effect. The process that occurs when employees become more efficient at complex production processes the more often they perform the task.

Loss leader. A product line that yields low profit (or a loss) but is retained in order to attract customers who might also purchase more profitable items.

M

Machine hour method. A method of applying factory overhead to production based on the number of machine hours used for a job or process.

Magnetic card reader. A machine connected to a remote computer terminal that automatically logs "on" and "off" labor time to the accounting department through the use of magnetic cards that employees swipe into this machine at the beginning and end of specific job assignments.

Make-up guarantee. An amount paid to employees under a modified wage plan when established production quotas are not met during a work period. The make-up guarantee is charged to the factory overhead account.

Management accounting. Focuses on both historical and estimated data that management needs to conduct ongoing operations and long-range planning.

Management by exception. As relates to variance analysis, it is the practice of examining significant unfavorable or favorable differences from standard.

Manufacturers. They convert raw materials into finished goods by using labor, technology, and facilities.

Manufacturing margin. The term commonly used in variable costing to designate the difference between sales and variable cost of goods sold.

Manufacturing cells. *See* Work centers.

Manufacturing (or production) costs. All costs incurred in the manufacturing process; the costs are classified into three basic elements: direct materials, direct labor, and factory overhead.

Manufacturing process. The activities involved in converting raw materials into finished goods through the application of labor and incurrence of various factory expenses.

Margin of safety. The amount that sales can decrease before the company will suffer a loss.

Margin of safety ratio. A relationship computed by dividing the difference between the total sales and the break-even point sales by total sales.

Mark-on percentage. A percentage of the manufacturing cost per unit that is added to provide for selling and administrative expense and profit.

Master budget. *See* Static budget.

Materials. The inventory account that represents the cost of all materials purchased and on hand to be used in the manufacturing process, including raw materials, prefabricated parts, and supplies.

Materials control. Procedures incorporated in the system of internal control that are designed to physically protect or safeguard materials (physical control) and to maintain the proper balance of materials on hand (control of the investment in materials).

Materials cost standard. A predetermined estimate of the cost of the direct materials required for a unit of product.

Materials ledger. *See* Stores ledger.

Materials price variance. The difference between the actual unit cost of direct materials and the standard unit cost, multiplied by the actual quantity of materials used.

Materials quantity (usage) variance. The difference between the actual quantity of direct materials used and the standard quantity for the actual level of production at standard price.

Materials (or stores) requisition. A form, prepared by authorized factory personnel and usually approved by the production department supervisor, to request materials from the storeroom; represents authorization for the storeroom keeper to issue materials for use in production.

Merchandisers. Wholesalers or retailers who purchase finished goods for resale.

Mixed costs. *See* Semifixed costs and Semivariable costs.

Modified wage plan. A wage plan that combines certain features of the hourly rate and piece-rate plans.

Moving average. An inventory costing method based on the assumption that materials issued at any time are withdrawn from a mixed group of like materials, and no attempt is made to identify materials as being from the earliest or most recent purchases. Under this method, an average unit price is computed each time a new lot of materials is received, and the new unit price is used to cost all issues of materials until another lot is received and a new unit price is computed.

N

Noncontributory plans. Pension plans that are completely funded by the employer.

Nonfinancial performance measures. These are performance measures that are used to evaluate operations, but that are not expressed in dollars, such as the percentage of defective units produced.

Nonvalue-added activities. Operations that include costs but do not add value to the product, such as moving, storing, and inspecting.

Non–volume-related activities. Activities performed that create overhead costs that are more a function of the complexity of the product being made rather than the number of units produced; examples are number of machine setups and product design changes.

Normal capacity. The level of production that will meet the normal requirements of ordinary sales demand over a period of time; frequently used for budget development because it represents a logical balance between maximum capacity and the capacity demanded by actual sales volume.

Normal losses. Units lost due to the nature of the manufacturing process. Such losses are unavoidable and represent a necessary cost of producing goods.

Not-for-profit service agencies. These include charities, governmental agencies, and some health care facilities that provide services at little or no cost to the user.

O

Observation (or account analysis) method. A technique used to classify a semivariable cost as either fixed or variable; involves examination and analysis of past relationships between the expense and production volume. Based on the observed pattern of cost behavior, a decision is made to classify the expense as either a fixed or variable cost, depending on which it more closely resembles.

Order costs. The costs incurred as a result of ordering materials; includes salaries and wages of employees involved in purchasing, receiving, and inspecting materials; communications costs, such as telephone, postage, and forms; and record-keeping costs.

Order point. The point at which an item of inventory should be ordered; occurs when a predetermined minimum level of inventory on hand is reached. Determining an order point requires consideration of usage, lead time, and safety stock.

Outliers. Nonrepresentative data points that may be wrongly selected when using the high-low method.

Overapplied (or overabsorbed) factory overhead. The amount by which applied factory overhead exceeds actual factory overhead expenses incurred; represented by a remaining credit balance in Factory Overhead.

Overtime pay. The amount earned by employees at the regular hourly rate for hours worked in excess of the regularly scheduled time.

Overtime premium. The additional pay rate earned for working hours in excess of the normal daily or weekly hours.

P

Payroll record. A form prepared each pay period showing the earnings of all employees for the period.

Payroll taxes. Taxes imposed on employers, including social security tax and federal and state unemployment taxes.

Peanut-butter costing. The practice of assigning costs evenly to jobs via an overhead rate when, in fact, different jobs consume resources in different proportions.

Pension costs. The costs incurred by an employer to provide retirement benefits to employees.

Performance report. A periodic summary of cost and production data that are controllable by the manager of a particular cost center.

Period costs. All costs that are not assigned to the product, but are recognized as expense and charged against revenue in the period incurred.

Periodic inventory system. A method of accounting for inventory that requires estimating inventory during the year for interim statements and shutting down operations to count all inventory items at the end of the year.

Perpetual inventory system. A method of accounting for inventory that provides a continuous record of purchases, issues, and balances of all goods in stock.

Piece-rate plan. A wage plan under which an employee is paid a specified rate for each unit or "piece" completed.

Planning. The process of establishing objectives or goals for the organization and determining the means by which the objectives will be attained.

Practical capacity. The level of production that provides complete utilization of all facilities and personnel but allows for some idle capacity due to operating interruptions, such as machinery breakdowns, idle time, and other inefficiencies.

Predetermined factory overhead rate. A percentage or amount determined by dividing budgeted factory overhead cost by budgeted production; budgeted production may be expressed in terms of machine hours, direct labor hours, direct labor cost, or units. The predetermined rate is an estimate used in applying factory overhead to production.

Price. In the context of variance analysis, refers to the cost of materials or the hourly wage rate for direct labor.

Prime cost. The combined costs of direct materials and direct labor incurred in manufacturing a product.

Process cost system. A method or system of cost accounting that is appropriate for manufacturing operations that produce continuous output of homogeneous products. Manufacturing costs are accumulated separately for each department and are recorded on a cost of production report.

Product costs. Costs that are included as part of inventory costs and expensed when goods are sold.

Production budget. A detailed plan indicating the number of units that must be produced during a specific period of time to meet sales and inventory requirements.

Production department. A department in which actual manufacturing operations are performed and the units being produced are physically changed.

Production department supervisor. The employee who is responsible for supervising the operational functions of a production department.

Production report. A report, used in a process cost accounting system and prepared by the department head, showing beginning units in process, number of units completed during the period, ending units in process, and their estimated stage of completion.

Production work teams. A recent concept where output is dependent upon contributions made by all members of the work crew or department.

Professional labor budget. A budget for which the budgeted hours required for each client service area are multiplied by the budgeted rate for each category to obtain the total wages expense for each category of professional labor.

Purchase order. A form, prepared by the purchasing agent and addressed to the chosen vendor, that describes the materials ordered, credit terms and prices, and the date and method of delivery; represents the vendor's authorization to ship goods.

Purchase price variance. The difference between the actual cost of materials and the standard cost.

Purchase requisition. A form, usually prepared by the storeroom keeper or employee with similar responsibility, that is used to notify the purchasing agent that additional materials are needed; represents the agent's authority to purchase materials.

Purchasing agent. The employee who is responsible for purchasing the materials needed for production. An individual in any organization who is responsible for the purchasing function.

R

Receiving clerk. The employee who is responsible for supervising incoming shipments of materials and making sure that all incoming materials are checked as to quantity and quality.

Receiving report. A form that is prepared by the receiving clerk for each incoming shipment of materials. The clerk identifies the materials, determines the quantity received, and records this information on the receiving report as well as the name of the shipper, date of receipt, and the number of the purchase order identifying the shipment.

Relative sales value. A basis for allocating joint costs proportionally based on the respective selling prices of the separate products.

Relevant range. The wide range of production volume in which the firm expects to operate.

Responsibility accounting. The assignment of accountability for costs or production results to those individuals who have the most authority to influence costs or production.

Retailers. A type of merchandiser who sells products or services to individuals for consumption.

Returned materials report. A form prepared to accompany materials being returned to the storeroom that had been previously requisitioned but were not used in production.

Return shipping order. A form prepared by the purchasing agent when goods are to be returned to the vendor.

Revenue budget. A budget that projects revenue to be received from client business.

S

Safety stock. The estimated minimum level of inventory needed to protect against stockouts.

Sales budget. A budget that projects the volume of sales both in units and dollars.

Sales mix. The relative percentage of unit sales among the various products made by the firm.

Scattergraph method. A method that estimates a straight line along which the semivariable costs will fall by drawing the line by visual inspection through the data points plotted on the graph.

Schedule of fixed costs. A listing of fixed overhead costs, such as depreciation, insurance, and property taxes; provides the source from which fixed costs can be allocated to the various departments. Since fixed costs are assumed not to vary in amount from month to month, a schedule can be prepared in advance for several periods; at the end of a period, a journal entry can be prepared to record total fixed costs from the information provided in the schedule.

Scrap (or waste) materials. By-products that are generated in the manufacturing process; usually, such materials have some value and their costs and revenues are accounted for separately.

Segment. A division, a product line, a sales territory, or other organizational unit that can be separately identified for reporting purposes and profitability analysis.

Segment margin. The term used in segment analysis for the excess of segment revenue over direct costs assigned to the segment; common costs are excluded in computing segment margin.

Selling and administrative expenses budget. A sales forecast that will affect the planned expenditure level for such items as sales force compensation, advertising, and travel.

Semifixed (or step) costs. Costs that tend to remain the same in dollar amount over a certain range of activity but increase when production exceeds certain limits.

Semivariable costs. Manufacturing costs that are some-what responsive to changes in production but do not change proportionally with increases or decreases in volume; examples include indirect materials, indirect labor, repairs and maintenance, and power.

Sequential distribution (or step-down) method. A method for allocating service department costs to production departments that recognizes the interrelationship of the service departments. Costs are first allocated, sequentially, to other service departments and then to production departments. The sequence may begin by distributing the costs of the service department that renders the greatest amount of service to all other service departments. Alternatively, the costs of the service department with the largest total overhead can be distributed first.

Service. An intangible benefit that does not have physical properties and is consume at the time it is provided; examples include consulting, transporting, and entertaining.

Service department. A department within the factory that does not work directly on the product but provides needed services to other departments; examples include a department that generates power for the factory, a maintenance department that maintains and repairs buildings and equipment, and a cost accounting department that maintains factory accounting records.

Shift premium. An additional rate of pay added to an employee's regular rate as compensation for working an evening or night shift.

Spending variance. The difference between the actual factory overhead for variable costs and the actual hours multiplied by the standard variable rate. *See also* Budget variance.

Split-off point. The point where joint products become separately identifiable; may occur during, or at the end of, the manufacturing process.

Spoiled units. Units of product with imperfections that cannot be economically corrected; they are sold as items of inferior quality or "seconds."

Stage of completion. The fraction or percentage of materials, labor, and overhead costs of a completed unit that have been applied during the period to goods that have not been completed.

Standard. A norm or criterion against which performance can be measured.

Standard cost accounting. A method of accounting for manufacturing costs that can be used in conjunction with either a job order or process cost accounting system. Standard costing makes it possible to determine what a product should have cost as well as what the product actually cost.

Standard cost card. Form used to summarize the standard quantities and costs of assembling, testing, and packaging a given product.

Standard cost system. A system that uses predetermined standard costs to furnish a measurement that helps management make decisions regarding the efficiency of operations.

Standard costs. The costs that would be incurred under efficient operating conditions and are forecast before the manufacturing process begins. The predetermined standard costs are compared with actual manufacturing costs incurred and are used by management as a basis for evaluating operating efficiency and taking corrective action, when necessary.

Standard production. The volume on which the initial calculation of standard costs is based.

Standard unit cost for factory overhead. The result of estimating factory overhead cost at the standard, or normal, level of production, considering historical data and future changes and trends.

Static (or master) budget. A budget that is prepared for only one level of activity.

Step costs. *See* Semifixed costs.

Step-down method. *See* Sequential distribution method.

Step fixed cost. Semivariable production cost that remains the same over a wide range of production (e.g., the salaries of factory supervisors).

Step variable cost. A type of semivariable cost that remains constant in total over a range of production and then abruptly changes.

Stockout. Running out of an item of inventory; may occur due to inaccurate estimates of usage or lead time or other unforeseen events, such as the receipt of damaged or inferior materials from a supplier.

Storeroom keeper. The employee who is responsible for the storing and maintaining of materials inventories.

Stores (or materials) ledger. A subsidiary ledger supporting the Materials control account in the general ledger. The individual accounts in the stores ledger are used to record receipts and issues of materials and show the quantity and cost of materials on hand.

Stores requisition. *See* Materials requisition.

Summary of factory overhead. A schedule of all factory overhead expenses incurred during a period; prepared from the factory overhead analysis spreadsheets, the schedule shows each item of overhead expense by department and in total.

Summary of materials issued and returned. A form used to record all issuances of materials to the factory, returns of materials previously requisitioned, and returns of materials to the vendors (sellers). The summary, when completed at the end of a period, provides the information needed to record the cost of materials for the period.

T

Target volume. The amount of sales volume needed, in units or dollars, to cover all costs and earn a certain amount of profit.

Theoretical capacity. The maximum number of units that can be produced with the completely efficient use of all available facilities and personnel.

Three-variance method. The analysis of factory overhead costs based on the computation of efficiency, capacity, and budget (spending) variances.

Throughput time. The time that it takes a unit to make it through the production process.

Touch labor. Category of factory payroll costs that can be traced directly to an individual job (also known as "direct labor").

Transferred-in costs. The portion of a department's total costs that were incurred by and transferred from a prior production department.

Trigger points. Points in the production process at which to record journal entries in a backflush system.

Two-variance method. The analysis of factory overhead costs based on the computation of the volume variance and the budget variance.

U

Under-and overapplied factory overhead. An account used to accumulate differences from period to period between actual and applied factory overhead. At the end of the year, the balance in this account may be closed to Cost of Goods Sold (if the amount is relatively small) or allocated on a pro rata basis to Work in Process, Finished Goods, and Cost of Goods Sold (if the amount is material).

Underapplied (or underabsorbed) factory overhead. The amount by which actual factory overhead exceeds applied factory overhead; represented by a remaining debit balance in Factory Overhead.

Unfavorable variance. The difference when actual costs exceed standard costs.

Unit cost. The cost of manufacturing one unit of product.

Units from the prior department. Units that have been completed as to the transferor department and that are raw materials as to the transferee department.

Usage. The quantity of materials used or the number of direct labor hours worked.

V

Vacation pay. An amount paid to employees during their vacation periods as part of the employees' compensation for services to the employer.

Variable costing. A method of accounting for manufacturing costs that charges the product with only the costs that vary directly with volume: direct materials, direct labor, and variable factory overhead.

Variable costs. Manufacturing costs that vary in direct proportion to changes in production volume; includes direct labor, direct materials, and some types of factory overhead.

Variable overhead efficiency variance. A measure of the change in the variable overhead consumption that occurs because of efficient or inefficient use of the cost allocation base, such as direct labor hours.

Variable overhead spending variance. A measure of the effect of differences in the actual variable overhead rate and the standard variable overhead rate.

Variance. The difference, during an accounting period, between the actual and standard or budgeted costs of materials, labor, and overhead.

Velocity. The speed with which units are produced in a manufacturing system. It is the inverse of the throughput time.

Vendor's invoice. A form, usually received from the vendor before goods are delivered, confirming a purchase of materials and representing a "bill" for the ordered goods. The purchasing agent should compare the invoice with the related purchase order to verify the description of materials, price, terms of payment, method of shipment, and delivery date.

Volume variance. The difference between budgeted fixed overhead and the fixed overhead applied to work in process; the result of operating at a level of production different from the standard, or normal, level.

Volume-related activities. Activities performed where all overhead costs are directly related to the volume produced; examples are direct labor hours and machine hours.

W

Waste materials. *See* Scrap materials.

Wholesaler. A type of merchandiser who purchases goods from manufacturers and sells to retailers.

Work centers. Combined manufacturing functions that were performed in individual departments in a traditional manufacturing system.

Work in process. The inventory account that includes all the manufacturing costs incurred to date for goods that are in various stages of production but are not yet completed.

Work shift. A regularly scheduled work period for a designated number of hours.

Index

A

B

C

D

E

F

M

N

O

P

T

U

V

W